HELLENIC STUDIES 23

Paradise Earned

Other Titles in the Hellenic Studies Series

Plato's Rhapsody and Homer's Music
The Poetics of the Panathenaic Festival in Classical Athens

Labored in Papyrus Leaves
Perspectives on an Epigram Collection Attributed to Posidippus
(P.Mil.Vogl. VIII 309)

Helots and Their Masters in Laconia and Messenia
Histories, Ideologies, Structures

Archilochos Heros
The Cult of Poets in the Greek Polis

Master of the Game
Competition and Performance in Greek Poetry

Greek Ritual Poetics

Black Doves Speak
Herodotus and the Languages of Barbarians

Pointing at the Past
From Formula to Performance in Homeric Poetics

Homeric Conversation

The Life and Miracles of Thekla

Victim of the Muses
Poet as Scapegoat, Warrior and Hero
in Greco-Roman and Indo-European Myth and History

Amphoteroglōssia
A Poetics of the Twelfth Century Medieval Greek Novel

Priene (second edition)

Plato's Symposium
Issues in Interpretation and Reception

http://chs.harvard.edu/chs/publications

Paradise Earned
The Bacchic-Orphic Gold Lamellae of Crete

Yannis Tzifopoulos

CENTER FOR HELLENIC STUDIES
Trustees for Harvard University
Washington, D.C.
Distributed by Harvard University Press
Cambridge, Massachusetts, and London, England
2010

Paradise Earned
   by Yannis Tzifopoulos
Copyright © 2010 Center for Hellenic Studies, Trustees for Harvard University
All Rights Reserved.
Published by Center for Hellenic Studies, Trustees for Harvard University, Washington, D.C.
Distributed by Harvard University Press, Cambridge, Massachusetts and London, England
Production: Ivy Livingston
Cover design and illustration: Joni Godlove
Printed in Ann Arbor, MI, by Edwards Brothers, Inc.

LIBRARY OF CONGRESS CATALOGING-IN-PUBLICATION DATA:
Tzifopoulos, Yannis.
   Paradise earned : the Bacchic-Orphic gold lamellae of Crete / by Yannis Tzifopoulos.
      p. cm. — (Hellenic studies series; 23)
   Includes index.
   ISBN 978-0-674-02379-6
   1. Inscriptions, Greek—Greece—Crete. 2. Goldwork—Greece—Crete—History.
   3. Burial—Greece—Crete—History. 4. Future life—Social aspects—Greece—Crete—History.
   5. Orpheus (Greek mythology) 6. Dionysus (Greek deity) 7. Future life in literature.
   8. Religious literature, Greek (Hellenistic)—Greece—Crete—History and criticism.
   9. Crete (Greece)—Antiquities. 10. Crete (Greece)—Religious life and customs. I. Title.
   II. Series.
   CN420.T95 2009
   938—dc22

                                                                                2009019736

Table of Contents

Contents

Acknowledgments

THIS WORK HAS INCURRED MANY DEBTS in the past years, which I gratefully and appreciatively acknowledge; for the work's shortcomings I alone am responsible.

First and foremost, I am immensely indebted to the colleagues who forthrightly informed me of their excavations, placed at my disposal all the necessary information of their intriguing findings, made every effort to facilitate my work in the Rethymno and Herakleion Museums, and undertook the time and trouble, among other far more pressing personal work and research, to prepare their reports of the archaeological context and chronology: Irene Gavrilaki for nos. 8 and 10–12; Stella Kalogeraki and Niki Tsatsaki for no. 9; Matthaios Bessios for nos. 13–15; Kalliopi Galanaki for nos. 18–19; Giorgos Rethemiotakis for no. 20; and the late Betty Psaropoulou, an expert in modern ceramics and head of the Center for the Study of Modern Ceramics in Athens, for no. 24 and the photograph.

No less is my debt to colleagues in the Archaeological Service for their permission to study and photograph the lamellae and the related inscriptions: the National Archaeological and the Epigraphical Museums in Athens, and Charalampos Kritzas, Io Zervoudaki, and Eleni Kourinou; the 25th Ephorate of Prehistoric and Classical Antiquities in Chania and Rethymno, and Maria Andreadaki-Vlazaki, Vana Niniou-Kindeli, Stavroula Markoulaki, Eva Tegou, Nota Karamaliki, and the staff Giorgos Nikoloudakis, Kostis Tsogas, Manolis Akoumianakis, Petros Fytros, Christos Alertas; the 23th Ephorate of Prehistoric and Classical Antiquities in Herakleion, and Alexandra Karetsou, Eva Grammatikaki, Nota Dimopoulou-Rethemiotaki, Antonis Vassilakis, Ioanna Serpetsidaki and Vasso Marsellou; the 24th Ephorate of Prehistoric and Classical Antiquities in Agios Nikolaos, and Vili Apostolakou and Alexandros Nikakis; the 27th Ephorate of Prehistoric and Classical Antiquities in Katerini, Pieria, and the director at the time, Polyxeni Adam-Veleni.

The photographs of these difficult objects were expertly made by Stephanos N. Stournaras, the late Stephanos Alexandrou, and Yannis Ploumidis Papadakis, and the drawings of nos. 8 and 9 by Amanda Kelly and Katerina Kaklamanou respectively. Photographs were also kindly provided by: the J. Paul Getty Museum, and then-Associate Curator John K. Papadopoulos (Figure 41: the lamella from Thessaly); the Toledo Museum of Art (Figures 42a–c: the Darius-painter krater); Matthaios Bessios (Figures 14–16); and Professor Petros Themelis (Figures 50a–c: the 'Herm' from Eleutherna). Finally, the map is a modified version of the one published by Katja Sporn (2002), to whom I am grateful.

The study of the Cretan lamellae is part of the ongoing project *Archive of Inscriptions of the Rethymno Prefecture*, which began in 1997 and was financially supported by: the Department of Philology and the Research Council of the University of Crete for the academic years 1998–2002; and the Loeb Classical Library Foundation Trustees, Harvard University, and the committee members Zeph Stewart, Richard Thomas, and Lloyd Weinreb for the academic year 2003–2004. To them all I am deeply grateful.

The Library of the University of Crete and its staff, especially Michael Tzekakis, Eleni Diamantaki, Pantelis Generalis, Kalli Karadaki, Yannis Lagamtzis, and Antonis Diamantakis have done their best to procure the necessary books and articles, especially during 2004–2005.

A number of colleagues have offered congenial settings in which portions of this work were presented: Dimitris Kyrtatas in Rethymno and Volos, Aphrodite Avagianou in Athens, Kostas Moutzouris in Chania, Maria Fragiadaki in Herakleion, Apostolos Pierris in Patras, and Sarah Iles Johnston and Fritz Graf in Columbus, Ohio. The audiences' reactions and criticisms in these places provided encouragement and stimulated new avenues of research.

At various stages of this work, I have had the privileged opportunity to exchange views and ideas on specific issues, sometimes in advance of publication, and receive judicious and provocative comments on drafts from Vili Apostolakou, Alberto Bernabé, Chryssa Bourbou, Walter Burkert, Radcliffe Edmonds III, Irene Gavrilaki, Fritz Graf, Sarah Iles Johnston, Thanassis Kalpaxis, Theokritos Kouremenos, Katerini Liampi, Nikos Litinas, Nannó Marinatos, Stavroula Oikonomou, Katerina Panagopoulou, Robert Parker, Alexis Politis, Christoph Riedweg, Yannis Sakellarakis, Kleanthis Sidiropoulos, Nikos Simandirakis, Maria Stamatopoulou, Eva Tegou, Petros Themelis, Kyriakos Tsantsanoglou, Dimitris Yatromanolakis, and especially Angelos Chaniotis, Stavros Frangoulidis, Maria Sarinaki, Nicholas Stampolidis, and Stephen Tracy.

Finally, Gregory Nagy, director of the Center for Hellenic Studies and editor of the Center's Hellenic Studies series, heartily and judiciously embraced this *golden project*; my sense of indebtedness to him, a true *parastates*, cannot be expressed in words. I am also deeply grateful to the Center's superb team, Leonard Muellner, Jill Curry Robbins, Zoie Lafis, Sam Mohlo, Benjamin Woodring, Emily Collinson, and Ivy Livingston, who all have been more than ideal and obliging in expertly preparing the manuscript for the Press; and to George Motakis, the computer expert in the Department of Philology in Rethymno, who efficiently and ingeniously solved numerous computer problems.

As I was reading and correcting the proofs in July 2007, two new incised *epistomia* have been unearthed in the site Mnemata (Figures nos. 24–27, pages 82–84), one of Eleutherna's cemeteries whence come the seven engraved *epistomia* of Crete (the section Topography below, and nos. 1–7, B3–8 and E1). Eva Tegou, in charge of the excavations conducted by the 25th Ephorate of Prehistoric and Classical Antiquities, graciously showed me the new finds, and kindly informed me of the progress since March 2007 of the ongoing excavations. As excavation is still in progress, which means that more may show up, we decided to present the new incised *epistomia*, which will become nos. B13 and B14 in group B, and their archaeological context in the near future.

Since the manuscript's submission, new important contributions came to my attention, unfortunately too late to be appropriately integrated into the present discussion: Franco Ferrari's, *La fonte del cipresso bianco. Racconto e sapienza dall'Odissea alle lamine misteriche*, Torino: UTET 2007; Alberto Bernabé's, *Poetae epici graeci testimonia et fragmenta*, pars II, fasc. 3: *Musaeus, Linus, Epimenides, Papyrus Derveni, Indices*, Berlin: W. De Gruyter 2007; Beryl Barr-Sharrar's, *The Derveni Krater: Masterpiece of Classical Greek Metalwork*, Ancient Art and Architecture in Context 1, Princeton: The American School of Classical Studies at Athens 2008; R. Drew Griffith's, *Mummy Wheat: Egyptian Influence on the Homeric View of the Afterlife and the Eleusinian Mysteries*, Lanham: University Press of America 2008; and Claude Calame's, *Poetic and Performative Memory in Ancient Greece: Heroic Reference and Ritual Gestures in Time and Space*, Washington, DC, and Cambridge, MA: Center for Hellenic Studies, 2008 (Chapter V: "Ritual and Initiatory Itineraries toward the Afterlife: Time, Space, and Pragmatics in the Gold Lamellae").

The work is respectfully dedicated *eis mnemósynon* to Nikephoros Tzifopoulos, Metropolitan of Chios, Psara, and Oinoussai, and Zacharias Tzifopoulos.

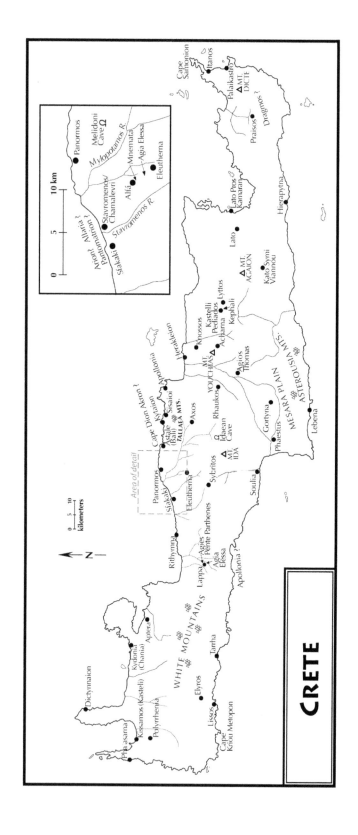

CRETE

Area of detail (inset map)

Panormos

Melidoni Cave Ω

Mylopotamos R.

Mnemata

Agia Elessa

Eleutherna

Stavromenos/ Chamalevri

Alfa

Arion? Allaria ?
Pantomatrion ?

Stavromenos/ Chamalevri

Stavromenos R.

Siakaki

10 km

0   5

Main map

Cape Sarhonion

Itanos

Palaikastro

MT. DICTE

Dragmos ?

Praisos

Lato Pros Kamaran

Hierapytna

Lato

MT. AGAION

Kato Symi Viannou

Lyttos

Kastelli Pediados

Acharna

Kephali

Knossos

Herakleion

Apollonia

MT. YOUCHTAS

Agios Thomas

ASTEROUSIA MTS.

MESARA PLAIN

Cape Dion Akron ?

Kysaion

Sisaioi

Astale (Bali)

TALLAEA MTS.

Axos

Rhaukos

Gortyna

Lebena

Idaean Cave Ω

Sybritos

MT. IDA

Phaestus

Panormos

Siakaki

Eleutherna

Soulia

Rithymna

Lappa

Agies Pente Parthenes

Agia Elessa

Apollonia ?

WHITE MOUNTAINS

Tarrha

Aptera

Kydonia (Chania)

Elyros

Dictynnaion

Kisamos (Kasteli)

Polyrrhenia

Lissos

Cape Kriou Metopon

Phalasarna

0   5   10
kilometers

← N

Preface

THE GREEKS WHO ON THE BRINK OF DEATH took with them to the grave a small gold incised lamella died content, feeling assured that special treatment awaited them in the Underworld. Such a statement is, of course, only a hypothesis, as there is no way to ascertain what the deceased themselves thought, or how content they were. This much, however, the texts on the lamellae clearly indicate. The individuals buried with the incised lamellae died with the belief that they 'earned' what we would call, for all intents and purposes, 'paradise,' the Persian word first used by Xenophon to refer to an "enclosed park, or pleasure-ground, always in reference to the parks of Persian kings and nobles." Only in late antiquity did the word acquire the meaning *garden of Eden, Paradise, the abode of the blessed*, eventually becoming identical with the ancient *Islands of the Blessed*.[1] The literally golden letters on the small lamellae were meant to ensure an equally golden afterlife.

The incised gold *epistomia* from Sfakaki, Crete, nos. 8 and 9 below, are the stimulus of the present study. Together with the previously published *epistomia*, nos. 1–7 below, and the three unincised ones, nos. 10–12 below, they comprise a distinct group representing the Cretan contribution to the small corpus of incised lamellae and *epistomia*, found in Italy, the Peloponnese, Thessaly, and Macedonia. Since the middle of the 1970s, the publication of engraved lamellae has been steadily growing, and the number of studies treating them has likewise increased. Thus the edition of the new *epistomia* from Sfakaki necessitated the simultaneous presentation of all Cretan lamellae, so that the new artifacts and texts might be presented within a greater context.

The incised lamellae and *epistomia*, however, have multiple contexts. First, they are grave-goods, and attention should be paid accordingly to their Cretan and Panhellenic archaeological contexts. Secondly, because they are also texts

---

[1] Xenophon *Anabasis* 1.2.7, 9; 1.4.10, 14, 17; *Cyropaedia* 1.3.14; 1.4.5, 11; 8.1.38; 8.6.12; *Hellenika* 4.1.15, 33; *Oeconomicus* 4.13-14, 21; LSJ, s.v.; and Chantraine 1980:857.

written in verse or rhythmic prose, their poetics, Cretan and Panhellenic, warrant discussion. Finally, their content presupposes performance of one or more rituals (Cretan and/or Panhellenic) which also deserve examination. These three distinctive contexts are all appropriate for the incised lamellae, a fact which raises rather than solves problems. Although many of these issues will become evident in the following chapters, a brief outline of the interpretative problems and the guidelines followed should be spelled out from the start.

If the archaeological and epigraphical context posits no great difficulty, the contexts of poetics and ritual are another matter. The texts on the lamellae and *epistomia* belong to the (sub)literary category of religious texts, but this is an all-encompassing category.[2] The texts of nos. 1–9 and nos. 13–25 below, as well as the unincised *epistomia* nos. 10-12, are all in different ways religious 'texts' and discourses on the afterlife: the Bacchic-Orphic hexametric and rhythmic texts, the unincised gold *epistomia*, the personal names of initiates, a hymn, an epigram, and the incised or painted *symbola* on clay fragments.[3] Already within this group a noteworthy difficulty arises, namely the yoking together of different genres with different sets of compositional techniques, structures, and aims. As Don Fowler has shown admirably in relation to Lucretius' 'didactic' poem:[4]

> [G]enres are unstable and leaky entities, ... *generic analysis ... has to take its place within wider systems of social construction ...* Didactic poetry [aside from its primary teacher-to-student aspect] has ... structural metaphors and implicit myths ... [which] are secondary elements of the genre ... The didactic journey through the text leads to other genres—above all epic—and to our configurations of travel

---

[2] Roland Baumgarten (1998), under the telling title *heiliges Wort, heilige Schrift,* and *hieroi logoi,* has presented an important contribution to the study of religious texts, such as oracles, 'orphic' literature, *hieroi logoi* in mystery cults, the two *hieroi logoi* supposedly by Pythagoras, and 'egyptianizing' sacred writings. This is a disparate miscellany, but it underscores the variety in form and objectives of what we might call religious texts. As Robert Parker (2000b) and Albert Henrichs (2003a and 2003b) have argued, the terms *hieros logos, hiera anagraphe, hieros chresmos, sacred writ,* and the like are not identical, just as the *theogonies, hymns, cult regulations, oracles,* and a number of other texts are different entities. They all, however, comprise what we would call a corpus of religious texts.

[3] On the variety of religious documents the place to start is Henrichs 2003b.

[4] Don Fowler 2000:218–219; for epic as an especially 'leaky genre,' see Martin 2005b; in relation to Poseidippos' epigrams Obbink (2005) entertains the idea of subliterary or occasional texts, i.e., texts composed for an occasion and not necessarily as part of a canon whose primary criterion is literariness; and 107n42.

in the ancient world ... If all didactic arguably has a plot of enlightenment, the meaning of "enlightenment" nevertheless changes in
history (my emphasis).

If the didactic nature of the texts on the lamellae is self-evident, the didactic
genre is not their place. The poetics of these texts are not bound by genres.

In investigating "wider systems of social construction," Dimitrios
Yatromanolakis and Panagiotis Roilos have put forward a useful interpretative
tool which they have dubbed *ritual poetics*. Ritual poetics emphasizes performance and its context, as well as poetics' discursivity, "the 'text'/discourse as
situated within a nexus of what we would call *textural interactions* with other
discourses."[5] Any given Greek linguistic product, *Greek* being a term "principally employed ... as an overarching *linguistic* category,"[6] may in different
historical and cultural moments appropriate, transform, interact with other
current or traditional discourses, or even, in this interaction, create 'new'
ones:

> Instead of subscribing either to the detrimentally misleading
> dogma of linear diachronic continuities or to the equally mono-
> lithic and politically-charged dogma of absolute discontinuities, our
> approach [i.e., ritual poetics] offers transhistorical, transcultural
> perspectives on the embeddedness of ritual patterns in broader
> cultural and sociopolitical discourses in different traditions of the
> Greek-speaking world. This exploratory enterprise puts emphasis
> on discontinuities and transformations across chronological and
> discursive boundaries. The diversity and volume of written records
> regarding ritual activities, whether religious or secular, actual or
> reinscribed in other cultural discourses, is exceptionally rich in the
> Greek language. The Greek case, therefore, with its abundant mate-
> rial full of diverse continuities and discontinuities and their, more
> often than not, ideologically-informed reworkings throughout a
> period of around three millennia offers an admittedly challenging
> but fertile ground for comparative explorations and debates.

Although ritual poetics runs the danger of over-simplifying and strives to
be all-encompassing, it nevertheless features some distinct advantages.[7] The

---

[5] Yatromanolakis and Roilos 2003:13 and 2004:5.
[6] Yatromanolakis and Roilos 2003:11–12 and 11–41; 2004:3–4 and 3–34.
[7] Yatromanolakis and Roilos (2004) provide an array of approaches from archaic to modern
Greece with fruitful results on "ritual textures and textures of sociocultural interaction as

emphasis on the cultural and sociopolitical discourses, and on the dynamic potential of ritual patterns, presents a hermeneutic tool well-suited for the incised lamellae and *epistomia*, especially the small Cretan corpus. The similarities and divergences displayed in the Cretan texts may have been due to different influences and/or concerns, as regards the discourse on afterlife and the practical matters of the ever-re-enacted ritual.

The cultural discourses on afterlife have been the focus of Lars Albinus' (2000) study. He has delineated a convincing picture of two competing discourses on afterlife in Greek literature from the archaic period onwards, the 'Homeric' and the 'Orphic'. Both discourses based their promises on *mnemosyne* and its intrinsic nature: the Homeric, inspired by the Muse, revitalizes the dead and the past through poetry and offers the eternal *kleos* of song;[8] the Orphic, being the Muse incarnate, preaches the continuity from mortal life to immortal death, the beginning of a new existence after death. Of necessity, Albinus' approach must put aside any differences within each discourse and emphasize the similarities in order to harmonize each discourse. But neither all persons initiated in mystery cults looking for reward after death were required to carry an incised lamella or *epistomion*; nor is there a unanimous voice in the Homeric discourse.[9] The 'Homeric' and 'Bacchic-Orphic' discourses on afterlife dominated and competed from the archaic period onwards,[10] but within each discourse divergences did exist, even if these did not weaken the overall premises of each discourse.

Rather than concentrating on similarities, Radcliffe Edmonds has focused on the divergences in the narratives of the lamellae's texts, and has argued cogently that the Underworld journey, depicted in the texts on the lamellae, is a mythic narrative. Instead of breaking it up into stages of an assumed ritual, he analyzes the narrative according to a tripartite nexus of obstacle-solution-result: the obstacle faced by the deceased, the solution provided by the lamella, and the result that the deceased hopes to obtain. Each time, the authors, although they employ traditional mythic elements for the obstacle, solution and result, reformulate these mythic elements, a process that reveals "the different conceptions about the afterlife, the different agendas and

---

interwoven nexuses of ever-reinvented negotiations of power capitals and *sēmansis*" (2004:34). For a similar example see the sections "In Search of a Context" and "Afterword."

[8] For the mnemonic techniques, applicable to both sets of texts, see Minchin 2001.

[9] Ledbetter 2003 presents an eloquent discussion of the divergent poetics within the Homeric discourse.

[10] Homeric and Orphic should be understood throughout as linguistic expedients (Calame forthcoming); and 120n80.

eschatological hopes."[11] Edmonds' approach offers new insights into the study of these texts and presents a strong case for their traditional mythic narrative, constantly changed and rearticulated with omissions and additions which underscore the different, perhaps personal approaches of the deceased towards death and the afterlife.

The mythic narrative and the Orphic discourse of the texts on the lamellae betray a constant interaction at the level of poetics. The texts also disclose a similar interaction at the level of ritual. Christoph Riedweg has shown convincingly how the different versions of the texts, in whatever way one chooses to classify them, may fit together in a religious discourse on the afterlife.[12] Employing the tools of narratology, Riedweg matches context and content, presenting a reconstruction of a *hieros logos* in six stages, which comprise all the texts. This reconstruction of some of the *legomena* and the presumed *dromena* of a ritual undoubtedly involved a *hieros logos*, from which may have derived the *synthemata* and *symbola*, the 'strange' expressions, of the texts, but as Albert Henrichs has demonstrated, the texts themselves may not have been a *hieros logos* proper: *hierologein* was a secret *logos* which explained the why and the how of words and actions.[13] The ritual context for the performance of the *legomena* and *dromena* has been postulated as an initiation into a mystery cult, or as a rite during the final stage of the funeral over the grave. But as with genres and poetics, rituals are also "unstable and leaky entities," and have their own dynamics. The simple fact that a ritual was constantly re-enacted for centuries and performed in different places argues against a unified model of the same ritual. As Angelos Chaniotis has aptly put it, "one cannot celebrate the same festival twice," especially when performers and receptors of festivals and rituals change constantly from century to century.[14] The owners of all the lamellae were initiates in a similar ritual, but it is rather unlikely that this ritual was re-enacted in an identical way from the fourth century BCE to the second century CE in all the places where a lamella or *epis-*

---

[11] Edmonds 2004:35–36 (the quotation from 36).

[12] Riedweg 1998 and 2002.

[13] Henrichs (2003a) allows for only one, *PGurob*, as a "more likely candidate for the designation *hieros logos*" (233n86 with previous bibliography), which may have survived from antiquity. He entertains as a second possibility the Orphic text whose commentary survives in *PDerveni*, provided this lost Orphic text is designated in the *PDerveni* commentary as a *hieros logos* or its author's activity as *hierologein*. Such is the case by the verb ἱερολογεῖσθαι restored in *PDerveni* column VII line 7 (and possibly in column VII line 2), for which see Kouremenos, Parássoglou, and Tsantsanoglou 2006:74–75, 171–173.

[14] Chaniotis 2002:43 (further cases in Chaniotis 2005b and 2005c); and also Frankfurter 2002, and Humphreys 2004.

tomion has been discovered: in Italy, Thourioi, Rome, Hipponion, Poseidonia, Petelia, and West Sicily; in Crete, Eleutherna and Sfakaki; in the Peloponnese, Elis and Aigeion; in Thessaly, Pharsalos, Pelinna, Pherai; and in Macedonia, Dion, Methone, Pydna, Aigai (Vergina), Agios Athanassios, Pella, Amphipolis, Kilkis.

In the case of the texts incised on the lamellae and *epistomia*, poetics, ritual, and the archaeological contexts go hand in hand, one informing or complicating the others. Fritz Graf and Sarah Iles Johnston (2007), in their attempt to present a coherent and sensible whole, articulate with good judgment these disparate and at times conflicting contexts: the myth of Dionysos and Orpheus, their poetics, eschatological discourses, Bacchic mystery cults, sacred texts, gold tablets. Along their lines, some of these issues will be addressed in what follows, and answers will be attempted, but definitive conclusions about the texts on the lamellae are yet to come. The nature of the evidence is such that a new find may overturn completely what at present we think we know for certain, or even what we assume is reasonable.

Chapter 1, the epigraphical edition, is divided into two sections. In the first, all the *epistomia* from Eleutherna and Sfakaki, Crete are (re)edited: nos. 1–9 comprise the incised and nos. 10–12 the unincised *epistomia*. In the second section, texts, related to the lamellae and *epistomia* and discussed in subsequent chapters, are (re)edited: nos. 13–15 comprise the two incised coins and the *epistomion* from Pieria in Macedonia, hitherto published in preliminary reports; nos. 16–17 the Hymn from the Diktaian Sanctuary in Palaikastro, and the epigram of Magna Mater from Phaistos respectively; nos. 18–23, and nos. 24–25 incised or painted clay *epistomia* found in Byzantine and modern Greek graves respectively. These texts, either because of usage or because of their content, present cases analogous to the gold lamellae. All translations of these (and all other ancient) texts are my own, unless noted otherwise.

Chapter 2 offers an extensive commentary on the *epistomia* from Crete, which also touches upon issues pertinent to the other incised lamellae. It comprises sections on the topography of Cretan *epistomia*, their lettering and engraving, dialect and orthography, meter, chronology, and finally on the material, shape and burial context, and usage of all the lamellae and *epistomia*.

In Chapter 3 the Cretan lamellae are placed within the small corpus of all lamellae published so far. The chapter is divided into three sections. First, an attempt is made at clarifying the nature of these incised objects, and a new classification is proposed for all lamellae and *epistomia*, which modifies the one suggested by Günther Zuntz (1971) and according to which all lamellae and *epistomia* are referred to throughout by letter group and number (Tables 1–2).

In the second section, the Cretan texts are analyzed in relation to the corpus of texts which connote a certain ritual and imply a secret *hieros logos*. Finally, the texts' composition and content are discussed in comparison to rhapsodic performances, which may have influenced those who transmitted the texts of the lamellae. Two distinct discourses on death and the afterlife appear from the archaic period onwards: one of them, promoted by epic poetry and later by tragedy, pronounces *kleos* as the only way to heroization and immortalization, thereby making genre the sole determinant of one's chances of gaining access to the Isles of the Blessed; the other proffers an alternative path to the Isles, *via* initiation into a mystery cult. If such initiations are sometimes implied in epic and dramatic poetry, it is only so they can be rejected or problematized, as Christiane Sourvinou-Inwood (2003) suggested. Oracles, another type of religious text, share a unique relationship with both types of discourses: although they adhere to the Homeric and Hesiodic outlooks on the afterlife, they nevertheless betray affinities with the texts on the lamellae in terms of structure, composition, and objective; in a sense, the texts on the lamellae pronounce a kind of "prophecy come true" on afterlife.

Chapter 4 focuses on Crete and its literary, archaeological, and epigraphical contexts. It is argued that in the literary works of non-Cretans from the archaic period onwards, the subject *Crete and the Cretans* becomes a literary topos, as it were, signifying a certain behavior, activity, or belief. This phenomenon implies that although the Homeric and Orphic discourses on afterlife were most prevalent, they were not the only ones. Indeed, the Cretan discourse was also significant, especially in matters of poetics and ritual. Regardless of whether the other discourses ended up rejecting, modifying, or integrating the Cretan topos, they all had to reckon with it and seriously acknowledge it. Later in the chapter, perceptions of *Crete and the Cretans* in non-Cretan literary works are compared to the actual archaeological and epigraphical evidence of Crete, and in particular to the evidence around the Idaean Cave. Greek perceptions of *Crete and the Cretans*, that is, of Cretan poetics, rituals, and religious matters, were not just a literary topic in mainly Athenian literary texts. There is strong evidence to suggest that in Crete, and especially around the Idaean Cave, to the south at Phaistos and to the north at Eleutherna (where we find the incised *epistomia*), poetics, rituals, and religious matters enjoyed a continuous development and exercised a lasting impact. The emerging context is fitting for, and may explain, not only the presence of the deceased buried with *epistomia* (incised or not), but also the deviant choices and ideologies in these texts, because of the various but similar in concept mystery cults and rituals in Phaistos, the Idaean Cave, and Eleutherna.

Instead of an epilogue, the concluding part presents a coda: further developments in the life of the burial custom of lamellae during the Byzantine and the modern Greek periods. The thin gold incised lamellae become clay fragments incised or painted with Christian symbols. Drawing parallels between the ancient and modern customs illuminates the discussion of the incised lamellae in two ways: first, such parallels present a necessary interpretative caveat regarding the issues of continuities and discontinuities, similarities and differences, and local and Panhellenic distinctions; more importantly, however, they forcefully evince the everlasting and persistent human quest to 'earn Paradise.'

Finally, an appendix features two Tables cataloguing all forty-four lamellae and *epistomia* published thus far. Table 1 modifies Zuntz's classification (1971), arranging the texts of the lamellae and *epistomia* into groups A through G according to their content. Information is provided concerning provenance, date, shape, accompanying coin(s), the deceased's gender, the manner of burial, and other goods recovered from the graves. In Table 2, the lamellae and *epistomia* and their texts are presented according to different criteria in three groups: 1) the twenty-three lamellae and *epistomia*, of which nineteen are engraved with brief texts (eight of them leaves, two coins, and a pseudo-coin?), and four *epistomia* with no texts; 2) the twenty-one lamellae and *epistomia* engraved with long texts (one of them two leaves); 3) all forty-four lamellae and *epistomia* according to their provenance: ten from Italy, twelve from Crete, five from the Peloponnese, five from Thessaly, and twelve from Macedonia.

1

Edition

THE GOLD *EPISTOMIA* OF CRETE

N̄ine Incised

Archaeological Context for nos. 1–7

T̄he provenance of the seven published *epistomia* is unknown. Margarita Guarducci, guided by Federico Halbherr's notes and drawings (IC II.xii [Eleutherna].31, p. 136) and by Domenico Comparetti's edition (1910:37–41), included nos. 1–3 and 7 in the epigraphical dossier of Eleutherna. Guarducci, however, published *epistomion* no. 4 in the *Loci Incerti*, since we know nothing of its provenance, except that it came from Mylopótamos (see the section "Topography"; for the publication history of all the lamellae, see Graf and Johnston 2007:50–65; Graf forthcoming-1 and forthcoming-2; Edmonds forthcoming-1).

The seller of incised *epistomia* nos. 5 and 6 insisted that they were found "rolled up in small cylinders in graves near Eleutherna" (Verdelis 1953–1954:vol. II, 56), giving no other specific information.

The Inscriptions

Because of the difficulties they present, the *epistomia* have been photographed anew for the present study, and for each *epistomion* are published a black-and-white photograph and a drawing (drawings of nos. 1–3 and 7 by Federico Halbherr are quite accurate with only a few minor oversights; drawing of no. 4 by Margarita Guarducci, with minor inconsistencies; drawings of nos. 5–6 by Nikolaos Verdelis).

1 (B3; Figures 1a–b) Eleutherna, National Archaeological Museum, Συλλογὴ Ἀγγείων 632

The rectangular paper-thin gold lamella is preserved in excellent condition with few wrinkles. There are no creases to indicate any previous folding or rolling.

9

a.

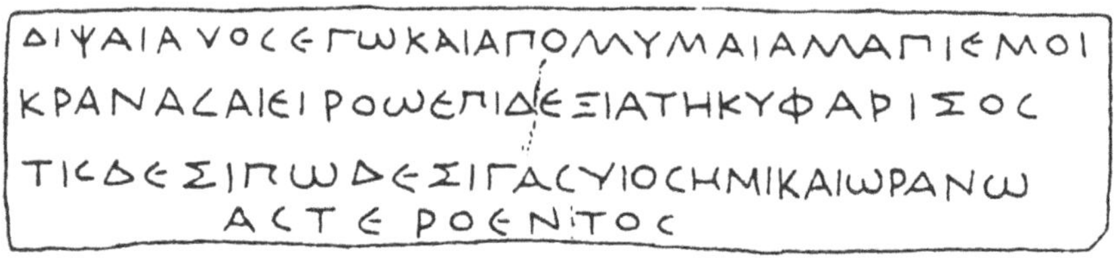

ΔΙΨΑΙΑ ΝΟⲤ ⲈΓⲰΚΑΙΑΠΟ ΛΥΜ ΑΙΑ Λ ΛΑΠΙ Ⲉ Μ ΟΙ
ΚΡΑΝΑⲤΑΙⲈ Ι ΡΟⲰ Ⲉ ΠΙⲆ Ⲉ ΞΙΑΤΗΚΥ Φ Α Ρ Ι Ⲭ Ο Ⲥ
ΤΙ ⲤⲆ Ⲉ ΞΙ Π Ⲱ Ⲃ Ⲉ ΞΙ ΓΑ Ⲥ ΥΙΟⲤΗΜΙΚΑΙ ⲰΡΑ Ν Ⲱ
ΑⲤΤ Ⲉ Ρ Ο Ⲉ Ν Τ Ο Ⲥ

b.

Figure 1a. Gold *epistomion* (no. 1), from Eleutherna. Athens, National Archaeological Museum, Συλλογή Ἀγγείων 632. H.0.01, W.0.056, Th. less than 0.0001, LH.0.0006–0.0015. III–I centuries BCE.

Figure 1b. Drawing of *epistomion* no. 1.

ΔΙΨΑΙΑΥΟⲤΕΓΩΚΑΙΑΠΟΛΛΥΜΑΙΑΛΛΑΠΙΕΜΟΙ
ΚΡΑΝΑⲤΑΙΕΙΡΟΩΕΠΙΔΕΞΙΑΤΗΚΥΦΑΡΙΖΟⲤ
ΤΙⲤΔΕΖΙΠΩΔΕΖΙΓΑⲤΥΙΟⲤΗΜΙΚΑΙΩΡΑΝΩ
ΑⲤΤΕΡΟΕΝΤΟⲤ

δίψαι αὖος ἐγὼ καὶ ἀπόλλυμαι· ἀλλὰ πιε<μ> μοι
κράνας αἰειρόω ἐπὶ δεξιά· τῇ, κυφάριζος.
3 τίς δ' ἐζί; πῶ δ' ἐζί; Γᾶς υἱός ἤμι καὶ Ὠρανῶ
ἀστερόεντος.

I am parched with thirst and I am perishing; but (give) me to drink from the ever-flowing spring to the right; there! the cypress. 'Who are you?' 'Where are you from?' I am the son of Earth and starry Sky.

Joubin 1893:121–124; Myres 1893:629; Comparetti 1910:37–40; Olivieri 1915:14–15 no. bA; IC II.xii [Eleutherna].31a (Guarducci); Zuntz 1971:362–364; Gallavotti 1978–79:356 notes 19–20; Colli 1981:4 [A 70a]; Cassio 1987:314–316; Cassio 1995:191–192; Riedweg 1998:397–398; Pugliese Carratelli 2001:78–79 no. IB1; Bernabé and Jiménez San Cristóbal 2001:265 no. 5a; Bernabé 2005:fr. 478; Graf and Johnston 2007:20–21 no. 10; Edmonds forthcoming-2.

The letters are carefully incised; the engraver tries to cover the entire surface of the lamella, respects word-divisions, and indents the last word in line four, making the text approximately centered.

Characteristic letter-shapes include the following: the alpha with a horizontal crossbar or a crossbar which leans in either direction; the rather wide eta with verticals straight or curving; the mu with leaning and sometimes curving verticals; the xi with a smaller middle horizontal stroke; the pi with straight or outward-curving verticals and with the right vertical smaller than the left; the upsilon either without a vertical or with a very tiny vertical; and the open, quasi-symmetrical omega. The sigma is either open or closed and is either lunate (C) or angular (<); the middle bar of the lunate or angular epsilon may be incised at some distance and extend well beyond the letter space; the shape Σ with quasi-lunate middle bars is used for -σσ-, which in nos. 4–6 below is engraved with the shape Z (for the shape Σ/Z = σσ in Crete see: *LSAG* 308 and Verdelis 1953–1954:59–60).

Line 1: δίψαι δ' αὖος Gallavotti trying to emend the hiatus, on account of the reading in no. 4 below. ΠΙΕΜΟΙ on the lamella; πιέμ μοι Comparetti; πιέ μοι Olivieri; πιê μοι Guarducci; πιêμ μ' ὄ(ν) (= οὖν) Gallavotti; πίε μοι Colli; πιέ<ν> μοι Cassio, Bernabé and Jiménez San Cristóbal, Bernabé, Graf and Johnston; πιέ<μ> μοι Zuntz, Pugliese Carratelli, Riedweg on account of no. 3 below. In this period one should expect πιῆν or πιεῖν (Bile 1988:239–242); the verb δότε should be understood as governing the infinitive (Cassio 1987, 1995), and ἀλλά as introducing "a break-off in the thought" and an appeal/exhortation with an impatient tone (Denniston 1950:13–15).

Line 2: ἐπιδέξια Gallavotti. ΤΗΚΥΦΑΡΙΣΟΣ on the lamella; τῆ(ι) Comparetti; τῆ<ι> Olivieri, Bernabé and Jiménez San Cristóbal, Bernabé; τῆ Guarducci; τῆ Zuntz, Gallavotti, Pugliese Carratelli, Riedweg; τῆ{ς}, Graf and Johnston. τῆ, the adverb of place, always with iota subscript in literary texts, may also be the old epic interjection τῆ (LSJ; I owe this idea to Kyriakos Tsantsanoglou).

Lines 2–3: κυφάριζος, ἐζί Gallavotti, Pugliese Carratelli; κυφάρισσος, ἐσί Comparetti (1910:38–39: for the sigma, the engraver used the shapes C and Σ interchangeably); κυφάρισος, ἐσί Olivieri, Guarducci (IC II.xii [Eleutherna].31a, p. 168: *littera sigma modo C modo Σ est*, but she later suggests that (p. 170), because in lamella no. 4 below the letter shape Z stands for -σσ-, perhaps we should understand the shape Σ as a relic of the archaic/classical *tsade* [*sampi*]); κυφάριΖος, ἐΖί Graf and Johnston; κυφάρισσος, ἐσσί Zuntz, Riedweg, Bernabé and Jiménez San Cristóbal, Bernabé.

2 (B4; Figures 2a–b) Eleutherna, National Archaeological Museum, Συλλογὴ Ἀγγείων 633

The rectangular, paper-thin gold lamella is preserved in excellent condition with minor wrinkles; at least two creases show that it was folded.

a.

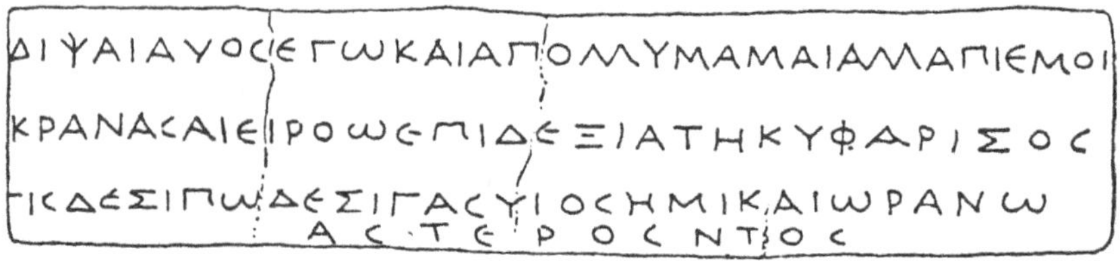

b.

Figure 2a. Gold *epistomion* (no. 2), from Eleutherna. Athens, National Archaeological Museum, Συλλογὴ Ἀγγείων 633. H.0.013, W.0.062, Th. less than 0.0001, LH.0.001–0.0015. III–I centuries BCE.

Figure 2b. Drawing of *epistomion* no. 2.

ΔΙΨΑΙΑΥΟΣΕΓΩΚΑΙΑΠΟΛΛΥΜΑΜΑΙΑΛΛΑΠΙΕΜΟΙ
ΚΡΑΝΑΣΑΙΕΙΡΟΩΕΠΙΔΕΞΙΑΤΗΚΥΦΑΡΙΣΟΣ
ΤΙΣΔΕΣΙΠΩΔΕΣΙΓΑΣΥΙΟΣΗΜΙΚΑΙΩΡΑΝΩ
ΑΣΤΕΡΟΣΝΤΟΣ

δίψαι αὖος ἐγὼ καὶ ἀπόλλυμα{μα}ι· ἀλλὰ πιε͂<μ> μοι
κράνας αἰειρόω ἐπὶ δεξιά· τῆ, κυφάριζος.
3   τίς δ' ἐζί; πῶ δ' ἐζί; Γᾶς υἱός ἠμι καὶ Ὠρανῶ
ἀστερό<ε>ντος.

I am parched with thirst and I am perishing; but (give) me to drink from the ever-flowing spring to the right; there! the cypress. 'Who are you?' 'Where are you from?' I am the son of Earth and starry Sky.

Myres 1893: 629; Comparetti 1910:37–40; Olivieri 1915:14–15 no. bB; IC II.xii [Eleutherna].31b (Guarducci); Zuntz 1971:362–364; Gallavotti 1978–79:356 notes 19–20; Colli 1981:4 [A 70b]; Cassio 1987:314–316; Cassio 1995:191–192; Riedweg 1998:397–398; Pugliese Carratelli 2001:80 no. IB2; Bernabé and Jiménez San Cristóbal 2001:266 no. 5b; Bernabé 2005:fr. 479; Graf and Johnston 2007:20–21 no. 11; Edmonds forthcoming-2.

The letters are carefully incised; the engraver covers the surface of the lamella, respects word-divisions, and indents the last word in line four in order to center the text.

For the letter-shapes, follow no. 1 above, with the following exceptions: the epsilon and sigma are lunate throughout, the verticals of the pi are of equal length, and the right half of the open omega is smaller than the left.

The text is identical to no. 1 above and the readings and corrections of previous editors are also the same.

Line 1: ΑΠΟΛΛΥΜΑΜΑΙΑΛΛΑΠΙΕΜΟΙ on the lamella.

Line 2: ΤΗΚΥΦΑΡΙΣΟΣ on the lamella.

Line 4: ΑΣΤΕΡΟΣΝΤΟΣ on the lamella.

3 (B5; Figures 3a–b) Eleutherna, National Archaeological Museum, Συλλογὴ Ἀγγείων 634

The rectangular paper-thin gold lamella is preserved in excellent condition, except for wrinkles and minor tears on top and bottom. At least two creases show that it was folded.

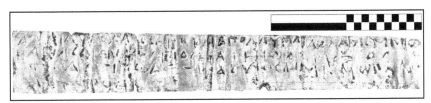

a.

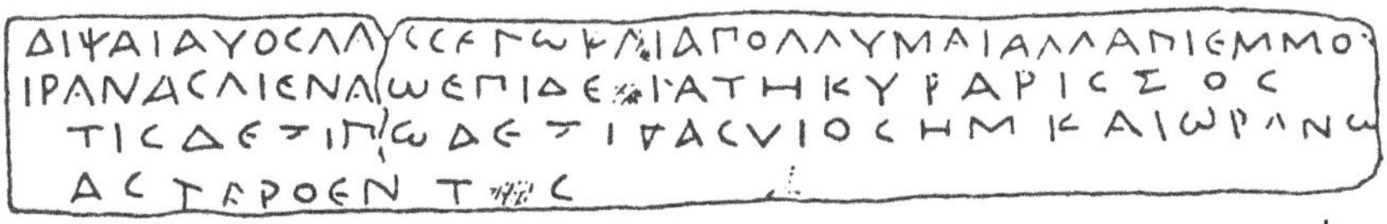

b.

Figure 3a. Gold *epistomion* (no. 3), from Eleutherna. Athens, National Archaeological Museum, Συλλογὴ Ἀγγείων 634. H.0.0075, W.0.054, Th. less than 0.0001, LH.0.0007–0.001. III–I centuries BCE.

Figure 3b. Drawing of *epistomion* no. 3.

ΔΙΨΑΙΑΥΟΣΑΑΥΟΣΕΓΩΚΑΙΑΠΟΛΛΥΜΑΙΑΛΛΑΠΙΕΜΜΟΥ
ΚΡΑΝΑΣΛΙΕΝΑΩΕΠΙΔΕ[.]ΙΑΤΗΚΥΦΑΡΙΣΣΟΣ
ΤΙΣΔΕΣΙΠΩΔΕΣΙΓΑΣΥΙΟΣΗΜΚΑΙΩΡΑΝΩ
ΑΣΤΕΡΟΕΝΤ[.]Σ

δίψαι αὖος {ααυοσ} ἐγὼ καὶ ἀπόλλυμαι· ἀλλὰ πιἐμ μου
κράνας <α>ἰενάω ἐπὶ δε[ξ]ιά· τῇ, κυφάρισζος.
3   τίς δ' ἐζί; πῶ δ' ἐζί; Γᾶς υἱός ἠμ<ι> καὶ 'Ωρανῶ
ἀστερόεντ[ο]ς.

I am parched with thirst and I am perishing; but (give) me to drink
from the ever-flowing spring to the right; there! the cypress.
'Who are you?' 'Where are you from?' I am the son of Earth
and starry Sky.

Myres 1893:629; Comparetti 1910:37–40; Olivieri 1915:14–15 no. bC; IC
II.xii [Eleutherna].31c (Guarducci); Zuntz 1971:362–364; Gallavotti 1978–79:356
notes 19–20; Colli 1981:4 [A 70c]; Cassio 1987:314–316; Cassio 1995:191–192;
Riedweg 1998:397–398; Pugliese Carratelli 2001:81 no. IB3; Bernabé and
Jiménez San Cristóbal 2001:265–266 no. 5c; Bernabé 2005:fr. 480; Graf and
Johnston 2007:22–23 no. 12; Edmonds forthcoming-2.

The lettering is sloppy and the engraver has made a few mistakes or omissions. He tries to cover the surface of the lamella, respects word-divisions, and
indents lines three and four by two-letter spaces.

For the letter-shapes, follow no. 1 above, with the following exceptions:
the middle bar of the alpha (in addition to being either horizontal or leaning)
is very small or leans to the left forming an angle; the mu's verticals are asymmetrical; the pi's horizontal sometimes slants downward; the open omega is
half the height of the other letters.

The text is identical to no. 1 above and the readings and corrections of
previous editors are also the same.

Line 1: ΑΥΟΣΑΑΥΟΣΕΓΩ on the lamella; of the upsilon the upper right
slanting and the tip of the vertical are visible; αὖος ἄλ[ι]ος ἐγὼ Comparetti;
αὖος [ἄλ.σσ] ἐγὼ Olivieri; {αὖος} δ' αὖος ἐγὼ Guarducci; αὖος {ΛΑΥΣΣ} ἐγὼ
Zuntz, Pugliese Carratelli, Riedweg, Bernabé and Jiménez San Cristóbal,
Bernabé; αὖος {λα.ος} Graf and Johnston. ΠΙΕΜΜΟΥ on the lamella; of the last
upsilon the upper left slanting remains.

Line 2: ΚΡΑΝΑΣΛΙΕΝΑΩ on the lamella; of the kappa the vertical and
a trace of the beginning of its middle lunate strokes are visible; <κ>ράνας

<α>ἰενάω Guarducci, Zuntz, Pugliese Carratelli, Riedweg, Bernabé and Jiménez San Cristóbal, Bernabé. ΕΠΙΔΕ[.]ΙΑ on the lamella; ἐπὶ δε<ξ>ιὰ Olivieri; ἐπὶ δε[ξ]ιὰ Guarducci, and all editors; ἐπιδέξια Gallavotti.

Line 3: ΗΜΚΑΙ on the lamella. Guarducci's (p. 169) suggestion that a ligature of Ι and Κ may have been intended in Κ, is rather unlikely, given the mistakes and/or omissions in lines 1–2.

4 (B6; Figures 4a–b) Eleutherna (Mylopotamos), Herakleion Archaeological Museum, Χρυσά 639.

The paper-thin gold lamella in the shape of the mouth is preserved in excellent condition, except for minor tears at the edges and wrinkles. At least two creases show that it was folded.

a.

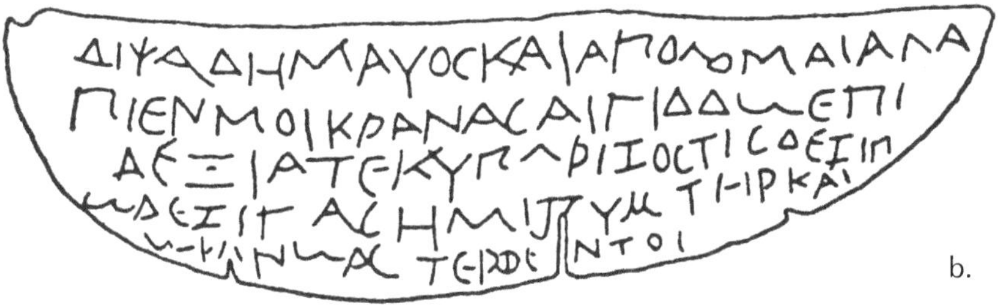

b.

Figure 4a. Gold *epistomion* (no. 4), from Eleutherna/Mylopótamos. Herakleion, Archaeological Museum, Χρυσά 639. H.0.012, W.0.045, Th. less than 0.0001, LH.0.001–0.002. III–I centuries BCE.

Figure 4b. Drawing of *epistomion* no. 4.

ΔΙΨΑΔΗΜΑΥΟΣΚΑΙΑΠΟΛΟΜΑΙΑΛΑ
ΠΙΕΝΜΟΙΚΡΑΝΑΣΑΙΓΙΔΔΩΕΠΙ
ΔΕΞΙΑΤΕΚΥΠΛΡΙΖΟΣΤΙΣΔΕΞΙΠ
ΩΔΕΖΙΓΑΣΗΜΙΓΥΑΤΗΡΚΑΙ
ΩΡΑΝΩΑΣΤΕΡΟΕΝΤΟΣ

δίψᾳ δ' ἠμ' αὖος καὶ ἀπόλ<λ>ομαι· ἀλ<λ>ὰ
πιὲν μοι κράνας ΑΙΓΙΔΔΩ ἐπὶ
3 δεξιά· τῆ, κυπ<ά>ριζος. τίς δ' ἐζί; π-
 ῶ δ' ἐζί; Γᾶς ἠμι ΓΥΑΤΗΡ καὶ
 Ὠρανῶ ἀστερόεντος.

I am parched with thirst and I am perishing; but (give) me to drink
from the ΑΙΓΙΔΔΩ spring to the right; there! the cypress.
'Who are you?' 'Where are you from?' I am of Earth, ΓΥΑΤΗΡ, and
starry Sky.

IC II.xxx [Loci Incerti].4; Zuntz 1971:362–364; Gallavotti 1978–79:356 notes
19–20; Colli 1981:4 [A 70d]; Cassio 1987:314–316; Cassio 1995:191–192; Riedweg
1998:397–398; Pugliese Carratelli 2001:82–83 no. IB4; Bernabé and Jiménez San
Cristóbal 2001:266 no. 5d; Bernabé 2005:fr. 481; Graf and Johnston 2007:26–27
no. 16; Edmonds forthcoming-2.

The lettering is sloppy and careless; some of the letters' strokes cross-
over or are joined to the next character, giving the impression of handwritten
style. There are a few mistakes or omissions. The engraver is trying to cover
the surface of the lamella and indents lines 3 and 5 by one letter-space, but he
does not respect word-divisions (lines 3–4 π|ῶ).

For the letter-shapes, follow no. 1 above, with the following exceptions:
for -σσ-, instead of the shape Σ, the shape Z is employed with a vertical middle
bar (see no. 1 above); of the alpha either one of the slanting strokes are overex-
tended, and the crossbar may be horizontal, leaning to the left or to the right,
or curvilinear; epsilons and sigmas are lunate throughout; the mu's verticals
are asymmetrical; the horizontal of the pi sometimes slants downward; the
upsilon has a vertical throughout; and the open omega is very short with only
a small curve for its right half.

The text is similar to no. 1 above and the readings and corrections of
previous editors are also the same; see also no. 9 below, and the sections "The
Cretan Texts in the Context of a Ritual and a *Hieros Logos*" and "The Cretan
Context of the Cretan *Epistomia*."

Line 1: δίψα<ι> Guarducci, Zuntz, Riedweg, Pugliese Carratelli, Bernabé
and Jiménez San Cristóbal, Bernabé, Graf and Johnston. ΑΠΟΛΟΜΑΙΑΛΑ on the
lamella, corrected by Guarducci; ἀπόλ<λ>υμαι· ἀλ<λ>ὰ Bernabé and Jiménez
San Cristóbal, Bernabé.

Line 2: ΑΙΓΙΔΔΩ on the lamella; αἰ<ε>ι<ρό>ω Guarducci, Zuntz, Pugliese
Carratelli, Riedweg, Bernabé and Jiménez San Cristóbal. Gallavotti (356 note

20): "non sarà αἰ<ε>ι<ρό>ω, ma piuttosto αἰ(ε)ιγάω, se la grafia non rispecchia addirittura un originario Ἀίδαο (in tal caso il verso sarebbe <u>enh</u>+<u>reiz</u>)." On account of the reading in no. 9 below and of the similarities between these two *epistomia*, I prefer not to emend the text, despite the engraver's sloppiness; the letters on the lamella are clear and it is not unlikely that some other epithet for the spring, so far unknown, may have been intended; if emendation be mandatory, then αἰγί{δ}ρω is far more preferable (proposed by Verbruggen 1981:90–91).

Line 4: ΗΜΙΓΥΑΤΗΡ on the lamella (Guarducci's drawing is not very accurate); of the dotted letters, the gamma could conceivably be a pi and the alpha could conceivably be an eta. The reading is a *locus desperatus* and a number of emendations have been proposed: ἦμι <θ>υ<γ>άτηρ Guarducci, Bernabé and Jiménez San Cristóbal, Bernabé, Graf and Johnston; ἦμι †τυμτηρ Zuntz; ἦμι γυήτηρ Gallavotti (356 note 20: "Sospetto uno scambio o un incrocio con *κυητήρ, nel senso di "concezione" (cf. κυήτωρ, κυητέριος); forse è un termine iniziatico, che nelle altre redazioni è stato saostittuto con υἱός oppure πάϊς)"; ἦμι γ<ενε>τὴρ (= γενέτης 'figlio'?) Pugliese Carratelli; ἦμι †γυητηρ† Riedweg. On the basis of the new text from Sfakaki, no. 9 below line 5 where: ἠμ{ο}ὶ μάτηρ (sic!) is clearly engraved on the *epistomion*, perhaps the reading: Γᾶς ἦμι, <μ>άτηρ, καὶ Ὠρανῶ ἀστερόεντος, was intended, with <μ>άτηρ understood as a vocative addressing Persephone who is asking the question (see further the sections "The Cretan Texts in the Context of a Ritual and a *Hieros Logos*" and "The Cretan Context of the Cretan *Epistomia*").

5 (B7; Figures 5a–b) Eleutherna, National Archaeological Museum, Collection Hélène Stathatos 292

The rectangular paper-thin gold lamella is preserved in excellent condition, except for minor tears on top and bottom. Many creases indicate that it was rolled up.

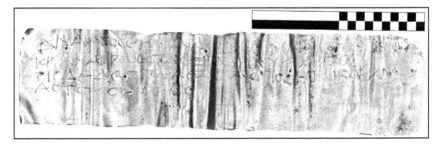

a.

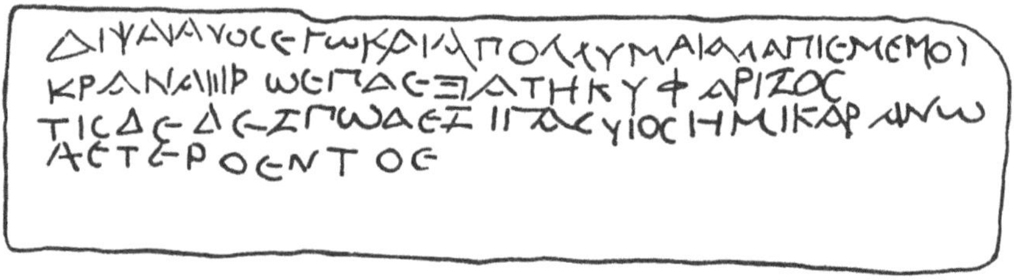

b.

Figure 5a. Gold *epistomion* (no. 5), from Eleutherna. Athens, National Archaeological Museum, Collection Hélène Stathatos 292. H.0.012, W.0.048, Th. Less than 0.0001, LH.0.001–0.002. III–I centuries BCE.

Figure 5b. Drawing of *epistomion* no. 5.

ΔΙΨΑΙΑΥΟΣΕΓΩΚΑΙΑΠΟΛΛΥΜΑΙΑΛΑΠΙΕΜΕΜΟΙ
ΚΡΑΝΑΙΙΙΡΩΕΠΔΕΞΙΑΤΗΚΥΦΑΡΙΖΟΣ
ΤΙΣΔΕΔΕΖΠΩΔΕΖΙΓΑΣΥΙΟΣΗΜΙΚΑΡΑΝΩ
ΑΣΤΕΡΟΕΝΤΟΣ

δίψαι αὖος ἐγὼ καὶ ἀπόλλυμαι· ἀλ<λ>ὰ πιὲμ {ε} μοι
κράνα<ς α>ὶ<ε>ιρ<ό>ω ἐπ<ὶ> δεξιά· τῆ, κυφάριζος.
3   τίς δ' ἐ{δε}ζ<ί>; πῶ δ' ἐζί; Γᾶς υἱός ἠμι κα<ὶ> Ὠ>ρανῶ
ἀστερόεντος.

I am parched with thirst and I am perishing; but (give) me to drink
from the ever-flowing spring to the right; there! the cypress.
'Who are you?' 'Where are you from?' I am the son of Earth
and starry Sky.

Verdelis 1953–1954:56–57 no. A, 59–60 (= Verdelis 1963:256–257 no. 173); Zuntz 1971:362–4; Gallavotti 1978–79:356 notes 19–20; Colli 1981: 4 [A 70e]; Cassio 1987:314–316; Cassio 1995:191–192; Riedweg 1998:397–398; Pugliese Carratelli 2001:84 no. IB5; Bernabé and Jiménez San Cristóbal 2001:266–267 no. 5e; Bernabé 2005:fr. 482; Graf and Johnston 2007:22–23 no. 13; Edmonds forthcoming-2.

The lettering is careful and the text covers only the upper two-thirds of the lamella. The engraver has made a few mistakes or omissions and respects word-divisions.

For the letter-shapes, follow no. 1 above, with the following exceptions: Z is incised with the vertical slanting to the left, instead of the shape Σ for -σσ- (see nos. 1, 4 above and no. 6 below); alpha's middle bar may also be curved, almost broken; the epsilon and sigma are lunate throughout; the verticals of the pi may also be of equal length; and the open omega is asymmetrical.

The text is identical to no. 1 above and the readings and corrections of previous editors are also the same.

Line 1: ΑΛΑΠΙΕΜΕΜΟΙ on the lamella; ἀλ<λ>ὰ πιêμ {ε} μοι Verdelis; πιêμ μ' ô(ν) (= οὖν) Gallavotti; ἀλλὰ πιέμ μοι Pugliese Carratelli, Riedweg; ἀλ<λ>ὰ πιέν {ε} μοι Cassio, Bernabé and Jiménez San Cristóbal, Bernabé.

Line 2: ΚΡΑΝΑΙΙΙΡΩΕΠΔΕΞΙΑΤΗ on the lamella; κράνα<ς αἰει>ρ<ό>ω ἐπ<ὶ> δεξιὰ τῆ<ι> Verdelis; κράνα<ς α>ἰ<ε>ιρ<ό>ω ἐπ<ὶ> δεξιὰ τῆ Pugliese Carratelli, Riedweg, Graf and Johnston; κράνας <α>ἰ<ε>ιρ<ό>ω ἐπ<ὶ> δεξιὰ τῆ<ι> Bernabé and Jiménez San Cristóbal, Bernabé.

Line 3: ΤΙΣΔΕΔΕΖΠΩ on the lamella; τίς <δέ> δ' ἐζ(ί) Verdelis; τίς δ' ἐζ<ί> Pugliese Carratelli; τίς δ' {εδ} ἐσσ<ί> Bernabé and Jiménez San Cristóbal, Bernabé, Graf and Johnston. ΚΑΡΑΝΩ on the lamella; κάρανῶ Verdelis; κα<ὶ 'Ω>ρανῶ Zuntz (363 note 6: ΚΑΡΑΝΩ in S[1] is hardly indicative of a krasis in pronouncing καὶ ὠρ-, which would spoil the dactylic rhythm; more likely the engraver skipped two letters), Pugliese Carratelli, Bernabé and Jiménez San Cristóbal, Bernabé; καὶ <'Ω>ρανῶ Graf and Johnston.

6 (B8; Figures 6a–b) Eleutherna, National Archaeological Museum, Collection Hélène Stathatos 293

The rectangular paper-thin gold lamella is in two joining pieces and is pre-served in excellent condition, except for minor tears and wrinkles. Many creases indicate that it was rolled-up.

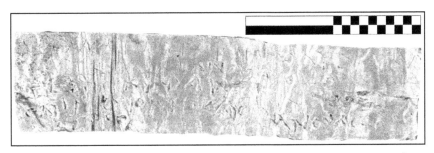

a.

b.

Figure 6a . Gold *epistomion* (no. 6), from Eleutherna. Athens, National Archaeological Museum, Collection Hélène Stathatos 293. H.0.012, W.0.048, Th. less than 0.0001, LH.0.001–0.002. III–I centuries BCE.

Figure 6b. Drawing of *epistomion* no. 6.

ΔΙΨΑΑΑΥΟΣΕΓΩΚΑΙΑΠΟΛΥΜΑΙΑΛ
ΛΑΠΕΜΜΟΚΡΑΝΑΣΑΙΕΝΑΩΕΠΙΔ
ΞΙΑΤΗΚΥΦΑΡΙΖΟΣΤΙΣΔΕΖΙΠΩ
ΔΖΙΓΑΣΥΙΟΣΙΜΙΚΑΙΩΡΑΝΩΑΣΤΕΡΟ
ΕΝΤΟΣΣ

δίψᾳ {α} αὗος ἐγὼ καὶ ἀπόλ<λ>υμαι· ἀλλὰ π<ι>ἐμ μο<ι> κράνας αἰενάω ἐπὶ δ-
3   <ε>ξιά· τῇ, κυφάριζος. τίς δ' ἐζί; πῶ
    δ' <ἐ>ζί; Γᾶς υἱός ἰμι καὶ Ὠρανῶ ἀστερό-
    εντος {σ}.

I am parched with thirst and I am perishing; but (give) me to drink
from the ever-flowing spring to the right; there! the cypress.
'Who are you?' 'Where are you from?' I am the son of Earth
and starry Sky.

Verdelis 1953–1954:58–60 no. B (= Verdelis 1963:257–258 no. 174); Zuntz 1971:362–4; Gallavotti 1978–79:356 notes 19–20; Colli 1981: 4 [A 70f]; Cassio 1987:314–316; Cassio 1995:191–192; Riedweg 1998:397–398; Pugliese Carratelli 2001:85 no. IB6; Bernabé and Jiménez San Cristóbal 2001:266–267 no. 5f; Bernabé 2005:fr. 483; Graf and Johnston 2007:24–25 no. 14; Edmonds forthcoming-2.

The lettering is sloppy and the lines are not straight; some of the letters' strokes cross over or are joined to the next character, giving the impression of handwritten style. There are a few mistakes or omissions. The engraver covers the surface of the lamella, but does not seem to respect word-divisions (line 2–3). In the beginning of lines 3 and 4, one letter space appears to have been left vacant.

For the letter-shapes follow no. 1 above, with the following exceptions: Z is incised with the vertical slanting to the left, instead of the shape Σ for -σσ- (see nos. 1, 4, and 5 above); the alpha may also be like a delta and its middle bar may be horizontal, lunate, broken, or leftward or rightward leaning (forming an angle); the epsilon and sigma are lunate throughout; the mu's right half is considerably smaller; the pi's horizontal is sometimes curved; the upsilon has a vertical throughout; and the open omega sometimes has a smaller right half.

The text is identical to no. 1 above and the readings and corrections of previous editors are also the same.

Line 1: ΔΙΨΑΑΑΥΟΣ on the lamella; δίψα<ι> δ᾽ αὖος Verdelis, Gallavotti; δίψα<ι> αὖος Pugliese Carratelli, Riedweg; δίψα<ι> {α} αὖος Bernabé and Jiménez San Cristóbal, Bernabé, Graf and Johnston. ΑΠΟΛΥΜΑΙ on the lamella; ἀπόλ<λ>υμαι Verdelis, Bernabé and Jiménez San Cristóbal, Bernabé, Graf and Johnston; ἀπόλλυμαι Pugliese Carratelli, Riedweg.

Line 2: ΠΕΜΜΟΚΡΑΝΑΣΑΙΕΝΑΩΕΠΙΔ on the lamella; there is no space after the final delta, where most editors add the missing epsilon; but there seems to be one letter-space in the beginning of line 3 where the epsilon could have been incised, although this would violate word-division. π<ι>ὲμ μο<ι> κράνας ἀενάω ἐπὶ δ<ε>|ξιὰ Verdelis; πιὲμ μ᾽ ὂ(ν) (= οὖν) κράνας ἀενάω ἐπιδέξια Gallavotti; π<ι>έμ μο<ι> κράνας αἰενάω ἐπὶ δ<ε>|ξιὰ Pugliese Carratelli, Riedweg, Graf and Johnston; π<ι>έγ μο<ι> κράνας αἰενάω ἐπὶ δ<ε>|ξιά Cassio, Bernabé and Jiménez San Cristóbal, Bernabé.

Line 4: ΔΖΙΓΑΣΥΙΟΣΙΜΙ on the lamella; on Verdelis' drawing, what appears as sigma after the alpha is only a crease; δ᾽ <ἐ>ζί; Γᾶς {σ} υἱός ἱμι Verdelis; δ᾽ <ἐ>ζί; Γᾶς υἱός <ἠ>μι Pugliese Carratelli, Graf and Johnston; δ᾽ <ἐ>σσί; Γᾶς υἱός ἦμι Bernabé and Jiménez San Cristóbal, Bernabé.

Line 5: ΕΝΤΟΣΣ on the lamella; -εντος {σ} Verdelis; -εντος Pugliese Carratelli, Graf and Johnston; -εντο{σ}ς Bernabé and Jiménez San Cristóbal, Bernabé.

7 (E2; Figures 7a–b) Eleutherna, National Archaeological Museum, Συλλογὴ Ἀγγείων 635

The left third of the rectangular paper-thin gold lamella is missing. The lamella is otherwise preserved in excellent condition, except for minor tears on top and bottom and wrinkles. There are no creases to indicate any previous folding or rolling.

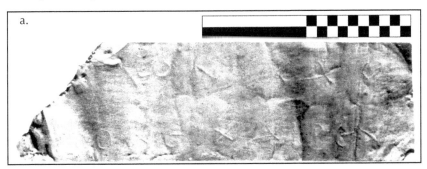

b.

Figure 7a. Gold *epistomion* (no. 7), from Eleutherna. Athens, National Archaeological Museum, Συλλογὴ Ἀγγείων 635. H.0.011, W.0.04, Th. less than 0.0001, LH.0.0015–0.002. III–I centuries BCE.

Figure 7b. Drawing of *epistomion* no. 7.

ΤΩΝΙΚΑΙΦ
ΟΠΟΝΕΙΧΑΙΡΕΝ

[Πλού]τωνι καὶ Φ-
[ερσ]οπόνει χαίρεν.

Greetings to Plouton and Persephone.

Myres 1893:629; Comparetti 1910:40–41; Vogliano 1913:269; Olivieri 1915:17–18; IC II.xii [Eleutherna].31bis; Zuntz 1971:384; Gallavotti 1988:28–31; Riedweg 1998:391; Pugliese Carratelli 2001:121–122; Bernabé and Jiménez San Cristóbal 2001:278–279 no. 15; Riedweg 2002; Bernabé 2005:fr. 495; Graf and Johnston 2007:24–25 no. 15; Edmonds forthcoming-2.

The lettering is very careful. The text is centered, as can be surmised from the right edge, where at least one letter-space is left vacant, and the engraver does not respect word-divisions.

For the symmetrical letter-shapes, follow no. 1 above, with the following exceptions: the alpha's middle bar is horizontal or slanting downward from the right; the epsilon is lunate; the pi's right vertical is smaller than the left and curves outwards.

The restoration is Guarducci's, and it is based on the dedicatory inscription from Lappa (IC II.xvi.10, Figure 8): Μεσσωμήδης | [Ἀ]ντιόχω θεᾷ Φ|[ε]-ρσοπόνῃ εὐχή[ν]. Comparetti reluctantly included the lamella in his corpus and suggested to restore two names ([Ἀρίσ]τωνι, [Κρί]τωνι, [Πλά]τωνι vel sim., and Φ[ιλ]οπόνης, Φ[ιλ]οκάλης vel sim.), who would have been ὁμόταφοι—a probable assumption. On the basis of the owner's information that the lamella was found in the same grave as nos. 1–3 above, Comparetti also suggested that the verb χαίρεν is to be understood in the same way as it is on the lamella from Thourioi (A4 line 6: χαῖρ<ε>, χαῖρε· δεξιὰν ὁδοιπόρ<ει>), as a salutation to the *mystai*. Vogliano (1913:269) suspected the names Plouton and Persephone and made restorations accordingly: [παρὰ Πλού]τωνι καὶ Φ|[ερσεφόναι ἀπ]οπόνει χαίρεν. Olivieri included the text in his commentary on χαῖρε on the lamella from Thourioi.

Figure 8. Inscription from Lappa (Argyroupolis): vow to Persephone. Rethymno, Archaeological Museum Ἐ(πιγραφές) 63.

8 (E5; Figures 9a–b) Sfakaki, Rethymno Archaeological Museum, Μ(ετάλλινα) 896, on display

Archaeological Context and Chronology by Irene Gavrilaki

The rescue excavations, undertaken by the 25th Ephorate of Prehistoric and Classical Antiquities from December 1988 to June 1989, revealed part of a Roman cemetery on the property of Markos Polioudakis in the Sfakaki region, approximately 8 km E of Rethymno and in close proximity to the better-known archaeological sites of Stavromenos and Chamalevri (Gavrilaki-Nikoloudaki 1988, Gavrilaki 1989 and 1991–1993, and the section "Topography"). The cemetery comprised twenty-six unlooted cist-graves and pit-graves and one pithos-burial, all of which were cut into a strip of land approximately 7 m wide in an E-W direction, only approximately 30 m from the shore. Cist-grave 1, which is well-preserved, was constructed out of rectangular slabs that had been used once before (as one of the covering slabs indicates). The skeleton was found in an extended supine position with the head to the E and leaning to the N towards the sea. Chryssoula Bourbou's study of the remains has shown that the deceased was a young adult 25–35 years old, and probably male. In addition to the *epistomion*, the few other grave-goods, gathered in the W-SW part of Cist-grave 1, consisted of: a small clay prochous (Π[ήλινα] 5198), a small bronze prochous (Μ[ετάλλινα] 938), a clay unguentarium (Π[ήλινα] 6624) and an aryballos-shaped lekythion (Π[ήλινα] 22561), two glass phialae (Ὑ[άλινα] 120, 217), a bronze strigil (Μ[ετάλλινα] 919), an obsidian flake (Λ[ίθινα] 685), and a bronze coin found on the skeleton's chest (Ν[ομίσματα] 665). The bronze coin, discovered on the skeleton's chest and studied by Kleanthis Sidiropoulos, is a diobolon of Augustus issued by the Alexandria mint in 30–28 BCE. It is a rare issue, the numismatic epilogue of the Ptolemies, minted immediately after the formal incorporation of Egypt into the Roman Empire. The appearance of this coin in Crete is even more rare, and all the more remarkable. Its state of preservation indicates that it was used for a few decades before it was placed in this grave. Judging from this coin, the other grave-goods, and the typology of the cemetery's graves, we can safely date Cist-grave 1 between the last quarter of the first century BCE and the first four decades of the first century CE.

The Inscription

The inscribed gold lamella, in the shape of the mouth, was discovered at the base of the skull. Perhaps its position on the lips of the deceased and its subsequent slide have caused the minor damages and the numerous wrinkles on the surface and at the edges of the lamella, especially at its left edge where the upper part is missing. This damage could also be due in part to earth falling inside the grave (drawing by Amanda Kelly).

a.

Figure 9a. Gold *epistomion* (no. 8), from Sfakaki. Rethymno, Archaeological Museum, Μ(ετάλλινα) 896. H.0.012 (left)–0.018 (center), W.0.075, Th. less than 0.0001, LH.0.002–0.004, Weight 0.4 g. 25 BCE–40 CE.

Figure 9b (facing page). Drawing of *epistomion* no. 8.

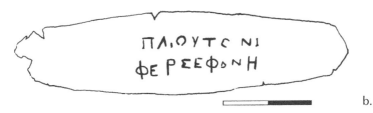

b.

ΠΛΟΥΤΩΝΙ ...
ΦΕΡΣΕΦΟΝΗ

Πλούτωνι ...
Φερσεφόνη.

(Greetings) to Plouton and Persephone.

Gavrilaki and Tzifopoulos 1998:343–355; SEG 46.1318; SEG 48.1227; EBGR 1998.89; Bernabé and Jiménez San Cristóbal 2001:279–280 no. 16l; Riedweg 2002; Bernabé 2005:fr. 494; Graf and Johnston 2007:26–27 no. 17; Edmonds forthcoming-2.

The letters are carefully engraved, although they appear pressed. The letters do not follow a straight line: in line 1 the pi and lambda lean to the left, and in line 2 the first two letters are cut considerably lower than the rest, which are aligned with the upper part of the rho. In both lines, there is a vacant area (the size of half a letter-space) between the second and third letters.

For the letter-shapes, follow no. 1 above, with the following exceptions: the epsilon is rectangular, the sigma has four bars, and the pi has verticals of equal length.

The names of the two deities appear to have been inscribed symmetrically in the middle part of the lamella (see no. 7 above). After the iota in line 1, it is very difficult to determine whether the traces are letter-strokes of the conjunction καί, or simply creases.

9 (B12; Figures 10a–b) Sfakaki, Rethymno Archaeological Museum, Μ(εtάλλινα) 2891, on display.

Archaeological Context and Chronology by Stella Kalogeraki and Niki Tsatsaki

From 1995 to 1996, a rescue excavation was carried out by the 25th Ephorate of Prehistoric and Classical Antiquities on the property of Michalis Pyrgaroussis, a plot to the east of and in close proximity to the property of Markos Polioudakis (no. 8 above). The excavation revealed one open burial and 29 cist- and tile-graves belonging to the same cemetery. The poorly-preserved Grave I is probably a tile-grave, as its construction is analogous to the other graves of this type. The grave-goods include: 32 clay unguentaria found in the middle and western parts of the grave; fragments of glass only in the western part; a bronze mirror in the eastern part; small bronze and gilt fragments, and the incised gold *epistomion*. The head of the deceased would normally lie in the eastern part of the grave as well, although no skeletal remains were recovered. The position inside the grave of these few grave-goods is, in all probability, not the original one, as the grave's condition indicates that it was disturbed. The only guidance we have in dating Grave I are the types of the unguentaria, the latest of which were in use in the second and perhaps early first centuries BCE.

The Inscription

The oblong gold lamella is preserved intact except for minor wrinkles and creases, caused no doubt by the grave's disturbance. No creases indicate that it had been folded or rolled up (drawing by Katerina Kaklamanou).

a.

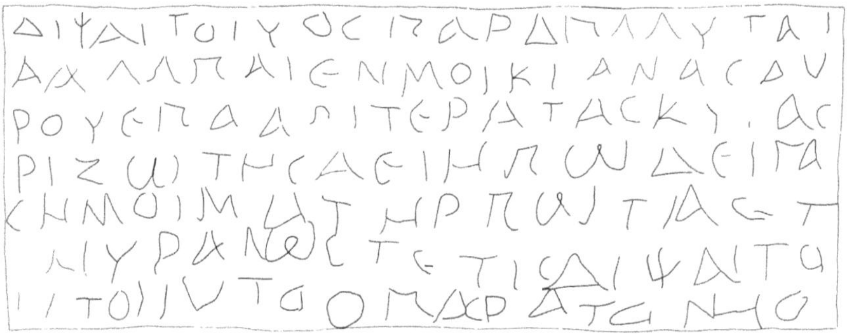

b.

Figure 10a. Gold *epistomion* (no. 9), from Sfakaki. Rethymno, Archaeological Museum, Μ(ετάλλινα) 2891. H.0.013, W.0.036, Th. less than 0.001, LH.0.001–0.002. II – early I centuries BCE

Figure 10b. Drawing of *epistomion* no. 9.

ΔΙΨΑΙΤΟΙΥΟΣΠΑΡΔΠΛΛΥΤΑΙ
ΑΛΛΛΠΑΙΕΝΜΟΙΚΡΑΝΑΣΑΥ
3 ΡΟΥΕΠΑΑΡΙΤΕΡΑΤΑΣΚΥΦΑΣ
ΡΙΖΩΤΗΣΔΕΙΗΠΩΔΕΙΓΑ
ΣΗΜΟΙΜΑΤΗΡΠΩΤΙΔΕΤ
6 .ΛΙΥΡΑΝΩΣΤΕΤΙΣΔΙΨΑΙΤΟ
ΙΛΤΟΙΙΥΤΟΟΠΑΣΡΑΤΑΝΗΟ.

δίψαι τοι <α>ῦος. παρ<α>π<ό>λλυται.
ἀλλ<ὰ> π{α}ιὲν μοι κράνας <Σ?>αύ-
3 ρου ἐπ’ ἀ{α}ρι<σ>τερὰ τᾶς κυφα{σ}-
ρίζω. τ<ί>ς δ’ εἶ ἢ πῶ δ’ εἶ; Γᾶ
ς ἡμ{ο}ί, μάτηρ· πῶ; τί; ΔΕΤ
6 [κ]αὶ <Ο>ὐρανῶ <ἀ>στε<ρόεντος>. τίς; δίψαι το-
ι ΛΤΟΙΙΥΤΟΟΠΑΣΡΑΤΑΝΗΟ.

Because of thirst you are (or surely he is/I am) parched. S/he is
perishing.
But (give) me to drink from the spring of <S>auros(?)
to the left of the cypress. 'Who are you?' 'Where are you from?'
Of Earth I am, mother. From where? And what . . .
And the (starry) Sky. Who (are you)? (Are) you thirsty?

. . . .

Papadopoulou 2000–01:289 (brief preliminary report of the rescue excavations); Bernabé 2005:fr. 484a (preliminary text); Graf and Johnston 2007:28–29
no. 18 (preliminary text); Edmonds forthcoming-2.

The lettering is very sloppy and jumbled, similar to that of nos. 3, 4, and 6
above. The engraver covers the surface of the lamella, does not respect word-
divisions in lines 4–5, and has made a few mistakes and omissions. The letters
from the second half of line 3 onwards grow increasingly larger. In line 7, the
lower parts of some of the letters give the impression that they have been cut,
almost as if with scissors, in the wrong place.

For the letter-shapes, follow no. 1 above, with the following exceptions:
the alpha's crossbar is horizontal or slanting to the left and forming an angle
(sometimes in the shape of delta); the vertical of the zeta slants to the left and
its horizontals curve; the pi's horizontal is also slanting to the right and the
right vertical is smaller than or equal in length to the left; the open omega
is tall and wide, either symmetrical or asymmetrical (with a narrower left or
right half).

The text is similar to nos. 1–6 above, particularly no. 4 (see further the sections "The Cretan Texts in the Context of a Ritual" and "The Cretan Context of the Cretan *Epistomia*").

Line 1: ΔΙΨΑΙΤΟΙΥΟΣΠΑΡΔΠΛΛΥΤΑΙ on the lamella. The first person pronoun is missing; instead of the conjunction καὶ and the verb in the first person singular, the verb is in the third person singular (παρ<α>π<ό>λυται). In no. 4 above, after δίψαι the particle δὲ is employed to eliminate the hiatus, and here τοι may be the particle: "let me tell you, look you, surely" (LSJ); I understand it, however, as the second person dative and punctuate after <α>ῦος, creating two sentences addressed to different audiences and perhaps uttered by different speakers.

Line 2–3: ΑΛΛΛΠΑΙΕΝΜΟΙΚΡΑΝΑΣΑΥ|ΡΟΥ on the lamella. For π{α}ιὲν see the readings in nos. 1–3 and 5–6 above, and in particular no. 4. Equally possible readings are: κράνας <Σ>αύρου or κράνας Αὔρου; in the other Cretan texts the spring's epithets are ἀείροος/ἀέναος, but in no. 4 above ΑΙΓΙΔΔΩ (perhaps to be emended to αἰγί{δ}ρω). If the text should conform to the one in nos. 1–3 and 5–6, then we may correct ΑΥ|ΡΟΥ to ἀ<ει>|ρ<ό>ου, the upsilon being another example of itacism (as in lines 4 and 5; so Bernabé, and Graf and Johnston). The genitive ending in ΟΥ, however, is inexplicable (compare lines 3–4, the genitive ending in Ω: κυφαρίζω). For κράνας <Σ>αύρου see Theophrastos, *Historia plantarum* 3.3.4: ἐν Κρήτῃ δὲ καὶ αἴγειροι κάρπιμοι πλείους εἰσί· μία μὲν ἐν τῷ στομίῳ τοῦ ἄντρου τοῦ ἐν τῇ Ἴδῃ, ἐν ᾧ τὰ ἀναθήματα ἀνάκειται, ἄλλη δὲ μικρὰ πλησίον· ἀπωτέρω δὲ μάλιστα δώδεκα σταδίους περί τινα κρήνην Σαύρου καλουμένην πολλαί. εἰσὶ δὲ καὶ ἐν τῷ πλησίον ὄρει τῆς Ἴδης ἐν τῷ Κινδρίῳ καλουμένῳ καὶ περὶ Πραισίαν δὲ ἐν τοῖς ὄρεσιν (I owe this reference to Angelos Chaniotis). Sauros is attested in the Peloponnese as a name of a ridge at the borders between Elis and Arcadia, where, as the story is recorded by Pausanias, a local criminal Sauros was pestering travellers and locals until Herakles killed him and buried him there (6.21.3–4: διαβάντων [δὲ] ποταμὸν Ἐρύμανθον κατὰ τὴν Σαύρου καλουμένην δειράδα τοῦ Σαύρου τε μνῆμα καὶ ἱερόν ἐστιν Ἡρακλέους, ἐρείπια ἐφ᾽ ἡμῶν· λέγουσι δὲ ὡς ὁδοιπόρους τε καὶ τοὺς προσοικοῦντας ὁ Σαῦρος ἐκακούργει, πρὶν ἢ παρὰ Ἡρακλέους τὴν δίκην ἔσχε. κατὰ ταύτην τὴν ἐπώνυμον τοῦ λῃστοῦ δειράδα ... τεσσαράκοντα δὲ ἀπὸ τῆς Σαύρου δειράδος ...; see also Frazer 1965:vol. 4, 92; and Papachatzis 1979:380–382). The name Σαωρέος, probably a translation from Shahur or Sahar, is attested in an inscription from Ghor Es-Safi, as the editors suggest (Meimaris and Kritikakou-Nikolaropoulou 2005:325–326 no. 236 line 3). Bechtel (1917:396–397) classes names beginning with Σα(υ)- under: Σαφι-, Σαφο-, -σάφων, a stem from a present Σάfω, but Sauros is not attested. Saurias, Sauron, Sauris and Sauritas are attested (LGPN I; II; IIIA; IV). The reading κράνας <Σ>αύρου, if not a reference to some unknown local tale, should rather be associated with Eleutherna's earlier name Σάτρα or Σάωρος attested in Stephanus, *Ethnica* s.v.: Σάτρα and Ἐλευθεραί (compare Herodianus s.vv. Ἐλευθεραί, Ἄωρος, and Ἀώρα; and Pape and Benseler 1959:188, 1340, 1354–55).

Line 3–4: ΕΠΑΑΡΙΤΕΡΑΤΑΣΚΥΦΑΣ|ΡΙΖΩ on the lamella; of the phi only the bottom tip of a vertical remains. The spring is at the left and not at the right, as in nos. 1–6. Instead of the interjection τῆ or adverb of place τῇ in nos. 1–6, the genitive is employed in its Doric form (Bile 1988: 89–90). For κυφα{σ}|ρίζω see the readings in nos. 1–6 above.

Line 4: ΤΗΣΔΕΙ on the lamella, apparently a misspelling for the iota.

Line 5: ΣΗΜΟΙΜΑΤΗΡΠΩΤΙΔΕΤ on the lamella; the dotted delta may also be an alpha. ΗΜΟΙ is confused either for εἰμί (nos. 1–3, 5–6; so Bernabé, and Graf and Johnston), in which case μάτηρ should be understood as vocative; or for ἐμοί, in which case it may equally be read: Γᾶ| {σ} <ἐ>μοί μάτηρ· πῶ; τί; ("Earth is my mother; from where? what? ..."). In the second half of the line the engraver is perhaps repeating by mistake the letters from the previous line 4 (ΠΩΔΕΙΓΑ), or this is another formula of the question-and-answer trial-scene. No. 4 line 4 above presents similar difficulties. (I am indebted to Christoph Riedweg, Alberto Bernabé, and Radcliffe Edmonds for suggestions on this and the following line.)

Line 6: .ΛΙΥΡΑΝΩΣΤΕ or .ΛΙΥΡΑΝΩΣΤΕ on the lamella. In the beginning of the line, there seems to be a vacant letter space; the dotted lambda-shape may equally be an alpha, lambda, or kappa: .ΑΙ, .ΛΙ, .ΚΙ, or, if combined with the following vertical, a nu or eta: .Ν, .Η. The dotted omega (in ligature with the previous nu?) may also be an omicron, hence perhaps also: <κ>αὶ <Ο>ὐρανός. Both readings are plausible and depend on what one reads in lines 4–5: the genitive Γᾶς (Bernabé, and Graf and Johnston), or the nominative Γᾶ.

Line 6–7: ΤΙΣΔΙΨΑΙΤΟ|.ΙΛΤΟΙΙΥΤΟΟΠΑΣΡΑΤΑΝΗΟ on the lamella. The first letters are engraved lower than the previous ΤΕ, as if it were a new beginning point. The string of letters appears to be a repetition of the beginning of the text by confusion or on purpose; the same text may have been incised several times on a large gold sheet which was then cut in the appropriate places: ΤΕ τίς; δίψαι το|ι is clear, and the remaining string of letters may have been an attempt for αὖος, παραπόλλυται, *vel sim*. This line, however, may also be a new formula of the question and answer process.

The Three Unincised

Archaeological Context and Chronology by Irene Gavrilaki

10 (G2; Figure 11) Sfakaki, Rethymno Archaeological Museum, Μ(ετάλλινα) 2887, on display. 1–50 CE

On the property of Markos Polioudakis, where the incised gold *epistomion* no. 8 above was found, another three unincised gold *epistomia* were also unearthed (see no. 8 above and nos. 11–12 below). Cist-grave 9 in an E-W direction was constructed by rectangular slabs; the skeleton of what was likely a male was found in a supine position with the head to the E; the bones of the thorax and the right hand were brittle on account of the grave's walls having caved in. The grave-goods were found around the feet from the knees down and consisted of: a clay prochous (Π[ήλινα] 5202), four glass cups ('Υ[άλινα] 192, 215, 216, 217), a glass phiale ('Υ[άλινα] 214), a bronze lekythion (Μ[ετάλλινα] 908), a bronze strigil (Μ[ετάλλινα] 918), and a silver coin (Ν[ομίσματα] 677). The glass phiale and the strigil suggest the first half of the first century CE as a date for Cist-grave 9. The *epistomion* (H.0.004–0.016, W.0.052, Th. 0.0001), rhomboid (in the shape of the mouth?) and similar to no. 8 above, only smaller, was found under the right part of the cranium and has suffered minor tears and wrinkles.

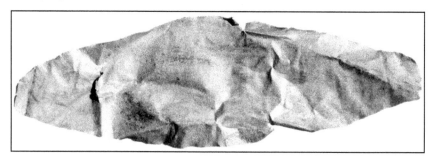

Figure 11. Gold *epistomion* (no. 10), from Sfakaki. Rethymno, Archaeological Museum, Μ(ετάλλινα) 2887.

11 (G3; Figure 12) Sfakaki, Rethymno Archaeological Museum, Μ(ετάλλινα) 897, on display. 50–100 CE

Another unincised *epistomion* was found in Cist-grave 4 (see also nos. 8 and 10 above and 12 below). The grave in an E-W direction was constructed by rectangular slabs and the skeleton of what was likely a female was found in a supine position with the head to the E. The grave-goods lay around the feet and consisted of: a clay kylix (Π[ήλινα] 5208), a clay prochous (Π[ήλινα] 6621), four clay unguentaria (Π[ήλινα] 6642, 6644, 6653 6654), a glass cup (Ύ[άλινα] 149), a bronze mirror (Μ[ετάλλινα] 906), a lead pyxis (Μ[ετάλλινα] 914), and bronze nails (Μ[ετάλλινα] 913a, b, 947a, b). The kylix, the prochous, and the glass cup suggest the second half of the first century CE as a date for this grave. The *epistomion* (H.0.016–0.018, W.0.053, Th. 0.0001) was found on the upper mandible of a cranium damaged by the fallen earth and the caving-in of the grave's northern wall. In excellent condition, the *epistomion* is oblong in shape with protruding corners and a net-like pattern covering the surface.

Figure 12. Gold *epistomion* (no. 11), from Sfakaki. Rethymno, Archaeological Museum, Μ(ετάλλινα) 897.

12 (G4; Figure 13) Sfakaki, Rethymno Archaeological Museum, Μ(ετάλλινα) 964, on display. 1–100 CE

A third unincised gold *epistomion* was found in Cist-grave 20 (see nos. 8, 10–11 above). The grave in an E-W direction was constructed by rectangular slabs and two skeletons were recovered in a supine position with the head to the W. They were placed successively, skeleton A buried later to the N, and skeleton B (an older burial, probably a female), to the S. The grave-goods were around the feet of the skeletons and consisted of: a clay prochous (Π[ήλινα] 5206), three aryballos-shaped lekythia (Π[ήλινα] 5207, 6628, one without an inventory number), a clay unguentarium (Π[ήλινα] 5216), a clay cup (Π[ήλινα] 5209), and a glass phiale (Ύ[άλινα] 136). A bronze coin was found on Skeleton A (Ν[ομίσματα] 682). The clay prochous, the unguentarium, the clay cup, and the glass phiale date the grave to the first century CE. The oblong *epistomion* (H.0.015, W.0.037, Th. 0.0001) was found in the bones of the cervix of skeleton B (probably a female). Between the legs of this skeleton were also discovered bronze foils (Μ[ετάλλινα] 963) which probably had originally plated a wooden pyxis. The *epistomion* is preserved in excellent condition, except for minor wrinkles, and its surface is covered by thin lines forming a chess-like pattern.

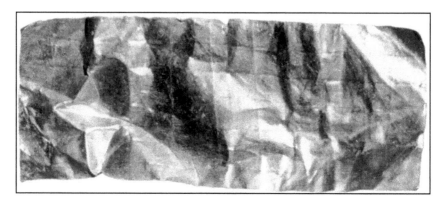

Figure 13. Gold *epistomion* (no. 12), from Sfakaki. Rethymno, Archaeological Museum, Μ(εтάλλινα) 964.

RELATED TEXTS

INCISED COINS AND *EPISTOMION* FROM PIERIA

13–14 (F8–F9; Figures 14–15) Pydna in Pieria (modern Alykes, Kitros), Thessaloniki Archaeological Museum, Πύ(δνα) 778.

Archaeological Context by Matthaios Bessios

Between 1984 and 1992, the 16th Ephorate of Prehistoric and Classical Antiquities undertook rescue excavations on the plot of K. Chryssochoidis at the site of Alykes, Kitros in Pieria. A total of eighty-two graves, which belong to the south cemetery of Pydna, were investigated. Two of the burials, nos. 8 and 29 (nos. 13 and 14 below respectively), contained gold coins of king Phillip II, which were found in the cranium area and were incised with the names of the deceased. In both cases the deceased were placed on wooden biers decorated with ivory, fragments of which were recovered. This similarity, and the fact that the two graves were very close to each other indicates that the deceased may have been members of the same family. Grave no. 8 (no. 13 below) is a pit-grave with red plaster covering the lower part of the pit, and yellow plaster the upper part. From the grave were recovered two bronze gilt wreaths and four clay vessels. Grave 29 (no. 14 below) is a cist-grave made of unburnt bricks covered with white plaster. The grave-goods comprise: a bronze ladle, a small bronze bell, a lead pyxis, and seven clay vessels.

13 The Inscription (F8; Figures 14a–b).

a.

b.

Figure 14. Gold coin (no. 13) incised with the name 'Andron,' from Pydna, Pieria. Thessaloniki, Archaeological Museum, Πύ(δνα) 778. (a. obverse; b. reverse). Diameter: 0.01, LH.0.001–0.002. 348–328 BCE.

The surface of the coin has been slightly smoothed in order to accommodate the incision of the deceased's name (in two lines) on both sides. The smoothness is visible in the upper half of the reverse, where the first four letters of the coin's legend: Φιλί|ππου are still visible, on top of which the name of the deceased Andron was incised. The lettering is neat, especially in line 1. The strokes curve slightly outward and are overextended in the letters alpha, delta, and nu; the shape of the omega on both sides is open and wide with long horizontals, almost as a triangle.

Obverse A   Ἄνδ-   Reverse B   Ἄνδ-
            ρων.   ρων.

14 The Inscription (F9; Figures 15a–b).

a.

b.

Figure 15. Gold coin (no. 14) incised with the name 'Xenariste,' from Pydna, Pieria. Thessaloniki, Archaeological Museum, Πύ(δνα) 778. (a. obverse; b. reverse). Diameter: 0.011, LH.0.0012–0.0028. 348–328 BCE.

The coin was smoothed so much that its obverse and reverse are barely visible; the name of the deceased is incised in two lines on the lower two thirds of the obverse; in line 2 the lower half of the right vertical of eta is missing due to lack of space; the lettering is similar to that of 13B above.

Obverse   Ξενα-
               ρίστη.

Bessios 1992:247; SEG 45.803; Riedweg 1998:389–398, and 2002; Bernabé and Jiménez San Cristóbal 2001:279–280 no. L16e; Bernabé 2005:fr. 496e; Graf and Johnston 2007:30–31 no. 20; Edmonds forthcoming-2.

These two coins incised with the names of a male and female deceased (nos. 13 and 14) are an eighth of a stater or trihemiobol and are dated by Le Rider (1977:244 no. 90a, pl. 84 no. 90a; and 1996:61–68 and pl. 6 no. 31). For Andron in Macedonia see Kanatsoulis (1955:18) and Tataki (1988:107 no. 179, 313, 336, 339; and 1998, 85, 145, 243); an Andron from Teos is related to Macedonia, see Berve 1926:vol. 2, 40 (= Kalléris 1988:618 note 4); the name is not found in Bechtel 1917:47–49 (see also LGPN I, II, IIIA, IIIB, IV). Xenariste is not found in Bechtel 1917:339–340 (see also LGPN I, II, IIIA, IIIB, IV).

The two engraved coins present a unique case, for which see the section "Usage." The incision of the names cannot technically be understood as a graffito on the coins (see e.g. Davesne and Le Rider 1989:304–316; BE 1992:126, 192); nor as an overstrike (see Le Rider 1975:27–56; Kraay 1976:12–13; Mørkholm 1991:13–14, 19–20; and Howgego 1995:89, 98).

15 (F3; Figure 16) Methone in Pieria, Thessaloniki Archaeological Museum, Πύ(δνα) 52.

Archaeological Context by Matthaios Bessios

The construction of a water-reservoir at the site of Palaiokatachas, Methone in Pieria resulted in rescue excavations undertaken by the 16th Ephorate of Prehistoric and Classical Antiquities. A number of graves, dated to the Classical, Hellenistic, and Roman periods, were unearthed. Among them, Cist-grave no. 2 (no. 15 below), made of unburnt mud-bricks, contained a female burial, as the name incised on the gold *epistomion* indicates. The deceased was placed on a bier whose front side was decorated with ivory depicting floral patterns at the borders and figures from the Dionysiac cycle at the center. The female deceased was carrying two gold earrings and two gold rings, while the incised lamella was placed on her body; the grave-goods also included: seven clay vessels, a bronze phiale, an iron scissor, and a bronze gilt wreath.

The Inscription

The lettering is careful and the letters are spread out to cover the surface of the *epistomion*; the strokes of the letters curve slightly outward and are over-extended in the letters alpha, lambda, and mu; the middle bar of alpha does not cross the left stroke; the mu's right vertical is half the size of the left; the omicron, half the size of the other letters, is incised in the middle of the line.

Figure 16. Gold *epistomion* (no. 15) incised with the name 'Phylomaga,' from Pydna, Pieria. Thessaloniki, Archaeological Museum, Πύ(δνα) 52. H.0.006, W.0.042, Th. less than 0.001, LH.0.0015–0.003. 325–300 BCE.

Φυλομάγα.

Bessios 1986:142–143; SEG 40.541, 45.777; Riedweg 1998:389–398, and 2002; Bernabé and Jiménez San Cristóbal 2001:279–280 no. L16h; Bernabé 2005:fr. 496h; Graf and Johnston 2007:44–45 no. 35. Edmonds forthcoming-2.

The date is based on the grave-goods. The name *Phylomaga/Phylomache* is attested in Attica (Bechtel 1917:459; *LGPN* II, 467).

16 (Figures 17a–g) Hymn from the Diktaian Sanctuary in Palaikastro, Crete, Herakleion Archaeological Museum, Ἐ(πιγραφές) 102, on display.

Four fragments of bluish limestone with white and yellowish veins were discovered in May 1904 during the excavations of the Diktaian sanctuary. Two of these fragments join and form the middle part of a large stele, at least 1.05 in height, according to Guarducci. She has also suggested that the hymn was first inscribed on side B, and, when the priests or magistrates discovered the numerous mistakes and the recklessness of the cutter, they had the hymn reinscribed on side A. That sides A and B are each the work of a different letter-cutter is evident, but the engraving process is not at all certain. The three fragments are inscribed on both sides, except for fr. c which is inscribed only on side B. The text printed below is that of Guarducci in IC III.ii [Dictaeum Fanum].2, which is a composite of both sides, with her corrections in Guarducci 1974b; as Perlman (1995:161), I print only the most probable restorations and modify accordingly the translation by Furley and Bremer (2001:vol. 1, 68–69).

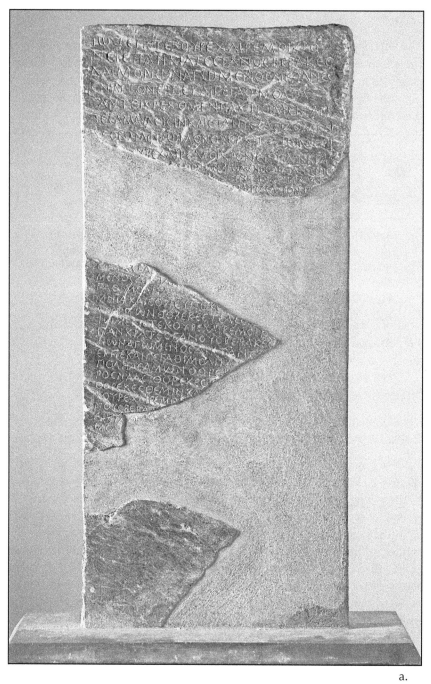

a.

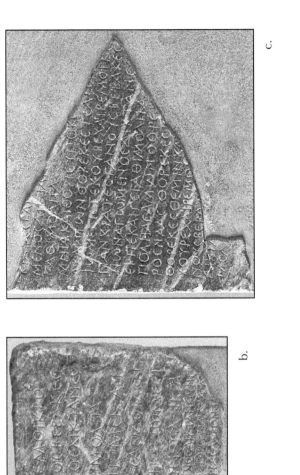

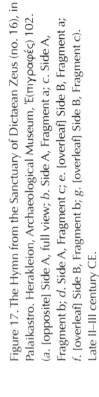

Figure 17. The Hymn from the Sanctuary of Dictaean Zeus (no. 16), in Palaikastro. Herakleion, Archaeological Museum, Ἐ(πιγραφές) 102. (*a*. [opposite] Side A, full view; *b*. Side A, Fragment a; *c*. Side A, Fragment b; *d*. Side A, Fragment c; *e*. [overleaf] Side B, Fragment a; *f*. [overleaf] Side B, Fragment b; *g*. [overleaf] Side B, Fragment c). Late II–III century CE.

e.

f.

g.

ἰὼ μέγιστε Κοῦρε, χαῖρέ μοι, Κρόνειε,	ἐπῳδός
πανκρατὲς γάνους, βέβακες δαιμόνων ἀγώμενος·	
Δίκταν ἐς ἐνιαυτὸν ἔρπε καὶ γέγαθι μολπᾷ.	
τάν τοι κρέκομεν πακτίσι μείξαντες ἅμ᾽ αὐλοῖσιν	στροφή α
5 καὶ στάντες ἀείδομεν τεὸν ἀμφὶ βωμὸν εὐερκῆ.	
ἰὼ μέγι[στε] Κοῦρε, χαῖρέ μοι, Κρόνειε,	ἐπῳδός
πανκρα[τὲς γάνους, βέβακες] δαιμόνων ἀγώμενος·	
Δίκταν ἐς ἐνι[αυτὸν ἔρπ]ε καὶ γέγαθι μολπᾷ.	
ἔνθα γάρ σε παῖδ᾽ ἄμβροτον ἀσπιδ[- - - -]	στροφή β
10 πὰρ Ῥέας λαβόντες πόδα κ[- - - - - -].	
[ἰὼ μέγιστε Κοῦρε, χαῖρέ μοι, Κρόνειε],	ἐπῳδός
[πανκρατὲς γάνους, βέβακες δαιμόνων ἀγώμενος]·	
[Δίκταν ἐς ἐνιαυτὸν ἔρπε καὶ γέγαθι μολπᾷ].	
[- - - - - - - - - - - - - -]	στροφή γ
15 [- - - - - - - - -]ας καλᾶς Ἀ̂ος.	
[ἰὼ μέγιστε Κοῦρε, χαῖρέ μοι, Κ]ρόνειε,	ἐπῳδός
[πανκρατὲς γάνους, βέβακες δαιμόνω]ν ἀγώμενος·	
[Δίκταν ἐς ἐνιαυτὸν ἔρπε κα]ὶ γέγαθι μολπᾷ.	
[- - - β]ρύον κατῆτος καὶ βροτὸς Δίκα κατῆχε	στροφή δ
20 [- - - - -]ηπε ζώ<ι>᾽ ἁ φίλολβος Εἰρήνα.	
[ἰὼ μέγιστε Κοῦρε, χαῖρέ μοι, Κρόνειε],	ἐπῳδός
πανκρατὲς γάν[ους, βέβακες δαιμόνων ἀγώ]μενος·	
Δίκταν ἐς ἐ[νιαυτὸν ἔρπε καὶ γέ]γαθι μολπᾷ.	
ἁ[μῶν δὲ θόρ᾽ ἐς ποί]μνια καὶ θόρ᾽ εὔποκ᾽ ἐς [μῆλα]	στροφή ε
25 [κὲς λάϊ]α καρπῶν θόρε κὲς τελεσ[φόρος οἶκος].	
ἰὼ μέγιστε Κοῦρε, χαῖρέ μοι, Κρ[όνειε],	ἐπῳδός
πανκρατὲς γάνους, βέβακες [δαιμό]νων ἀγώμενος·	
Δίκταν ἐς [ἐνιαυτὸν] ἔρπε καὶ γέ]γαθι μολπᾷ.	
[θόρε κὲς] πόληας ἁμῶν, θόρε κὲς ποντο<π>όρος νᾶας,	στροφή στ
30 θόρε κὲς ν[έος πο]λείτας, θόρε κὲς θέμιν κλ[ειτάν].	
[ἰὼ μέγιστε] Κοῦρε, χαῖρέ μοι, Κρόνειε,	ἐπῳδός
πανκρατὲς γάνους, βέβακ[ες δαιμόνων ἀγώ]μενος·	
Δίκταν ἐς ἐνι[αυτὸν ἔρπε καὶ γέγαθι] μολπᾷ.	

Io! most mighty youth, I salute you, son of Kronos,
almighty splendour, who stand as leader of the company of gods!
Come to Dikta at this New Year's Day and take delight in the
music,
(I) which we weave for you with harps, adding the sound of oboes,
which we sing having taken our stand around your well-walled altar.
Io! most mighty youth etc.
(II) For here it was that with their shield[s - - -]
received you, immortal babe out of Rhea's hands, and [- - -]
Io! most mighty youth etc.
(III) [- - -] of the fair Dawn.
Io! most mighty youth etc.
(IV) [- - -] plentiful each year, and Justice ruled over mortals;
[- - -] living beings [- - -] by Peace which goes with prosperity.
Io! most mighty youth etc.
(V) [Come on, Lord! leap up for our he]rds and leap up for our
fleecy [sheep];
leap up also [for the harvest] of corn, and for [our houses that
there be] offspring.
Io! most mighty youth etc.
(VI) [Leap up also] for our cities, leap up also for our seafaring ships;
leap up also for the y[oung ci]tizens, leap up also for famous *themis*.
Io! most mighty youth etc.

translation Furley and Bremer 2001:vol. 1, 68–69

Bosanquet 1908–1909:339–356; Harrison 1908–1909; Murray 1908–1909:357–365; IC III.ii [Dictaeum Fanum].2; Guarducci 1974b:32–38; Perlman 1995:161; Furley and Bremer 2001:vol. 1, 65–76, vol. 2, 1–20 (with full bibliography and with extensive commentary); Morante Mediavilla 2006 (on the Hesychian gloss γάνος).

The inscription is dated by Guarducci to the third century CE on the basis of the letter forms, but the late second century CE cannot be excluded. The *opinio communis* agrees that the inscription is a copy of the hymn, which originally must have been composed in the late classical period, the fourth or the third century BCE. This is evidenced by the hymn's metrical form and also by its linguistic and stylistic features, which are summarized by Furley and Bremer (2001:vol. 1, 69–70, vol. 2, 3–4).

17 (Figure 18) The Epigram of Magna Mater from Phaistos, Herakleion Archaeological Museum, Ἐ(πιγραφές) 43.

The local poros-stone, found in Agios Ioannis, near Phaistos, is decorated around its three sides, except for the bottom, by a double frame in relief, and its inscribed surface measures: H.0.275, W.0.41. The letters are inscribed with the help of guidelines 0.02 in height; and the interlinear space only between lines 1 and 2 is 0.007, which in the following lines is kept to a minimum. Red paint is clearly visible in the letters' strokes. The metrical units, five dactylic hexameters and a sixth pentameter, are indicated below by vertical lines.

Figure 18. The Epigram of Magna Mater (no. 17), from Phaistos, Crete. Herakleion, Archaeological Museum, Ἐ(πιγραφές) 43. Dimensions: H.0.37, W.0.52, Th.0.15 (top)–0.17 (bottom), LH.0.013–0.02. II century BCE.

θαῦμα μέγ᾽ ἀνθρώποις
πάντων Μάτηρ πρo͜δίκνυτι· |
τοῖς ὁσίοις κίνχρητι καὶ οἳ γον-
εἀν ὑπέχονται, | τοῖς δὲ π-
5   αρεσβαίνονσι θιῶν γέν-
ος ἀντία πράτει. ᵛ | πάντε-
ς δ᾽ εὐσεβίες τε καὶ εὔγλωθ-

{ἰ}οι πάριθ' ἁγνοὶ ᵛ | ἔνθεον ἐς
Μεγάλας Ματρὸς ναόν,
10   ἔνθεα δ' ἔργα | γνώσηθ' ἀ-
θανάτας ἄξια τῶδε ν-
αῶ. ᵛᵃᶜᵃᵗ

A great marvel for humans
the Mother of all performs by example (in advance):
for the *hosioi* she divines and (for those)
who maintain (stay within) their race;
but for the transgressors of the race of gods
she does the opposite.
Every pious and eloquent (or sweet to the ear)
come pure to the holy
temple of the Great Mother,
and you will learn the divine works
of the immortal (Mother), worthy of this very temple.

IC I.xxiii [Phaistos].3; SEG 50.933bis; 44.731bis; Pugliese Carratelli 2001:86–87; Bernabé 2005:135–136 fr. 568 F; Martínez Fernández 2006b:155–164 no. 23.

The lettering is not very careful, except for the first two lines, and suggests, according to Guarducci, the second century BCE, but the later third or the early first centuries should not be excluded. Characteristic letter shapes include: the broken-bar alpha, the theta with a dot or a short horizontal, the mu, nu, pi, and upsilon with verticals which curve slightly outward, the four-bar sigma, and the open omega. According to Bile (1988:227 note 298), the dialectic forms in the epigram may be purposeful archaisms, appropriate for a religious text (see further the section "A Cretan Context").

Line 2: ΠΡΔΙΚΝΥΤΙ on the stone; Guarducci read *paene certe* a small painted omicron between rho and delta, above them in the interlinear space, which I was unable to see; πρ<ο>δίκνυτι Pugliese Carratelli.

Line 3: ΤΟΙΟ corrected by the cutter to ΤΟΙΣ; ΚΙΝΧΡΗΤΙ on the stone, κίνχρητι Guarducci, κίν<κ>ρητι Pugliese Carratelli, Bernabé.

Line 6: πράτ<τ>ει Pugliese Carratelli; a space for a letter and a half separates the two sections of the epigram.

Line 7–8: ΕΥΓΛΩΘ|ΙΟΙ on the stone, εὔγλωθ|{ἰ}οι Guarducci, εὔγλωθ|<τ>οι Pugliese Carratelli, Bernabé, ευγλωθ|ιοι for εὔγλωτοι Bile (1988:84, 146–147 n295), Martínez Fernández.

Line 8: a space for a letter and a half separates the words ἁγνοὶ and ἔνθεον.

Line 9: NEON corrected by the cutter to NAON.

Line 10: of the theta a clear trace of the upper left and bottom right of a circular letter; γνωσῆθ' Guarducci, Bernabé, Martínez Fernández, γνώση[θ]' Pugliese Carratelli.

EPISTOMIA IN BYZANTINE GRAVES

18–19 (Figures 19, 20, 21a–b) Kastelli Pediados, site Kephali.

Archaeological Context by Kalliopi Galanaki

Between April 12 and July 31, 2002, excavations were undertaken by the 23rd Ephorate of Prehistoric and Classical Antiquities and the archaeologists Kalliope Galanaki, Deukalion Manidakis, and Yanna Triantaphylidi at the site of Kephali, a low hill to the SE of the village Kastelli Pediados. Around the top of the hill in an area of 24 m (N-S) by 21 m (E-W), 39 roughly-built cist-graves and eleven open burials were excavated, the majority of which had no grave-goods. Cist-grave 25, in the W edge of the cemetery on the hilltop, was dug into the natural rock in an E-W direction and was covered by six, uneven schist-slabs. Its dimensions are 1.23 by 0.22 in the west-end and 0.35 in the east-end. Inside the grave, two burials were uncovered and a few ostraca, three of which were glazed with greenish, gray-greenish, and yellowish color. In the W part of the grave a partly preserved skeleton (burial no. 39) was recovered in a supine but contracted position with the cranium and the legs bent towards the S; the hands were bent at the elbows and were touching the knees. In the E part of the grave bones of another skeleton (burial no. 40) were recovered that probably belonged to an earlier burial. The gender of both skeletons is not recoverable. In addition to the very few ostraca, a small iron ring near the legs of deceased no. 39 and the engraved pottery fragment (no. 18 below) were recovered from the grave's interior. Outside the grave, near the SW stone, a small bronze lamella attached to a ring was found. The engraved fragment no. 19 below was recovered from the surface survey of the cemetery.

18 The Inscription (Figures 19–20), Kastelli Pediados, site Kephali, Herakleion Archaeological Museum, Π(ήλινα) 31847.

The ostracon was found covering the mouth of the deceased in burial no. 39 (Figure 19), a findspot indicating that it was undoubtedly used as an *epistomion*. It is from the body of a medium sized clay vessel and the usual acclamatory text is incised with clumsy letters which are overlined, a sign of abbreviation (Figure 20).

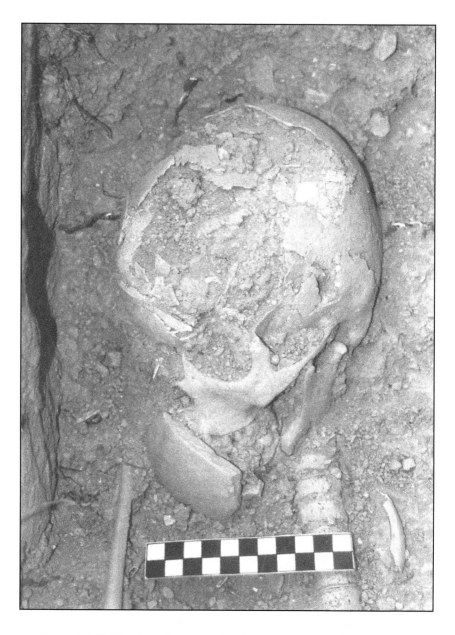

Figure 19. Skull with ostracon covering the mouth (no. 18), from Burial 39, Kephali archaeological site, Kastelli Pediados. Herakleion, Archaeological Museum.

Figure 20. Engraved ostracon (no. 18), from Burial 39, Kephali.
Herakleion, Archaeological Museum, Π(ήλινα) 31847. H.0.075, W.0.069,
Th.0.009, LH.0.003–0.008. Late V–VII centuries CE.

'Ι(ησοῦ)ς ^{cross} Χ(ριστό)ς
ν(ι)^{cross}κ(ᾷ)
3 φ(ῶς) ^{cross} Χ(ριστοῦ)
φ(έγγε) ^{cross} π(ᾶσι)
θεω.

Jesus Christ
conquers.
Light of Christ
light for all
...

Line 5: what is intended by θεω is not certain.

19 The Inscription (Figure 21a–b), Kastelli Pediados, site Kephali, Herakleion Archaeological Museum, Π(ήλινα) 31846.

A tile ostracon was recovered from the surface of burial no. 26 on top of a schist-plaque. Because it was not found inside a grave, it may not be classified as an *epistomion*, but it could have come from one of the cemetery's graves, or it could even have been discarded as an item not good enough for use. On side A the usual acclamatory text, abbreviated, is inscribed with clumsy letters which are overlined; on side B, various scratches look like drawings.

a.

Figure 21. Incised clay tile (no. 19), from Burial 26, Kephali archaeological site, Kastelli Pediados. Herakleion, Archaeologial Museum, Π(ήλινα) 31846. (*a*. obverse; *b*. reverse). H.0.105, W.0.10, Th.0.027, LH.0.008–0.015. Late V–VII centuries CE.

Side A   Ἰ(ησοῦ)ς ^{cross} Χ(ριστό)ς
           ν(ι)^{cross}κ(ᾷ).

           Jesus Christ
           conquers.

Side B   *drawings (possibly a fish and an ivy-leaf).*

b.

20 (Figure 22) Kastelli Pediados, Herakleion Archaeological Museum, Π(ήλινα) 32069.

Archaeological Context by Giorgos Rethemiotakis

On August 10, 1988, excavations were undertaken by the 23rd Ephorate of Prehistoric and Classical Antiquities on the plot of the nursery in Kastelli Pediados. The inscribed ostracon was found in the surface layer of the processional *dromos* and the stepped altar or *exedra* of the 'Minoan central building' amidst pottery dating from Minoan to the late and post Byzantine period. This landfill was formed during the construction of the Venetian castle for which material from the site or from nearby sites was used. Scattered burials were found in the plot, two of which were 'protected' by the landfill in the NE corner-tower of the Venetian castle. The supine skeletons of unknown gender were laid in pits dug into the Minoan landfill with no grave-goods. This indicates that these burials must antedate the construction of the Venetian castle in the late Byzantine period and probably should be associated with the burials excavated in the site Kefali (nos. 18 and 19 above), whose graves may have provided the material needed for the construction of the Venetian tower. Although the findspot of the tile is not known, in all probability it too may have been employed either as an *epistomion* or as a grave-good in one of the burials in this site, as nos. 18 and 19 above.

The Inscription

The tile is broken all around and engraved with crosses: lines 1–4 feature three crosses per line, lines 5–7 have two, and lines 8–9 have one; in each pane of each cross, overlined letters are inscribed, an indication that they are Christian acclamations in abbreviated form.

1 ’Ι(ησοῦ)ς cross Χρ(ιστός)c   5 φ(ῶς) cross Χ(ριστοῦ)   9 κ() cross χ()
  νιcrossκᾳ̃   φ(έγγε) cross π(ᾶσι)   .( ) cross .( )
  Χ(ριστός)? cross Χ(ριστός)?   ε( ) cross .( )   θ(εός)? cross θ(εός)?
4 Χ(ριστός)? cross Χ(ριστός)? 8 ε( ) cross ( )   12 θ(εός)? cross θ(εός)?
        13 σ(ωτήρ)? cross σ(ωτήρ)?   15 τ( ) cross .σ( )
        14 σ(ωτήρ)? cross σ(ωτήρ)?   16 π( ) cross γ( )
             17 σ( ) cross γ( )ς?
             18 .( ) cross τ( ).

        Jesus Christ   Light of Christ   ...
        conquers.   light for all
        Christ   ...   god

Christk ... god
  Soter   ...
  Soter   ...
    ...

Figure 22. Incised clay tile (no. 20), from an unknown burial, Kephali archaeological site, Kastelli Pediados. Herakleion, Archaeological Museum, Π(ήλινα) 32069. H.0.143, W.0.095, Th.0.018, LH.0.005–0.012. Late V–VII centuries CE.

The dates of nos. 18–20 above cannot be ascertained, but usually the Cretan inscriptions of the proto-Byzantine period are dated to the late fifth, sixth, and seventh centuries.

The inscriptions in all these cases (nos. 18–20) are acclamatory Christian prayers, some of which are attested in Crete for the first time. Not all of them are certain, hence the question marks. Similar texts are also found elsewhere in Crete (Bandy 1970:9–13; Diamantis 1998:314; and Tzifopoulos 2000:243–244 no. 2, 253–254 nos. 13–15); in the columns of the Parthenon (Orlandos and Vranousis 1973:83 no. 90, 92 no. 105, 121 no. 154); in Aphrodisias (Roueché 1989:180 no. 129ii, 182–3 no. 134vi, 185 no. 139ii); and in the island of Syros (Kiourtzian 2000:22, 148 no. 73, 154–155 no. 83, 160–161 no. 90).

21 Square of Cypriote Fighters (Governor's Residency), Thessaloniki.

Ioannis Kanonidis (1990:262–263) conducted a rescue excavation in the square of Cypriote Fighters (Governor's Residency) in Thessaloniki, during which a number of Byzantine graves came to light, dated to the thirteenth century CE. In two graves the cranium of the deceased was found on a stone-cushion and in two other graves, the deceased's faces were covered with tiles set on stones around their craniums.

22 Basilica of Glykys in Epiros.

Dimitrios Pallas (1971:140–141) excavated the Basilica of Glykys in Epiros, dated to the fourteenth century CE. Equal care for covering the head of the deceased, noted in no. 21 above, is also attested in the tile-graves, the dominant type of the graves around this Basilica: the deceased in graves 8 and 9 had tile-covers only over their heads; in grave 8 the cranium was surrounded by clay ostraca; in grave 10 the female deceased was found with a tile sherd near the head and shoulder; in grave 11 only the deceased's head and chest were covered by a tile (1971:plate 176γ right tile).

23 Episcopal Church and Residence in Kitros, Pieria.

Efterpi Marki (1990) excavated the episcopal church and residence in Kitros, Pieria. Graves of the bishop(s) or the clergy have come to light beneath the floor of the thirteenth century CE basilica, which attest, as in nos. 21–22 above, the same care for covering the head with clay tiles.

Figure 23. Burial of Charalambos Tsigkos (no. 24), Mandamados, Lesbos.

Modern Greek Examples

24 (Figure 23) Funeral in Mandamados, Lesbos.

Betty Psaropoulou (1986), who founded the Center for the Study of Modern Ceramics in Athens and its Museum, came across a number of customs in different parts of Greece during her research and study of ceramic workshops. On November 8, 1990, while on a research trip to study the ceramic workshops in Mandamados, Lesbos, she was told by Stelios Stamatis of the funeral of Charalambos Tzigkos and was allowed to take a photograph (see also Giannopoulou and Demesticha 1998:74–75). Just before inhumation, an ostracon from a clay pot of the house, broken and painted with a cross, was placed on the mouth. Stamatis also told her that the burial shroud for dressing the body was perforated with wax (compare English 'cerecloth') which was later formed into a cross and placed in the deceased's mouth.

25 Philotheos Holy Monastery, Mount Athos.

In Mount Athos the burial custom of covering the face of deceased monks with clay ostraca, incised or painted with a cross or the acclamation: Ἰ(ησοῦ)ς Χρ(ιστὸς) νικᾷ, is still practiced, as Efraim notes, Archimandrite and Abbot of the Philotheos Holy Monastery (1990:85 with photographs).

2

Commentary on *Epistomia* nos. 1–12

Topography

L AMELLAE NOS. 1–7 WERE RECOVERED FROM GRAVES in the extensive cemetery to the north-northwest of Eleutherna, the city's north entrance, but the exact location of their discovery is unknown. Theodoros Triphyllis, Consul of Austria-Hungary in Rethymno came to acquire nos. 1–3 and 7 and showed them to André Joubin,[1] John L. Myres,[2] and Federico Halbherr[3] before his collection of antiquities ended up in the National Archaeological Museum.[4] He told these men that the lamellae came from graves in Eleutherna, assuring them further that they came "from the same grave,"[5] a rather unlikely piece of information.[6] Halbherr, who visited the site and inquired about the lamellae's provenance, was told by locals that they came from the large cemetery at the north entrance of Eleutherna which reaches the modern villages Lagká (Λαγκά, 'Ravine') and Alfá (Αλφά, 'Limestone').

Thus Margarita Guarducci, drawing on Halbherr's notes, included four lamellae in the epigraphical dossier of Eleutherna, because they were found *non longe ab Eleutherna et quid loco* Alphá (*ita Halbherr, in schedis; qui de hoc a nonnullis loci illius incolis se certiorem factum esse adfirmat), in sepulcreto aliquot ...*[7] The lamella in Herakleion Museum was published by Guarducci among the

---

[1] Joubin (1893:121–124) apparently saw only no. 1.

[2] Myres 1893:629.

[3] Comparetti 1910:37–41; IC II.xii [Eleutherna].31, p. 136.

[4] Theodoros Triphyllis served also as a representative of the Austrian Lloyds and had in his possession antiquities from the Idaean Cave which he likewise showed to people visiting Rethymno and Herakleion; for these see Sakellarakis 1998:54–55, 58, 64, 69, 72, and 187 (for a brief biography).

[5] See Myres 1893; Comparetti 1910:41.

[6] As Guarducci (1974a:13) has suggested.

[7] IC II.xii.31, p. 168; see also IC II.xii.31bis, p. 170.

inscriptions of *Loci Incerti*, because *in Cretae regione* Mylopótamos *appellata reperta est (e quo potissimum loco prodierit non constat)* ...[8] Chances are, however, that as Guarducci proposed later,[9] this lamella (no. 4 above) came from the same cemetery as nos. 1–3. In fact, it is probable that nos. 5 and 6 in the Hélène Stathatos Collection also came from this cemetery, since they were all found, according to the seller, "in graves near Eleutherna."[10]

Although no systematic excavations have been undertaken and sufficient evidence is therefore lacking, the extensive Hellenistic-Roman cemetery in the sites Mnemata (Figures 24–27, pages 82–84) and Agia Elessa (Figures 29–33, pages 85–87) appears to be the most likely candidate for the provenance of the seven Cretan *epistomia* (see Acknowledgements above).

Some years ago, a brief rescue excavation revealed a Roman bath (Figure 28, page 84) in close proximity to Agia Elessa.[11] The site is called Mnemata (Μνήματα, 'Graves'; Figure 24, page 82), because the graves to the south and east of the village Alfá are still visible (Figures 25–27, pages 83–84), whereas Agia Elessa (Ἁγία Ἐλέσα or Ἐλεοῦσα, 'Holy Elessa or Virgin Mary the Compassionate or Saint Helen and Constantine'; Figure 29, page 85) is nothing more than a Roman chamber-tomb with larnakes that was later converted into a small church (Figures 30–33, pages 85–87).[12] This fact may account for the locals' insistence, upon being questioned by Halbherr, that the lamellae came from the same grave, i.e. from a Roman chamber tomb with more than one larnax (Figures 30 and 32–33, pages 85–87). A similar example may be observed in ancient Lappa (modern Argyroupolis; see map, opposite page 1). In the Roman cemetery to the east of the city, one chamber-tomb became the small church of Agies Pente Parthenes (Ἅγιες Πέντε Παρθένες, 'Holy Five Virgins'; Figures 34–37, pages 87–89) and another tomb was converted into the Agia Elessa church (Figures 38–39, pages 89–90).[13]

The sites Mnemata (Figures 24–28, pages 82–84) and Agia Elessa (Figures 29–33, pages 85–87) to the north-northwest of Eleutherna are located on hilly terrain approximately 200 m above sea-level, on the borders of the modern villages Lagká and Alfá.[14] The graves are cut on top of a hill. The west hillside is very steep due to erosion (Figures 26–27, 29, pages 83–85). Thanassis Kalpaxis

---

[8] IC II.xxx.4, p. 314.

[9] Guarducci 1974a:13.

[10] Verdelis 1953–1954:vol. II, 56.

[11] Banou 1994–1996:290–291.

[12] For the saints to whom these country-churches are dedicated, see 204n177. I am indebted to Eva Tegou for our visits to these sites and our discussions.

[13] For these graves, see Gavrilaki 2004; and the section "A Cretan Context."

[14] A modern limestone quarry is located just to the south of the village.

and Niki Tsatsaki have studied the sites and the chance finds from some of the looted graves dated from the late fourth to the second centuries BCE, and they have suggested that this cemetery was probably used by the inhabitants of the Nesi hill in Eleutherna, whose remains are dated within the same period.[15] This extensive cemetery lies within the wider area of Eleutherna, the ancient city at the northern foothills of Mount Ida. As the excavations by the Department of History and Archaeology of the University of Crete have shown,[16] Eleutherna's settlement pattern emerges as one of many 'neighborhoods' at some distance from each other, what van Effenterre has called "un habitat polynucléaire."[17] Nicholas Stampolidis has convincingly argued that the graves to the east and west of the two streams of Eleutherna, which eventually flow north into the river Geropótamos, are located at Eleutherna's natural passages from the north.[18] The village Lagká is located approximately 2 km to the north-north-west of Eleutherna and the village Alfá approximately 4 km, the latter roughly at the midpoint of the approximately 10 km distance from Eleutherna to the north shore (see map, opposite page 1).

Lamellae nos. 8–12 come to us from rescue excavations which have revealed part of the Hellenistic-Roman cemetery in Sfakaki on the north shore.[19] It seems certain that this cemetery belonged to the settlement that has been excavated in the villages Stavromenos and Chamalevri. It is therefore reasonable to assume that this settlement, most probably within the wider area of Eleutherna, would or should bear some similarities to Eleutherna in terms of political, social, economic, and religious matters. From the religious dimension, at least, we find support for this ostensible overlap in the fact that the nine incised *epistomia* form a distinct group (albeit not a homogeneous one) and consequently must be studied as texts related to, even if not actually produced in, the city of Eleutherna.

The exact location, however, of the ancient cities on the north shore of Crete from Rhithymna to Herakleion remains vague. It is difficult to deter-

---

[15] Kalpaxis and Tsatsaki 2000; Kalpaxis et al. 1994.

[16] See the archaeological reports of the excavators Petros Themelis for Eleutherna's Sector I, Thanassis Kalpaxis for Sector II, and Nicholas Ch. Stampolidis for Sector III in *Kretike Estia* 2 (1988), 3 (1989–1990), 4 (1991–1993), 5 (1994–1996), 9 (2002); and also van Effenterre et al. 1991; Themelis 2000a, 2002, 2004a, 2004c; Kalpaxis et al. 1994; Kalpaxis 2004; Stampolidis 1993, 1994, 1996a, 2004a, 2004c.

[17] van Effenterre 1991:29; Perlman 1996:252–254; Themelis 2002:29; Themelis 2004a:48–49; Stampolidis 2004a:68–69.

[18] Stampolidis 1993:21–23, 29–31; 1994, 142–147; 2004a.

[19] Tsatsaki 2004 studies the Hellenistic pottery from a number of graves excavated in Sfakaki and Stavromenos.

mine the territories of Cretan cities in antiquity, as they shifted from period to period on account of various economic, social, and political changes.[20] Nevertheless, we can be certain that Eleutherna's territory extended to the north shore in the modern villages of Stavromenos, Chamalevri, Sfakaki, and Panormo, where one or possibly two of the city's harbors must have been. The ancient cities(?) Allaria, Arion (Ariaioi), Pantomatrion, Panormos, and the site Dion Akron are variously associated with Eleutherna and with the north shore of this part of the island (see map, opposite page 1).

Dion Akron, a site mentioned in a text prescribing that Eleuthernaean *dromeis* serve in this promontory-outpost(?),[21] has been placed on modern Cape Stavros, west of Sisai, probably an ancient dependent city.[22] Stampolidis has suggested persuasively that it should instead be placed somewhere between modern Panormo and Bali (ancient Astale), Dion Akron probably being Eleutherna's east border with Axos.[23]

Stylianos Alexiou places Panormos in modern Agia Pelagia, ancient Apollonia, and locates Arion in Stavromenos/Chamalevri, and Pantomatrion in modern Panormo (Castel Mylopotamo), although this does not exclude the possibility of an Eleuthernaean harbor in the area with some other name, presently unknown.[24] In Panormo's vicinity, the Melidoni Cave, the *Tallaeum Antrum* dedicated to Hermes in the Roman period, may have served as a

[20] Faraklas et al. (1998) and Xifaras (2002) study the territories of the ancient Cretan cities on the basis of the geophysical morphology, although this is only one of the criteria, admittedly crucial, that should be taken into consideration for a city's territory; for the shifting of borders, see e.g. Chaniotis 1996a:pl. 3; and 2001a.

[21] van Effenterre 1991:17–21 (SEG 41.739); van Effenterre and Ruzé 1995:346–347 no. 98.

[22] SEG 25.1022 (Alexiou 1966): on an altar-base or a horos the genitive plural Σισαίων is inscribed, the inhabitants of Sisa or Sisai (Andreadaki-Vlazaki 2004:43 prints the name of the city as: ΣΙΣΑ, and notes that it is inscribed on a Hellenistic stele); van Effenterre 1991:17–21; Bile 1988:59 no. 74. Stefanakis (1998:97–101) reviews the topography of the coastline, places Kytaion northwest of Sisai, at the Almyrida bay, as in the *Barrington Atlas* pl. 60 (cf. map, opposite page 1), and associates the area with Axos.

[23] Stampolidis 1993:50–52; 1994:154–5; 2004a; 2004c:71–72. For Astale see Litinas 2006. In the *Barrington Atlas* pl. 60 (cf. map, opposite page 1), Dion Akron is placed with a question mark in modern Bali. It is not at all certain where the borders were between the two major cities of the area, Eleutherna and Axos, especially from one century to the next; for discussion and previous bibliography, see Faraklas et al. 1998:77–86; Stefanakis 1998; Perlman 2004b:1153–1154, no. 950 and 1158–1160 no. 957. For Axos, see further: Mandalaki 2006, Monaco 2006, Aversa 2006, Kelly 2006, Tzifopoulos 2006b, Martínez-Fernández 2006a, Sidiropoulos 2006, Kefalidou 2006, Sporn 2006, Tegou 2006.

[24] Alexiou 2002a, 2002b, 2002c, and 2006; Perlman 2004b:1150–1151 no. 946; and compare Stampolidis 1993:50–52; 1994:154–155; and 2004a. For a number of ancient Apollonias in Crete (among them Eleutherna), and the problems of their location, see Kitchell 1977:196–211; and the section "A Cretan Context."

border sanctuary between Eleutherna and Axos, although its exact role may have changed from one period to the next. From the Roman period onwards, it appears that caves regain their attractiveness as potential sites for cult places and sanctuaries.[25] During the Imperial period, however, Eleutherna was privileged over Axos by the emperors,[26] and her territory may have been extended again to include the Melidoni Cave—although, under Roman rule, what such control meant is unclear.

Other equally convincing possibilities for Pantomatrion, Allaria, and Arion (Ariaioi) include the modern villages of Sfakaki, Chamalevri, and Stavromenos, all of which lie 8–10 km east of Rethymno,[27] the area where one of Eleutherna's ports was probably located, and the area which most probably served as the city's western border with Rhithymna. We do not have sufficient evidence for determining the eastern border of Rhithymna's territory, nor can we ascertain whether or not this territory was fixed throughout the centuries. Guarducci included in the epigraphical dossier of Rhithymna a small number of inscriptions from this region.[28] Albeit of no help in identifying the ancient settlement, at present these texts comprise the area's epigraphical dossier, together with the two incised *epistomia* from Sfakaki and a new inscription from Chamalevri that corroborates the existence of a *hieron* and most probably a city.[29] The continuing excavations by the 25th Ephorate are gradually bringing to light extensive settlements in this region,[30] but unfortunately the

---

[25] For cave-sanctuaries and their territories, see Tzifopoulos 1999 (SEG 49.1215, 1216, 1235, 1250); Sporn 2002:231–232 and 346–348; Niniou-Kindeli 2002; di Branco 2004; and Melfi 2006. For sanctuaries and poleis' territories, see Baldwin Bowsky 2001a; Chaniotis 2006c; and the section "A Cretan Context."

[26] Baldwin Bowsky 2006.

[27] For topographical identifications, see Kitchell 1977:117–128; Stampolidis 1993:50–52; 1994:154–155; 2004a; Perlman 1996:282–285 and 2004b:1149–1150 no. 944; Stavrianopoulou 1993; Faraklas et al. 1998:77–86; Faure 2000b; Chaniotis 2001a:323; and Sporn 2002:224–247.

[28] IC II.xxiv.1ab from Stavromenos; IC II.xxiv.12 from Pigi (east of Rhithymna); to these add SEG 23.580 from Nea Magnesia (SE of Stavromenos); two unpublished fragments from Stavromenos; and the Iouliane of Pantomatrion who died in Egypt (Bernand 1984); for the epigraphical dossier of the Rethymno Prefecture, see Tzifopoulos 2006a.

[29] The new text from Chamalevri records the restoration of a temple (ἱερόν), which, however, as Angelos Chaniotis noted (SEG 51.1180), need not mean only temple or sanctuary, and lists the names of the *kosmoi* in charge (see Martínez-Fernández, Tsatsaki and Kapranos 2006). For the evidence that a sanctuary existed at the site Manousés, see Hood, Warren, and Cadogan 1964:64–65; and Scheiring, Müller, and Niemeier 1982:45 (I am indebted to Epaminondas Kapranos and Niki Tsatsaki for discussing this text with me).

[30] Thus far, the evidence indicates settlements of four periods: 2000–1900, 1400, 1200–1100 BCE, and from the fourth century BCE onwards; for the ongoing excavations in this area, see Andreadaki-Vlazaki 1995, 1994–1996, 2002, 2004; Andreadaki-Vlazaki and Papadopoulou 1997; and Tegou 1998, 2002.

evidence is still too inconclusive to allow for identification with any known ancient settlement.

Nonetheless, the topography of the graves within the Hellenistic-Roman cemetery in Sfakaki, although the cemetery's limits remain unknown, does not support the idea that a special burial place was set aside for those deceased bearing lamellae and *epistomia*. The idea, unanimously accepted, that within a cemetery there may have been reserved areas for particular burials, appeared after the publication of an inscription from Kyme. This text, however, inscribed in five lines on a block from a large chamber-tomb and dated to ca. 450 BCE, prohibits burial inside the tomb of those not initiated in the Bacchic mysteries,[31] a case similar, if not identical, to the ἀραὶ ἐπιτύμβιοι.[32] The text does not imply a special area within the cemetery designated for burial of Bacchic initiates, but forbids burial inside the specific chamber-tomb on whose block it was inscribed. If another *bebaccheumenos* passed away, presumably the chamber-tomb might be re-opened for the new burial, but the main purport was that this tomb should not be re-opened and violated for the interment of just anybody. In turn, this should not lead to the conclusion that all prohibitions and curses against violation of the grave imply that the deceased was an initiate; only that the deceased with ἀραὶ ἐπιτύμβιοι and his family for some reason were strongly against re-opening of the grave or its violation.

The idea that a special burial place was set aside is not evident in the partly excavated cemetery in Sfakaki. Of the fifty–six, only five graves contained an *epistomion* (nos. 8–12): Grave 4 (no. 11 above) is immediately to the west of Grave 1 (no. 8 above), and Graves 9 (no. 10 above) and 20 (no. 12 above) are in relative proximity, but Grave I (no. 9 above) is some distance away. At present, it does not appear that a specific area within the excavated part of the cemetery was reserved for *mystai*,[33] as is also the case in the Amphipolis cemetery, where of more than 1600 graves excavated, only one contained an engraved lamella (D4).[34] If there were ever a choice for a burial plot within a

---

[31] *LSAG* 239, 240 and pl. 48 no. 12; and Sokolowski 1962:202–203 no. 120 (SEG 36.911): οὐ θέμις ἐν|τοῦθα κεῖσθ|αι <ε>ὶ μὲ τὸν βε|βαχχευμέ|νον. Dickie 1995a:86; Oikonomou 2002:49–50; Parker and Stamatopoulou 2004.

[32] Strubbe 1991; for imprecations in epigrams from Asia Minor Strubbe 1997; for a curious example of such a text from Lappa (Argyroupolis), Crete, see the section "A Cretan Context." Figures 30, 32–33, 37 show aptly how the Kyme prohibition should be understood.

[33] Oikonomou (2002:49–50) has noted that the graves whence the incised lamellae from Pella and Elis, are in the cemetery's outer limits.

[34] Malama 2000 and Malamidou 2006. A comparable case, albeit at another level, is the dedicatory inscription from Meneis in Bottiaia, Macedonia together with the *horos*, delimiting the area of a funerary-sanctuary with a small temple, dated after the early third century CE

cemetery, or if designated areas ever existed, the topographical indications are inconclusive; they do suggest, however, that most probably such choices may not have been based on a distinction or aggregation according to wealth, religious conviction, and so forth.

Lettering—Engraving

The letters on the small and extremely thin gold foils were incised by a small, sharp instrument, without the engraver tearing the foils. The letters in no. 8 above are an exception, as they seem to have been pressed. It is not certain whether these lamellae were first cut to their present size and then incised, or whether the texts were engraved first in longer foils and then cut with scissors accordingly, perhaps for mass-production.[35] At least some unincised *epistomia* appear to have been cut with scissors, not always successfully, after they have been decorated.[36] Nor can the possibility be ruled out that some of these gold foils originally had some other use and that, when the occasion arose, they were cut and incised or vice versa.

The need to keep the lamella steady for incision and for the laying-out of the text most likely explains the indention and the spaces left vacant in all the lamellae and can further offer some hints about the lamellae's preparation.[37] Nos. 4, 5, and perhaps 6 were probably incised in their present size. The text of no. 4 is etched following the mouth-shape of the foil without care for a neat layout. In nos. 5 and 6 on the other hand, there seems to have been a miscalculation regarding the text to be engraved relative to the surface area available on the foils: in no. 5 the text is crammed on the upper two-thirds with enough space left empty below the text for one or two more lines; in no. 6 the same amount of letters as no. 5 fills in almost the entire surface, as the characters are slightly taller, and the lines are meandering.

The layout of nos. 1–2 (and to a lesser extent, no. 3) is careful and ordered, the lines are straight, and syllabification is respected. Symmetry in incising the letters from left to right in no. 7 is more important than word-division,

---

(Chryssostomou 1999–2001 and 2000). It is not certain, as Chryssostomou emphasizes, if these *mystai* were those of Liber Pater, the Thracian or Macedonian Dionysos, or a syncretism of the two or three deities, or even of the chthonian Dionysos, even though no lamellae were recovered. The topography of this sanctuary with its adjacent graves is so far unique. For a brief overview of necropoleis in Macedonia, see Rhomiopoulou 2006.

[35] Zuntz 1971:353; Kyriakos Tsantsanoglou (*personal communication*).

[36] Oikonomou 2002:15–16.

[37] For the Pelinna leaves, see Tsantsanoglou and Parássoglou 1987:5.

whereas in no. 8, the two words are centered. The text in no. 9 is laid out differently, although from the middle of line 4 onwards, the letters become larger in order to fill the space which otherwise would have been left empty. Even so, the last line is incised in such a way that the lamella gives the impression that it had been cut after incision, as if one had cut(?) the foil carelessly and without knowing where exactly it should be cut; such an inference can perhaps explain the text's abrupt break off.

The lettering (see nos. 1–9 above), with minor idiosyncrasies and sometimes with different shapes within the same text, is basically similar in all lamellae, except in no. 8. In nos. 1, 2, 5, 7, and 8, the style of the letters is very careful and ordered, with very few mistakes—the work of an experienced, if not a professional(?) engraver. In nos. 3, 4, 6, and 9, on the other hand, the lettering is sloppy and offhand, perhaps the work of an amateur. Comparetti, based on an analysis of lettering, layout, and orthography, suggested that lamellae nos. 1 and 2 were apparently incised by the same engraver and that no. 7 is very similar to nos. 1–2, a conceivable case accepted by Guarducci.[38] These types of assessments, however, are hard to prove and the differences in the style of the letters, although minute (see nos. 1–3, 7 above), do not support such attributions. Engraving objects as small as lamellae was difficult and demanding, and resulted in numerous shapes for individual letters (see the section "Chronology").

Dialect—Orthography

In terms of orthography and dialectic forms, the texts appear consistent and follow the rules of the Cretan-Doric psilotic dialect:[39] the infinitive ending in -εν in nos. 1–6 and 9 πιῆν, and in no. 7 χαίρεν;[40] the 1st person singular of ἠμί in nos. 1–6 and 9;[41] in nos. 1–6, the genitive singular in ω = ου, but also in the beginning of Ὠρανῶ and in the interrogative πῶ = πόθεν;[42] the shapes Σ or Z for -σσ- in the word κυφάριζος and in the 2nd person singular ἐζί of εἰμί (the shape Σ, according to Guarducci, is perhaps a relic of the archaic/classical *tsade* (*sampi*), turned 90 degrees counterclockwise).[43] In nos. 1–3, 5–6, and 9, the aspiration of the word κυφάριζος is not uncommon, nor are the two forms

---

[38] Comparetti 1910:39, 41; Guarducci in IC II.xii.31, p. 168.
[39] Bile 1988:213 with n241.
[40] Bile 1988:240–242; Cassio 1987:314–316; 1995:191–192.
[41] Bile 1988:92–94, 226.
[42] Bile 1988:96–98, 186, 213 with n241.
[43] *LSAG* 308; Bile 1988:143–146; Guarducci in IC II, p. 170.

for Persephone's name: Φερσοπόνη in no. 7, with metathesis of aspiration, is a rarer form than Φερσεφόνη in no. 8 with two aspirates, the normal spelling (together with the Attic form Φερρέφαττα) in pre-Roman Attic inscriptions.[44]

The orthographic variations of the texts in nos. 1–6 do not present major difficulties; perhaps Verdelis (1953–1954:57) is correct in describing the engravers of nos. 5–6 as having only a mediocre knowledge of grammatical rules. The only noteworthy case of variation involves the epithet for the spring: in nos. 1–2 and 5, it is αἰειρόω, and in nos. 3 and 6 (the more problematic texts in terms of letter-style and engraving) αἰενάω. Olivieri (1915:15) inferred that αἰέναος must be the older form whose glosseme αἰείροος became the more comprehensible one, but Guarducci (IC II, p. 170) suggested that either one may have been in the archetype, if such a text ever existed. Zuntz (1971:363) noted the perfect suitability of αἰέναος, preserved in the faulty texts, as opposed to the more problematic αἰείροος.

Although the text on lamella no. 9 is similar to nos. 4–6 in terms of orthography, amateurism, and dialectic forms, it nevertheless stands out in comparison to the others because it presents significant dialectic and textual divergences. Instead of using either one of the epithets αἰέναος or αἰείροος, it employs a new and unexpected word <Σ>αύρου or Αὔρου for the spring, and as a consequence strongly suggests that the epithet in no. 4 ΑΙΓΙΔΔΩ deserves more thought before emendation. Because of ignorance (or error?), the location of the spring in no. 9 changes from right to left, and the epic τῇ followed by the nominative becomes the article of the noun in the genitive. In this text, both endings of the genitive singular -ου and -ω are present in <Σ>αύρου, κυφαρίζω, <Ο>ὐρανῷ; and instead of the epic ἐζί (ἐσσί) used in the other texts for the 2nd person singular of the verb εἰμί, the classical form εἶ is employed. If the verb's change may be justified as a later simplification of the less intelligible and more archaizing form ἐζί, the *spring of* <S>*auros* is a unique instance (it is mentioned only once, in Theophrastos' *Historia plantarum* 3.3.4, in reference to the Idaean Cave), and perhaps a reference that may even antedate the form αἰέναος, which Olivieri has argued is the more pristine form (see the section "The Cretan Context of the Cretan *Epistomia*"). Lastly, the latter part of the text of no. 9 is another unique instance and is thus equally difficult to account for: if not a hodgepodge, it appears to prompt further questions and answers regarding the stichomythia and the currently known narrative scenes (see the section "The Cretan Texts in the Context of a Ritual and a *Hieros Logos*").

---

[44] Bile 1988:139–141; 2000:56–57; Threatte 1980:449–451; Matthaiou and Papadopoulos 2003:46–47, no. 18; for the epic Περσεφόνη Richardson 1974:170.

Meter

The brief texts on nos. 7–8 are not metrical, but it is uncertain whether the two words were completely without rhythm, if any rhythm were intended. The layout of the remaining texts nos. 1–6 and 9 creates rather than resolves metrical problems. In nos. 1–3 and 5, the text's layout appears to have been prearranged according to its metrical form, which presumably was recognized as such by the engraver and perhaps also by the buyer/recipient who placed the order. Their knowledge, however, of the hexameter or of its rhythm, if any, was only nominal, as αἰειρόω in line 2 is not analyzable in dactyls. Any knowledge in these matters, then, was probably limited to the recognition of a line as metrical by its incised form on the foil. The text in nos. 4, 6, and 9 (the most problematic ones), however, testifies that such a prerequisite or demand was not necessary in certain cases and that the engraver was sometimes free to incise the text as he pleased.

Even so, and despite the mystery surrounding this process, the text which the engravers of all seven lamellae, except no. 9, strive to etch either from memory or by copying, is in its Cretan-Doric dialect the following:

> δίψαι αὖος ἐγὼ καὶ ἀπόλλυμαι· ἀλλὰ πιὲμ μοι
> κράνας αἰενάω ἐπὶ δεξιά· τῇ, κυφάριζος.
> 3 τίς δ᾽ ἐζί; πῶ δ᾽ ἐζί;
> Γᾶς υἱός ἠμι καὶ Ὠρανῶ ἀστερόεντος.

Zuntz suggested that the text "evidently consists, in the main, of three hexameters which are, however, oddly expanded." The third hexameter may have originally comprised the question, attested in the Homeric epics in its brief form τίς πόθεν εἶς, and line 4, which may have originally been without the expendable anyway υἱός (or παῖς), in light of the variation in nos. 4 and 9; hence the original must have been a perfect hexameter: τίς πόθεν εἶς; Γᾶς ἠμι καὶ Ὠρανῶ ἀστερόεντος. Zuntz also noted the perfect suitability to meter and context of αἰέναος, preserved in the faulty texts (nos. 4 and 6), in contrast to αἰειρόω, "a rare word not unsuitable in itself but ruinous to the metre—unless indeed one supposes Ionic (or Lesbian) αἰΐ to have been expelled by local αἰεί."[45]

Interestingly, in the Homeric epics the question is never employed in an Underworld context (e.g. in the *Nekyia*). When asked,[46] and depending on the

---

[45] Zuntz 1971:363; compare Janko 1984:99–100.
[46] Zuntz 1971:362. As the Homeric epics attest, this question formula may be expanded, contracted, and modified accordingly; its expanded version: τίς πόθεν εἶς ἀνδρῶν; πόθι τοι πόλις

way it is answered, the question almost always involves actual or metaphorical death or danger. In the battlefield, Achilles asks Asteropaios this question and kills him (*Iliad* 21.150); Diomedes asks the question to Glaukos, who is saved, however, on account of the previous hospitality (*Iliad* 6.123). In scenes of hospitality, the person asked the question reveals his identity only in ideal circumstances, as in the meeting of Telemachos with Nestor (*Odyssey* 3.71). In all other circumstances, the person faces two choices: either to answer earnestly and face imminent danger, as Odysseus realizes, when he replies to Polyphemos (*Odyssey* 9.504);[47] or to answer with a Cretan tale (*Odyssey* 13.253–286, 14.191–359, 19.164–202). The same pattern is followed in two of the *Homeric Hymns* where the question occurs. In the *theoxenia* scene, Demeter is asked the question and replies with a Cretan tale (*Homeric Hymn to Demeter* 113); and the Cretans, after being overtaken by Apollo as a pirate, reveal their true identity (*Homeric Hymn to Apollo* 452),[48] but as a consequence, change it, by becoming priests of Apollo at Delphi (as their failed *nostos*, which amounts to death, indicates). In all of these instances, the inquirer is in a privileged position, whereas the fate of the person inquired is sealed by the way he chooses to answer. If he passes the test, then his earlier precarious position is overcome.

This epic strategy is adopted in the texts of the lamellae. The inquirer is in power, and the question-and-answer test, so familiar from the epic world, allows the *mystes*, by answering honestly and as taught during initiation, to acquire a new identity in the Underworld, to bypass death, and to begin a new life after death. The fact that the Homeric question in line 3 may be thematically insignificant perhaps led Zuntz to deny the possibility that line 3 may also be in "rhythmical prose"—his own well-chosen term used in discussing the *symbola* or *synthemata* of the initiate's deification in the texts of group A.[49] And yet both questions in line 3 meet his criteria for "rhythmical prose": they are parallel, and they have an equal number of syllables and accents (two long syllables and a short, – – ◡, which may in fact be two palimbacchiacs, a Dionysiac[?] meter).[50] In addition, these 'questions' follow, in a more moderate way, the pattern of grammatical, phonetic, syntactic, and semantic parallelism specified in relation to the Pelinna text by Charles Segal and Calvert Watkins. Watkins has further suggested that "the strophic alternation of metrical long

---

ἠδὲ τοκῆες, in *Odyssey* 1.170, 3.71, 7.238, 9.252, 10.325, 14.187, 15.264, 19.105, 24.298). I am indebted to Maria Sarinaki for her comments.
[47] Frangoulidis 1993.
[48] See further the section "A Literary Cretan Context."
[49] Zuntz 1971:341 and 382n1.
[50] Tessier 1987:238; Riedweg 2002:464–465.

lines and non-metrical short lines closely recalls the liturgical pattern of the Vedic Asvamedha."[51] For the metrical form in line 4, Gallavotti and Tessier have proposed a combination of a reizianum and an enhoplion,[52] but it seems that the line's dactylic rhythm (actually five dactyls) harkens back to that in lines 1–2, especially if υἱός is read ⌣⌣ as in epic.[53]

The text in lamella no. 9 presents metrical difficulties in the initial foot of the first hexameter, and these problems only worsen in line 2 with the change of the spring's epithet (Σαύρου/Αὔρου) and the spring's location ἐπ᾽ ἀριστερά. Such difficulties are comparable to the ones in texts nos. 1–2, and 4–5, where the epithet αἰειρόω is employed.

These difficulties notwithstanding, the majority of these brief texts comprise two dactylic hexameters (1–2) with a spondee only in the first foot, a line in the ritual's rhythmical prose – – ⌣, and a fourth line again in dactylic rhythm. The new, bacchiac rhythm in line 3 changes the dactylic hexameter and at the same time announces the change of speaker, who initiates the brief stichomythia, but also signals a change of epic expectations.[54] At the level of meter and epic conventions, the change in rhythm may also indicate the new way of achieving immortality. Whereas epic poetry cannot promote any way of transcending death besides *kleos* (through which a mortal can become a hero through the epic poetry itself), the texts on the lamellae introduce another way, alien to epic poetry, but all the while employing the tricks of the epic craft. The epic model of immortality, expressed in dactylic hexameters (lines 1–2), is undermined first by the bacchiac rhythm of line 3 (the inquirer) and then by the dactylic rhythm of line 4 (the initiate), both of which pronounce an alternative route to immortality through initiation into a mystery cult.

Chronology

Based on lettering, orthography, and a comparison with the Italian lamellae, Comparetti accepted Halbherr's dating of Cretan *epistomia* nos. 1–3 to the

---

[51] Segal 1990; Watkins 1995:279. For dialectical, syntactical, and metrical observations on the text from Hipponion, see Iacobacci 1993 and Giangrande 1993. On the subject of magical texts, Christidis' (1997) discussion is applicable to the texts of the gold lamellae, as they betray almost the same aspects of the magical texts, although they cannot be classified with them; see further 93–94nn3–4.

[52] Gallavotti 1978–79:356–357; Tessier 1987:236.

[53] Janko 1984:99.

[54] Dramatic *stichomythiae*, albeit in the same metrical form, show likewise different sound-patterns and rhythm in the exchange of two speakers; for their competitive nature in various performance settings, see Collins 2004:3–60.

second century BCE, a date also accepted by Guarducci for no. 4.[55] By contrast, on the basis of a palaeographic study of the letter-forms and orthography of nos. 5–6 (which he compared to the previously published nos. 1–3 and 7), Verdelis proposed a date no later than the middle of the third century BCE for all seven texts, nos. 1–7.[56] *Epistomia* nos. 1–7 lacked any archaeological context; consequently, any effort at dating them had to be based on palaeographic criteria, which involve personal criteria as well. The result was the two different dates for the Cretan *epistomia*. *Epistomia* nos. 8–9, however, discovered during rescue excavations and thus less difficult to date because of other grave-goods, accentuate vividly the precariousness of strict reliance on palaeographic criteria.[57] If *epistomion* no. 8 were to be dated exclusively on palaeographic grounds, then the letter-forms would certainly indicate the third, if not the late fourth century BCE. And yet, the bronze coin and the other grave-goods offer a secure date for the grave between the last two decades of the first century BCE and the first half of the first century CE. In like manner, although the grave was found disturbed, *epistomion* no. 9 cannot have been placed inside the grave before the second or even the early first century BCE.

The chronological inconsistency between letter-forms and other grave-goods in the case of *epistomion* no. 8 raises an issue seldom touched upon in discussions of the incised gold lamellae and *epistomia*. Dating is most often not absolute but relative to various factors: e.g. the date of the artifacts' manufacture may not always coincide with the period in which they were used as grave-goods, except of course for the exclusively *entaphia*-artifacts. In the case of *epistomion* no. 8, it appears that either the engraver wished to use more archaic-looking letter-forms, or, rather unlikely, the incision of the *epistomion* took place during the third century BCE, and it somehow came to the possession of the deceased, or his family and was employed for his burial sometime between 25 BCE and 40 CE.[58]

It must be emphasized that the dates for these texts incised on the Cretan *epistomia* indicate only the time when the *epistomia* were placed in the graves. As has been noted, those *epistomia* discovered in rescue excavations at Sfakaki seem to fall within the second or first centuries BCE and the first century CE (based on the graves' typology and other grave-goods), whereas nos. 1–7 may

---

[55] Comparetti 1910:39; IC II.xii [Eleutherna].31a–c, 31bis; II.xxx [Loci Incerti].4.

[56] Verdelis 1953–1954; Guarducci 1974a:13.

[57] Tracy (2003, 1995, 1990a, 1982, 1975) has repeatedly advocated restraint in dating inscriptions on the basis of palaeographic criteria alone.

[58] Compare the Petelia text, its provenance, and the related discussion in Zuntz 1971:284, 355–356; and Guarducci 1974a:8–11.

be dated to the third-first centuries BCE. The texts themselves, however, may actually antedate even the third century BCE. The dialectic and metrical forms of the Cretan texts are usually referred to as 'archaisms' and/or local translations of the *Ur-Text*. This "aura of archaic sanctity," as Zuntz described it,[59] is conveyed by all of the incised *epistomia*. More specifically, in the Cretan texts, the major factors in evaluating archaism are not only the lettering in no. 8 and the dialectic and orthographic forms in all nine texts (which, after all, may have been the original ones translated into a more acceptable Panhellenic epic *Kunstsprache*), but also the combination of the dactylic rhythm with the rhythmic prose of the two questions (and possibly more than two, as implies no. 9 above) that are preserved verbatim in nos. 1–6 and 9 (B3–8 and 12) and in the lamella from Thessaly (B9 and Figure 41, page 91). Furley and Bremer have indicated that in dating the inscribed hymn from Palaikastro (no. 16 above), three separate issues must be distinguished: the date of the inscription, the date of the hymn, and the date of the cult behind the hymn.[60] Likewise, these three different aspects should be distinguished in dating the epigram from Phaistos (no. 17 above), and in dating all of the incised lamellae and *epistomia*. In particular, the fact that the Cretan *epistomia* may be dated somewhere between the third century BCE and the first CE does not necessarily bespeak the date of the texts' composition, or the date of the ritual behind the *epistomia*, which undoubtedly antedates the placement of the *epistomia* in the graves. How far back one should go in assigning a date to the text's composition, or to the ritual's appearance on the island (whether it be the third, fourth, or even fifth century BCE) cannot be determined.

Material

All twelve *epistomia* from Eleutherna and Sfakaki, like the majority of the lamellae so far published, are paper-thin foils of gold. The only exception to this rule is one foil of silver from Poseidonia (D1).[61] There are also three cases where, instead of a gold foil, two gold coins (nos. 13–14 above; F8, F9), and a small gold disc are employed (F12). Gold, on account of its natural properties and qualities, became a symbol for eternity and life after death; the practice of depositing gold objects in graves is, as Zuntz keenly observed, "unlikely

---

[59] Zuntz 1971:342n1.
[60] Furley and Bremer 2001:vol. 1:69–70, vol. 2:3–4.
[61] For the two silver lamellae also discovered in Thourioi, see Zuntz 1971:291n1; Riedweg 1998:390.

to have been a mere ostentation of riches, just as its opposite, the dark and heavy lead, was used to promote destruction and death. It does not, in fact, seem unreasonable to assume that the Orphic lamellae were consciously devised as a positive counterpart to the traditional *defixiones*."[62] The texts on the gold lamellae are literally and metaphorically gold because of their valuable promise for access to a golden world,[63] and because "both the immortalizing gold and the ivy-leaf shape reinforce their message by the physical form of their medium," as Segal aptly put it for the Pelinna lamella.[64]

Shape—Burial Context

Cretan *epistomia* nos. 1–3, 5–7, 9, and 11–12 are oblong, whereas nos. 4, 8, and 10 are ellipsoid, in the shape of the mouth, indicating their use as an *epistomion*. This word has become a *terminus technicus* at least among the majority of Greek archaeologists, who have no difficulty in identifying paper-thin gold foils as *epistomia*,[65] using as a definitive criterion the position of the foils inside the grave.

The custom, however, of covering the mouth or the whole face of the deceased did not start with the incised lamellae, nor did it end in late antiquity as nos. 18–25 above indicate. The *epistomia* date from the end of 5000 BCE until the second and third centuries CE, and their shapes are relatively few: oblong, rhomboid, ellipsoid in the shape of the mouth, and (very rarely) rectangular or triangular. The decorative motifs of the unincised *epistomia*, embossed or engraved, vary greatly.[66] The majority of these artifacts were thought to be jewelry, which formed part of the body's *kosmos*, until Pierre Amandry

---

[62] Zuntz 1971:285–286 with n4.

[63] Zuntz 1971:285–286; Tortorelli Ghidini 1995a; Bodel 2001, 23; Despoini 1996 and 1998; Oikonomou 2002:25.

[64] Segal 1990:414–415; see also Ricciardelli 1992. For poetic references to gold and the utopian and eschatological worlds in the archaic period, see especially Brown 1998.

[65] Oikonomou (2004:91–92), instead of the word *epistomion* she employed earlier (2002), defines these objects as "burial jewels: the custom of mouth bands" (Νεκρικά κοσμήματα: τα ελάσματα κάλυψης του στόματος), on account of the meaning of ἐπιστοματίζω and the like (LSJ). Interestingly, however, the noun derived from this verb is the feminine *epistomis*, whereas *epistomion* appears not to have been a word in antiquity, as a search in *Thesaurus Linguae Graecae* has shown.

[66] Oikonomou (2002:17–21, 43; 2004) has gathered all the information of 239 published lamellae, the majority in gold and only 8 in silver, which may be classified as *epistomia*, and studied this custom diachronically. For jewelry from the Neolithic period and its symbolism, if any, see the sensible remarks of Demakopoulou 1998; and Kyparissi-Apostolika 1998; 2001:155–166; for Greek and Roman jewelry in general, see Higgins 1961. For a brief, online overview of Greek burial customs, see: http://www.ims.forth.gr/joint_projects/e-mem/burial_customs-gr.htm.

suggested that the lamellae are descendants of the Mycenaean gold masks.[67] Instead of covering the whole face of the deceased, people gradually employed (for economic and perhaps for more practical reasons) smaller foils for the forehead, eyes, mouth, and ears.[68] Aikaterini Despoini (1998) has shown incontrovertibly, under the telling title *Gold epistomia*,[69] that, as the excavations of the cemetery at Sindos in Macedonia during 1980–82 and subsequent discoveries in graves throughout Macedonia testify, the paper-thin gold foils, which were found near the cranium or even on the chest of the skeleton where some of these may have slipped (and which were described earlier as diadems or pectorals), had been used as *epistomia*, mouth-bands. Shape and motif of these *epistomia* do not appear to be important factors, except that these mouthbands, rectangular, oblong, or rhomboid, approximate the shape of the mouth. The drawing by Arnold von Salis (Figure 40, page 90) offers an idea of the way in which these *epistomia* were fastened behind the head with a string passing through holes on either end.[70] Despoini, however, suggested that in all probability they were sewed on the garment that eventually covered the head, but, as not all *epistomia* bear marks of a needle, they may have been simply put on the mouth or on the chest of the deceased. The grave-goods in some of these graves, which are published, do not delineate a recurrent pattern so as to substantiate a distinct burial custom for those deceased bearing an *epistomion*, incised or not.[71] As a result, the reasons for this custom or its presence in different areas and especially in different times cannot be ascertained, despite

[67] Amandry 1953:37; Laffineur (1980:364–366) accepts as *epistomia* only those foils in the shape of a mouth; Oikonomou 2004:102–103.

[68] For gold masks and gold foils covering the eyes and other body-parts, recently discovered in graves at Archontiko near Pella, Macedonia, and dated to the archaic period, see Chryssostomou and Chryssostomou 2001 and 2002. Another mask of solid gold, weighing more than half a kilogram, portraying a face with closed eyes and robust expression, has been unearthed in the outskirts of Shipka Peak, near the town of Kazanlak, Bulgaria by a team of archaeologists led by Georgi Kitov (2005); see also Williams 2006; for a second gold mask discovered by the same archaeologist in a Thracian mound near the village of Topolchene, the municipality of Sliven, see the reports in: http://dsc.discovery.com/news/2007/07/16/mask_arc.html?category=archaeology; and in: http://www.novinite.com/view_news.php?id=83027.

[69] Despoini had excluded this group of gold artifacts from her earlier study *Ancient Greek Gold Jewelry* (1996).

[70] von Salis 1957:98 Abb. 8; see also Vermeule 1979:14; Garland 1985:23–24, 138; and Kurtz and Boardman 1994:210–213. Recently, from four graves of male warriors in Sindos, dated in the sixth century BCE, gold *epistomia* were recovered in a unique shape which, according to the excavators, is reminiscent of the archaic smile (Keramaris, Protopsalti, and Tsolakis 2002:233–234, 239 no. 3); they also look almost identical to von Salis' drawing reproduced in Figure 40 (page 90). For unincised epistomia, dated to the archaic period, see also Skarlatidou 2007, 30, 34, 58–59.

[71] Oikonomou 2002:6, 43–44, and 2004.

Lucian's satire of this custom wherein the deceased is unable to open his mouth and speak, as his jaws are tied up by the cloth.[72] To state the obvious: people in different periods and in different areas felt the need to cover the face or, more specifically, the mouth of the deceased.

There is, however, a special category that deserves attention: the incised or unincised lamellae in the shape of certain leaves, a word which sometimes is also employed for the incised lamellae to describe thinness, regardless of shape.[73] Some of these leaves were used as *epistomia*, but not exclusively. Unfortunately, the excavators' preliminary reports seldom provide detailed information regarding the exact findspot of these gold leaves or of their accompanying grave-goods (Tables 1–2). Even when such information is provided, few students have paid attention to the archaeological context of the lamellae, in order to understand shapes, material, usage, and texts.[74] It is therefore worthwhile to survey briefly the evidence for the grave-goods, where available, accompanying each of the nine incised leaves and each of the remaining thirty–five incised lamellae which have been published, in order to gain a general picture, especially on the issues of shape, context, and usage.

Only eight (D2, E3, F2, F4, F5, F6, F7, F11) incised gold leaves have been found so far in graves in Macedonia and in the north-northwest Peloponnese. The ninth leaf may have been written on in ink, now lost, as Pavlos Chryssostomou (1992) has proposed (G1). What emerges from the excavators' reports is that, except for the unambiguous ivy leaves from Pelinna (D2) and for Philemena's myrtle leaf from Elis which is also employed as a *danake* (F7),[75] the shape of the remaining seven leaves is either unknown or described as laurel or almond-shaped. In his study of the shapes of the incised leaves that have been published, Matthew Dickie has argued convincingly that the literary sources and the archaeological record allow for only a few trees to be represented by

---

[72] Lucian *On mourning* 19.16–20: ὥστε μοι νὴ τὴν Τισιφόνην πάλαι δὴ ἐφ᾽ οἷς ἐποιεῖτε καὶ ἐλέγετε παμμέγεθες ἐπῄει ἀνακαγχάσαι, διεκώλυσε δὲ ἡ ὀθόνη καὶ τὰ ἔρια, οἷς μου τὰς σιαγόνας ἀπεσφίγξατε.

[73] Parker and Stamatopoulou (2004:n1) clarify the conventional use of the word. Actual (ivy-) leaves, incised with just a name, were also used as 'mantic votes,' as the scene on the krater by the Sisyphos painter in Munich indicates, for which see Tiverios 1985:49–56, pl. 5–6; for the ivy of liberation, see Lewis 1990.

[74] Notable exceptions are: Zuntz 1971; Guarducci 1974a; Bottini 1992; Graf 1993; Dickie 1995a; Bernabé and Jiménez San Cristóbal 2001; Oikonomou 2002; Salskov Roberts 2002; and Parker and Stamatopoulou 2004.

[75] Themelis 1994; on the name Philemena, see Zoumbaki 2005:354–355. Greek archaeologists employ the word *danake* for foreign coins or pseudo-coins with no monetary value; the word denoted foreign coins, perhaps Persian according to the Lexicographers: Pollux *Onomastikon* 9.82.9–83.5; Suda s.v.; Hesychius s.v.; Photius s.v.

these gold leaves: primarily myrtle and ivy, and less often olive.[76] All three are evergreen trees associated with fertility, vegetation, and the chthonian aspects of Dionysos, Demeter and Persephone, Aphrodite, and also perhaps Athena. As Dickie discovered, and as Davaras, Despoini, and Kaninia also stressed in their studies of gold wreaths,[77] there is an insurmountable difficulty in distinguishing especially between myrtle-, laurel- and sometimes olive-leaves. This may be due to the shape of these leaves, all of them being oblong with differences in details which the ancient goldsmiths could not or did not care to reproduce. The goldsmiths may have been interested simply in a more schematic representation, letting the customer decide, or as Dickie aptly put it, letting the "context determine which plant was imagined to be represented."[78]

There is, however, further evidence corroborating Dickie's interpretation of these as myrtle-leaves, instead of laurel- or almond-shaped leaves, when the other grave-goods are taken into consideration. Together with the Poseidippos leaf (E3)[79] were recovered clay gilt myrtle-berries from a wreath and forty-one clay gilt pebbles in the shape of acorns, forty-six bone astragaloi, and a clay figurine of a female. The leaf of Philoxena (F6) was accompanied by clay myrtle-berries from a wreath and bronze gilt leaves, whereas Philon's leaf (F5) was found with twelve lance-shaped leaves apparently from a gold wreath. The ivy-leaves from Pelinna (D2) were discovered with: a *danake* with gorgon in the deceased female's mouth; a coin of Antigonos Gonatas; a diadem-like wreath of lead stem; gilt clay berries and gilt bronze myrtle-leaves with a gold ornament in the cranium; nearby a clay aryter; a clay bowl and two gold spirals ending in snake-heads; near the feet another clay aryter with a lamp inside it, a clay unguentarium, two bowls and a shallow skyphos; by the feet a bronze lebes with the bones of a neonate, probably the case of a baby and its mother having died in childbirth; and on the cover slab of the marble sarcophagus two clay bowls and fragments of a third, a clay feeder, and a clay figurine of a comic actor sitting on an altar.[80] The grave-goods recovered

---

[76] Dickie 1995a:84–86.

[77] Davaras 1985:180–182; Despoini 1996:26; and Kaninia 1994–1995:105 with nn21–22.

[78] Dickie 1995a:86.

[79] For Poseidippos (I retain the orthography of the name on the lamella E3 from Pella) and the probability that he may have been related to his Pellaean namesake poet in Alexandria, see Dickie 1994, 1995a, 1995b, 1998; Rossi 1996. For the Alexandrian poet's work, see the essays in Acosta-Hughes, Kosmetatou, and Baumbach 2004, and in Gutzwiller 2005a; for Poseidippos' references to initiates in mystery cults in his funerary epigrams, Dignas 2004; Clay 2004:84–86; and for Poseidippos' *sphragis,* Gutzwiller 2005b:317–318.

[80] The description of this important burial follows that of Parker and Stamatopoulou (2004), who set the record straight. Salskov Roberts (2002:16) notes that "it is most likely that the two

together with the unincised olive(?)-leaf (G1) are two gold myrtle-wreaths together with the bones wrapped in purple gold cloth inside the larnax which was placed inside a marble sarcophagus.

Statistically, these graves are few, but it seems that together with the gold leaf, the deceased was also 'crowned' by myrtle- and/or oak-wreaths (E3, F6, G1), either of pure gold or gilt clay. Given that laurel-wreaths in the archaeological record of Macedonia are scarce, because, as Despoini observed, laurel was the sacred tree of Apollo, whose relations with the dead and the Underworld were virtually non-existent,[81] and given that, in two cases, myrtle-wreaths were found together with the incised gold-leaves (E3, F6), it is rather unlikely that these leaves were meant to represent laurel-leaves. This is most probably also the case with the leaf from Aigeion (F5), although the possibility of the existence of different kinds of leaves cannot be ruled out, as the discovery of the 'olive'-leaf indicates (G1).

A more or less similar picture emerges from the archaeological context of the remaining sixteen lamellae which have brief texts (Tables 1–2) and are either rectangular, 'leaf'-, or mouth-shaped. Three graves with lamellae engraved with brief texts stand out specifically because of their grave-goods. In the grave of Phylomaga (no. 15 above; F3) the accompanying goods were: ivory fragments of the bier's decoration representing floral patterns and figures of the Dionysiac cycle,[82] two gold finger-rings, and a bronze gilt wreath. Bottakos (F10) was buried with a bronze gilt wreath with berries; outside the grave to the northeast a trapezoid construction was found, apparently for the funeral supper (a similar case in D4, E5), and to the northwest of this construction were unearthed pottery fragments, traces of *enagismos* in later times, and

---

depositions were contemporaneous and made about 275 BC" (14); she associates, as indications that the deceased were initiates in Bacchic mysteries (16–17), the Maenad terracotta statuette with 'similar' ones found in Lokroi, South Italy (tomb 934), and in Sennaia, Phanagoria, South Russia, "where the influence of Dionysiac cult is noticeable, e.g. in Olbia, where some bone plaques from the 5th century BC with inscriptions referring to Dionysos have been found" (17).

[81] Savvopoulou (1995:399, 404 no. 14), however, publishes a laurel-wreath from a grave in Europos. Despoini (1996:26) explains that the oak-wreaths in Macedonia are related to Zeus, whose cult was boosted by the Argead dynasty, whereas olive-wreaths appear in graves of Amphipolis (and perhaps Potidaia), colonies of Athens, and are therefore associated with Athena. She offers excellent photographs of wreaths recovered from graves: a rare one of ivy (Despoini 1996:47 pl. 1; add also Adam-Veleni 2000); four of myrtle (Despoini 1996:48 pl. 2, 52 pl. 5, 53 pl. 6 (zoom of pl. 5) and 54 pl. 7); two of oak (Despoini 1996:49 pl. 3 and 50–51 pl. 4); and one of olive (Despoini 1996:55 pl. 8); to these add also Kallintzi 2006:148 pl. 20.1; Skarlatidou 2007:82–83; on wreaths in Macedonia, also Tsigarida 1999.

[82] A great number of fragmentary biers recovered from Macedonian graves were decorated with Dionysiac motifs and themes, for which see Sismanidis 1997:especially 212–215.

a bronze gilt wreath with gilt clay berries. Inside Euxena's grave (F1),[83] fragments of gold foils from a diadem were found.

Finally, of the nineteen remaining lamellae with long texts (Tables 1–2), four stand out in terms of their burial context.[84] Three burials at Thourioi (A1–3) yielded no offerings, except for the small hollows in the four corners of the chamber of grave 1, filled with ashes of bones and plants, indicating funeral sacrifices. The remaining two, however, are unique (A4, C1), in that the tumulus above the grave was nothing more than deposits of eight strata, each consisting of ashes, carbon and burnt pottery sherds topped by earth above, a strong indication of rituals, sacrifices, and hero-worship of the dead buried inside. Outside the grave only a few small black vases were found, and inside the chamber, where the cremation took place and the remains were simply covered by a white sheet which disintegrated when touched by the excavators, were found bronze locks of the coffin, two silver medallions on the chest decorated with 'female heads' (reminiscent of the head of Persephone to be found in images on the Apulian vases), a few small pieces of gold from the dress' decoration, and two small wooden boxes with inlaid palmettes. The two gold lamellae were discovered one inside the other, A4 folded nine times and placed inside C1, which was folded like an envelope. The Petelia lamella (B1), according to Zuntz, was somehow recovered from its grave at a later period, rolled up, and clipped off, in order to fit in a gold case with chain attached, dated to second–third century CE; the final product was an amulet used for its "outstanding magical virtue."[85] Lastly, the lamella from Pharsalos (B2) was discovered with two other small objects inside a hydria-urn which in turn had been placed inside a round limestone container. The urn, manufactured exclusively for burial use, is decorated at the base with ivy-leaves and anthemia, and below the neck-handle there is a representation of the 'abduction' of Oreithyia by Boreas, a scene essentially similar, according to Verdelis, to the abduction of Persephone by Plouton.[86]

This brief survey of the graves and their respective goods leads to some important points concerning the overall burial context of each grave.[87] In

[83] Papathanassopoulos 1969; Zoumbaki 2005:169.

[84] Guarducci 1974a:8–18; and Parker and Stamatopoulou 2004.

[85] Zuntz 1971:355–356. For a gold engraved amulet encased, see Maltomini 2006.

[86] Verdelis 1950–1951; Parker and Stamatopoulou 2004. Scullion (1998) discusses the cathartic aspect of Dionysos' *mania* in the fifth stasimon of Sophocles' *Antigone*; Cullyer (2005) argues that the north wind blowing from Thrace is an allusion to the Thracian god (the Delphic Dionysos), in addition to that of Lykourgos, which sweeps through the house of Labdakos.

[87] There will always be an interpretative tension between textual and archaeological evidence and the methodological attempts to make sense of them both; see Morris 1987; the essays in

Macedonia, where more than half of the lamellae and *epistomia* discovered are incised with only a few words and where no lamellae and *epistomia* have been found bearing a longer text, shape did not matter, or so it appears. The *epistomia* of Hegesiska, Poseidippos, Philoxena, and the blank leaf (F11, E3, F6, and G1) are myrtle- or olive-leaves, as (most probably) are the ones from the Peloponnese (F2, F4, F5, F7). The shape of the remaining lamellae with short texts is either rectangular or rhomboid. There are also three extraordinary cases in Pieria, two gold coins employed instead of lamellae in Pydna (F8, F9), and another in the shape of a coin (a pseudo-coin?) in Dion (F12).

In certain cases, the deceased was crowned with wreaths of gold or of gilt clay, which were less expensive (E3, F5, F6, F10, G1),[88] or, in two instances, with a diadem (D2 and F1). In seven cases, the deceased appear to have received offerings, sacrifices, and *enagismoi* in some form of ritual after burial, with Timpone Grande standing out perhaps as a case of a local hero-cult (A1–4, C1, D4, E5, F10).[89] There are also four cases in which Dionysiac overtones emerge, irrespective of the text incised on the gold lamellae: D2 was accompanied by a clay figurine of a comic actor seated-on-altar in addition to the two incised ivy-leaves placed over each breast of the buried female; in the Timpone Grande at Thourioi, two medallions with a female head looking like the Persephone on the Apulian vases were placed on the chest of the deceased (A4, C1);[90] the Pharsalos hydria bears a representation of the 'abduction' of Oreithyia by Boreas, which reminds the excavator of the more familiar one of Persephone by Plouton and which "prepares and complements the text on the lamella" (B2);[91] finally, ivory fragments from the bier's decoration in Methone represent figures from the Dionysiac cycle (F3).

The presence of gold or gilt clay wreaths inside a grave in addition to an engraved *epistomion* seems to defy explanation. Despoini has noticed that relatively few wreaths have been found in the hundreds of graves in Attica,

---

Small 1994; Sourvinou-Inwood 1995, especially 413–444; Georgoulaki 1996; and below, page 76n101.

[88] See also Vermeule 1979:13–15.

[89] For these trapezoid constructions or *exedrai* used for rituals after burial, see Tsimbidou-Avloniti 1992; Savvopoulou 1992; and Malama 2000 and 2001. These *exedrai*, however, are not exclusively for deceased with incised or unincised lamellae, as they are also found elsewhere, e.g. in the Europos cemetery (Savvopoulou, Giannakis, and Niaouris 2000), and in other parts of the Amphipolis cemetery (Malama 2000 and 2001).

[90] Graf 1993:254–255.

[91] Ricardo Olmos in Bernabé and Jiménez San Cristóbal 2001:310–313, 313. Salskov Roberts (2002:20–21) draws on Richter's (1946:361–367) study of hydriae with related subjects, Dionysos and Ariadne, and Dionysos with a satyr, all symbolizing love and marriage.

despite the frequent references in literature and in inscriptions to honors individuals received, sometimes including a gold wreath, and other times including a myrtle crown after initiation at Eleusis.[92] Most of these, as with the gold athletic wreaths,[93] would have been dedicated to the appropriate god after the celebration and some would have ended up in graves. The number of wreaths, however, recovered from graves in Macedonia, indicates, according to Despoini, that the crowned deceased, reenacting the *persona* of either 'an athlete' or 'a symposiast' or (less likely in Macedonia) 'a honored citizen,' would have certainly expected to attain eternal life among the blessed.[94] The metaphor of the foot-race and the crowning of the victorious 'athlete' is employed in lines 9–10 of the lamella from Thourioi (A1): ἱμερτῶ δ' ἐπέβαν στεφά|νο ποσὶ καρπαλίμοισι. According to Zuntz,[95] the line is spurious because it is repeated in lines 12–14 of the same lamella, even though he admits that *stephanos*, the normal prize of victors, is appropriate for the occasion, and that it is used elsewhere, again metaphorically, to denote purpose and distinction. Bernabé and Jiménez San Cristóbal have discussed in more detail the literary references to events for which a wreath was employed and have concluded that the wreath-metaphor, rich in symbolism, may at the same time stand for mystic initiation, athletic triumph, and symposium.[96] But what about the deceased (especially in Macedonia) in whose graves both an incised *epistomion* and a wreath have been recovered?[97] Is it sheer coincidence, or is this *steph-*

---

[92] Despoini 1996:26–28; Guarducci 1973, 1975, 1977. Dickie (1995a:84–86) suggests that the myrtle crowns are reminiscent of Eleusinian initiation, but Parker and Stamatopoulou (2004) rightly stress that the texts on the lamellae defy any one association with a specific mystery cult; also Parker 2005:327–368, 360–361n159. Chaniotis (2005c:50–55) argues that *stephanosis* accommodated a variety of purposes from the Hellenistic period onwards with different symbolism and meaning. Scafuro (2005) discusses instances in inscriptions, which prescribe that wreaths were to be dedicated to gods, and that statues of gods were to be crowned by wreaths. Günther (2003) examines the crowning with wreaths of the prophets in inscriptions from Didyma as an immortalizing self-representation.

[93] Kefalidou 1996 for representations of athletes in iconography.

[94] Despoini 1996:28.

[95] Zuntz 1971:319n2.

[96] Bernabé and Jiménez San Cristóbal 2001:165–173, 241; also Guthrie 1993:180–182; Graf and Johnston 2007:127–128. Seaford (1986:23–25) discusses the roundness of the wreath and the association of its origin with Prometheus. Kokkinia (1999) associates the ritual of roses (*rhodismos*) over the grave during the Roman period with the *rosalia* and *parentalia*, and also with the wreaths offered to the dead in Greece.

[97] Wreaths or parts of them, most often gilt clay but also gold, are very often recovered from graves in Macedonia and are usually dated to the Hellenistic period, as can be seen by a perusal of the archaeological reports published in the volumes *Το Αρχαιολογικό Έργο στη Μακεδονία και Θράκη*. For two probable cases in Athens, see Theochari 2003; for Cretan cases, see Figure 44 (pages 194) and page 195n146.

anosis nothing more than the material sign of the lines in the Thourioi text A1? Does this connote not only a metaphorical but also an actual event of the initiation? Would this burial practice in Macedonia thus allow us to associate the texts of group A with the ones in groups B and E? Whatever the case, the coincidence is indeed remarkable.

Likewise, the overall picture of "Men and Women, Rich and Poor" (to borrow Graf's title[98]) that emerges from the graves where lamellae and *epistomia* have been found is not clear, as the evidence is inconclusive and perhaps misleading. In terms of gender, males and females are equally equipped with the necessities for their eternal trip. There is no evidence to suggest any preferences, besides the usual, of males or females regarding certain types of offerings or concerning the texts incised. In terms of affluence, richer graves may give an impression of a 'Dionysiac context,' while poorer graves may allude to an 'Orphic/Pythagorean' one. The archaeological finds in the graves at Thourioi (A1–4, C1) are moderate if not austere in comparison to the finds in some graves at Macedonia, but grave-goods at Thourioi may have been of less importance as compared to the tomb's actual construction and the later ritual over the tumuli. Even so, as Themelis and Touratsoglou have shown convincingly with regard to the Derveni grave, generalizations and *prima facie* conclusions should be resisted. The discovery of the papyrus in Derveni grave A led to the conclusion that the deceased was an Orphic follower. The richness, however, and the strong Dionysiac character of the grave's archaeological context stand in sharp contrast to the Orphic-Pythagorean austere life and to its more moderate means.[99] As has become evident only recently, 'Orphism' and Dionysos are not, after all, mutually exclusive. The graves with a lamella at Hipponion, Thessaly, and Sfakaki constitute an intermediate stage between the 'rich' burial customs in Macedonia and the 'poor' ones in

---

[98] Graf 1993:255.

[99] Themelis and Touratsoglou 1997:148–149; see also Nilsson 1985, especially 116–147; Burkert 1987; Oikonomou 2002:48–49; Most 1997b; and Kouremenos, Parássoglou, and Tsantsanoglou 2006:3–5. For the funerary architecture in Macedonia, see Guimier-Sorbets and Morizot 2006. Salskov Roberts (2002:23 and 27–28) is overstating her case, when she notes that: "initiates of mystery cults were apparently not allowed spectacular tomb-gifts apart from the small gold foil with the formula essential to gain new life, but vessels like water-jugs, skyphoi, and lamps in plainware seem to have been characteristic for these burials, presumably because they were thought to be important at various stages in the Beyond and they may be indications of the beliefs of the buried people even when written evidence is missing. The funeral regulations of Delphi and Keos ... show that it was often ordinary household vessels that were used for burials. These plain containers might be invested with symbolic meaning by the actual placing in the tomb or by the rites performed at the deposition."

Thourioi.[100] The grave-goods recovered from the five graves with an *episto-mion* in the Sfakaki cemetery indicate that the deceased were of moderate means; these five graves are not among the richest of the 56 excavated at Sfakaki so far, but they are richer than the pit-graves. The overall picture of the undisturbed graves is that of a careful and well-ordered burial but with no extravagance.

Usage

A key issue related to the lamellae's shape and apparently a matter of impor-tance to those buried with an *epistomion* was the placement of the lamella inside the grave. Some are found near the cranium or the mouth (A4, C1, E4, F7, F8, F9), others on the chest (B10[101], D2, D3?, D4), or, less often, close to hand (A1–3, F3). What is striking is that the so-called Charon's obol or *danake* was placed inside the mouth, at least from the second half of the fifth century BCE onwards,[102] but it was also placed in the hand, on the chest, or simply anywhere inside the grave, a practice that Guarducci associated with the incised lamellae.[103]

Not all graves, however, contained a coin, and not all graves with an *epistomion* contained coins—these two facts imply a differentiation in burial

---

[100] Parker and Stamatopoulou (2004) note the wealthy burial context of a deceased with an incised lamella, but this is not the case in Sfakaki.

[101] Salskov Roberts (2002:23) probably by oversight notes that it was found "rolled up," for which see Pugliese Carratelli 2001:44. Salskov Roberts (2002:22–26), in her discussion of grave-goods from the Hipponion tomb offers a number of interpretations, plausible enough, which, however, must perforce remain hypotheses. For example, she suggests that "the two skyphoi and the lamp found outside the Hipponion tomb may show a final rite of libation performed after the closing of the tomb. The lamp may be taken to show that this also in Magna Graecia took place before daybreak, as prescribed for Attica ... Inside the tomb there was also a lamp placed in the left hand of the skeleton, this presumably meant to illuminate the path in Hades ... The jug, as well as the small hydriae, might well be thought to come in useful in carrying out the procedures in the Underworld with the two springs and a lake. Finally, there were some bronze fragments of a ring (or clasp?) with an oval disc placed on the left shoulder and at the right elbow a small bronze hemisphere, perhaps part of a bell—to announce the new arrival?" (23–24). Likewise, for the graffiti on the skyphos from Hipponion, on the back side of two of the bone plaques from Olbia, and on two Etruscan bowls she proposes that "it is possible to see this as a version of the Zeta taken to be a symbol of the tearing to pieces, which seems to have played an essential part in Bacchic/Orphic cult" (26); Lévêque (2000) identifies the Zeta with Zagreus. For the toys of Dionysos in myth and ritual, see Tortorelli Ghidini 2000b; for toys in graves at Abdera, see Papaïkonomou 2006.

[102] For the use of burial-coins in graves of Macedonia, dated in the middle fifth century BCE, see Misaïlidou-Despotidou 1995:315; Chryssanthaki-Nagle 2006.

[103] Guarducci 1974a:8–18.

practices and funerary ideology. Placing a coin in a grave is not a widespread phenomenon within the ancient Greek necropoleis. This practice should therefore not be associated exclusively with Charon's Greek myth, because it does not fit entirely well with this myth, and because it is also attested in other cultures where the Charon myth does not exist. The first evidence of this practice, so it appears, comes from the famous scenes of Aristophanes' *Frogs* between Dionysos, Xanthias, and Heracles (lines 139–140), and between Dionysos, Xanthias, and Charon (lines 170–270). The ferryman transports the dead for a fee to the Underworld, where, instead of the fee, Dionysos is forced to pay in kind, 'working' as an oarsman, a theme that will be later developed and expanded. There is no doubt that this was an actual practice at the time of Aristophanes—otherwise the scene's jokes and hilarity would be pointless—but this does not confirm how widespread it was, nor does it answer why only a rather small group of people practiced it. Although she does not discuss the issue of the burial-coin practice, Christiane Sourvinou-Inwood has argued convincingly that Charon the ferryman and Hermes Chthonios emerge as *psychopompoi* in art already by ca. 500 BCE.[104] This indicates shifting attitudes and ideologies in the archaic period as new needs arose, either from a development of a more individualistic attitude towards and concern for death, the afterlife, and its rituals, or from the emergence of a polis system which looked to control burial practices as well as funerary rituals and ideology.

Keld Grinder-Hansen (1991) proposed to replace expressions like "Charon's/Charonian obol/fee/coin" with the less ideologically-charged "death/burial-coin" or the like, whereas Susan Stevens rightly stressed that references or allusions to "Charon's obol" in a variety of texts are guided by different aims, all of which imply a connection between poverty and death, as the obol is the cheapest denominator. Thus, this expression is employed for humor or an ironic look at the vanity of conventional views on the afterlife, but it also signals the replacement of alimentary goods in the grave in exchange for the nourishment of the soul as it begins its journey. When the coin is placed inside the mouth immediately after death, it may especially denote "a rite of passage rather than burial practice."[105] This interpretative variety is also exhibited in the archaeological record and, according to Stevens, it comes from a belief rooted in the religious-magical significance and intrinsic value of coins on account of their 'invisible' power. This burial

---

[104] Sourvinou-Inwood 1995:303–361, especially 353–356; and also Vermeule 1979:4–5, 211–212; Seaford 2004a:162–165.
[105] Stevens 1991:221.

practice or rite of passage was "a way for the living to communicate with the dead, to promote life among the dead, while the door to the other world was still open."[106] Renata Cantilena has correctly remarked that change in terminology provides a more accurate description of the facts, but does not solve the essential problem of explaining the funerary ideology, if any, behind this burial practice.[107] Placing a coin in a grave has indeed been explained in many different ways: it may or may not indicate the affluence of the deceased and his or her social status as another burial offering; it may constitute a symbolic payment or recompense facilitating the passage from life to death; it may also have been used as a talisman to protect the dead or as an amulet for protection of the living against the dead; or even, as Rhode had proposed,[108] as a *pars pro toto*, symbolizing the transference of the dead's wealth to the living members of his family.[109]

These explanations, alongside with others that account for economic, political, and social circumstances, need not account for every coin in every grave. They simply bring to the fore some of the ideas and symbolism that people may or may not have had in relation to the burial-coin practice. Sourvinou-Inwood's recommendation of "more complex and ambivalent categories" to replace a "dichotomy belief/not belief of the Greeks in the myth of Charon" which is "culturally determined and misleading"[110] is applicable *mutatis mutandis* to the practice of the burial-coin, and arguably to the use of the gold lamellae and *epistomia* as well. In particular, there are cases (D2, D4, E4, F2, F4, F5, F7, F8, F9, F12?, G1) where both a lamella and a coin or pseudo-coin accompany the deceased, but there are cases where only a lamella is found, and when it functions also as an *epistomion*, the lamella apparently takes over the coin's duties altogether.

For these difficult issues, the excavated part of the Sfakaki cemetery may serve as a test case for a rule of thumb. Of the 56 burials excavated so far, five graves contained gold lamellae (nos. 8–12 above; B12, E4, G2–4). All of them, regardless of shape ('mouth,' rectangular, rhomboid), were *epistomia*, i.e. they were found in the mouth or near the cranium, and in one case, a bronze coin

---

[106] Stevens 1991:223–227 and 229.

[107] Cantilena (1995:165–166) in her introduction to the Proceedings of the Conference: *Caronte - Un obolo per l'aldilà*, published in *Parola del Passato* 50 (1995) 165–535; in this special issue, see also the contributions, important for the present discussion, by Parise 1995; Mugione 1995; Cerchiai 1995; Bragantini 1995; Torraca 1995; Cerri 1995; Tortorelli Ghidini 1995a; and Pontrandolfo 1995.

[108] Rhode 1987:306–307.

[109] Grinder-Hansen 1991:215; Stevens 1991:227–228; and Cantilena 1995.

[110] Sourvinou-Inwood 1995:355.

was found on the chest of the deceased (no. 8 above; E4). One is dated between the third and early first centuries BCE and four are dated to the first century CE, and they comprise three groups of gold lamellae, just as the *epistomia* from Macedonia, Thessaly, and South Italy (Tables 1–2): unincised (group G), incised with a few words (group E), and incised with a long text (group B).

The *epistomia* from Sfakaki together with their grave-goods demonstrate similarities in burial customs—whether this might also indicate familial relations of the deceased must remain a conjecture—but at the same time, they militate against generalizations. Of the twenty-six graves studied so far, including those with *epistomia* nos. 8, and 10–12 above, twenty-two contained burial-coins, but of the four graves with *epistomia*, in only one grave was a coin discovered on the chest of the young male (no. 8 above; E4). This may be accidental, but it may also be that the deceased with *epistomion* no. 8 and his relatives felt strongly about the burial-coin practice, whereas the deceased with nos. 10–12 (G2–4) probably employed these three unincised *epistomia* as pseudo-burial-coins, because of their intrinsic value, and at the same time perhaps as unincised tokens of initiates for passage and transfer to a special place of the Underworld.

Margarita Guarducci was the first to realize the similarities between the custom of placing a coin in the mouth and the customs seemingly surrounding some of the *epistomia*.[111] Accordingly, she postulated a practical explanation. On account of its shape and the fact that it is not folded, lamella no. 4 above (B6) was probably placed at the right hand, as the Thourioi lamellae (A1–3), whereas lamellae nos. 1–3 above (B3–5), on account of their being folded, were probably placed inside the mouth, the safest place of the body. Guarducci's suggestion encountered Zuntz's scepticism,[112] because *epistomia* nos. 1–3 above (B3–5) were not unearthed during systematic excavations. Puzzled, however, by the fact that some lamellae were found folded or rolled up, so as to 'become coins' and fit into the mouth in order to 'put the right words on the tongue,' Zuntz allowed for the possibility that some of these may have been later employed as amulets. There is, however, no substantial evidence whatsoever that these were put inside cases, except for the curious case of the Petelia lamella (B1), and for the reports of the Eleutherna sellers for nos. 5–6 above (B7–8).[113] In like manner, Petros Themelis (1994) suggested for the gold myrtle-leaf incised with the female deceased's name (F7) that, since no coin

---

[111] Guarducci 1939; IC II, p. 314–315; and especially 1974a:8–18.
[112] Zuntz 1971:335–336n2.
[113] See 93–94nn3–4.

was found inside the grave and the leaf was discovered under the cranium, the incised myrtle-leaf may have also served as a *danake*.

Guarducci's and Themelis' cautious suggestions are corroborated by three unique (thus far) examples in Macedonia, which bring together the use of the burial-coin practice with the mystic *symbola*. Matthaios Bessios (nos. 13–14 above; F8, F9; Figures 14–15) reports the discovery of two gold coins of Philip II incised with a male and a female name: Andron and Xenariste, respectively; the coins were found in the mouths of the deceased, buried in two almost identically decorated graves.[114] Dimitrios Pantermalis has published from Macedonian Grave V in Dion a photograph of a small gold disc on which the name Epigenes was incised with dotted letter-strokes (F12).[115] Coins on which personal names are incised are extremely rare: either because of a lack of a gold foil, or lack of time, or for some other reason, the relatives(?) of Andron, Xenariste, and perhaps Epigenes employed two gold coins and a small gold disc (as a token or as a pseudo-coin?) on which they engraved the names. These three examples appear to combine (in a manner so far unique) the burial-coin with the gold lamella practices.[116] A comparable but not entirely similar case is presented by a gold rectangular tablet with an inscription addressing Serapis, found inside a skull in a cinerary urn in Columbarium III at Rome. Although it is not Orphic, this phylactery, with its address to Serapis, presents (according to David Jordan) a curious case of either a Charonian obol or a mystic *symbolon*.[117]

The ambiguity between a burial-coin practice and a mystic *symbola* lingers, and the Sfakaki *epistomia*, two of them incised with different texts and three unincised, only increase the difficulty in approaching the problem. In spite of all the information they yield, evidence remains inadequate and a number of practical problems persist. Answers to the questions below would seem crucial in accounting for the differentiation; at the moment, unfortunately, we can only answer them with conjectures:

1) When were the lamellae procured and prepared? Did this happen upon initiation or perhaps some time later, but still in advance of the initiate's death?

---

[114] Bessios 1992:247.

[115] Pantermalis 1999:271 (SEG 49.703).

[116] Bernabé (2005:75–79 496 F) is cautious and does not include the three names incised on the coins and the gold disc in the group of the other lamellae with short texts, but he mentions Andron and Xenariste at the endnote (78), among other texts suspect of being 'Orphic'; so, too, Graf and Johnston 2007:28, without the names.

[117] Jordan 1985a:162–167.

2) However inexpensive these gold foils were, some money was needed for their preparation, especially if the lamella was incised by an expert. Was cost a serious factor? The extremely low rate of their survival, when considering the thousands of graves excavated, does not corroborate Zuntz's statement that these were "articles of mass-production."[118] The number of coins recovered from graves eclipses the number of incised lamellae unearthed, and in turn, the occurrences of graves with coins are far outnumbered by instances of graves excavated with no coins at all.

3) Who was entrusted with the actual placement of the *epistomion* on the deceased, and according to whose instructions? Was it a family-member or perhaps another initiate? Was the incised lamella placed at the last minute before inhumation? It is true that all family-members need not have been initiates, but they could not have been excluded from the burial ceremony, let alone the preparation of the body.

4) Do all *epistomia* and lamellae, whether incised or unincised, point to the same or to a similar burial custom of initiates?

5) What was the intended position of the incised *epistomia*? Was the inscription meant to be facing the mouth of the deceased, or was it meant to face the mourner/Underworld deity?[119] Furthermore, as far as intended positioning is concerned, what are we to make of the *epistomia* which were found folded or rolled up inwards, so as to make reading the letters an impossible task; or those found on the chest or in the hand of the deceased?

6) Who engraved the long, supposedly 'secret' texts, if an initiate scribe or itinerant priest were not available? Were these texts copied from a pre-existing text or incised from memory?

The nature of the evidence surrounding the five *epistomia* from the graves at Sfakaki allows only for assumptions and educated guesses in these matters. In spite of the graves' similarities in terms of place, date, and content, no conclusive and convincing explanations may be offered regarding burial customs and rituals, and their funerary ideology. The five *epistomia* from Sfakaki attest that differentiation in burial customs may have been both a diachronic and a synchronic phenomenon, and they seem to embrace diversity or individualization, as Sourvinou-Inwood (1995) has argued, rather

---

[118] Zuntz 1971:353.

[119] Lead, bronze, and clay lids of funerary urns have been found in Arta and Ambrakia, inscribed with single names on the inside of the lid, as if meant to be read by the deceased inside the urn (Miliadis 1926:63–77; Daux 1955:267; Tsirivakos 1965:355–360, pl. 423; and Oikonomou 2002:40–42). These curious instances may or may not be connected with the gold tablets on which single names are inscribed, but they underline the inadequacy of our evidence.

than homogeneity. Among the five graves at Sfakaki comprising a deceased buried with an *epistomion*, three different practices are evident. This variety suggests that, even though these people were inhabiting the same area, practiced similar burial customs, became *mystai* in a Bacchic-Orphic cult promising life after death, and lived one sometime between the third and the early first century BCE (B12), another between 25 BCE and 40 CE (E4), and three in the first century CE (G2–4), they nevertheless developed a more personal attitude towards death.

Figure 24. Mnemata archaeological site, Eleutherna/Alfá, view from the north.

Figure 25 (facing page, above). Graves cut in the rock on top of the hill, Mnemata.

Figure 26 (facing page, below). Graves at the edge of the hill, Mnemata.

Figure 27. Graves cut at various levels, Mnemata.

Figure 28. Roman bath and cistern(?), Tou Papa o Kolumpos archaeological site, Eleutherna/Alfá.

Figure 29. Agia Elessa archaeological site, Eleutherna/Alfá, view from the north.

Figure 30. Larnakes cut into the rock, Agia Elessa.

Figure 31. Roman chamber tomb, exterior, Agia Elessa.

Figure 32. Roman chamber tomb, converted into the small church of Agia Elessa.

Figure 33. Interior, Roman chamber tomb, Agia Elessa.

Figure 34. Pente Parthenes archaeological site, Lappa (modern Argyrou-polis), view from the south.

Figure 35. Chamber tombs at various levels, Pente Parthenes.

Figure 36. Graves, with Church of Pente Parthenes beyond.

Figure 37. Interior, Roman chamber tomb, converted into the Church of Pente Parthenes.

Figure 38. Site of the Church of Agia Elessa (Lappa), from the west.

Figure 39. Exterior of graves, Agia Elessa (Lappa).

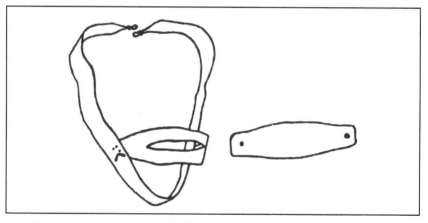

Figure 40. Conjectured method for fastening an *epistomion* to the mouth of the deceased.

Figure 41 (opposite). Engraved gold lamella, thought to be from Thessaly. Malibu, CA, The J. Paul Getty Museum, Villa Collection, 75.AM.19.

3

The Cretan *Epistomia* in Context

The Corpus of the *Epistomia*: Nature and Classification

THE ENGRAVED LAMELLAE are objects *sui generis*[1] and appear to defy categorization. In order to expedite the study and understanding of these artifacts, Zuntz attempted to set standards for the classification, which have changed as more texts have been published since 1971.[2] More importantly, however, Zuntz contributed decisively to the clearing-up of a number of misconceptions. He argued that the gold lamellae are neither curse-tablets (*defixiones*), nor phylacteries, nor amulets—all of these are incised in metals, curse-tablets usually in lead, and phylacteries and amulets in virtually any available metal or precious stone.[3] These items, he contended, are similar to lamellae in their symbolic writing but not in their function and aim. Zuntz also suggested tentatively that the gold leaves may have "afforded the model" for the phylacteries, as is shown by the Petelia lamella (B1): the lamella was recovered at a later period from the grave in which it had been placed, and it was then put in a gold case with a chain attached, apparently in order that it might be worn as an amulet.[4] This finding, of course, may or may not imply

---

[1] Zuntz 1971:285.

[2] Cole 1980; and Graf 1993.

[3] Zuntz 1971:278–286. For magic, *defixiones*, and amulets, see the collection of essays in Faraone and Obbink 1991, Christidis and Jordan 1997, and Mirecki and Meyer 2002; see also Gager 1992; Kotansky 1991 and 1994; Graf 1997; Jordan 1997a; Johnston 1999:71–80; Dickie 2001; Collins 2003; Johnston 2004b. For a small number of phylacteries on lead, see Giannobile and Jordan 2006. For updates of new editions, see Jordan 1985b, 1997b, 2000; to which add Grammatikaki and Litinas 2000; and Maltomini 2006. For later exorcisms and *defixiones* in Cretan manuscripts, see Spyridakis 1941–1942. See also 120n79 and 132n122.

[4] Zuntz 1971:284 and 355–356; and Guarducci 1974a:8–11. Kotansky (1991:114–116 and 122) in his discussion of the lamellae notes: "the fact that the tablet had once been rolled up or folded suggests that at some point an 'Orphic' tablet could have been used, like the Phalasarna tablet, as a personal amulet. One might speculate, then, that the widespread use of the gold and silver phylacteries was indeed patterned after the 'Orphic' *lamellae*, that is, that the protection of

that the person wearing it was also an initiate and that s/he understood what was written on it. At any rate, Cretan *epistomia* nos. 5–6 above (B7–8), which, according to the seller, were found rolled up inside cylindrical gold cases, cannot be a paradigm case (even though Verdelis accepts the seller's report) because of the circumstances of their acquisition. These *epistomia* do not come from systematic excavations, and it is very likely that the seller would have also presented the gold cylinders (had there been ones) in order to increase the price.[5]

The two lamellae (A4 and C1) from Timpone Grande, excavated systematically, and five lamellae bearing the *chaire* formula (E1–5) suggest instead that these small engraved objects served as an *epistula*.[6] According to Zuntz,[7] the envelope-like lamella (C1) is nonsensical and cannot be associated with the text on the lamella found inside it. From his own transcription, however, this "Triballian rather than Greek" text, as he calls it, appears to have some relevance to the other, more 'public Orphic' texts that have survived. As Bernabé and Jiménez San Cristóbal have shown convincingly,[8] the envelope-like lamella is comparable to other texts of this sort, the *Gurob* and *Derveni Papyri*, and the bone tablets of Olbia, texts which perhaps should be included within the same group C. In fact, by virtue of its being 'more public,' it may have been used as an 'envelope' in order to protect (because of its 'value' [?] or 'secrets' [?]) the 'less public' but much more crucial text.

---

the recently dead from the dangers of the Underworld may have been, or gradually became, a desideratum for the living folk as well" (115). Although Zuntz (1971:353) may have overdone it with the analogy of Catholicism and has been rightly criticized (Kotansky 1991:114–116; Kingsley 1995:308–316; Edmonds 2004, 40), and although there may have been "a blurring of the distinction between protection in the present life and in the hereafter" (Kotansky 1991:116), nevertheless, the texts engraved on the gold lamellae and *epistomia* suggest otherwise, as their usage, function, and purpose is in no way similar or comparable to the phylacteries, amulets, and curse tablets, so far discovered, (compare the prescriptions *for the living* in the *lex sacra* from Selinous; SEG 43.630 and Jameson, Jordan, and Kotansky 1993); they do not aim at protection for staying alive or for averting evil spirits in this life above the earth, but they provide knowledge and serve as memory-tags for the proper road in the afterlife when in the Underworld. This distinction need not, in fact should not, as Kotansky rightly argues, imply a degeneration of an original 'pure' prototype religion into the alleged secondary and 'magical' creations, as Zuntz's discussion implies. Bernand (2003:415–432) concludes his discussion of Greek magicians with the gold engraved lamellae as specimens of magic; Rangos (2003:143–145) calls them phylacteries; for Robert Fowler (2000:320) they are a special instance of favorable reception in the other world, although he stresses the difficulty in discussing ancient Greek magic and religion separately.

[5] Guarducci 1974a:13, and the sections "Shape-Burial Context" and "Usage."
[6] Guarducci 1974a:12.
[7] Zuntz 1971:344–354.
[8] Bernabé and Jiménez San Cristóbal 2001:183–200; Bernabé 2005:492F; and Betegh forthcoming.

Five lamellae with short texts (E1–5) appear to be employing or implying the standard opening of a letter, which consisted of the name of the sender in the nominative, the addressee in the dative, and the infinitive χαίρειν.[9] Either as an infinitive of command or as object of an understood λέγω, χαίρειν must "mean something like 'Tell Persephone' or 'This is for Persephone's attention'";[10] or "greetings (or I say greetings) to Persephone (and Plouton/Despotes)," this being the most natural form of address by the deceased upon meeting the Lords of the Dead.[11] Moreover, Christiane Sourvinou-Inwood has convincingly argued that *chaire* is employed in addresses only to 'the living,' i.e. living humans, the gods, and the heroes, and, if addressed to the deceased (especially before the fourth century BCE), the deceased must have been seen as heroized/deified dead, because *chaire* "was felt to include the wish 'be well/rejoice'."[12]

The five incised lamellae and the envelope-like lamella of Thourioi may have used the typical beginning of an *epistula* as a model. The lamellae were found variously at the mouth, the chest, and the hand. In the cases where these gold lamellae were used as *epistomia*, the mouth of the deceased was, as it were, 'uttering' the appropriate words;[13] the lamellae found on the chest or near the hand of the deceased probably performed the duty of an *epistula* to be read by the deceased and/or the Underworld power, or even by an intercessor on his/her behalf. In the case of the lamellae, the *epistula*-style address would

---

[9] LSJ *s.v.* III1c: "inf[initive] alone at the beginning of letters, Κῦρος Κυαξάρῃ χαίρειν (sc. λέγω)." For this epistolary formula, see Gerhard 1905:27–65; the examples from a variety of epistolary papyri of the third century BCE to the third century AD (familial, business, and official letters, petitions, complaints, applications) collected by Exler 1976:23–68; and the remarks by Llewelyn 1998:122–128. For addresses in Greek prose in general, see Dickey 1996; for the origins of the *chaire* salutation, see Wachter 1998; for *chaire* in hymns and inscriptions Rossi 1999, Day 2000, and Depew 2000; for its use in the New Testament, see Konis 2006.

[10] Dickie 1995a:82.

[11] As proposed by Guarducci 1985:385–397. Gallavotti (1978–79:348n16; 1988:28–31) has argued instead that this brief text is not a salute to the gods of the Underworld, but an exhortation to the deceased to "rejoice either in the divine presence of Plouton and Persephone, or in some divine favor," a plausible, but unlikely interpretation, in light of the longer texts which present a dialogue between the deceased and the Underworld deities. The expression *Greetings* also includes a wish for "joy and well-being," as Sourvinou-Inwood (1995:180–216) cogently demonstrated.

[12] Sourvinou-Inwood 1995:207 and especially 195–197 where she comments on A4; Rossi 1999; Day 2000:47; and Depew 2000:62–63. García (2002) has shown that the *chaire* formula in the *Homeric Hymns* belongs to symbolic action, the moment of its utterance being the moment of god's epiphany. Martin (2007) adds that *chaire* anticipates the transformation of the deceased from *anthrôpos* to *theos*, before we are told so explicitly later in the texts on the lamellae.

[13] Dickie 1995a:83; Gallavotti 1988:28–31; Guarducci 1974a:15–17; Zuntz 1971:335–336n2.

be delivered in person by the deceased; the message itself, perhaps because it would be easily understood, is not spelled out in detail on the majority of the lamellae. Marisa Tortorelli Ghidini has discussed the character of these lamellae and has also addressed the beginning and end of the few long texts (B1, B10–11) and their symbolic nature as "passports for the afterlife." She suggested that these objects are simply carriers of the non-material words, which when incised on gold materialize literally as well as figuratively as gold signs/words (χρύσεα γράμματα).[14] Although there is ample information that the use of books was important in mystery cults,[15] it is generally agreed that the long texts show signs of oral transmission of the mystic doctrine,[16] and that the engraving was done from memory. Nevertheless, the incision itself, and the choice of what (and how much of the) text to engrave on the lamella required some level of literacy, especially if one assumes that the lamellae incised with the long texts in clumsy and careless lettering may have been engraved by an amateur scribe privy to the mysteries, still learning and still making orthographical mistakes. The fact that some lamellae were folded or rolled up, and some texts were abbreviated may also have been one way to preserve a certain secrecy, a secrecy very successfully guarded in antiquity.[17]

These and other practical problems further imply that the texts themselves on these gold lamellae (and especially on the *epistomia*[18]) need not carry as much significance as modern commentators would like to impute to them—perhaps the unincised lamellae were just as able as the incised to accomplish their function effectively. If so, all of the unincised gold lamellae in the shape of the mouth, rhombus, oblong, or the leaves of ivy, myrtle, and olive (whose presence in a grave cannot be explained in any other way, e.g. as dress-ornaments, and which were found near the cranium or on the chest and therefore were used as *epistomia*), all of these may in fact have been employed as tokens for the Underworld deities to recognize the *mystai*, but they were left unincised either because of secrecy or for other reasons and practical problems, or perhaps because the letters on them did not matter much (at least not as much

---

[14] Tortorelli Ghidini 1995a:468–482.

[15] Burkert 1985:286–301, 296–297; Parker 1996:43–55, especially 54–55; and Henrichs 2003a and 2003b.

[16] Dickie 1995a:82; Segal 1990:413; Janko 1984:89–91; Riedweg 2002:478–479; Henrichs 2003a and 2003b.

[17] Johnston (2004a:108–109) distinguishes between absolute and relative secrecy, the latter of which is applicable to the mysteries.

[18] Compare, however, Zuntz 1971:353.

as they matter to us).[19] John Bodel has best articulated the aims of symbolic epigraphy:[20]

> The purpose of this sort of inscribed writing was not to preserve or to convey information but *to effect an action through its physical presence*; *its function* was not descriptive or commemorative but, in the useful information of the anthropologist Stanley Tambiah, *persuasive and performative*: the ritual of inscribing was meant to encourage the result it described. *Sometimes words were of secondary importance* to the delivery of the objects that carried them (21) ... The *material* on which the text was inscribed or the *place* in which the object was located or the way in which the inscription was displayed *had nothing to do with its legibility* but was dictated instead by *some extratextual function* it was meant to serve (24) (my emphasis).

All of the lamellae, regardless of shape, placement, and text, are σύμβολα, or συνθήματα, the word employed in two of the lamellae in reference to their own texts (D3, B11).[21] This self-definition as "signs or tokens by which one infers a thing" (LSJ) is by far the most apt one to start making some sense of these objects. These performative and metaphorical signifiers challenge interpretations and defy classification and they will continue to do so for as long as the non-material signifieds/referents, the ritual *teletai*, fail to appear in the archaeological record.

Either in spite of or because of these constraints imposed by the nature of the evidence, attempts have been made to group these texts, in order to facilitate discussion about the objects and their texts. Günther Zuntz classified the lamellae according to their content into three groups under the letters A, B, and C; he excluded, however, all lamellae with short texts, like Eleutherna's no. 7 above (E1).[22] After the publication of the texts from Hipponion (B10) and especially those from Pelinna (D2), it became clear that Zuntz's groups A and B were not as airtight as Zuntz himself thought. But, as the classification was convenient and facilitated discussion of the texts, scholars continued

---

[19] E.g. see Keramaris, Protopsalti and Tsolakis (2002:234, 239 no. 4) for an unincised *epistomion* in a fifth century BCE grave whose goods suggest a Dionysiac context: decoration of ivy-leaves on the neck of the attic krater, and a Dionysiac depiction on a small black-figure lekythos.

[20] Bodel 2001:19–24; see further Skouteri-Didaskalou 1997; Chatzitaki-Kapsomenou 1997; Frankfurter 2004; and Graf and Johnston 2007:134–136 (the proxy-texts). The performative aspect is the only one shared by curse-tablets, amulets, phylacteries, and the gold lamellae for which see Obbink forthcoming; Calame forthcoming; and 93–94nn3–4.

[21] See also *PGurob* (Hordern 2000); and Riedweg 2002.

[22] Zuntz 1971:281–305, 328–329, 333, 344–364.

to use it, while the Pelinna texts were placed in a separate group under the initial letter of their provenance, P[elinna]. Christoph Riedweg (1998:Anhang; 2002) accepted Zuntz's (and Graf's 1993) groups and presented the texts on the lamellae as those already published (A), those published in preliminary form (B), and the short texts not taken into serious consideration in previous discussions of the lamellae (C).[23] Giovanni Pugliese Carratelli (2001) employed a different set of criteria and divided the long texts (excluding the short ones except one) into three groups and subcategories within each group: the first includes texts with the *symbola* "I am the child of Earth and Starry Sky" (B10, B1, B2, B11; B3–8, B9; A5); the second texts where divinities are invoked (A2, A3; A1, A4, D2; E1, D3); and the third texts of uncertain character (magical?) (C1). Alberto Bernabé and Ana Jiménez San Cristóbal (2001) treat the entire corpus as a more or less homogeneous set of texts and attempt to arrange all the pieces of the puzzle into one 'original' from which derive the abbreviated texts on the lamellae; thus, they number the texts on the lamellae continuously (1–16) and in a descending order from the longer one (B10) to those with only one word (the texts in groups F, E, and D1). Spiros Rangos (2003) reverses Zuntz's classification: group A becomes the lamellae of *mnemosyne*; B the lamellae of purity; A4 the lamella of the blessed *pathema* (group C); the two Pelinna texts the lamellae of *nun* (group D); and the short texts E2, and F4–F5 in their own separate groups, the latter comprising the *mystai* category. Susan Cole (2003) kept Zuntz's groups, and she placed all the brief texts in group D, and the fragmentary or unincised lamellae in group E. Finally, Fritz Graf and Sarah Iles Johnston (2007; and Graf forthcoming-1) present the texts according to their geographical distribution, a classification choice that has its advantages as well as its disadvantages. In their discussion, however, they group them into purity, *mnemosyne*, and proxy texts, the latter being the short texts (here groups E, F, and G).

The geographical criterion is essential and is the golden rule of epigraphy, expounded constantly and most eloquently by Louis Robert: inscriptions, before all else, belong to and should be understood within their *local context* first and foremost, and then within wider contexts of similar texts from other areas—an approach that will be evident in the next chapter.[24] Nonetheless, and without denying the fact that all these texts, long and short, are interrelated but at the same time exhibit certain differences, and local divergences,

---

[23] Edmonds 2004; and Parker and Stamatopoulou 2004.

[24] For an interesting discussion of the lamellae's geographical distribution, see Cole forthcoming.

the texts of this small corpus are classified here into seven groups, according to their content. The first three groups are those identified by Zuntz, to which four more are added in order to accommodate old, new, and perhaps forthcoming texts.[25] These comprise (Table 1):

A   five texts; the so-called 'purity' texts, because purity is singled out; this does not imply in any way that the other *mystai* buried with an incised or unincised lamella or *epistomion* were not 'pure';

B   twelve texts; the so-called '*mnemosyne*'- or Underworld-topography-texts;

C   one text; the so-called Orphic texts; this group should perhaps also include all related texts: the Olbia bone tablets, Bacchic inscriptions from Olbia, *PGurob*, Edict of Ptolemy IV Philopator;[26] and also *PDerveni*, *PAntinoopolis* I 18 (= MP³ 2466), *PChicago* Pack² *1620*;[27] a few of Poseidippos' epigrams (Dignas 2004); the *Orphic Hymns*, and other related *Orphica*, among which epigrams of *mystai* (West 1983 and Bernabé 2005);

D   texts in which Dionysos and/or Persephone (and/or Demeter), or other deities are present by name or by epithet (D1–5; Cole 2003:202–205 groups P1/2 and B12);

E   texts in which the *chaire*-formula is employed or implied in addressing the Underworld deities, either Plouton or Persephone by name or epithet, or both (E1–5; Cole 2003:202–205 group D);

F   all remaining lamellae with brief texts, i.e. the deceased's name, the word μύστης, or a combination thereof (F1–12; Cole 2003:202–205 group D);

G   four unincised lamellae: one from Pella whose letters might have been in ink, hence now lost; and nos. 10–12 above from Sfakaki (G1–4; Cole 2003:202–205 group E). These four lamellae were dubbed *epistomia* by the excavators who suggested that, for all intents and purposes, they served as tokens of initiates for the Underworld, just as the engraved

---

[25] In *Archaeological Reports* (1988–1989:93) it was reported that from a Hellenistic cist-grave in Sourada, Lesbos were recovered: "a gold diadem with Heracles' knot flanked by stylized Aeolic capitals; parts of a gold pendant of semiprecious stones; gold olive leaves; an incised gold sheet with an Orphic text; a pendant with gold beads; silver coins; and a series of statuettes of young men." This unpublished text has been included provisionally in the corpus of the lamellae's texts (Gavrilaki and Tzifopoulos 1998:348 n20; Graf and Johnston 2007:28). Although the grave-goods present a very interesting case in relation to the above discussion, the text incised on the gold lamella is not a 'Bacchic-Orphic' text, as Angelos Matthaiou (who is going to publish the text) informs me.

[26] These four are included in the Appendices of Graf and Johnston (2007:185–190), as Additional Bacchic Texts, related to the discussion of the texts on the gold lamellae.

[27] For the curious text of a column of this papyrus, see Niafas 1997.

ones did. In light of the discussion above (sections "Shape—Burial Context" and "Usage"), it is almost impossible to determine when an *epistomion*, if unincised, is also a token/passage to the Underworld and should therefore be included in discussions of the engraved texts. This is the reason for not including in this group, at present, a great number of *epistomia*, mainly from graves in Macedonia, but a few also from Crete (see the section "A Cretan Context"), most of which have been published in preliminary reports. There must have existed some reason for placing these items on the mouth of the deceased, but before we claim that these unincised lamellae or *epistomia* functioned in a manner similar to the incised ones, more evidence is needed, and the aforementioned issue of the presence of gold or gilt wreaths and/or coins and other grave-goods in Macedonian graves, and elsewhere, should be accounted for. Both the Pella and the Sfakaki *epistomia*, however, present strong indications that they were employed in the same way and toward the same end as the engraved ones, i.e. as tokens for the initiates' passage to the Underworld.

Be that as it may, it cannot be stressed enough that these categories should not be understood as airtight, as their texts are interrelated and complement one another. The above classification constitutes one important objective in the study of these texts, which is based primarily on their strong similarities (the stemmatological approach). Another objective, equally worth the effort as the next chapter ("The Cretan Context") will show, is to shift the emphasis from similarities to divergences, and, instead of one central document behind these texts, to entertain the possibility that within the same Bacchic-Orphic discourse on afterlife and even within the same group of texts existed simultaneously dominant and peripheral ideas and texts (in Crete, twelve texts that belong to three different groups), for which local or even individual cultic and religious considerations may be accountable.

Table 1 also provides information regarding: provenance, date, the deceased's gender, shape, accompanying coin(s), manner of burial and other goods recovered from the grave. This information may be found in the excavators' preliminary reports and *editiones principes;* more detailed information about these sources is listed below each Group's respective Table. The texts printed follow the orthography of the engraver (with very few editorial corrections), and are based on the editions by Riedweg (1998:389–398 and 2002); Bernabé and Jiménez San Cristóbal (2001:257–281); Bernabé (2005:indicated by a B following the number in parenthesis); Graf and Johnston 2007:4–49; and Edmonds forthcoming-2.

In Table 2, all forty–four lamellae and *epistomia* are grouped in descending chronological order according to two different criteria: the text's size, and their provenance. These groups comprise: 1) twenty–three lamellae and *epistomia* with short or no texts, of which eight leaves, two coins, and one a pseudo-coin; 2) twenty–one lamellae and *epistomia* with long texts, of which one is two leaves; and 3) all of the lamellae and *epistomia* according to their provenance: ten from Italy, twelve from Crete, five from the Peloponnese, five from Thessaly, and twelve from Macedonia.

The Cretan Texts in the Context of a Ritual and a *Hieros Logos*

Following the proposed classification, the nine incised and the three unincised Cretan *epistomia* recovered from graves of Eleutherna's wider region fall into three different groups: B comprises the seven long texts; E the two brief ones; and group G the unincised *epistomia*.[28] It seems that, within approximately the same area and during a relatively short period of time, people sharing more or less the same beliefs and ritual practices acted in divergent, more individual ways, a behavior that remains a mystery.

In terms of content, the three unincised *epistomia* nos. 10–12 above (G2–4), provided they fulfill the same function, may be understood as implying a content analogous to the texts in groups B and E, or even perhaps analogous to the texts of the other groups. Their being left blank need not present a problem, as this would be a perfect, if extreme, example of symbolic epigraphy.

The two short texts (E1, E4) address Plouton and/or Persephone with the verb χαίρειν, incised or understood. On account of Plouton's presence, these *epistomia* have not traditionally been classed with the other incised lamellae and *epistomia* B3–8, B12 (nos. 1–6 and 9 above). According to Guarducci, the appearance of Plouton here may have been due to a conflation of Orphic beliefs, as expounded in the gold *epistomia* with the long texts, with some sort of local cult and ritual in Eleutherna, chief among them the mystery cult of Cretan Zeus in the Idaean Cave. Zuntz accepted this explanation with the modification that the conflation of Orphic beliefs was not with a local, but with a general tradition;[29] Graf, on the other hand, drew attention to this inscription as one of the "signals that the classification [sc. of the lamellae by Zuntz in groups A

---

[28] For a preliminary discussion, see Tzifopoulos 1998b and 2002.
[29] Zuntz 1971:384.

and B] was not watertight."[30] It is hard to deny that Plouton's role is kept very much in the background in the long texts of group B (in the texts of group A he is addressed euphemistically) but, at the same time, his presence is always implied as the husband of Persephone and Lord of the Underworld. Zuntz, as it turns out, was right. Plouton's presence is due not to a local but to a general tradition, as more pieces of evidence that have since appeared (E4, E5) testify.

Until recently, the known examples from Macedonia addressed only Persephone (E2 and E3), but a new lamella (E5) contains a text where Plouton alone is addressed as *despotes*.[31] Moreover, the Apulian volute-krater, attributed to the workshop of the Darius painter whose themes and motifs are usually inspired from dramatic works, presents a unique narrative scene (Figures 41a–c [pages 104–105]): Hades with sceptre in his left hand is seated upon a throne inside his palace and extends his right hand to Dionysos, who, coming from the right side, 'grasps' it with his right hand; to Hades' left side, Persephone is standing with a torch in her hands, and Hermes is holding a caduceus and resting against one of the columns of the palace. This central scene is surrounded by Dionysiac figures: the maenads Acheta and Persis, a Paniskos approaching Cerberus, and Actaeon, Pentheus and Agaue. On the back side are portrayed: a young male nude inside a *naiskos* holding a stick and a phiale in his hands and a drapery over his arm; a seated youth with branch and fillet; a woman approaching with a bunch of grapes and a phiale; a seated woman with fan and cista; and a nude youth running up with wreath and phiale. The connection with Euripides' *Bacchae*, noted by Trendall and Cambitoglou, and the scene's eschatology are evident enough.[32] The dominant role of Plouton, previously attested only in two Cretan texts (E1 and E4), is corroborated by E5 from Macedonia, and is also evident on the main narrative

---

[30] Graf 1993:250–251.

[31] Petsas 1967a, 1967b; Hatzopoulos 2002, 2006, and 2008.

[32] The krater was found in Tomb 33 at Timmari (Basilicata) and was acquired by the Toledo Museum of Art (1994.19). Since its publication by Trendall and Cambitoglou (1992:508 no. 41a1), it has attracted much attention and rightly so: Graf 1993:256; Johnston and McNiven 1996:25–36, pl. 1; Avagianou 2002 in relation to Thessalian inscriptions to Hermes Chthonios. Kefalidou (2005–2006) discusses afresh the iconography and she tentatively suggests for the painter's inspiration some dramatic work like the *Minyas* or *Nostoi* or even another painting such as Polygnotos' in the Knidian Lesche at Delphi. Chicoteau (1997; SEG 47.1509; EBGR 1997.76) discusses a similar interaction with and/or influence of Orphic-Dionysiac beliefs on a fresco in a Roman catacomb. For depictions of the Underworld in Apulian vases, see Schmidt (1991, 1996, and 2000, the Toledo scene in pages 96–97); and Carpenter forthcoming. For Bacchic themes, see Rauch 1999; for Dionysos' depictions on coin-legends, see Franke and Marathaki 1999; and Ruotolo 2005; for Dionysos' depictions on seals and gems Overbeck and Overbeck 2005.

scene of the Apulian krater. Plouton's prominence here does not jibe well with the tradition in which Persephone was the key-figure, but it accords perhaps with another, final (?) stage of the initiate's Underworld journey, in which final approval and consent depended ultimately on the Lord of the Dead.

The crucial element of the scene, however, is Dionysos' intercession on behalf of his initiate, as it presents visually what the texts D2–5 and B10 only hinted at: the god himself served as the initiate's guide to the place reserved for *mystai*, and as the advocate that perhaps actually uttered the deceased's words incised on the gold lamellae (D2). With this in mind, the manner in which the 'grasping' of hands between Hades and Dionysos takes place is unusual, to say the least.[33] The gesture has been understood as a handshake, but has also been interpreted as a means of "alerting the audience."[34] In a normal handshake, however, the thumb is visible in the iconography. Furthermore, Hades is not a god in the habit of shaking hands. The gesture as portrayed in the Toledo krater looks as if something is being given by Dionysos to Hades, but for such a gesture there are no parallels. Eurydice Kefalidou has studied *katabaseis* and *anodoi* of Dionysos and has concluded that, in the iconography, even when objects are exchanged secretly, these objects are portrayed, so that the viewer would not misunderstand the message. She does, however, refer to two other parallel cases of unusual 'handshakes': Dionysos and Apollo, and Hades and Amphiaraos. According to Kefalidou, these scenes present variants of the normally expected 'handshake,' the *dexiosis* scene implying welcome and mutual recognition of power. It is very difficult to determine whether the gesture meant anything more than this. What complicates the situation even further is the strong possibility that the deceased in whose grave the Toledo krater was found may not have been a *mystes* in a manner comparable to those buried with a gold lamella or *epistomion*.[35]

Turning to the longer texts, all seven Cretan *epistomia* in group B present two motifs: a) a deadly thirst that is quenched by drinking from a specific, revitalizing spring whose location appears to be an important factor; and b) the recognition of the deceased's identity through certain questions and answers. Taken by themselves, these texts are not readily comprehensible; they must be placed within the context of the other long texts in group B, and must also be understood relative to those in groups A and D from Italy and Thessaly, as they appear to present a synopsis of these texts.

[33] I owe this observation to Charalambos Kritzas' discerning eye.
[34] For the former, Trendall and Cambitoglou 1992:508; and Johnson and McNiven 1996; for the latter, Boegehold 1999:25–26; and compare Carpenter forthcoming.
[35] Kefalidou 2005–2006.

a.

Figure 42. Apulian volute-krater by the Darius Painter. Toledo, OH, Toledo Museum of Art, 1994.19. (*a*. obverse, Underworld scene with Dionysiac figures; *b*. obverse, detail, Hades and Persephone in their palace; *c*. reverse, youth in *naiskos*).

b.

c.

Regarding the synoptic character of the Cretan texts (nos. 1–6 above; and the similar one from Thessaly B9; Figure 41 [page 91]), Zuntz commented:[36]

> [The Cretan lamellae] are inscribed in the local dialect and spelling [and] contain extracts from originals in the traditional epic *Kunstsprache* which luckily are preserved; the transposition into the local dialect, then, is a secondary feature. And what happened at Eleutherna could have happened also at Thourioi.

Zuntz further proposed that the Cretan texts contain the absolute minimum form (what he termed "the cardinal words") of the longer, expanded versions, but concluded:[37]

> The Cretan text, however solid and primordial its substance, cannot be taken for the original of the expanded versions. First, because of its informal imperfections. This combination of perfect poetry with completely unmetrical prose cannot possibly represent the primitive form of conveying this eschatological vision; nor obviously, is it in the least likely to have been done, originally, in a local Cretan dialect. The obvious vehicle would have been the traditional epic *Kunstsprache*, retranslation into which indeed can afford a cure for the most striking irregularity: namely the question in prose ('v. 3'); but not for all (unless indeed one were to rewrite the whole *ad lib.*).

And yet, only a few pages earlier, in his discussion of the 'rhythmical prose' in the announcement of the deceased's deification (a quality he denied line 3 of the Cretan texts), he adduces two analogies: Philostratos' narrative of the visit of Apollonius of Tyana in Diktynna's temple in Crete, and Lucian's legend about the suicide of Peregrinus Proteus during the Olympic games of 166 CE. In drawing these analogies, Zuntz awards the dialect a distinct importance: "The Doric dialect in both these legends is remarkable. It seems to have conveyed, in this late period, an aura of archaic sanctity."[38]

It is impossible to find a reasonable explanation for the synoptic character of some of the texts in the B series, the seven from Crete, and B9 from Thessaly (the only one, so far, outside the island; Figure 41 [page 91]).[39] For

---

[36] Zuntz 1971:339–340n1.

[37] Zuntz 1971:381–382.

[38] Philostratos *Apollonius of Tyana* 8.30; Lucian *The Passing of Peregrinos*; Zuntz 1971:341–342, the quotation from 342n1.

[39] As John Papadopoulos, at the time Associate Curator at the Getty Museum, informed me, the Thessalian provenance of this lamella is not completely secure.

that matter, it is just as difficult to find any suitable explanation in this regard for all of the lamellae with brief texts. We find an analogous situation in the modern period surrounding the expression "I await for the resurrection of the dead" (προσδοκῶ ἀνάστασιν νεκρῶν), which is inscribed on grave plaques in modern Greek cemeteries. This sentence is taken from the Eastern Orthodox Church's Creed which is heard during the Divine Liturgy and sums up in three words all the Christian teachings and dogmas. The faithful, who know the whole Creed, will have little trouble understanding the sentence's context, its implications, and the ritual during which it is uttered; to non-believers, on the other hand, it is incomprehensible, if not absurd (see the section "Afterword"). The identical repetition of the same formulae and motifs (except for the two questions in rhythmical prose) proves beyond doubt that these lamellae belonged to the same tradition which was responsible for the four long texts in the same group: B1, B2, B10, B11. Both Martin West and Richard Janko, in their very useful attempts at reconstructing an archetype from the texts in group B, have assumed that this archetype was probably composed orally in Homeric diction and hexameters and that it gradually was transformed, region by region, in successive centuries.[40] Similarly, Charles Segal has demonstrated the repetitive, rhythmic, and formulaic qualities of these texts and their suitability for oral performance during a funerary ritual, without excluding the possibility of a performance during an initiation rite.[41] He also emphasized that the texts' similarity implies not *ad hoc* compositions, but copies of preexisting poetic texts. Dirk Obbink, however, argued that the authors of these texts are not "producing at best a derivative hodgepodge of formulae pirated from the language of earlier, canonized poems. The texts of the gold leaves are poetry, but they are neither arbitrarily, nor affectedly, nor derivatively so ... [S]ome type of ritual (probably funerary or initiation) is closely connected with the performance and ritual context of [this] poetry ..."[42] Such a ritual, as Watkins argues, constitutes, "in a word, liturgy."

What exactly this ritual pertained to has recently been a subject of inquiry, especially by Christoph Riedweg, who has shown convincingly how the different pieces (the texts, in whatever way one chooses to classify them) may fit together in a sacred discourse on the afterlife. Cogently employing the tools of narratology, Riedweg matched context and content and presented a reconstruction of a ritual and its sacred text and *hieros logos* in six stages, a

---

[40] West 1975; and Janko 1984 and forthcoming.
[41] Segal 1990:413–414.
[42] Apud Watkins 1995:281; and for these texts as "non-parasitic ritual utterances," Obbink forthcoming, and 2n4.

reconstruction which comprises all of the texts (2002:470–471; the texts are referred to below by letter group and number in Tables 1–2):[43]

I) The death of the *mystes* and the *katabasis* of the soul to the Underworld (the subjects of these texts, as indicated in A4 line 1; B1 lines 13–14; B10 lines 1–2; and B11 lines 1 and 3).

II) The topography in Hades, the motif of thirst, and the encounter with the guards of the spring, all mainly exhibited in detail only in the texts of group B (A5 lines 3–4 may be an allusion to the spring); we may also add to this stage D3 and D5, and the texts of groups E, F, and G.

III) The meeting with Persephone and the other gods, which may take different forms: a) the elaborate address in the texts of group A; b) D2A lines 5–7, D2B lines 6–8, and D4–5; c) the question and answer (which may also be asked by Persephone and Plouton when the deceased greets them in the group E-texts) of B3–9, B12, D3, D5; and the texts of groups E, F, and G.

IV) Mystic *symbola* for entrance in the reserved place: A1 lines 15–16; A4 lines 5–6; the answers in the B series, B11 line 19; D2A lines 7–13; D2B lines 9–15; D3, D4, D5; and (?) the texts of groups E, F, and G; these small 'cryptic' phrases, some of which are reminiscent of *PGurob*, may have been part of the *hieros logos* proper, the holy and therefore secret discourse.

V) The place that awaits the deceased *mystes* and her/his new status (*makarismos* and 'deification/heroization'): A1 lines 14–15; A2 lines 10–11; A3 lines 12–13; A4 lines 4–8; A5 lines 5–6; B1 lines 10–11; B2 line 8 (the name Asterios); B9 line 6; B10 lines 15–16; B11 line 2 and 15; D2AB lines 1–4 and 11–15, D5.

VI) The final exhortation of the *mystes* in A4 lines 2–3.

This is a conceivable reconstruction of a ritual which may lie behind the texts of all groups, and which implies a *hieros logos*. The ritual may have been either an initiation rite during which the *mystes'* Underworld journey was reenacted, the *persona loquens* thereby being the hierophant; or the ritual may have been a rite following the *mystes'* death over the grave, in which case

---

[43] Riedweg 1998, 2002: 470–471. Bernabé's and Jiménez San Cristóbal's (2001), Graf's and Johnston's (2007), and Graf's (forthcoming-2) extremely helpful commentaries present a more or less similar set of stages. For *hieroi logoi*, see 2n2. For the symbiosis of myth and ritual Buxton 1994:145–165; for the tension between ritual and myth, see Calame 1995:186–201; Waldner 2000; Bremmer 2004; Graf 2004b; for both myth and ritual as manifestations of symbolic processes, see Calame 1996. For the emotional experience of the mourner's physical contact with the deceased and for the tension in funerary rituals, see Chaniotis 2006b:219–226.

the speaker is an 'omniscient author' directing the deceased *mystes* in order to effect his passage into the Underworld. Either ritual may have re-enacted and rehearsed the actual journey the *mystes* would make when in the Underworld.

We should remember, however, that the synoptic Cretan *epistomia* seem to suggest that these initiation stages need not be spelled out in great detail (nos. 1–9 above; and E- and F-texts) or even spelled out at all. The unincised *epistomia* (nos. 10–12 above and group G) perhaps present the absolute minimum a *mystes* would need for the Underworld journey, what Graf and Johnston call the "proxy tablets":[44] a gold, paper-thin, 'mouth'-shaped lamella (which might be placed at or inside the mouth, the chest, or the hand). This is symbolic epigraphy *par excellence*, especially if secrecy were crucial, as those not privy to the ritual and initiation would hardly have a clue as to what these 'symbols'/'tokens' meant, implied, and brought about.

The engraved *epistomia* of Crete can be placed within this six-stage ritual: nos. 1–6 and 9 of group B in stage II (the topography of Hades and the encounter with the guards protecting the spring) and also in stage III (the question and answer dialogue, which is a *symbolon* both for drinking from the spring and also for the *mystes'* recognition by Persephone and Plouton). Nos. 7–8 above (E1 and E4) belong to stage III (the encounter of the deceased with Persephone and the other gods whom they address with *chaire* and receive the reply: "who are you?"), but they should also be understood as tokens recognized by the guards of the spring from which the deceased had to drink before addressing Persephone and the other gods. All of the engraved *epistomia* of Crete, except B12 and B6, present the deceased talking and describing his extreme and deadly thirst and his request to drink from the ever-flowing (ἀέναος or ἀείροος) spring to the right. The request is granted after the question by the guards: "who are you? where are you from?" is answered by the deceased with the *symbolon*: "I am the son of Earth and starry Sky."[45]

---

[44] Graf and Johnston 2007:134–136.

[45] Betz forthcoming. According to Bremmer (1999:81), "traditionally an impossible statement for a human," who, however, relates it with "probably the final stage of the process of reincarnation." It is worth noting that the expression usually employed in the Homeric epics, εὔχομαι εἶναι (for which see Muellner 1974) is absent from the texts of the lamellae (Herrero de Jáuregui forthcoming-2; and the sections "In Search of a Context" and "The Cretan Context of the Cretan *Epistomia*"). Kingsley (1995:250–277) sees Herakles as the model behind these texts, concentrated around Thourioi, and those of Empedokles: the only human who attained divine status after death, an alias Dionysos. Herakles' heroization/deification, however, is of a different scale, as he went to Olympos and not the Underworld, and Thourioi cannot serve as an example for Crete, Macedonia, and Thessaly; see also 204n177.

This dramatic narrative is changed in the new text B12 (no. 9 above). It begins with the third person verb and changes in line 2 to the first person, not unlike A5, where lines 1–3 belong to an intermediary introducing the deceased to Persephone and Plouton. In this case, then, the following parties seem to be present: the omniscient hierophant/deceased, the guards, an intermediary, Persephone (who initiates the dialogue by describing the deceased's condition: "because of thirst you (are) parched"), and some sort of audience (as the statement: "s/he is perishing" cannot be an address to the deceased who replies: "but (give) me to drink"). Thus, the new text seems to explicate line 13 of B10: "they (i.e. the guards of the spring) will tell for you (on your behalf) to the queen of the Underworld (that you are the son of Earth and starry Sky," etc.); this *symbolon*, the deceased's identification, is to be found in B10 lines 10–12. The guards cannot act on their own accord before Persephone is notified and grants permission to the deceased to drink from the spring. Moreover, this same exchange, which in the long texts of group B is taking place between the deceased and the guards, may also take place when the deceased meets Persephone and Plouton. If μάτηρ in line 5 of B12 is understood as a vocative addressing Persephone, and if accordingly the reading of B6 line 4 may also be emended to: <μ>άτηρ (a palaeographically sound emendation), then stages II and III may have included:

> Guards: "Who are you? Where are you from?"
> Deceased: "I am (the son) of Earth and starry Sky."

The *mystes*, after the guards get permission from Persephone, drinks from the spring, and moves on to encounter Persephone and Plouton:

> Deceased: "Greetings to Persephone and Plouton" (E1, E4, and the other texts of the group).
> Persephone/Plouton: "Who are you? Where are you from?" (B3–8);
> Deceased: "Earth is my mother, and (starry) Sky" (B6 lines 3–5, B12 lines 4–6); or, "I am of Earth, mother, and starry Sky" (B6 lines 3–5, B12 lines 4–6), and
> "I have this everlasting gift of Mnemosyne" (A5 lines 3–5).

If lines 5–7 of B12 are not mistakes by the engraver, it is possible that the dialogue between Persephone and the deceased was longer (see also the texts in group D which present a variety of responses):

> Deceased: "of Earth I am, mother."
> Persephone/Plouton: "Where are you from? What ...?"

Deceased: "And (starry) Sky."
Persephone/Plouton: "Who? Thirst ... you?" (perhaps something like A5 lines 3–5).

These deviant readings in the *symbola* of B6 and B12 do not create any serious obstacles in understanding the gist of what was intended. They may present different choices of text for incision on the *epistomia* of the kind we encounter in Macedonia, Thessaly, the Peloponnese, and Rome, where only the name, or the word *mystes* anonymously, or a few words are chosen to be incised.

Most intriguing and challenging is the reading in lines 2–4 of the new text B12 (no. 9 above), because, when compared to the other Cretan texts (B3–5 and B7–8), it appears to contradict the topography in Hades.[46] The spring is named as the *spring of Sauros/Auros*, a name instead of the epithets ἀ(ι)είροος (B3–4 and B7), ἀ(ι)έναος (B5 and B8), and the curious ΑΙΓΙΔΔΩ (B6 line 2); and the fountain's location in B12 is noted as being to the left of the cypress, something so far unique in all the texts of group B. In all other Cretan texts (B3–8), the location of the spring and the cypress is clearer: the spring is to the right, and the cypress is disassociated from it (κράνας ... ἐπὶ δεξιά· τῇ, κυφάριζος, "from the ... spring to the right; there! the cypress"; or, if a comma is placed after δεξιά, and τῇ is understood as the locative relative pronoun: "from the ... spring to the right, where the cypress"). Guarducci's easiest solution for B6 was to emend the problematic reading ΑΙΓΙΔΔΩ to αἰ<ε>ι<ρό>ω, one of the two epithets of the spring attested in B3–4, B7. This emendation may likewise be accepted for the problematic reading in the new text B12: <Σ>αύρου or Αὔρου into ἀ<ει>ρό<ω>. If emended, these deviations in the texts of B12 and B6 may be eliminated, and thus the two texts may be made to conform to the other long texts especially from Crete, but also from Thessaly and Italy. But perhaps before emendation of both divergent texts is considered final, other plausible options should also be entertained, in particular the possibility that these divergences may have been influenced by local (or individual) cultic and religious considerations. It may not be a coincidence, or the engravers' mistake, that both texts present divergent readings in the same places: the *symbolon*, and the location of the cypress and the spring. The process by which a minor detail was allowed to creep into the dominant version, if such a text was ever in circulation, can only be guessed at (see the section "The Cretan Context of the Cretan *Epistomia*").

Turning to the longer texts of group B for clarification, the matter becomes more confused. B2 lines 1–3, B10 lines 2–5, and B11 lines 4–7 all

---

[46] Cole 2003:193–217.

concur: the spring to the right near which there is a white/bright[47] cypress is not to be approached by the *mystes*, because there come down/plunge the souls of the deceased to become cold (ἔνθα κατερχόμεναι ψυχαὶ νεκύων ψύχονται)[48]—whether or not this plunging also implies drinking is not certain. The deceased is advised to move ahead (πρόσθεν in B10 line 6; restored in B11 line 8; πρόσσω in B2 line 3) in order to find the lake of Mnemosyne whose cold water, after the recognition scene, the *mystes* will have to drink for his/her rebirth. The motif of thirst is not unique in these texts. As Emily Vermeule aptly put it, "the dead in many cultures are rumored to be thirsty, and our communication with them is more commonly by toast and libation than by food."[49] In the Homeric epics, Tantalus' thirst is one of the worst forms of punishment after death (*Odyssey* 11.582–592). Viewed in this light, the lamellae and *epistomia* seem to be offering an alternative for the initiates: thirst can be quenched and Tantalus' predicament can be avoided.[50] B1 and B9 are different: in B1 lines 1–4, the spring and the white cypress near it are to the left, whereas the direction towards the second spring is vague: "you will find another one, the lake of," etc. (εὑρήσεις δ' ἑτέραν ...); in B9 lines 2–3, the *mystes* asks for permission to drink from "the ever-flowing spring to the right (near? where?) a white/bright cypress," associating the correct spring with the wrong tree. Thus, the syntax in B12 is so far unique: the cypress in the genitive is governed by the adverbial expression of place. The spring and the cypress are connected and seem to serve as nothing more than marks or signs for the *mystes* in his way through the Underworld, at least in the Cretan texts.

The Underworld topography presented by the texts, especially the choice of the cypress (not a chthonic tree in literature), its epithet *leuké*, and the location of the spring to the left- or right-hand-side, has always been a puzzle. In Homeric epic, the cypress appears only once, on the island of Calypso, Ogygia (*Odyssey* 5.64), and its eschatological symbolism there is ambiguous. Calypso's

---

[47] Bernabé and Jiménez San Cristóbal (2001:45, 44–49) correctly point out that the epithet bears both meanings at the same time. Comparetti (1910:34) understood the *leuké* cypress as identical to the white poplar (in Greek *leúke*), because of its chthonic associations (Harpokration 192: ... οἱ τὰ Βακχικὰ τελούμενοι τῇ λεύκῃ στέφονται διὰ τὸ χθόνιον μὲν εἶναι τὸ φυτόν, χθόνιον δὲ καὶ τὸν τῆς Περσεφόνης Διόνυσον ...); but Guthrie (1993:182 and 192n16) was skeptical; see further Guarducci 1972; Pugliese Carratelli 2001:57–58; Graf and Johnston 2007:108–109.

[48] Dieterich 1969:95-100; Guthrie 1993:177–178; Nagy 1979:167–171; Tortorelli Ghidini 1992 (her suggestion to read ψυχοῦνται, i.e. the souls receive a *psyche* and become alive, requires to understand differently the drinking from a specific spring); Bernabé and Jiménez San Cristóbal 2001:49–58.

[49] Vermeule 1979:57–58 (the quotation in 57).

[50] I am indebted to Maria Sarinaki for drawing this to my attention.

island is a kind of paradise, an isle of the blessed, which threatens Odysseus' *kleos*.[51] The hero, near the end of his wanderings, is presented with two ways to gain immortality: Calypso's unepic and therefore misleading way, and the one he chooses, which leads to his death but ensures his epic *kleos*. The texts on the lamellae appear to invest the cypress with a new(?) and distinct symbolism that becomes one of their central themes and trademarks. Calypso's island in the *Odyssey* and the texts on the lamellae share the cypress, but the idea expressed by this tree is different in the two contexts: in the lamellae it is a tree in the Underworld, and symbolizes, together with the motif of thirst, the choice the *mystes* faces; in the *Odyssey* it is an ambivalent symbol on the island of Calypso. The tree in the texts of the lamellae is explicitly the limen not only of the Underworld, but of the special place within the confines of the Underworld, reserved for the *mystai*, and it is intimately connected with the motif of thirst. This distinct symbolism may have influenced the later or contemporary practice of making coffins of cypress-wood (a practice Thucydides noted in Athens 2.34.3: *larnakas kyparissinas*).[52] After death, the *mystes* faces choices which will determine her/his condition in Hades. S/he must choose the proper direction, wherever that may be (although the deictic τῇ emphatically points to a direction[53]), and s/he must drink from the appropriate spring.

---

[51] For the cypress tree and its ambivalent symbolism, see Crane 1988:16 and 25 with nn13–14. Although the presence of cypress in the Underworld is uncommon or non-existent (Olck 1901; compare Graf and Johnston 2007:108–109), poplars are not (112n47); in the *Odyssey*, they are present in Calypso's island (5.238–240), in Scheria in the grove of Athena (6.291–294, compare 7.105–106), in the island of the Cyclops (9.140–142), at the entrance to the Underworld, in the grove of Persephone (10.509–510); and on Ithaca (17.208–210); for Scheria as a kind of Elysium and the Phaeacians as ferrymen see Cook 1992; for 'katabatic' associations, see Martin 2007:15–17 and passim; and the section "The Cretan Context of the Cretan *Epistomia*." Generally both Circe and Calypso have "strong associations with the Underworld," and both endanger Odysseus' *kleos* (Tracy 1990b:57–58 and 9n5; Slatkin 2005); on Circe's Near Eastern parallels, see Marinatos 2000:32–44. Nagler (1996, especially 142–149) argues that Circe and Calypso, both with prophetic powers, live close to the *axis mundi*; Bakker (2001:345–346) notes that, through the symbol of the tall-as-the-sky trees and that of the axis, the "domestic paradise (of Penelope) feeds on (the) mythic paradise (of Calypso and Circe);" see further Nakassis 2004:221–223.

[52] For such a larnax covered with silver-plates from Macedonia, see Tsimbidou-Avloniti 2000. Plato (*Laws* 741c–d) proposes to write down in detail laws and regulations for the priestesses' future reference to the "memories of cypress" (*kyparittinas mnemas*); compare the comments in *FGrHist* IV A 3 F22 (1026: Hermippos of Smyrna), pages 249–252 on the symbolism of the cypress and its 'Pythagorean' associations; and see further the section "Afterword."

[53] On deictics in the Homeric epics, see Bakker 1997:71–91; 2005:71–91; on time, temporality, and deixis in epic, see Bakker 2005:92–113. The process of composition of the texts on the lamellae is reversed, in comparison to Bakker's arguments for the Homeric epics, as the afterlife is revealed in the present, but remains to be materialized in the future.

The deviations in the texts of group B do not portray a neat topography of Hades and many attempts have been made to accommodate the differences.[54] If the directions in the texts mattered, then a few of the deceased carrying these texts would have certainly been in for a surprise.[55] The cypress (and also the (black) poplar) and the spring are mythic stock-elements, which, as Edmonds has argued, do not illustrate a clear-cut operative dichotomy of left and right, but they can signify different things in particular texts, "first and second, or near and far."[56] This accounts well for the divergent readings in the B group texts, but the deviant readings particularly in B12 and B6 may have been due also to local cultic and ritual considerations (see the section "The Cretan Context of the Cretan *Epistomia*").

Be that as it may, even if this ritual context for understanding the Cretan *epistomia* (incised and unincised) is plausible enough to be accepted, the fact remains that, within the same area and within a period of four centuries—and

---

[54] Zuntz (1971:368–393) and Guarducci (1974a:18–21) have commented extensively on the variant readings and have presented parallels from Egypt and the Near East; Delia (1992) relates the motif of thirst with sepulchral texts inscribed: δοί σοι ὁ Ὄσειρις τὸ ψυχρὸν ὕδωρ, and concludes that "the 'B' texts, which are indisputably Pythagorean, reflect this philosopher's debt to Egypt." Merkelbach (1995:34–36 and 477–478, and 1999) and Burkert (2004b:71–98) also find Egyptian parallel motifs in the texts, as does Assmann (2005: especially 206–208), but the symbolism behind these motifs is not the same, as in the lamellae the water of the two springs stands for *lethe* and *mnemosyne* respectively (I follow Mourelatos' [2002:12–13] distinction between motif and theme borrowed from the visual arts: the former connotes the 'form' a topic takes in literature, the latter the 'idea' expressed by this 'form'). For convergences and divergences, see especially the balanced discussion by Dousa (forthcoming). For the Egyptian gods in Greece Bommas 2005. For Crete and Egypt in particular, see Karetsou 2000; and Karetsou, Andreadaki-Vlazaki, and Papadakis 2000; Haider 2001 for the Keftiu on a papyrus; and 154n3, 190n129. For Hittite analogies and differences, see Bernabé forthcoming. Chaniotis (2000) rightly emphasizes that the Underworld is not portrayed as antithetical to the world above earth (*Gegenwelt*), but rather as an imaginary *other*-world, with familiar topography (*Jenseits*). Graf (1974:79–94) discusses the Place of the Reverend, the Elysium, and the Isles of the Blessed, for which see also Nagy 1979:189–190; Griffith 2001; Assmann 2005:232–234 and 389–392; Janda 2005; Santamaria Álvarez 2006. Cairon (2006) discusses a rather detailed description of Elysion in a 3rd century CE epigram, reminiscent of the Christian paradise. For the mythic narratives of Underworld journeys, see further Schmidt 1991; Cole 2003; and Edmonds 2004:46–52; for the journey as being primarily, but not exclusively, by boat, see Kritzas 2004:especially 1096–1102 with the previous bibliography. Instructions for the dead are also a motif in present-day laments of Mordovia for which see Jordan 2001.

[55] Cole 2003:209.

[56] Edmonds 2004:46–55, 50, and 51–52. According to Edmonds, this implies an *askēsis* practiced in life that helps the deceased to make the right decision in the Underworld, "practices characteristic of the Pythagoreans and other countercultural groups," as the Pythagoreans and Plato's myth of Er in the *Republic* indicate. Seaford (2004a:263–264) sees an adaptation by Parmenides of the distinction between the right and the wrong road to express the difference between himself and the ignorant; see further 175n86.

therefore one may assume within the same group of people—the evidence points not towards homogeneity, as is expected, but towards diversity. A comparison of the texts in Table 2 grouped according to provenance is impressive. Three different methods are in operation amongst the deceased buried in the Sfakaki cemetery (representing groups B, E, and G), all with the same purpose in mind, thus demonstrating that apparently not all initiates felt the same way on the matter. Is this evidence for what Sourvinou-Inwood (1995) has called an 'individualization,' a more personal attitude towards death? Is this evidence for more than one ritual and its implied *hieros logos* expounded by traveling priests? Is each deceased or family member picking and choosing what s/he remembers from the ritual and the *hieros logos*, as they were perhaps allowed to do, because there were no strict prohibitions? Is this what s/he understands as most important for the final journey? Alternatively, is this evidence that the deceased or family member bought the engraved lamella without being able, or did they not care, to check the text? These issues must perforce remain open.

In Search of a Context: Rhapsodizing and 'Prophesying' the Afterlife

In light of the foregoing discussion, it is evident that the corpus of the forty-four lamellae and *epistomia* (incised and unincised) presents a ritual and a *hieros logos, in parte* or *in toto*, but exactly what kind of ritual and *hieros logos* is still a matter of debate. The *opinio communis* concurs only in one thing: these texts relate a ritual and/or mystery cult whose emphasis is on afterlife. Despite scrutiny, the texts' origin and context remain elusive, because of the nature of the evidence. Interpretations abound, however, and the study of these texts has generated arguments relating the engraved lamellae to *Orphica, Pythagorica, Eleusiniaca, Bacchica,* and even *Orphicodionysiaca*.[57] Although few scholars today, if any, would maintain the exclusively Eleusinian or Pythagorean character of these texts, consensus is, expectedly, not within reach.

---

[57] The best concise and cogent exposition on this is Parker 1995:483–510 with earlier bibliography; and Bremmer 1994b:84–97. See further Picard 1961; Nilsson 1985; Graf 1993; Brisson 1995; Burkert 1993 and 1998; Riedweg 1998 and 2002; Cole 1980, 1993, 2003; Bremmer 1991, and 2002:11–26; Sorel 2002; Rangos 2003; Bernabé and Jiménez San Cristóbal 2001 and forthcoming; Calame 2002; the new and updated edition of the *Orphica* by Bernabé 2005 (see also Bernabé 2000); Edmonds 2004; Parker and Stamatopoulou 2004; and Graf and Johnston 2007. For a historiographical approach to Orpheus and Orphism, Pythagoras and Dionysos, see Cosi 2000. For the literary presence and exploitation of Orpheus' myth, see Segal 1989. The influence exerted by 'Orphic literature' is even evident in a Jewish-Hellenistic imitation (Riedweg 1993).

As Walter Burkert has shown definitively, mystery cults appeared in Greece as early as the sixth century BCE, if not earlier, and shared many common characteristics that make it difficult to distinguish clearly among them.[58] Their interaction influenced both their discourse and practical matters. Without discrimination regarding religious convictions, gender, age, social or economic status, or nationality (only those who committed murder were discriminated against), initiation was open and tolerant. The *mystes* could decide at will to be initiated into as many mysteries as s/he wished to, in the hope of personally receiving rewards in this life or after death. In many mysteries, secrecy was enforced and revelation of the *arrheta* and *aporrheta* was severely punished. As it turns out, the oral and apparently written teachings concentrated on a *hieros logos* and involved both *legomena* and *dromena*,[59] but evidence for the procedure is scanty or totally absent, except for one thing which was allowed to be revealed: the impact the mysteries had on the initiates (hence the allusions in literary texts). Through initiation, the *mystes* acquired a special relationship with the divine, what Burkert calls "the extraordinary experience." This experience transformed her/his views on matters of life and death, as is shown by the epithets ὄλβιος, εὐδαίμων, μάκαρ, and ὅσιος employed for *mystai*,[60] epithets otherwise reserved only for gods and heroes.

The common ground shared by all mystery cults is the main obstacle in the search for a religious context regarding the lamellae's texts. The texts on the lamellae are consistently referred to as Orphic or Bacchic with Pythagorean influences (often between inverted commas or with the qualification 'so-called'), despite facts which seem to militate against these epithets: Orpheus is found nowhere in these texts; the deceased's regeneration does not necessarily entail *metempsychosis* (or at least the *metempsychosis* Pythagoras

---

[58] Burkert 1985:276–304; and 1987:passim; Pakannen 1996:13–21 and 65–71; the essays in Cosmopoulos 2003; and Johnston 2004a. For *telete, myesis,* and *mystagogos,* see Simms 1990. Price (1999:108–125) rightly calls them "elective cults," as does Mikalson in his chapter on Greek religion and the individual (2005:180–197, 180), but his discussion of the Eleusinian mysteries is grouped together with four other major (but less elective) cults (Athena Polias at Athens, Zeus Olympios at Olympia, Apollo Pythios at Delphi, Dionysos Kadmeios at Thebes), because Eleusis gradually acquired Panhellenic prominence (68–132), as opposed to Dionysiac mysteries which could be performed anywhere. Arnaoutoglou (2003:19–30 and 159–163) discusses the private religious associations in Hellenistic Athens and their 'marginality,' for which see also Parker 1996:328–342.

[59] Henrichs 1998 and 2000 (where he demonstrates that in rituals the *dromena* are more prominent than the *legomena,* unlike in tragedies where the latter are more prominent than the former); Graf and Johnston 2007:94–164; Riedweg 1998; Faraone forthcoming-1.

[60] For these epithets, see de Heer 1969 and McDonald 1978:10-36. On views of death and the afterlife around the Mediterranean, see the essays in Bremer, van den Hout, and Peters 1994.

and Empedokles meant);[61] evidence for Orphic rites depends more or less on the lamellae's texts, which thus portray Orphism as interested primarily if not exclusively in eschatology. Marcel Detienne has described Orphism, Dionysiac cult(s) and ritual(s), and Pythagoreanism as *chemins de déviance*, pieces of one and the same system which refused or protested against the main sociopolitical religious practice of the polis.[62] Yet, as Edmonds rightly pointed out, *déviance* is rather relative, in that many or all of the deceased with the incised lamellae could have followed traditional social and religious practices within their poleis.[63] Noel Robertson has even suggested that the Orphic ideas and rites originated from the public cults and rituals of the Mother and Dionysos already performed in various Greek cities.[64] Although it remains uncertain whether rituals and stories of the Mother and Dionysos, which unfold together, predate the Orphic ones, or whether their genesis can be assigned to the people's concern for vine's and grain's fertility in nature alone, Robertson correctly points out the common ground shared by these rituals and the traditional character of the Orphic practices.

Jan Bremmer may eventually be proved correct in his formulation of the dynamic interaction between these mystery cults: "Orphism was the product of Pythagorean influence on Bacchic mysteries in the first quarter of the fifth century, but despite their similarities both movements also displayed many differences."[65] Until more evidence comes to light, we might follow Susan Cole's succinct and sensible advice: "it seems safe to assume that the texts on the tablets—short, contradictory, heterogeneous, and unpredictable—are more likely the product of *independent groups* supervised by *inspired leaders than the result of a particular philosophical movement*" (my emphasis).[66] As it is, these groups' interaction and interdependence are best explained by Burkert:[67]

> Bacchic, Orphic, and Pythagorean are circles each of which has its own centre, and while these circles have areas that coincide, each preserves its own special sphere. The nomenclature is based on different principles: mystery ritual, literature marked by the

---

[61] For Pythagoras, see Kahn 2001 and Riedweg 2005 with previous bibliography. For Empedokles, see Kingsley 1995, Riedweg 1995, and Casertano 2000. On early Pythagoreanism, see also Pierris 1992.

[62] Detienne 1975, 2001, and 2003:155–157.

[63] Edmonds 2004:43.

[64] Robertson 2003:218–240; on Mother Earth and some misconceptions, see Georgoudi 2002.

[65] Bremmer 2002:24.

[66] Cole 2003:207.

[67] Burkert 1985:300; Graf and Johnston 2007:especially 137–164.

name of an author, and a historically fixed group with their master; Dionysos is a god, Orpheus a mythical singer and prophet, and Pythagoras a Samian of the sixth century. Within the sphere of *Orphica*, two schools may perhaps be distinguished, an Athenian-Eleusinian school which concentrated on the bestowal of culture allegedly to be found in the Demeter myth and the Eleusinian mysteries, and an Italian, Pythagorean school which took a more original path with the doctrine of the transmigration of the souls. Orphic and Bacchic coincide in their concern for burial and the afterlife and probably also in the special myth of Dionysos Zagreus, while Orphic and Pythagorean coincide in the doctrine of metempsychosis and asceticism. However that may be, the difficulties of precise demarcation should not lead to a denial of the phenomena themselves.

Orphic literature, Pythagorean philosophy, and Dionysiac cult(s) and ritual(s) are different contexts in which the texts on the lamellae may be placed (in some more readily than in others). Much depends on whether we emphasize the similarities or the differences among the texts.[68] Even Burkert's careful formulation of the interactive yet independent nature of these contexts needs modification. For example, the 'Athenian-Eleusinian school' has not as yet produced an incised gold lamella, unless the initiates were employing perishable material, and some certainly did, like the deceased of grave A at Derveni.[69] Italy,[70] Crete, the northwest Peloponnese,[71] Thessaly, and Macedonia also appear as other 'schools' which partake one way or another in Orphic, Pythagorean, and Bacchic ideas about personal needs in this life and in the hereafter, but with distinct characteristics.[72] If the northwest Peloponnese,

---

[68] Tortorelli Ghidini (2000a) attempts such a comparison and suggests that the texts' basic couples are: mother/son, Persephone/Bacchios, and Mnemosyne/bacchoi, the last being deified under Pythagorean influence.

[69] This absence in Athens presents an anomaly and a puzzle, according to Parker (2005:368).

[70] For Dionysos in Italy, see Casadio 1995; for Italian mysteries, influenced by Bacchic and Orphic cults and those of Demeter and Persephone, see Poccetti 1995 and 2000; Maddoli 1996; and Hinz 1998; for eschatologies in Magna Graecia, Tortorelli Ghidini 1995b and Dettori 1996; for Thourioi in particular, Burkert 1975; for the archaeology of eschatology in Magna Graecia, Bottini 2000.

[71] For Dionysos in Argos, Corinth, Sicyon, and Troezen, see Casadio 1994 and 1999; for Dionysos in Sparta, Stibbe 1991.

[72] Oikonomou (2004:102–105) entertains the possibility that the incised *epistomia* from the northern Peloponnese and Crete may be associated with the Macedonian presence in these areas, and Macedonian direct or indirect influence, a less probable possibility for Crete which presents a case more complicated than the cities in the northern Peloponnese.

and to some extent also Crete (see the section "A Cretan Context"), presents a rather homogeneous picture, at least so far, the five texts on Thessalian lamellae are astonishing in their diversity (B2, B9, D2, D3, D5). Likewise, the twelve Macedonian lamellae are not the only evidence concerning views on the afterlife in Macedonia,[73] as testify a number of discoveries: the theo-/ cosmogonic commentary on *PDerveni*;[74] the outstanding paintings in the *Judgment Tomb* at Leukadia,[75] and at the *Tomb of Persephone* at Vergina;[76] the cist-tomb at Agios Athanassios, in which there was discovered a silver-plated cypress-*larnax* with the pregnant mother's bones wrapped in purple gold inside, as well as ivory fragments from the bier's decoration (a bier which, at least in one of its zones, was of a Dionysiac character), and a painting on one of the walls portraying a wooden box with two scrolls of papyri on top;[77] the discovery of a number of clay figurines in rooms of a house in Pella, dated to the second century BCE, representing snakes, grapes, eggs, and a horseman, and finally, fragments of clay statuettes of Dionysos, Persephone, Aphrodite, and the Mother of Gods, all probably associated with the cult(s) of Dionysos, aimed at both the living and dead.[78] All of these discoveries offer yet more examples of other 'schools' within Macedonia, independent or interrelated with the 'school(s)' manifest in the texts on the lamellae and *epistomia*. Lastly, Olbia, the only area that has offered concrete evidence for the existence of a group of people calling themselves Orphics, is probably yet another, different

---

[73] On cults and rites of passage in Macedonia, see Hatzopoulos 1994 and 2006. Rizakis and Touratsoglou (2000) discuss only monuments above the grave; for altars as grave markers, see also Adam-Veleni 2002:161–197 and 219–256. Lioutas (1997:636–637; SEG 49.814) publishes a fragmentary stele from Thessaloniki, probably a catalogue of the members of a Dionysiac *thiasos*, dated to the second half of the second or the third century CE; the left column records the male and the right the female members.

[74] Betegh (2004:56–68 and passim) argues in favor of the papyrus' function in a funerary ritual, not unlike the one implied for the gold lamellae. See also Bernabé 2005 (and 2002b, where he argues that the theogony is Orphic), and compare Most 1997a; Kouremenos, Parássoglou, and Tsantsanoglou 2006:2–4, who suggest that the deceased may have been (a soldier) from Thessaly.

[75] Petsas 1966; Miller 1992; Rhomiopoulou 1997; Brécoulaki 2006; and Kottaridou 2006.

[76] Andronikos 1994:especially 129–134 for a comparison of wall paintings in Macedonian tombs; Brécoulaki 2006; and Kottaridou 2006.

[77] Tsimbidou-Avloniti (2000:553) wonders if this may allude to the woman's musical activity; for another painted tomb in this area, see Tsimbidou-Avloniti 2006.

[78] Chryssostomou 1996–1997; Chryssostomou argues that these artifacts are evidence for the everyday life and popular ritual(s) in second-century BCE Pella. For Dionysos in the city of Drama, see Koukouli-Chryssanthaki 1992; for Dionysos' sanctuary in Aphytis, near a spring and a cave, see Voutiras 2000; for *thiasoi* of the cult of Egyptian gods in Philippoi, see Tsochos 2002; for Dionysos' various identities and associations in Macedonia, see Hatzopoulos 1994.

'school': the famous bone-plaques were not found inside a grave, but in the area of the eastern temenos, and their graffiti imply views on the afterlife (even if the graffiti are not connected *stricto sensu* with the afterlife).[79]

And yet, even if the texts on these lamellae are labeled as Bacchic with Orphic and Pythagorean influences and are thus securely placed within this religious-philosophical-literary context, it is by no means certain that all of those interred with the lamellae and *epistomia* (engraved or not) shared all or some of the views expressed in the Bacchic ritual, the 'Orphic rites,' and the Pythagorean teachings. Understanding and appreciation of the *Homeric Hymns*, for example, is not enhanced and intensified because of their label *Homeric*, nor will our understanding or appreciation of the Orphic rhapsodies or the incised lamellae ever increase merely because they are entitled Orphic or Bacchic. As Edmonds has argued, Orphic may have been nothing more than a descriptive title for quickly and easily distinguishing between Homer/Homeric/Hesiod/ lyric poetry/drama on the one hand, and everything else on the other.[80] The search for a context for these texts is helpful and illuminating if only because it brings to light the complicated and dynamic interaction of ideas on matters of life and death. We must keep in mind, however, that this context search is not the only fruitful approach for the study of these texts, especially when

---

[79] Bernabé 2004:463–465 F; Vinogradov 1991; Burkert 1994a; Vinogradov and Kryžickij 1995:116–117; Dubois 1996:154–155 no. 94a–c; Lévèque 2000; Seaford 2004:108–109. Lebedev (1996a:271, 275) argues convincingly that the bone-plaques were kleromantic and were probably owned by Pharnabazos (see also Lebedev 1996b for the Demetreion in Olbia and the gods worshipped therein; and 132n122, 149n157). For Orpheus and his cult in Thrace, see Theodossiev 1994–1995, 1995, 1996, 1997, and 2002; and Fol 2004. Three individuals bear the name Orpheus in Odessos, the most recent of whom dedicates an inscribed wheel to Herakles *kallinikos* (Sharankov 2001:176nn23–24). Mastrocinque (1993; SEG 43.677, 45.1488) studies a hematite ear-ring of unknown provenance inscribed: Ὀρφεός | Βακκι|κός on either side of a man hanging on a cross surrounded by the moon and seven stars (of which there are three more examples).

[80] Edmonds 2004:102–104; and 4n10. For the *Orphic rhapsodies* the standard is West 1983, and Bernabé 2005; see also Albinus 2000:101–152; Betegh 2004:138–152. Rudhardt (1991, and especially 2002) presents compelling arguments on the attempt in *Orphic Hymns* to combine the Homeric and Orphic views of Dionysos through the use of multiple epithets for the god's double identity, a son of both Semele and Persephone (also 129n106). For neoplatonic and neopythagorean allegorical developments of 'Homer' and 'Orpheus' and their philosophical and religious importance in late antiquity, see Lamberton 1986; Brisson 1995 and 2002; Athanassiadi 2005:33–34. The author of *PDerveni* (column VII) is also involved in explaining the *riddling* works (*ainigmata*) of Orpheus, for which see Tsantsanoglou 1997:121–122; Most 1997b; Betegh 2004:362–364; and Kouremenos, Parássoglou, and Tsantsanoglou 2006:75, 172–173. Yunis (2003:195–198) compares the *PDerveni* author and the rhapsode Ion in Plato, both of whom are distinguishing between poetic experience in performance and poetic interpretation through critical reading.

the evidence is inadequate.[81] Both the *Homeric Hymns* and the lamellae's texts appear to have been anonymous products of approximately the same era, the archaic and early classical periods in Greece, during which, with the emergence of the polis, many crucial developments took place in art and literature and in the political, social, and economic spheres. This was a period full of exciting and provocative ideas, but a period also poorly documented.[82]

What the texts on the lamellae and *epistomia* present is an outlook on and prospect of an afterlife very much different from the one presented in the texts of Homer, Hesiod, and the archaic poets. At the same time, however, the texts on the lamellae present a narrative of the afterlife very well versed in the traditional mythic elements and compositional techniques.[83] Edmonds has recently studied the Underworld journey as a mythic narrative. These "roadmaps of *déviance*," as he calls the lamellae's mythic narratives, if viewed from the "locative order of Greek polis religion," show that "these marginal, countercultural figures appeal to a different standard to evaluate themselves and their society, one centered not on the existing pattern, but on an ideal pattern located elsewhere in space or time."[84] Although Edmonds readily admits the problems in "defining countercultural religion in the context of a religious system like the ancient Greek, which had no real orthodoxy as it is understood in the Judaeo-Christian tradition,"[85] it is not only the term *countercultural religion* that is problematic. Equally problematic are terms like *polis religion* (behind which usually lies Athens) and *marginal*.[86] Admittedly, mainstream or everyday

---

[81] Particularly relevant are Clay's (1989:88) remarks in relation to the study of the *Homeric Hymns*: "classical philology has always regarded itself primarily as a historical discipline. The question a classicist initially asks of a text is not what does it mean, but when was it composed and by whom. In dealing with anonymous texts of unknown date, these questions become the focus of inquiry. Clues are sought everywhere, and lack of evidence becomes a goad to ingenuity."

[82] For a persuasive discussion of the emerging cults from the protogeometric period onwards and their instrumental role in the social and political formation and redefinition, see de Polignac (2000). Papachatzis (1990) distinguishes, in a somewhat oversimplistic way, between public and popular religion: the former being more of a literary creation which the polis adopted; the latter being addressed to individuals stressed religious purification, which allowed initiation into mystery cults, thus alleviating fear of death and securing a blessed afterlife. For developments in Athenian religion in particular, see Parker 1996.

[83] Cole 2003; Albinus 2000; and di Benedetto 2004 for the Petelia and Hipponion texts.

[84] Edmonds 2004:41–43 and 108–109.

[85] Edmonds 2004:41. Detienne 2003:155–157 on Orphics as renouncers and as fleeing civic institutions and values such as sacrifice and meat-eating. Compare Henrichs 2003a, 2003b, 2004a; and Graf and Johnston 2007:137–184.

[86] On the problems raised by these terms, and the ramifications entailed, see Cole 1995; Burkert 1995, 2001a, and 2001d; for Crete in particular, see Chaniotis 2001a; for an instructive discussion of sacred and profane, see Bremmer 1998. Sourvinou-Inwood's (2000a and 2000b) discussion of

life in a Greek polis *vis à vis* the *bios Orphikos* or *Pythagorikos* was different than the ordinary way of life within a Greek polis. It is not at all certain, however, if in the case of the latter the difference should be understood as protesting against and countering the polis religion and the cultural system it entailed.[87]

Solon's famous reply to Kroisos' question concerning who is the most *olbios* (a word not associated with mystery cults in the Herodotean context) helps clarify the different perspectives from which polis-religion and private initiation were approached (at least by the time of Herodotus) (1.30–31). As Seth Benardete has argued cogently, the Athenian case of Tellos excludes the divine and its criteria are highly political, as the individual is perceived first and foremost as a member of the polis; the Argive example of Kleobis and Biton concentrates on the *oikos* and the divine and ignores political criteria to the point of becoming non- or even antipolitical, as the individual is a member not of the polis but of the human race.[88]

The two Herodotean examples of *olbiotes* are incompatible because they are based on different premises. And yet, as neither Athens stopped worshipping gods nor Argos ceased to exist as a city-state, these examples suggest that a polis could not, or did not care to, enforce a homogeneous religious system; hence these "varying forms, trends, or options within the one disparate yet continuous conglomerate of ancient religion."[89] Graf and Johnston rightly argue against the categorization of these groups as marginal; they replace the idea of marginality with a concept of supplementarity. Even this

---

polis religion provides the groundwork at least for Athens, but I am not so certain if "non-institutionalized sectarian discourse of the Orphic type … may have been perceived as lying outside the authority of the polis discourse" (2000b:55); for private initiations in Athens alongside public cults of Dionysos, and Athenian beliefs in afterlife, see Parker 2005:325, 363–368. Redfield (1991) has shown that certain doctrines about death and the afterlife may go hand in hand with polis religion, as the examples of Sparta and Lokroi in South Italy demonstrate. De Polignac (1996) argues that the two kinds of social expression, i.e. self-identity and status, are complementary and at times competitive. Frankfurter (1998 and 2002) suggests that in terms of the spatial model center/periphery the dynamics of ritual expertise are fluid and are negotiated constantly between local and peripheral ritual experts, between ritual experts inside and outside the community, between literati and less so ritual experts, and so on. Johnston (2002) examines sacrifice mentioned in magical papyri and concludes that the experts followed traditional patterns of ritual in a creative, and perhaps individualistic way. Cole (2004) discusses in detail the evidence for distinguishing between human and divine space for different uses, a process in which gender as articulated in ritual is significant.

[87] This is not to deny that such cases existed, at least in Athens, as Parker (1996:161–163) has demonstrated, but Athens need not, in fact should not, be the model for other cities and other parts of the Greek world.

[88] Benardete 1969:133–134.

[89] Burkert 1987:4.

notion of supplementarity, however, provides only partial answers, because, as Graf and Johnston point out, the evidence is scanty and perplexing at best.[90] Initiation that promises a blissful afterlife is indeed supplementary to the 'mainstream' attitude about the afterlife. The new lamella from Pherai (D5), however, strongly suggests that the rule was the more the better, as some *mystai* apparently needed additional assurances while alive and their initiation into a second mystery cult supplemented the first. It appears that the 'deviant' ideas expressed in the texts of the lamellae laid emphasis on the individual rather than on the community (whichever community that may have been). Each and every incised lamella and *epistomion* should not be viewed as a representative expression, the mouthpiece of that community, because, in spite of similarities, the texts' divergences also point towards individuation. These individuals expressing ideas such as those in the texts of the lamellae and *epistomia* are on the margins or the periphery of the polis-religion, in the same way as the Sophists, Socrates, Euripides, Plato, and others: their views are 'peripheral' to but at the same time interactive with the 'polis ideological system.'[91]

The ideas on the afterlife expressed in the corpus of the lamellae and *epistomia* may therefore be viewed as part and parcel of the religious ideas *within* the polis where they compete in order to attract the individual's attention. They aim at offering a more personal rather than collective identity as far as one's postmortem state is concerned. Although one might imagine that this clash between personal and collective identities may sometimes result in conflict, this supplementary arrangement promoted by the corpus of the lamellae and *epistomia* is not perforce mutually exclusive or nullifying. This 'dual identity' may easily explain the fact that a number of texts from the archaic period onwards betray, in various degrees, influences of Orphic ideas, ideas that seem to permeate everything in these periods as if by osmosis. The ideas of the Underworld presented in the texts of the lamellae are not alien to Greek thinking; they refer to an *illo tempore*, a golden age when humans and gods lived together before their subsequent estrangement,[92] a utopian ideal located in another permanent world, that of the dead. For this other world the

---

[90] Graf and Johnston 2007:178–184.

[91] Sally Humphreys (2004) provides a challenging argument, with much of which I am in agreement, of the competitive interaction, development, and rearticulation of rational and irrational discourses of thought, of public and private attitudes towards intellectuals and religion, of ritual showing resilience to accommodate new needs and developments (especially 51–76, and 223–275 on the metamorphoses of the Athenian Anthesteria).

[92] Edmonds 2004:43–44.

texts on the lamellae offer hope, and they promote endurance for the hardships of the present life on earth.

Two contemporary but conflicting discourses on the afterlife may be distinguished in the archaic period. One comprises views on afterlife as expressed in the works of Homer, Hesiod, and in lyric and dramatic poetry; the other comprises the Orphic, Pythagorean, Bacchic, and Eleusinian views, which may be found in the mystery cult(s). We might call these discourses the Homeric and the Orphic, although it is important to remember that the distinction is somewhat arbitrary, because within each discourse, an array of differing and sometimes opposing views and approaches is evident.[93]

The Homeric view of the afterlife in the *Iliad* and the *Odyssey* is rather gloomy and pessimistic, as the Underworld is portrayed in unflattering terms. Odysseas Tsagarakis revisited the issues concerning the Homeric *Nekyia* and concluded that, in the so-called 'Review of Hades,' two themes are conflated, a *nekyomanteion* and a *katabasis*.[94] The two differing views about the fate of the *psyche* after death may be explained in parallel to the two ways of burial within the epic, inhumation and cremation: the latter, favored by the poet, may have supported the idea of a "*bodiless psyche* in Hades, a mere *eidolon* of its former self"; the former supports the idea rather of the *psyche's* 'physical' existence in Hades, an arrangement which allows the activities of one's earthly life to

---

[93] For these two (and more) discourses on afterlife, see Graf and Johnston (2007:94–136), who point out that according to the sources the souls in the Underworld are judged as the bad, the good, and the good-plus; although I do not differentiate between the good and the good-plus, the three groups show clearly the differences encountered within the same discourse on death, either the Homeric or the Orphic. See further Rhode 1987; Farnell 1995:373–402; Guthrie 1993:148–171; Calame 1991; Redfield 1991; Pierris 1996:3–68, 113–192; and Albinus 2000. West (1983) illustrates the divergences of the hubbub of books within Orphic poetry (his stemma on page 264 gives an idea of how things may have worked between Homeric and Orphic). Johnston (1999:3–35, 36–81) provides a critical overview of the relation between the living and the dead in narrative and non-narrative sources respectively, and she doubts if Homer was aware of other views about the dead, except those he presented. Seaford (2004:219–230) proposes to view this distinction as a split in cosmogonic accounts of the archaic period: "on the one hand *impersonal* 'philosophy', and on the other hand the bizarrely *personal* Orphic cosmogony and anthropogony that reflect to some degree the re-creation of the self in mystic initiation" (225). Papagiorgis (1995:93–106) rightly emphasizes that the Homeric epics do not identify the sacred with the gods who cannot save humans from death. For the texts on the lamellae in relation to Pindar, Lloyd-Jones 1990 is the place to start; for the complexities of *kleos* in Pindar, Currie 2005:71–84; in particular for *Olympian 2*, see Iakov 2005; for *Isthmian 6*, Faraone 2002 (Pindar's praise poetry can provide a special kind of happiness that can persist even in the Underworld); for Pindar's fr. 133, Edmonds forthcoming-4; and Herrero de Jáuregui forthcoming-1 (Pindar as bridging the two discourses). For afterlife in Pindar, Simonides, and archaic poetry, Bremmer 1994a; Bremer 1994; Brown 1998.

[94] Crane 1988:93–96; Tsagarakis 2000:105–119 (and also 1995a, 1995b, and 1997).

be paired with appropriate punishments in the Underworld. Even the Elysian and the Asphodel Meadows, places for heroes, the privileged deceased of epic, are somewhat vague and do not have a well-defined topography; at least not yet, because epic poetry would have compromised its very existence. In that respect, it is no surprise that the epithet μακάρτατος is employed by Odysseus in order to characterize a person's excellence among all humans alive or dead.[95]

Likewise, Hesiod attempts in the *Theogony* (lines 717–819) to throw light on the shadowy Underworld, Tartaros. In the final act of Zeus' consolidation of power and his making a *kosmos* of all parts of the universe, Tartaros acquires a geography. This geography, however, is articulated by its monstrous inhabitants, those dangerous to Zeus' reign. Among them, humans cannot as yet have a place.[96] It seems that epic poetry bypasses consciously the issue of life after death. The description of Tartaros is followed by the catalogue of Zeus', Poseidon's, and Ares' divine marriages, some of which have a happy end for the humans involved (Semele, Ariadne, Dionysos, and Herakles are deified, for instance). The next catalogue of heroes married to goddesses does not present an example of deification, but interestingly it begins with Demeter and Iasion in Crete and ends with Odysseus' offspring by Circe and Calypso,[97] choices that Odysseus and the poet faced and rejected in the *Odyssey*.[98]

In Hesiod's *Works and Days* (lines 106–201), on the other hand, the manner of death/mode of existence in the afterlife is one of the key criteria (alongside the living condition) in explaining the gradual deterioration and worsening progression of the five races of humans (symbolized as metals) over time.[99]

---

[95] Tsagarakis 2000:25–26, 97, 117 (and 1995a, 1995b, and 1997); Albinus 2000:86–89; and compare Bremmer 1994a and 2002. For *makartatos*, see the convincing discussion in Dova 2000. For Polygnotos' *Nekyia* at Delphi, its relation to the Homeric one, and its association with mysteries, see Manoledakis 2003:186–187 (Orpheus), 189–190 (Thamyris), 196–202 (the uninitiated into Orphic mysteries, according to the author), 208–220 (mysteries in general); Polygnotos' work seems thus to combine in visual terms a synthesis of the Homeric and Orphic discourses. For the different and problematic interpretative approaches to pictorial narratives, see Stansbury-O'Donnell 1999 and Ferrari 2003.

[96] West 1983; Guthrie 1993:82–86; and Clay 2003:12–30.

[97] See 113n51.

[98] On the inclusion of the Cretan heroine Ariadne and of Demeter's union with Iasion on Crete in the section of the *Theogony* following the description of Tartaros, see Sarinaki forthcoming.

[99] The bibliography on the races of men is immense; see the discussion by Bezantakos 2006:114–134, and Tsagalis 2006:193–209, both with previous bibliography. West (1978; 1997b:312–319) discusses Anatolian influences. Fontenrose (1974) examines the criteria of work and *dike* in distinguishing the races, which may bring to mortals a golden life and a place in the Isles of the Blessed. Vernant (1976:29–91) proposes a synchronic and diachronic dimension of the ages. Nagy (1979:151–172) focuses on the heroes whose afterlife resembles the one narrated

The first golden race (lines 109–126) consists of humans living as gods, and their death is like sleep overcoming them after which: "they become *daimones* upon the earth, guardians of mortals" (δαίμονες ἐσθλοί, ἐπιχθόνιοι, φύλακες θνητῶν ἀνθρώπων, Most 2006). The humans of the silver race (lines 127–142) are babies that never reach adulthood; *hybris* and violence reigns, but when these humans die they are called: "*makares* mortals beneath the earth" (ὑποχθόνιοι μάκαρες θνητοί, Most 2006). The bronze race (lines 143–155) is ruthless and horrible and is therefore self-destroyed by *hybris* and war; once annihilated by black death, its members, nameless, enter the house of Hades (Hesiod's reference to this house here is the first of its kind). The fourth race of heroes and demigods (lines 156–173) is bellicose like the bronze race, but it is also more just, and so when they die: "they become *olbioi* heroes and dwell with a spirit free of care in the islands of the *Makares* beside deep-eddying Ocean" (καὶ τοὶ μὲν ναίουσιν ἀκηδέα θυμὸν ἔχοντες | ἐν μακάρων νήσοισι παρ' Ὠκεανὸν βαθυδίνην, | ὄλβιοι ἥρωες, Most 2006). Lastly, the race of iron (lines 174–201), the poet's and 'our' race, is described as a constant and continuous mixture of good and evil, by which is effected the abolition of rules and attitudes (the fundamental ingredients for instituting a family, a polis, or a society). The extinction of this race is forthcoming, but the poet does not even speculate on how this extinction will come about, nor does he venture to imagine the condition of its members in the afterlife.

This schematic summary of the five Hesiodic races suggests two contradictory views on the afterlife: a favorable and desirable one, symbolized by gold and silver, whose human members become gods above the earth and *makares* under the earth; the other, an unfavorable and undesirable one, symbolized by bronze and iron, introduces Hades and anonymity. The heroes and demigods stand in between, as they share characteristics with the gold/silver races and the bronze/iron races. They are called *olbioi* and reside in the

---

in the *Aethiopis* but not the *Iliad*. Sourvinou-Inwood (1997) sees the myth through the ancients' cultural perceptions as a simultaneous movement up- and downward. Most (1997a) reconstructs the passage within Greek epic tradition, fully adapted to the didactic message of the *Works and Days* to Perses, as Edwards (2004) also stresses. Clay (2003:81–99) underlines Hesiod's emphasis on mortality in the creation of the successive races, which are experiments by trial and error. Calame (2004) argues for the temporal and spatial structure of the races and for Hesiod's utopian proposition, evident especially in Aristophanes, which cannot materialize through the social institutions, but only through rituals for an afterlife. Instead of the parallels Calame adduces from *Daniel* (2, 1–3, 7), I would argue that Hesiod portrays the gold, silver, and heroic races with characteristics found in the Orphic beliefs, which he rejects in favor of Olympos: what the mysteries profess is a hoax, because a golden age can no longer be attained; see further Brown (1998) who views the golden age as an 'other world,' utopian or eschatological, well attested in archaic poetry as a whole, but particularly in Pindar and Simonides.

islands of the *makares*, a status attained through a 'bronze and iron' living condition and manner of death. The gold and silver races bear characteristics not unlike those of the initiates in the lamellae's texts. It appears that Hesiod integrates the Orphic view only to reject it: as the gold and silver races are removed to the remotest past, the efficacy of contemporary mystery cults is denied. Within the narrative of the five races, Hesiod eliminates the contradiction between the two views on afterlife by presenting them not as contemporary but in a chronological sequence. He relegates the most desirable race(s) *in illo tempore*, when distinctions were blurred, and, as the condition of successive human races gradually worsens, he places the least desirable at *hic et nunc*. The mystery cults and their golden promises, as the race of the heroes implies, did exist once upon a time, but no more; only epic poetry can assure *kleos aphthiton*.[100]

That these two views seriously concerned people from the archaic period onwards is also attested by Herodotus. In addition to Solon's reply to Kroisos mentioned above, the historian also incorporates the human races into the second half of book one, but he employs a different narrative strategy. Seth Benardete has argued convincingly that by changing the Hesiodic criterion of chronological sequence and succession, Herodotus presents the human races as co-existing *hic et nunc* on the surface of the earth, and not as bygone races, except that of iron, distinguished also by their postmortem condition:[101]

> The surface of the earth presents together all the Hesiodic ages, which are not distinguished so much by what metals they use as by their customs ... Herodotus is not unaware of the changes time brings in human happiness as well as in customs and inventions, but he sees in customs something more permanent than he could find in empires and wars. Customs form the horizon within which these historical events occur, and without which they could not be understood.

---

[100] Nagy 1979:151–210; 2005; and Herrero de Jáuregui (forthcoming-1) on *kleos* and *mnemosyne* in the living and the dead as expounded in epic poetry and the texts on the lamellae.

[101] Benardete 1969:27–30 (the quotation from 29): in Herodotus' narrative the Hesiodic races partly correspond to the 'golden' Massagetai, the 'silver' Persians, the 'heroic' Spartans, the 'bronze' Karians, the 'iron' Lydians. This correspondence is of course schematic, in order to drive home the argument, as these people also reveal other shared characteristics in the historian's narrative. For the *eschata* and the golden age having the same limits and betraying similar if not identical characteristics (gold, automatic growth, and counter-*hypo-hyper*-civilization), see Romm 1992:especially 9–81; and Nakassis 2004. For the political and cultural potential of utopias in Rome, see Evans 2003.

Herodotus employs geographical criteria and the various metals in order to imply that the Hesiodic races, distinguished by their use of metals and presented by Hesiod in chronological succession, actually exist synchronically in different parts of the known world. In Herodotus, the metals are symbolic vehicles reflecting the various races' customs and habits, which, according to the historian, are the actual differentiating factors, but which betray characteristics similar to the Hesiodic races. Hesiod opts for one of the two views on afterlife: he removes the golden race from the *hic et nunc* and relegates it to a time forever lost, allowing no possibility of the golden period's return, not even in the Underworld. Herodotus opts for none or for both views on afterlife (in book 2 Egypt presents a different challenge): he 'harmonizes' them by changing Hesiod's criteria of chronological succession and genealogy into those of geographical distribution and recontextualizes in his narrative all the human races as existing contemporaneously in different parts of the known world.

And yet, although there is no way of ascertaining if Hesiod was consciously responding to 'unepic' ideas, it is safe to assume (as the narrative of the *Works and Days* and Herodotus' Book 1 certainly indicate) that, in the archaic period, two views on the afterlife competed for attention. The 'Homeric/Hesiodic' one presented a gloomy and pessimistic outlook on the hereafter. The 'Orphic' one, which Homer ignored but Hesiod could not and therefore integrated in the manner discussed above, proposed to alleviate the fear of death and to offer endurance for the daily hardships.[102] This 'Orphic' view also promised a differentiated status of the individual after death—that of a hero and god, as if s/he were a member of the Hesiodic golden, silver, or heroic races. The difference between the two discourses and the Orphic opposition to Homeric *kleos* may be seen in the semantic shift of the otherwise innocent Homeric/Hesiodic epithet ἀστερόεις. In Homer, it is regularly an attribute of the sky, with two exceptions:[103] the *thorax* of Achilles' first panoply (16.134); and Hephaistos' abode when Thetis visits to ask for the second panoply (18.370). The epithet's cosmological associations emphasize the limitations of Achilles' and Hephaistos' status which in their case may be overcome through

---

[102] Gera (2003:53) notes the Homeric and Hesiodic distinction between the language of gods and men, which, not only in Orphic writings, as Gera argues, but in mysteries in general "becomes a distinction between common language and mystical speech." See also Maurizio 1995 and 1997. For the language criterion in the narrative of Herodotus, see Munson 2005.

[103] Nine times in the *Iliad* (4.44, 5.769, 6.108, 8.46, 15.371, 16.134, 18.370, 19.128, 19.130), and four times in the *Odyssey* (9.527, 11.17, 12.380, 20.113).

art (the panoply and the palace), a metaphor for epic poetry itself.[104] These two exceptions of the epithet in Homer reflect the epic perception of *kleos* and immortality.

In Hesiod, there are no surprises, except that the first occurrence of the epithet matches the formula which (in a modified form) becomes the *symbolon* in the group B texts:[105]

Theogony 106: οἳ Γῆς ἐξεγένοντο καὶ Οὐρανοῦ ἀστερόεντος,

B1, B3–12: "I am of Earth and starry Sky,"

and

B2: "my name is Asterios."

Whereas in epic the epithet's symbolism of immortality conforms to the overall strategy for *kleos*, in the group B-texts, the epithet evokes the epic immortality but rejects the human limits set in the epic. The heroization/ divinization process of humans does not require the subtlety of epic poetry and its *kleos*. The same formula that Hesiod employs for the divine genealogy becomes in the group B-texts the mortal initiate's *symbolon* for attaining immortality the 'Orphic' way: through *Eukles* ('beautiful *kleos*'), Hades' euphemistic epithet, and through *Eubouleus* ('beautiful *boule*'), a euphemism for Zeus/Dionysos (and perhaps also Hades),[106] a way which transforms the epic symbols of immortal *kleos* into a more concrete immortality: the *mystes* is reborn and acquires the status of a hero/god in the afterlife.

This 'unepic' view, contemporary with the Homeric one, was not only an opinion held by the nascent mystery cults of the archaic period. If, as Richard Martin has argued cogently,[107] epic and Orphic material shared the medium by which they became known, that being *performance*, and if, as will be argued, they also shared the epic techniques of composition, then much that is explained in discussions of literary texts as an interpolation or influence of

---

[104] For the discussion of this epithet I am indebted to Maria Sarinaki. For the comparison of heroes to heavenly bodies and their association with divinity, see Hardie 1985; for Achilles and Hephaistos, see Hubbard 1992, where he argues for the self-referential character of the shield.

[105] For this line, see Obbink forthcoming. The epithet occurs nine times in the *Theogony* (106, 127, 414, 463, 470, 685, 737, 808, 891), and one in the *Works and Days* (548).

[106] For the divinities in the texts of the lamellae, see Graf and Johnston 2007:123; and Bremmer forthcoming. For the linguistic play of epithets in *Orphic Hymns*, see Hopman-Govers 2001; and 120n80.

[107] Martin 2001, to whom I owe the 'rhapsodizing' of this section. For competitive rhapsodic performances, see also Collins 2004:167–222; Burgess 2004; and Skafte Jensen 2005.

Homer or Orpheus and vice versa may be nothing more than the mutual and dynamic interaction of competitive discourses on the afterlife. One performer of Homeric rhapsodies might allude to or even quote from other contemporary versions, versions which would become more and more well known and widely circulated upon performance.[108] In this manner, a rhapsode of Homeric material would respond to the 'competitive pressure' of other rhapsodes performing Orphic 'unepic' material.[109] Thus, the *Nekyia*, in which 'Orphic traces' have been detected,[110] may be viewed as an attempt by the *Odyssey* poet/performer to appropriate motifs and themes that became popular through a performance of an Orphic *katabasis* or another, less Homeric *Nekyia*. Although evidence for this scenario is only circumstantial, as Martin admits, one must concede that things become much easier to explain and understand if placed within the tradition of epic poetry.

Two prominent examples may serve to highlight such a process, the golden amphora for Achilles' bones (*Iliad* 83a, 83b; *Odyssey* 24.73–75), and Telemachos' trip to Crete (*Odyssey* 1.93a and 285a). Casey Dué has argued convincingly that the presence or absence of the gold amphora is not simply a matter of interpolation, but a signaling of alternative poetic performances which may affect the outlook of the whole poem and its focus on Achilles' mortality. The amphora "points to a critical dichotomy in how the Achilles story ends ..., whether he will achieve immortality through cult or pass into obscurity in the underworld."[111] This may serve as a prolepsis of events in the *Aethiopis*,[112] but one wonders if this is not also an allusion to the alternative conception of the afterlife, the one evident in the texts of the gold lamellae and *epistomia*, particularly because the amphora is made of gold and serves as a gift from Dionysos to Thetis, a gift touted by Thetis because of Hephaistos' craftsmanship (*Odyssey* 24.73–75).[113]

---

[108] Martin 2001:25; and 2007.

[109] Martin 2001:29; and 2007.

[110] Diodorus 1.96.2; Crane 1988:87 and 110n15–17; Tsagarakis 2000:25n72.

[111] Dué 2001:45 and passim. Nagy (1979:208–209) correctly in my view sees the Dionysiac model of regeneration applied to the immortalization of Achilles, but I would argue that the hero-cult is not the only kind of immortality, even within the confines of epic tradition, that was known to the poet/performer.

[112] Rengakos 2006:17–30 with previous bibliography.

[113] Christos Tsagalis (2002) has explained the very few allusions to Dionysos in the *Iliad* as indications of the Theban epic tradition and its appropriation, adaptation, and assimilation by the Homeric poet; his suggestion that the Theban epic tradition was older than the *Iliad* does not affect my argument, as both traditions could very well have enjoyed contemporary and antagonistic performances mutually interacting.

An analogous case is that of the athetized verse which complicates Telemachos' information-gathering journey concerning his father's *nostos*. Nestor in Pylos, Menelaos and Helen in Sparta, and Idomeneus in Crete, all three appear to have been traditional destinations, but at some point Crete was eliminated.[114] The reasons for this are not self-evident. And yet, one wonders if the Athenian propaganda was not compounded by what Crete represented in the geometric and archaic period.[115] Gregory Nagy (2001 and 2004a) has presented compelling arguments, even though the evidence remains tenuous, for the two ancient theories of Homeric composition and performance, articulated by Aristarchos in Alexandria and Krates in Pergamon. In the editions produced, Aristarchos favored Peisistratid and Athenian recension, and the Pergamene Krates favored the Ionian recension with Orphic elements. In this light, Homer's *Iliad* and *Odyssey* constitute only one of the forms of epic poetry, the Homeric, as Nagy argues, with which interacted and competed the Hesiodic, Cyclic, and Orphic forms.[116] Such a scenario is not completely out of the question, in spite of the lack of evidence. As Richard Hunter has shown convincingly, a similar interaction and competition is embedded in the *Orphic Argonautica*. Orpheus is presented as an Odyssean figure wandering from didactic to traditional epic and thus exhibits a generic consciousness and tension between Homer and Hesiod, which creates a new literary space.[117]

Epic as "super-genre" betrays both expansiveness and pervasiveness, as Martin has argued,[118] and the performance of rhapsodies is only one factor, albeit a crucial factor because it provides the context. The Homeric and the Orphic views on afterlife competed through mutual and dynamic interaction, a process that eventually led to two distinct discourses on death and the after-

---

[114] On the Cretan tales, see further 155n9.

[115] See the section "A Literary Cretan Context."

[116] Nagy 2005:80–81 and 2004b:3–128; Finkelberg (2006) discusses the regional centers of learning and book production, influenced by the social and historical context. Böhme (1992) argues that the poet/composer of the *Iliad* and the *Odyssey* in their present form may have been a member of the γένος Λυκομιδῶν in Phlya, Attica, who traditionally were associated with Orpheus, Demeter, and hymnic poetry.

[117] Hunter 2005. Collins (forthcoming) studies the B-texts and the poetry of Theocritus for models and copies. For Apollonius Rhodius', Valerius Flaccus', Silius Italicus', and the *Orphic Argonautica,* Nelis (2005) postulates a pre-Apollonian theogony and cosmogony; for Apollonius Rhodius and Crete, Nikolidaki 2003.

[118] Martin 2005b:17–18 and passim. Martin (2007) and Herrero de Jáuregui (forthcoming-1 and 2) present cogent discussions of the texts on the lamellae and epic poetry. For the epic Cycle, see Burgess 2005. For epic and other genres, Dalby 1998; Garner 2005. Rengakos (2006:17–30, 158–180) discusses the dynamic interaction of various traditions within Homeric epic in terms of narratology and poetics. For the Hellenistic developments, see Fantuzzi and Hunter 2005; and Rengakos 2006:181–204.

life, but not without discordant voices within them. If Homeric rhapsodizing provided a context, 'prophesying' and oracular poetry influenced the technique and composition of the texts on the lamellae and *epistomia*.[119] This is not to suggest (or even imply) that the texts on the gold lamellae should be viewed as oracles or oracular poetry, although Orpheus (i.e. his head after his death on Lesbos and his xoanon made of cypress-wood in Leibethra) sung oracles among other things,[120] and Dionysos was himself not completely devoid of oracular powers.[121] Both oracular texts and the texts on the lamellae belong to the same sub-literary genre of religious texts that have an emphasis on the written word; nevertheless, oral transmission and ritual performance also played a significant part, and all of these parameters may have been engaged by the same individual, as the cases of Pharnabazos in Olbia, Timarete in Pella, and the author of *PDerveni* imply.[122] Since Homer, oracles and oracular poetry constituted another kind of written religious document, a text not necessarily attached to any mystery cult, but certainly involving a ritual. These oracles, whatever their specific role and relation, were seen as something very important, as can be surmised from testimonies about oracle collections. To name only one example,[123] the Athenian Onomakritos was involved with the Peisistratids at the end of the sixth century BCE, and according to the scholia,

---

[119] Edmonds (forthcoming-3) also compares the lamellae's texts and surviving oracles and argues for traditional compositional techniques; I had not seen his discussion, when working on this aspect of the texts, but I discovered that our approaches and conclusions are basically in agreement. For prophetic speech, see Christidis 1996. Maurizio (1997) argues convincingly that the corpus of oracles and their narratives may be viewed as oral performances, not unlike Homeric poetry.

[120] On Orpheus as prophet after death, see Graf 1987; on the Thracian and Macedonian versions of Orpheus' death and prophecy, Papachatzis 1986 and Gartziou-Tatti 1999; and on oracular heads, see Faraone 2004 and 2005, who suggests a necromantic ritual behind these stories.

[121] On Dionysos and prophecy, see Chirassi Colombo 1991: the prophecy of Apollo is controlled by, and is integrated in the polis, that of Dionysos concerns the individual and extends beyond the limits of the polis, a statement partly true for Athens where most of Dionysos' cults and rituals were integrated. For Dionysos' presence at Delphi, see also Fontenrose 1980:374–394; West 1983:150–154; and Dietrich 1992.

[122] For Pharnabazos as magician, diviner of Hermes, and *orpheotelestes*, who may also have been the owner of the bone-plaques in Olbia, see Lebedev 1996a; for Timarete, see Voutiras 1998; and 93–94nn3–4, 120n79, 149n157. In *PDerveni* column V reference is made to oracles, but also to dreams, both of which are not misunderstood in what they say about Hades' *deina* (Kouremenos, Parássoglou, and Tsantsanoglou 2006:70–71 and 161–166). Betegh (2004:364–370) correctly in my view understands the interpretative method followed by the *PDerveni* author as similar to that of interpreting oracles, but this need not be different from allegorical interpretations (see also 120n80).

[123] For names and oracle collections, one of them reportedly by Epimenides, see Rosenberger 2001:166–172; and Bowden 2003:264–265.

he was an interpolator of Homer's *Nekyia*. According to Christian writers, Onomakritos purportedly had in his possession books of oracles by Musaios and *chresmoi* by Orpheus, along with prophecies and ritual directives he had composed himself. This information has led Martin to suggest that he probably was a rhapsode employing Orphic material in his compositions.[124]

The texts on the gold lamellae and the surviving oracles, when compared and contrasted in terms of form, structure, and compositional technique, show affinities, although each presents its own distinct 'prophetic/mantic' vision. The main characteristics of the texts on the lamellae may be summarized as follows (Tables 1–2):

1) The meter in the majority of the texts is the dactylic hexameter (although not without problems), or the rhythmic prose which, according to Watkins,[125] may go as far back as the Hittite texts, especially the enigmatic formulas in the texts from Thourioi and Pelinna (A1–3, A4, D2, and perhaps D3).

2) The language is basically that of epic poetry, if not Homeric, then at least "sub-Homeric as seen in Hesiod and the *Homeric Hymns*."[126] The Doric elements observed are statistically negligible and may have been due to the dialect of the *mystes* and/or the itinerant priest.

3) The verbs employed in all texts are either in the future or the present tense. The former, as Riedweg proposed, may imply that, when spoken during the initiation-ritual, the text referred to the future time, when the *mystes* will have began the journey (A1–3, B1, B2, B10); the latter, according to Janko, serves as *praesens propheticum*.[127]

4) The structure in some of the texts follows the pattern "when X, then Y" (Fontenrose's "condition precedent") (A4, B10),[128] and includes prohibitions (B1, B2, B10), commands (B1, B2, B10, D1–2), enigmatic formulas (A1–3, A4, D1/2, D3), and a *makarismos* (in all except B2, B3–9).

Similar characteristics may also be observed in some of the oracles that have survived from antiquity, all of which have been collected and examined on strict methodological grounds by Joseph Fontenrose, who concluded that none of them can be accepted as genuine. Six oracles have been chosen (four of

---

[124] Martin 2001; Fontenrose 1981:157 and 162; Nagy 2004a; Graf and Johnston 2007:70; Edmonds forthcoming-3. Martínez Nieto (2001) concludes that the fragments of Musaios' cosmo-/theogony present an Orphic-Eleusinian version of Thracian origin, introduced by Musaios in sixth-century BCE Athens.

[125] Watkins 1995:279.

[126] Janko 1984:98.

[127] Janko 1984:96.

[128] Fontenrose's (1981) term *condition precedent* is employed by Edmonds (forthcoming-3).

which come from Herodotus' narrative[129]) which may illustrate their conventional techniques of composition. The reference to Fontenrose's collection includes page and oracle numbers with capital letters indicating the category of the oracle: H for Historical and Q for Quasi-historical.[130] The expressions underlined betray the points of contact between the oracles and the texts on the lamellae and *epistomia* mentioned above:

1. Herodotus 1.55.2, Fontenrose 302 Q101, 185 (Parke and Wormell 2004, no. 54).

<u>ἀλλ' ὅταν</u> ἡμίονος βασιλεὺς Μήδοισι γένηται,
<u>καὶ τότε, Λυδὲ ποδαβρέ,</u> πολυψήφιδα παρ' Ἕρμον
<u>φεύγειν μηδὲ μένειν, μηδ' αἰδεῖσθαι κακὸς εἶναι.</u>

But when the Medes have a mule as king,
just then, tender-footed Lydian, by the stone-strewn Hermus
flee and do not stay, and do not be ashamed to be a coward.

translation Godley 1920–1925

2. Herodotus 1.67.4, Fontenrose 298 Q90, 173 (Parke and Wormell 2004, no. 33).

<u>ἔστι τις</u> Ἀρκαδίης Τεγέη λευρῷ ἐνὶ χώρῳ,
<u>ἔνθ'</u> ἄνεμοι πνείουσι δύω κρατερῆς ὑπ' ἀνάγκης,
καὶ τύπος ἀντίτυπος, καὶ πῆμ' ἐπὶ πήματι κεῖται.
<u>ἔνθ'</u> Ἀγαμεμνονίδην κατέχει φυσίζοος αἶα·
τὸν σὺ <u>κομισσάμενος</u> Τεγέης ἐπιτάρροθος <u>ἔσσῃ.</u>

There is a place Tegea in the smooth plain of Arcadia,
where two winds blow under strong compulsion;
blow lies upon blow, woe upon woe.

---

[129] For a concise overview of oracles, see Johnston 2004c. On different forms of divination in Herodotus, see Harrison (2000:122–157), who correctly emphasizes Herodotus' religious beliefs and concerns as central in the *Histories*; Harrison (2003) even suggests that the *Histories* may be thought of as 'prophecy in reverse'; for Herodotus as manipulator of signs, see Hollmann 2005; for the historiographical uses of oracles especially in book 1, see Kindt 2006 and Barker 2006. Bowden (2005:67–73) argues convincingly that Delphi and its oracles, genuine or not, played a very important role in Herodotus (if excessive), and especially in Athenian politics (40–64 and 88–133). For the political role of oracles and divination in Aeschylus' *Persae*, Athanassaki 1996; for their gradual decline in matters political Parker (2000a) suggests that it may be in part due to new skills developed and secular modes of divination, like rhetoric.

[130] The other two categories of Fontenrose (1981) are L(egendary) and F(ictional) oracles. This classification and the distinction between authentic and non-authentic oracles (Parke and Wormell 2004) are not vital for the present discussion, and both are rightly questioned and criticized by Maurizio (1997).

There the life-giving earth covers the son of Agamemnon;
bring him back, and you shall be lord of Tegea.

translation Godley 1920–1925

3. Herodotus 5.92.2, Fontenrose 288 Q61, 183 (Parke and Wormell 2004, no. 8).

ὄλβιος οὗτος ἀνὴρ ὃς ἐμὸν δόμον ἐσκαταβαίνει,
Κύψελος Ἠετίδης, βασιλεὺς κλειτοῖο Κορίνθου,
αὐτὸς καὶ παῖδες, παίδων γε μὲν οὐκέτι παῖδες.

That man is fortunate who steps into my house,
Cypselus, son of Eetion, the king of noble Corinth,
he himself and his children, but not the sons of his sons.

translation Godley 1920–1925

4. Clement of Alexandria, *Stromateis* 6.3.29, Fontenrose 317 Q148, 193 (Parke and Wormell 2004, no. 96).

ὦ Δελφοί, λίσσεσθ᾽ ἀνέμους καὶ λώιον ἔσται.

Delphians, pray to the winds, and it will be/become better.

Herodotus 7.178.1 (prose version):

Δελφοὶ δ᾽ ἐν τούτῳ τῷ χρόνῳ ἐχρηστηριάζοντο τῷ θεῷ ὑπὲρ ἑωυτῶν
καὶ τῆς Ἑλλάδος καταρρωδηκότες, καί σφι ἐχρήσθη ἀνέμοισι
εὔχεσθαι· μεγάλους γὰρ τούτους ἔσεσθαι τῇ Ἑλλάδι συμμάχους.

In the meantime, the Delphians, who were afraid for themselves
and for Hellas, consulted the god. They were advised to pray to the
winds, for these would be potent allies for Hellas.

translation Godley 1920–1925

5. IG II^2 5006ab, CE 117–138, Fontenrose 264 H66, 189 (Parke and Wormell 2004, no. 466).

Φοῖβος Ἀθηναίοις Δελφοὺς ναίων τάδε [εἶπεν]·
ἔστιν σοὶ παρ᾽ ἄκρας πόλεως παρὰ [τὸν Προπύλαιον],
οὗ λαὸς σύμπας κλήιζει γλαυκώ[πιδα Ἀθήνην],
Δήμητρος Χλοίης ἱερὸν Κούρη[ς τε μακαίρας],
οὗ πρῶτον στάχυς εὔξη[ται - - - - - -]
ς πρότεροι πατ[έρες - - - - - - - - -]
ἱδρυσα[- - - - - - - - - - - - - - - - -]
[- - - - - - - - - - - - - - - - - - - -]ν

[- - - - - - - - - - - - - - - -] ἀπαρχάς
[- - - - - - - - - - - - - - -]ς ἁγνοῦ
[- - - - - - - - - - - - - - τ]έχναισιν
[- - - - - - - - - - - - - -] ἀνιούσης
[- - - - - - - - - - - - - - θ]ρεπτά
[- - - - - - - - - - - - - λώι]ον ἔσται
[- - - - - - - - - - - - - - - - - - - -].

Phoibos, who dwells in Delphi, said to the Athenians the following:
by the Propylaia on the Akropolis, where all the Athenians celebrate in song [Athena] with gleaming-eyes, there is the sanctuary
of Demeter Chloia and Kore [Makaira], ... it will be [better].

6. Demosthenes *Against Meidias* (21.51–52), Fontenrose 253 H28, 187 (Parke and
Wormell 2004, no. 282).

ἴστε γὰρ δήπου τοῦθ' ὅτι τοὺς χοροὺς ὑμεῖς ἅπαντας τούτους καὶ τοὺς
ὕμνους τῷ θεῷ ποιεῖτε, <u>οὐ μόνον κατὰ τοὺς νόμους τοὺς περὶ τῶν
Διονυσίων, ἀλλὰ καὶ κατὰ τὰς μαντείας</u>, ἐν αἷς ἁπάσαις ἀνηρημένον
εὑρήσετε τῇ πόλει, ὁμοίως ἐκ Δελφῶν καὶ ἐκ Δωδώνης, χοροὺς
ἱστάναι κατὰ τὰ πάτρια καὶ κνισᾶν ἀγυιὰς καὶ στεφανηφορεῖν.
ἀνάγνωθι δέ μοι λαβὼν αὐτὰς τὰς μαντείας.

ΜΑΝΤΕΙΑΙ.

<u>αὐδῶ</u> Ἐρεχθείδησιν, ὅσοι Πανδίονος ἄστυ
ναίετε καὶ πατρίοισι νόμοις ἰθύνεθ' ἑορτάς,
<u>μεμνῆσθαι</u> Βάκχοιο, καὶ εὐρυχόρους κατ' ἀγυιὰς
<u>ἱστάναι</u> ὡραίων Βρομίῳ χάριν ἄμμιγα πάντας,
καὶ <u>κνισᾶν</u> βωμοῖσι κάρη στεφάνοις πυκάσαντας.

<u>περὶ ὑγιείας θύειν καὶ εὔχεσθαι</u> Διὶ ὑπάτῳ, Ἡρακλεῖ, Ἀπόλλωνι
προστατηρίῳ· <u>περὶ τύχας ἀγαθᾶς</u> Ἀπόλλωνι ἀγυιεῖ, Λατοῖ, Ἀρτέμιδι,
καὶ κατ' ἀγυιὰς <u>κρατῆρας ἱστάμεν καὶ χοροὺς καὶ στεφαναφορεῖν</u>
καττὰ πάτρια θεοῖς Ὀλυμπίοις πάντεσσι καὶ πάσαις, †ἰδίας† δεξιὰς
καὶ ἀριστερὰς ἀνίσχοντας, καὶ <u>μνασιδωρεῖν</u>.

If, men of Athens, I had not been a chorus-producer when Meidias
treated me in this way, one would have condemned his actions only
for insolence. As it is, I think it would be proper to condemn them
for impiety too. You know of course that you hold all these performances of choruses and hymns for the god, not only in accordance
with the laws about the Dionysia, but also in accordance with the

oracles, in all of which you will find it ordained for the city, from Delphi and from Dodona alike, to establish choruses in accordance with tradition, to make streets smell of sacrifice, and to wear crowns. Please take and read the actual oracles.

ORACLES

I declare to the sons of Erekhtheus, all you who dwell in Pandion's town and direct festivals by inherited laws, to remember Bakkhos, and all together to establish a thanksgiving to Bromios for ripe crops along the broad-spaced streets, and to make a smell of sacrifice on the altars, covering your heads with crowns.

For health, sacrifice and pray to Zeus the highest, Heracles, and Apollo the protector; for good fortune, to Apollo of streets, Leto, and Artemis. Along the streets establish bowls of wine and choruses, and wear crowns, and in accordance with tradition raise your right and left hands to all the Olympian gods and goddesses and remember their gifts.

translation MacDowell 2002

The structure and composition of these six oracles is mainly based on five themes, themes which are presented either independently or in combination:[131]

1) salutation, either honorific or deprecatory (in 1, 3, 6 above);
2) assertion of mantic authority (in 3, 5, 6 above);
3) the formula "when X then Y," or condition precedent (in 1, 2, 5 above);
4) the message, which may include a prediction in the indicative 'prophetic' present or in the future tense, or a command, recommendation, prohibition in the iussive, (in all except 3 above, where it is implied);
5) explication, i.e. statements intended to justify, elaborate, clarify, or expand the message or some other theme of the oracle (in all except 4 above).

According to Fontenrose (1981):

Oracular poetry has conventions of content and poetic expression, patterns and formulae both flexible and fixed. These are due in

---

[131] Fontenrose's (1981:177–180) sixth theme, "restatement of the question asked," which is not found in the texts of the lamellae, is excluded.

part to the genre itself, in part due to the meter employed. Since the dactylic hexameter was the epic meter, we may expect to find epic echoes in verse oracles (186) ... Authentic verse oracles differ in style and content from the traditional oracles of folk narrative, poetry, chresmologues' compositions, and oracle collections. They are simple in structure, short, mainly confined to the message, not much embellished with formulae ... and not strongly epic in diction or manner. But traditional oracles are a genre of poetry. The original composition of this kind purported to be the pronouncements of seers, who were also poets (195).

The similarities in form, structure, and compositional technique between the texts of the six oracles and the texts on the lamellae are obvious enough.[132] That the majority of oracles were composed in verse (more specifically, in dactylic hexameter, with a few in iambic trimeter) does not bear on the issue of their authenticity, nor does it imply that they were poetic compositions from the beginning, since there were many responses in prose as well. On this issue, Fontenrose is following Plutarch, who devoted a treatise on *The Oracles at Delphi No Longer Given in Verse* (402d–e):

> But they established the cult of the Muses as associates and guardians of the prophetic art (τὰς δὲ Μούσας ἱδρύσαντο παρέδρους τῆς μαντικῆς καὶ φύλακας) in this very place beside the stream and the shrine of Earth, to whom it is said that the oracle used to belong because of the responses being given in poetic and musical measures. And some assert that it was here that the heroic verse was heard for the first time (ἔνιοι δὲ καὶ πρῶτον ἐνταῦθά φασιν ἡρῷον μέτρον ἀκουσθῆναι): "Birds, contribute your feathers, and bees, bring wax as your portion." Later Earth became inferior to the god and lost her august position.
>
> translation Babbitt 1936

If the Chaironeian is to be trusted,[133] then the poetic composition of oracles was due to the shrine of the Muses and to their cult established near the spring. *Hypothesis* A to Pindar's *Pythians* (Drachmann, page 2, see below, pages 141–142) adds further that Dionysos was responsible for the dactylic meter in the Delphic *nomos*. Thus, the Greek perception that the Pythia spoke in

---

[132] Versnel 2002 presents an eloquent account of the magical texts' poetics, "the art of making poetry and the art of creation."
[133] Rosenberger 2001:172–176; and especially Bowden's (2005:33–38) discussion.

verses, or that the hexameter was an invention by the Pythia is only that, a perception.[134] The Greeks thought that the hexameter was the meter of oracles and oracular poetry, and this conception must have been cultivated through Delphic propaganda. It may have been only natural to follow in the path of Homer, Hesiod, and epic poetry and to adopt their well-established techniques and methods of structure and composition. More importantly, Homer's and Hesiod's precedents would have been more than influential, as the case of the Presocratic philosophers (who employed the same medium for their works in terms of form) amply illustrates. The dactylic hexameter, once sanctioned by Delphi as the oracular medium which led to the oracles' wide circulation and prestige, was, so it seems, also adopted by the composers of the texts on the lamellae and *epistomia*, together with the techniques and methods of structure and composition, found in oracular poetry.

In addition to metrics and form, the texts on the lamellae show further similarities with the oracles: in their (sub)epic diction; in their formula "when X then Y" (Fontenrose's "condition precedent"); in their prohibitions and commands in the present or future indicative or in the iussive; in their salutation or *makarismos*; in their assertion of authority by the deity; and in their explication or expansion or contraction of the text. These similarities are certainly conventional, but at the same time they constitute a convenient medium of structural and technical methods that proved successful in transmitting a divine message. Thus, the oracles and the texts on the lamellae and *epistomia*, as they employ the same medium and techniques of composition, represent different groups of the same (sub)literary genre of religious texts.

Beyond form and technique, however, there is another more crucial element shared by these two groups of oracular and mystic texts, the terms *mantis*, *prophetes*, and *mania*. The equation of Dionysos with prophecy[135] and of Apollo with ecstasy might seem disturbing and paradoxical, especially after Friedrich Nietzsche's *Birth of Tragedy*. Macrobius, in the *Saturnalia* (1.18.6), contending that Euripides considered Apollo and Dionysos one and the same god, quotes a fragment from Euripides' *Likymnios* (fr. 477 N): δέσποτα φιλόδαφνε Βάκχε, παιὰν Ἄπολλον εὔλυρε (*Lord, lover of laurel, Bacchus, paean*

---

[134] Bowden 2005:33–38. On an etymology for the dactylic hexameter, see Nagy 2004b:144–156.

[135] For Dionysos, a perplexing divinized human or humanized divinity, also called *Bacchos* just like his followers, see in general Otto 1991; Jeanmaire 1951; Detienne 1979, 1989, 2001, 2003; Burkert 1985:161–167, 293–304; Seaford 2006; Lekatsas 1985:189–192 for the relation of Apollo and Dionysos, and Lekatsas 1996 for the divine infant, to which compare Carpenter 1993 for depictions of Dionysos beardless. Daraki (1997) somewhat exaggerates the relation between Dionysos and Mother Earth, for which compare Henrichs 1990, and Sourvinou-Inwood 2005.

Apollo with the fair lyre); and, in order to show that Aeschylus also held the same view, he adds a line from Aeschylus' *Bassarai* (fr. 86 Mette): ὁ κισσεὺς Ἀπόλλων, ὁ βακχ<ε>ιοσόμαντις (*Apollo of the ivy [crowned with ivy], the Bacchic mantis, or the mantis inspired by Baccheios*).[136] Likewise, on a second–third-century-CE papyrus (an anthology of hymns to Aphrodite, Artemis-Hekate, Apollo, and Dionysos) there is a number of astonishing but fragmentary elements which seem to juxtapose again, presumably in a complementary way, Apollo and Dionysos (*PChicago* Pack² 1620, column X): line 5 μύσσται, line 8 μαντικὸν προφήτην, line 13 μαντικὲ παιάν, line 14 Διόνυσε.[137] The surviving evidence is not always as clear-cut as we would like it to be. These fragments apparently call into question the polar conflict between a prophecy-associated Apollo and an ecstasy-associated Dionysos which, since Nietzsche,[138] has systematically dominated western thought.

The two fragments Macrobius quotes, however, are not the only evidence regarding this matter. Plutarch, an authority on Delphic matters, testifies to Dionysos' presence at Apollo's prophetic shrine during the winter (*The E at Delphi* 388e–389c):

> If, then, anyone ask, 'What has this to do with Apollo?', we shall say that it concerns not only him, but also Dionysos, whose share in Delphi is no less than that of Apollo (ἀλλὰ καὶ πρὸς τὸν Διόνυσον, ᾧ τῶν Δελφῶν οὐδὲν ἧττον ἢ τῷ Ἀπόλλωνι μέτεστιν). Now we hear the theologians affirming and reciting, sometimes in verse and sometimes in prose ... And as for his turning into winds and water, earth and stars, and into the generations of plants and animals, and his adoption of such guises, they speak in a decep-

---

[136] Seaford (2005) discusses the mystic light, a symbol of both Apollo and Dionysos, which Orpheus saw when in the Underworld, and concludes that "Orpheus as author of mystic discourse was claimed by groups who were (or were imagined as) in opposition: adherents of Dionysos and Pythagorean adherents of Apollo" (606).

[137] Niafas (1997) has suggested an epiphany and a mystic initiation ritual as the context for this fragment, particularly because of Dionysos' presence which is felt and experienced through earthquake, thunder, and lightning (mainly in Euripides' *Bacchae*). Barbantani (2005) comments on columns I–IV, the hymn to Aphrodite-Arsinoë.

[138] Dietrich (1992) and Clay (1996 and 1997) discuss the complementary role of Apollo and Dionysos at Delphi; see also Guthrie 1993:41–48. On Orpheus and Dionysos in the Aeschylean lost tetralogy, see Jouan 1992; di Marco 1993; in Euripides' *Rhesos*, see 228n264; on the complementary nature of the therapeutic aspects of the couple, see Terzakis (1997:169–214). On a number of modern misconceptions about Dionysos stemming from Nietzsche, among others, see especially Henrichs 1993a; Obbink 1993; Jameson 1993; Detienne 2001 and 2003 (who is preparing a study of the Delphic odd couple); Sourvinou-Inwood 2005; and Edmonds forthcoming-3.

tive way of what he undergoes in his transformation as a tearing apart, as it were, and a dismemberment (τὸ μὲν πάθημα καὶ τὴν μεταβολὴν διασπασμόν τινα καὶ διαμελισμὸν αἰνίττονται). They give him the names of Dionysos, Zagreus, Nyctelios, and Isodaites; they construct destructions and disappearances, followed by returns to life and regenerations—riddles and fabulous tales quite in keeping with the aforesaid transformations (Διόνυσον δὲ καὶ Ζαγρέα καὶ Νυκτέλιον καὶ Ἰσοδαίτην αὐτὸν ὀνομάζουσι καὶ φθοράς τινας καὶ ἀφανισμούς, εἶτα δ' ἀναβιώσεις καὶ παλιγγενεσίας οἰκεῖα ταῖς εἰρημέναις μεταβολαῖς αἰνίγματα καὶ μυθεύματα περαίνουσι). To this god also sing the dithyrambic strains laden with emotion and with a transformation that includes a certain wandering and dispersion (ᾄδουσι τῷ μὲν διθυραμβικὰ μέλη παθῶν μεστὰ καὶ μεταβολῆς πλάνην τινὰ καὶ διαφόρησιν ἐχούσης). Aeschylus, in fact, says (fr. 355 N): "Fitting it is that the dithyramb with its fitful notes should attend Dionysos in revel rout (μιξοβόαν ... πρέπει διθύραμβον ὁμαρτεῖν σύγκωμον Διονύσῳ)." But to Apollo they sing the paean, music regulated and chaste ..., but to Dionysos a certain variability combined with playfulness, wantoness, seriousness, and frenzy (τῷ δὲ μεμιγμένην τινὰ παιδιᾷ καὶ ὕβρει [καὶ σπουδῇ] καὶ μανίᾳ προσφέροντες ἀνωμαλίαν). They call upon him (ἀνακαλοῦσιν): "Euoe Bacchus who incites womankind, Dionysos who delights 'mid his honours fraught with frenzy" (fr. Lyr. Adesp. 131: εὔιον ὀρσιγύναικα μαινομέναις Διόνυσον ἀνθέοντα τιμαῖς), not inappositely apprehending the peculiar character of each transformation. But since the time of the cycles in these transformations is not equal, but that of the one which they call 'Satiety' (κόρον) is longer, and that of 'Dearth' (χρησμοσύνης) shorter, they observe the ratio, and use the paean at their sacrifices for a large part of the year (τὸν μὲν ἄλλον ἐνιαυτὸν παιᾶνι χρῶνται περὶ τὰς θυσίας); but at the beginning of winter they awake the dithyramb and, laying the paean to rest, they use the dithyramb instead of it in their invocations of the god (ἀρχομένου δὲ χειμῶνος ἐπεγείραντες τὸν διθύραμβον τὸν δὲ παιᾶνα καταπαύσαντες τρεῖς μῆνας ἀντ' ἐκείνου τοῦτον κατακαλοῦνται τὸν θεόν).

translation Babbitt 1936

Hypothesis A to Pindar's *Pythians* (Drachmann, page 2) relates an interesting version of the successive occupants at Delphi, not very different from the catalogue of the gods of Delphi the Pythia presents in the *parodos* of Aeschylus' *Eumenides* (lines 1–29): before Apollo, Nyx, Themis, Dionysos, and then Pytho gave oracles at the site.[139] There seems to be an orderly transfer of prophetic power from Nyx, to Themis[140] (who sang oracles), and then to Dionysos, who began giving *themistes* (according to *Themis*?) from the tripod, although no reason is given for the necessity of this succession. Python took over the tripod from Dionysos violently, and in turn, the serpentine prophet was killed by Apollo who celebrated the Pythian Games and restored the order. The new Apolline order, according to *Hypothesis A*, took into consideration all previous occupants and created epithets and nouns which recalled the oracle's history: *iambos*, because of Python's abuse of Apollo; *daktylon*, because Dionysos is believed to have prophesied from the tripod first; *Cretan* from Zeus; and *Metroon*, because Delphi is Earth's oracle.

At any rate, the Delphians themselves were so proud of their 'odd couple' that they had Dionysos and the Thyiads sculpted on the west pediment of Apollo's temple, and on the east pediment, Apollo's arrival at the site with his entourage: Leto, Artemis, and the Muses. It may also be safely assumed that the Delphians were instrumental in the composition by Philodamos of Skarpheia of the Paean in honor of Dionysos, in the middle of the fourth century BCE. In it, the god is summoned as *Paean Soter* and in the *ephymnion*, quite unexpectedly, we hear both the Bacchic cry *euhoi* and the Apolline *ie Paian*:[141] εὐοῖ ὦ ἰὸ Βάκχ', ὦ ἰὲ Παιάν.

These fragmentary pieces of evidence present not a polar conflict between Apollo and Dionysos, or between prophesy and ecstasy, but a sort of fusion of the two at Delphi,[142] an Apollo masked as Dionysos and/or a Dionysos

---

[139] For Aeschylus' *Eumenides*, see Sommerstein 1989. On the Delphic myths and Apollo's predecessors, see Dempsey 1918:1–37; Allen, Halliday, and Sikes 1936:197–200; Fontenrose 1980; Lloyd-Jones 1976; Clay 1989:61–74, 1996, and 1997; Sourvinou-Inwood 1987 and especially 2005:162–168 (who argues that the myth of Apollo's absence and Dionysos' presence during the winter was a later invention, probably after the oracle had gone into radical decline); Avagianou 2000 (on Ephorus' version of the foundation of the oracle); Suárez de la Torre 2002; and Chappell 2006:339–341.

[140] On Themis and her prophetic powers, see Berti 2002.

[141] Furley and Bremer 2001:vol. 1:121–128, vol. 2:52–84, with previous bibliography; and add Schröder 1999. On the earliest epigraphical attestation of *euhoi* (ca. 510 BCE), see Anderson 2005; *euhai* and *eiau* were incised on the mirror of Demonassa, daughter of Lenaios, at sixth-century BCE Olbia (West 1983:156).

[142] According to Clay (1996 and 1997) the fusion of the two gods may be due to the influence the *Dionysiac Technitai* exerted on the Delphic priesthood, which led to the incorporation of the most threatening god Dionysos into the Apolline oracle; I am not so sure, however, that this fusion is a product of the fourth century BCE and not an earlier one (see also Dietrich 1992;

masked as Apollo.[143] The complementarity of the two is obvious enough, and their common ground seems to have been *mania*:[144] Apollo prophesied through the manic/mantic Pythia, and Dionysos' initiates became *bacchoi* through *mania* and *teletai*. The Apolline cult and the Dionysiac ritual appear to have had an equal share in ecstasy through the manic possession of the individual, be it the Pythia or Dionysos' *manteis* and *prophetai*.

The semantic interrelation of the terms *mantis, prophetes, chresmologos,* and *mania* is best elaborated by Euripides in the *Bacchae* and by Plato in his *Timaeus*.[145] In the *Bacchae*, Teiresias, Apollo's seer and an expert in distinguishing between *mantis* and *prophetes*, promotes the new cult of the Stranger/ Dionysos. He is the only one employing the word *mantis* and *mantike* to describe Dionysos and the god's art, as well as his own art. This implies—and this is an *argumentum ex silentio*—that Teiresias cannot be a *mantis* of Dionysos, but only his *prophetes* (*Bacchae* 298–301, 367–368):[146]

> ΤΕΙ. μάντις δ' ὁ δαίμων ὅδε· τὸ γὰρ βακχεύσιμον
> καὶ τὸ μανιῶδες μαντικὴν πολλὴν ἔχει·
> ὅταν γὰρ ὁ θεὸς ἐς τὸ σῶμ' ἔλθηι πολύς,
> λέγειν τὸ μέλλον τοὺς μεμηνότας ποιεῖ.

> This god is also a prophet: for the bacchic and the manic have much mantic power: for when the god enters abundantly into the body, he makes the maddened speak the future.
>
> Seaford 1996

Guthrie 1993:238–240; Calame 1996:364–369; and Loraux 2002:54–80). Stewart (1982) discusses the sculptural representation of Dionysus in pseudo-Apolline, and Apollo in pseudo-Dionysiac manner. Detienne (2001; 2003:125–136, 152–164) has proposed Orpheus as the intermediary for the Apollonian Dionysos and/or Dionysiac Apollo, who appears to have been associated both with Apollo, as a musician and poet with lyre in hand, and with Dionysos, as his victim and later as creator of initiatory *teletai*. Detienne offers a number of brilliant and thought-provoking ideas, but his overall reconstruction of Orpheus and Orphism is only partially supported by the sources presently known.

[143] To borrow from the title of Carpenter and Faraone (1993); Detienne 2003:164.

[144] What Stewart (1982:214) has called μανία σώφρων.

[145] Interestingly the verb Thucydides employs twice for *chresmologoi* is ἀείδω (2.8.2 and 2.21.3), but in 8.1.1 he lumps *manteis* and *chresmologoi* together. For a succinct distinction between *mantis* and *chresmologos*, see Fontenrose 1981:152–158; Bowden 2003; Dillery 2005; for the role and history of seers, see Bremmer 1996; for their presence in Athens Parker 2005:116–135.

[146] Roth (1984) discusses the 'sophistic' Teiresias in the *Bacchae* and emphasizes that the gulf between seers and intellectuals is a modern view, influenced by our distinction between secular and religious activities.

ΤΕΙ. Πενθεὺς δ' ὅπως μὴ πένθος εἰσοίσει δόμοις
  τοῖς σοῖσι, Κάδμε· <u>μαντικῆι μὲν οὐ λέγω</u>,
  τοῖς πράγμασι δέ.

May Pentheus not bring grief to your house, Kadmos. It is not prophecy that I say this, but by the facts.

Seaford 1996

Kadmos, in order to characterize himself, and the Chorus, referring to the promoters or preachers of Dionysos' *teletai*, both employ the term *prophetes* (*Bacchae* 210–211, 550–552):

ΚΑ. ἐπεὶ σὺ φέγγος, Τειρεσία, τόδ' οὐχ ὁρᾷς,
  ἐγὼ <u>προφήτης</u> σοι <u>λόγων</u> γενήσομαι.

Since you cannot see this light, Teiresias, I will become interpreter to you with words.

Seaford 1996

ΧΟ. ἐσορᾷς τάδ', ὦ Διὸς παῖ
  Διόνυσε, <u>σοὺς προφήτας</u>
  ἐν ἁμίλλαισιν ἀνάγκας;

Do you see these things, O son of Zeus, Dionysos, your proclaimers in struggles against constraint?

Seaford 1996

In the discourse of the *Bacchae*, it appears that *mantis* is the god-inspired person and *prophetes* the interpreter, the intermediary, the preacher of what the god is divining through the *mantis*.[147]

This distinction between *mantis* and *prophetes* is also evident in Plato's *Timaeus*.[148] The philosopher explains the placement of the liver near the soul's part for the natural appetites (*epithymetikon*) and its function as the body's

---

[147] Papadopoulou (2001) argues convincingly that Teiresias and the Stranger present two different forms of prophecy: Teiresias rationalizes in order to define the nature of the new god, as when he used to interpret signs and oracles, although I am not certain that this should indicate that the prophet "speaks not through his prophetic knowledge, but through his human reasoning" (31); the Stranger does not rely on oracles and signs; he is a prophet of a 'new' kind, knowing full well the essence of the Bacchic rites; he is simultaneously human and divine, as the *mystai* believe after initiation. Segal (1986:304–305) sees a similar process at work in Sophocles' *Oedipus Tyrannus* (412–414), where Teiresias reveals Oedipus' hidden identity.

[148] For the following discussion I am indebted to Dodds (1951:64–101), and especially Nagy (1990a; 1990b:162–168). For a general overview of oracles and prophesies in the Eastern Mediterranean, see the essays in Heintz 1997.

oracle, through which gods can send messages to the body. In discussing this, he broaches the subjects of prophesy, ecstasy, and divination (*Timaeus* 71e–72b):[149]

> And that God gave unto man's foolishness the gift of divination (μαντικήν) a sufficient token is this: no man achieves true and inspired divination (μαντικῆς ἐνθέου καὶ ἀληθοῦς) when in his rational mind, but only when the power of his intelligence is fettered in sleep or when it is distraught by disease or by reason of some divine inspiration (ἐνθουσιασμόν). But it belongs to a man when in his right mind to recollect and ponder both the things spoken in dream or waking vision by the divining and inspired nature (μαντικῆς τε καὶ ἐνθουσιαστικῆς φύσεως), and all the visionary forms that were seen, and by means of reasoning to discern about them all wherein they are significant and for whom they portend evil or good in the future, the past, or the present. But it is not the task of him who has been in a state of frenzy, and still continues therein, to judge the apparitions and voices seen or uttered by himself; for it was well said of old that to do and to know one's own and oneself belongs only to him who is sound of mind. Wherefore also it is customary to set the tribe of prophets to pass judgment upon these inspired divinations (τὸ τῶν προφητῶν γένος ἐπὶ ταῖς ἐνθέοις μαντείαις κριτὰς ἐπικαθιστάναι νόμος); and they, indeed, themselves are named "diviners" (μάντεις) by certain who are wholly ignorant of the truth that they are not diviners but interpreters of the mysterious voice and apparition (τῆς δι' αἰνιγμῶν οὗτοι φήμης καὶ φαντάσεως ὑποκριταί), for whom the most fitting name would be "prophets of things divined" (προφῆται δὲ μαντευομένων δικαιότατα ὀνομάζοιντ' ἄν). For these reasons, then, the nature of the liver is such as we have stated and situated in the region we have described, for the sake of divination. Moreover, when the individual creature is alive this organ affords signs that are fairly manifest, but when deprived of life it becomes blind and the divinations it presents are too much obscured to have any clear significance.
>
> translation Bury 1929

---

[149] Kalfas 1995; and Pierris 1996:195–214. For Plato's pronouncements in the *Republic* as prophetic Virvidakis 1996. On the complex issue of Orphism and the Presocratics, see Burkert 1968 and Bernabé 2002a; for the Orphic and anti-Orphic Plato, see Kingsley 1995:112–132; Cosi 2000:146–150; and for the terminology of the mysteries employed by the philosopher Riedweg 1987.

According to Plato's discussion, a *mantis* is someone possessed by god, who has god inside, and therefore speaks from an altered or special mental state, a state of *mania*, which explains the *mantis'* failure to remember his own words. The *prophetes* and the *chresmologos* on the other hand, is an interpreter, a preacher, a judge of the divinely inspired mantic pronouncements. Yet divine *mania* is not of one kind, but rather, as Plato explains, there are four types: mantic, telestic, poetic, and erotic, represented by Apollo, Dionysos, the Muses, and Aphrodite/Eros respectively (*Phaedrus* 265b; compare also 244a–245a). This clear definition of the semantics of the two words has led Gregory Nagy to infer that, at Delphi, the *mantis*-Pythia would have been in control of the content, the sacred medium, whereas the *prophetai* would turn the divinely inspired content of the Pythia into the oracular medium of poetic form, as described above.[150] Although this "division of labour" is not evident in the sources, as Lisa Maurizio has argued,[151] the role of the male priests at Delphi cannot have been very different from the picture Plato presents, that is, as interpreters of the cryptic and enigmatic divine language of the Pythia. To what extent (if any) this process of interpreting involved tampering with the form, is anybody's guess.

This procedure, *mutatis mutandis*, should also be envisioned for the composers of the texts on the lamellae and *epistomia*, who have been called *bricoleurs*.[152] The mantic pronouncements (ascribed to Orpheus and Musaios), circulating in written form and through performances since at least the fifth century BCE, would have been the object of interpretation and preaching by *manteis* and *prophetai*, both of whom people trusted. Among them there were also fakes, *agyrtai*, who tried to earn a living by playing on people's superstitions and fears, and *orpheotelestai*, a group criticized and ridiculed by Theophrastos and Plutarch.[153] Plato had already set the standard for this in his

---

[150] Nagy 1990a:61; 1990b:166.

[151] Maurizio (1995:70 and passim) proposes to view the Pythia's *mantike* similar to Cassandra's; see also Connelly 2007:72–81. Maurizio (1997) argues convincingly that the Delphic oracles and their framing narratives are best understood as oral performances, the first consultation being the first oral performance, after which followed the second in the city, and also more, each time reformulating and recomposing appropriately the original. Mazzoldi (2002) has proposed that Aeschylus' Cassandra in the *Agamemnon* combines the dual nature of *mantis* and *prophetes*, as two distinct phases may be detected respectively: the ecstatic and visionary in contact with the divinity, during which ritual cries and invocations are heard and clairvoyance takes place without mediation; and the conscious in contact with the humans, during which clairvoyance takes place with mediation and rational prophetic utterances are issued. On how Delphi worked, see further Bowden 2005:12–39.

[152] Edmonds 2004:4; Graf and Johnston 2007:70–95.

[153] Theophrastos *Characters* 16.11 (translation Rusten and Cunningham 1993): "he goes to the

harsh critique and reprobation of false *manteis* and *prophetai* in the *Republic* (364b–365a):

> But the strangest of all these speeches are the things they say about the gods and virtue, how so it is that the gods themselves assign to many good men misfortunes and an evil life, but to their opposites a contrary lot; and *agyrtai* and *manteis* go to rich men's doors and make them believe that they by means of sacrifices (θυσίαις) and incantations (ἐπῳδαῖς) have accumulated a treasure of power from the gods that can expiate and cure with pleasurable festivals any misdeed of a man or his ancestors, and that if a man wishes to harm an enemy, at slight cost (μετὰ σμικρῶν δαπανῶν) he will be enabled to injure just and unjust alike, since they are masters of spells and enchantments (ἐπαγωγαῖς τισιν καὶ καταδέσμοις) that constrain the gods to serve their end. And for all these sayings they cite the poets as witnesses (μάρτυρας ποιητάς), with regard to the ease and plentifulness of vice ... And others cite Homer as a witness to the beguiling of gods by men ... And they produce a bushel of books of Musaios and Orpheus (βίβλων δὲ ὅμαδον παρέχονται Μουσαίου καὶ Ὀρφέως), the offspring of the Moon and of the Muses, as they affirm, and these books they use in their ritual (καθ᾽ ἃς θυηπολοῦσιν), and make not only ordinary men but states believe that there really are remissions (λύσεις) of sins and purifications (καθαρμοί) for deeds of injustice, by means of sacrifice and pleasant sport (διὰ θυσιῶν καὶ παιδιᾶς ἡδονῶν) *for the living*, and that there are also special rites *for the defunct*, which they call *teletai*, that deliver us from evils in that other world (αἳ τῶν ἐκεῖ κακῶν ἀπολύουσιν ἡμᾶς), while terrible things await those who have neglected to sacrifice (μὴ θύσαντας δὲ δεινὰ περιμένει).

> translation Shorey 1937, modified

Initiators of Orpheus every month to be inducted with his wife—if she has no time, he takes his children and their wet-nurse" (καὶ τελεσθησόμενος πρὸς τοὺς Ὀρφεοτελεστὰς κατὰ μῆνα πορεύεσθαι μετὰ τῆς γυναικός—ἐὰν δὲ μὴ σχολάζῃ ἡ γυνή, μετὰ τῆς τίτθης—καὶ τῶν παιδίων). Plutarch *Sayings of Spartans* 224e (translation Babbitt 1931): "this is his retort to Philip, the priest of the Orphic mysteries, who was in the direst straits of poverty, but used to assert that those who were initiated under his rites were happy after the conclusion of this life; to him Leotychidas said, 'You idiot! Why then don't you die as speedily as possible so that you may with that cease from bewailing your unhappiness and poverty?'" (πρὸς δὲ Φίλιππον τὸν ὀρφεοτελεστὴν παντελῶς πτωχὸν ὄντα, λέγοντα δ᾽ ὅτι οἱ παρ᾽ αὐτῷ μυηθέντες μετὰ τὴν τοῦ βίου τελευτὴν εὐδαιμονοῦσι, 'τί οὖν, ὦ ἀνόητε' εἶπεν, 'οὐ τὴν ταχίστην ἀποθνῄσκεις, ἵν᾽ ἅμα παύσῃ κακοδαιμονίαν καὶ πενίαν κλαίων;') For this group, see Graf and Johnston 2007:178–184.

This passage is usually read as representing a negative critique against itinerant priests, or *charismatics*,[154] be they *magoi, agyrtai, orpheotelestai, manteis, chresmologoi*, or *prophetai* (some of whom may indeed have been local or Panhellenic jokes). The distinctions usually drawn among these religious practitioners are abolished by Plato so as to emphasize the message. Interestingly, however, Plato refers to two kinds of needs that peoples and cities have, and then addresses the way in which these false religious practitioners accommodate their preaching to suit those needs. The first need involves an interest in this life: people want assurances and blessings during their lifetime. The second need of people is what happens to them after death. This kind of itinerant preaching by self-appointed *magoi, agyrtai, orpheotelestai, manteis, prophetai* is not difficult to imagine, regardless of the validity of their teachings. At least this much is evident also in *PDerveni* whose author presents a critical attitude similar to Plato's. In *PDerveni* columns V–VII, XI and XIII, the subject also appears to be eschatology, but its interpretation is far from certain due to the fragmentary preservation. The didactic posture of the person speaking is evident, but the attitude towards the *magoi*, whether positive or negative, is not. However one understands the author of *PDerveni*, a *telestes, mantis*, or philosopher-poet,[155] what needs to be emphasized is that *mantike*, as everything else, had both true and false interpreters and practitioners, who catered people's needs. Perceptions are difficult to grasp, but a bad poet does not make poetry bad, just as a bad *mantis, prophetes, orpheotelestes, agyrtes, magos* does not make these arts bad by definition. Both Plato and the *PDerveni* author, although their views cannot be taken as representative or mainstream, try to distinguish between true and false religious practitioners.[156] Graf and Johnston

---

[154] Burkert 1987:30–53.

[155] For discussion of these columns and the problematic identity of their author, *orpheotelestes* or *physikos*, see Obbink 1997; Kahn 1997; West 1997a; Tsantsanoglou 1997; Janko 2001:18–24; Betegh 2004:74–91; and Kouremenos, Parássoglou, and Tsantsanoglou 2006:45–59, 70–75, 82–83, 86–87, 161–174, 186–189, 193–197. Torjussen (2005) argues that Dionysos was most probably absent from the commentary whose author used Orpheus as an authority. For the reference to Herakleitos' poetry by the *PDerveni* author and the interaction between the philosopher and 'Orphism,' see Sider 1997; for Herakleitos and the mysteries, see also Schefer 2000 and Drozdek 2001. Granger (2000) convincingly argues that the foolish and ignorant are portrayed by Herakleitos as living a life like the Homeric dead souls. Seaford (2003b) discusses the unity of opposites in mystic initiation, Presocratic thought, archaic poetry, and in Aeschylus' tragedies, particularly the *Oresteia*.

[156] Betegh (2004:80) understands Plato's attitude as negative and that of the *PDerveni* author as positive; for a discussion of this passage and the one in *Laws* 909a-b, see also Voutiras 1998:123–127 and Kouremenos, Parássoglou, and Tsantsanoglou 2006:45–59; for the νυκτερινός σύλλογος, Larivée 2003.

propose that the authors of the texts on the lamellae and *epistomia* may have been local or itinerant *orpheotelestai*, a term which combines all (or almost all) the religious activities mentioned by Plato. According to Andrei Lebedev's hypothesis, Pharnabazos, the diviner of Hermes, and Aristoteles were two such individuals, both magicians and *orpheotelestai*, at work in Olbia, and, because of competition, they were writing curse-tablets against one another. In a parallel case, Emmanuel Voutiras has proposed that Timarete from Corinth most probably was an itinerant female magician active in fourth century BCE Pella.[157]

Be that as it may, at least as far as the *Bacchica* are concerned, the two kinds of human needs, illuminated by Plato, are evident in the sources. The Dionysos of Euripides' *Bacchae* preaches Bacchic *teletai*, which concentrate on maenadism and Bacchic blessings during this life.[158] As Susan Cole has shown convincingly, the epitaphs of Bacchic initiates from Asia Minor, Thrace, Macedonia, Thessaly, Boeotia, the Peloponnese, Rhodes and Rome, dated from the third century BCE to the third century CE, present the expected Dionysiac motifs: the vine, the wine, and the symposium; children dying young and parents at a loss by the death of their children; people despairing at the prospect of death.[159] These initiates ask Dionysos to help and save them now, while they are alive on earth and not after death, and they even accuse and chastise the god for having failed to protect their children or themselves from death.

The Dionysos of the texts on the lamellae and *epistomia* promises to remove the fear of death from those initiated in another(?) Bacchic mystery cult which promised life after death. The texts on the lamellae and *epistomia* may be thought of as 'prophetic or oracular' texts, in that their content, the divine message, taught during initiation, will materialize only after the *mystes*

---

[157] Graf and Johnston 2007:90–96, 158–164, 178–184; Lebedev 1996a; Voutiras 1998:90–111; and 120n79, 132n122.

[158] Dodds 1960; Bierl 1991:177–218, and compare Iakov 2004; Thomson 1999. Seaford (1996:35–44 with earlier bibliography; and 2004:305–311) suggests that in the *Bacchae* Euripides dramatizes maenadism, polis-festivals of Dionysos, and the Dionysiac mysteries, among which the gold lamellae, the Derveni papyrus, and the bone plaques from Olbia. Segal (1982) also sees the possibility that the *sparagmos* of Pentheus may recall that of Dionysos/Zagreus (48–49), or later that of Orpheus (74–76). On the differing views of Dodds and Seaford, see the convincing arguments by Henrichs (1984a and 1993a). On maenadism in particular, see Dodds 1951:64–101 and 270–282; 1960:xi–xx; and compare Henrichs' redress (1978, 1984a, 1984b, 1995), and Bremmer 1984. On *sparagmos* as a fertility rite, see Halm-Tisserant 2004. On Bacchic *teletai* and Dionysos' multiple associations with other divinities, see Nilsson 1985; Merkelbach 1988:7–134; Burkert 1993; Bierl 1991; and Ricciardelli 2000.

[159] Cole 1993. For prayers in facing death in which a gradual development of ideas of immortality is evident, see Intrieri 2002; and also 198–200n162, 206n185. For epitaphic epigrams of initiates into a mystery cult, see also Avagianou 2002 (Pherae = Bernabé 2004, 466 F); Karadima-Matsa and Dimitrova 2003; and Dignas 2004.

crosses the threshold of Hades. In that sense, Dionysos masked as Apollo or Hades, or Apollo and Hades masked as Dionysos, are not paradoxes, as Dionysos is one of the few gods that defies categorization and definition and partakes in more than one clearly defined sphere of human activity and human needs.

At Delphi, Dionysos is a chthonian *lover of laurel and paean Apollo*, and Apollo becomes *the Bacchic mantis of the ivy*. The divine *mania* of Euripides' *Bacchae*, with its positive and negative consequences, is transformed at Delphi through Dionysos into the mantic *mania* of Pythia and Apollo.[160] Both gods purportedly know what the future holds, but Apollo's knowledge of the after-life is very limited, if not non-existent. He was asked only once, in 262 CE or a little later, by the neoplatonist Amelios to reply to the question: "where has the soul of Plotinos gone?"[161] Apollo, through his manic/mantic Pythia and through his oracles, accommodates those who simply want to know what the future holds, while they are alive. This is also true of the Dionysos in the *Bacchae* and the inscriptions of his initiates *above the grave*. But Dionysos also accommodates those who want to know the future of their existence after death and who care very much about it. These initiates take with them into the grave the gold lamellae and *epistomia* (incised or unincised). Masked as a Hades, or being one and the same with Hades (Herakleitos fr. 15: ὡυτὸς δὲ Ἀΐδης καὶ Διόνυσος, ὅτεωι μαίνονται καὶ ληναΐζουσιν), or masked as an Apollo (according to Aeschylus, Euripides, and Philodamos of Skarpheia), Dionysos ensures the hopes of this group of initiates for a special postmortem treat-ment and promises their transformation after death into a hero and even a god.

Dionysos as *bacchos*; Dionysos as *mantis* and prophet; Dionysos as trans-former of humans after death into heroes and gods; Dionysos as *telestes* and poet; Dionysos as initiator of rituals and poetics—these are but a few of the many *personae* this god had in Greece (at least as many as Orpheus had: the Argonaut, the foreigner, the singer, the magician, the initiator, the husband of Eurydice).[162] Trying to make sense out of this complex divinity with the frag-mentary information which has survived is not an easy task, as the interpreta-tive tools at our disposal are still too Apolline to deal with matters Bacchic.

---

[160] For positive *mania* in a Christian context (First Epistle to the Corinthians 14.23), see Chester 2005.

[161] Fontenrose 1981:164–165. Questions concerning the dead were of course numerous (in all 54 oracles), but they were related to: appeasing the dead, establishing a cult to the dead, and proper burial, as Johnston (2005) has shown. Yet, they *never* addressed the afterlife, except in the case of Amelios.

[162] Graf and Johnston 2007:165–174.

4

The Cretan Contexts

A Literary Cretan Context

THE NINE INCISED AND THREE UNINCISED *EPISTOMIA* OF CRETE, dated between the third century BCE and the first CE, bear witness to a mystery cult(s) and ritual(s) in Eleutherna and Sfakaki, both located in the area to the north of the Idaean Cave. Attempts have been made to place these texts within a Cretan context, but what this context should consist of remains a puzzle, as the evidence is insufficient and accentuates the problems of interpretation. Before delving into the search for a Cretan context regarding the texts on the *epistomia*, it is important to state the obvious: due to their nature, the sources for Crete (literary texts (mostly non-Cretan), inscriptions, and the archaeological record) have always been controversial, as they are of varying quality. This issue persistently plagues scholars of Crete. One question that constantly arises is: to what extent, if at all, is a synthesis of all the evidence attainable? And consequently, does the portrait of Crete and the Cretans that emerges during the archaic period actually reflect the ideas and beliefs of Cretans, untainted by Greek prejudices and perceptions?[1] We will first establish the literary Cretan context, i.e. how Crete and the Cretans are presented in literary works (mostly by non-Cretans); and then (either in contrast or accord with this background) a Cretan context will be established for the texts on the lamellae on the basis of the archaeological and epigraphical evidence.

The sources concerning Crete and the Cretans have been problematic since antiquity and betray both strengths and weaknesses. The tension between literary and archaeological/epigraphical evidence is hardly new. Diodorus, writing in the first century BCE, warned his readers (5.80.4):[2]

---

[1] Maria Sarinaki is addressing these problems in her dissertation "The Literary Cretan Goddess" with emphasis on the literary context of the Cretan goddesses. Morris 1992 presents an eloquent account of Crete and the Orient from the late Bronze Age onwards.

[2] Sporn (2002:21) subscribes to the same warning in the beginning of her study of Cretan

ἐπεὶ δὲ τῶν τὰ Κρητικὰ γεγραφότων οἱ πλεῖστοι διαφωνοῦσι πρὸς ἀλλήλους, οὐ χρὴ θαυμάζειν ἐὰν μὴ πᾶσιν ὁμολογούμενα λέγωμεν· τοῖς γὰρ τὰ πιθανώτερα λέγουσι καὶ μάλιστα πιστευομένοις ἐπηκολουθήσαμεν, ἃ μὲν Ἐπιμενίδῃ τῷ θεολόγῳ προσσχόντες, ἃ δὲ Δωσιάδῃ καὶ Σωσικράτει καὶ Λαοσθενίδᾳ.

And since the greatest number of writers who have written about Crete disagree among themselves, there should be no occasion for surprise if what we report should not agree with every one of them; we have, indeed, followed as our authorities those who give the more probable account and are the most trustworthy, in some matters depending upon Epimenides who has written about the gods, in others upon Dosiades, Sosikrates, and Laosthenidas.

translation Oldfather 1939

The historian's reliability is contested, but at least here we are told that the discussion of Cretan matters comes from at least four different sources (after being filtered through the writer's own criteria of plausibility and trustworthiness): Epimenides, Dosiadas, Sosikrates, and Laosthenidas are authors whose works he presumably had at his disposal, works that have not survived except in meagre fragments. This does not exclude the possibility that the historian employed other sources as well, but he chose to mention by name only these four. It is important to consider the use of these four sources in relation to Diodorus' entire section of the Cretan account, in which the following passage focuses on the mystery cults in Crete (5.77.3–8):

Such, then, are the myths which the Cretans recount of the gods who they claim (μυθολογοῦσι) were born in their land. They also assert (λέγοντες) that the honours accorded to the gods and their sacrifices and the initiatory rites observed in connection with the mysteries (τιμὰς καὶ θυσίας καὶ τὰς περὶ τὰ μυστήρια τελετάς) were handed down from Crete to the rest of men, and to support this they advance the following most weighty argument, as they conceive it (τοῦτο φέρουσιν, ὡς οἴονται, μέγιστον τεκμήριον): the initiatory rite which is celebrated by the Athenians in Eleusis, the most famous, one may venture, of them all, and that of Samothrace, and the one practised in Thrace among the Cicones, whence Orpheus came

sanctuaries and cults during the Classical and Hellenistic period; for this passage, see also Guthrie 1993:110–117.

who introduced them—these are all handed down in the form of a mystery, whereas at Knossos in Crete it has been the custom from ancient times that these initiatory rites should be handed down to all openly; and what is handed down among other peoples as not to be divulged, this the Cretans conceal from no one who may wish to inform himself upon such matters. Indeed, the majority of the gods, the Cretans say (φασί), had their beginning in Crete and set out from there to visit many regions of the inhabited world, conferring benefactions upon the races of men and distributing among each of them the advantage which resulted from the discoveries they had made. Demeter, for example, ... Aphrodite ... Apollo ... Artemis ... And similar myths are also recounted by the Cretans regarding the other gods, but to draw up an account of them would be a long task for us, and it would not be easily grasped by our readers (παραπλήσια δὲ μυθολογοῦσι καὶ περὶ τῶν ἄλλων θεῶν, περὶ ὧν ἡμῖν ἀναγράφειν μακρὸν ἂν εἴη, τοῖς δ' ἀναγινώσκουσι παντελῶς ἀσύνοπτον).

translation Oldfather 1939, modified

In the first century BCE, Diodorus, following his four Cretan sources, relates the Cretan opinion concerning the institution of mystery cults in Crete and in the rest of Greece, which is the most probable and trustworthy opinion according to his own criteria. Demeter's mystery cult at Eleusis, the Kabeiria at Samothrace, and the mysteries in Thrace (whence Orpheus revealed and taught them), all three feature secret performances (μυστικῶς) under prohibitions (ἐν ἀπορρήτῳ); at Knossos, on the other hand, the rituals are performed openly (φανερῶς), and without anything being hidden from inquiring individuals (μηδένα κρύπτειν τῶν βουλομένων τὰ τοιαῦτα γινώσκειν). The historian then chooses only four divinities out of the Cretan pantheon, Demeter, Aphrodite, Apollo, and Artemis, allowing them to serve as representative cases for his statement; he concludes that he could go on and on about the other Cretan divinities, relating the stories about them he found in his Cretan sources, but he would then have created a narrative impossible to follow and conceive (παντελῶς ἀσύνοπτον).

Diodorus' information cannot be validated and there are many ways to interpret his words, although he is careful enough to state that his account is nothing more and nothing less than what his Cretan sources relate. Nevertheless, the fact that Epimenides, the legendary Cretan *theologos* of the archaic period, is mentioned among his sources primarily on religious matters suggests that texts of the archaic period may elucidate Diodorus' statement

153

concerning the Cretan claim that Crete had been the provenance of mystery cults in Greece.[3]

Both in the Homeric epics and in the *Homeric Hymns to Demeter* and *to Apollo,* Crete and the Cretans occupy a special place. In the Homeric *Iliad,* the Cretan contingent under Idomeneus and his *therapon* Meriones receives due attention as one of the largest forces of the Achaeans.[4] Meriones, being the

---

[3] The location of Crete in the Mediterranean basin and its intermediary role in transit and communication with the Near East and Egypt contributed decisively to the island's special place. Burkert (1992, 2004b, 2005a), and West (1997b) present an impressive account of parallels between the Greeks and their Eastern neighbors, which strongly suggest an *Eastern Mediterranean koine,* or according to Nagy (2005:75) a *lingua franca.* For a brief definition of ancient Mediterranean religion, see Graf 2004a. Marinatos (2000) argues that Odysseus' and Menelaus' journeys lead to paradisiac places; she even proposes that Odysseus' journey probably resulted from Greek, Near Eastern, and Egyptian motifs, and therefore may be termed a "cosmic journey" (2001); and in her forthcoming book's Chapter IX she argues that the pictorial narratives on Cretan *larnakes* should be viewed as a Minoan version of the later Greek iconography of Elysion (for which see also 114n54). That such a *koine* did exist is evident in the archaeological record, for which see the discussions in Stampolidis and Karetsou 1998; Karageorghis and Stampolidis 1998; Stampolidis 2003a, 2003b, 2003c; and Stampolidis and Karageorghis 2003; for Crete and Egypt, 190n129. Objects and people traveled extensively, and with them traveled shapes, motifs, and ideas as well. The difficulties that arise are: 1) whether or not this exchange was unidirectional, always from east and south to west and north; and 2) what kind of influences these interconnections exerted, because objects and motifs are one thing, but the ideas and symbols behind them are completely another; e.g. the Semitic origin of the Greek alphabet is undeniable, but the Greek alphabet itself and its consequences in Greece and the Mediterranean is beyond comparison (Teodorsson 2006:169–175). Hodos (2006) argues convincingly that, in his case studies of the regions of North Syria, Sicily, and Africa, adoptions and/or adaptations involved a dynamic process of constant modification and reinterpretation of customs, practices, beliefs, and traditions. (Similar issues are raised by the evidence which dates from the late Republic into late antiquity, for which see the important discussion by Moatti 2006.) Lebessi and Muhly (2003) have shown convincingly the fundamental ideological differences of some oriental artifacts found in Kato Symi. Similar conclusions are reached by Bakker (2001) in his comparison of *Gilgamesh* and the *Odyssey,* two works which develop in parallel and betray constant interaction and significant modification. Cook (2004) has presented convincing evidence that the description of Alkinoos' palace in *Odyssey* 7 is modeled on Assyrian palatial architecture. Bachvarova (2005) has argued cogently that Homeric poetry cannot be assumed to have been a direct imitation of any Near Eastern epic, but that "it is safe to surmise that Homeric poets, at some point in history, were in contact with an offshoot of the Near Eastern epic tradition" (153); see further Robertson 1990:424–426; 1991:60–62. For Homer and the Near East, see Morris 1997. For rituals in the Mediterranean from the Hellenistic period onwards, relevant to matters Cretan, and the problems their study presents Chaniotis 2005b, 2005c, 2002; and Kaizer 2006.

[4] In the Catalogue of Ships, the Cretans under Idomeneus contributed 80 ships (*Iliad* 2.645–652), the same number of ships that Argos-Tiryns under Diomedes sent (*Iliad* 2.559–568), whereas the first two in size were Mycenae under Agamemnon with 100 ships together with 60 of Arcadians (*Iliad* 2.569–580, 603–614), and Pylos under Nestor with 90 (*Iliad* 2.591–602). For an overview of Crete in Homer, see Sherratt 1996; for poetry in Minoan Crete, see Tsagarakis 2006;

younger, is awarded by the poet the Achillean epithet "swift of foot" (with the necessary change in the formula) (13.249: πόδας ταχύ); he wins the archery contest by defeating the far superior archer Teucer (23.850–883), and is second to Agamemnon without contest in the javelin-throw (23.884–897).[5] Moreover, before the funeral games, Meriones and his men are chosen by Agamemnon as experts in gathering the timber from Mount Ida in the Troad and in building the pyre for Patroklos' funeral.[6] Interestingly enough, in the *Odyssey*, where Meriones is absent, Achilles is no longer the dominating hero, and Odysseus is performing one of his three 'Cretan tales/lies,' the poet attributes the Achillean formula "swift of foot" (twice in the same passage) to Orsilochos the son of Idomeneus, who surpassed in swiftness all Cretans.[7]

Beyond the Cretan marks of distinction in running, archery,[8] and ambush (as emphasized in these scattered passages of the Homeric epics), the famous Cretan tales/lies present an intriguing case that has puzzled commentators.[9]

---

for topographical and historical details, see Aposkitou 1960 and Willetts 1962:120–137. For the hundred cities of Crete in the *Iliad* and the ninety in the *Odyssey* and on the issue of their *politeia*, see Strataridaki 1988-1989:159–160; Tsagarakis 1989; Perlman 1992; Gehrke 1997; and Link 2002.

[5] The πόδας ὠκύς formula is reserved almost exclusively for Achilles and, much less frequently, for the goddess Iris. In the *Iliad*, in addition to Meriones, the formula swift-footed (πόδας ταχύς) is awarded, only once in each case, to: Aineias (13.482), the hare in the simile where Menelaos is likened to an eagle (17.676), and Antilochos (18.2). For this formula in the *Iliad*, see Dunkle 1997 with earlier bibliography.

[6] Stampolidis (1996:121–122 and passim) presents a detailed and generally convincing comparison of Homer's description of Patroklos' pyre and pyre A in Eleutherna's necropolis.

[7] In one of Odysseus Cretan tales: *Od.* 13.259–261: φεύγω, ἐπεὶ φίλον υἷα κατέκτανον Ἰδομενῆος, | Ὀρσίλοχον πόδας ὠκύν, ὃς ἐν Κρήτῃ εὐρείῃ | ἀνέρας ἀλφηστὰς νίκα ταχέεσσι πόδεσσιν.

[8] For running and the Cretan *dromeis*, see Tzifopoulos 1998a; for archery Skoulikas, 2000; for Meriones as *therapon* of Idomeneus in the *Palatine Anthology*, see Steinbichler 1995. For Cretan traits as a literary *topos* in the Hellenistic epigrams, see Vertoudakis 2000a and 2000b.

[9] For convincing discussions of these problematic tales/lies and their poetics, see: Clay (1983:84–89), who stresses the literary links between Meriones and Odysseus; Haft (1984), who examines the poetics of Odysseus' Cretan tales, the similarities of Odysseus, Idomeneus, and Meriones, and Homer's strategy in his narrative of *Odyssey*'s second half; Maronitis (1999:226–252), who argues that the first tale/lie to Athena is programmatic for the following ones; Grossardt (1998), who studies in detail the tales as tests of the characters involved, the tales' narrative function, their self-referential poetics, and their reception in later texts; Sherratt (1996:89), who stresses the verisimilitude of the stories, in spite of their false frame, and distinguishes two earlier discourses in which Cretans held a prominent place, a heroic world evident in the *Iliad*, and a "'real' (contemporary and 'historically' remembered) world," which "appears as something of an anti-Phaeacia" (92); and Sarinaki forthcoming, who discusses the Cretan tales in light of Odysseus' mention of Ariadne in the *Nekyia* (*Odyssey* 11.321–325). For the Athenian myths and rituals which shaped and crystallized the *Odyssey*, see Cook 1995; and Calame 1996:98–112.

In the guise of a Cretan, a guise perhaps anticipated by the end of the *Nekyia* where Cretan Ariadne is mentioned, Odysseus presents himself to Athena (Book 13),[10] Eumaios (Book 14), and Penelope (Book 19), and performs three different tales. The composition of these tales mirrors that of the *Odyssey* itself and invites comparison, in terms of poetics, with the poet of the *Odyssey*.[11] The reasons for Odysseus' undertaking the guise of a Cretan in his successful poetic enterprise are not self-evident. They are explained either in literary and mythological terms, or as traditional material, or as alternative poetic compositions in which Crete and the Cretans held a more prominent place.[12] In terms of alternative compositions, the Cretan tales present a metaphorical trip to Crete, one of Telemachos' destinations usually athetized (*Odyssey* 1.93a and 285a). The poet of the *Odyssey*, because of performance interaction, was perhaps forced to incorporate in his work traditional and alternative poetic material about Crete, but chose to downplay the Cretan presence, because he was aiming at a Panhellenic audience.[13]

And yet, it seems that one of the most effective poetic *personae* during the archaic period is that of a Cretan.[14] In the *Homeric Hymn to Demeter* (lines 120–132), the goddess, in a move similar to Odysseus', adopts the guise of an old woman from Crete. Abducted by pirates (ληϊστῆρες, 125), she uses her best persuasive skills to gain entrance to the house of Keleos.[15] This may indicate an alternative Cretan *Hymn*, which may also imply Demeter's non-Eleusinian origin and, more importantly, her late arrival at Eleusis, where another powerful female, Kore/Persephone, already presided.[16] Apart from literary or

---

[10] See also 155n9.

[11] See especially Walsh 1984:3–21.

[12] Reece (1994) suggests a parallel *Cretan Odyssey* that accounts for the inconsistencies in the narrative of the tales/lies, for which compare Burkert 2001b; for an *Aetolian Odyssey*, see Marks 2003. Faure (2000a), while provocative and interesting, undermines his case by over-enthusiastic arguments for *Odysseus the Cretan*; Malkin (1998) argues that the *Odyssey* may also present a protocolonization. Nagy (2004b:39) understands these variants "as multiforms stemming form oral traditions localized in Crete."

[13] See the section "In Search of a Context: Rhapsodizing and Prophesying the Afterlife."

[14] On Cretan Homers and on Cretan alterity, variation, and fictionality, see Martin 2005a.

[15] Grossardt 1998:227–253; Parker 1991; Richardson 1974.

[16] Suter 2002:147–148; also Graf 1974; and Clinton 2003. Clay (1989:265) suggests that "Eleusis always offered a potential antagonism to Olympos, and its doctrine posed a possible threat to the Olympian *theologoumenon*, as is abundantly confirmed by the later adoption of Eleusis by the anti-Olympian Orphics and other sects. As a whole, the *Hymn to Demeter* may be understood as an attempt to integrate, and hence absorb, the cult of Demeter and the message of Eleusis into the Olympian cosmos." For the authorship of the *Hymn to Demeter* Clinton 1986. On *eleus-in* from *eleuth-in*, the ceremonial "going," the procession, see Robertson 1998:568–572. On the transmission of the cult of Demeter Eleusinia, see Bowden 2009.

historical considerations,[17] however, the fact remains that Demeter chooses the Cretan *persona* in her tale/lie in order to present herself to the daughters of Metaneira. Moreover, in Hesiod's *Theogony*, Demeter's mating with the hero Iasion takes place in Crete,[18] and it is possible that this is also the place where Demeter's sexual encounter with Zeus occurred, as Hesiod's narrative may imply: the expression ἐς λέχος ἦλθεν (912) is employed only for the mating of Zeus and Demeter,[19] whereas in all other sexual encounters of Zeus, the females either go to Zeus' chamber or the location is altogether unspecified.

In the *Homeric Hymn to Apollo* a similar, possibly even more curious case is presented.[20] The god, searching for people to minister his newly built temple at Delphi (line 389: ἀνθρώπους ὀργιόνας), chooses Cretans on board a ship who are sailing either for trade or for piracy and who already know the *iepaian*-song and dance (lines 500, 516–519). In addition to associating the Cretans with themes of trade and piracy[21] (as did the poets of the *Hymn to Demeter* and of the *Odyssey*), the poet of the *Hymn to Apollo* also relates that the Cretans are already *orgiones* and *paieones*. Apollo is not following in the steps of Odysseus and Demeter in imitating a Cretan poetic *persona*. He does imitate, however, Cretan 'activities': of piracy,[22] when disguised as a dolphin he takes

---

[17] Clay (1989:228n79) suggests: "there is no reason to find a reference to a Cretan origin of the Demeter cult here," although earlier she argued cogently that "the hymn-poet assumes a knowledge of this common version on the part of the audience and has deliberately modified it" (224); so also Mylonas 1961:16-19; Willetts 1962:151; Richardson 1974:188 ad v. 123. Suter (2002, especially in chapters 2, 6, 7, and 8) presents convincing arguments for the complex issues raised by the *Hymn*.

[18] *Theogony* 969-974 (see Richardson 1974; Clay 1989; Suter 2002; and Sarinaki forthcoming): Δημήτηρ μὲν Πλοῦτον ἐγείνατο δῖα θεάων, | Ἰασίῳ ἥρωι μιγεῖσ' ἐρατῇ φιλότητι | νειῷ ἔνι τριπόλῳ, Κρήτης ἐν πίονι δήμῳ, | ἐσθλόν, ὃς εἶσ' ἐπὶ γῆν τε καὶ εὐρέα νῶτα θαλάσσης | πᾶσαν· τῷ δὲ τυχόντι καὶ οὗ κ' ἐς χεῖρας ἵκηται, | τὸν δὴ ἀφνειὸν ἔθηκε, πολὺν δέ οἱ ὤπασεν ὄλβον. The *hieros gamos* of Demeter and Iasion, according to Avagianou (1991:165-175), "forms a marginal alternative to Zeus' and Hera's sacred marriage" (175).

[19] The location of Demeter's bed is not specified purposefully (*Theogony* 912-914): αὐτὰρ ὁ Δήμητρος πολυφόρβης ἐς λέχος ἦλθεν· | ἣ τέκε Περσεφόνην λευκώλενον, ἣν Ἀιδωνεὺς | ἥρπασεν ἧς παρὰ μητρός, ἔδωκε δὲ μητίετα Ζεύς.

[20] For Apollo and Crete, see Swindler 1913; Willetts 1962; Burkert 1985:143-149; Sporn 2002:319-323; for Crete and Delphi, Guarducci 1943-1946; for Delphi and the *Hymn to Apollo*, see Chappell's (2006) scepticism.

[21] For trading and piracy, see the discussion in Miller 1986:95-96 with nn244-245; de Souza 1999; Perlman 2000; and Chaniotis 2004.

[22] Kurke (2003:99n49) suggests that Apollo's choice of Cretan *traders* and *pirates* "may represent an implicit acknowledgement—even within the high tradition—that the activities of Delphic priests are somehow akin to those of brigands or pirates"; similarly, Sherratt 1996. On Cretan involvement in colonizing, see Perlman (2002), who proposes to view within this context the choice of Cretans in the *Hymn to Apollo*; and Stampolidis 2006. The Cretan expertise in economic activities and transactions is of course only one of their characteristics.

over the Cretan ship,[23] and of trade, when after his epiphany a *quid pro quo*
understanding is reached between the god and the Cretans. The Cretans in
this *Hymn* are portrayed in the same way as they were in Demeter's tale to the
daughters of Metaneira, but their traits emphasized by the poet are similar
to those of Demeter, *orgiones* and *paieones*. Apollo's search is very specific. He
is looking for a group of humans for his temple at Delphi who excel in two
areas, *orgia* and the *paean*.[24] The words *orgiones* and *paieones* are relatively rare
in Greek literature and their semantics have caused trouble, but as epithets of
the Cretans, their simplest and most straightforward meaning must be 'those
who perform *orgia* and *paeans*.' The meaning of *orgiones* is relatively clear. It is
usually associated with Demeter, Dionysos, and mystery cults in general, as its
etymology is related to *orgia*, the word employed by Demeter herself to denote
her gift to the Eleusinian kings (*Hymn to Demeter* 273, 476). The word *orgia* may
have also denoted Meriones' activity in *Iliad* 23, his expert knowledge of the
burial ritual.[25]

The equally rare epithet *paieones* is more problematic. In the *Hymn
to Apollo*, the phrase Κρητῶν παιήονες (518) can only be referring to Cretan

---

[23] On Apollo Delphinios, see Willetts 1962:262–264, and Graf 1979. On the Delphic priesthood, see
Parke 1940; Parke and Wormell 2004:17–45; Fontenrose 1981:196–232; Miller 1986:91–110; Clay
1989:74–91; Bowden 2005:14–25. Athenaios relates that the dolphin, Apollo metamorphosed
into one in the *Hymn to Apollo* (as Dionysos metamorphosed the sailors in the *Hymn to Dionysos*),
was thought of as a sacred fish by the author of the *Telchiniake Historia* (*Deipnosophistai* 7.18):
τίς δ' ἐστὶν ὁ καλούμενος ἱερὸς ἰχθύς; ὁ μὲν τὴν Τελχινιακὴν ἱστορίαν συνθείς, εἴτ' Ἐπιμενίδης
ἐστὶν ὁ Κρὴς ἢ Τηλεκλείδης εἴτ' ἄλλος τις, ἱερούς φησιν εἶναι ἰχθύας δελφῖνας καὶ πομπίλους.
ἐστὶ δ' ὁ πομπίλος ζῷον ἐρωτικόν, ὡς ἂν καὶ αὐτὸς γεγονὼς ἐκ τοῦ Οὐρανίου αἵματος ἅμα τῇ
Ἀφροδίτῃ. On the importance of the dolphin in the cult of Melikertes/Palaimon, viewed in a
Dionysiac context, see Seelinger 1998.

[24] Clay (1989:79) emphasizes the poet's presentation of the Cretans as "anonymous, unheroic
representatives of mankind in general"; so also Miller 1986:96–99.

[25] For the etymology, see LSJ; and especially Chantraine 1980, s.v. ὄργια, who notes that the word
may be related to ἔρδω, but also to ὀργή and ὀργάω; and Clay 1989:242 with n120 (she also
points out that (252) "as enumerated by Hades Persephone's future *timai* have nothing to
do with either the Mysteries or initiation or, to be sure, with Orphic notions of punishment
after death"; this, however, is Hades', or Olympos', and not Demeter's perspective and understanding of the final arrangement, as lines 272–274 and 476–482 indicate). Motte and Pirenne-
Delforge (1992) clarify the uses of the term, but place the mystery cult of Cretan Zeus in the
Hellenistic period (138). Ustinova (1996) discusses the social reasons for the Athenian *orgeones*
during the pre-archaic and archaic periods; Arnaoutoglou (2003:31–37, especially 33–34) in his
study of the Athenian religious associations of the Hellenistic period, among them the *orgeones*,
notes that the word in poetic contexts means "some kind of priesthood," or later in relation to
Demeter and her mysteries, "the persons performing these rites"; but "the occurrences in the
4th-century law courts speeches point to ... their [*orgeones*'] role as contexts of solidarity and
sociability for their members" (37).

singers (and dancers) of paeans,[26] whereas ἰηπαιήον' ἀείδειν/ἄειδον (500, 517) means 'sing/were singing the (choral) song *iepaian*,' probably in paeans or cretics.[27] In its immediate context, the *iepaian* serves as a marching song for the Cretans' anabasis from Krisa to Apollo's temple at Delphi, with Apollo leading the way and playing the phorminx.[28] But what the poet intends by employing this word is not immediately clear. This scene has been compared with good reason to the earlier ones in the *Hymn*, at Delos (lines 146–178) and on Olympos (lines 186–206), as the verbal echoes are strong (especially 201–202 ~ 515–516). And yet, the poet in those scenes is narrating performances of *aoide* and *hymnos* by the Deliades and the Ionians at Delos, and by the Muses and Apollo on Olympos. The *iepaian*-song and dance is completely absent from those scenes.[29]

Likewise, the Cretan *paieones* whom Apollo is bringing to Delphi are not 'healers' or performers of purification-rites. George Huxley suggested that the name *Paiawon* in a Linear B tablet from Knossos is understood as primarily an earlier healing divinity identified with Apollo for the first time in Crete.[30] The Homeric epics are familiar with the Egyptian Paieon, distinct from Apollo, who knows cures for everything and is the ancestor of all Egyptians (*Odyssey* 4.227–232). In the *Iliad*, Paieon heals and helps escape from death the two most deadly divinities: Hades (5.398–402) and Ares (5.899–900).

---

[26] For this meaning, see Huxley 1975:119–120, with discussion of previous literature; and Watkins 1995:511–512. For the genre of the paian, see now the definitive study of Rutherford 2001:3–182 with complete previous bibliography; he translates, however, this phrase as 'Cretan healers' (24), although earlier he notes (15–16): "... I remain unconvinced that the earliest παιᾶνες were simply healing-songs." For the poetics and juxtaposition of *paian* and *threnos*, see Loraux 2002:54–80. For *orgiones* and *paieones* Arnaoutoglou (2003:37) allows for the possibility of importation from Crete of certain rites of purification, as suggested by Defradas (1972).

[27] Huxley 1975:121–122. Clay (1989:84n200) briefly notes the connection between the paean and paeonic meter and Crete; see further Rutherford (2001:24–29 and 76–79) on the meters of the paean-song, closely connected with the cretic and the bacchiac whose place of origin was thought to have been Crete; and Furley and Bremer 2001:vol. 1:78–82. Watkins (1995:510–511) analyzes the paean in *Iliad* 22.391–394 in paroemiacs and translates the phrase "Sing the paean-cry 'Hail Healer'" (511–512).

[28] The lyre is not the exclusive instrument for the paeans, as Archilochos' fr. 121W (αὐτὸς ἐξάρχων πρὸς αὐλὸν Λέσβιον παιήονα) indicates (Rutherford 2001:66 and 18–23). The verb παιανίζω in Modern Greek indicates the marching-song played by a band for those participating and marching in a parade.

[29] Rutherford (2001:29) suggests that what the Deliades sing and perform is a paean, although the poet does not use the word; for the human and divine choreography in the two scenes, see Peponi 2004.

[30] Huxley 1975; Stampolidis 2006. On healing and purification, see the fundamental study of Parker 1983. For healing in epic and lyric poetry, and for Machaon, see Martin 1983:26–31, 60–65; for the Minoan and Mycenaean healers, Arnott 2002.

The healing aspect of Apollo, however, is not part of the *Homeric Hymn's* poetics and its Panhellenizing agenda, unless by synecdoche or metonymy the 'bow' may also be taken to denote 'healing' because of the wounds it incurs,[31] or unless purification-rites may be included among the *orgia* performed by the Cretan *orgiones*. Immediately following his birth, Apollo pronounces his *timai* (131–132): εἴη μοι κίθαρίς τε φίλη καὶ καμπύλα τόξα, / χρήσω δ' ἀνθρώποισι Διὸς νημερτέα βουλήν. If Apollo's *timai*, his archery and song-*hymn*-poetry (which are also shared by Cretans in Homer and in the *Hymn to Demeter)* are articulated in the beginning of the *Hymn* and in the Delian part respectively, the Delphic section should pertain to the god's oracular power. For the appropriation of the latter, however, in the Delphic part, Apollo employs the two *timai*, acquired and displayed in the first half of the *Hymn*. The Pythoktonia is achieved thanks to Apollo's skill with the bow. Apollo's prophetic power is introduced and celebrated by the *iepaian*-song and dance,[32] a specific and new(?) kind of poetry, after which follows Apollo's pronouncement of his first oracle (lines 532–544).[33] In these lines, where the god describes how his oracle will be administered, an allusion to a Cretan motif and theme has also been suggested. Apollo reveals to the stunned Cretans that their livelihood will henceforth depend on the knife, with which they will be sacrificing sheep (lines 535–536). This ritual knife, an allusion to the proverbial *Delphike machaira*, has been associated with the ritual gold knives Cretan young men are carrying on the shield of Achilles (*Iliad* 18.590–602).[34] In all probability, the Delphic sacrificial knife is the Homeric knife of a Cretan ritual dance; at Delphi, the dance becomes the ritual dance of the *iepaian*, whereas the knife of the ritual dance acquires another ritual use, that of a sacrificial knife.

In *Hypothesis A* to Pindar's *Pythians* (quoted above, 141–142), a slightly different version is narrated regarding the history of Delphi, a version which the poet of the *Hymn to Apollo* appears to be suppressing. Not only are the female occupants absent from the *Hymn*, but so is Dionysos and his contri-

---

[31] So Rutherford 2001:15–16; he discusses the military or quasi-military contexts of Paiawon/Paian and the *iepaian*-song, in which the 'healing' aspect originally belonged. In Homer things are different and Apollo is associated with healing: Martin 1983; and Burkert 1985:144–145.

[32] Watkins (1995:511–512) understood the *iepaian*-song as a victory-response to the Pythoktonia, which he associated with other Indo-European poetry; see further Rutherford 2001:15–17. For performance contexts of the *paian* genre, which is not always related to Apollo as the dithyramb is not exclusively Dionysiac (Zimmermann 1992), see Rutherford 2001:23–90.

[33] For this first oracle of Apollo, see Miller 1986:110 and Clay 1989:85–92.

[34] Martin 1983:87–93 with earlier bibliography. Kurke (2003:86–90) discusses the proverbial *Delphic machaira* and Aesop's critique of the Delphic "parasitic dependence on sacrificial offerings" (87). For the vignette's Minoan associations, see Lonsdale 1995 with previous bibliography.

bution to the way oracles were given. Instead of Nyx, Themis, and Dionysos, the poet presents the Cretans as experts in the *iepaian*-song and dance and as *semantores*. Can they stand as representatives of the previous owners of Delphi, especially Dionysos, the famous bridegroom of Ariadne and Crete? Is Crete mentioned first in the *Hymn* as a possible birthplace of Apollo (*Hymn to Apollo* 30) only due to geographical reasons?[35] The paionic rhythm, which Apollo must learn and with which he is henceforth identified (see the passage from Plutarch quoted above, 140–141), is closely associated with—if not a derivation of—the bacchiac rhythm, and, according to the *Hypothesis A*, Dionysos was responsible for the dactylic rhythm as well.

Be that as it may, the *iepaian*-song and dance within the *Hymn's* context may be both an epinician paean, celebrating victory in combat, and a special poetic composition articulating and 'inviting,' among other things, Apollo's oracles of Zeus. In this respect, the etymologies of the god's name and of Pindar's *Paeans* are revealing. On the basis of Burkert's suggestion that Apellon is related to the Doric *apellai*,[36] Nagy has proposed that scholars take into account the relation of the name Apellon to *apeilé* and *apeiléo*. Thus, Apollo may be viewed as (Nagy 1994:7):

> the god of authoritative speech, the one who presides over all manner of speech-acts ... the god of poetry and song. The god of eternal promise, of the eternity of potential performance, he is the word waiting to be translated into action.

Ian Rutherford, in his indispensable introduction to Pindar's *Paeans*, has shown convincingly that *paiaon* in all probability arose within military or quasi-military contexts. He notes that "prophecy is of great importance in Pindar's articulation of the παιάν" and "if more of Pindar's *Paianes* survived, we might expect to find more examples of the relationship between song and prophecy."[37] It appears that the poet of the *Hymn to Apollo* is trying to appropriate and integrate the paeanic activity of the Cretans into the *Hymn's* narrative for the institution of the Delphic oracle, perhaps an activity antagonistic to the epic tradition and to Olympian discourse.

---

[35] Allen, Halliday, and Sikes (1936:205) note that "Crete, Athens, and Delos are connected by the legend that Theseus, on his return from killing the Minotaur, instituted the festival of Apollo at Delos ... But ... the mention of Crete and Athens here is due to geographical rather than to mythological reasons."

[36] Burkert 1975 and 1985:144–145; see also Rutherford 2001:16–17.

[37] Rutherford 2001:173 and 174.

It is not unreasonable, therefore, to assume that what the poet in the *Hymn* intended with the epithet *paieones* was nothing more than 'singers (and dancers) of paeans', an activity which invites and stimulates Apollo to make manifest Zeus' oracle. Already earlier, the poet related in less problematic terms the special characteristics of the Cretans on board the ship, which Apollo thought were best suited for the job (lines 393–396): Κρῆτες ... οἵ ῥά τ' ἄνακτι / ἱερά τε ῥέζουσι καὶ ἀγγέλλουσι θέμιστας / Φοίβου Ἀπόλλωνος χρυσαόρου, ὅττι κεν εἴπῃ / χρείων ἐκ δάφνης ("Cretans ... the ones who perform sacrifices for the god, and who announce the rulings of Phoibos Apollo of the golden sword, whatever he says when he gives his oracles form the bay tree," translation West 2003). This is an elaborate description of the traits needed to serve Apollo at Delphi, a description succinctly stated by the epithets *orgiones, paiaones,* and *semantores*. For, when Apollo pronounces the first oracle in the final arrangement, where he calls the Cretans, and the priesthood that will succeed them at Delphi, σημάντορες (line 542), he must be referring back to the detailed description of lines 393–396. The Cretans are not only performers of sacrifice (*orgiones*), and singers and dancers of paeans which invite Apollo's prophecies (*paiaones*), but they are also 'announcers of Apollo's themistes and oracles', i.e. *semantores*, those who 'make a *sema* (hence masters, governors), 'prophets' and 'seers', people who interpret, translate, and communicate in an intelligible manner the divine signs.[38] It does not seem to be a mere coincidence that the poet of the *Hymn to Demeter* employs the same word when Demeter narrates her tale/lie to Metaneira's daughters and describes her Cretan abductors as ὑπερφιάλους σημάντορας, "arrogant makers of signs/signals, leaders" (line 131).[39] And this very verb σημαίνω was Herakleitos' choice for Apollo's oracular function in his famous fragment (93 D-K): "the Lord, whose oracle is at Delphi, neither speaks, nor conceals, but offers signs (ὁ ἄναξ, οὗ τὸ μαντεῖόν ἐστι τὸ ἐν Δελφοῖς, οὔτε λέγει οὔτε κρύπτει ἀλλὰ σημαίνει).[40]

Thus, the Cretans, in addition to their expertise in archery and running, trade and piracy, appear also as *orgiones, paieones, and semantores*, performers

---

[38] The word is usually taken to refer only to those priests of Apollo who will come after the Cretans; if so, the role of the Cretans described earlier in lines 393–396 makes no sense and Apollo's first oracle must come true as soon as the performance of the hymn ends so that there is no time for the Cretans to exercise any such activity, as the word *semantores* denotes: Allen, Halliday, and Sikes 1936:266–267; Miller 1986:110 and 91–110; Clay 1989:85–87; West 2003 s.v.; Athanassakis 2004 s.v.

[39] Richardson (1974:190) notes that in the *Hymn to Demeter* the sense of the epithet is "presumably 'my arrogant overlords'"; West (2003 s.v.) translates "those imperious ruffians."

[40] Nagy 1990a:62–64; 1990b:162–168.

and interpreters of rites, paeans, and signs/signals. Evidence for prophecy in Crete is almost non-existent, but for Cretan *manteis* in the archaic period, there is some indirect evidence. Later sources report that Cretan poets and seers were active in traveling abroad, especially as experts in music and healing; the poet of the *Hymn to Apollo* appropriates the musical aspect but suppresses the healing dimension. According to one version of the Delphic myth, after the Pythoktonia, Apollo went for his purification to Karmanor in Tarrha (modern Agia Roumeli).[41] The oracle at Claros, according to local legend transmitted by Pausanias (7.3.2), was instituted by the Cretan Rhakios and his group, who settled in Colophon, where a group of Thebans and Teiresias' daughter Manto later arrived after being expelled by the Argives who took over Thebes; Rhakios married Manto and they had a son Mopsos.[42]

Moreover, in his narrative on the institution of the Pythian games, Pausanias presents an astonishing 'prehistory' (10.7.2–3):

> The oldest contest and the one for which they first offered prizes was, according to tradition (μνημονεύουσι), the singing of a hymn to the god. The man who sang and won the prize was (λέγεται) Chrysothemis of Crete, whose father Carmanor is said to have cleansed Apollo. After Chrysothemis, says tradition (μνημονεύουσι), Philammon won with a song, and after him his son Thamyris. But they say (φασί) that Orpheus, a proud man and conceited about his mysteries (σεμνολογίᾳ τῇ ἐπὶ τελεταῖς καὶ ὑπὸ φρονήματος τοῦ ἄλλου), and Musaeus, who copied Orpheus in everything, refused to submit to the competition in musical skill. (3) They say (φασί) too that Eleuther won a Pythian victory for his loud and sweet voice (μέγα καὶ ἡδὺ φωνοῦντα), for the song that he sang was not of his own composition (ἐπεὶ ᾄδειν γε αὐτὸν οὐχ αὑτοῦ τὴν ᾠδήν). The story is (λέγεται) that Hesiod too was debarred from competing because he had not learned to accompany his own singing on the harp (ἅτε οὐ κιθαρίζειν ὁμοῦ τῇ ᾠδῇ δεδιδαγμένον). Homer too came to Delphi to inquire about his needs, but even though he had

---

[41] Pausanias 2.7.7, 2.30.3; *Hypothesis* C to Pindar's *Pythians* (Drachmann p. 4) names Chrysothemis and not Karmanor as Apollo's purifier at Tarrha; Huxley 1975:122–124; Burkert 1992:42–46, 62–64; Sarinaki forthcoming.

[42] For another Manto (both appropriately named so, as their fathers were *manteis*) daughter of the *mantis* Polyidos (about whom Euripides wrote a tragedy), and other prophetesses, see Lyons 1999; she argues that their identity is flexible and open so as to become the communicative vehicle of god's prophecy.

learned to play the harp (καὶ κιθαρίζειν διδαχθέντι), he would have found the skill useless owing to the loss of his eye-sight.

translation Frazer 1965

Pausanias is very careful in his narrative. The repetition of verbs like μνημονεύουσι, λέγεται, and φασί indicates that all of this information belongs to the sphere of tradition (not exclusively oral) which is based on what people 'remember, say, allege.' Even so, the names included in and excluded from this legendary proto-victors-list at the Pythia are remarkable. The games originally started as a competition of hymns sung to Apollo and the first winner who was awarded a prize in the contest was Chrysothemis, son of Karmanor who purified Apollo, a name that might also serve as the god's epithet, the gold-*themis*-one.[43] After Philammon and his son Thamyris, the Thracian representatives, tradition mentioned two dissenting competitors rather than winners, none other than Orpheus and his follower Musaios. They refused to participate, because they were proud and conceited about the mysteries, which they presumably regarded as more crucial than a musical competition. Eleuther, the eponymous hero of Eleutherna and one of the Kouretes,[44] was next in this catalogue and introduced a novelty in the games: his winning the prize was completely on account of his singing performance, as the hymn he sang was composed by another poet, unlike, we may assume, the previous victors who performed their own compositions. Finally, Hesiod and Homer conclude this proto-catalogue as failures in the new contest: the former was refused admission to the competition, because he could not sing his hymn to the accompaniment of the kithara; the latter, although he had learned the new tricks of the trade, discovered the uselessness of playing the kithara, because of his blindness.

Admittedly, Pausanias' evidence is late and may have been filtered through the intervening centuries. A similar categorization, however, is found in Aristophanes' *Frogs*. Aeschylus argues for the utility of poetry and refers to the example set by noble poets of old: Orpheus and Musaios, Hesiod and Homer (1030–1036). He then contrasts this poetry with Euripides' poetry, specifically that which deals with Cretan matters (1039–1044). Pausanias' narrative indicates that, because of the institution of the Pythia, Delphi was instrumental during the archaic period in issues of musical competitions and poetics in

---

[43] The word, however, not attested as an epithet, is a name, for which see Bechtel 1917:472 and 580; and LGPN I, II, IIIA, IIIB, IV.

[44] On Kouretes as *oikistai* of various Cretan cities, see Strataridaki 1988–1989:160; Guizzi 2001:283–303; 2003; and for Eleuther, the section "The Cretan Context of the Cretan *Epistomia*."

general.[45] The legendary names in Pausanias' mythistoric catalogue appear as representatives of three distinctive trends in the poetics of the archaic period, rivaling one another in terms of form, content, and performance (not unlike Plato's four kinds of divine *mania* in *Timaeus*): Homer and Hesiod represent the epic tradition; Orpheus and Musaios stand for religious poetry; Chrysothemis, Philammon-Thamyris, and Eleuther, who are absent from Aristophanes' *Frogs* (see below) may stand in between epic, religious, and lyric poetry, genres which appear to hold a prominent place also in Crete. In that respect, Homer's and Hesiod's failure at Delphi and the corresponding success of the Cretan poets is remarkable.

Scattered pieces of information also imply that Crete was the homeland of other legendary figures who excelled in musical poetic compositions and dances, activities which were employed for purifications as well as other purposes. Pyrrhichos from Kydonia is, according to some sources, the inventor of the pyrrhic dance.[46] Nymphaios, from the same city, is mentioned together with Terpander, Thaletas of Gortyn, Tyrtaios, and Alcman, who, as *iatroi* and *kathartai*, visited Sparta according to a Delphic oracle in order to cleanse the city.[47] In particular, Thaletas of Gortyn, according to some Delphic oracle (κατά τι πυθόχρηστον), was called to Sparta as a traveling seer around 670 BCE in order to prevent a disease or plague and to cure Sparta, which he did successfully through his music;[48] the Cretans considered Thaletas to be the inventor of paeans and other local *odai*.[49] These pieces of information are late, but they

---

[45] For these and other Delphic activities, see de Araújo Caldas 2003 with the previous bibliography; for other oracles, see Rosenberger 2001.

[46] Stobaeus 4.2.25: καὶ τὴν ἐνόπλιον πυρρίχην ἐκπονοῦντες, ἥντινα πρῶτος εὗρε Πύρριχος Κυδωνιάτης [Κρὴς] τὸ γένος. According to Strabo, however, who is using Ephorus, *Koures* was the inventor (10.4.16): ἀσκεῖν δὲ καὶ τοξικῇ καὶ ἐνοπλίῳ ὀρχήσει, ἣν καταδεῖξαι Κουρῆτα πρῶτον, ὕστερον δὲ καὶ συντάξαντα τὴν κληθεῖσαν ἀπ' αὐτοῦ πυρρίχην (Lonsdale 1993:148–168); see also 166n50, 210n196. This dance survives today in the *pyrrhichios* (*Masherae*, Μαχαίρια or Ti *Masherí*, Τι Μαχαιρί') of the Greeks from Pontos, and in Ανωγειανός πηδηχτός, a rare Cretan dance at the village Anogeia.

[47] Aelian *Varia historia* 12.50: Λακεδαιμόνιοι μουσικῆς ἀπείρως εἶχον· ἔμελε γὰρ αὐτοῖς γυμνασίων καὶ ὅπλων. εἰ δέ ποτε ἐδεήθησαν τῆς ἐκ Μουσῶν ἐπικουρίας ἢ νοσήσαντες ἢ παραφρονήσαντες ἢ ἄλλο τι τοιοῦτον δημοσίᾳ παθόντες, μετεπέμποντο ξένους ἄνδρας οἷον ἰατροὺς ἢ καθαρτὰς κατὰ πυθόχρηστον. μετεπέμψαντό γε μὴν Τέρπανδρον καὶ Θάλητα καὶ Τυρταῖον καὶ τὸν Κυδωνιάτην Νυμφαῖον καὶ Ἀλκμᾶνα. Swindler 1913:48–53.

[48] Ps-Plutarch 1146b10–1147c1; Huxley 1975:122; Burkert 1992:42–46, 62–64; Rutherford 2001:24–26.

[49] Strabo 10.4.16 quoting Ephorus: ὡς δ' αὕτως καὶ τοῖς ῥυθμοῖς Κρητικοῖς χρῆσθαι κατὰ τὰς ᾠδὰς συντονωτάτοις οὖσιν οὓς Θάλητα ἀνευρεῖν, ᾧ καὶ τοὺς παιᾶνας καὶ τὰς ἄλλας τὰς ἐπιχωρίους ᾠδὰς ἀνατιθέασι καὶ πολλὰ τῶν νομίμων· καὶ ἐσθῆτι δὲ καὶ ὑποδέσει πολεμικῇ χρῆσθαι, καὶ

form part of the same traditions found in the *chorós* of Ariadne on Achilles' shield, fashioned by Hephaistos like the one by Daidalos in Knossos.[50]

Moreover, Eleutherna in particular (whence the twelve incised and unincised *epistomia*) was allegedly the home of Linos, one of Apollo's sons, and of Diogenes son of Apollothemis (*the themis of Apollo*), a physicist in the Ionian tradition and the last Presocratic alongside Democritus. Eleutherna is also reported to have changed its name to Apollonia, presumably in order to honor Apollo, although this name is not corroborated by the epigraphical evidence and it is possible that both names were employed interchangeably in nonepigraphical texts.[51] In Eleutherna, as Athenaios reports, Ametor (*the motherless one*) composed for the first time erotic *odai* to the accompaniment of the kithara and thus became the eponym of the Ametoridai.[52] The Ametoridai, like(?) the Homeridai (or Homeristai),[53] probably continued this tradition in their city and

---

τῶν δώρων τιμιώτατα αὐτοῖς εἶναι τὰ ὅπλα (Huxley 1975:122; Lebessi 1989; Burkert 1992:42–46, 62–64; and Rutherford 2001:24–26).

[50] *Iliad* 18.590–594; on the destructive potential of Ariadne's *chorós,* see Rinon 2006:10–12; on the association between the dance of Ariadne and the Dionysiac motifs on the shield see Sarinaki forthcoming; on the shield's poetics and audiences, see Hubbard 1992, Stanley 1993, Becker 1995, and Scully 2003 with previous bibliography; on the poetics of *choreia,* see Ladianou 2005. For the possible association of the dance with the labyrinth, see Obsomer 2003; and 165n46, 210n196. Kritzas (1992–1993:282–289) discusses in detail, and provides convincing parallels to, an inscription from the sanctuary of Asclepius in Lebena, Crete, dated to the second half of the second and early first century BCE, which records that the *neokoroi* moved from the precinct's adyton the *chorós,* a special construction for performances of dance and musical hymns, near the sanctuary's spring, sacred probably to Nymphs; see also Lonsdale 1993:114–121; for the *chorós* in Sparta see Kourinou 2000:114–124.

[51] Stephanus *Ethnica* 106 s.v. Ἀπολλωνία: κγ´ Κρήτης, ἡ πάλαι Ἐλεύθερνα, Λίνου πατρίς. ἐκ ταύτης ὁ φυσικὸς Διογένης, for whom see also: Diogenes Laertius 9.57: Διογένης Ἀπολλοθέμιδος Ἀπολλωνιάτης, ἀνὴρ φυσικὸς καὶ ἄγαν ἐλλόγιμος. ἤκουσε δέ, φησὶν Ἀντισθένης, Ἀναξιμένους. ἦν δὲ τοῖς χρόνοις κατ᾽ Ἀναξαγόραν. τοῦτόν φησιν ὁ Φαληρεὺς Δημήτριος ἐν τῇ Σωκράτους ἀπολογίᾳ διὰ μέγαν φθόνον μικροῦ κινδυνεῦσαι Ἀθήνησιν. For the cities in Crete named Apollonia, see Kitchell 1977:196–211. Diogenes was a contemporary of Anaxagoras and taught in Athens in the second half of the fifth century BCE, but Kirk, Raven, and Schofield (1988:431) prefer Miletos' colony Apollonia in the Euxine Pontus; compare Janko 1997 with previous bibliography, who discusses all previous proposals about the *PDerveni* author and concludes that he may have been either Diogenes, or one of his pupils, or Diagoras of Melos (Janko 2001); Burkert (1997) also finds affinities between Diogenes and the *PDerveni* author; see further Betegh 2004:306–321; and Kouremenos, Parássoglou, and Tsantsanoglou 2006:28–59.

[52] Athenaios *Deipnosophistai* 14.42: ἄλλοι δὲ πρῶτόν φασιν παρ᾽ Ἐλευθερναίοις κιθαρίσαι τὰς ἐρωτικὰς ᾠδὰς Ἀμήτορα τὸν Ἐλευθερναῖον, οὗ καὶ τοὺς ἀπογόνους Ἀμητορίδας καλεῖσθαι. Guizzi 2006; Stampolidis (2006) suggests that these may have been 'orphans' or foreigners (ἀ-μητρίς), whom the city encouraged to devote their lives to music, poetry, and *teletai,* whereas the non-orphaned children of the citizens were led to apply themselves to war and politics.

[53] Burkert 2001c and 2001d on Homeridai and Kreophyleioi.

abroad, as their name became a Cretan epithet denoting: *Cretan purificators and/ or kithara players* (ἀμητορίδας· καθαριστὰς Κρῆτες, ἢ κιθαριστάς). This explanation in an entry by Hesychius reveals what the poet in the *Hymn to Apollo* only hinted at when using the words *orgiones, paieones,* and *semantores.*

In the late seventh and early sixth centuries BCE, another Cretan, the most famous but equally enigmatic, Epimenides of Knossos or Phaistos,[54] under whose name a few fragments have survived, was also involved in activities similar to those not only of Karmanor and Thaletas, but also of Hesiod, the epic tradition, and the Presocratics. An intriguing and very active personality during the archaic period, he was presumably instrumental in much of the Greek perception of Crete and the Cretans, as the testimonia and the handful of fragments from his works indicate. The majority of the sources are admittedly late, the most extensive narrative being Plutarch's *Solon* and Diogenes Laertius'. But they all stress two areas of Epimenides' expertise, primarily in religious matters (Diodorus' passage above), but also in matters of poetics and their political ramifications. In the sources, the epithets employed to describe Epimenides are impressive: θεῖος, θεοφιλής, and θεοφιλέστατος ἀνήρ, ἱδρυτὴς ἱερῶν καὶ τελετῶν, ἱερεύς of Zeus and Rhea and Nymphs, νέος Κούρης, ῥιζοτόμος, μάντις, καθαρτής.[55] He is also ἐποποιός, νομοθέτης, and σοφός; composer of a *Theogony*, and many works in the epic manner (ἔγραψε δὲ πολλὰ ἐπικῶς· καὶ καταλογάδην μυστήριά τινα καὶ καθαρμοὺς καὶ ἄλλα αἰνιγματώδη),[56] which may have been antagonistic to Homer's and Hesiod's. Additionally, he is sometimes one of the Seven Sages,[57] whom Xenophanes crit-

---

[54] For fragments and testimonia, see *FGrHist* 457 (Jacoby); Strataridaki 1988:12–32, and 1991:207–217. Mele, Tortorelli Ghidini, Federico, and Visconti 2001, a collection of the 1999 proceedings of a seminar on Epimenides, brings up to date and presents a systematic and definitive discussion of all the issues surrounding this important Cretan sage and the impact his work may have had. For Diogenes Laertius' biography, see Gigante 2001. West's (1983:39–61) discussion of Epimenides and other legendary poets signifies that these mythistorical figures appear to have been in between Homeric and Orphic poetry and discourse; for Pamphos, also Durán 1996.

[55] Plato *Laws* 642d–e; Aristotle *Athenaion Politeia* 1; Diogenes Laertius 1.109; Plutarch *Solon* 12; *Suda*; Hershbell (2007) argues that Plutarch never visited Crete, but instead used Plato's text for matters Cretan. For Epimenides' contribution in matters funerary at Athens, see Garland 1989:4–5.

[56] Albeit a late source, the *Suda*'s characterization of a number of Epimenides' works as *riddling* recalls the *PDerveni* author who employs the same word and cognates to refer to the work of Orpheus (see 120n80). Willetts (1962:311) and Casadio (1994:173) view Epimenides as the Cretan Orpheus. For Epimenides' *Theogonia*, see Bernabé 2001, Breglia Pulci Doria 2001, and Arrighetti 2001; for the corpus *Epimenideum*, Mele 2001 and Tortorelli Ghidini 2001; for his expertise in *rhizotomia* and diet, Capriglione 2001.

[57] On the seven sages as traveling 'performers of wisdom,' see especially Martin 1993; for the Hellenistic catalogues of sages, see Broze, Busine, and Inowlocki 2006.

icized together with Thales and Pythagoras.[58] Epimenides' fame seems to have reached its peak when, in the beginning of the sixth century, the forty–sixth Olympiad (596–592 BCE), Delphi ordered him and gave him specific instructions how to purify Athens from the *Kyloneion agos* caused by the Alkmeonids.[59] His involvement in Athenian politics and his other reported travels serve as telling signs of his achievements and his status outside Crete, and his overall influence during the archaic period.

Concerning the foregoing discussion on perceptions of Crete and of the Cretans in literary sources, two specific contributions of Epimenides to the discourse on poetics and religious matters during the archaic period need to be emphasized.[60] The first relates to the rather well-known proverbial expression on Cretans always being liars.[61] This is already foreshadowed in Odysseus' and Demeter's tales/lies in the *Odyssey* and the *Hymn to Demeter* respectively. It may imply that this Cretan trait was widely known, but Epimenides appears to have been a crucial intermediary before this theme is quoted and commented upon by Callimachus and by the Apostle Paul.[62]

Callimachus, employing the traditional hymnic motif 'how to hymn you,' since people say you were born in Crete and Arcadia, apostrophizes

---

[58] For references to Epimenides' 'non-religious' activities, see Diogenes Laertius 1.109, 9.18, and Plutarch *Solon* 12.

[59] Diogenes Laertius 1.109–110; Herodotus 5.71; and Thucydides 1.126.2–127.1. Johnston (1999:279–286) proposes convincingly to view Epimenides' activity in Athens as similar to that of a *goes*. For the standard definition of *agos* and *miasma*, see Parker 1983:1–17; Burkert 1992:41–87; for the Athenian perspective in these sources, see Tortorelli Ghidini 2001, Federico 2001, Visconti 2001; for Epimenides' other visits, Lupi 2001.

[60] For Epimenides as magus, miracle-man, and shaman the sources again are late; Apuleius (*Apologia* 27: *partim autem, qui providentiam mundi curiosius vestigant et impensius deos celebrant, eos vero vulgo magos nominent, quasi facere etiam sciant quae sciant fieri, ut olim fuere Epimenides et Orpheus et Pythagoras et Ostanes, ac dein similiter suspectata Empedocli catharmoe, Socrati daemonion, Platonis* τὸ ἀγαθόν); Iamblichus (*Life of Pythagoras* 135–136 = Porphyry, *Life of Pythagoras* 2: μεταλαβόντας Ἐμπεδοκλέα τε τὸν Ἀκραγαντῖνον καὶ Ἐπιμενίδην τὸν Κρῆτα καὶ Ἄβαριν τὸν Ὑπερβόρειον πολλαχῇ καὶ αὐτοὺς τοιαῦτά τινα ἐπιτετελεκέναι. δῆλα δ' αὐτῶν τὰ ποιήματα ὑπάρχει, ἄλλως τε καὶ ἀλεξανέμας μὲν ὃν τὸ ἐπώνυμον Ἐμπεδοκλέους, καθαρτὴς δὲ τὸ Ἐπιμενίδου, αἰθροβάτης δὲ τὸ Ἀβάριδος); and Suda (s.v.). See especially the discussion in Dodds 1951:141–143; and Scarpi 2001. Kingsley's (1995) elaborate portrayal of Empedokles may also be applied, *mutatis mutandis,* to Epimenides, whose life and writings are parallel to the Sicilian sage. Svenbro (2002:204–216) discusses the proverbial *skin of Epimenides*, attested in the Suda, which does not separate the *corpus humain* from the *corpus écrit,* 'tattooed' with letters concerning *apotheta,* i.e. things secret or about mysteries (LSJ s.v. 2); on the skin guarded as a repository of written prophetic texts, see Dillery 2005. Verbruggen (1981) is overly cautious and assigns all information concerning Epimenides to inventions of the Hellenistic period, mainly Euhemerus and company; compare Chaniotis 1986, Grossardt 1998:282–293.

[61] For κρητίζειν and its variants, and other proverbs about Cretans, see Nikolaïdes 1989; and 177n89.

[62] Strataridaki 1988:21–26; 1991:217–223; Grossardt 1998:282–293.

(*Hymn to Zeus* 8–9): 'Κρῆτες ἀεὶ ψεῦσται'· καὶ γὰρ τάφον, ὦ ἄνα, σεῖο | Κρῆτες ἐτεκτήναντο· σὺ δ' οὐ θάνες, ἐσσὶ γὰρ αἰεί.[63] Callimachus challenges the Cretan belief in Zeus' death and rebirth, and the Cretans' construction of Zeus' tomb, variously located in Ida and Dikte.[64] Although only the Cretans are credited with this belief, in the rest of Greece (as well as in the East and in Egypt) such a belief was not completely unacceptable. Some gods, but never Zeus, followed nature's cycle of reproduction and fertility. Among them, Dionysos was prominent, who, according to Herodotus (2.42.2, 144.2), was none other than the Egyptian Osiris.[65] The Cretan challenge to Olympian orthodoxy, Zeus Kretagenes, is none other than the chthonic Dionysos in the rest of Greece, one of the gods encountered in the gold incised lamellae.[66] The Cretan paradox,[67] an eternal divinity that nevertheless dies and is reborn, is explained away by Callimachus as *the biggest lie ever told by Cretans*.[68] Callimachus quotes the beginning of Epimenides' hexameter, a poem within a poem, in order to establish firmly his poetry, first within the genre,[69] and then in relation to his predecessors, among whom is Epimenides (both an epic poet and a representative of Cretan poetics in general).[70]

---

[63] For the discussion of Callimachus, I am indebted to Sarinaki forthcoming.

[64] Clemens *Stromateis* 1.14.59. For the *Hymn to Zeus*, see McLennan 1997; Hopkinson 1984; Haslam 1993; Depew 1993; for poetic and divine performance, Henrichs 1993b; and for its geography, Sistakou 2005:92–98; for Callimachus' *Hymns* and the Homeric and epigraphical ones, see Vamvouri Ruffy 2004; for Callimachus' utilization of Cretan myths and rituals and his knowledge of matters Cretan, see Chaniotis 2001b; and 204n177, 218–219 with n231. For Hesiod's narrative incorporating more than one tradition of Zeus' birth in various Cretan caves, see O'Bryhim 1997. Sometimes Mount Youkhtas is also mentioned in the secondary bibliography as Zeus' birth-place for which see Zoes 1996:337–398; Sakellarakis and Sapouna-Sakellaraki 1997:49–51; and Karetsou 2003; for the literary use of this theme from the fourth century BCE onwards, see Kokolakis 1995a and 1995b; West 1997b; and Postlethwaite 1999.

[65] The Argive tradition for Ariadne mentions Dionysos Κρήσιος (Pausanias 2.23.7–8), for which see the discussion in Casadio 1994:123–222; and Piérart 1996. For Herodotus and his treatment of Egyptian religious ideas, see Zographou 1995. Zeus Kretagenes and his cult, supposedly brought by Cretan immigrants in the Seleucid empire, was adopted by Seleukos as one of the most important royal gods (Mastrocinque 2002). See further Willetts 1962:199–227; Verbruggen 1981; Chaniotis 1986; Kokolakis 1995a and 1995b; Postlethwaite 1999; on the distinction between Olympian and Chthonian, see Scullion 1994, and on heroic and chthonian, Scullion 2000a.

[66] For Epimenides and Orpheus as mythic poets, victims of the Muses, and scapegoats, see Compton 2006:174–180.

[67] Strataridaki (1998:352–358) discusses the narrative of Theopompus of Chios (*FGrH* 2 B 115 F76a) on Epimenides' sleep which lasted fifty-seven years, where the idea of time as a relative quantity is introduced; time "passes with different rates for different people" (158).

[68] For Epimenides' line, see 172n76.

[69] Depew 1993:72–73 on the ambiguity of the *Hymn's* claim to truth.

[70] See below, 173–175.

In a different vein, the Apostle Paul in his Epistle to Titus quotes the whole hexameter from Epimenides' work of oracles(?), in order to scoff at the attitude of all the Cretans towards his disciple Titus and his preaching (1.12–13):[71] εἶπέν τις ἐξ αὐτῶν (scil. τῶν Κρητῶν), ἴδιος αὐτῶν προφήτης· 'Κρῆτες ἀεὶ ψεῦσται, κακὰ θηρία, γαστέρες ἀργαί·' ἡ μαρτυρία αὕτη ἐστὶν ἀληθής. Titus, the first bishop and founder of a Christian community in Crete, probably at Gortyn, got himself into trouble trying to proselytize the pagan Cretans of the first century CE. He is thus admonished by Paul and advised how to argue his case and accomplish his extremely daunting task against the Cretans, renowned (even by their own prophet) as liars, ugly wild beasts, and idle bellies. Clement of Alexandria, however, when he mentions Epimenides in his catalogue of the Seven Sages, opens a parenthesis and refers to Paul's statement in order to prove that some Greek prophets knew part of the 'real truth' that pagan gods were not immortal after all. Thus, Clement advises, Greek texts may be used without shame, because Paul (First Epistle to the Corinthians 15.32–34) acted similarly on another occasion and quoted a Euripidean trimeter, when preaching to the Corinthians about the resurrection of the dead.[72]

Unfortunately, neither Callimachus nor Paul is of any help regarding the context of Epimenides' hexameter, even though Clement's argument is rather straightforward. There is no way of determining whether the new context is compatible with the old, or whether the work of Epimenides, from which comes the hexameter, also treated issues of truth and lying. For this is the reason why both Callimachus and Paul are utilising Epimenides' hexameter in the first place, a situation where a Cretan mouth undermines and subverts Cretan claims to truth: Callimachus for the purpose of undermining the preposterous story about Zeus' death and for the poets' lies about Zeus' sphere of influence; Paul for the purpose of establishing Cretan unreliability in general.

---

[71] According to Hieronymos' commentary on Paul's Epistle to Titus (VII p. 606 Migne), which implies that the commentator had Epimenides' book of oracles in his library: *dicitur autem iste versiculus in Epimenidis Cretensis poetae oraculis reperiri ... denique ipse liber Oraculorum titulo praenotatur.*

[72] *Stromateis* 1.14.59.2–4: οἱ δὲ Ἐπιμενίδην τὸν Κρῆτα [ὃν Ἑλληνικὸν οἶδε προφήτην,] οὗ μέμνηται ὁ ἀπόστολος Παῦλος ἐν τῇ πρὸς Τίτον ἐπιστολῇ, λέγων οὕτως· "εἶπέν τις ἐξ αὐτῶν ἴδιος προφήτης οὕτως· 'Κρῆτες ἀεὶ ψεῦσται, κακὰ θηρία, γαστέρες ἀργαί·' καὶ ἡ μαρτυρία αὕτη ἐστὶν ἀληθής." ὁρᾷς ὅπως κἂν τοῖς Ἑλλήνων προφήταις δίδωσί τι τῆς ἀληθείας καὶ οὐκ ἐπαισχύνεται πρός τε οἰκοδομὴν καὶ πρὸς ἐντροπὴν διαλεγόμενός τινων Ἑλληνικοῖς συγχρῆσθαι ποιήμασι; πρὸς γοῦν Κορινθίους, οὐ γὰρ ἐνταῦθα μόνον, περὶ τῆς τῶν νεκρῶν ἀναστάσεως διαλεγόμενος ἰαμβείῳ συγκέχρηται τραγικῷ "τί μοι ὄφελος;" λέγων, "εἰ νεκροὶ οὐκ ἐγείρονται, φάγωμεν καὶ πίωμεν· αὔριον γὰρ ἀποθνήσκομεν. μὴ πλανᾶσθε· 'φθείρουσιν ἤδη χρηστὰ ὁμιλίαι κακαί.'" For discussion of more references to Epimenides in patristic texts, see Tortorelli Ghidini 2001:70–74.

Interestingly, however, the composition of Callimachus'/Epimenides' hexameter echoes the one in Hesiod's *Theogony*, where again the issue of lies and truth surfaces. In the poet's *Dichterweihe*, the Muses scorn the shepherds (26–28):

> ποιμένες ἄγραυλοι, κάκ' ἐλέγχεα, γαστέρες οἶον,
> ἴδμεν ψεύδεα πολλὰ λέγειν ἐτύμοισιν ὁμοῖα,
> ἴδμεν δ' εὖτ' ἐθέλωμεν ἀληθέα γηρύσασθαι

field-dwelling shepherds, ignoble disgraces, mere bellies: we know how to say many false things similar to genuine ones, but we know when we wish to proclaim true things.[73]

translation Most 2006

These lines by the Muses are not unique; they are also employed in Odyssean poetics. Before Odysseus/Aithon performs his third Cretan tale/lie in front of Penelope, he has an exchange with the suitors, who chastise his *gaster* in a manner like the Muses censure the shepherds (*Odyssey* 18.364 and 18.380 respectively).[74] Immediately after the tale, the poet describes Odysseus' performance exactly as Hesiod's Muses describe their poetry (19.203): ἴσκε ψεύδεα πολλὰ λέγων ἐτύμοισιν ὁμοῖα. Odysseus' poetics in the *Odyssey* and the poetics of the Muses in the *Theogony* are part and parcel of the same tradition. Furthermore, Hesiod's and Epimenides' lives, before their divine instruction, were parallel. Both were shepherds who encountered the divine and were transformed. But unlike the Boeotian, who became a poet, the Cretan, entering a cave, became mysteriously, among other things, a poet, *kathartes*, founder of sanctuaries (most beloved by the gods), a diviner, and above all else a new *Koures*,[75] a Cretan Zeus.

Although the *persona loquens* is unknown, Epimenides' hexameter, *the Cretans are always liars*, which looks like a sophistic argument in terms of its logical construction, may very well betray the Cretans' emphasis on the ambivalence of poetics and, in particular, Epimenides' own poetics. This statement, provided that it refers to *the biggest Cretan lie ever told*, that Zeus dies and

---

[73] Leclerc 1992; for Epimenides' literary *Theogonia* in comparison to that of Hesiod's Arrighetti 2001:222–223 and passim.

[74] On this line, see Katz and Volk 2000 with the previous bibliography; Pucci 1977; Pratt 1993; and Sarinaki forthcoming. On Aithon/Odysseus, a good heroic name that applies to the situation the hero faces with interesting connotations, see the cogent analysis of Levaniouk 2000. Ross (2005) argues that the use of *barbarophonos* language in early epic is a marker of a nascent Panhellenism, alterity, or of exotic places and people (among them Crete).

[75] Diogenes Laertius 1.109–115.

is reborn every year, is liable to be interpreted in at least two ways: *prima facie*, the Cretans are always liars, so Zeus is eternal; or self-referentially, the Cretans are always liars; I, Epimenides, am a Cretan, so do not believe anything I say; Zeus dies and is reborn.[76] Neither Callimachus nor Paul, however, understood Epimenides' hexameter self-referentially, that is as a programmatic statement of Cretan poetics that are at work in Odysseus' and Demeter's tales in the *Odyssey* and in the *Hymn* respectively; nor did they understand it as a general programmatic statement concerning the poetics of Homer, Hesiod, and the *Hymns'* poets.

The second important element in Epimenides' career is his relation to Delphi and his expertise in prophecy, although only Paul and other Christian Fathers call him a *prophetes*, probably in order to associate him with the more familiar, and therefore easier to understand, Biblical prophets.[77] Both Pausanias (2.21.3) and Aristotle (*Rhetoric* 1418a21–26) employ the verb *manteuomai* for one of Epimenides' activities,[78] and Diogenes Laertius calls him <προ>γνωστικώτατον (1.114).[79] However rare, this epithet mainly refers to the Hippocratic *prognosis*,[80] a process very much like Epimenides' divinatory activity. Among the various reports on how Epimenides cleansed Athens, Diogenes Laertius notes (1.110): οἱ δὲ τὴν αἰτίαν εἰπεῖν τοῦ λοιμοῦ τὸ Κυλώνειον ἄγος σημαίνειν τε τὴν ἀπαλλαγήν.[81] *Semainein* is exactly the verb employed by Herakleitos for Apollo's activity at Delphi, whereas *semantores* is the word Apollo uses to describe his Cretan (proto-) priests, and the word Demeter uses to describe her Cretan abductors in the gods' respective *Hymns*. But this is not all. Epimenides' prophetic power is of a particular kind, as Aristotle comments in his *Rhetoric*, taking into account Epimenides' own writings (1418a21–26):[82]

---

[76] On this line, see Strataridaki 1991; Leclerc 1992; Tortorelli Ghidini 2001:70–74; Catarzi 2001; and Casertano 2001.

[77] Tortorelli Ghidini 2001:73–74. On Epimenides' prophecy to the Athenians about the Persian danger (Plato *Laws* 642d–e; compare 707b–c), see Pugliese Carratelli 1974 and Viviers 1995.

[78] Strataridaki (2003) discusses the etymology of the name Epimenides from *mania*.

[79] For the emendation proposed by Reiske, see Gigante 2001:16.

[80] LSJ s.v.; the results of a *Thesaurus Linguae Graecae* search are indicative as the word and cognates appear mainly in medical authors.

[81] On disease as pollution, see Parker 1983:2; Sophocles' *Oedipus Tyrannus* is also revealing for the limits of human knowledge, a topic hotly debated by the Presocratics (Liapis 2003). See further Gigante 2001:16; Tortorelli Ghidini 2001:74–75.

[82] Loscalzo (2003) briefly discusses Aristotle's comment on Epimenides' non-prophetic activity in relation to Hesiod's *Theogony* 31–32, the latter of which he translates "le cose che sarebbero state e quelle che furono" (363); compare, however, Clay (2003:65–67): "the things that will be in the future and have been in the past are the eternal things, that is, the *genos aien eonton*" (66), in comparison a few lines later to *ta eonta*, the human race.

Deliberative speaking is more difficult than forensic, and naturally so, because it has to do with the future; whereas forensic speaking has to do with the past, which is already known, even by diviners (ὃ ἐπιστητὸν ἤδη καὶ τοῖς μάντεσιν), as Epimenides the Cretan said; for he used to divine (ἐμαντεύετο), not the future (περὶ τῶν ἐσομένων), but only things that were past but obscure (περὶ τῶν γεγονότων μὲν ἀδήλων δέ).

translation Freese 1926

Aristotle's aside concerning the way in which Epimenides understood *mantike* may also be relevant to Delphi, or to any divinatory activity. Lisa Maurizio has argued convincingly that:[83]

the presence of Mnemosyne and the Underworld in the prophetic geography at Delphi links oracular knowledge about the future to the past and an otherwordly place ... Mnemosyne at Delphi makes evident the simultaneity of past, present and future at Delphi, just as oracles do in narrative ... The presence of the Underworld, then, emphasizes Delphi's already other-worldly dimensions, removing it further in space and time from its geographical and historical surroundings.

Moreover, Plutarch calls Epimenides (*Solon* 12.1): θεοφιλὴς καὶ σοφὸς περὶ τὰ θεῖα τὴν ἐνθουσιαστικὴν καὶ τελεστικὴν σοφίαν, a statement best elucidated in Plato's *Timaeus* and *Phaedrus* on *mania* quoted above (144–146), and in Cicero's *de divinatione* (1.xviii.34). Plutarch's *enthousiastic* and *telestic* wisdom of Epimenides, i.e. wisdom acquired through a god entering the body and through initiation rites, is explicated by Cicero's account of the two kinds of divination, the one with and the other without art. The former relies on rational conjecture and observation (*observatione, coniectura*), Plutarch's telestic wisdom; the latter on an esoteric movement of the spirit that happens while dreaming or through *mania* (*concitatione quadam animi aut soluto liberoque motu futura praesentiunt*), Plutarch's *enthousiastic* wisdom. Oracles received from the casting of dice constitute a third category, because, Cicero conjectures, these too require some divine action for the dice to fall in the way they do. Cicero, however, *contra* Aristotle, groups Epimenides together with Bacis and the

---

[83] Maurizio 1999:154–155 and passim for the complementarity of Delphic narratives and ritual conventions. I would only add that Dionysos' presence at Delphi during the winter is the concrete manifestation of the otherworldly dimension of Delphi and another expression of the intimate relation between Underworld and prophecy.

Sybil, all three being representatives of the dreaming and manic prophecy (*per furorem*), but at the same time, he emphasizes that all oracles, regardless of the way acquired, need their *interpretes*, just like poetry needs its *grammatici poëtarum* (philologists), whose activity thus comes very close to that of the seers, and ultimately to that of the divine spirit.

The case of Epimenides, sometimes seen as one of the Seven Sages, appears to be unique. A late source (Maximus Tyrius *Dissertations* 10.1) relates a detail not mentioned in either of the longer accounts on Epimenides (Diogenes Laertius and Plutarch): the Cretan sage and seer fell into a deep, deathlike sleep that lasted a number of years inside a cave, where he had a dream. During this dream, he underwent instruction by the gods he met and talked with, of whom two are mentioned by name, Aletheia and Dike. Epimenides' sleeping experience produces a metamorphosis. The mortal Epimenides appears not to have simply attained the status of a hero, as does Hesiod in Oinoe, but to have become Zeus himself; hence his title *(new) Koures*. This detail about Epimenides inspired Marcel Detienne's persuasive discussion of the workings of *aletheia*, *lethe*, and *mnemosyne* and their complementary nature during the archaic period. *Aletheia*, *lethe*, and *mnemosyne* relate in a special manner to Epimenides' self-instruction during his dream in the cave, and to Hesiod's Nereus, the old man of the sea. Three different spheres dominate archaic society and archaic thought: poetry, prophecy, and justice. As Detienne argues: "Poet, diviner, and king of justice were certainly masters of speech, speech defined by *the same concept of Aletheia*" (my emphasis).[84] Epimenides is presented as the flesh and blood of what Detienne calls the "philosophico-religious sects" and participates in a unique way in the archaic discourse on poetics, prophecy, and politics.[85] This discourse is based on the opposition of *lethe* versus *mnemosyne*, an opposition concretely represented by the poets/composers of the texts on the gold lamellae and *epistomia* as a topography with two springs/lakes whose water when drunk effects either *lethe* or *mnemosyne* respectively (Detienne 1996:124):

> While the conversation with Aletheia signified Epimenides' gift of second sight, similar to that of a diviner, it also confirmed a *melete* whose goal was to escape time and attain a level of reality char-

---

[84] Detienne 1996:67, 53–67.

[85] 'Sect' may be a misleading word in that it may imply homogeneity and unison of a specific group of people who promote the same views and teachings (Detienne 2003:156–157 repeats this); the texts on the gold lamellae, however, suggest otherwise, as has been argued above; see further Burkert 1982; and Graf and Johnston 2007:94–164.

acterized by its opposition to Lethe. Once he entered into *contact with Aletheia, Epimenides acceded to an intimacy with the gods strictly analogous to the divine status of the initiate of the "tablets of gold," when he is able to drink the fresh water of Lake Memory.* The level of Aletheia is divine: it is characterized by intemporality and stability (my emphasis).

Detienne further observes similarities between the thought of Epimenides and Parmenides (both of whom stand close to this godlike state), but he also points to a major difference:[86]

The magus had lived apart from the polis, on the periphery of society, but the philosopher, by contrast, was subject to the urban regime and therefore to the demands of publicity. He was obliged to leave the sanctuary of revelation: the gods gave him Aletheia, but at the same time, his truth was open to challenge if not to verification.

And yet, Detienne's dichotomy between magus and philosopher is neither as strong nor as categorical as his previous distinction between *lethe* and *mnemosyne*. Except for his instruction while dreaming inside the cave, Epimenides appears nowhere to be living "apart from the polis and on the periphery of society, in a revelatory sanctuary."[87] On the contrary, he is participating, traveling, cleansing, conversing, and performing in Crete, in Athens, and probably elsewhere. Richard Martin has argued persuasively in his study of the Seven Sages that, in addition to special skill and knowledge in poetry, religious matters, and politics, there is a fourth hallmark of all the Seven Sages: performance, defined as:

public enactment, about important matters, in word or gesture, employing conventions and open to scrutiny and criticism, especially criticism of style. Performance can include what we call art. But as can be shown by the ethnographic record, it can also include such things as formalized greetings exchanged by chieftains, rituals,

---

[86] Detienne 1996:130–133 (the quotation from page 133). Epimenides and his activities are much closer to Empedokles than Parmenides, according to Kingsley's (1995) argument for Empedokles. Mourelatos (2002, especially 1–50) argues that Parmenides was a child of his epoch: he worked within the epic tradition and was influenced by the ideas current in the archaic period, transforming, altering and presenting his own original proposal through the journey of the Kouros; see also Cassio 1996; and 114n56.

[87] Giangiulio (1995) discusses the tension within the polis between Pythagorean wisdom and Apollonian religion.

insult duels, and the recitation of genealogies. Some megaperformances involve several of these smaller types.

Martin 1993:115–116

Performance is by nature agonistic and therefore presupposes more than one sage competing with another, whence the group of the Seven Sages. Their tradition in Greece may be paralleled with the ones in the Babylonian epic of Gilgamesh and in the Sanskrit Vedas.[88] Indeed, it seems that the Sages' activity, whether political, poetical-musical-philosophical, or religious, required a competitive performative approach which publicly showcased their expert opinions, opinions not always or exclusively directed against fellow-sages. This was a risky business for the emerging polis, which was trying to integrate these 'masters of truth' by transforming them into:

> such civic bodies as the *gerousia* in Sparta or the *exegetai* in Athens. At the same, an extrapolitical form of the institution (sc. of the Seven Sages) could have continued to function at common sanctuaries such as Didyma and Delphi, in a form that emphasized sacrificial expertise and, hence, generalized "moral" teaching.

Martin 1993:123

Martin also proposes, using Nagy's (1990b:143–145) model of "Panhellenizing-internationalizing," that:

---

[88] Martin 1993:120–123. Detienne (1996:119–120 and 205nn73–74) advanced the following formulation: "At the end of the sixth century, certain circles in Greece witnessed the birth of a type of philosophical and religious thought absolutely opposed to that of the Sophists. The thought of the Sophists was secularized, directed toward the external world, and founded on *praxis*, while the other was religious, introverted, and concerned with individual salvation. Whereas the Sophists, as a particular type of individual and as representative of a certain form of thought, were the sons of the city, and their aim, within an essentially political framework, was to influence others, the magi and initiates lived on the periphery of the city, aspiring only to an altogether internal transformation. The diametrically opposed aims of the two groups were matched by their radically different techniques. While the mental techniques of sophistry and rhetoric marked an abrupt break with the forms of religious thought that preceded the emergence of Greek reason, the philosophicoreligious sects, in contrast, adopted procedures and modes of thought that directly prolonged earlier religious thought. At this level, among the values that *mutatis mutandis* continued to play the same important role as in earlier thought, memory and *Aletheia* held a recognized position." This is only partly true, however, as it is based primarily on the polis criterion, according to which philosophicoreligious thought allegedly paid little, if any, attention to politics. But the Athenian dramatic festivals, during which prophets and *manteis* performed, the meetings of the Areopagus Council, the Eleusinian Mysteries, the *exegetai*, and so on, are these not philosophicoreligious discourses at the heart of the city? In the Roman period things are complicated even further, as Chaniotis (2003) shows.

the competition among sages (as local ritual experts) in a tribal context would have been incompatible with the ideological strains in the emerging polis that encouraged unification and hierarchy. Therefore, it could be "internationalized" into a long-distance competition between, for instance, the local "sages" such as Solon and Thales, who earlier had "competed" only with other wise men of their own region.

Martin 1993:123

Where do these trends of rationalizing, secularizing, hierarchizing and internationalizing-Panhellenizing within Greek poleis leave Epimenides? The Cretan presents his own poetic compositions, rivaling(?) the Homeric and Hesiodic ones, and he proposes a Cretan or Epimenidean method concerning oracles and divination. His prophetic *sophia* that earned him fame beyond Crete is based on astutely observing the past, especially the events' latent dimensions which have ramifications for the present, and his intimate association with Koures may have been responsible for the proverbial "mouth of the Kouretes."[89] This concept of divinatory practice may very well have been Epimenides' criticism of Delphic hyperbole and propaganda, although, in all the sources, he appears to comply fully and in every detail with Delphic demands and pronouncements. That Epimenides was critical *vis à vis* Delphi, especially concerning the Delphic *omphalos*, is recorded by Plutarch (*The Obsolescence of Oracles* 409e–f):[90]

The story is told (μυθολογοῦσιν), my dear Terentius Priscus, that certain eagles or swans, flying from the uttermost parts of the earth towards its centre, met in Delphi at the *omphalos*, as it is called; and at a later time Epimenides of Phaistos put the story to test (ἐλέγχοντα τὸν μῦθον) by referring it to the god and upon receiving a vague and ambiguous oracle (χρησμὸν ἀσαφῆ καὶ ἀμφίβολον) said: "Now do we know that there is no mid-centre of earth or of ocean; yet if there be, it is known (δῆλος) to the gods, but is hidden (ἄφαντος) from mortals."

translation Babbitt 1936

---

[89] The proverb in *CPG* I: Diogenianus v.60: Κουρήτων στόμα· ἐπὶ τῶν μαντεύεσθαι ὑπισχνουμένων· τοιοῦτοι γὰρ οὗτοι; and in *CPG* II: Apostolius ix.95, where it is added: μαντικοὶ γὰρ οἱ Κρῆτες; and 168n61.

[90] Defradas 1972:102–110; Sourvinou-Inwood 1987:233–235.

The famous story that Delphi is the navel of the earth, absent from the *Homeric Hymn to Apollo*, was decided by the meeting at the so-called *omphalos* of two birds flying in opposite directions, whence the oracle of Apollo. According to Epimenides' *elenchos*, this story is also found wanting. There is no such thing as a middle point, an *omphalos* of the earth or of the sea; and even if there were, it would be visible only to gods and not mortals. The other famous stone at Delphi, related in the *Theogony* (497–500), is the one Rhea gave to Cronus instead of Zeus and which, after Cronus regurgitated it, was then placed at Delphi as a *sema*.[91] The two stories seem parallel. What is striking is that this two-hexameter-declaration constitutes Epimenides' reply to an ambiguous and dubious oracle he received from Delphi. This is unique, as there is no other metrical response to a Delphic oracle, on account of the oracle's ambiguity and uncertainty (which are traits of Apollo's speech *par excellence*). It is clear that in his reply, the Cretan sage is posturing against and competing with the Delphic priesthood and their propaganda.[92] The *omphalos* story may have been an attempt at minimizing, or at severing Delphi's Cretan connections, among which the stone/Zeus *sema* was an old and revered object, sanctioned by epic poetry. After all, as the story goes,[93] Epimenides was self-styled Aiakos and son of Selene, while his fellow-Cretans hailed him as the *(new) Koures*.

Be that as it may, during the archaic period, a formative period in many respects, 'Crete and the Cretans' acquired various characteristics that in later times became canonized.[94] 'Crete and the Cretans,' so it appears, evolved into a *topos* or trope of sorts in literary texts and the reasons for this are many and multidimensional.

First, 'Crete and the Cretans' is convenient. The island is located in the middle of nowhere, at a reassuring and safe distance that may be perceived both as a center-point in the Mediterranean and part of the periphery of mainland Greece, as the poet of the *Odyssey* aptly puts it (19.172–173): Κρήτη τις γαῖ' ἔστι μέσῳ ἐνὶ οἴνοπι πόντῳ, | καλὴ καὶ πίειρα, περίρρυτος.

---

[91] For the Boeotian tradition (Pausanias 9.2.7; 9.41.6), see West 1966:301.

[92] For the legendary Aesop's critical stance towards Delphi, see Kurke 2003.

[93] Diogenes Laertius 1.114–115; Plutarch *Solon* 12.7; Aelian *De natura animalium* 12.7.

[94] Morris (1992:150–194 and passim) eloquently discusses Crete's place in the emerging Greek world, for which Athens, especially after the Persian Wars, was instrumental: "the creation of Athens through mythology not only involved amplifying a scanty local tradition, but appropriating or undermining other mythologies" (386). For the Kimonian monuments, see Castriota 1992:58-63; on the relation of Crete and Athens, especially as regards the Persian Wars, see Viviers 1995; and for economic pressure on Crete by the nascent Athenian Empire after the Persian Wars, see Erickson 2005.

Secondly, 'Crete and the Cretans' is or may easily become a wonderland because of its distance and its real or imaginary antiquity, "une terre aussi exemplaire que marginale" (Calame 1996:233): mortals meet gods by habit; gods die and are buried; mortals proclaim their divine status (Minos, Aiakos, Rhadamanthys and Epimenides receiving special treatment and stories); strange creatures live there, like the Minos-bull; what the rest of the Greeks call "mysteries" are not mysteries there at all.

Finally, the Cretans inhabiting a large and mountainous island assume all the concomitant virtues and vices: running, archery, ambush, trade, and piracy. These traits, which also imply outside contacts, naturally force the Cretans to 'construct' an exceptional image of themselves, of their beliefs, and of their land, all in a unique way; hence their epithets *orgiones, paieones, and semantores*. Morris argues that, "at some point, Crete exported religion as well as craftsmanship and constitutional reforms."[95] The Cretans, if Pausanias' mythistoric narrative of the institution of the Pythian games is to be trusted, appear to have been unique in combining two, if not all three, otherwise distinct 'genres'/discourses in vogue during the archaic period: *orgia, paeans,* and *theo-cosmogonies*, or sacred, lyric, and epic poetry, all emblematic of the activities of the legendary Epimenides.

Be it real or imaginary, this is the perception of 'Crete and the Cretans' emerging from the texts discussed above, a perception that appears to continue well into the fourth century BCE, as is attested by Plato's *Cretan city* and Aristotle's works.[96] 'Crete and the Cretans' is one of the repositories for the performance of discourses on sacred-secular poetics and music,[97] and on politics and religious matters, but it differs from comparable discourses elsewhere in Greece. These discourses in Crete, so it appears, did not undergo (or the Cretans did not care to let them undergo) a process of rationalization, secularization, and internationalization-Panhellenization that other Greek poleis, principally Athens, experienced. These processes appear to have been too Athenian to accommodate matters Cretan.

How real or imaginary this perception was and to what extent, if any, it influenced Greek affairs are legitimate questions to ask, but answers to them must inevitably remain speculative. This tension between real and imaginary is particularly true in the case of Euripides' manipulation of 'Crete and the

---

[95] Morris 1992:170.

[96] Panagopoulos 1981 and 1987; Mandalaki 2000.

[97] The distinction between secular and sacred/religious poetry was not drawn in antiquity, as Parker (1996:77–78) has shown.

Cretans' in a number of tragedies he presented in the Athenian theatre in the second half of the fifth century BCE. *Cretans, Cretan Women, Polyidos,* and (to an extent) *Hippolytos* are compositions which either are based on or employ Cretan mythological topics and themes. Aeschylus and Sophocles did not shy away from 'Cretan' material, but only titles of their works survive: *Cretan Women* (Aeschylus), and *Manteis* and *Kamikoi* (Sophocles).[98]

The *Hypothesis* dates Euripides' *Hippolytos* to 428 BCE, and the *Cretan Women* (the first tragedy in the tetralogy that closed with *Alcestis*) to 438 BCE, while the *Cretans* is dated between 442 and 432 BCE.[99] For the present discussion, Euripides' *Hippolytos*, performed after the *Cretans* and the *Cretan Women*, is interesting for two reasons. First, the tragedian seems to employ, in a tangential manner, all of the conventional and expected perceptions of 'Crete and the Cretans' developed in the archaic period: sailing, lascivious women, and lying. To this list, Elizabeth Craik has added references to 'Cretan' initiation rites into manhood, citizenship, and marriage, in which Artemis and Zeus held a prominent place.[100] Admittedly, these references may show a 'Cretan tinge' in the *Hippolytos*, especially in relation to Phaedra, but they are definitely not decisive. The tragedians, especially Euripides, improvise within the literary context of a particular tragedy and, in certain cases, even 'invent' rituals and cults. Thus, in *Hippolytos* 141–150 the Chorus' references to Pan, Hekate, the Korybantes, and the Mountain Mother as divinities that may have 'possessed' Phaedra, and to Diktynna, whose rites Phaedra may have neglected, in order to

---

[98] Collard, Cropp, and Lee 1995:53–59, especially 59; Calame 1996:98–112; Mills 1997:223–225; and Cozzoli 2001:9–18; on the *Kamikoi*, see Zacharia 2004.

[99] In her valuable and extensive commentary Cozzoli (2001:9–11) revisited the dating issue and proposed this decade.

[100] Craik 2002:59–65; she argues that (65): "Euripides shows the same interest in, and knowledge of, the practices, especially cult practices, of distant places as is evinced in the later *Helen* and *IT.* Here Phaidra's Cretan background is the starting point for allusive deployment of a wide range of Cretan cult practice, highly relevant to Hippolytos' tragedy; this extra dimension enhances the intellectual appeal, emotional charge and poetic texture of the play." The fact that Artemis was worshipped in various Cretan cities and under various cultic epithets cannot be direct evidence for Euripides' *knowledge of* Cretan cultic practice, as Sporn's (2002:383–384) table for Artemis-Britomartis-Diktynna worship in Crete reveals. The myths, however, of the exclusively Cretan deities, like Ariadne or Diktynna/Britomatis, may indeed have had wider circulation. Compare Willetts' (1962:185) careful formulation about the cult of Artemis Orthia, Limnatis, Agrotera, and Craik's (2002:61) discussion. Craik (2002:60), however, rightly corrects Barrett (1964:390 with n5), who comments that lines 1252–1254: οὐδ' εἰ γυναικῶν πᾶν κρεμασθείη γένος | καὶ τὴν ἐν Ἴδηι γραμμάτων πλήσειέ τις | πεύκην, refer to Mount Ida not in Crete but in the Troad; not only the stories about Epimenides and Zeus' Cave on Ida, but Euripides' own *Cretan Women, Cretans,* and *Polyidos* support the reference to Cretan Ida. For *Hippolytos*, see Walker 1995:Chapter 4 and Mills 1997:186–221.

explain Phaedra's behavior, perhaps point to 'Cretan' connections. But which connections and what kind of connections are totally beyond recovery. As Scot Scullion and Francis Dunn have shown convincingly in relation to Euripidean aetiologies,[101] tragedy and ritual, especially Euripidean tragedies and cult practices, are not always what they seem to be at first glance. Their interconnection and interdependence are so intertwined that they are not easily detectable, except in very general and not always useful terms.[102] The second issue that *Hippolytos* raises, relevant to the present discussion, is in the *agon* between father and son, when Theseus apostrophizes (*Hippolytos* 952–954):

> ἤδη νυν αὔχει καὶ δι' ἀψύχου βορᾶς
> σίτοις καπήλευ' Ὀρφέα τ' ἄνακτ' ἔχων
> βάκχευε πολλῶν γραμμάτων τιμῶν καπνούς.

Now you may plum yourself, now by a vegetable diet play the showman with your food, and with Orpheus for your lord hold your covens and honour all your vaporous screeds.

translation Barrett 1964:342

Barrett is certainly right in stressing that Hippolytos is not a vegetarian Orphic, but Theseus is using the expression as a tag rather than implying that

---

[101] Scullion (2000b) and Dunn (2000) suggest a variety of explanations for the presence of aetiologies in Euripidean drama, a great number of which are purely Euripidean inventions composed according to known rituals and cults.

[102] Moreover, Scullion (2002:136–137) has argued convincingly that: "tragedy is full of ritual, rituals of all sorts, rituals connected with the full range of Greek divinities. It parodies, distorts, subverts, and probably even invents rituals as well as reflecting them. But it is not itself ritual, unless by a very broad definition that would classify any form of theatre as ritual, and it is not a form of cult for the god Dionysos or for any other gods in connection with those festivals it was produced. In this sense the Greek gods are all on the same footing in tragedy, and earn their keep in it by fulfilling a dramatic function. Politics and religion and the politics of religion all come within the tragedians' compass, but the ritual approach often narrows and distorts our view of these things rather than opening them up to scrutiny, and these days it bids fair to distort our understanding not only of drama but of the politics of Greek religion and the civic discourse of democratic Athens." For the political and metatheatrical dimension of Dionysos, see Bierl 1991; for tragedy's exploitation of Dionysiac motifs and themes for its own purposes, see Schlesier 1993; Seaford 1993; and Zeitlin 1993; for the prominence of ritual, especially in Euripides' *Bacchae*, see Seaford 2003a; for Aeschylus and the mysteries, see Tiverios 2004; for Sophocles and the mysteries, Seaford 1994; and for *Oedipus at Colonus* and Eleusis, Calame 1998 and Markantonatos 2002:167–220; for Euripides' *Hypsipyle*, Burkert 1994b; for Orphic incantations in Euripides, Faraone forthcoming-2. For the problematization of religious issues in Euripides and the interplay and interconnections between the ritual and the tragic matrix, see Lloyd-Jones 1998; Sourvinou-Inwood 2003:291–458 (for *Hippolytos* 326–332, and briefly for *Bacchae* 402–403); and Easterling 2004.

his son is actually a follower of Orpheus.[103] Theseus does say, however, that his son is 'acting as a *bacchos*.' To Theseus' mind, the arguments and lifestyle of Hippolytos are similar to those people whom the Athenian authors classified under the rubric 'Orphics.'

Euripides' treatment of 'Crete and the Cretans' becomes even more frustrating in the *parodos* of the *Cretans*. In these few lines, quoted by Porphyry on the subject of meat-abstinence, the Chorus addresses Minos and introduces itself as follows (*Cretans* fr. 472 Collard et al. = fr. 1 Cozzoli):[104]

> Φοινικογενοῦς τέκνον Εὐρώπης
> καὶ τοῦ μεγάλου Ζηνός, ἀνάσσων
> Κρήτης ἑκατομπτολιέθρου·
> ἥκω ζαθέους ναοὺς προλιπών,
> 5 οὓς αὐθιγενὴς στεγανοὺς παρέχει[105]
> τμηθεῖσα δοκοὺς Χαλύβωι πελέκει
> καὶ ταυροδέτωι κόλληι κραθεῖσ'
> ἀτρεκεῖς ἁρμοὺς κυπάρισσος.
> ἁγνὸν δὲ βίον τείνομεν ἐξ οὗ
> 10 Διὸς Ἰδαίου μύστης γενόμην,
> καὶ νυκτιπόλου Ζαγρέως βούτης[106]
> τὰς ὠμοφάγους δαῖτας τελέσας,
> Μητρί τ' Ὀρείᾳ δᾷδας ἀνασχὼν
> μετὰ Κουρήτων
> 15 βάκχος ἐκλήθην ὁσιωθείς.
> πάλλευκα δ' ἔχων εἵματα φεύγω
> γένεσίν τε βροτῶν καὶ νεκροθήκας
> οὐ χριμπτόμενος,[107]
> τήν τ' ἐμψύχων
> 20 βρῶσιν ἐδεστῶν πεφύλαγμαι.

Child of Europa born to Phoenix and of great Zeus, lord over Crete of the hundred cities! To come here I have left the most holy temple, its roof furnished by cypress grown on the very site and cut with

---

[103] Barrett 1964:342–345.

[104] Collard, Cropp, and Lee 1995:58–61; Cozzoli 2001:57–58. On Porphyry's *Life of Pythagoras* and the sage's initiation, see Makris 2001:212–224.

[105] Cozzoli (2002:57) prints lines 5–8 differently with slight changes in the meaning: οἷς αὐθιγενὴς τμηθεῖσα δοκὸς | Χαλύβωι πελέκει στεγανοὺς παρέχει | ... | ... κυπαρίσσου.

[106] Cozzoli (2002:58) prints the manuscript reading: βροντὰς for which see her commentary (85–87); βούτης is also present in *Hippolytos* 537, albeit as an adjective (Barrett 1964:261).

[107] Cozzoli (2002:58) prints a lacuna before the participle.

Chalybean axe into beams and brought together with bonding ox-glue into exact joints. Pure is the life I have maintained since I became an initiate of Idaean Zeus and a herdsman of nocturnal Zagreus, after performing feasts of raw flesh; and holding aloft torches to the Mountain Mother among the Kouretes I was named a celebrant after consecration. In clothing all of white I shun both the birth of mortals and the laying-places of the dead, which I do not approach; and I have guarded myself against the eating of living food.

translation Collard, Cropp, and Lee 1995, modified

This is unique and extraordinary, and the *opinio communis* is succinctly stated by Collard, Cropp and Lee (1995:67):

[Euripides] is mingling elements of ritual from various times and places, some poetic in provenance, some no doubt contemporary, in order to engage and impress his audience, and to establish for the Chorus a religious authority from which they may comment on the actions of both Pasiphae and Minos, and perhaps Deadalus.

And yet, the lexicon and motifs of the *parodos*, when compared to that of the texts on the lamellae, reveal astonishing affinities, even if they diverge in symbolism. The cypress is employed by Euripides for the construction of the most holy temple (compare *Hippolytos* 1252–1254), where initiatory rites of some sort take place. The 'priests' of the Chorus assert that they have become: *mystai* of Idaean Zeus after initiation; *boutai* of Zagreus after performing feasts of raw flesh; and *bacchoi* after praying with torches to the Mountain Mother among the Kouretes. These 'priests,' furthermore, wear white cloths, avoid polluting activities having to do with birth and death, and take care not to eat 'living' foods. Euripides seems to be appropriating techniques and motifs from mystery cults for his dramatic performance on stage. For at one and the same time, the members of this Chorus claim to be initiated into the mystery cults of Idaean Zeus, Dionysos Zagreus,[108] and the Mountain Mother, and they further claim to be followers of 'Orphics' and Pythagoreans.

---

[108] The equation Zagreus-Dionysos is attested in Callimachus (*Aetia* fr. 43 line 117), but depictions of Dionysos' birth on Attic vases are dated from 470 to 435 BCE, for which see Beaumont 1995:341; Camassa 1995; and Carpenter 1997. Compare the critical remarks on the Zagreus myth by Edmonds (1999 with extensive bibliography), Bernabé's reply (2002b), and Graf and Johnston 2007:66–90. Sourvinou-Inwood (2005:169–189, especially 170–171) argues that: "Zagreus ... was one of the transformations of the divine persona of a Minoan deity ... [and] would have been perceived as the Cretan Dionysos."

A similar, but *not comparable*, case is evident in the *parodos* of the *Bacchae* where Euripides presents "Dionysos at large" (64–169).[109] After the *prooimion*, the Chorus begins with the blessings of the god's followers, which contain all the catchwords found in mystery cults (72–77):[110]

> ὦ μάκαρ, ὅστις εὐδαί-
> μων τελετὰς θεῶν εἰ-
> δὼς βιοτὰν ἁγιστεύει
> καὶ θιασεύεται ψυ-
> χὰν ἐν ὄρεσσι βακχεύ-
> ων ὁσίοις καθαρμοῖσιν.

O blessed is he who, truly happy, knowing the initiations of the gods is pure in life and joins his soul to the thiasos in the mountains performing Bacchic ritual with holy purifications.

translation Seaford 1996

Then, the Chorus enumerates Dionysos' association with Cybele and her *orgia* in Phrygia (τά τε ματρὸς μεγάλας ὄργια Κυβέλας θεμιτεύων, 78–79); his double birth by Semele in Thebes and by Zeus (88–98); the newborn's *stephanosis* by the Moirai, and the customs of the Thebans (99–119); and Dionysos' connection with the Kouretes, Rhea, and (Cretan) Zeus, on account of the invention of the tympanon (120–134):

> ὦ θαλάμευμα Κουρή-
> των ζάθεοί τε Κρήτας
> Διογενέτορες ἔναυλοι,
> ἔνθα τρικόρυθες ἄντροις
> βυρσότονον κύκλωμα τόδε
> μοι Κορύβαντες ηὗρον·
> βακχείαι δ᾽ ἅμα συντόνωι
> κέρασαν ἡδυβόαι Φρυγίων
> αὐλῶν πνεύματι ματρός τε Ῥέας ἐς
> χέρα θῆκαν, κτύπον εὐάσμασι βακχᾶν·
> παρὰ δὲ μαινόμενοι Σάτυροι
> ματέρος ἐξανύσαντο θεᾶς,

---

[109] The expression is the English title of Detienne 1989. For the *Bacchae*, see 143–144nn146–148, 149n158, 181n102.

[110] According to Seaford (1981 and 1996:157), this alludes to the texts on the lamellae, although any reference to the afterlife is nowhere to be found in the *Bacchae*, and although all *makarismoi* need not refer to mystery initiations and discourses on afterlife.

ἐς δὲ χορεύματα
συνῆψαν τριετηρίδων,
αἷς χαίρει Διόνυσος.

Oh lair of the Kouretes and sacred Zeus-begetting haunts of Crete,
where the triple-helmeted Korybantes in the cave invented for me
this hide-stretched circle. And in the intense bacchic dance they
mixed it with the sweet-shouting breath of Phrygian pipes, and put
it in the hand of mother Rhea, a beat for the bacchants' cries of joy.
And the frenzied satyrs obtained it from the mother goddess, and
attached it to the dances of the biennial festivals in which Dionysos
rejoices.

translation Seaford 1996

Kouretes; Zeus' begetters; Korybantes; Phrygian and Bacchic music; Mother
Rhea; Satyrs and dance—all, and much more, are brought together by Dionysos
one way or another.[111] Even Orpheus joins the Dionysiac crowd in the second
stasimon, but this time he plays his magical music in Pieria, another place
where Dionysos left his mark. In the *Bacchae*, however, these references to
Dionysiac *teletai* throughout the Greek world present only one of the Dionysiac
discourses, whose emphasis concentrates on the blessings of maenadism and
of becoming a *bacchos* during this life.[112]

If the *Bacchae* and the *Cretans* present an upsetting and unconvincing
amalgam, what Sourvinou-Inwood has called "the problematizing of religious
matters," the recent text from Pherai (D5) "in its austerity and *sophrosyne*"[113]
offers corroborating evidence: "send me to the *thiasoi* of *mystai*; I have been
initiated both to the *orgia* of Demeter Chthonia and to the *teletai* of the

---

[111] On the intimate relation between music and ecstasy and its representation on vases, see
Somville 1992; in Plato Moutsopoulos 1992. For the revolution in aulos music and its consequences, see Wallace 2003.

[112] Segal (1982:176–177) indicates that the participants in the rite of the *parodos* are "antithetical
to the polis in every way;" this is true in terms of the play's structure, but it should be emphasized that the same participants are also members of the polis, at least as soon as Thebes will
become such a polis by the end of the *Bacchae*, where many Dionysiac identities coexist; see
also 143–144nn146–148, 149n158, 181n102.

[113] Parker and Stamatopoulou 2004. A similar case of at least a double initiation is presented
by the epigram of the Athenian Isidoros, son of Nikostratos, a mime by profession and an
initiate in the Eleusinian and Samothracian mysteries (Karadima-Matsa and Dimitrova 2003).
Fountoulakis (2002) argues convincingly that in *Mimiamb* 8.66–79 Herondas appropriates
themes and images from Dionysiac myth and ritual in order to present the mime as a genre of
dramatic poetry and literary merit, conferring poetic authority and fame.

Mountain Mother." Dionysos is absent from the text,[114] but elsewhere, especially in Euripides, he is associated with the Mountain Mother. The Chorus in the *Bacchae* presents as many associations of Dionysos as possible, or local discourses on *Bacchica*. The *parodos* of the *Cretans*, although its context is missing, probably presents a different, non-Athenian Dionysiac discourse. The words, names, and motifs in the *Bacchae* and the *Cretans* may be the same, but the Dionysiac discourses are not. The characteristics of the *Cretans'* Chorus are, in a sense, similar to those Theseus is employing for his son Hippolytos, quoted above, but with a Cretan tinge. To a great extent, this Chorus is not far removed from the deceased buried with the gold lamellae and *epistomia*, whose texts, when brought together, form a similar *asymmetrical* corpus in terms of their ritual(s), their mystery cult(s), and their local or Panhellenic considerations.

Euripidean fondness for matters 'Cretan' comes up again in Aristophanes' *Frogs*, when Aeschylus and Euripides compete for the chair of tragedy by quoting representative specimens of each other's tragedies. Among the many issues debated, Aeschylus confronts Euripides for presenting unholy marriages on stage and for collecting Cretan monodies, which he inserts in his tragedies. The commentators explain that this is due to Crete's association in the sources with mimetic dancing and to Euripides' fondness for using Cretan myths, especially sexually immoral Cretan heroines.[115] Later on, when push comes to shove, these allegations become specific and center on the issue of truth and falsehood, on concealing and revealing. Aeschylus explains that by unholy marriages he meant stage-productions of prostitutes like Stheneboea and Phaedra; Euripides replies that he only presented on stage the truth about Phaedra.[116] Euripides' reply is ironic, as he plays on the theme 'Cretans are always liars' by claiming that he is staging the truth about a Cretan woman.

An example of Euripides' Cretan monodies is also 'staged' when Aeschylus quotes in parodic fashion one such Euripidean monody in lines 1329–1364 (in all likelihood from one of Euripides' 'Cretan' tragedies).[117] The

---

[114] Unless we accept the restoration by Graf and Johnston (2007:38) at the end of line 1 of this text: [Βάκχου]; Parker and Stamatopoulou 2004 prefer simply [τε or καὶ], or [ἰδοῦσα].

[115] *Frogs* 849–850: ΑΙ. Ὦ Κρητικὰς μὲν συλλέγων μονῳδίας, | γάμους δ' ἀνοσίους εἰσφέρων εἰς τὴν τέχνην; Dover 1997, 174–175; Sommerstein 1996, 231; Collard, Cropp, and Lee (1995:55) quote Dover's judicious handling; and Cozzoli 2001:113–116.

[116] *Frogs* 1043: ΑΙ. Ἀλλ' οὐ μὰ Δί' οὐ Φαίδρας ἐποίουν πόρνας οὐδὲ Σθενεβοίας; 1052: ΕΥ. Πότερον δ' οὐκ ὄντα λόγον τοῦτον περὶ τῆς Φαίδρας ξυνέθηκα;

[117] See the comments by Dover 1997:174–175, 217–219; Sommerstein 1996:230–231, 277–280; Collard, Cropp, and Lee 1995:55, 58–59, 66; and Cozzoli's (2002:67 fr. 8, 113–116) careful argumentation, with full references to the sources on 'Cretan' monodies; she concludes that the ascription by the Scholiast is probable but in no way certain.

'Cretan' colouring of this text is unmistakable, and its music would probably also have had a distinct Cretan character (the rhythm in lines 1356–1360 is the cretic).[118] In this ridiculous incident concocted in paratragic mood by the comic poet, Night holds a prominent place. Mountain Nymphs and Mania as well as Diktynna, Artemis, and Hekate (just as in the *Hippolytos*) are called upon for help. Line 1356: ἀλλ᾽, ὦ Κρῆτες, Ἴδας τέκνα, is a fragment from the *Cretans* according to the scholiast,[119] which is followed expectedly by a reference to Cretan archery and ambush: τὰ | τόξα <τε> λαβόντες ἐπαμύνατε, τὰ | κῶλά τ᾽ ἀμπάλλετε κυκλούμενοι τὴν οἰκίαν (1357–1358). These references conform to common general perceptions of 'Crete and the Cretans,'[120] as has been seen above in the literature of the archaic period and in Euripides' plays.

Aristophanes continues his paratragic play to the bitter end, when Dionysos twice replies to Euripides' pleas for a fair judgment with Cretan 'Euripidean' expressions. First, in *Frogs* 1471, the first half of the line: ἡ γλῶττ᾽ ὀμώμοκ᾽, Αἰσχύλον δ᾽ αἱρήσομαι, is Hippolytos' famous line (612: ἡ γλῶσσ᾽ ὀμώμοχ᾽, ἡ δὲ φρὴν ἀνώμοτος). And a little later, Dionysos quotes another Euripidean fragment, this time from another 'Cretan' tragedy, the *Polyidos* (fr. 638): τίς δ᾽ οἶδεν εἰ τὸ ζῆν μέν ἐστι κατθανεῖν, | τὸ κατθανεῖν δὲ ζῆν κάτω νομίζεται. This rhetorical question is employed twice in the *Frogs*, first by Aeschylus, when he attacks Euripides for staging immoral women who philosophize[121]: 'life is not life' (*Frogs* 1082: καὶ φασκούσας οὐ ζῆν τὸ ζῆν;), and then by Dionysos in *Frogs* 1477–1478, appropriately modified into the ridiculous: "τίς δ᾽ οἶδεν εἰ τὸ ζῆν μέν ἐστι κατθανεῖν," | τὸ πνεῖν δὲ δειπνεῖν, τὸ δὲ καθεύδειν κῴδιον.[122] Interestingly, Dionysos' paratragic reply from *Polyidos* is the final blow. Euripides is 'convinced,' shuts up, and is not heard from anymore in the play. This outcome still remains a puzzle,[123] perhaps because the context

---

[118] Dover 1997:246; Sommerstein 1996:279. The monody's rhythm (lines 1329–1364), however, is not consistent throughout, as the meters comprise a potpourri: Dover 1997:245–246; Sommerstein 1996:277–280.

[119] Collard, Cropp, and Lee 1995:58 fr. 471 = Cozzoli 2001:67 fr. 8.

[120] See below, 224n252.

[121] *Frogs* 1054–1055: ΑΙ. Μὰ Δί᾽, ἀλλ᾽ ὄντ᾽· ἀλλ᾽ ἀποκρύπτειν χρὴ τὸ πονηρὸν τόν γε ποιητήν, | καὶ μὴ παράγειν μηδὲ διδάσκειν.

[122] It is not beyond doubt that this is a fragment from *Polyidos*, as the same idea is expressed in Euripides' two *Phrixos* plays; see Dover 1997:196 and 230; and Sommerstein (1996:253–254 and 293) who argues for *Polyidos*. It is interesting that a similar idea is alluded to in Callimachus' *Hymn to Zeus* 60–65, where Callimachus challenges another 'poetic lie,' namely that Zeus' sphere of influence, Olympos, was obtained by lot, as if the world of the living was equivalent to the world of the dead without any difference.

[123] For recent discussions with previous bibliography, see Heiden 1991; and compare Lada-Richards 1999, especially 321–329.

surrounding this fragment is unknown. The aporetic stance, however, of the *Polyidos*-line looks very close to what Epimenides would have put forward. Nor is this stance far removed from the promises of all mystery cults,[124] especially the texts on the gold lamellae and *epistomia*, which profess death to be the beginning of a new kind of life.

The non-Cretan literary context concerning matters Cretan is remarkably consistent. 'Crete and the Cretans' are credited and portrayed as experts in archery, ambush, running, sailing, piracy, but also as expert performers of discourses on poetics (and lying) and music, on politics and philosophy, and on religious matters. The *parodos* of Euripides' *Cretans* and Diodorus' narrative on mysteries in Crete (5.77.3) elaborate, in a sense, the Cretan epithets *orgiones*, *paieones*, and *semantores*, epithets that could aptly describe Epimenides' activities. The Cretan sage, in particular, appears to have been a major influence in archaic times, as his works seem to combine both the Homeric and the Orphic views about the world above and below. The *Cretans' parodos* is a controversial fragment and, because of its missing context, the extent of Euripides' manipulation of this Chorus with extraordinary qualities cannot be ascertained. Pasiphae's escapades, which yielded monstrous results, may have required Euripides' purposeful mingling of these mystery cults within the tragedy's context, in order to create an almost divine Chorus that could handle them. What may safely be assumed, however, is that the *Cretans' parodos* and Diodorus' narrative of mystery cults in Crete are complementary. The Cretans themselves believe that the cults of Eleusis, Samothrace, and Orphic Thrace are one and the same. They all satisfy the same human need and manifest a single belief and principle, life after death. Euripides presents 'distinctive' mystery cults and rituals being 'fused.' But perhaps in Crete all these activities of the priests *were* indeed fused, or were thought to respond to the same

---

[124] Polyidos, the Argive *mantis*, brought back to life Glaukos, the son of Minos, who forced him to teach his son the art of divination. Glaukos eventually became a Knossian hero with chthonic associations, not unlike Trophonios and Amphiaraos. For the myth, see Willetts 1962:60–67; for an analysis of Glaukos' myth according to the Cretan ritual of initiation from puberty into adolescence and adulthood, and the motifs shared with other Panhellenic analogues, see especially Muellner 1998; I would not exclude, however, a mystery cult in which death and rebirth were prominent, especially in light of the important place of the honey in the myth, "at the threshold between life and death" (26), a case which would indicate exploitation of Glaukos' story both from the point of view of the Orphic, and the Homeric discourse on afterlife ("the road to immortality and glory is on a mystical, wide-eyed path through death and beyond it, not by way of resurrection," Muellner 1998:27). Hoffmann (2002) interprets the scene on the Glaukos Attic cup in the British Museum as representing an initiation into mysteries "pertaining to immortality and enlightenment, the two terms being synonymous with self-knowledge at a higher level of comprehension" (85); and 204n177.

needs, as Diodorus' narrative implies and as Epimenides' activities attest. They could perform *orgia* and *teletai* for the mystery cults of Idaean Zeus, (Dionysos) Zagreus, and the Mountain Mother, and at the same time claim to be following Orphic and Pythagorean instructions. After all, it was not at all unlikely that one person could have been initiated in all three cults (perhaps even more, as the new text D5 demonstrates), and at the same time claim to have been a devotee of Orpheus and Pythagoras, as Burkert has argued.[125] And perhaps this phenomenon was all the more common in Crete.

A Cretan Context

Perceptions of 'Crete and the Cretans' in non-Cretan literary works of the archaic period and of the fifth century BCE did exist, but, as the case of Euripides has demonstrated, these perceptions are embedded in a literary context. Attempts at identifying in the archaeological and epigraphic record of Crete the particular cults that show up in the literary context may be judged worthwhile, even if daunting. The fact that in an inscription a specific god or goddess is recorded does not necessarily constitute evidence for a Cretan cult in general, but evidence for a cult of the specific city, whence the inscription. Nor can an inscription concerning a specific god or goddess necessarily be used as evidence for confirming the 'Cretan' rites and rituals alluded to in literary texts, because influences may have been at work in both directions, and because chances are that the author of the texts had not read the particular inscription, but may have had indirect or general knowledge of its information. Attempting to identify in the epigraphical and archaeological record the rituals and cults attested in a 'literary' work is problematic: Euripides' aims are specific, and he certainly did not intend to advertise and promote local Cretan ritual and cult practice. Moreover, evidence for the specifics of local rituals and cults is almost non-existent and thus seldom enhances understanding of Cretan (or any other) rituals, let alone of the interrelation and interdependence between literary non-Cretan texts and the archaeological and epigraphic record.

These limitations, inherent in the archaeological and epigraphical record, caution against overstatements and simplifications. A careful and sensible study of the Cretan archaeological and epigraphical record and of what it *does* have to offer, as regards the Cretan *epistomia*, may be a promising approach.[126]

---

[125] Burkert 1987:12–29.
[126] Strataridaki (1988 and 1988–1989) discusses the fragmentary literary evidence of Cretan historians; Antonelli (1995) discusses the Minoan connections of Dionysos; Tsagarakis (2001 and 2006) offers a brief overview of Cretan literature.

The evidence indicates that mystery cults and rituals, pertinent to the ones implied by the texts on the *epistomia*, existed in Crete in certain chronological periods,[127] but especially from the third–second centuries BCE onwards.[128] Their form and their content, however, are unknown.[129] Similarities and differences between literary perceptions and the archaeological/epigraphical record may complement, correct, or even (perhaps) disprove one another, especially as far as the twelve gold *epistomia* are concerned. And this may imply a dynamic interaction, especially from the late Hellenistic period onwards: non-Cretan literary perceptions of 'Crete and the Cretans,' well-established by the fifth century BCE, may have exerted their influence on Cretan habits and customs; and Cretan traditions concerning poetics and discourses on death may have influenced non-Cretan perceptions.

Before attempting to place the twelve *epistomia* within their specific Eleuthernaean context, it is useful to review the record of the island for parallels concerning mystery cults and burial practices. The twelve Cretan *epistomia* are not the only ones found in Crete. A number of unincised gold lamellae, some of which the excavators call *epistomia*, have also been discovered in graves of the Roman and Imperial period:[130]

---

[127] For a convincing discussion of the evidence from the Iron age and the archaic period, see Morris 1992:150–194.

[128] A remarkable example of the proliferation of cults and mysteries in the late Hellenistic period is the altar of Dionysos in Kos, dated in the middle of the second century BCE, with scenes from the life of Dionysos, some of them rare and unique: Dionysos' *katharsis* by Rhea in Phrygia, scenes from a peaceful Dionysiac *thiasos*, and victorious battle(s) of a Dionysiac army against barbarians (Stampolidis 1987); for the Rhodian Dionysion, see Konstantinopoulos 1994–1995; for the presence of the cult of Egyptian gods in Rhodes and Kos since the Hellenistic period for political and economic reasons, see Bosnakis 1994–1995.

[129] I have resisted throughout to refer to the Minoan period for (dis)continuities of religious ideas and practices, because the evidence is at best conjectural, as will become evident (for the literature on the subject, see 114n54, 154n3; for perceptions of Crete in the literature of the eighteenth and nineteenth centuries, before Arthur Evans, see Pope 2003; and Hamilakis and Momigliano 2006). There is simply no way in determining what the Cretans thought from the archaic period onwards about their Minoan past, or about their 'common Anatolian/Eastern Mediterranean' tradition, or how for that matter they re-interpreted that past. Nilsson 1950 and Willetts 1962 are the classic; see also Rutkowski 1986; Georgoulaki 2002; Sporn 2002; and Prent 2005. For the archaeological gap of the late archaic and classical periods, see Erickson 2000, 2002, 2004, and 2005, who presents evidence that fills in this gap; for the rise of the polis in central Crete Kotsonas (2002) suggests the sixth century BCE, while Xifaras (2002) and Prent (2005) the proto-geometric and geometric periods.

[130] The inscribed gold leaf from Lissos (Platon 1958:466) should not be associated with the Bacchic-Orphic Cretan *epistomia*, as Bultrighini (1993; SEG 45.1319) suggested, since it is a dedication to Asclepios, for which see Martínez-Fernández 2003 (BE 2004.254).

1) In Epanochori of Selinos, within the territory of ancient Elyros. According to Vana Niniou-Kindeli, the larger-than-life size *epistomion*(?) may have been also the middle part of a diadem for the forehead of the deceased, since two more large gold bands were found near the cranium which were fitted together, as is indicated by the holes they bear.[131]

2–3) In graves of the cemetery in Kasteli of Kissamos, near ancient Polyrrhenia, which are unpublished; the first, according to the excavator Yannis Tzedakis (1979:394) may also have been a leaf from a wreath; the second is larger than the usual 'mouth'-size.[132]

4) From a grave of the extensive Roman cemetery in the site Agia Elessa of ancient Lappa (modern Argyroupolis; Figures 38–39 [pages 89–90]) an *epistomion*, gold leaves, and a round gold foil (a pseudo-coin?) with *gorgoneion* were recently handed over to the 25th Ephorate (compare the grave-goods of D2 in Table 1).[133]

5) From grave no. 16 in the extensive Roman cemetery of ancient Lato pros Kamaran (Figure 43); the grave was found disturbed; among the grave-goods were also found two figurines of Leda and one of a nude female, and two clay theatrical masks.[134]

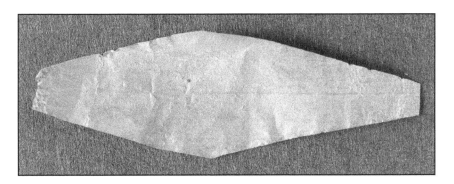

Figure 43. Unincised gold lamella, from Grave 16, Lato pros Kamaran. Agios Nikolaos, Archaeological Museum, 7437.

---

[131] Niniou-Kindeli 1987.

[132] Vana Niniou-Kindeli 1993, to whom I am also indebted for permission to see these two *epistomia*, and for her discussing them with me.

[133] I am indebted to Irene Gavrilaki for showing and discussing with me this find; for the site Agia Elessa in Eleutherna, see the section "Topography." For *gorgoneia* associated with Dionysos, see Csapo 1997:256–257; for clay gilt *gorgoneia* from a *kline*, see Savvopoulou 1995:399; and Tsimbidou-Avloniti 2006:328 with n26.

[134] Agios Nikolaos Museum 7437. Kostis Davaras 1985:205 no. 16/7, plate 56β figure 2 and drawing in 133 fig. 2; the figurines and masks, 203–206 no. 16, figure 27–28, plate 56β–57αβγ.

At present, these four (or five) gold *epistomia* cannot be included in the same group with the ones from Eleutherna and Sfakaki, because their findspot inside the graves alone cannot determine their exclusive use as *epistomia* and therefore corroborate their association with any mystery cult or ritual. They do indicate, however, that the custom of *epistomia* or mouth-size gold bands, for whatever reasons they were employed, was not restricted to the vicinity of Eleutherna. Even though these cannot be classed in the same group G with the unincised ones from Sfakaki and Pella, it may not be completely irrelevant to mention briefly the gods and goddesses attested in the wider areas, whence these unincised *epistomia*, deities whose presence may imply some kind of rituals.

In Kastelli of Kissamos, Zeus Kretagenes is mentioned among the *patroi* gods in a fragmentary inscription,[135] but Dionysos is also prominent: a 'House of Dionysos,' named so after its mosaics which depict scenes of the Dionysiac cycle, and part of a second house with an Orpheus mosaic have come to light, both from the Imperial period; additionally, a head of a statue of Dionysos has been unearthed and is now in the Museum of Chania.[136]

In Lappa (modern Argyroupolis), in addition to a statue of Dionysos in the Rethymno Museum dated to the third century BCE, and the asylia decree with Teos, (inscribed on the wall of Dionysos' temple at Teos and dated ca. 200 BCE),[137] Persephone alone received an *ex voto*.[138] There is also an intriguing example of a statue base from a *heroon*, on which was inscribed:[139] χαῖρε, Διομήδη Συμβρίτιε, | χαίρετε πάντες; and of a *defixio* with an ἀρά, placed inside the same grave, above which stood Diomedes' *heroon*.[140] The only available information about the texts' provenance comes from its first

---

[135] IC II.viii.8, lines 5–6.

[136] Markoulaki 1995, 1994, 1987a, and 1987b for the House of Dionysos; also Markoulaki, Christodoulakos, and Fragonikolaki 2004; Drosinou 1992 for the Orpheus mosaic; and Niniou-Kindeli 1991–1993 for heads of Dionysos in the Chania Museum. For what it is worth, it should also be noted that Dionysos together with Zeus is attested in Linear B tablet KH Gq 5 from Chania (Tzedakis, Hallager, and Andreadaki-Vlazaki 1989–1991; and also Hallager, Andreadaki-Vlazaki, and Hallager 1992). For the cults in Polyrrhenia and its environs, see Sporn 2002:283–290, for Dionysos 286. For Cretan mosaics, see Guimier-Sorbets 2004 and Sweetman 2004. For the image of Orpheus in mosaics and his association with a variety of gods, among them Dionysos, see Jesnick 1997.

[137] IC II.xvi.3 (for a similar decree between Teos and Eleutherna, 219n244); for these texts, see Rigsby 1996:280–325; and Kvist 2003.

[138] No. 7 above (IC II.xvi.10) and Figure 8 (page 23).

[139] IC II.xvi.27.

[140] IC II.xvi.28; on these kinds of curses, all of them public and therefore ἐπιτύμβιοι, see Strubbe 1991 and 1997.

editor.[141] Guarducci suggested that the first inscription, a hexameter verse which, however, presents metrical problems in the name and city-ethnic, is composed according to the *chaire*-formula, well attested in other epigrams. In light of the *heroon* mentioned in the *defixio* and the rites probably performed on the spot, perhaps the *chaire-chairete* exchange may also be interpreted in a way analogous to the one in some of the lamellae (A4, E-texts).[142] It should also be noted that the *defixio's* purpose, to avert desecration of the *heroon*, must definitely have failed: the text could be read by the Underworld divinities alone, as the grave's looter would have discovered too late. The reason why Diomedes from Sybritos (another ancient city where Dionysos' presence is prominent[143]) acquired after death a *heroon* in Lappa remains a mystery.

The extensive cemetery in Lato pros Kamaran (Agios Nikolaos) exhibits interesting burial practices.[144] In grave no. 8, in addition to a silver burial-coin, the male deceased is crowned with a gold olive-wreath (rather than laurel) attached to the cranium (Figure 44a–b). Kostis Davaras, after extensive reflection on all possible interpretations, proposes we view the deceased as a real athlete, since among the grave-goods a strigil and an aryballos were also found; or, at any rate, he proposes we view the deceased as someone whom his relatives wanted to bury as an athlete.[145] Since in Macedonia wreaths are found in an increasing number every year, perhaps other explanations should

---

[141] Kalaïssakis (1892) notes that the base and the *defixio* were chance finds by an anonymous inhabitant who was plowing his field; Kalaïssakis appears not to have seen the objects himself, but to have received in Chania transcriptions from which he published the inscriptions; few other Cretan magic texts are attested: from Phalasarna (IC II.xix.7, and Brixhe and Panayotou 1995); Knossos (Grammatikaki and Litinas 2000); and a possible amulet from Gortyn (Bessi 2004). On Lappa, see Gavrilaki 2004; and Sporn 2002, 255–257 (she correctly places the gods and goddesses of the *defixio* under *Incerta und Dubitanda,* but she misses the *heroon*); and Sporn 2004, 1112–1115 for a relief depicting Nymphs; Tzifopoulos 2007. For the *heroon* in Aptera, see Martínez-Fernández and Niniou-Kindeli 2000–2001; Niniou-Kindeli and Christodoulakos 2004. On *heroa* and tomb cults, see Antonaccio 1995; Snodgrass 2000; Themelis 2000b; Pirenne-Delforge and Suarez de la Torre 2000; Boehringer 2001; Ekroth 2002; and Bremmer 2006; for the Roman *heroa* in Miletos, see Weber 2004. In particular, for the cults of poets, see Clay 2004:63–93.

[142] See the section "The Cretan Texts in the Context of a Ritual and a *Hieros Logos*."

[143] Sporn 2002:247–252, 334 with previous bibliography; Perlman 2004b:1187–1188 no. 990; and Tzifopoulos forthcoming-2.

[144] For the cults of Lato, Lato pros Kamaran, and environs, see Sporn 2002:61–75; and very briefly Apostolakou 2003. An epigram relates a dedication of a statue to Hermes Kyllanios and Kypharissita (IC I.xvi.7 reads: Πανὶ as restored by Guarducci, but see Voutiras 1984); the epithet Kypharissitas is so far unique in Crete, but, it is probably analogous to the other epithet of Hermes, Kedritis (Daux 1976; Voutiras 1984), attested in inscriptions from the Kato Symi Viannos sanctuary, for which see below.

[145] Agios Nikolaos Museum (7355). Davaras 1985:171–190, 188.

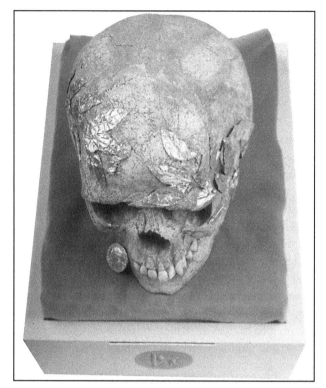

a.

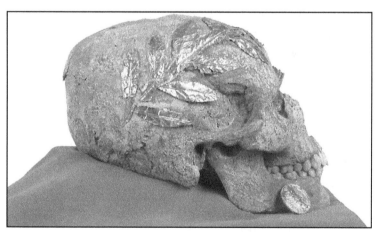

b.

Figure 44. The 'crowned' deceased: skull with gold olive-wreath, from Grave 8, Lato pros Kamaran. Agios Nikolaos, Archaeological Museum, 7355. (a. view from above; b. right side of skull).

also be entertained for this *stephanosis* in grave no. 8.[146] Moreover, grave no. 16, from which comes the gold unincised lamella, was not the only grave with figurines[147] and clay theatrical masks as grave-goods. In grave no. 2, a plot for the burial of a female, a figurine of Dionysos and a young Satyros and no less than eight smaller than life-size theatrical masks have been discovered. Davaras rightly discussed these masks in relation to the ones found in Knossos and essentially accepted Bieber's and Carington Smith's suggestion for an eschatological interpretation of theatrical masks inside graves:[148] the deceased become members of a divine *thiasos* and are therefore apotheosized.

Knossos is one of the places for which there are strong indications of some kind of rituals and mystery cult activity.[149] Carington Smith discussed the theatrical mask and the other grave-goods of the Roman chamber tomb in Monasteriaki Kephala, two other masks from a nearby Roman rock-cut tomb, and two more housed in the Herakleion Museum. Some of these masks betray strong Dionysiac aspects and some are very similar to the ones in the fresco of the Villa of the Mysteries in Pompeii.[150] Carington Smith therefore proposed that "the people in our tomb seem to have been devotees of a type of mysticism which owed something to the chthonic deities,"[151] who, in the case of Knossos, can be none other than Demeter-Kore and their mysteries. In addition to the villa of Dionysos, and Demeter's sanctuary (where rites and rituals either of the Eleusinian or Thesmophoria type would have taken place),[152] there are dedicatory inscriptions to these goddesses, dated to the Roman period. One inscription is to Demeter alone,[153] and another is to Persephone

---

[146] See the sections "Shape-Burial Context" and "Usage." Wreaths in Crete are rare and after Davaras' publication two more have also been found in Hellenistic graves of Kydonia: Pologiorgi 1985:165–168 pl. 60b and c (a clay-gilt myrtle wreath with gilt berries); and Markoulaki and Niniou-Kindeli 1982 and 1985.

[147] For a somewhat overstated association of lines 10–12 of text A1 with figurines of a certain type, see Fridh-Haneson 1987.

[148] Davaras 1985:139–157, 153–157; Bieber 1930; Carington Smith 1982:286–289. For the marble theatrical masks in the National Museum, most of them not funerary, see Zoumbaki 1987.

[149] For rituals and cults in Knossos and its environs, see Sporn 2002:111–140 and Prent 2005:514–518.

[150] Carington Smith 1982:287–289. For the Roman mausolea in Knossos and Gortyn, see Vassilakis 2004.

[151] Her suggestion that these chthonic deities "were perhaps first invoked in sixth-century-B.C. Rhodes" (Carington Smith 1982:288) is not necessary, as the Idaean Cave, Phaistos, and the Diktaian Cave lay far closer to Knossos.

[152] Paton 2004 with earlier bibliography; Coldstream 1973; and especially Sporn 2002:118–122; Suter 2002:169–191; and Trümpy 2004.

[153] IC I.viii.16: [- - -] | λήδου | τοῦ υἱοῦ Δά|ματρι | εὐχὰν | καὶ χα|ριστῆον; for the last two words in Cretan inscriptions, see Ghinatti 2004:65–66.

alone where the word πρόοδος in line 2 appears problematic, although it probably refers to a cult title, not unlike the analogous epithets Hekate receives in the *Hymn to Demeter* (line 440).[154] In the village of Agios Thomas, approximately 20 kms south of Knossos, a dedication to Demeter and Kore is inscribed within a tabula ansata chiseled on the rock (Figures 45–46).[155] An inscription of unknown provenance and not included in Guarducci's *Inscriptiones Creticae* was published as sepulchral by Ricci from a drawing made by Halbherr given to him by Antonios Alexandridis (Figure 47): Μ. Ἀντώνιος Κλω|διανὸς Εὐβούλῳ | χαριστήριο[ν]. The text appears to be an *ex-voto* (χαριστήριον) to Euboulos whose cult is so far unique for Crete.[156] Eubouleus is the euphemistic name of Zeus/Hades/Dionysos in the A-texts of the lamellae, but in Cretan mythistoric tradition, Euboulos is the son (or one of the sons) of Karmanor (who cleansed Apollo after the Pythoktonia), the grandfather of Britomartis, and a brother(?) of Chrysothemis, victor in the Pythia (unless Chrysothemis is another name for Euboulos).[157] Finally, the statue of a new Egyptian god

---

[154] IC I.viii.21: Νωνία Ἀνχαρία | πρόοδος Κόρης. | *folium*. Halbherr thought that *proodos* may be a cognomen, but Guarducci proposed with scepticism a cultic term and emended the word accordingly to πρό<π>ο<λ>ος with a question mark, although Halbherr's drawing is clear and so gross a mistake by the cutter would be rather unlikely. The word, followed by the genitive *Kores*, should probably be related to a procession (LSJ s.v. 2) for Kore, in charge of which(?) was Nonia, or the term denotes that Nonia was literally *going on before Kore* during a ritual; the word denotes procession in inscriptions from Asia Minor (IEphesos 122 line 7; 1133 line 15; IPanamara 244 lines 13 and 40; 258 line 29; IStratonikeia 310 lines 13 and 40; http://erga.packhum.org/inscriptions/). For the comparable case of the Corinthian Timarete, *propolos Enodias*, in an epigram from Pella, see the convincing discussion of Voutiras (1998:90–111); for the possible presence of this expression in a fragmentary epigram by Poseidippos, see Dignas 2004:181.

[155] IC I.xxxi [Loci Incerti].2: θεαῖς Δήμητρι καὶ Κόρῃ | Λαρκία Ἄρτεμεις | ἐκ τῶν ἰδίων *folium* (rho and eta in *Kore* in ligature).

[156] Ricci 1893:304–305 no. 13; Baldwin Bowsky 2002b:35n21 (SEG 52.826). Chaniotis (SEG 52.880) notes that the Knossian or even Cretan provenance of the inscription is not certain, and that the cult of Euboulos is unattested in Crete (for the name, see Bechtel 1917:170 for Εὐβούλιος, Εὐβουλίδης, and 613 Εὐβουλία; and LGPN I, II, IIIA, IIIB, IV). For the word χαριστήριον in Cretan inscriptions, see Ghinatti 2004:65–66.

[157] Pausanias (1.14.2–3) notes an Eubouleus, the son of the Argive hierophant Trochilos and brother of Triptolemos in his narrative of the different versions on Triptolemos' ancestry, the Athenian and the Argive, which depended on different sources, among them the poetry of Musaios and Orpheus. In this section Pausanias also relates a statue of Dionysos at the Odeion's entrance; a temple of Demeter and Kore above the nearby Enneakrounos; and the statues of Triptolemos and seated Epimenides in front of the Athenian Eleusinion, where he digresses to narrate Epimenides' dream in the cave and to refer to another Cretan purifier, Thaletas of Gortyn. For Triptolemos and the mysteries, see the fragmentary papyrus *PAntinoopolis* I 18 (= MP^3 2466), where the collocation of λειμών, μυρρίνην, ὦ Τριπτόλεμε, σοι νῦν μεμυηκ[-], τὴν κόρην εἶδον, οὐδὲ τὴν Δή[μητραν], [-]λυπημενην, νεικοφόρους βα[σιλεῖς], μυστικόν, present a puzzle.

and two proxeny decrees deserve to be mentioned. The former, dated to the second century CE, is a unique syncretism of three Egyptian divinities, Imhotep, Osiris, and Aion, and its provenance is unknown.[158] The Knossian proxeny decrees, dated to the second century BCE, honor visiting poets and musicians on account of their performance. Menekles, son of Dionysios, from Teos, in addition to his duties as ambassador, performed on the *kithara* beautiful compositions of Timotheos, Polyidos, and of old Cretan poets; Menekles' performance, as another inscription from Priansos relates, also included a potpourri of various epic, lyric, and historiographical compositions on Crete, gods, and heroes.[159] Likewise, the *grammatikos* Dioskourides from Tarsos, son of Dioskourides and adopted son of Asklepiodoros, composed an *egkomion* according to the poet (presumably Homer?) extolling the Cretan nation, but he sent his pupil, Myrinos from Amisos, son of Dionysios, a composer of poems and music, to perform it in front of the *kosmoi* and the Knossian assembly to their delight and approval.[160]

Beyond Knossos, Lato pros Kamaran, Lappa, Kissamos, and Kydonia, the evidence from four more locations contributes to the subject at hand in a more significant way. The *Hymn* from the sanctuary of Diktaian Zeus in Palaikastro, the sanctuary of Hermes Kedrites and of Aphrodite in Kato Symi Viannos, the epigram in the sanctuary of Magna Mater at Phaistos, and the Idaean Cave, all present strong evidence for ritual activity and mystery cults (Chaniotis 2006c), analogous to those implied by the texts on the Cretan *epistomia*.

---

[158] Vassilika 2004.

[159] IC I.viii.11 lines 7–11: ἀλλὰ καὶ ἐπε|δείξατο Μενεκλῆς μετὰ κιθάρας πλεονάκις τά τε | Τιμοθέω καὶ Πολυίδω καὶ τῶν ἀμῶν ἀρχαίων ποιη|τᾶν καλῶς καὶ ὡς προσῆκεν ἀνδρὶ πεπαιδευμέ|νωι. The proxeny decree of Priansos (IC I.xxiv.1 lines 6–13): ἀλλὰ | καὶ ἐπεδείξατο Μενεκλῆς μετὰ κιθάρας τά τε Τι|μοθέου καὶ Πολυίδου καὶ τῶν ἀμῶν παλαιῶν ποιη|τᾶν καλῶς καὶ πρεπόντως, εἰς<ή>νεγκε δὲ κύκλον | ἱστορημέναν ὑπὲρ Κρήτας κα[ὶ τ]ῶν ἐν [Κρή]ται γε|γονότων θεῶν τε καὶ ἡρώων, [ποι]ησάμενο[ς τ]ὰν | συναγωγὰν ἐκ πολλῶν ποιητᾶ[ν] καὶ ἱστοριαγρά|φων.

[160] IC I.viii.12 lines 2–20: Διοσκουρίδης Διοσκουρίδου, καθ' ὑοθεσίαν δὲ Ἀσκλη|πιοδώρου, Ταρσεύς, γραμματικός, διὰ τὴν εὔνοιαν ἂν | ἔχει πορτὶ τὰν ἀμὰν πόλιν συνταξάμενος ἐγκώ|μιον κατὰ τὸν ποιητὰν ὑπὲρ τῶ ἀμῶ ἔθνιος ἀπήστελ|κε Μυρῖνον Διονυσίου Ἀμισηνόν, ποιητὰν ἐπῶν καὶ με|λῶν, τὸν αὐτοσαυτῶ μαθετάν, διαθησιόμενον τὰ | πεπραγματευμένα ὑπ' αὐτῶ· ὑπὲρ ὦμ Μυρῖνος πα|ραγενόμενος παρ' ἀμὲ καὶ ἐπελθὼν ἐπί τε τὸς κόσμος | καὶ τὰν ἐκκλησίαν, ἐμφανία κατέστασε διὰ τᾶν ἀκροα|σίω]ν τὰν τῶ ἀνδρὸς φιλοπονίαν τάν τε περὶ τὸ | ἐπιτάδουμα εὐεξίαν· ὁμοίως δὲ καὶ τὰν εὔνοιαν ἂν | ἔχει πορτὶ τὰν πόλιν, ἀνανεώμενος αὐτ<ὸ>ς τὰν προγο|νικὰν ἀρετάν, δι' ἐγγράφω ἐπ[έδει]ξε καὶ τοῦτο πε|δὰ πλίονος σπουδᾶς καὶ φιλοτ[ιμί]ας τὸν ἀπολογισ|μὸν πο{ι}ιόμενος, καθὼς ἐπέβαλλ[ε] ὑπὲρ ἰδίω παιδε[υ]|τᾶ· ἐφ' ὧν καὶ τὸ πλῆθος τῶν πολιτᾶν ἀκούσαντεν | τὰ πεπραγματευμένα καὶ τὰν [ὅ]λαν αἵρεσιν τῶ ἀν|δρός, ἂν ἔχων τυγχάνει εἰς τὰν ἀμὰν πόλιν ἀπεδέ|ξατο μεγάλως ... A similar case, where Thaletas is mentioned, is presented by two inscriptions of Mylasa, for which see Chaniotis 1988.

Figure 45. Location of inscription to Demeter and Persephone, Agios Thomas.

Over a hundred years ago, a very important but controversial text was discovered in the temple of Diktaian Zeus in Palaikastro near Itanos,[161] a hymn *kletikos*,[162] an appeal to the god to come and appear (no. 13 above and Figures

---

[161] Perlman (1995) has revisited all previous interpretations, literary and religious, and proposed, because of its similarities to the civic oath of Itanos (IC III.4.8), to place this text in a Hellenistic historical and political context: the *Hymn* is an annual petition to the god for Justice and Peace in the social and political strata of the city, without which the blessings of prosperity and well-being are invalidated. Chaniotis (1996a:129 and 187n1134) suggested that the cities, comprising an amphictyony, were probably involved in the hymn's ritual. MacGillivray, Driessen, and Sackett (2000) presented the chryselephantine statuette and interpreted it as the very cultic statue of Megistos Kouros to whom the hymn is addressed: the statuette "was the personification of the youthful male god who arrived from the Underworld to herald the beginning of the Harvest: Diktaian Zeus, associate with Egyptian Osiris, and immortalized as Orion" (169). See further in MacGillivray, Driessen, and Sackett 2000 especially the articles by Robert Koehl, Charles Crowther, Stuart Thorne, Alexander MacGillivray, and Hugh Sackett; and compare Alonge 2005 who argues against the identification of the Hymn's Zeus with the Minoan youthful god. For a useful summary of interpretations, see Furley and Bremer 2001:vol. 1:69–76. On Palaikastro and the cult, see Sporn 2002:45–49 and Prent 2005:532–550.

[162] Depew (2000:61–65 and 69–77) and Furley and Bremer (2001:1–62) discuss the problematic

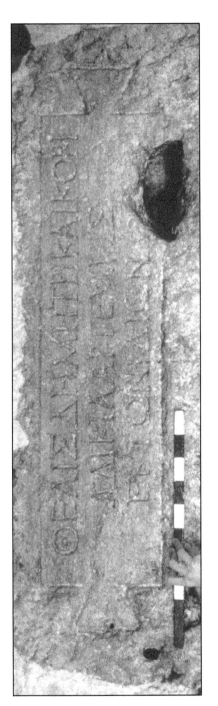

Figure 46. Inscription on stone: vow to Demeter and Persephone, Agios Thomas.

ΜΑΝΤωΝΙΟCΚΛω
ΔΙΑΝΟCΕΥΒΟΥΛω
ΧΑΡΙCΤΗΡΙΟ///

Figure 47. Inscription: vow to Euboulos, from the environs of Knossos.

17a–g [pages 36–38]). The fifth and sixth strophes comprise a catalogue of objects, all of which are to be affected positively by the god's activity (the text is printed as in Furley and Bremer 2001, vol. 2, 2):

ἀ[μῶν δὲ <u>θόρ' ἐς</u> ποί]μνια
καὶ <u>θόρ'</u> εὔποκ' <u>ἐς</u> [μῆλα]
[<u>κἐς</u> λάϊ]α καρπῶν <u>θόρε</u>
<u>κἐς</u> τελεσ[φόρος οἴκος].
[<u>θόρε κἐς</u>] πόληας ἀμῶν,
<u>θόρε κἐς</u> ποντο<π>όρος νᾶας,
<u>θόρε κἐς</u> ν[έος πο]λείτας,
<u>θόρε κἐς</u> θέμιν κλ[ειτάν].

Strikingly, the expression θόρ' ἐς (θρῴσκω εἰς) is employed for the god's activity, which dominates the two strophes by strong anaphora. Guarducci proposed to understand the activity of the god "*non saltantem ... sed insil-ientem*"; West pointed out examples which supported the translation 'spring up'; and Furley and Bremer, following West, translated the verb "leap up" and summarized the expression's possible associations: "either with a renewal of the god's birth ... or with the fertilizing power of the god, the verb being also used for the sexual activity of the male: 'mounting.'"[163]

The same expression, however, is also used in the text from Pelinna, Thessaly (D2A lines 7–10, D2B lines 9–11): ταῦρος εἰς γάλα ἔθορες, αἶψα εἰς γάλα ἔθορες, κριὸς εἰς γάλα ἔπεσες (in A4 line 5: ἔριφος ἐς γάλα ἔπετες). Perlman has noted the discrepancy between the two texts' contexts and the expression employed: in the *Hymn*, fertility is important and receives emphasis, in D2 the "ritual matrix ... does not stress fertility."[164] Tsantsanoglou and Parássoglou (1987:13) were puzzled by the expression on the lamella from Pelinna and argued that:

> the picture of a soul rushing, like a new-born kid, to suck the milk of bliss is rather felicitous after the idea expressed in the words νῦν ἔθανες καὶ νῦν ἐγένου, but what are we to make with ταῦρος and κριός? Bulls and rams do not rush to milk—it is not *their* idea of bliss. Are the new formulas hyperbolic and grotesque variations

---

distinctions between the genres of hymn and prayer; see further Versnel 1981; Bremer 1981; and Furley 1995.

[163] Guarducci in IC III.ii [Dictaeum Fanum].2, commentary (pp. 16–17); West 1965:157–158; and Furley and Bremer 2001:vol. 2:16–17.

[164] Perlman 1995:162n11.

of an original ἔριφος-phrase? In such a case, do they allude to the conduct of the defunct who, in his mature age and after his symbolic rebirth, behaves like a new-born animal? Or should we rather posit the possibility that deification involves a mystic union with a theri-omorphic god, Dionysos in particular?

Tsantsanoglou and Parássoglou preferred the latter explanation (supported by the evidence for the bull-phrase) and pointed out the lack of parallels for the ram-phrase.

It seems, however, that the semantics of the phrase imply a fusion of two motifs: the erratic jumping movements of a newborn, as well as the over-whelming charge of an animal when attacking. The verb θρῴσκω is almost a technical term for describing the birth and the first movements of a god or hero.[165] In Hesiod's *Theogony* 281: from Medusa's head ἐξέθορε Χρυσάωρ τε μέγας καὶ Πήγασος ἵππος. In the *Homeric Hymn to Apollo* 119: Apollo ἐκ δ᾽ ἔθορε πρὸ φόως. In the *Homeric Hymn to Hermes* 20: Hermes μητρὸς ἀπ᾽ ἀθανάτων θόρε γυίων. In *PDerveni* 8F: αἰδοῖον κατέπινεν, ὃς αἰθέρα ἔκθορε πρῶτος.[166] In the *Homeric Hymn to Demeter* 430, Persephone narrates Hades' rush towards her from the opening of the earth: τῇ δ᾽ ἔκθορ᾽ ἄναξ κρατερὸς πολυδέγμων Hades, who, albeit not newly born, moves suddenly and overwhelmingly to accom-plish the abduction.

In the Homeric epics, attestations of this verb are numerous (there are far more occurrences in the *Iliad* than in the *Odyssey*), all of which describe the movement of the heroes or gods in battle or in action, and more specifically, the way in which they jump from the chariot or rush towards the enemy.[167] These movements are sometimes likened in similes to those of animals (the lion, the dog, the eagle) attacking their prey, or to the movement of the sea.[168] One instance in which both verbs are employed (as in the text from Pelinna) is Hector's overwhelming attack, likened to that of a wave crushing a swift ship (*Iliad* 15.623–625): αὐτὰρ ὃ λαμπόμενος πυρὶ πάντοθεν ἔνθορ᾽ ὁμίλῳ, | ἐν

---

[165] For the verb θρῴσκω in the texts of the lamellae, see also Alonge 2005.

[166] On this line and its interpretative problems, see Calame 1997:66–72; Burkert 2004b:89–96; Betegh 2004:113; Bernabé 2004, 8 F; and Kouremenos, Parássoglou, and Tsantsanoglou 2006.

[167] Greeks on Trojans or vice versa: *Iliad* 8.252, 11.70, 12.462, 14.441, 15.380, 15.573, 15.582, 15.623, 16.770, 20.381, 21.233, 21.539 (Apollo), *Odyssey* 17.233 (Odysseus); jumping from chariot: *Iliad* 8.320, 10.528, 16.427, 23.509; lot jumping out: *Iliad* 7.182, 23.353, *Odyssey* 10.207; Athena's landing *Iliad* 4.79; Iris' sea-landing 24.79; *Odyssey* 23.32 (Penelope from bed, at the moment when she identifies the beggar as Odysseus [23.25–31], and not earlier when Eurykleia announces to her Odysseus' return [23.4–9], for which see Winkler 1990:156–157).

[168] Similes: *Iliad* 5.161 (lion on cattle), 15.577 (dog on young deer), 16.773 (flying arrows), 21.18 (Achilles like a *daimon*); *Odyssey* 22.303 (eagles on birds; compare *Iliad* 16.427–430).

δ᾽ ἔπεσ᾽ ὡς ὅτε κῦμα θοῇ ἐν νηΐ πέσῃσι | λάβρον ὑπαὶ νεφέων ἀνεμοτρεφές.[169] In that respect, bulls and rams may not rush towards milk as newborns, but the verbs employed, θρώσκω and πίπτω, are exactly the ones to describe their fierce attacks, as both a bull and a ram charge in the same unidirectional way. Epic poetry seems aware of the verb's semantics, especially its relation to new beginnings, be it birth or rebirth, or a particular and decisive movement.

What this movement pertained to is best illustrated in the invocation of Dionysos by the women of Elis, preserved in Plutarch's *Greek Questions* (299a–b), an invocation which "may be the oldest extant Greek cult song": "come, hero Dionysos, to the pure temple of Elis' people accompanied by the Graces, to the temple storming on your bovine foot, worthy bull."[170] Furley and Bremer emphasize the relation of the hymn to sacrifice, as the women "address simultaneously the animal which is going to be sacrificed and acquire quasi-heroic status, and the god Dionysos himself"; this relation is further exemplified in a scene depicted on a vase in which Hermes leads a sacrificial procession comprising a bull adorned for sacrifice, Apollo singing with a lyre, and Dionysos following behind.[171] Moreover, Furley and Bremer discuss the Austrian excavations under the direction of Veronica Mitsopoulos-Leon, which have revealed the agora of ancient Elis and the adjacent theatre and temple of Dionysos. At the theatre's western corner, tombs, dated to the eleventh century BCE, were found intact, and under the center of the innermost row of the theatre's seats an underground room was discovered, and at its bottom a bull-skull lying on clay fragments with horns and forehead looking east. Mitsopoulos-Leon associated the astonishing finding with the hymn; Furley and Bremer were "tempted to ask: is it possible that in this theatre the local population worshipped a heroised bull?"; and Scullion found the association "quite arbitrary" because *boukrania* are found in a variety of contexts, and the temple rather than the theatre would be a more appropriate site "for regularly recurring cultic offerings."[172] The coin-

---

[169] The modern Greek expression έπεσε με τα μούτρα στο φαγητό, στη δουλειά, literally "he fell with his face to food, to work," likens the way someone is eating or working to an unnatural action, someone eating and working in an unnatural and unexpected way.

[170] Furley and Bremer 2001:vol. 1:369: ἐλθεῖν, ἥρω Διόνυσε, | Ἀλίων ἐς ναὸν | ἁγνὸν σὺν Χαρίτεσσιν | ἐς ναὸν τῷ βοέῳ | ποδὶ θύων. | ἄξιε ταῦρε (they translate ἥρω as *Lord* on the basis of Mycenaean Greek ἥρα/ἥρως being equivalent to 'Lady/Lord,' vol. 2:374–375). For extensive commentary, and the previous bibliography, see Furley and Bremer 2001:vol. 1:369–372 and vol. 2:373–377; and Scullion 2001.

[171] Furley and Bremer 2001:vol. 1:372; and LIMC s.v. Dionysos no. 514.

[172] Mitsopoulos-Leon 1984; Furley and Bremer 2001:vol. 1:371 with epigraphical evidence; Scullion (2001:217n57): "one might think rather [the *boukranion*] as a one-time offering to guarantee the water supply."

cidence of the eleventh-century-BCE tombs and this subterranean chamber-tomb(?), adjacent to the theatre and the nearby temple of Dionysos in the agora of Elis, is remarkable, and begs yet another question: might this coincidence also be related to the other reported tomb of Dionysos in Apollo's temple at Delphi, and the reported tomb of Zeus inside the Idaean Cave?

More importantly, for the verb θύω Furley and Bremer rightly point to the Palaikastro hymn's θρῴσκω, since both imply a similar movement of the two(?) divinities.[173] The movement implied by these verbs, combined with the expression τῷ βοέῳ ποδί, suggests, as Scullion has remarked, "a god described as a bull in the context of ecstatic dancing; dancing that produces the bliss of communion with a powerful god, who has both ecstatic and destructive madness in his gift."[174] It should be noted that in the Palaikastro hymn's fragmentary second strophe (lines 9–10), the feet also appear, undoubtedly for the description of the Kouretes' ritual dancing, while the chorus sings the hymn standing around the altar. Furthermore, among the scenes on vases where Dionysos and a bull appear, two depict the god riding on a bull: in one, Dionysos has a double axe and rhyton in his hands; in the other, he is pouring a libation from a kantharos.[175] The motifs of the bull (or ram or kid), the ecstatic ritual dancing, the theme of purity, and the mysteries in the two hymns from Elis and Palaikastro and in the texts of the lamellae (groups A and D) are manifestations of a divinity in ritual contexts whose aims may differ. In that respect, Dionysos' epithet *heros* in the hymn from Elis may not be as problematic, as only humans are or become heroes, at least in epic poetry. Or, it should be as problematic as the expressions: "you have become god, now you died and now you are reborn, you will reign along with other heroes," all of which refer to the *mystes'* new status in the A-texts (which stress purity), in B1 and by implication in the B-texts (which stress drinking from the water of *mnemosyne*), and in the D2-text (which stress milk and wine).[176] The *mystai* of Dionysos become identical with him, i.e. they become *bacchoi*, just as the god in his earthly manifestations becomes a bull, a ram, or a kid, and in the cult song from Elis is addressed as *heros*. These animals were selected because their movements (which were perhaps consciously imitated by Dionysos' followers)

---

[173] Furley and Bremer 2001:vol. 2:376–377.

[174] Scullion 2001:217.

[175] LIMC s.v. Dionysos no. 435 and 436; and Furley and Bremer 2001:vol. 1:372.

[176] Calame (forthcoming) in his semiotic analysis of the dialogue in the texts on the lamellae and *epistomia*, and in hymns and prayers concludes that in both sets of texts there is an interesting interplay in the roles: poet—addressee (man/woman)—god; see further Parker 1983:281–307; Velasco Lopez 1992; and Graf and Johnston 2007:128–129.

came close to the movements of the ecstatic ritual dance, through which communion with god and the god's epiphany were effected.

The god in the Palaikastro hymn is called to "rush towards" cattle, sheep, trees, the *oikoi*, the poleis, the ships, the young citizens, *themis*, with the same energy that a newborn would, or in the manner a bull or ram might charge, in order to effect fertility and growth. In the texts of the lamellae, the deceased, after her/his rebirth, is exhorted with a similar energy to "rush towards milk," the essential food for the survival of newborn babies, whatever 'food' represented in the mystery cult context. Interestingly, in Callimachus' *Hymn to Zeus* (48–50), the young god is nourished on the milk of the goat (and *not* the nymph) Amaltheia and on the honey of the *melissa* Panakris, named after *Panakra* ("the top of Mt Ida"). This nourishing formula for the supreme god is unique in literature and not at all divine. Milk and honey, with the addition of wine, are also prominent features in Euripides' *Bacchae* (142–143), where the Dionysiac miracles have been understood as a paradisiac condition; honey may also endow someone with prophetic skills according to the *Homeric Hymn to Hermes*; and "the land of milk and honey" (γῆ ῥέουσα γάλα καὶ μέλι) is repeatedly promised in the Septuagint, but never in the New Testament.[177] Again these coincidences are remarkable, but they should not imply necessarily that the Palaikastro hymn (and Callimachus' *Hymn to Zeus*, the *Bacchae*, the *Homeric Hymn to Hermes*, and the Septuagint) are Orphic documents.[178] It does indicate, however, that the Cretan composer of the Palaikastro hymn, just as the composer of the Elis hymn, was well versed in the epic and hymnic tradition, within which the texts on the lamellae and *epistomia* are also solidly placed. Both share this peculiar

---

[177] The interpretation of the milk and honey formula as paradisiac and divine nourishment started with Usener (1902) and Dieterich (1911:96–97), who were criticized by Bonner 1910. On Callimachus, see 169n64. On the milk formula as regenerative in the heroization/divinization process, see Graf 1991:93–95; 1980; Faraone forthcoming-1; for the formula's Near Eastern perspective López-Ruiz forthcoming; and for Pythagorean connections, Iakov forthcoming; Kingsley (1995:264–272; also 109n45); and Petridou (2004), who, extending Kingsley's argument, suggests that it probably refers to an adoption initiation ritual in the Persephone cult, particularly as the texts from Thourioi and Pelinna imply, although in the texts the 'adopted' initiates are called *bacchoi*. For the formula in Alcman fr. 56P, see Schlesier 1994; for honey's prophetic powers, see Scheinberg 1979; and 188n124; in the Septuagint and the New Testament, see Derrett's (1984) and Kelhoffer's (2005) convincing discussion. Stampolidis (2004a:140–141) has associated these expressions (the nourishing power of milk without which babies die) with the modern custom, especially in Crete and the Aegean islands, to dedicate small country churches to Holy Milk (Ἅγιο Γάλα), Saint Milkwoman (Ἁγία Γαλα(κ)τοῦ), or Saints like Agios Stylianos ("he who supports and strengthens"), and Eleutherios ("he who frees"), all associated with birth and the protection of babies (see also page 54).

[178] Aly 1912:471–472 and 477–478; but compare Nilsson (1950:546–547n47): "I cannot find any traces of Orphism which Aly ... makes responsible for the hymn."

expression chosen to express a ritual and cultic activity, most probably the ecstatic and orgiastic ritual dance that looked similar to the erratic movements of young animals and babies, especially when in need of nourishment.

The sanctuary of Hermes Kedritis and Aphrodite in Kato Symi Viannos at an altitude of 1135 m on the southern slopes of Mount Dikte was an interstate destination of continuous worship from the Minoan Old Palace period onwards, as the excavations by Aggeliki Lebessi have established.[179] In attempting to assess the nature of the rituals and cults in the sanctuary, Lebessi has studied the bronze plaques and figurines and their iconography, items which were dedicated by young and mature male members of aristocratic clans. They represent scenes from a ritual initiation of youths into adulthood: youth in adorant posture, nude males bearing arms, a ritual involving a cup, a self-flagellation purificatory ordeal, the hunting of a wild goat, the sacrifice of animals, the playing of the phorminx and the flute.[180] The presence of both Hermes and Aphrodite indicate that in the sanctuary coexisted rituals and cults of fertility, of adulthood initiation, and of marriage. This divine couple appears endowed with both chthonic and vegetative aspects, which were not conceived of as distinct. Hermes in particular has been identified with the piled stones, *hermakes,* where both chthonic and fertility powers dwelled.[181]

An epigram from Phaistos (no. 17 above and Figure 18 [page 41]),[182] the city south of the Idaean Cave and close to Gortyn, was set up in the temple of Magna Mater. This text has been commented upon briefly but convincingly by Giovanni Pugliese Carratelli, who associated it with the Cretan incised *epistomia* (the text is printed below in its hexametric form with verticals indicating line-divisions on the stone):[183]

---

[179] Lebessi 1981; for the bronze animal statuettes, see Schürmann 1996; see further for the site and its cults Sporn 2002:85–89; and Prent 2005:565–604. For the sanctuary's late archaic and classical period relations with nearby Aphrati, see Erickson 2002.

[180] Lebessi 1985 and 2002.

[181] Burkert 1985:156–157. Lebessi (1985:163–187, especially 176–177) correctly emphasizes that there is no longer any need to distinguish between the phallos of Hermes and that of Dionysos, as both are fertility symbols *par excellence*. The phallos on the Herms emphasizes first and foremost Hermes' vegetative fertility that gradually diminished, as Dionysos took over and monopolized the symbol. For an interesting discussion of the opposition in the *Homeric Hymn to Hermes* of the lyre from the shell of a tortoise (and its chthonic power, as it can accomplish the return from the Underworld) and the tomb-stone (as the liminal symbol blocking the return from the Underworld), see Svenbro 1992; as Battos' petrification does not occur in the *Hymn,* but instead the old man later reappears 'talkative,' I would suggest that the tomb-stone is capable of *récit,* but of a different kind than that of the lyre.

[182] For cults and rituals in Phaistos and environs, see Sporn 2002:195–218; Prent 2005:519–523.

[183] Pugliese Carratelli 2001:86–93, 87.

θαῦμα μέγ' ἀνθρώποις | πάντων Μάτηρ προδίκνυτι: |
τοῖς ὁσίοις κίνχρητι καὶ οἳ γον|εὰν ὑπέχονται,
5   τοῖς δὲ π|αρεσβαίνονσι θιῶν γέν|ος ἀντία πράτει. ⱽ
πάντε|ς δ' εὐσεβίες τε καὶ εὔγλωθ{ι}οι πάριθ' ἀγνοί ⱽ
10   ἔνθεον ἐς | Μεγάλας Ματρὸς ναόν, | ἔνθεα δ' ἔργα
γνώσηθ' ἀ|θανάτας ἄξια τῶδε ν|αῶ.

The epigram is divided either into two or three parts, as the empty spaces on the stone indicate after the verb πράτει, and after ἀγνοί. In the first case (3:3), the first three hexameters state the ways of the goddess; the latter three invite all who are "pious" and "eloquent" or "sweet to the ear" to enter the temple "pure" and learn the divine works. In the second case (3:1:2), the fourth hexameter forms the central portion of the epigram, where there is also a change from the third person of the first three hexameters to the second, while the last two hexameters form an elegiac couplet (the problematic sixth line is not a hexameter, but a pentameter).[184] The shift in metrical rhythm and in the person of the verbs is not alien to compositional techniques of funerary epigrams and of the texts on the lamellae and on the Cretan *epistomia*, especially B12 (no. 9 above). The Phaistian epigram therefore invites comparison with these texts, which unveils almost identical compositional techniques, but different discourses on death, as each set of texts aims at a different target. The great miracle in line 1 is picked up again in the concluding lines 10–12, where it is explicated as the god-inspired *erga* worth performing in this temple. The pentameter highlights the transition from the ways of the goddess in the first part to the invitation to the pious in the second and complements the shift of the verbs from third to second person.

The first part of the epigram (especially the second and third hexameters) is difficult to understand. The first verb προδίκνυτι, "show by example, show first, make known beforehand" (LSJ), clearly indicates an oracle and/or a cultic place where mysteries ("a great miracle") are performed. The verb's semantics allude to the ritual and performative aspect of the text itself,[185]

---

[184] A similar metrical change is observed in Isyllos' *paian* to Apollo and Asclepius: whereas lines 10–27 and 29–31 are hexameters, a pentameter is interjected in line 28 which forms an elegiac couplet with line 27 (I owe the reference and discussion to Maria Sarinaki); on Isyllos' *paian*, see Furley and Bremer 2001:vol. 1:180–192 (the text on 182), vol. 2:227–240.

[185] For δείκνυμι as a term of performance, semantically close to σημαίνω and his relation to *kleos*, see Nagy 1990b:217–221; and Lateiner 1989:13–51; for the monumental character of Herodotus' *prooimion*, as *apodexis* and the use of deictics, a case analogous to funerary inscriptions, see Bakker 2002:30–31nn64, 65 with earlier bibliography; for the funerary epigram and Homeric epic, see Létoublon 1995; and especially Day 2000; Depew 2000; for *threnoi*, 159n26.

and the deictic at the end, τῶδε ναῶ, emphasizes forcefully the performative present, the *hic et nunc* performance of the ritual.[186] The goddess' foreknowledge and divination (κίνχρητι)[187] is exclusively reserved for the *hosioi* and for those who literally "put themselves under/within their generation" (LSJ), and who "maintain their origin" (lines 3–4). But to those who transgress the divine generation, the goddess performs the opposite, i.e. does not foretell or divine. Cautiously but correctly, Pugliese Carratelli associated the two sentences, οἳ γονεὰν ὑπέχονται and παρεσβαίνοσι θιῶν γένος, both of which must refer to the same confession, none other than the one encountered in the B-texts of the lamellae and *epistomia*, where the deceased introduces him/herself as: "the son of Earth and starry Sky" (Γῆς παῖς εἰμι καὶ Οὐρανοῦ ἀστερόεντος); and in two of the B texts, s/he also adds: "my name is Asterios" (B2: Ἀστέριος ὄνομα); and "my generation is from heaven" (B9: αὐτὰρ ἐμοὶ γένος οὐράνιον).

What kind of mystery cult and ritual is behind this epigram is not clear, although tempting suggestions have been proposed. Pugliese Carratelli emphasized the relation between this text and Euripides' *parodos* of the *Cretans*, where "divine works" are also performed in honor of the triad: Zeus, (Dionysos) Zagreus, and Mountain Mother. Behind these cults and rituals, according to Pugliese Carratelli, may lie an interrelation between a Cretan Dionysiac mystery cult and an "Orphic-Pythagorean belief about Mnemosyne," because only through Memory can the initiates accomplish the divine message: to remain within and not to transgress their divine origin. Otto Kern had suggested the presence of Orphics in Crete. Nicola Cucuzza associated the epigram with the *ekdusia* of Leukippos and the initiatory rites of ephebes as well as with the fertility ritual of Rhea and/or Lato Phytia at Phaistos. And Katja Sporn cautiously proposed to leave the matter open, as the available evidence does not corroborate the identification between Magna Mater and Leto or Rhea (or even Cybele for that matter).[188]

What this epigram does demonstrate is a Phaistian mystery cult, similar in concept to the cult and rituals behind the *Cretans' parodos*, performed in

---

[186] Bakker 1997:28–29 and 78–80.

[187] Chantraine 1980:1274 s.v. χράομαι; Bile (1988:227n298) Attic κίχρησι; Pugliese Carratelli (2001:87–88) and Martínez Fernández (2006b:162) χρήιζει or χρᾶι.

[188] Pugliese Carratelli 2001:90–91; Kern 1916; see also Chaniotis 1987 and 1990; Tortorelli Ghidini 2000a:40–41; Cucuzza 1993; Sporn 2002:202. Papachatzis (1993) suggests that Rhea's Hesiodic myth was attributed to the cult of Phrygian Magna Mater, who was also associated with chthonian Demeter and/or Kore; Borgeaud (2001) discusses the diachronic development of Magna Mater/Kybele. On the *ekdusia*, see Lambrinoudakis 1971 and Leitao 1995.

honor of Zeus, (Dionysos) Zagreus, and the Mother Oreia (who by analogy is closer to Magna Mater than to Rhea or Leto).[189] These two cults also appear similar in concept to the mystery cult(s) behind the texts of the gold *epistomia* discovered in the wider area of Eleutherna, but also in Pherai, Thessaly (text D5 in Table 1). Moreover, in this epigram the priest/poet employs the verbs προδίκνυτι and κίνχρητι to denote the activity of the goddess, verbs that recall Epimenides' divinatory activity which is not associated with that of Apollo. Magna Mater, inside her god-inspiring temple, reveals the only god-inspiring deeds that count. She pronounces '*the oracle*' of life and death answering the awe-inspiring question 'what happens when humans die?'

Phaistos and Eleutherna lie on opposite sides of Crete's most famous site in antiquity, the Cave of Zeus on Mount Ida,[190] where a mystery cult and rituals were also performed (although of what kind remains a mystery). It would be quite astonishing, however, if the mystery cult and rituals in the Cave were very different from what the Phaistian epigram, the twelve Eleuthernaean *epistomia* and Euripides' *Cretans* imply.[191] The Cave, located at an altitude of

---

[189] The evidence is scanty, but at present these female deities seem to be separate, although Lekatsas (1985:172–189) understands all the female divinities associated with Dionysos as *personae* of Magna Mater.

[190] For worship on mountains in general, see Langdon 2000 with previous bibliography. For the Greek imagination towards mountains and caves, see Buxton 1992 and 1994:80–96 and 104–108. For Thracian sacred mountains, see Theodossiev 1994–1995, 1995, 1996, 1997 and 2002. For Ida, in particular, and for possible cultic activity near Ida's top, see Kritzas 2006. Although the mountains' shape and form do not appear in Greek writers to have had a religious significance (Langdon 2000:463), it should be noted that, as one looks up from below, both Ida in Crete and Olympos in Macedonia have the same conical shape; in Olympos' case this is not the summit (Mytikas 2.917 m), but the peak Profitis Ilias (2.787 m) from the east, and the peak Agios Antonios (2.817 m) from the northwest, where Hellenistic remains of Zeus' sanctuary have been unearthed (Kyriazopoulos and Livadas 1967); Höper 1992; and Pantermalis 1999:19–29 with excellent photographs of the peaks; for Olympos' topography, see Kurz 2003. For the cult of Zeus on Olympos, see Voutiras 2006. For late Bronze Age cemeteries on the northwest slope of Olympos, below the peak Agios Antonios, at an altitude of 1.000–1.100 m, see Poulaki-Pantermali (1987 and 1990), who suggests that the stone seals found on the chest of the deceased were most probably phylacteries with magical qualities, not unlike the ones described in Orpheus' *Lithica*, who is closely related with the area. Soueref (2002) has excavated graves dated to the late archaic period, in which together with an *epistomion* amber beads were found inside or on the deceased's mouth. Clay fragments or small stones are also found as covers of the eyes, the head and other body parts in graves, dated to the late seventh and sixth century BCE, in Thermi near Thessaloniki, in Vitsa Epirus, and in Akanthos (Allamani, Chatzinikolaou, Tzanakouli, and Galiniki 1999:155–156n7 with the references); and compare the section "Afterword."

[191] Lekatsas (1985:77–79) identifies Cretan Zeus with Dionysos and discusses his association with caves; Psaroudakis 1999–2000 studies the often-neglected relation of Dionysos with metals, which are mined in caves, and the 'magical' world of technology.

approximately 1500 m, has intrigued visitors and students alike. Literature concerning the location and its enticing qualities and mesmerizing effects stretches back to the ancient times. The recent excavator Yannis Sakellarakis has presented solid evidence confirming continuous worship from the Minoan period until well into the fourth century CE:[192]

> As is to be expected, the sanctuary particularly prospered during certain periods when it received Panhellenic offerings and at other times worship shows signs of decline. Most frequently worship was transformed, a subject of particular importance for religion, to blend other divinities, chiefly in later times ... The origin of the singular worship of Cretan Zeus, the god who was born and died every year, lies in the prehistoric, Minoan deity, the young god who personified the yearly birth and death of the vegetation cycle, despite the lack of archaeological proof. *This evidence is now explicit and unquestionable*, and furthermore indicates the extent and dynamism of Minoan worship which preceded ... Fortunate, too, are the names of the neighbouring mountain tops, one of which is called Tympanatoras, which alludes to an act of worship, namely the beating of the drums by the Kouretes at the birth of Cretan Zeus (my emphasis).

The findings are overwhelming and more will definitely come to light, as excavations have resumed at Zominthos, a late Minoan site close to the Idaean Cave, perhaps the last stop from the north and east roads leading to the Cave.[193]

Conclusive evidence has not been found for the worship of the triad and the mysteries found in the *parodos* of Euripides' *Cretans*, except for Zeus Idaios,

---

[192] Sakellarakis 1988:209, 212–213, and 214 respectively. The bibliography is extensive: for the recent excavations, see Sakellarakis 1983, 1988–1989; Chaniotis 1987, 1990, 2001a, 2001b, 2006a, and forthcoming (for the inscriptions from the recent excavations), who rightly calls the Idaean Cave "eine überregionale Kulthöhle"; Sporn 2002:218–223; and Prent 2005:565–604. Verbruggen (1981) raised doubts about the nature of Zeus Kretagenes and proposed not to view this god as a dying and being reborn young god; but compare Chaniotis 1986; Kokolakis 1995a, 1995b; and Vikela 2003. In particular, for the possibility of the presence inside the cave of Zeus' throne, see Sakellarakis 2006, who presents an informed array of this object's ramifications in the cave's cult and ritual; for iron finger-rings with very interesting, if intriguing, depictions, see Moustaka 2004; for the depictions on 'shields' and phialae, see Galanaki 2001 and 2006; for the possible production in Eleutherna of some orientalizing artifacts recovered from the cave, see Goula 2006; for the cave during Neolithic times, Mandeli 2006; for the cave's Minoan period, Vassilakis 2006, and for the Roman period, Melfi 2006; for the cave's literary uses in Latin texts, Braccesi 2004 and George 2006.

[193] Sakellarakis and Panagiotopoulos 2006 with the earlier bibliography.

mentioned in a number of treaties between Cretan cities as their guarantor.[194] Some of the artifacts are associated with ephebic initiation rites and fertility, while others indicate worship of more deities in addition to Zeus.[195] Motifs on the bronze art works from the Idaean Cave, dated from the ninth century BCE to the archaic period, include the *potis* and *potnia theron*, ritual dancing and musical processions, warriors and hunters, and female divinities enthroned or lying on a couch. These motifs have been clarified by Popi Galanaki, who argues that one of them, the *potis theron* motif, is reminiscent of the later mystery cult of Zeus Idaios and Dionysos Zagreus.[196]

The very few texts from the Cave that have been published and those whose publication is forthcoming include: some inscribed pottery sherds and numerous lamp signatures;[197] a dipinto;[198] a fragmentary text on stone, perhaps a dedication by or in honor of an Emperor;[199] and a bronze cauldron with a dedicatory inscription by Phaistos son of Sybrita dated to ca. 490–480 BCE.[200] A dedication to Zeus Idaios of the Imperial period is engraved on a clay *tabula ansata*(?) by Aster son of Alexandros (IC I.xii.1, Figure 48; on the back side the letters ΔΙ are probably Zeus' name again in the dative): Δὶ Ἰδαίῳ | εὐχὴν | Ἀστὴρ Ἀ|λεξάν|δρου. A gold lamella with a curious text (perhaps a phylactery although its presence in the Cave is not easily explainable) was tentatively suggested by Halbherr to be a gnostic formula, and by Guarducci to be an "*inscriptio abracadabrica?*" (IC I.xii.8, Figure 49; line 4 is inscribed ἐπὶ τὰ λαιά): [- -]ΙΟΥΩΗ | [- -]ΩΑΙΙΗ | [-   - φυλ]|άσσου. And a dodecahedral cube made of rock crystal and dated to the first century CE, is engraved with a letter or number on all twelve sides.[201] Its presence in the Idaean Cave is not easy to explain, as a number of different reasons may account for its find-spot, but Chaniotis rightly associates it with divinatory activities which may have taken place in the Idaean Cave, where Cretan Zeus was prominent, as the legends about Epimenides also indicate.[202] He cautions, however, that, if

---

[194] Chaniotis 1996a:70; Sporn 2002:222–223.

[195] Sporn 2002:220–221; for the terminology of initiation in Cretan inscriptions, see Bile 1992.

[196] Galanaki 2001:39–44 and passim; also compare Pappalardo 2001 and 2004; for the dancing motifs, see also 165n46, 166n50.

[197] IC I.xii.4–7; Sapouna 1998:91–117 (SEG 48.1212); Chaniotis 2005a:103–107.

[198] Baldwin Bowsky 1999:325 no. 67 (and 2004:117–118); and Chaniotis forthcoming, no. 12: Δειπόνιος, the Roman name Dip(p)onius of a magistrate or manufacturer, not necessarily a Knossian (SEG 52.826).

[199] IC I.xii.2: [- -].ΚΩ[- - -] | [- -]Τ.ΙΟ[- - -] | [- -] υἱός [- - -] | [- -]ΟΣΥΠ[- -] | [- -]Ν[- - -].

[200] Chaniotis 2002:55 (SEG 44.714).

[201] Chaniotis 2006a.

[202] Chaniotis 2006a. Capdeville (1990) has argued for an oracle in the Cave, but compare Chaniotis' remarks. A parallel case is the sanctuary of Trophonios at Lebadeia, near Delphi, which appears

Figure 48. Inscription on clay *tabula ansata*: vow to Zeus Idaios, from the Idaean Cave.

Figure 49. Engraved gold lamella (possibly a phylactery?), from the Idaean Cave.

an oracle existed in the Idaean Cave, it need not have been either permanent or continuous. The gold foil with the curious text and the dodecahedral cube are intriguing pieces of evidence, as both admit a variety of explanations, but a connection with the activities, oracular and/or ritual, in the Cave seems the most probable.

Finally, a late, but very important inscription from Samos provides significant information about the mysteries on Ida:[203]

> Ἥρη παμβα[σίλεια, Δι]ὸς μεγάλου παράκ[οι]τι
> εἴλαθι κάμὲ <u>φύλαττε</u>, σαόπτολι, σὸν λάτριν ἁγνόν.
> ἄρτι γὰρ ἱρὰ Διεὶ ῥ[έξ]ας Κρήτησιν ἐν ἄντροις
> Ἴδης ἐν σκοπέλοισι λάχον γέρας ἐκ βασιλῆος
> 5 Νήσων, τὰς πέρι πόντος ἁλίκτυπος ἐστεφάνωκε,
> ἡγῖσθαι, Πλούταρχος, ἔχων πατρὸς οὔνομα κλεινόν,
> [Οὐρανίοις] σὺμ π[ᾶσι]ν ἐμὸν βασιλῆα <u>φύλασσε</u>.

Hera, queen of all, wife of great Zeus, saver of cities, be merciful and protect me, your pure worshipper. For I have just performed sacrifices to Zeus in the Cretan Cave on Mount Ida, and the king appointed to the office of leader of the Islands, which the wave-sounding sea garlands, me, Ploutarchos, the glorious name of my father; protect my king with all the Ouranian gods.

Ploutarchos son of Ploutarchos, the *clarissimus* proconsul of Achaia under Constans, has been identified by Louis Robert and Angelos Chaniotis as the *praes insularum* under Julian the Apostate, who addressed to Ploutarchos a brief letter and therefore the text is dated to 361–363 CE.[204] Chaniotis has discussed the language of the inscription which employs key words: λάτριν ἁγνόν, ἄρτι ἱρὰ Διεὶ ῥέξας Κρήτησιν ἐν ἄντροις Ἴδης ἐν σκοπέλοισι, suggestive of the sacrifice and initiation in the mystery cult performed in the Cave,

---

to have been regarded both as an oracle and as a mystery cult, where divinatory practice depended upon *Lethe* and *Mnemosyne*; Bonnechere 2003a and 2003b; Maurizio 1999. Ustinova (2002) discusses mythical figures with prophetic traits and their association with subterranean places in the southern Balkans. She also argues that Apollo's epithet *pholeuterios* in Histria on the Thracian Black Sea coast should rather point to the god's oracular activities in dens and caves as well (Ustinova 2004).

[203] Chaniotis 1987, 1990.

[204] Athanassiadi 2005 is fundamental for Julian. Di Branco (2004:12n46) identifies Ploutarchos as the son of Ploutarchos who made two dedications to Asclepius in Epidauros (IG IV.1² 436–437), dated to 307/308 CE, and consequently dates the Samos inscription to the age of Constantine the Great; see also Melfi 2006.

even at so late a date. Ploutarchos employs the epithet *hagnos*, which is found also in the Phaistian epigram and in the A-texts; line 1, on the other hand, is a variant of the *Orphic Hymn to Hera* (*Hymn* 16 Kern, line 2), although the epithet παμβασίλεια is employed for other female deities as well in the *Orphica*, all or some of whom may be understood as other identities of Magna Mater.[205] Interestingly, albeit not unexpectedly, the Samian inscription begins and ends with the same verb, φύλασσε with which the curious text on the gold foil from the Idaean Cave appears to end. Even though the verb, like the epithets above, is very common in amulets and phylacteries, the possibility that the lamella may have been incised with some other kind of text (dedicatory? hymnic?) cannot be ruled out (perhaps like the C1-text in Tables 1–2).

More importantly, however, Ploutarchos' initiation and sacrifice in the Idaean Cave before assuming office, the Palaikastro hymn, and the evidence we have from the treaty oaths of the Hellenistic period, where Zeus Fidatas is present among the gods to whom the parties swear, suggest that the mysteries and rituals of the Idaean Cave were not simply religious activities without any political or social impact. That such was the case not only in Crete but also elsewhere is further corroborated by an analogous incident in seventh-century BCE Lesbos,[206] attested in Alcaeus' fragment 129V. As Anne Pippin Burnett has demonstrated in her excellent discussion on "the disintegrating faction,"[207] this fragment presents a *persona loquens*, none other than the faction formed by Alcaeus, Pittakos, and other Lesbian aristocrats to overthrow Myrsilos, who is speaking at the moment when Pittakos has defected and the members of the group are running to safety in a precinct as suppliants. The members of this faction had sworn an oath to either kill Myrsilos or themselves die, which Pittakos' treason has broken. As Burnett points out, the fragment starts out as a solemn prayer of supplication and turns into a solemn curse: "though it is in actuality a sympotic performance, not a ritual denunciation, the poet has found ways to give it a sense of supernatural efficacy."[208] The oath which the group swore is itself worth a closer look. It is witnessed by a specific triad of

---

[205] A *hieros gamos* between Zeus and Hera in Crete, specifically in the vicinity of Knossos, is attested only in Diodorus (5.72.4), for which see Verbruggen 1981; and Avagianou 1991:71–73. Zeus' marriage to Europa is discussed by Lambrinoudakis (1971:298–301) as a type of *hieros gamos*, which results in the death of the male Talos through the foot, a result comparable to "the Cretan mystery cult of Zagreus" (301); Lambrinoudakis' study shows that the foot or its parts appear to be connected with rituals, especially in mystery cults (for Pythagoras' gold thigh, 365–368).

[206] Chaniotis 1996a:68–76.

[207] Burnett 1983:157–163.

[208] Burnett 1983:160–161.

deities, whom the poet calls upon again, now that the secrecy of their plot is revealed to Myrsilos by Pittakos' defection. Zeus Antiaios/Suppliant (129V line 5: ἀντίαον), Hera Aeolian Mistress, famed mother of all (lines 6–7: Αἰολήιαν κυδαλίμαν πάντων γενέθλαν), as well as Dionysos Kemelian and Omestes (lines 7–9: κεμήλιον ... Ζόννυσσον ὠμήσταν) are called upon to hear the prayer and to "send the oath's indwelling curse after Hyrras' son—the Fury we invoked the day we swore ..."[209] Burnett comments on the specific epithets of the triad: "Zeus is addressed from a posture of mortal humility, as Antiaios; Hera from a stance of racial pride, as the birth-source of all; Dionysos from a mirroring position of noble ferocity, as Omestes." Dionysos' first epithet is problematic and a number of emendations have been proposed, the most recent one associating this epithet with an obscure entry in Hesychius: †καμαν τὸν ἀγρόν. Κρῆτες; whence "Dionysos of the fields."[210] This triad has been associated with a Prehellenic group like the analogous triad of Herakles-Hera-Dionysos in Samos, in which the two male divinities are also young. Burnett argues that "if this (sc. association) is correct, the Lesbian cult will have been peculiar in its substitution of a powerful, chthonian Zeus of Suppliants for the second consort, usually likewise a youth."[211]

The traits of this triad are not very far removed from those of certain deities of the Idaean Cave, especially the Euripidean triad: young Zeus Kretagenes also as guarantor of treaties, Mater Magna or Oreia as the fertility goddess *par excellence*, and Dionysos Zagreus as the perfect hunter.[212] It is significant that both Alcaeus and Euripides employ for Dionysos two epithets, one referring to his raw nature, the other to the fields and hunting, and it is further illuminating that the members of the faction call upon as witnesses a divine triad closely related with mystery cults and rituals. This does not imply a secret society in seventh-century BCE Lesbos initiated into the mysteries of Zeus, Hera, and Dionysos, and sworn to overthrow the tyrant. The distinctiveness, however, of the Alcaean fragment and its Cretan connection (however obscure, and admittedly tenuous) bring to the fore a dimension of mystery cults and rituals usually overlooked. Alcaeus manipulates and activates all

---

[209] Translation by Burnett (1983:157–158) of Alcaeus fr. 129V lines 13–15: τὸν Ὕρραον δὲ πα[ῖδ]α πεδελθέτω | κήνων Ἐ[ρίννυ]ς ὥς ποτ' ἀπώμνυμεν | τόμοντες ...

[210] By G. Tarditi apud Burnett (1983:162n9), who also notes a connection of this epithet to the Linear B *ke-me-ri-jo* found in the Pylos tablets; see further Graf 1985:74–78. Picard (1946:463–465) had associated the epithet with κεμάς, -άδος, "the fawn," and with Dionysos' epithet Eriphios. Quinn (1961) has proposed Cape Phokas as a possible site for this temenos, whence the dedicatory inscription to Dionysos ΒΡΗΣΑΓΕΝΗΣ (IG XII.2 478).

[211] Burnett 1983:160–162, 161n8.

[212] Chantraine 1980:396; Pugliese Carratelli 2001:90–91.

available means (literally and figuratively) for his sympotic and political poetic performance, and among them initiation cults and rituals and their political dimension hold a prominent place, as they are intimately interrelated.

The Idaean Cave and its activities emerging from the fragmentary evidence—mystery cult, rituals and sacrifices, oracular pronouncements, all with important political and social ramifications—must have dominated central Crete, and the impact must have been lasting.

North of the Idaean Cave, Eleutherna and its environs, the provenance of the nine incised and three unincised gold *epistomia*, provides enough evidence to support the view that these *epistomia* may not have been out of context, especially from this particular part of the island. Chance finds and the excavations by the University of Crete over the last twenty years have brought to light structures, artifacts and especially inscriptions that demonstrate continuous but fluctuating habitation since the late Neolithic period. Sanctuaries and public buildings from the late Geometric and Archaic to the Hellenistic and Roman periods have been excavated on the hills Pyrgi and Nesi[213] and also at the site Katsivelos.[214]

The intra-mural necropolis at Orthi Petra, dated from the ninth to perhaps the end of the sixth century BCE, attests to a variety of burial practices which demonstrate a developing ideology and self-consciousness of the city's inhabitants during this period.[215] The necropolis comprises a number of remarkable finds:[216] the Orthi Petra itself, a huge stone-pessos around which the cemetery itself gradually developed; the pyre A of the warrior with the beheaded skeleton at its corner (an example reminiscent of Patroklos' pyre and Achilles' revenge in Homer, as Stampolidis has argued);[217] the lady of Auxerre and a second Kore of Eleutherna, most probably grave monuments;[218] and a

---

[213] Kalpaxis 2004.

[214] Themelis 2002 and 2004a.

[215] This is also the case in the Prinias-stelai, dated to the seventh century BCE; they were fitted on the outer walls of grave monuments in the necropolis of ancient Rhizenia or Apollonia (modern Patela of Prinias) and were engraved with male and female figures representing all social classes, in an impressive posture and with iconographic elements that "may characterize the figures ... as 'heroic,' in the secular sense of the word," according to Lebessi 1976:176 and passim; see also Sporn 2002:176–177 and Palermo 2001.

[216] Stampolidis 2004a:116–138; and Stampolidis 2001 for the burial practices in the necropolis; Erickson (2006) argues for burial austerity in sixth century Eleutherna. For offerings in graves of the geometric-orientalizing period, see Lefèvre-Novaro 2004.

[217] Stampolidis 1996a; 2004a:127–129; 2004c:69–70.

[218] As argued by Stampolidis 2004b:235–236 nos. 252–253; in Eleutherna workshops of sculptors did exist, but how early is debatable; in the Hellenistic period Eleuthernaean artists also worked abroad (Stampolidis 1993:50; 1994:153; 2004a:70–71; Papachristodoulou 2000; Themelis

cenotaph or *heroon*, a public burial monument to 'the unknown warrior,' as it were, inside which were discovered no skeletal remains, but only a baetyl, and on whose roof probably stood as akroteria or cornices the ten shield-bearing warriors, none other than the ten Kouretes, among them no doubt Eleuther himself (after whom the city was named). If the excavator is correct, what may have begun in Eleutherna as an intra-mural burial monument of one or more aristocratic clan-members who claimed their ancestry from one or more of the Kouretes, became gradually by the sixth century BCE the city's most prominent and 'official' necropolis.[219] What rituals and burial rites, if any, were performed at the necropolis and whether the necropolis continued to function as such in the Hellenistic and Roman periods are at present open questions.

Moreover, from 400 BCE onwards, the epigraphical record of Eleutherna together with other finds provides strong indications about the presence of certain divinities who may suggest the existence of cults and rituals relevant to the texts on the *epistomia*.[220]

Apollo was apparently one of the major divinities of the city. The silver and bronze coins, issued by Eleutherna's mint and dated from the middle of the fifth to the middle of the second centuries BCE, carry on the obverse Apollo laureate. On the reverse, two legends appear: in one Apollo is standing nude and is holding a sphere and a bow in his hands; in the other, nude Apollo with bow and quiver and a sphere in his right hand[221] is seated on an *omphalos* with a lyre beside it.[222] The latter coin-legend in particular alludes clearly not only to the hunter-motif, but also to the motifs of prophecy and music, associated in the literary record with Epimenides and Eleutherna.[223] The god's

---

2002:17–18). For the problematics of describing statues and especially the Lady of Auxerre, see Donohue 2005:131–143, 202–221.

[219] Stampolidis 2004a:137–138; 2004b:234–235 nos. 250–251.

[220] For Eleutherna and environs, see Stampolidis 2004a; Sporn 2002:234–244.

[221] This is variously described as a round object, a stone, a rock, a disc.

[222] Sidiropoulos 2004; Furtwängler and Spanou 2004; Stampolidis 2004b:161–162 nos. 24–26; *SNG Kopenhagen* 429–436; Le Rider 1966:105; Svoronos 1890:128–136, 131–135 nos. 2–34. The coin-legends of neighboring Axos include (Sidiropoulos 2006): Apollo with tripod; ivy-crowned Dionysos and tripod with thunderbolt; Zeus Agoraios or Idaios; later, Apollo with quiver and bow, Zeus, Hermes, and the more rare Dionysos with bee or fly; Zeus, tripod, and on top of tripod thunderbolt; Zeus Idaios, Kretagenes, Agoraios, Korybantes, eagle.

[223] It should be noted that a rock and a tree form the scenery, where communication with the divine, and poetic and/or prophetic inspiration, are achieved, as Hesiod's proverbial apostrophizing indicates (*Theogony* 35): ἀλλὰ τίη μοι ταῦτα περὶ δρῦν ἢ περὶ πέτρην; O'Bryhim (1996) and West (1997b:431) adduce Near Eastern parallels where birth from a tree and a rock is mentioned. In Minoan times a similar scenery appears in what Nannó Marinatos (2004) calls scenes of epiphany (for a similar scene on a seal, see also Papadopoulou 2006, 147–149), and

epithets include: Δελφίνιος (in two inscriptions), Βιλκώνιος, and Σασθραῖος.[224] Furthermore, a very fragmentary text from ca. 500 BCE, which Guarducci tentatively calls *lex ad kitharoedos*, may be a regulation regarding the location within the city where the *kitharistai* might live (according to Paula Perlman's cautious reconstruction),[225] but it cannot be taken in itself as evidence for foreign-residents in the city.[226] Perlman (2004:112) is correct in stressing that the legendary figures of poetry and music from Eleutherna and this single fragmentary attestation are not proof for the city being a center of music and poetry. But perhaps there is more to this than an intriguing coincidence. If these legendary stories predated this inscription, and if the coin-legends are therefore later than the inscription or at the least contemporary with it, then the Eleuthernaeans were conforming to their legends for obvious reasons. If, however, the stories were later inventions and postdate the inscription, then Eleuthernaean perceptions of themselves were projected onto these legends, which for some reason became widespread beyond the island—hence their attestation in non-Cretan literary texts.

Zeus' presence at Eleutherna is attested in the epithets Fidatas, Thenatas, and possibly Skyllios in two fragmentary treaties from the third century BCE,[227] as Ὕψιστος in a small altar,[228] and as Πολιάο[χος], Μα[χανεύς?] in the calendar of sacrifices dated to 150–100 BCE.[229]

In the same calendar-of-sacrifices inscription, the cult of the Materes is also attested for the first time, as is [?Δάματερ Μεγάλα?]ρτος, and probably a month Damatrios. Eutychia Stavrianopoulou has argued convincingly that this inscription is the missing evidence that the Materes-cult in Engyon Sicily orig-

Burkert (2004a:19 and passim; 2005b) tentatively describes as "some form of 'divination.'" For the line's use in Plutarch's *Consolation to his Wife* 608c, see Alexiou 1998.

[224] van Effenterre 1991:26–30 (SEG 41.743; BE 1992.360); Chaniotis 1995:16–27; 1996a:190–195 no.6 (SEG 45.1258; 46.1206; BE 1996.324, 332; 1998.318); Themelis and Matthaiou 2004 (SEG 52.852).

[225] Perlman 2004a:109–112. The inscription reads: κιθαριστᾶν, and not Guarducci's (IC II.xii.16Ab line 1): κι[θ]αριστὰς (van Effenterre and Ruze 1995:118–119 no. 26 read κι(θ)αριστὰς). The text is very difficult to read, because the stone was reinscribed without erasing completely the previous text; thus, the strokes of both texts are visible at places. See also Stampolidis 2004a:69–70; and Guizzi 2006.

[226] Presence of Anatolians is attested in the necropolis as three Phoenician cippi have been found, for which see Stampolidis 2003a; 2004b:135, 238 no. 257; 2004c:67–68.

[227] See 217n224; on Zeus' epithets, see Verbruggen 1981:138–141 with earlier bibliography; Psilakis (2002) relates the epithet Skyllios with σκυλλίς, the 'vine-shoot' according to Hesychius.

[228] Sporn (2002:241 and 244) follows the reading in Themelis (1989–1990:266; SEG 39.958): Ὑέτ[ιος], but see Tzifopoulos forthcoming-1.

[229] Stavrianopoulou 1991 (SEG 41.744); on Zeus Machaneus, see Verbruggen 1981:129–130; and Martin 1983:76–84.

inated in Crete in the area around the Idaean Cave. Who these Materes were is not clear. Their identification with Demeter and Kore is an easy solution, but the literary evidence does not support it and it is not certain that the number of the Materes was two. Stavrianopoulou has recognized in them the Nymphs, mentioned in the context of the Idaean Zeus-cult, Amaltheia and Melissa. She has also argued for a connection of their cult with the locality Pantomatrion or Amphimatrion, thus probably named after them, north of Eleutherna in the area of modern Stavromenos, Chamalevri, and Sfakaki whence the five *epistomia* (see map, opposite page 1).[230] Sporn, although in agreement, is sceptical about the specific identification of the Materes with Amaltheia and Melissa (compare also Callimachus' version above).[231] In the same calendar of sacrifices, a Nymph (Λύμφα<ι>) is also to receive a sacrifice, and in the treaty between Eleutherna and Rhaukos, the last divinities mentioned in the oath are: [κ]αὶ Λύμφας καὶ θιὸνς πάντ<α>[νς]. It appears, therefore, that the cult and ritual of the Nymph(s) is rather distinct from that of the Materes, who may thus be identified with the Magna Mater of Phaistos, the Mater Oreia of Euripides, and/or Rhea, Leto, Hera, or some other Magna Mater figure present in the Idaean Cave.

Persephone and/or Demeter or even a chthonian Aphrodite were most likely worshipped in a sanctuary at the site Elleniko on the hill SE of the modern village.[232] In the calendar of sacrifices mentioned above, Artemis is to receive offerings in her *adyta* ([ἐς τ]ὰ ἄδυτ<α> τὰ Ἀρτέ[μιδος]),[233] while the epithet ἀγρο[τέραι], if the restoration is correct, most probably refers to this goddess; she is also included in the oath of the treaty between Eleutherna and Rhaukos without epithet, followed by Velchanos (Fέλχανος).[234]

In the site Katsivelos, the excavated Hellenistic temple was dedicated to Aphrodite and Hermes, as the discovery of a small *naiskos* with the couple in relief and the statue of Aphrodite and Pan demonstrate.[235] Aphrodite is also included in the oaths of the two fragmentary treaties, together with Ares and

[230] Stavrianopoulou 1991 and 1993; Pugliese Carratelli 2001:90–91; Larson 2001:185–188; and the section "Topography."

[231] Sporn 2002:239–240; and 168–169n64, 204n177; on maiden triads, see further Scheinberg 1979; Larson 2001. For Cretan reliefs depicting Pan and Nymphs, see Sporn 2004.

[232] Stampolidis 2004a:57. For Aphrodite, see Pirenne-Delforge 1994, and Budin 2003; for Aphrodite and Dionysos, see Pingiatoglou 2004.

[233] Stavrianopoulou (1991:33 and 38 (SEG 41.744) reads): [ἐς τ]ὰ ἄδυττα <τὰ> Ἀρτέ[μιδος], but on the stone: ΑΑΔΥΤΙΤΑΑΡΤΕ.

[234] Themelis and Matthaiou 2004 (SEG 52.852). Artemis is missing from what survives from another treaty (217n224).

[235] Themelis 2002; 2004a; 2004b:183 no. 78 (*naiskos*), 178–180 no. 71 (statue); and 2006:16–36.

Hermes.[236] Additional finds from this site also include: a statue of a Muse; a marble head of Aphrodite or a Nymph;[237] a statuette of a billy goat; a statuette and a small lead-plaque of Aphrodite; three ivory plaques decorated with mythological scenes from Achilles' life (dated to the fourth century CE);[238] two gold cylindrical phylacteries, one dated to the second century CE, the other to the sixth century CE;[239] a demonic figure, an apotropaic figurine, and what is probably a magic ringstone.[240]

Until recently, the existence of a Dionysiac cult and ritual in the city was conjectured on the basis of a statue group of Dionysos and Silenos in the Rethymno Museum;[241] a few coins which depicted a bunch of grapes issued by Eleutherna;[242] and two inscriptions, a fragmentary text dated to the sixth or fifth century BCE, which preserves the name of the month Dionyssios,[243] and the asylia-treaty between Eleutherna and Teos, dated *paulo ante* 201 BCE and inscribed on the wall of Dionysos' temple at Teos. Although much in this text is probably legalistic formulae,[244] the reference to a cult or ritual of Dionysos implied is undeniable (although of what kind remains a conjecture). The common ground between the two cities is their attitude towards Dionysos, who in this case acts also in a political capacity, not unlike Zeus Poliaochos, Apollo, and Zeus Idaios/Fidatas in the treaties between Cretan cities.

A number of artifacts, most of them dated from the second century BCE onwards, provide additional indications for the presence of Dionysos and his

---

[236] For the inscriptions, 217n224.

[237] Tegou 2004:147 no. 1.

[238] Themelis 2002; and 2004b:181 no. 72 (Muse), 182 no. 77 (billy-goat), 184 no. 81 (Aphrodite small statue), 218 no. 191 (Aphrodite small plaque), 231–232 no. 248 (ivory plaques).

[239] Yangaki 2004 with an addendum of known phylacteries; and Themelis 2004b:nos. 219 and 411; Themelis 2002:60 and 62 figure 67, 78 figures 88–89.

[240] Themelis 2004b: nos. 87 (Themelis 2002:74, 76 figure 84), 224, 246 respectively.

[241] Sporn 2002:239 with n1768.

[242] Eleutherna, Sybritos, and Kydonia were the only three cities of Crete that issued coins whose legends employed Dionysiac motifs; Marangou-Lerat 1995; and Perlman 2004a:102–103.

[243] IC II.xii.9 line 2, as restored by van Effenterre and Ruzé 1994:114–117 no. 25: Διονυσσίαν νεμογ[ηίαν]; see also Bile 1988:154n334; and Sporn 2002:239. The month Dionyssios is attested so far only in Praisos (IC III.vi [Praisos].7A line 14; and Trümpy 1997:195), and Sybritos (Tzifopoulos forthcoming-2).

[244] IC II.xii.21, especially lines 19–29: ... δεδόχθαι τοῖς κόσμοις καὶ τᾶι πόλει τῶν Ἐλευ|θερναίων ἀποκρίνασθαι Τηίοις φίλοις καὶ οἰκείοις | οὖσιν διότι τά τε περὶ τὸν Διόνυσον καὶ αὐτοὶ σεβό|μεθα καὶ τὸν ὑμὸν δᾶμον ἀσπαζόμεθά τε κὴ|παινίομεν διότι καλῶς καὶ ἱεροπρεπῶς καὶ κατα|ξίως τῶ θεῶ διεξάγοντες οὐ μόνον καθὼς πὰρ τῶν | προγόνων παρέλαβον διαφυλάσσοντες, ἀλλὰ καὶ | πολλῶι μᾶλλον προσαύξοντες, ἕνεκεν ὦν καὶ πὰρ' ἁ|μίων τὰ σεμνὰ καὶ τίμια δίδοται τῶι θεῶι καὶ Τηίοις | καὶ τάν τε πόλιν αὐτῶν καὶ τὰν χώραν ἱερὰν καὶ ἄσυ|λον ἀποδείκνυμεν καὶ πειρασόμεθα συναύξειν; and 192n137.

entourage at Eleutherna. A fragment of a marble vessel, depicting a Maenad in the characteristic stance of ecstasy and dated between the first century BCE and the first century CE, is undoubtedly part of a Dionysiac scene and is reminiscent of the Dionysiac scenes on the Derveni krater.[245] There is also a bronze lamp, dated between the second century BCE and the second CE, in the shape of a panther; on the beast rides Dionysos, holding in the right hand a *thyrsos* (now lost) and in the left a branch of ivy.[246] Additionally, in the Katsivelos site were excavated: a clay dramatic mask dated to the first century CE; a clay figurine of Ganymedes carrying wine, dated to the second century CE; and a clay-figurine of Papposilenos, dated to third century CE.[247] All of these artifacts display Dionysiac motifs and themes.

The most remarkable find, however, comprises the three 'Herms' of Pentelic marble unearthed during the excavations of the Protobyzantine Basilica's narthex. In second use, without their heads, inset hands, and genitals, the 'Herms' were placed as lintels of the narthex's doors. A head with two faces looking in opposite directions found in the small bath northwest of the Basilica joins with one of the 'Herms' and, as a result, one of these is almost complete, as it is missing only the inset hands and genitals. The excavator Petros Themelis dates the 'Herms' to the years of Hadrian or Septimius Severus and regards their craftsmanship and quality as comparable to that of the Herms found in the Panathenaic Stadium, an exquisite piece of work imported from Athens, and a unique example for Crete (Figures 50a–b).[248] The Eleutherna example, however, is not truly a Herm (hence the quotes for all three). The one whose head has been recovered depicts Dionysos and Ariadne crowned with an ivy-wreath and wearing a band. So far, this is one of the rarest representations in the Hellenic world and a quite unexpected find at Eleutherna. The few rare 'Herms' of Dionysos depict the god on one side as a youth, and on the other as a bearded adult. Themelis has suggested that the original, in all likelihood, was a fourth century BCE bronze work(s) by Praxiteles, which was used as a model for later copies. He compares the Eleutherna copy with the scene of the couple on the bronze kalyx-krater B1 from Derveni tomb B, and also with Dionysos on the western pedimental sculpture of Apollo's temple

---

[245] Yiouri 1978; Barr-Sharrar 1982; Themelis and Touratsoglou 1997.

[246] Tegou 2004:147 no. 2 (Maenad), 151 no. 8 (lamp).

[247] Themelis 2004b:210 nos. 162, 163 and 164.

[248] Rethymno Museum (Λ[ίθινα] 2579 stele + Λ[ίθινα] 2377 head with two faces); Themelis 2002:96–99; 2004b:185–186 no. 86; and 2006:37–45; for beardless Dionysos, Carpenter 1993. For Herms of Dionysos in Macedonia, see Koukouli-Chryssanthaki 1992:81.

at Delphi.[249] The features of the two heads are nearly identical, and perhaps, instead of Dionysos and Ariadne, the Herm may have represented Dionysos and Apollo, or even a double Dionysos. All three identifications seem equally plausible. Whichever may be correct, it is clear that Dionysos is connected with a divinity intimately associated with poetry, either Apollo or Ariadne, who in the literary record have overlapping spheres.[250] If, however, its identification with the Delphic odd couple is correct, this 'Herm' would visually represent most eloquently the true nature of the two gods: being identical, but looking in different directions, they share an intimate relationship often alluded to in the literary works, as shown above. Be that as it may, the reasons and the purpose for this costly enterprise of commissioning three 'Herms' from an Athenian workshop and transporting them to Eleutherna, remain elusive.

The Cretan Context of the Cretan *Epistomia*

The evidence presented so far indicates that literary perceptions of 'Crete and the Cretans' is not simply a matter of literature. Despite its piecemeal and sketchy nature, the evidence reveals that the epithets *orgiones, paiaones,* and *semantores* applied to Cretans during the archaic period are not outright literary fabrications. Especially regarding the texts on the Cretan gold *epistomia*, the context which produced them is not only similar to that of other texts incised on gold lamellae from Italy, the Peloponnese, Thessaly, and Macedonia. There is also a Cretan context that emerges, as the evidence suggests a variety of mystery cult(s) and rituals in Phaistos, in the Idaean Cave, and in Eleutherna (where the Cretan gold *epistomia* were found). As is the case with the texts on the lamellae, there is both similarity and divergence amongst the evidence from Phaistos, the Idaean Cave, and Eleutherna. It seems as if there was a renaissance of cults and rituals in these and in other places in Crete from the third century BCE until the late fourth century CE, notably after the Roman conquest and the organization of the island as a Roman province. Martha Baldwin Bowsky has argued cogently that the Romans took a partic-ular interest in realigning and reorganizing the regional zone between Mount Ida and the White Mountains (see map, opposite page 1), so that finally Gortyn and the Diktynnaion were connected via Sybritos, Eleutherna, Lappa, and

---

[249] For the Delphic couple and its representation in sculpture, see pages 139–150 with notes. For a sanctuary of Apollo (*kitharoidos*), in which Artemis and Dionysos were also worshipped, in Western Macedonia, see Karamitrou-Medessidi 2000.

[250] For Ariadne, see 155n9, 166n50, 169n65.

a.

Figure 50. Double-sided Herm from Eleutherna, Sector I. Rethymno, Archaeological Museum, Λ[ίθινα] 2579 (stele) and 2377 (double-sided head). (*a.* the Herm complete; *b.* the head's two faces)

Aptera. As a result Eleutherna was privileged over Axos, despite the latter's proximity to the Idaean Cave:[251]

> Eleutherna ... thanks to its strategic position along routes of trade, transit, and communication, which facilitated mobility both among the Roman population resident within Crete and from outside the island ... became the dominant Roman city west of Mt. Ida, a commercial hub strategically located along one of the island's principle east-west arteries of communication and also at a critical point in one of the north-south corridors that characterized Roman Crete.

In fact, the extensive necropolis (the place from which the gold *epistomia* were recovered) is located near this very west-east artery, which turns south near Sfakaki by the seashore, and winds through Viran Episkopi, Eleutherna, and Sybritos, finally reaching the Roman capital Gortyn (see map, opposite page 1).

---

[251] Baldwin Bowsky 2006:267; Baldwin Bowsky and Niniou-Kindeli 2006; for the Roman reorganization of the island and its ramifications, see further Viviers 2004; Sonnabend 2004; and Baldwin Bowsky 1995, 1999, 2001a, 2001b, 2002a, 2002b, 2004a, 2004b, and forthcoming.

During the Roman and Imperial periods, the Cretans apparently revitalized and emphasized the long-standing perceptions about their island and themselves, chief among them the perceptions surrounding the Idaean Cave and its rituals and mystery cult(s). Milena Melfi has observed that during the Classical and Hellenistic period, when Crete was plagued by internal strife, the artifacts from the excavations in the Idaean Cave are few and indicate a decline, but from the Imperial period onwards, the number of artifacts increases remarkably. This suggests, as she argues, that in the first centuries CE the Idaean Cave, among other places on the island, became a fashionable destination, mainly among neoplatonic circles, which, however, may have been only one of the crucial factors.[252] Both the Diktynnaion[253] and the sanctuary at Palaikastro (where, in this very period, arose the need to reinscribe a new copy of the *Hymn to Megistos Kouros*, no. 16 above) are also marked examples (see map, opposite page 1).

Moreover, the evidence from Eleutherna corroborates that this was the city's golden period (and, after the Minoan period, the entire island's for that matter), and it may very well provide the missing answers for the renaissance of old cults and rituals from the third century BCE onwards throughout the island, but chiefly around Mount Ida. The Cretan context sketched above, the evidence from the area around the Idaean Cave, to the south at Phaistos, and to the north at Eleutherna, does point to intensive and continuous ritual and cultic activity. In all probability, the priesthood in the Idaean Cave and the neighboring cities (Phaistos-Gortyn, Knossos, Axos, Eleutherna) exploited to their advantage the Roman interest and tried to accommodate the needs of the people frequenting cult-places.[254] Such a context is fitting for, and may explain, not only the presence of the deceased buried with incised *epistomia*, but also the deviant choices and ideologies in these texts, because of the various but similar in concept mystery cults and rituals in Phaistos, the Idaean Cave, and Eleutherna.

---

[252] Melfi 2006; Di Branco 2004; and 57n25. For two lamps from the Melidoni and Amnissos Caves with unique depictions of *taurokathapsia*, dated to the Roman period, see Sapouna 2004. The Minoan bull-leaping has also been variously associated with Theseus' myth, for which see Scanlon 1999.

[253] For the Diktynnaion and its funding activities, Tzifopoulos 2004; Sporn 2001; and Baldwin Bowsky 2001a, 2001b, and forthcoming; Baldwin Bowsky and Niniou-Kindeli 2006. Andreadaki-Vlazaki (2004:39) notes that the 'mile-stone' from Viran Episkopi indicates a Diktynnaion in this area. For the Asclepeion at Lebena, Melfi 2001 and 2004; Girone 2004; and Di Branco 2004.

[254] I purposefully avoid the term *pilgrimage* as it is loaded with the semantics of the Judeao-Christian tradition; in spite of recent arguments, it is not at all certain that ancient *theoria* was, or was meant to be, also a *proskynesis*, the Greek word denoting "pilgrimage." For recent treatments, see Coleman and Elsner 1995; Dillon 1997; Elsner and Rutherford 2005.

The piecemeal nature of the evidence, however, advises caution, and the dedication by Aster, son of Alexander may illustrate the point. It may indeed be far fetched to argue that Aster son of Alexander was not his true name—a rare name in any case[255]—but instead the name he received after initiation into the mystery cult in the Idaean Cave. If we wanted to speculate in this regard, however, we might notice that the name Aster is reminiscent of: 1) the *mystes* from Pharsalos who identifies himself as: Ἀστέριος ὄνομα (B2); 2) the *mystai* of the B-texts, who identify themselves as: Γῆς παῖς καὶ Οὐρανοῦ ἀστερόεντος; 3) the entry of Hesychius: Ἀστερίη· ἡ Κρήτη καὶ ἡ Δῆλος οὕτως ἐκαλοῦντο (and of Herodianus: Χθονία· οὕτως καλεῖται ἡ Κρήτη); as well as the mountain Ἀστερουσία to the southwest;[256] and 4) Asterion or Asterios or Asteros, the mythical childless king of Crete to whom Zeus gave Europa in marriage and who reared Zeus' and Europa's children Minos, Rhadamanthys, and Sarpedon. All of these are perhaps nothing more than bewildering coincidences, as may be the minor role assigned to two divinities named Astraios and Asterie in Hesiod's *Theogony* (376 and 409 respectively).[257]

Even so, and given the Cretan context(s) sketched above, the deviant readings in the *symbolon* and particularly in the topography of the *epistomia* B12 (no. 9 above) and B6 (no. 4 above), before they are dismissed as rather simple palaeographical oversights or mistakes, deserve serious consideration as significant variant readings. The expression: *I am of Earth, mother, and starry Sky* (Γᾶς ἠμι, <μ>ἁτηρ, καὶ Ὠρανῶ ἀστερόεντος), may have undergone a small change, perhaps because of the cult of Magna Mater or the Materes, so as to be in concert both with local cult and with the Bacchic-Orphic mystery cult on afterlife. The *mystes* addressing her/his reply to the *mother*, none other than Persephone in a Bacchic-Orphic mystery cult, or the Magna Mater or the Materes in their mystery cult, would thus have it both ways, not unlike the *mystes* in D5, or the Chorus in the *parodos* of Euripides' *Cretans*. This much at least, in spite of the problems in grammar and meter, is an equally plausible understanding of the *symbola* in B6 and B12.

---

[255] Bechtel, and LGPN I, II, IIIA, IIIB, IV.

[256] According to the entries in Stephanus *Ethnica* 139; Herodianus *De prosodia catholica*, 3.1 (p. 293); and Eustathius *Ad Iliadem* 1.518. 21–26. For the late sources, see Verbruggen 1981:149–151 with earlier bibliography.

[257] Unless these divinities have a minor role, precisely because their names were important in poetry rivaling Hesiod's epic (Asterie was also the original name of Delos; see West 1966:270 and 281). Willetts (1962:166–167) discusses the ancient sources; according to Pausanias (2.31.1) Minos had also a son Asterion whom Theseus defeated, if Asterion is not another name for Minotauros, for which see Lambrinoudakis 1971:301, 343–344. For a later development of Asterios' myth in Nonnos and Dionysios, see Vian 1998 with previous bibliography.

The topographical variants in B12 and B6 are more intriguing and challenging. In particular, B12 lines 2–3 mention "the spring of Sauros/Auros" (κράνας <Σ>αύρου or κράνας Αὔρου), and B6 line 2 mentions "the spring of ΑΙΓΙΔΔΩ" (κράνας ΑΙΓΙΔΔΩ). Both texts deviate from all other texts in group B from Eleutherna, Thessaly, and Italy, texts in which the spring is either simply ever-flowing, divine, or bearing ice-cold water (ἀείροος, ἀέναος, θεία, or ψυχρὸν ὕδωρ), whose water the deceased must drink; or there will not be a spring but instead a lake of Mnemosyne (λίμνη Μνημοσύνης). If the reading in B12 is not a nonsensical topographical mistake, then "the spring of Sauros/Auros" should be related to the only other attestation for such a spring on Mount Ida. Theophrastos, in his narrative on black poplars (αἴγειροι, some of which bear fruit and some not) records that in the Idaean Cave and its environs, most of the black poplars bear fruit. He locates one at the entrance to the Cave, another smaller one nearby, and, at a distance of twelve stades from the entrance (approximately 2200 m) he notes many poplars around "some spring called of Sauros" (*Historia plantarum* 3.3.4: ἐν Κρήτῃ δὲ καὶ αἴγειροι κάρπιμοι πλείους εἰσί· μία μὲν ἐν τῷ στομίῳ τοῦ ἄντρου τοῦ ἐν τῇ Ἴδῃ, ἐν ᾧ τὰ ἀναθήματα ἀνάκειται, ἄλλη δὲ μικρὰ πλησίον· ἀπωτέρω δὲ μάλιστα δώδεκα σταδίους περί τινα κρήνην Σαύρου καλουμένην πολλαί).[258]

There is no way of determining the source of Theophrastos' information. In the Nida plateau at the foot of the Cave, a number of springs are interspersed. One of them, "Christ's spring" (πηγὴ τοῦ Χριστοῦ) has been identified as Theophrastos' so-called "spring of Sauros" by Spyridon Marinatos and Eleutherios Platakis.[259] A second spring called "Partridge-water" (Περδικόνερο) was used by Sakellarakis' team during excavations in the 1980s (*personal communication*). Sauros, "the lizard-man," and especially Auros are not very common names, and this well accounts for Theophrastos' scepticism: περί τινα κρήνην Σαύρου καλουμένην. It is almost as if the author himself does not believe what he is writing (the manuscript tradition is sound and presents no difficulties in this sentence). And yet, a close parallel may be found in the name of the Nymph Saora or Aora after whom the city of Eleutherna was originally named, as the grammarians note:[260]

---

[258] For this passage, see also Stampolidis 1996b; 1998a:114–116; 1998b.

[259] Apud Sakellarakis 1983:419 and n3.

[260] Bechtel 1917, *LGPN* I, II, IIIA, IIIB, IV, LSJ, and Chantraine 1980, s.v. The form *Sauros* is already attested in a Linear B tablet from Knossos as a name: *Saurijo* (see Chantraine 1980:991). For Satra, see Stampolidis 1993:24–25; 1994:143–144; 2004d; van Effenterre 1991:29; Themelis 2002:11–14; 2004a:48. There is a Roman name Σάτριος/*Satrius*, relatively uncommon in Greek nomenclature (see Baldwin Bowsky 1995:272–273; SEG 45.1239). Another intriguing

Stephanus, *Ethnica* s.v.: Σάτρα· πόλις Κρήτης, ἡ μετονομασθεῖσα Ἐλεύθερνα· ὁ πολίτης Σατραῖος. And s.v. Ἐλευθεραί· ἔστι καὶ Κρήτης ἀπὸ Ἐλευθῆρος ἑνὸς τῶν Κουρήτων, ἥτις καὶ Σάωρος ἐκαλεῖτο ἀπὸ Σαώρης νύμφης.

Herodianus, s.v. Ἐλευθεραί· πληθυντικῶς λεγόμενον· ἔστι καὶ Κρήτης ἀπὸ Ἐλευθῆρος ἑνὸς τῶν Κουρήτων, ἥτις καὶ Σάωρος ἐκαλεῖτο ἀπὸ Σαώρης νύμφης. And s.v. Ἄωρος· πόλις Κρήτης ἀπὸ Ἀώρας νύμφης· ἐκαλεῖτο καὶ Σάωρος. And s.v. Ἀώρα ἢ Σαώρα· νύμφη, ἀφ' ἧς Ἄωρος ἢ Σάωρος πόλις Κρήτης μετονομασθεῖσα Ἐλευθεραί.

Satra, a city in Crete, which changed the name to Eleutherna; the citizen is called Satraios. Eleutherai, a city in Crete, named after Eleuther, one of the Kouretes, which used to have also the name Saoros/Aoros after a nymph Saora/Aora.

Nymphs gave their names to springs and cities, and in the epigraphical record of Eleutherna, they are included in treaties and in the calendar of sacrifices, as noted above. Moreover, the inhabitants' name Satraios is also a local epithet of Apollo, attested in the oath of a fragmentary treaty dated to the third century BCE.[261] The form Σασθραῖος provides the original name of the nymph (Σάσθρα), which perhaps the grammarians changed first to Σαστραῖος and then to Σατραῖος. Satra, in all probability, should be associated with the Iranian root χšαθρα, whence the Old Persian χšαθρα-pavan and satrap, literally "kingdom/fatherland protector"; alternately, it may have originated from a form Sat(a)ra or Sat(u)ra, after syncopation, from a root Sat- (Ksat-) which meant "free, master, ruler," or even "fatherland."[262] If the grammarians are to be trusted, then it appears that the two names may have been understood as similar in meaning; hence the change into a Greek and more intelligible name, Ἐλεύθερνα/Ἐλευθεραί.

This is not all, however. Things become even more complicated by a piece of evidence dated to at least the middle of the fifth century BCE which presents another remarkable coincidence.[263] Herodotus, in his narrative of Xerxes'

---

coincidence is the form of the month at Lato: *Sartiobiarios*, "a strange-sounding foreign word," according to Robertson (2002:26–27), for which see Chaniotis 1996a:322–323 no. 55 A22, B16 (= IC I.xvi.4 line 22); 1996b; and Trümpy 1997:193–194.

[261] van Effenterre 1991:29; Faraklas et al. 1998:78; and Chaniotis 1996a:190–195 no. 6 (SEG 46.1206).

[262] Chantraine 1980, s.vv. *satrapes* and *saturos*; LSJ s.vv. *satres, satra, satrap-*. Stampolidis (1993:24–25; 1994:143–144; 2004d) calls the root *sat-* ("free, master, ruler") Thraco-Pelasgian and entertains the possibility of *Sat(a)ra* being related to the Linear B toponym *Katara*.

[263] I owe this reference to Nicholas Stampolidis, who has also suggested that the name of the

march through Thrace, enumerates the Thracian tribes that were forced to follow Xerxes' army, naming only one exception, the tribe named *Satrai* (7.110). According to the historian (7.111.1), *Satrai* were the only Thracian tribe he knew up until his own time who had completely avoided subjection and had remained always free (ἐλεύθεροι). Herodotus attributes this freedom to their unparalleled military valor (τὰ πολέμια ἄκροι) and to their habitat high in the mountains, covered with every kind of forest and with snow (ἴδῃσί τε παντοίῃσι καὶ χιόνι συνηρεφέα). Among these mountains was Mount Pangaion which they especially minted for gold and silver (7.112). Moreover, high up on their mountainous territory, they possessed the oracle of Dionysos, whose prophets were from a group of *Satrai* called *Bessoi*, and whose female *promantis* divined in exactly the same way as the priestess at Delphi (πρόμαντις δὲ ἡ χρέωσα κατά περ ἐν Δελφοῖσι, καὶ οὐδὲν ποικιλώτερον 7.111.2).[264] What is remarkable is that Herodotus' narrative appears to relate the name of the tribe to their attributes, just as in the lexicographers' entries it is implied that the two names Satra/Eleutherna (Eleuther) had the same meaning, or that at least their meaning was understood as similar or identical. Two more details are also striking: the tribe's expertise in warfare, which apparently secured their free status, and its forested habitation (ἴδῃσί παντοίῃσι), described in a way that recalls *Ida* (the name given to the highest mountain in Crete because of its being forested), in whose Cave Cretan Zeus, alias Thracian or Greek chthonian Dionysos, was worshipped.

Be that as it may, the coincidence is remarkable. Even if it may not point to some kind of connection between Cretans and Thracians (a matter still up for debate), this coincidence does imply that in two areas the toponym *Sasthra/ Satra* underwent parallel interpretations.[265] Meaning either 'free/sovereign,'

---

    tribe *Paiones*, inhabiting the area west of Mount Pangaion, may have something to do with the Cretan *Paiawones*, perhaps due to migrations during the late Bronze or the early Iron Age. On *ide/Ida*, a prehellenic word of uncertain etymology, see Chantraine 1980:s.v.; and Willetts 1962:143–144.

[264] Fontenrose (1981:228–229) relates this oracle to the one at Amphikleia in Phocis, where a male *promantis* served Dionysos, and he assumes that it was a healing oracle through dreams and incubation, just like the one at Amphikleia, although Herodotus clearly relates it to Delphi; see Harrison 2000:150n105; Detienne 2003:163–164; and Connelly 2007:80 on the prophetess' direct inspiration from the god, as in the Delphic model. On Orpheus, Apollo, and Dionysos in Euripides' *Rhesos*, see especially Markantonatos 2004; Liapis 2004; and Fantuzzi 2006.

[265] Another intriguing coincidence is found in the modern names of the cities *Eleuthero(u)polis* and *Eleutherai* in the wider area of ancient *Satrai* (for the area of ancient Pieria, see Pikoulas 2001); and in the name of the village Satres (Σάτρες) in the Thracian Prefecture of Xanthi. And one should also keep in mind that Dionysos entered Attica from the Boeotian *Eleutherai* (for the story and the sources, see Farnell 2004:vol. 5, 226–239).

or 'fatherland/kingdom,' *Sasthra/Satra* or the like, after it was changed to *Eleutherna*, may have been retained as a name of one of Eleutherna's districts or neighborhoods, where Apollo's worship was prominent and ancestral links were thriving.[266] This much has been suggested by Henri van Effenterre for the other epithet of Apollo, *Bilkonios*, derived from *Bilkon*, perhaps the name of Eleutherna's western hill Nesi, where Apollo's presence could also have been prominent.[267]

Could *Sasthra/Satra* and *Eleuther/Eleutherna* have been Eleuthernaean re-inventions of the past, especially promoted from the late Hellenistic period onwards,[268] when people began flocking to the city and the neighboring renowned Cave-sanctuary on Ida? The stories could presumably have been about a Nymph named so and so, who had an escapade with Apollo in such and such a place, whence the epithet of Apollo and the name of the spring on Mount Ida. And about Eleuther, one or the most important of the Kouretes and a victor at the Pythia, there could also have been stories, about how he took such and such an action on behalf of the baby-god, and came down from Ida to such and such a place, whence the new name of the city. Such mythistorical creations, or "archaeologies," as Claude Calame (2003) would call them, would more than sanction Eleuthernaean presence in the Idaean Cave and its lucrative administration. The Eleuthernaeans apparently employed in certain periods for their own political, social, economic, and religious purposes some or all of the names for their city, names far more numerous than for any other Cretan city: Satra/Sasthra, Saoros/Saora, Aoros/Aora, Apollonia, Eleuther, Eleutherai, Eleuther(r)a, Eleuthernai, Eloutherna, Eleuthenna, Eleutherna. These names variously reflect the inhabitants' prejudices and ideology regarding self-awareness of their past and self-identity.

Eleutherna's distance from the Nida plateau and from the Idaean Cave (today approximately an hour and a half by car, but in antiquity probably a full day's walk up the mountain) should not present an insurmountable difficulty, as a modern example aptly illustrates. The pasture of the Nida plateau (or at least the majority of it) belongs today to the village of Anogeia, located at a distance of 21 kms to the north, and not to the village of Vorizia, located at a

---

[266] Until 2002 in Greek cities the districts or neighborhoods were given in most cases the names of the parish-churches dominating the district, according to which the voting catalogues were prepared.

[267] van Effenterre 1991:29–30; but evidence for such an identification does not exist and Chaniotis (1996a:191–192 and 195; BE 1996.332, 324) rightly argues against it.

[268] Baldwin Bowsky 2000 argues that the Cretans responded to Roman influence by revitalizing local traditions.

much closer distance of 8.5 kms to the south.[269] Whoever wished to visit the Idaean Cave and return could not have done so in one day, but had to spend at least one night, and probably more if s/he also wished to be initiated. The Nida plateau is scattered with Roman remains which no doubt belonged to structures for the accommodations of the visitors,[270] much like the ones excavated in the Diktynnaion. As the Idaean Cave was an interstate sanctuary (whether this was the case all along or if it only happened gradually is unclear) whose logistics and priestly responsibilities were administered by the citizens of Gortyn/Phaistos, Knossos, Axos, Eleutherna, and perhaps other cities, it is only natural that these citizens who had to spend a considerable number of days or months in the Nida plateau would have their own lodgings somewhere near the Cave. An analogous case, *mutatis mutandis*, is the so-called *thesauroi* of cities in the sanctuaries at Delphi and Olympia, which housed and protected the city's dedications to the god. The principle behind the *thesauroi* is similar. The sanctuary authorities permit cities to build within the precinct their own *oikiskoi* as dedications to the god, in which the city also housed and protected its smaller offerings. Likewise, in the Nida plateau, albeit not within the precinct itself (its borders can only be guessed at), the neighboring cities would have to come to terms and divided up the space proportionately(?), presumably to everybody's benefit. If such an amiable agreement, as described, ever existed, the evidence for it is wanting, as is information about the sanctuary's administration. In fact, evidence to the contrary is presented by the fate of the interstate sanctuary of Diktaian Zeus in eastern Crete. Disputes between the neighboring cities Itanos, Dragmos, Praisos, and Hierapytna about their borderline and about the control of the arable land and pastures of the sanctuary were fierce and long-lasting, and eventually ended each time with the annihilation of one of the parties involved, until the Romans reorganized the island as a province.[271]

With names sounding so strange (Saoros and Aoros), no wonder Theophrastos was sceptical about the spring's name. Theophrastos' reading and that in B12 (no. 9 above) are in all likelihood related to the 'older' name of Eleutherna, Saoros, and the name of the spring can be nothing other than the "spring of Saoros/Sauros/Eleutherna" on the Nida plateau. This would imply that the area around this spring 'belonged' to Eleuthernaeans, where presumably they would have camped when visiting the sanctuary, or would have built more permanent lodgings.

---

[269] Sakellarakis 1983:418.
[270] Sakellarakis 1983:passim; Melfi 2006.
[271] Guizzi 2001 with previous bibliography.

B12 thus provides a strong link between Eleutherna and the Idaean Cave and the mystery cult initiations performed there sometime from the third century BCE onwards, if not earlier. More importantly, however, if the "spring of Eleutherna" in the Nida plateau did exist (and at present there is no compelling reason to doubt that it did—whether it is the "Christ's spring" which Marinatos and Platakis identified as Theophrastos' so-called "spring of Sauros" or one of the other springs in the plateau), then the Underworld illustrated in the texts on the Cretan gold *epistomia* (and perhaps also in those of the other gold lamellae) gains a significant dimension. It is commonly assumed that initiation into a cult comprised the *legomena*, *dromena*, and *deiknymena*. The texts on the lamellae and *epistomia* provide some of the dialogue and the action, but what kind of performance there was, and what was shown to the initiates is anybody's guess.[272] The drama, reenacted constantly for each initiation and supposedly with minimal changes, must have also included some kind of scenery for the Underworld journey. Some persons, the priest(s?), would have acted out the roles of the guards of the spring/lake, and perhaps also those of Dionysos, Hermes(?), Demeter/Mater Oreia/Persephone, and Hades. The whole ritual performance should have been so impressive as to be inculcated into the initiate who thus would have no trouble during the 'actual journey' *recognizing the cypress and the spring*, and *remembering the symbola dialogue*.

What is astonishing, provided this reading and its scenario are plausible, is that an actual spring, the "spring of Eleutherna/Sauros/Saoros" in text B12 and its surrounding scenery may have been used as a 'prop' during the deceased's initiation. If so, this may also account for the 'wrong' topography of the spring to the left of the cypress, as "the spring of Eleutherna/Sauros" on Ida may have been actually to "the left of a cypress-tree." In that respect, if the reading in B6 line 2: κράνας ΑΙΓΙΔΔΩ does not refer to some topographical detail unknown so far, then κράνας αἰγί{δ}ρω, "the black-poplar spring," is equally, if not more, acceptable, as Verbruggen had proposed.[273] For "the black-poplar spring" may also have been another epic element appropriated by the composer of this particular text (and perhaps of other texts), and given a new and very specific symbolism. Although the cypress is absent from Circe's detailed instructions to Odysseus, poplars are not. A tree (black poplar) and a spring are part of Persephone's grove at the entrance to the Underworld, and a tree and a spring also appear on the islands of Calypso (cypress and poplar), the Cyclops, Scheria,

---

[272] See 116n59.
[273] Verbruggen 1981:90–91; and 112n48.

and Ithaca (poplars).[274] The scenery of the Nida plateau included poplars, as Theophrastos attests in the passage quoted above, but also the famous cypress-trees, exported throughout the Mediterranean, near which springs were flowing.[275] The cypress and the spring are mythic stock-elements, as is also the black poplar, which, as Edmonds has argued, do not illustrate a clear-cut operative dichotomy of left and right, but can signify different things in particular texts.[276] This accounts well for the divergent readings in the B group texts, but B12 and B6 may add another significant explanation of a more mundane nature. It appears that during initiation, a kind of Underworld scenery and atmosphere was created for the reenactment and performance of the ritual. This may indeed sound far-fetched, but is not unprecedented, as Merkelbach's documentation of the small ritual acts performed during the initiation ritual into the cult of Isis and Sarapis shows.[277] This 'stage' for the performance of the ritual had to be plausible enough and had to represent as closely as possible the Underworld scenery as imagined by the 'priesthood,' for which sometimes real props, ready at hand, had to be employed, and which from place to place would expectedly be tinted with a local coloring.[278] Thus, the Underworld illustrated in the texts of the gold lamellae and *epistomia* is a unique combination not only of mythic stock-elements, but also of 'real' ones, a combination conveniently present on the Nida plateau, the *black-poplar*, a *spring*, and a *cypress*, which may account for the divergent topographical hints in these texts. The world above, more familiar and less dangerous, lends to the world below some real objects, a *cypress* nearby the *spring of Eleutherna/Sauros*, and *the black-poplar spring*, in order to render it less threatening, and thus more easily attainable.

The deviant readings in texts B12 and B6 (and E1, E4, and G2–4 for that matter) from Crete may present a case of local (or individual), and therefore 'peripheral,' influences on the Bacchic-Orphic discourse of afterlife, and not another typical case of an engraver's mistake. To judge from the present state of the evidence, it may not be sheer coincidence that both texts present divergent readings in the same places, the *symbolon*, and the location of the cypress and the spring. The Cretan context(s) of mystery cults and rituals, especially

---

[274] For these Odyssean passages, 112n48, 113nn51–52.

[275] Willetts 1962:143–144; Chaniotis 1993; 1999:208–209; Perlman 2000:145–146.

[276] Edmonds 2004:46–55.

[277] Merkelbach 1995:147–181, 328–331, 343–346; the small ritual acts include impersonation of gods by priests, theatrical devices, machines, etc.

[278] Graf and Johnston (2007:109–111) explain the topographical divergence in B12 as a probable innovation by an *orpheotelestes*, claiming that *his* is the correct knowledge of the Underworld topography; this need not exclude a local context for the incised *epistomion*, unless the *orpheotelestes* was an iterant.

the context sketched above for Phaistos, the Idaean Cave, and Eleutherna, amply illustrates that, especially from the third century BCE onwards, mystery cult(s) and eschatological beliefs, similar in concept to the one expressed in the texts on the *epistomia*, were in vogue and flourishing. These were not always and in all areas of the island peripheral or central to the polis religion, but apparently coexisted side-by-side not only with Olympian religious ideas but also with other cults and rituals. Nor was there one central Bacchic-Orphic doctrine which prescribed specifically how the Underworld journey should be accomplished, and how the promised life after death should come true.

Within the small group of the twelve incised and unincised *epistomia* there is evident differentiation. Different *mystai* felt differently and expressed their beliefs and attitudes in differing, more individual(?) ways, as the shapes of the *epistomia*, the burial-coin practice, and the choice of the words to be incised strongly suggest. Although the majority of the *mystai* conform to the general and therefore central ideology of eschatological beliefs as expressed in the long texts from Italy and Thessaly, two *mystai* insist on engraving in texts B6 and B12 a local and therefore peripheral version of the Underworld topography, not to mention the two *mystai* addressing Plouton and Persephone (E1, E4), and the three who do not engrave anything but leave the matter completely blank to be filled in accordingly (G2–4). Why are the specific details of topography so significant for the two *mystai*? Have these two *mystai* been initiated in the Idaean Cave on the Nida plateau, whereas the other ten elsewhere? Is this a local change of the Underworld narrative topography, or were similar attempts also made elsewhere but so far are unknown?

These are legitimate questions that show the limitations imposed by the evidence. Crete, located in the periphery of Greece, and Phaistos, the Idaean Cave, and Eleutherna and environs, in turn peripheral centers on the island, provide strong evidence against hasty emendation of both deviant texts so as to make them conform to their similar Cretan examples. They strongly argue for further research on these texts, particularly the possibility that they could have been influenced by local (or individual) idiosyncrasies. Religious attitudes and ideologies not only within a polis but also within a specific group of *mystai*, as is the case at Sfakaki, need not, or could not, always conform to identical practices. The evidence from Eleutherna and Sfakaki, reveal an interpretative tension and dynamic interaction between local and Panhellenic, central and peripheral, rituals and mystery cults, burial practices and ideologies, and discourses on afterlife.

The probable "springs of Eleutherna/Sauros, of the black poplar, and of the cypress" near the Idaean Cave, and the evidence from the excavations of the city suggest that Eleutherna and its environs remained a stronghold for a mystery cult and ritual with chthonic associations and beliefs in the after-life from the late Hellenistic period until well into the fifth century CE. This long-lasting survival and the slow conversion of this area's inhabitants to Christianity must have been one of the reasons, if not the main reason, for the early establishment of a bishopric at Eleutherna, in order to win over gradually the population. This process does not appear to have been violent, as Themelis has concluded on the basis of the excavations of the Basilica. Building material for its construction was taken mostly from the adjacent sanctuary of Hermes and Aphrodite, and from the *Sebasteion*, which, although not yet located, most certainly existed (as the Imperial dedicatory and honorary inscriptions indicate). Perhaps the *Sebasteion* was in some other locale, where the three Dionysiac 'Herms' were also erected.[279] The church was built sometime between 430 and 450 CE, as the mosaic inscription in the Narthex commemorates its foundation and records as the founder the bishop Euphratas, who participated in the Ecumenical Synod of Chalkedon in 451 CE.

The mosaic inscription also records the Saint to whom the Basilica was consecrated, none other than the archangel Michael, the Christian psycho-pomp. To the eyes of the area's inhabitants he would not have looked that much different from Hermes and Dionysos, the psychopomps with whom they were already familiar. Whatever appeared non-offensive was appro-priately incorporated into the new Basilica (the three 'Herms' being the most elaborate example) and the new ritual and cult, a process that appar-ently was crowned with success. The excavations have yielded impressive remains,[280] which provide strong evidence for a thriving bishopric in the first Byzantine period. Although the Basilica appears to have been destroyed for some unknown reason in 641–668 CE or immediately thereafter, after which it was simply abandoned, this need not imply any major setback for the bish-opric. The sources mention only one other bishop of Eleutherna in addition to Euphratas, Epiphanios,[281] who participated in the Ecumenical Synod of Nicaea in 787 CE. In the second Byzantine period 961–1210/1 CE, the bishopric

---

[279] Themelis 2000a, 2002, 2004a; for the transition from the Imperial to Protobyzantine period, see Themelis 2004c; for the coins, Sidiropoulos 2000; for the inscriptions, Tzifopoulos 2000. As Chaniotis (2005b:146–147) notes, the reasons for turning pagan temples into churches are not the sacredness of the site, but its pagan and anti-Christian symbolism which have to be cleansed and re-consecrated; Lalonde (2005) argues against continuity, borrowing, or contact from ancient to Christian cult and ritual.

[280] Themelis 2004b:187 no. 88: a very rare seventh century CE portable icon of Christ.

[281] This bishop's epithet ἀνάξιος is not necessarily pejorative, as Themelis (2002:22 and 2004a:70) has suggested; it most probably indicates humility.

of Eleutherna apparently ceased to exist. This may have been caused by the site's decline, although churches continued to be built and the population did not abandon the site altogether.[282] The bishopric at Eleutherna, however, may have ceased because its purpose was accomplished: to convert the inhabitants into Christians. Another bishopric was instituted in the area of Mylopotamos/Aulopotamos (Aulopotamos still being part of the modern bishopric's titulature), an area north of the Idaean Cave, where three more bishoprics are known to have been active: one at ancient Axos, one at Episkopi immediately east of Eleutherna and north of Axos, and one at A(g)rion, which some have located at the north shore of Eleutherna (where ancient Pantomatrion, and modern Sfakaki, Chamalevri, and Stavromenos are located; see the section "Topography" and the map, opposite page 1). The institution of all these bishoprics cannot have been haphazard. They bespeak the lasting religious effects in the area north of the Idaean Cave, where, for many centuries, mystery cult(s) thrived and rituals were performed.

---

[282] Themelis 2002:24–25; and 2004a:79–80; Kalpaxis 2004; Tsougarakis 1987:402–403; 1988:230–231, 323–326.

Afterword

Old Habits Die Hard or New Customs Follow Old Paths?

THE SOPHISTICATED BURIAL RITES AND CUSTOMS presented above are obviously not unique to ancient Greece. The burial–coins, the wreaths, and the gold lamellae and *epistomia*, incised or unincised, are items ingeniously devised by humans to help them face the most terrifying fact of life. They attempt to solve practical problems and at the same time come to terms with the fear of death, as Plato aptly described it (*Republic* 330d–331a).

Two modern examples may suffice to accentuate the interpretative problems that other discourses about death raise.

First, suppose that archaeologists a thousand years from now excavate the crypt under Saint Peter's Basilica in the Vatican, in which the Popes are buried, and suppose that they reopen Pope John-Paul's II tomb. Under the inscribed marble slab is found a casket of oak-wood, inside which is a coffin of zinc, inside which is yet another coffin, this time of cypress-wood, engraved with a cross and an 'M.' In addition to the bones—the white silk veil over the face, the pontificals, and the bishop's hat placed on the chest may not have survived the intervening years—the archaeologists discover inside the last coffin a small bag of various commemorative medals from the pontificate of the deceased, imprinted with dates, and sealed in a lead tube a parchment which briefly summarizes the life and papacy of John Paul II.[1] If these were the only pieces of evidence, attempts at interpreting them and placing them into some kind of context would certainly run wild. Why cypress, zinc, and oak? What of the medals or burial-coins? What of the written parchment and its biographical narrative, and why inside a lead tube?

---

[1] Internet websites for the burial of Pope John Paul II on April 8, 2005: http://www.cnn.com/2005/WORLD/europe/04/08/pope.funeral/index.html; http://news.bbc.co.uk/1/hi/world/europe/4424477.stm.

And secondly, suppose that you were given and asked to write a commentary on the following poem/song of the American Indian Tewa tribe (produced by the music group Apurimac (1998) in Greece, and quoted in Modern Greek and English from the compact disc's leaflet):

Πείτε του ήλιου να φανεί και να χαμογελάσει
να τραγουδήσουν τα πουλιά στα πράσινα λειβάδια
πείτε του ήλιου να φανεί και να μας αγκαλιάσει
όπως μας αγκαλιάζουνε του αργαλιού τα δώρα.
Μάνα Γη Μάνα Γη
Ουρανέ Πατέρα Ουρανέ
τα παιδιά σας είμαστε.
Το άσπρο φως του πρωϊνού ας είναι το στιμόνι
το κόκκινο του δειλινού ας είναι το υφάδι
και οι σταγόνες της βροχής τα ασημένια κρόσια
κι ύστερα όλα τα χρώματα απ' το ουράνιο τόξο.

Won't you tell the sun to rise and shine
for the birds to sing down at the prairies
and embrace us with his glorious light
just as we're enwrapped in the warm loom's gifts.
Mother Earth, o Mother
Father Sky, o Father
'tis your children calling you.
Let the white morning light be the shuttle
let the purple of the dusk be the woof
and the raindrops be the silver fringes
with all the colours of the rainbow.

This poem/song from the Tewa tribe is entitled, after its refrain, "Mother Earth." Does this refrain, so strongly reminiscent of the new identity of the deceased in the B-texts, imply the presence of Orphics among the Tewa tribe, or are the Tewa influenced somehow by Bacchic-Orphic eschatological beliefs?

The questions asked in the two examples sound absurd, because they are not questions that the evidence permits to be asked. They ignore the context of the motifs, and the ideas and symbolism behind them. The ancient Greek incised lamellae and *epistomia*, the Tewa tribe's song, and the Catholic burial ritual of Pope John Paul II eloquently illustrate distinct attitudes towards and conceptions of death. And yet, despite their distinct underlying ideology of death, the external manifestations in all three instances present points of contact, not because of influence, but simply because human beings react to death and try to understand it in ways that look much alike. The context of all three cases *is not, cannot be,* comparable: Greek mystery cults, American Indian ideology and beliefs, Christian dogma. Their objective, however, to remove the fear of death by referring to a common source for all humans and/or by promising a special status for humans after death, and their means to achieve this objective disclose similarities. Thus these three cases manifest a "cultural interaction and transformation of discourses" on death which *do not depend on one another,* nor do they need to. In different historical contexts and cultures, they articulate the continuities, discontinuities, and transformations that human discourses on death have experienced.[2]

Furthermore, these two deliberately extreme cases, the burial ritual of Pope John Paul II and the Tewa tribal song, also serve as a forceful caveat for the Greek case. In certain areas of Greece, customs of *epistomia* (nos. 18–25 above), death-coins, and wreaths are still evident; there are also verbal reminiscences in popular poetry and songs (δημοτικά τραγούδια), especially in the laments (μοιρολόγια) and in the Eastern Orthodox Requiem. The Byzantine and modern Greek practices and customs, when and if compared with analogous ones from antiquity, run the serious risk of being drawn into the unending and vehement debate on Greek cultural continuities and discontinuities from antiquity to the present; hence the question mark of this section's title: either old habits die hard, or new customs instinctively follow old and time-honored paths, and new discourses are created. The Byzantine and modern Greek examples presented in nos. 18–25 above can be, and more often than not are, explained in terms of historical and cultural continuities or discontinuities with strong arguments for and against. This is an approach, however, which by definition leads to an impasse. It is far better to approach the Greek examples (ancient, Byzantine, and modern) as discourses on death in their own right, ones which utilize ritual patterns and poetic techniques, or "ritual poetics," for their own distinctive discourse on death, regardless of the historical gaps (which cannot be filled in anyway).[3]

---

[2] Yatromanolakis and Roilos 2003 and 3nn5–6.

[3] For the term, 3nn5–6. Guthrie (1993:261–271) concludes his study with the vexing issue of Orphism and Christianity; compare Zizioulas' (2003) and Stroumsa's (forthcoming) convincing arguments for the mutual influences and interconnections and the dynamic interaction between Judaism, Hellenism, and Christianity from the second century BCE until the early third century CE. That borrowings may be detected does not imply that the symbolism and discourse were also borrowed; *on the contrary,* dynamic interaction may lead to new discourses. For peculiar analogies with early Christianity and Gnostics, see Betz forthcoming.

Nos. 18–20 above date from the first Byzantine period, nos. 21–23 from the middle Byzantine, and nos. 24–25 from the modern era (Figures 19–23 [pages 44–47, 49, 51])). They are clay fragments, incised or painted, and they all document death-related rituals and customs which address a practical need when preparing the body of the deceased for burial: how to close the mouth. And yet the solution devised is highly unusual and unexpected. (The usual and expected practice, which has been followed throughout history across the globe and continues to be followed today, is to bind shut the lower jaw; compare Figure 40 [page 90], and the section "Shape—Burial Context").

Nikolaos Politis also notes that, in order to avert evil spirits, a tile or ostrakon incised or painted with a cross, pentacle, the inscription Ἰ(ησοῦ)ς Χ(ριστὸ)ς νικᾷ, or even with the name of the deceased (compare Figures 19–22 [pages 44–47, 49]) and 23 [page 51], dated to the first Byzantine period and 1990 respectively), is placed on the mouth of the deceased just before inhumation.[4] In Western Macedonia and Thrace, in particular, a coin called *peratikion* ("transporting-fee") is placed on or inside the mouth when the body is prepared, either as a phylactery or, according to a popular song, as Charon-fare to transport the deceased across the river which divides the worlds of the living and the dead.[5] Coins may also be placed on the chest or in the pockets of the deceased's clothing, and other gifts may be brought and placed in the coffin "for the long journey and to give them to those whom s/he meets," as the usual explanation runs.[6] In Archangelos Rhodes, a quite different object is placed inside the mouth: a small seal used for the consecrated bread, incised with a cross and wrapped in a kerchief.[7]

These are elaborate ways of dealing with a practical need, which are subsequently invested with the appropriate symbolism. Eurydice Antzoulatou-Retsila has studied in detail the "proofs of memory" (τεκμήρια μνήμης) which mostly concern the living, specifically the practice of bringing to the deceased flowers, wreaths, and evergreen plants of various kinds, sometimes covering

---

[4] Politis (1931), Sygkollitis (1934), and Megas (1940:166–205) are the basic works for modern Greek burial rites and customs, which are elaborated by Danforth (1982), Anagnostopoulos (1984), Alexiou (2002), and Antzoulatou-Retsila (2004).

[5] Politis 1931:330–333.

[6] Sygkollitis 1934:401–402 (tile), 392 (coins and silverware); Megas 1940:178, 183–184; Danforth 1982:40; Alexiou 2002:99 (tile), 72 and 91 (coin). Danforth and Alexiou mention only coins, but Antzoulatou-Retsila (2004:145–152) records various other 'gifts,' as I also personally witnessed in villages of Western Macedonia. It is also customary in the burial of clergy to place the book of Psalms on the chest of the deceased. For modern Greek beliefs in the magic qualities of metals, see Papamichael 1962–1963.

[7] Information kindly provided by Giorgos Diakonikolaou; see also Politis 1931:336n4.

the entire coffin (except for the face) with them. These gradually became large wreaths with ribbons on which the names of the dedicants were painted. There is also one case from Kydonies in Asia Minor, in which people used to dedicate flowers βαρακωμένα, i.e., after moistening the flower, they glued extremely thin gold foil on its leaves.[8] It is tempting to associate this practice with the ancient *stephanosis*, but no one who dedicates a wreath to honor the deceased does so (nor, if they do, is the symbolism the same). The modern practice is invested with new meaning and is transformed in order to accommodate two realities: firstly, Christian teaching, in accordance with which the deceased is wreathed as was Christ or as would be a victor of the hardships of life who is now entering the true life in Christ; secondly and more importantly, the social need of the dedicant to express respect and gratitude and to exhibit these feelings publicly by physical and tangible means, sometimes to the point of creating a spectacle. Such a gesture may be a last attempt to communicate with the deceased, but at the same time it emphasizes life and especially the life of the dedicant.

From her comparative study of funeral practices, Margaret Alexiou has concluded that the similarities between ancient and modern Greek funerary practices—"survivals," as she calls them—are impressive.[9] Although discrepancies between the official position of the Church and the attitude of people in the villages may have been a reality at least during the Protobyzantine period, it appears that under Ottoman occupation, the two traditions, the Christian and the pagan, became fused in Greece. Instead of a survival, however, this process points rather to a new discourse on death for whose synthesis various elements and motifs are appropriated and transformed, acquiring new meaning and symbolism. These motifs are common to humanity, especially to those groups which live in rural societies, and are not exclusively Greek. Ancient Greek laments and their modern counterpart, *moirologia*, reveal 'a common tradition' for the synthesis of these songs: their structure and morphology, the techniques, motifs, metaphors, and formulae employed suggest, according to Alexiou, the survival and transformation of beliefs kept alive from antiquity to the present day.[10] And yet these shared elements, constantly reworked in a creative manner and sometimes dynamically transformed, do not form "one common tradition," as implied by Alexiou's analysis

---

[8] Antzoulatou-Retsila 2004:133.
[9] Alexiou 2002:106–108. For a theological perspective of Hellenism, Judaism, and Christianity, see Zizioulas 2003; and Paraskevaidis 2005.
[10] Alexiou 2002:221–322 and 326–327.

of the evidence, but at least two 'common traditions.' If removed from their Greek context, they represent eschatological beliefs which may be encountered throughout the world—it is only for brevity's sake that they have been referred to in the previous chapters as the Homeric view of death and the Orphic view of life after death.

Loring Danforth has commented extensively, from an anthropological perspective, on the death-related rituals he observed in a village in Western Macedonia. Although much has changed since his research trip in 1979 and much more is bound to change in the future, several key elements of the death-rituals nevertheless remain evident. Concentrating on all stages of the rites and rituals from the moment of death until the exhumation of the deceased's bones, his approach reveals a discourse on death which appropriates and transforms motifs, metaphors, and powerful symbols from both the official Eastern Orthodox Requiem and orally transmitted popular songs, including laments (μοιρολόγια). As convincingly unveiled through Danforth's words and encapsulated in Alexander Tsiaras' extraordinary photographs of each stage of ritual, this discourse is an attempt "to mediate the opposition between life and death."[11] Danforth studies these death-rituals as rites of passage. The exhumation-ritual, in particular, is a reversal of the burial-ritual and thus, according to Danforth, an attempted or imperfect resurrection or a partial victory over death (35–69). To an outside observer, the pile of bones in an ossuary may be testimony that death is irreversible, that the opposition between life and death cannot be resolved, and that the material world cannot be transcended. The exhumation-ritual, however, when it occurs (in some areas, only when another relative dies and the grave-plot is needed for the new burial) is the final arrangement of the dead on earth as far as the living are concerned. The relatives, especially the women, are released of all their weekly and monthly duties to the dead following the exhumation. In terms of Danforth's rite-of-passage analysis, however, the exhumed deceased remains in a liminal state, in keeping with the Orthodox Church's ritual and teachings that the resurrection of the dead will occur with the Second Coming of Christ.[12] Thus the Church prescribes Memorial Services up to three years after death, a period after which relatives are advised to remember their dead on special Saturdays dedicated by the Church to the souls of the dead (ψυχοσάββατα) and especially during the week before Easter, the Good Friday, and the Pascha-Saturday. It should be noted here that in some villages of Western Macedonia

---

[11] Danforth 1982:32.
[12] Anagnostopoulos (1984:320–347) discusses the liminal state of the deceased.

and in Kozani, the area's capital city, the ceremony for Christ's resurrection (Ἀνάσταση) is held at midnight not inside the Church, but in the city's main cemetery.

Another mediation of this opposition discussed by Danforth is the singing of laments.[13] Their imagery and metaphors verbalize loss and bereavement by expressing them in 'poetic' terms and therefore creating a more 'rationalized' medium of communication between the living and the dead—an attempt which also fails, in that the opposition between life and death ultimately remains, even gaining added validity. The *moirologia* finalize loss and separation, but in the meantime the relatives grow exhausted and satisfied by the mourning process. Finally, according to Danforth,[14] religious and social modes of behavior enable the living to continue both their lives and their relationship with the dead, a relationship which, despite this elaborate discourse, in the end remains an open "wound that never heals"[15] and the exclusive prerogative of women.

These specific discourses created to come to grips with death are Greek, but the views on death and life after death, the Homeric and Orphic dichotomy, are not a uniquely Greek phenomenon. Furthermore, the opposition between life and death, between earth and the underworld, and between death and immortality—none of these is an issue that agonizes only Greeks. As Danforth has aptly put it in anthropological terms:[16]

> The religious perspective that is generated by the performance of death rites can be maintained most easily at the level of subjective reality. Subjectively we are able to deny death and maintain the fiction of our own immortality or of the continued existence, in some form, of significant others who have died. However, as this subjective reality is externalized and objectified during the course of social interaction, problems arise; contradictions begin to appear ... An individual who subjectively maintains a religious perspective, in which the death of a particular significant other is denied, is confronted with an objective reality in which the other members of his society, who are still alive and who have not been so powerfully affected by the death, adopt a common-sense perspective

---

[13] Danforth 1982:71–115.
[14] Danforth 1982:117–152.
[15] Compare Psychogiou (2003) on the crucial role of women as intermediaries between the living and the dead, exemplified in the preparation of the boiled wheat.
[16] Danforth 1982:32.

towards death and are able to accept it. The contradiction between the religious perspective and the common-sense perspective, between subjective reality and objective reality, between the denial and acceptance of death, can never be fully resolved. As far as our experience of death is concerned, the movement between these two perspectives will always be hampered by this contradiction. This results in an ambivalent attitude toward death, one in which we can neither accept nor deny it fully.

Death-related rites and rituals and discourses on death employ every available means in their attempts to invalidate the inherently human contradiction. In the case of the Greeks, these attempts are particularly elaborate discourses on death which make the most out of ritual patterns and poetics.

The popular, orally-transmitted *moirologia* eloquently articulate the contradictions between life and death, between culture and nature. They emphasize the theme of irreplaceable loss and separation, also evident in the motifs of marriage and journeying employed, and the theme of the natural cycle of birth and death, the return to nature, all complemented by powerful antithetical images and creative metaphors. These images and metaphors contrast food and its absence (even the corpse becomes earth's food); water is contrasted to the thirst of the deceased; light in life is contrasted to darkness in death; the season of spring, when all of nature is in bloom, is contrasted to wintertime, when all in nature dies, and to the harvest (as Charon reaps human-crops).[17] They allude also to evergreen plants and trees (especially the cypress), to birds (because they cross the boundaries of the upper and lower worlds more easily and swiftly), and to other animals as well.[18]

These motifs, themes, and metaphors may be compared and contrasted with analogous ones found in ancient Greek laments and discourses on death. The fact that the laments exhibit what has been called the Homeric view of death has led Alexiou to discuss the B1-text on the lamella from Petelia, Italy, in her concluding section on water and thirst; specifically, she associates the B1-text's motifs of the spring of Lethe and Mnemosyne, of the cypress, and of the deceased's thirstiness with those encountered in the *moirologia*.[19] Though the motifs may be identical, however, their different contexts, ancient and modern, invest them with entirely different symbolism and meanings. The

[17] Information kindly provided at Chania by Christoforos Sklavenitis about *moirologia* on the island of Leukas that refer to departure.
[18] Alexiou 2002:298–321; Danforth 1982:71–115.
[19] Alexiou 2002:323–326.

collections of *moirologia* lack any suggestions of the Orphic view of life after death[20] which is evident in the texts of the gold lamellae and *epistomia*. The motifs are therefore employed in the *moirologia* in order to create powerful images of the absence of life after death and the unnatural status of the dead. A few examples suffice to reveal the diametrically different associations which the themes, motifs, and metaphors of the lamellae and *epistomia* acquire in *moirologia*. The cypress exhibits an ambiguous eschatology in Homer, but in the lamellae it serves clearly as an eschatological place-marker near two springs/lakes;[21] in the *moirologia*, by contrast, it is employed either in metaphor (the deceased is likened to the tree) or as a marker for water in general, near the entrance to Paradise.[22] While in both cases the cypress represents a limen, actual or metaphorical, the new status awaiting the deceased in each case is markedly different. Likewise, the thirst-motif in the lamellae is meant to emphasize the choice the *mystes* faces as he decides which spring/lake to drink from, a choice which will affect his future condition in Hades; in the *moirologia*, however, thirstiness only accentuates the unnatural state of the dead, who do not drink and are not instructed to do so, because in fact they cannot. Moreover, Alexiou admits that the forgetfulness-and-memory motif of the texts on the lamellae has no convincing parallels in the *moirologia*, as the living are rather encouraged in the laments to remember the dead and not forget them.[23] In the lamellae, on the other hand, the motif belongs exclusively to the dead, who must remember which of two springs/lakes to drink from in order to be reborn. Alexiou's concluding remarks that these motifs are intertwined and reflective of ancient eschatological beliefs[24] thus require modification.

The absence in the *moirologia* of an Orphic view of life after death is not at all surprising, if other discourses on death are brought into the picture. The

---

[20] Saunier (1999) is the most accessible and offers a complete overview of *moirologia* drawn from previous collections (Fauriel 1999:301–302 was able to discover only two brief *moirologia*); see also Politis 1932. The south-central Peloponnese, Mani, Tsakona, and Sparta, have been studied more than other areas (Passagianis 1928, Scrometakis 1994, and Katsoulakos 2001); on *moirologia* as social protest Caraveli 1986 and 159n26. For Cretan *mantinades* on the subject of death see Jeannaraki 2005:142–148; and Tsouderos 2002. Anagnostopoulos (1984) provides a detailed study of the eschatology in surviving popular songs; and Kapsomenos (2000–2001) discusses the ideas on life and death in Cretan popular songs.

[21] See above the section "The Cretan Texts in the Context of a Ritual and a *Hieros Logos*" and 112nn47–48, 113nn51–52, 114n54.

[22] Antzoulatou-Retsila 2004:206; on the Underworld topography and the existence of the deceased there as depicted in popular songs see Anagnostopoulos 1984:269–319.

[23] Alexiou 2002:324–325. On forgetfulness in *moirologia*, see Saunier 1999:111–135.

[24] Alexiou 2002:326.

Eastern Orthodox Church Requiem *par excellence*, a very important text that has not received due attention, may fill in this gap.[25] It is composed of parts in narrative form, solos, and choral chants, through which the central dogma, the resurrection of the dead, is communicated. This dogma is summarized in the verse of the Creed: "I await the resurrection of the dead" (προσδοκῶ ἀνάστασιν νεκρῶν), a verse more often than not inscribed on tombstones as the deceased's own proclamation. Thus the deceased implies that s/he has not really died, but 'lives' in this liminal state until the Second Coming of Christ and the final judgment, a view analogous to the ancient Orphic view of death. These analogies, however, are shown to be limited and superficial when the motifs, themes, and symbols are studied within their contexts. After all, with the gold lamellae and *epistomia*, the deceased is immediately reborn into a new, heroic, if not outright divine, existence, but s/he remains forever in the Underworld, just like Hades, and is not transferred to Olympos, the other divine dwelling.

The ritual ceremony of a funeral in the Eastern Orthodox Church is divided into three stages.[26] The first takes place in the house of the deceased person, where the priest arrives to escort the deceased to the church; the second is the performance of the Requiem inside the church; and the final one occurs over the grave in the cemetery. In the first and the last stages, i.e., at the house before the formation of the funeral procession and at the grave where the procession ends, the priest performs the small Requiem, called τρισάγιον ("thrice-holy"), for the deceased, always mentioned only by her/his first name. The *trisagion* is also chanted over the grave after a three-, nine- and forty-day period, after a year, and after three years, or whenever the relatives visit the grave and ask the priest literally to "throw 'down' a *trisagion*" (να ρίξει ένα τρισάγιο), i.e., chant while looking downwards at the grave from within which the deceased 'may be listening.' At the intervals of forty days, a year, and three years, a Memorial Service is held inside the church, comprising the *trisagion* together with a number of benedictory chants (εὐλογητάρια) that are also chanted during the Requiem.

---

[25] I am using the official text of the Greek Orthodox Church (Νεκρώσιμοι καὶ ἐπιμνημόσυνοι ἀκολουθίαι). Unlike Danforth (1982), Alexiou (2002) gives the impression that she avoids references to this text, perhaps because of its uncertain date, although some of its parts and its music are believed to be compositions of John from Damascus, and although numerous other liturgical texts are employed throughout (compare also Alexiou 2004); see further Anagnostopoulos 1984.

[26] See Politis 1931; Sygkollitis 1934; Danforth 1982; Alexiou 2002. Bloom (2006) discusses the modern fear of death and loss, which in the early period of Christianity was assuaged by the most common prayer and exchange among them: "*remember death*" (sc. ἔχε) μνήμη θανάτου.

The *trisagion* begins and ends the funerary procession and thus frames the main Requiem ceremony held inside the church. It is composed of several steps: 1) The priest chants for the repose and protection of the deceased's soul in God's blessed life (φυλάττων ... εἰς τὴν μακαρίαν ζωὴν τὴν παρά σοι φιλάνθρωπε); for its repose among the righteous souls (μετὰ πνευμάτων δικαίων) that have already died; and for its repose in the place where are all those deceased who are Holy (ὅπου πάντες οἱ Ἅγιοί σου ἀναπαύονται). For God alone is immortal (ὅτι μόνος ὑπάρχεις ἀθάνατος), and it is God who went down to Hades and released the sorrows that were binding humans (Σὺ εἶ ὁ Θεὸς ἡμῶν, ὁ καταβὰς εἰς Ἅιδην, καὶ τὰς ὀδύνας λύσας τῶν πεπεδημένων); finally, the Virgin Mary is invoked to intercede on behalf of the deceased. 2) The congregation answers the priest's prayers in narrative form for the repose of the deceased's soul and for the forgiveness of her/his sins, the last one of which states:

ὁ Θεὸς τῶν πνευμάτων καὶ πάσης σαρκός, ὁ τὸν θάνατον καταπατήσας, τὸν δὲ διάβολον καταργήσας, καὶ ζωὴν τῷ κόσμῳ σου δωρησάμενος· αὐτός, Κύριε, ἀνάπαυσον τὴν ψυχὴν τοῦ/τῆς ... ἐν τόπῳ φωτεινῷ, ἐν τόπῳ χλοερῷ, ἐν τόπῳ ἀναψύξεως, ἔνθα ἀπέδρα πᾶσα ὀδύνη, λύπη καὶ στεναγμός ... ὅτι σὺ εἶ ἡ ἀνάστασις, ἡ ζωή, καὶ ἡ ἀνάπαυσις τοῦ κεκοιμημένου δούλου σου ... Χριστὲ ὁ Θεὸς ἡμῶν ...

God of spirits and of all flesh, who trampled upon death and annulled the devil and offered life to your world, You Lord place the deceased *in a place of light, in a verdant place, in a place of refreshing cold, where there is no pain, sorrow, and groaning* ... You, Christ our God, are the resurrection, the life, and the repose of your deceased servant ...

3) At the conclusion of the *trisagion,* the priest invokes Christ once more: "our true God, You have the power over both the living and the dead, because You are the eternal king and You resurrected from the dead" (ὁ καὶ νεκρῶν καὶ ζώντων τὴν ἐξουσίαν ἔχων ὡς ἀθάνατος βασιλεύς, καὶ ἀναστὰς ἐκ νεκρῶν, Χριστὸς ὁ ἀληθινὸς Οεὸς ἡμῶν ...) and concludes with the prayer: "may your memory be eternal, our blessed and unforgettable brother/sister" (αἰωνία σου ἡ μνήμη, ἀξιομακάριστε καὶ ἀείμνηστε ἀδελφὲ/-ἡ ἡμῶν).

Once the *trisagion* is over, the funeral procession is formed and reaches the church inside which the Requiem is performed. It is more elaborate than the *trisagion*, but contains the same mix of narrative and chant, in which the same motifs, images, and symbols are further amplified. Portions of Psalm 118 are chanted in three different modes of Byzantine music. At the end of each, the priest offers prayers for the repose of the deceased, and he does the same at the intervals between the benedictory chants (εὐλογητάρια). Three of these are chanted on behalf of the deceased (with the deceased as *persona loquens*) and the other three on behalf of the congregation. The first is as follows:

> τῶν Ἁγίων ὁ χορὸς εὗρε πηγὴν τῆς ζωῆς καὶ θύραν Παραδείσου·
> εὕρω κἀγὼ τὴν ὁδὸν διὰ τῆς μετανοίας· τὸ ἀπολωλὸς πρόβατον ἐγώ
> εἰμι· ἀνακάλεσαί με, Σωτήρ, καὶ σῶσόν με.

> *The choir of the Saints has found the spring of life and the gate to Paradise;
> and I have found the way* through repentance; I am the lost sheep,
> Savior, recall me and save me.

In the following benedictory chants, the deceased acknowledges how s/he was brought to life by God's hand and image and is now returning back to the earth from which s/he was taken, praying for a return to God's *homoiosis*, so that the ancient beauty may be reclaimed. These abstractions receive further elaboration. After praying to God the Lord and Compassionate for pity and cleansing, the deceased asks to be given her/his much-desired place and to be made again a citizen of Paradise. On behalf of the deceased, the congregation chants for her/his repose and placement in Paradise, where the choirs of the Saints and the Righteous will shine forth like leading lights (ἐκλάμψουσιν ὡς φωστῆρες). They proclaim their faith and pray to Mary, through whom they discovered Paradise, because she gave birth to Christ. Finally, they conclude: Christ, place the soul of your servant among the Saints, where there is no pain, no sorrow, no groaning, but life without end (ζωὴ ἀτελεύτητος).

The atmosphere and context created by these chants and prayers is not as poignant and gloomy as in the *moirologia*. Instead, the motifs and themes of the Requiem are so far developed in a manner analogous, but *not* comparable, to the Orphic view about life after death as exhibited in the texts on the lamellae and *epistomia*: anticipation of eternal life in Paradise among the Saints and the Righteous, in a verdant place, full of light and refreshingly cold. Strictly speaking, however, nowhere in the Requiem is the deceased called a Saint or one of the Righteous, because such a designation must await the final judgment at Christ's Second Coming.

Things change dramatically, however, in the next section of the Requiem, when hymns called *idiomela*, "with their own melody," are chanted in all eight modes of Byzantine music. It is not only the change of musical modes (a phenomenon acoustically evocative and impressive in itself) but the themes touched upon and commented upon in each hymn that are surprising and unexpected, given what has been heard so far. Significantly, all hymns (thirteen in all, but seldom all chanted) conclude with the same theme: a prayer to Christ *philanthropos*, who has called back the deceased, for her/his repose among the Saints and the Righteous, in the place which is the home of all who are jubilant (ἔνθα πάντων ἐστὶν εὐφραινομένων ἡ κατοικία), in the blessedness that never grows old (ἐν τῇ ἀγήρῳ μακαριότητι), in the land of the living (ἐν χώρᾳ ζώντων).

The beginnings of these hymns employ motifs and especially themes that one would usually encounter in the *moirologia* and in the Homeric view of death. Although cumbersome, it is worthwhile summarizing the themes elaborated in this part of the Requiem (paragraphs indicate the beginning of a new hymn and the change of musical mode):

Nothing in life remains without pain; there is no eternal glory; all is weaker than shadows and more deceiving than dreams; death is the end of everything.

Humans wither like flowers, pass by like a dream, and dissolve; when the trumpet blows just as in a self-inflicted earthquake, all dead will be resurrected and hasten to meet Christ for the final judgment.

Oimoi, the soul in tears is struggling to depart from the body and there is no one compassionate around; the soul looks to and begs the Angels to no avail, stretches its hands to humans and no one helps; life is short.

All human things that do not exist after death are futile; money and fame/glory are obliterated.

The mystery of death is indeed the most horrendous; how by God's will the soul is violently separated from the body and its harmony is ruptured and the most natural bonding of coalescence (συμφυΐα) is severed!

Where are the endeavors of humanity, where is the fantasy of short-lived things, where is gold and silver, where are the flood and turmoil of suppliants? All is dust, all is ashes, all is shadows.

I remembered the prophet who said, I am earth and ashes (ἐμνήσθην του προφήτου βοῶντος· Ἐγώ εἰμι γῆ καὶ σποδός); and then I went to the graves, saw the naked bones, and wondered: who is he, a king or a soldier, a rich man or a poor man, a righteous man or a sinner?

My beginning and my *hypostasis* was Your command and You have created me from invisible and visible nature, my body from earth, my soul from your divine and life-giving afflatus.

I mourn and lament (θρηνῶ καὶ ὀδύρομαι) when I realize death and see lying in the grave the beauty created for us according to God's image, amorphous, inglorious, without form; what a miracle, what a mysterious thing is happening to us, how did we surrender to decay, how were we conjugated to death?

Your death o Lord brought about immortality (πρόξενος ἀθανασίας); for if You were not placed in a tomb, Paradise would have never been opened.

Mother of our God, *hagne* Virgin, gate of *Logos*, intercede for the soul of the deceased to be pitied.

This part of the Requiem (and the following section called μακαρισμοί, "Beatitudes," not always chanted) is usually referred to as the Church's official *threnos* for the deceased, and people call it, not unjustly, the Church's *moirologia*. The threnodic posture is emphasized in the beginning of two of the hymns by the use of οἴμοι and the expression θρηνῶ καὶ ὀδύρομαι. More importantly, however, all of the motifs and themes of the *moirologia*, employed in the composition of these benedictory hymns and beatitudes, generate a very gloomy and poignant context. A Homeric view of death and afterlife is self-evident as their themes and ideas are reminiscent of the archaic epic and lyric poetry, the *Iliad*, Archilochos, Mimnermos, Solon, Simonides, and Pindar. But there is a striking and momentous development in the new context: they all conclude, in spite of all this horror and gloom, with a petition for the deceased's soul to be assigned a special place in the land of the living.

The mood of the Requiem changes again momentarily as what is heard emphasizes life after death: the road you (sc. the deceased) are walking today is blessed, because a place of rest has been prepared for you (μακαρία ἡ ὁδός, ἧ πορεύει σήμερον, ὅτι ἡτοιμάσθη σοι τόπος ἀναπαύσεως). Two passages are read from Paul's First Epistle to the Thessalonians (4.13–17) and from the Gospel of John (5.24–30) and more prayers are offered, as in the *trisagion* quoted above. At the close of the Requiem, when hymns are chanted in the most affecting modes of Byzantine music, the motifs and themes harken back to those in the Requiem's middle section, its *threnos*. Three of these final hymns are chanted on behalf of the congregation, and one very moving—and therefore seldom chanted—hymn on behalf of the deceased (s/he is the *persona loquens* describing what has happened and where s/he is going). They exhort the congregation to mourn, pay its last respects, and kiss the deceased for the last time, as this is the moment of final and irrevocable separation. While these are chanted and the congregation acts accordingly, the Requiem draws to a close and the procession towards the grave is formed.

Over the grave, the priest again performs the *trisagion*, the coffin is lowered into the grave, and the priest sprinkles the deceased with oil and wine, making the symbol of the cross and reciting verse 9 from Psalm 50: "sprinkle me with hyssop and I will be cleansed, wash me and I will be more white/bright than snow" (ραντιεῖς με ὑσσώπῳ, καὶ καθαρισθήσομαι, πλυνεῖς με, καὶ ὑπὲρ χιόνα λευκανθήσομαι). He then picks up earth from the ground, spits in it, and sprinkles the deceased with it, again making the symbol of the cross and saying: "the earth of the Lord and its fulfillment, the *oikoumene* and all who dwell in it; you are earth and you will depart to earth" (τοῦ Κυρίου ἡ γῆ καὶ τὸ πλήρωμα αὐτῆς, ἡ οἰκουμένη καὶ πάντες οἱ κατοικοῦντες ἐν αὐτῇ. Γῆ εἶ καὶ εἰς γῆν ἀπελεύσει). These last words appear to be an abbreviation of a longer version found in the funeral service for monks on Mount Athos (Paisios 1935:57): "yawning earth welcome him who was made of you by the hand of God; he is returning to you who bore him; for God welcomed what was according to his image, you welcome what is your own" (γῆ χανοῦσα ὑπόδεξαι τὸν ἀπὸ σοῦ πλασθέντα, χειρὶ Θεοῦ τὸ πρότερον· πάλιν δὲ ὑποστρέφοντα πρὸς σὲ τὴν τεκοῦσαν· τὸ γὰρ κατ᾽ εἰκόνα ὁ κτίστης προσελάβετο, σὺ δὲ ὑπόδεξαι τὸ ἴδιον). In some areas of Greece, those present also throw earth or flowers, and the priest or one of the relatives places the tile or ostrakon on the mouth or the chest of the deceased, painted or inscribed with a cross or the inscription Ἰ(ησοῦ)Σ Χ(ριστὸ)Σ νικᾷ (Figures 19–23 [pages 44–47, 49, 51]). Those present then wash their hands, have some bread, drinks (water and cognac), and *kollyva* (boiled wheat sometimes with nuts, almonds, pomegranate seeds, raisins, sugar, etc.).[27] The closest relatives return to the deceased's house for a simple meal, called μακαρία ("blessed") or παρηγοριά ("comforting, consoling"), which promotes a *quid pro quo* relationship: the meal is offered so that the relatives will comfort the family members and offer best wishes for them and the deceased: "may God forgive her/him" (Θεὸς σχωρέσ᾽ την/τον), "may her/his memory be eternal" (αἰωνία της/του ἡ μνήμη), "may you live and remember her/him" (νὰ ζήσεις νὰ τὴν/τὸν θυμᾶσαι).

This long but necessary digression on the Eastern Orthodox funeral ceremony, instituted for the burial of its members, reveals a very elaborate discourse on death involving ritual, music, and poetics. By its motifs and themes, it appears to share beliefs and practices with the Homeric and the Orphic discourses on death and the afterlife, but it also, of course, exhibits

[27] For an eloquent discussion of the intimate relation of *moirologia* and *kollyva* see Psychogiou 2003.

differences. Necessary changes are visible in the custom of the *epistomia*, as examples nos. 18–25 above indicate. The material is clay, symbolizing literally and figuratively the priest's final words, as more than once in the Requiem gold, silver, and all riches are declared meaningless after death, whereas the gold lamellae and *epistomia* were meant to symbolize literally and figuratively the golden life after death. The cypress and the refreshingly cold place stand out among the motifs and themes, but so does a gloomy outlook on the after-life as elaborated in epic and archaic poetry. Albrecht Dieterich long ago noted the coincidence of the *psyxis*,[28] but in the Orthodox Requiem, it refers to the place and not the water. Whereas the cypress and the cold water are inti-mately linked in the texts on the lamellae as markers (either topographically or for Mnemosyne), in the Requiem the refreshing cold describes a place, and in the *moirologia* the cypress is either a limen or a metaphor for the appearance of the dead. Moreover, whereas in antiquity, according to the *opinio communis*, the Homeric view was the public and official one and the Orphic the private and unofficial, the Orthodox Requiem is the official and public discourse on death whereas the *moirologia* occupy the private, more personal sphere. All of these elements, however, are invested with a new and completely different symbolism within their new ritual context, the Orthodox discourse on death and the afterlife.

In that respect, the benedictory hymns, the beatitudes, and the hymns at the end of the Requiem are quite revealing. In the beginning of each hymn, various aspects of human helplessness in the face of death are highlighted and presented in a very realistic and repugnant manner, as if they were didactic attempts to teach a hard lesson to the congregation and the deceased, who are 'chanting' and 'entering in dialogue' with one another and with God. At each hymn's conclusion, the only recourse left to human helplessness is Christ and the resurrection of the dead, an option that somewhat mitigates the horrific mood. Thus the motifs and themes, evident also in the *moirologia*, which may be characterized as the Homeric view of death, are rearticulated and recontextualized in a new Orthodox frame of reference, and acquire new and completely different meanings and symbolism. They become the human and the official perspective on death, characterized by limited capacity and knowledge, and within their new context are undermined and proven wrong, or at least proven only partially true. The threnodic posture in the Requiem is as gloomy and hopeless as that found in *moirologia*, whose inherent danger is thus disarmed, at least temporarily. This extraordinary dialogue between

---

[28] Dieterich 1969:94–100.

the Requiem and the *moirologia* within the Orthodox ritual context in a sense attempts, if not to eliminate the private and unofficial *threnos*, the *moirologia* (an attempt almost impossible), at least to appropriate them, 'expose' their limitations and dead-endedness, and to check and channel their unsettling portrayal of death into more restrained, comforting, and especially less threatening avenues.

Discourses on death have a long and fascinating history and will continue to intrigue us because they represent human nature *par excellence*. In most cases, human perceptions and attitudes towards death and the ritual and poetic discourses created thereby concern the living and their endless struggle to come to terms with this most profound fact of life. The Greek case, in very different historical periods, has produced challenging discourses on death: the Homeric, the Orphic, the *moirologia*, the Orthodox Requiem. As Kostis Papagiorgis eloquently put it: "humans had a hunch *how* to die and *why* to die, [but] now any relation to this fact is lost."[29] Each of them grapples creatively and dynamically with the most elemental question of humanity: the mystery of death, or rather the mystery of life and its values. The Byzantine and modern Greek examples of clay *epistomia* are comparable to the gold *epistomia* and lamellae of ancient mystery cult(s) and ritual(s), but only in a superficial and trivial manner, as their context is dramatically different. Both discourses, however, employ similar or identical motifs and themes within their distinct contexts, and bear witness to how the same elements may lead to completely different symbolisms and meanings. According to the Homeric discourse, the *moirologia*, and sections of the Orthodox Requiem, life is worth living, because death is unbearably final. According to the Orphic discourse, an immediate 'new' birth and a 'new' and blessed life after the deceased's inhumation or cremation is promised. The discourse of the Eastern Orthodox Requiem is neither Homeric, nor Orphic, nor like that of the *moirologia*, in spite of the apparent attempt at mediation between them. The motifs and themes acquire new meaning and symbolism, they are sanctioned by official authority, and they pronounce a new alternative: new life in Christ and a paradisiac repose, which however must await Christ's Second Coming, the resurrection of the dead, and the final judgment.

These Greek discourses on death, their rituals, and their poetics evince significant endeavors to come to grips with death. Even if human life and human death will always remain in irresolvable opposition, and even if all attempts at mediation between life and death eventually fail, the Greeks hold a

---

[29] Papagiorgis 1995:115 and passim.

prominent place among human cultures for doing their part in confronting the issue in their own hallmark way: performing poetics, rituals, and discourses that earn paradise.

Appendix 1

Group A Texts

A1   Thourioi, Italy, Timpone Piccolo: eight hexameters, and the last line in prose (indicated by a vertical line).
Bibliography: Zuntz 1971, 281–305, 328–329, 333, 344–364; Riedweg 1998, 389–398, and 2002; Pugliese Carratelli 2001, 102–103, no. IIB1; Bernabé and Jiménez San Cristóbal 2001, 270–271 no. L9; Bernabé 2005, fr. 488; Graf and Johnston 2007, 12–13 no. 5; Edmonds forthcoming-2.

A   ἔρχομαι ἐκ κοθαρῶ<ν> κοθαρά, χθονί<ων> βα-
σίλεια, | Εὐκλῆς Εὐβολεύς τε καὶ ἀ-
θάνατοι θεοὶ ἄλλοι· | καὶ γὰρ ἐγὼν
ὑμῶν γένος ὄλβιον εὔχομαι
5   εἶμεν, | ἀλλά με μόρα ἐδάμασε
καὶ ἀθάνατοι θεοὶ ἄλλοι καὶ ἀσ-
στεροβλῆτα κεραυνῶι, | κύκλο
δ’ ἐξέπταν βαρυπενθέος ἀργα-
λέοιο· | ἱμερτõ δ’ ἐπέβαν στεφά-
10   νο ποσὶ καρπαλίμοισι, | δεσποί-
νας δὲ ὑπὸ κόλπον ἔδυν χθονί-
ας βασιλείας, | ἱμερτõ δ’ ἀπέβαν
στεφάνο ποσὶ καρπασίμοι-
σι· "ὄλβιε καὶ μακαριστέ, θεὸς δ’ ἔ-
15   σηι ἀντὶ βροτοῖο," | ἔριφος ἐς γάλ’ ἔπετο-
ν.

A2   Thourioi, Italy, Timpone Piccolo: six hexameters, and the last line a pentameter? (indicated by a vertical line).
Bibliography: Zuntz 1971, 281–305, 328–329, 333, 344–364; Riedweg 1998, 389–398, and 2002; Pugliese Carratelli 2001, 98–99, no. IIA1; Bernabé and Jiménez San Cristóbal 2001, 271–272 no. L10a; Bernabé 2005, fr. 489; Graf and Johnston 2007, 14–15 no. 7; Edmonds forthcoming-2.

B   ἔρχομα<ι> ἐκ <κ>α<θα>ρῶ<ν> {σχονων}
        καθαρά, χ<θ>ονίων βασίλ{η}ει<α>, |
        Εὖκλε καὶ Εὐβουλεῦ {ι} καὶ θεοὶ δαίμον-
        ε<ς> ἄλλοι· | καὶ γ<ὰρ> ἐγὼν ὑμῶν γένο<ς> εὔχομα-
 5   ι ὄλβιο<ν> εἶναι· | πο<ι>νά<ν> δ' ἀνταπέ{ι}τε<ι>σ' {ει}
        ἔργω<ν> ἕνεκα οὔτι δικα<ί>ων· |
        εἴτε με μόρα ἐδαμάσατο
        εἴτε ἀστεροπῆτι κ<ε>ραυνῶν, |
        νῦν δ' ἱκέτ<ης> ἥ>κω {ι} πα<ρ'> ἀγνὴ<ν> Φε<ρ>σε-
 10 φόνεαν, | ὥς με {ι} πρόφ<ρ>ω<ν> πέ<μ>ψη<ι>
        ἕδρα{ι}ς ἐς εὐαγέ{ι}ω<ν>.

A3   Thourioi, Italy, Timpone Piccolo. Incised on both sides Ca–Cb: six hexameters, and the last line a pentameter? (indicated by a vertical line).

Bibliography: Zuntz 1971, 281–305, 328–329, 333, 344–364; Riedweg 1998, 389–398, and 2002; Pugliese Carratelli 2001, 100–101, no. IIA2; Bernabé and Jiménez San Cristóbal 2001, 272–273 no. L10b; Bernabé 2005, fr. 490; Graf and Johnston 2007, 14–15 no. 6; Edmonds forthcoming-2.

Ca   ἔρχομαι ἐκ <κ>αθαρῶ<ν> καθ<αρά, χθ>-
        ο<νίων> βασίλ<ει>α, | Εὖκλε {υα} κα<ὶ> Εὐ-
        βολεῦ καὶ θεοὶ ὅσοι δ<αί>μο-
        νες ἄλλο<ι>· | καὶ γὰρ ἐ<γ>ὼ ὑ-
 5   <μῶν> γένος εὔχομα<ι> ε<ῖ>να<ι>
        ὄλβιο<ν>· | ποινὰν <δ'> ἀ<ν>ταπ-
        έτε<ισ'> ἔργω<ν> ἕνεκ'> ὅτι δικ-
Cb   α<ί>ων· | ^ν ἔτ<ε> με μοῖρα <ἐδάμασσ'>
        ἔτ' <ἀσ>τεροπῆτι {κη} κερα-
 10 υν<ῶι>, | ^ν νῦν δ' <ἱ>κ<έτης> ἥκω
        {ιικω} παρὰ Φ<ερ>σεφ<όνειαν>, |
        ὥς {λ} με <π>ρόφ<ρων> πέ[μ]ψε<ι> {μ}
        ἕδρας ἐς εὐ<α>γ<έων>.

A4   Thourioi, Italy, Timpone Grande: five hexameters, and two lines in prose (indicated by a vertical line).
Bibliography: Zuntz 1971, 281–305, 328–329, 333, 344–364; Riedweg 1998, 389–398, and 2002; Pugliese Carratelli 2001, 112–113, no. IIB2; Bernabé and Jiménez San Cristóbal 2001, 268–270 no. L8; Bernabé 2005, fr. 487; Graf and Johnston 2007, 8–9 no. 3; Edmonds forthcoming-2.

> ἀλλ' ὁπόταμ ψυχὴ προλίπηι φάος Ἀελίοιο,
> δεξιὸν Ε.ΟΙΑΣ δ' ἐξι<έ>ναι πεφυλαγμένον
> 3   εὖ μάλα πάν[τ]α· | χαῖρε παθὼν τὸ πάθη-
> μα τὸ δ' οὔπω πρόσθε ἐπεπόνθεις· | θεὸς ἐγ-
> ένου ἐξ [.] ἀνθρώπου· | ἔριφος ἐς γάλα
> 6   ἔπετες, | χαῖρ<ε>, χαῖρε· δεξιὰν ὁδοιπόρ<ει> |
> λειμῶνάς τε ἱεροὺς καὶ ἄλσεα
> Φερσεφονείας.

A5   Rome: four hexameters (indicated by a vertical line).
Bibliography: Zuntz 1971, 281–305, 328–329, 333, 344–364; Riedweg 1998, 389–398, and 2002; Pugliese Carratelli 2001, 96–97, no. IC1; Bernabé and Jiménez San Cristóbal 2001, 273 no. L11; Bernabé 2005, fr. 491; Graf and Johnston 2007, 18–19 no. 9; Edmonds forthcoming-2.

> ἔρχεται ἐκ καθαρῶν καθαρά,
> χθονίων βασίλεια, | Εὔκλεες Εὐβου-
> 3   λεῦ τε, Διὸς τέκος ἀγλαά, ἔχω δὲ | Μνημο-
> σύνης τόδε δῶρον ἀοίδιμον ἀνθρώ-
> ποισιν, | Καικιλία Σεκουνδεῖνα, νόμωι
> 6   ἴθι δῖα γεγῶσα.

Group A

	Provenance	Date BCE	Gender	Shape	Position in grave	Coin	Burial and grave-goods
A1	Thourioi, Italy, Timpone Piccolo	IV c.	unknown	rectangular unfolded	close to hand	no	Inhumation. A tumulus of three strata: in the first more than ten persons carelessly interred; in the second fragments of pottery; in the third gravel mixed with sand and lime. In the lower third stratum, three graves were found (nos A1–3). In the four corners of the chamber of Cist-grave 1 small hollows filled with ashes of bones and plants, indications of funeral sacrifice; no mention of a coffin; no other offerings
A2	Thourioi, Italy, Timpone Piccolo	IV c.	unknown	rectangular folded once	close to hand	no	Inhumation. Under the tumulus (A1 above) Cist-grave 3: no mention of a coffin; no other offerings
A3	Thourioi, Italy, Timpone Piccolo	IV c.	unknown	rectangular unfolded	close to hand	no	Inhumation. Under the tumulus (A1 above) Cist-grave 2: no mention of a coffin; no other offerings

	Provenance	Date BCE	Gender	Shape	Position in grave	Coin	Burial and grave-goods
A4	Thourioi, Italy, Timpone Grande	IV c.	male?	rectangular folded nine times and placed inside no. C1 below which was folded like an envelope	near the cranium	no	Inhumation (partial cremation). Above the grave: a tumulus of 8 strata, each consisting of ashes and carbon and burnt pottery sherds topped by earth above, an indication of worship of the inhumed dead as a hero with rituals and sacrifices. Ouside the grave: a few small black vases. Inside: bronze locks of the coffin, two silver medallions on the chest decorated with female heads, similar to the ones of Persephone on Apulian vases, a few small pieces of gold from the dress' decoration, two small wooden boxes with inlaid palmettes. The cremation took place in situ and the remains were simply covered by a white sheet which disintegrated when touched by the excavators
A5	Rome, Italy	II c. CE	female	unknown	unknown	unknown	Not known

Group B Texts

B1   Petelia, Italy: fourteen hexameters (indicated by a vertical line). Bibliography: Zuntz 1971, 281–305, 328–329, 333, 344–364; Riedweg 1998, 389–398, and 2002; Pugliese Carratelli 2001, 67–72, no. IA2; Bernabé and Jiménez San Cristóbal 2001, 263–264 no. L3; Bernabé 2005, fr. 476; Graf and Johnston 2007, 6–7 no. 2; Edmonds forthcoming-2.

> εὑρήσσεις δ' Ἀίδαο δόμων ἐπ' ἀριστερὰ κρήν-
> ην, | πὰρ δ' αὐτῆι λευκὴν ἑστηκυῖαν κυπάρισσον· |
> ταύτης τῆς κρήνης μηδὲ σχεδὸν ἐμπελάσειας· |
> εὑρήσεις δ' ἑτέραν, τῆς Μνημοσύνης ἀπὸ λίμνης |
> 5   ψυχρὸν ὕδωρ προρέον· φύλακες δ' ἐπίπροσθεν ἔασιν· |
> εἰπεῖν· «Γῆς παῖς εἰμι καὶ Οὐρανοῦ ἀστερόεντος, | αὐτὰρ ἐμ-
> οὶ γένος οὐράνιον· τόδε δ' ἴστε καὶ αὐτοί· | δίψηι δ' εἰμὶ αὔ-
> η καὶ ἀπόλλυμαι· ἀλλὰ δότ' αἶψα | ψυχρὸν ὕδωρ προρέ-
> ον τῆς Μνημοσύνης ἀπὸ λίμνης.» | καὐτ̣[ο]ί σ[ο]ι δώσουσι
> 10 πιεῖν θείης ἀπ[ὸ κρή]νης, | καὶ τότ' ἔπειτ' ἄ[λλοισι μεθ'] ἡρώε-
> σσιν ἀνάξει[ς, | Μνημοσύ]νης τόδε <ἔ>ρ[γον· ἐπεὶ ἂν μέλληισι]
> θανεῖσθ[αι - - - - - -] τόδε γραψ[- - - - - - - -]
> versus a dextra in margine sursum legendus:
> τ̣ο̣γλωσ̣ει̣π̣α σκότος ἀμφικαλύψας.

B2   Pharsalos, Thessaly: ten hexameters (indicated by a vertical line). Bibliography: Zuntz 1971, 281–305, 328–329, 333, 344–364; SEG 45.634, 46.656; Riedweg 1998, 389–398, and 2002; Pugliese Carratelli 2001, 73–75, no. IA3; Bernabé and Jiménez San Cristóbal 2001, 264–265 no. L4; Bernabé 2005, fr. 477; Graf and Johnston 2007, 34–35 no. 25; Edmonds forthcoming-2.

> εὑρήσεις Ἀΐδαο δόμοις ἐνδέξια κρήνην, | πὰρ δ' αὐτῆι
> λευκὴν ἑστηκυῖαν κυπάρισσον· | ταύτης τῆς κρήνης
> 3   μηδὲ σχεδόθεν πελάσηισθα· | πρόσσω δ' εὑρήσεις τὸ Μνη-
> μοσύνης ἀπὸ λίμνης | ψυχρὸν ὕδωρ προ<ρέον>· φύλακες
> δ' ἐφύπερθεν ἔασιν· | οἱ δέ σ' εἰρήσονται ὅ τι χρέος
> 6   εἰσαφικάνεις· | τοῖς δὲ σὺ εὖ μάλα πᾶσαν ἀληθείην
> καταλέξαι· | {ιι} εἰπεῖ<ν>· "Γῆς παῖς εἰμι καὶ Οὐρανοῦ
>   ἀστ<ερόεντος>, |
> Ἀστέριος ὄνομα· δίψηι δ' εἰμ' αὖος· ἀλλὰ δότε μοι |
> 9   πιεν ἀπὸ τῆς κρήνης."

B3   Eleutherna, Crete: first two hexameters, and last two in prose(?).
Bibliography: Above no. 1; Zuntz 1971, 281–305, 328–329, 333, 344–364;
Riedweg 1998, 389–398, and 2002; Pugliese Carratelli 2001, 78–79 no.
IB1; Bernabé and Jiménez San Cristóbal 2001, 265 no. L5a; Bernabé 2005,
fr. 478; Graf and Johnston 2007, 20–21 no. 10; Edmonds forthcoming-2.

> δίψαι αὗος ἐγὼ καὶ ἀπόλλυμαι· ἀλλὰ πιε͂<μ> μοι
> κράνας αἰειρόω ἐπὶ δεξιά· τῆ, κυφάριζος.
> 3   τίς δ' ἐζί; πῶ δ' ἐζί; Γᾶς υἱός ἠμι καὶ Ὠρανῶ
>   ἀστερόεντος.

B4   Eleutherna, Crete: first two hexameters, and last two in prose(?).
Bibliography: Above no. 2; Zuntz 1971, 281–305, 328–329, 333, 344–364;
Riedweg 1998, 389–398, and 2002; Pugliese Carratelli 2001, 80 no. IB2;
Bernabé and Jiménez San Cristóbal 2001, 266 no. L5b; Bernabé 2005, fr.
479; Graf and Johnston 2007, 20–21 no. 11; Edmonds forthcoming-2.

> δίψαι αὗος ἐγὼ καὶ ἀπόλλυμα{μα}ι· ἀλλὰ πιε͂<μ> μοι
> κράνας αἰειρόω ἐπὶ δεξιά· τῆ, κυφάριζος.
> 3   τίς δ' ἐζί; πῶ δ' ἐζί; Γᾶς υἱός ἠμι καὶ Ὠρανῶ
>   ἀστερό<ε>ντος.

B5   Eleutherna, Crete: first two hexameters, and last two in prose(?).
Bibliography: Above no. 3; Zuntz 1971, 281–305, 328–329, 333, 344–364;
Riedweg 1998, 389–398, and 2002; Pugliese Carratelli 2001, 81 no. IB3;
Bernabé and Jiménez San Cristóbal 2001, 266 no. L5c; Bernabé 2005, fr.
480; Graf and Johnston 2007, 22–23 no. 12; Edmonds forthcoming-2.

> δίψαι αὗος {ααυοσ} ἐγὼ καὶ ἀπόλλυμαι· ἀλλὰ πιὲμ μου
> κράνας <α>ιενάω ἐπὶ δε[ξ]ιά· τῆ, κυφάρισζος.
> 3   τίς δ' ἐζί; πῶ δ' ἐζί; Γᾶς υἱός ἠμ<ι> καὶ Ὠρανῶ
>   ἀστερόεντ[ο]ς.

B6   Eleutherna, Crete: lines 1–3a hexameters, and lines 3b–5 in prose(?)
(indicated by a vertical line).
Bibliography: Above no. 4; Zuntz 1971, 281–305, 328–329, 333, 344–364;
Riedweg 1998, 389–398, and 2002; Pugliese Carratelli 2001, 82–83 no.
IB4; Bernabé and Jiménez San Cristóbal 2001, 266 no. L5d; Bernabé 2005,
fr. 481; Graf and Johnston 2007, 26–27 no. 16; Edmonds forthcoming-2.

δίψᾳ δ' ἤμ' αὖος καὶ ἀπόλ<λ>ομαι· ἀλ<λ>ὰ
πιὲν μοι | κράνας ΑΙΓΙΔΔΩ ἐπὶ
3   δεξιά· τε͂, κυπ<ά>ριζος. | τίς δ' ἐζί; π-
ῶ δ' ἐζί; Γᾶς ἤμι ?ΓΥΑΤΗΡ? καὶ
Ὠρανῶ ἀστερόεντος.

Line 2: αἰγί{δ}ρω?; αἰ<ε>ι<ρό>ω Guarducci, et alii. Line 4: <μ>άτηρ?;
<θ>υ<γ>άτηρ Guarducci, et alii.

B7   Eleutherna, Crete: first two hexameters, and last two in prose(?).
Bibliography: Above no. 5; Zuntz 1971, 281–305, 328–329, 333, 344–364;
Riedweg 1998, 389–398, and 2002; Pugliese Carratelli 2001, 84 no. IB5;
Bernabé and Jiménez San Cristóbal 2001, 266–267 no. L5e; Bernabé 2005,
fr. 482; Graf and Johnston 2007, 22–23 no. 13; Edmonds forthcoming-2.

δίψαι αὖος ἐγὼ καὶ ἀπόλλυμαι· ἀλ<λ>ὰ πιε͂μ {ε} μοι
κράνα<ς α>ἰ<ε>ιρ<ό>ω ἐπ<ὶ> δεξιά· τῆ, κυφάριζος,
3   τίς δ' ἐ{δε}ζ<ί>; πῶ δ' ἐζί; Γᾶς υἱός ἠμι κα<ὶ> Ὠ>ρανῶ
ἀστερόεντος.

B8   Eleutherna, Crete: first two hexameters, and last two in prose(?) (indi-
cated by a vertical line).
Bibliography: Above no. 6; Zuntz 1971, 281–305, 328–329, 333, 344–364;
Riedweg 1998, 389–398, and 2002; Pugliese Carratelli 2001, 85 no. IB6;
Bernabé and Jiménez San Cristóbal 2001, 266–267 no. L5f; Bernabé 2005,
fr. 483; Graf and Johnston 2007, 24–25 no. 14; Edmonds forthcoming-2.

δίψᾳ {α} αὖος ἐγὼ καὶ ἀπόλ<λ>υμαι· ἀλ-
λὰ π<ι>ε͂μ μο<ι> | κράνας αἰενάω ἐπὶ δ-
3   <ε>ξιά· τῆ, κυφάριζος. | τίς δ' ἐζί; πῶ
δ' <ἐ>ζί; | Γᾶς υἱός ἰμι καὶ Ὠρανῶ ἀστερό-
εντος {σ}.

B9   Thessaly: lines 1–3 two hexameters, and lines 4–6 in prose(?) (indicated
by a vertical line).
Bibliography: Breslin 1977; SEG 27.226bis; Riedweg 1998, 389–398, and
2002; Pugliese Carratelli 2001, 94–95 no. IB7; Bernabé and Jiménez San
Cristóbal 2001, 266–267 no. L6; Bernabé 2005, fr. 484; Graf and Johnston
2007, 24–25 no. 14; Edmonds forthcoming-2.

δίψαι αὖος ἐγὼ κἀπόλλυμαι·
ἀλλὰ πίε μου | κράνας αἰειρόω
3   ἐπὶ δεξιὰ λευκὴ κυπάρισσος. |
τίς δ' ἐσί; πῶ δ' ἐσί; | Γᾶς υἱός εἰμι
καὶ Οὐρανοῦ ἀστερόεντος· |
6   αὐτὰρ ἐμοὶ γένος οὐράνιον.

B10   Hipponion, Italy: sixteen hexameters.
Bibliography: Foti and Pugliese Carratelli 1974; SEG 26.1139, 27.674,
28.775bis, 34.1002, 37.778, 40.824, 42.903, 43.647, 44.809, 45.1440,
46.1318, 47.656, 52.951; EBGR 1996.33; Riedweg 1998, 389–398, and
2002; Sacco 2001; Pugliese Carratelli 2001, 39–66 no. IA1; Bernabé and
Jiménez San Cristóbal 2001, 258–261 no. L1; Bernabé 2005, fr. 474; Graf
and Johnston 2007, 4–5 no. 1; Edmonds forthcoming-2.

Μναμοσύνας τόδε ΕΡΙΟΝ ἐπεὶ ἂμ μέλλεισι θανέσθαι
εἰς Ἀΐδαο δόμος εὐέρεας, ἔστ' ἐπὶ δ<ε>ξιὰ κρένα,
πὰρ δ' αὐτὰν ἐστακῦα λευκὰ κυπάρισος,
ἔνθα κατερχόμεναι ψυκαὶ νεκύον ψύχονται·
5   ταύτας τᾶς κράνας μεδὲ σχεδὸν ἐνγύθεν ἔλθεις·
πρόσθεν δὲ ἑευρέσεις τᾶς Μναμοσύνας ἀπὸ λίμνας
ψυχρὸν ὕδορ προρέον· φύλακες δὲ ἐπύπερθεν ἔασι·
τοὶ δέ σε εἰρέσονται ἐν φρασὶ πευκαλίμαισι
ὅ τι δὲ ἐξερέεις Ἄϊδος σκότος ὀρφέεντος·
10 εἶπον· «ὑὸς Γᾶς ἐμι καὶ Ὀρανῶ ἀστερόεντος.
δίψαι δ' ἐμ' αὖος καὶ ἀπόλλυμαι· ἀλ<λ>ὰ δότ' ὄκα
ψυχρὸν ὕδορ πιέναι τὲς Μνεμοσύνες ἀπὸ λίμ<ν>ες.»
καὶ δέ τοι ἐρέοσιν {ι} ἡυποχθονίοι βασιλεί<αι>·
καὶ δέ τοι δόσοσι πιὲν τᾶς Μναμοσύνας ἀπὸ λίμνας·
15 καὶ δὲ καὶ σὺ πιὸν ἡοδὸν ἔρχεα<ι> ἅν τε καὶ ἄλλοι
μύσται καὶ βάχχοι ἱερὰν στείχοσι κλεινυί.

B11   Entella?, West Sicily: twenty one hexameters in two columns (lines
1–14, and 15–21).
Bibliography: Riedweg 1998, 389–398, and 2002; SEG 44.750, 48.1236bis,
50.998; BE 2000.93; EBGR 1997.138; Pugliese Carratelli 2001, 76–77
no. IA4; Bernabé and Jiménez San Cristóbal 2001, 258–261 no. L2;
Bernabé 2005, fr. 475; Graf and Johnston 2007, 16–17 no. 8; Edmonds
forthcoming-2.

col. I

   [- - - - - - - ἐπεὶ ἂν μέλ]λησι θανεῖσθαι
   [- - - - - - - - - - - - μ]εμνημέ<ν>ος ἥρως
   [- - - - - - - - - - - -] σκότος ἀμφικαλύψας,
   [- - - - - - - - - - ἐπὶ] δεξιὰ λίμνην,
5 [πὰρ δ᾽ αὐτῆι λευκὴν ἐστη]κῦαν κυπάρισσον,
   [ἔνθα κατερχόμεναι ψυ]χαὶ νεκύων ψύχονται·
   [ταύτης τῆς κρήνης μη]δὲ σχεδὸν ἐ<μ>πελάσ<ασ>θαι·
   [πρόσθεν δὲ εὑρήσεις τῆς] Μνημοσύνης ἀπὸ λίμνης
   [ψυχρὸν ὕδωρ προρέον·] φυλακοὶ δ᾽ ἐπύπε<ρ>θ<εν ἔ>ασιν·
10 [τοὶ δέ σε εἰρήσονται ἐνὶ] φρασὶ πευκαλίμησιν
   [ὅττι δὴ ἐξερέεις Ἄϊδος σκότο]ς ὀρφ{ο}νήεντο<ς>·
   [εἶπον· «ὑὸς Γῆς εἰμι καὶ] Οὐρανοῦ ἀστερόεντος.
   [δίψαι δ᾽ εἰμ᾽ αὖος καὶ ἀπόλλ]υμαι· ἀλλὰ δότε μ{μ}οι
   [ψυχρὸν ὕδωρ πιέναι τῆς] Μνημοσύνης ἀπὸ λίμνης·

col. II

15 αὐτὰρ ἐ[μοὶ γένος οὐράνιον· τόδε δ᾽ ἴστε καὶ αὐτοί.»]
   καί τοι δὴ [ἐρέουσιν ὑποχθονίωι βασιλείαι]·
   καὶ τότε τ[οι δώσουσι πιεῖν τῆς Μνημοσύνης ἀπὸ λίμνης]·
   καὶ τότε δ[ὴ - - - - - - - - - - - - - - - -]
   σύμβολα φ[- - - - - - - - - - - - - - - - -]
20 καὶ φε[- - - - - - - - - - - - - - - - - - -]
   σεν[- - - - - - - - - - - - - - - - - - - -].

B12   Sfakaki, Crete: lines 1–4a two hexameters, and lines 4b–7 in prose(?) (indicated by a vertical line).

      Bibliography: Above no. 9; Bernabé 2005, fr. 484a; Graf and Johnston 2007, 28–29 no. 18; Edmonds forthcoming-2.

   δίψαι τοι <α>ῦος. παρ<α>π<ό>λλυται.
   ἀλλ<ὰ> π{α}ιὲν μοι | κράνας <Σ?>αύ-
3 ρου ἐπ᾽ ἀ{α}ρι<σ>τερὰ τᾶς κυφα{σ}-
   ρίζω. | τ<ί>ς δ᾽ εἶ ἢ πῶ δ᾽ εἶ; Γᾶ-
   ς ἠμ{ο}ί, μάτηρ· πῶ τί ΔΕΤ
6 [κ]αὶ <Ο>ὐρανῷ <ἀ>στε<ρόεντος>. τίς; δίψαι το-
   ι ΛΤΟΠΥΤΟΟΠΑΣΡΑΤΑΝΗΟ.

Lines 2–3: or κράνας Αὔ|ρου; lines 4–6: Γᾶ {σ} <ἐ>μοὶ μάτηρ· πῶ; τί ΔΕΤ | <κ>αὶ <Ο>ὐρανός. τε τίς;.

264

Group B

	Provenance	Date BCE	Gender	Shape	Position in grave	Coin	Burial and grave-goods
B1	Petelia, Italy	IV c.	female?	rectangular, rolled in cylinder?	unknown	unknown	Not known; the lamella itself was found folded up inside a gold cylindrical case with a chain attached, dated to the II–III c. CE
B2	Pharsalos, Thessaly	360–340	male?	rectangular (folded twice?)	inside a hydria-urn	no	Cremation. A limestone round container in which a bronze hydria-urn with a representation below the neck-handle of the 'abduction' of Oreithyia by Boreas and ivy-leaves and anthemia at the base; inside the urn the ashes, a small bronze ring and a small skyphos
B3	Eleutherna, Crete	III–I c.	unknown	rectangular, folded	unknown	unknown	unknown (above no. 1)
B4	Eleutherna, Crete	III–I c.	unknown	rectangular, folded	unknown	unknown	unknown (above no. 2)
B5	Eleutherna, Crete	I.I–I c.	unknown	rectangular, folded	unknown	unknown	unknown (above no. 3)
B6	Eleutherna, Crete	III–I c.	unknown	*epistomion*, folded?	unknown	unknown	unknown (above no. 4)
B7	Eleutherna, Crete	III–I c.	unknown	rectangular, rolled in cylinder?	unknown	unknown	unknown (above no. 5)

Group B, cont.

	Provenance	Date BCE	Gender	Shape	Position in grave	Coin	Burial and grave-goods
B8	Eleutherna, Crete	III–I c.	unknown	rectangular, rolled in cylinder?	unknown	unknown	unknown (above no. 6)
B9	Thessaly	350–320	unknown	unknown	inside a hydria	unknown	Cremation. Bronze hydria-urn
B10	Hipponion, Italy	ca. 400	female?	rectangular, folded four times	on upper part of chest (hung by perishable material?)	unknown	Inhumation in tile-covered grave. Outside: a clay lamp and two skyphoi, one of them with a graffito. Inside: to the right of cranium a small clay jug and to the left bronze fragments of a ring with an incised representation; at the right elbow a hydria and a bronze semi-sphere with a hole of a bell(?); on the pelvis a skyphos; at the left hand a gold finger-ring; a clay lamp, a hydria and two clay lekythoi to the left and right of the left thighbone
B11	Entella?, West Sicily	III c.?	unknown	rectangular	unknown	unknown	unknown
B12	Sfakaki, Crete	II–early I c.	unknown	rectangular, unfolded	unknown	unknown	Inhumation in tile-grave, looted (above no. 9). Thirty-two clay unguentaria, fragments of glass, a bronze mirror, small bronze and gilt fragments

Group C Texts

C1 Thourioi, Italy, Timpone Grande.
Bibliography: Zuntz 1971, 281–305, 328–329, 333, 344–364; Riedweg 1998, 389–398, and 2002; Pugliese Carratelli 2001, 125–127, no. III1; Bernabé and Jiménez San Cristóbal 2001, 273–277 no. L12; Bernabé 2005, fr. 492; Graf and Johnston 2007, 10–11 no. 4; Betegh forthcoming; Edmonds forthcoming-2.

Πρωτογόνῳ<ι> ΤΗΜΑΙΤΙΕΤΗ Γᾶι ματρὶ ΕΠΑ Κυβελεία<ι>
Κόρρα<ι> ΟΣΕΝΤΑΙΗ Δήμητρος ΗΤ
ΤΑΤΑΙΤΤΑΤΑΠΤΑ Ζεῦ ΙΑΤΗΤΥ ἀέρ ΣΑΠΤΑ Ἥλιε, πῦρ δὴ πάντα
ΣΤΗΙΝΤΑΣΤΗΝΙΣΑΤΟΠΕ νικᾶι Μ
ΣΗΔΕ Τύχα ΙΤΕ Φάνης, πάμνηστοι Μοῖραι
ΣΣΤΗΤΟΙΓΑΝΝΥΑΠΙΑΝΤΗ σὺ κλυτὲ δαῖμον ΔΕΥΧΙ
Σ πάτερ ΑΤΙΚ παντοδαμάστα
ΠΑΝΤΗΡΝΥΝΤΑΙΣΕΛΑΒΔΟΝΤΑΔΕΠ ἀνταμοιβή
ΣΤΛΗΤΕΑΣΤΛ
5 ΤΗΜΗ ἀέρ Ι πῦρ ΜΕΜ Μᾶτερ ΛΥΕΣΤΙΣΟΙΛ·ΕΝΤΑΤΟ Νῆστι Ν
νύξ ΙΝΗΜΕΦ ἡμέρα ΜΕΡΑΝΕΓΛΧΥΕΣ
ἐπτῆμαρ ΤΙ νήστιας ΤΑΝ Ζεῦ ἐνορύττιε? καὶ πανόπτα, αἰέν
ΑΙΜΙΥ* μᾶτερ, ἐμᾶς ἐπ-
ἄκρουσον ΕΟ εὐχᾶς ΤΑΚΤΑΠΥΑΡΣΥΟΛΚΑΠΕΔΙΩΧΑΜΑΤΕΜΑΝ
καλ{η}ὰ Δ ἱερὰ ΔΑΜΝΕΥΔΑΜΝΟΙ
ΩΤΑΚΤΗΡ ἱερὰ ΜΑΡ Δημῆτερ, πῦρ, Ζεῦ, Κόρη, Χθονία
ΤΡΑΒΔΑΗΤΡΟΣΗΝΙΣΤΗΟΙΣΤΝ
ἥρως ΝΗΓΑΥΝΗ φάος ἐς φρένα ΜΑΤΑΙΜΗΤΝΝΤΗΣΝΥΣΧΑ
μήστωρ εἶλε Κούρην
10 αἶα ΦΗΡΤΟΝΟΣΣΜΜΟ·ΕΣΤΟΝ ἀέρ ΤΑΙΠΛΝΙΛΛΥ ἐς φρένα
ΜΑΡ*ΤΩΣ.

This group perhaps should also include:
The *Olbia Bone-Tablets* (SEG 28.659–661, 41.621, 42.720, 46.950; West 1983; (Graf and Johnston 2007, 185–190, "Additional Bacchic Texts no. 1"); and perhaps add also SEG 28.1651, 36.694, 52.731bis; EBGR 2003.123;
Bacchic Inscriptions from Olbia (Graf and Johnston 2007, 185–190, "Additional Bacchic Texts no. 2");
PGurob 1 (Hordern 2000; Bernabé 2005, fr. 578; Graf and Johnston 2007, 185–190, "Additional Bacchic Texts no. 3");

Edict of Ptolemy IV Philopator, *COrdPtol* 29 (= BGU VI 1211 = SB III 7266; Graf and Johnston 2007, 185–190, "Additional Bacchic Texts no. 4");

PDerveni (Betegh 2004; Bernabé 2005, frr. 470–473; Kouremenos, Tsantsanoglou and Parássoglou 2006);

Poseidippos' epigrams (Dignas 2004);

PChicago Pack[2] *1620* (Niafas 1997);

PAntinoopolis I 18 (= MP[3] 2466);

The Orphic Hymns (West 1983), and other *Orphica* in Bernabé 2005;

Other related *Orphica* (including epigrams of mystai) in Bernabé 2005.

Group C

	Provenance	Date BCE	Gender	Shape	Position in grave	Coin	Burial and grave-goods
C1	Thourioi, Italy, Timpone Grande	IV c.	male?	above no. A4	above no. A4	above no. A4	above no. A4

Group D Texts

D1   Poseidonia (Paestum), Italy.
Bibliography: IG XIV 665; Riedweg 1998:389–398, and 2002; Bernabé and Jiménez San Cristóbal 2001:273–277 no. L12; Bernabé 2005, fr. 496m; Edmonds forthcoming-2.

τᾶς θεὸς τ<ᾶ>ς παιδὸς ἐμί.

D2   Pelinna, Thessaly: two hexameters followed by four prose lines and one hexameter (indicated by a vertical line).
Bibliography: Tsantsanoglou-Parássoglou 1987; SEG 37.497, 39.505, 42.530, 45.632, 46.654, 47.753; Riedweg 1998:389–398, and 2002; Pugliese Carattelli 2001:116–120 no. IIB3; Bernabé and Jiménez San Cristóbal 2001:267–268 no. L7a, b; Bernabé 2005, fr. 485–486; Graf and Johnston 2007:36–37 no. 26a, b; Edmonds forthcoming-2.

A   νῦν ἔθανες
καὶ νῦν ἐγ-
ένου, τρισόλβ-
ιε, ἄματι τῶιδε. |

5 εἰπεῖν Φερσεφόν-
  αι ϛ' ὅτι Β<άχ>χιος αὐτὸς
  ἔλυσε. | τα{ι}ῦρος
  εἰς γάλ<α> ἔθορες, | αἶ-
  ψα εἰς γ<ά>λα ἔθορες, |
10 <κ>ριὸς εἰς γάλα ἔπεσ<ες>.
  οἶνον ἔχεις εὐ-
  δ<α>ιμονα τιμ<ὰ>ν |
  κἀπ<ι>μέν-
  ει σ' ὑπὸ
15 γῆν τε-
  λέα ἄσ<σ>α-
  περ ὄλ-
  βιοι ἄλ-
  λοι.

B νῦν ἔθανε<ς>
  καὶ νῦν ἐ-
  γένου, τρισόλ-
  βιε, ἄματι
5 <τῶι>δε. |
  <ε>ἰπεῖν Φερ-
  σεφό<ναι σ'> ὅτι Βά<χ>χιο-
  ς αὐτὸς ἔλυσε. |
  ταῦρος εἰ<ς> γάλα ἔ-
10 θορ<ε>ς, κριὸς εἰς γάλ<α>
  ἔπεσε<ς>. | οἶνον ἔ-
  χεις εὐδαι-
  μον<α>
  τιμ-
15 μ<ά>ν.

D3 Pherai, Thessaly.
  Bibliography: Chryssostomou 1998:210–220; Tsantsanoglou 1997:116–
  117 lines 1–3; SEG 45.646, 47.758; BE 1997.285, 1999.285, 2000.401;
  EBGR 1996.40, 1997.380, 1998.57; Riedweg 1998:389–398, and 2002;
  Pugliese Carattelli 2001:123–124 no. IIC2; Bernabé and Jiménez San
  Cristóbal 2001:277–278 no. L13; Bernabé 2005, fr. 493; Graf and Johnston
  2007:38–39 no. 27; Edmonds forthcoming-2.

σύμβολα, Ἀν<δ>ρικε-
παιδόθυρσον, Ἀνδρικεπα-
3   ιδόθυρσον, Βριμώ, εἴσιθ<ι>
ἱερὸν λειμῶνα, ἄποινος
γὰρ ὁ μύστης.
6   ΓΑΠΕΔΟΝ *(written upside down).*

Tsantsanoglou: ἀν<δ>ρικὲ (or ἀν<δ>ρὶ κὲ), παῖ, δὸ<ς> (or δὸ) θύρσον.

D4   Amphipolis, Macedonia.
Bibliography: Malama 2000:55–70; Malama 2001:117–118; Bernabé 2005, fr. 496n; SEG 51.788; BE 2003.378; EBGR 2001.118 (line 3 restored by Chaniotis); Graf and Johnston 2007:40–41 no. 30; Edmonds forthcoming-2.

εὐαγὴς ἱερὰ Διονύ-
σου Βαχχίου εἰμί,
3   Ἀρχεβού[λ]η
Ἀντιδώρου.

D5   Pherai, Thessaly: two hexameters.
Bibliography: Parker and Stamatopoulou, 2004; Graf and Johnston 2007:38–39 no. 28; Edmonds forthcoming-2.

πέμπε με πρὸς μυστῶ<ν> θιάσους· ἔχω ὄργια [Βάκχου? / τε? / καὶ?]
Δήμητρος Χθονίας, τέλη καὶ Μητρὸς Ὀρεί[ας].

Group E Texts

E1   Eleutherna, Crete.
Bibliography: Above no. 7; Riedweg 1998:389–398, and 2002; Pugliese Carattelli 2001:121–122 no. IIC1; Bernabé and Jiménez San Cristóbal 2001:277–278 no. L15; Bernabé 2005, fr. 495; Graf and Johnston 2007:38–39 no. 27; Edmonds forthcoming-2.

[Πλού]τωνι καὶ Φ-
[ερσ]οπόνει χαίρεν.

E2   Aigai (Vergina), Macedonia.
Bibliography: Petsas 1961–1962:259; Riedweg 1998:389–398, and 2002; Bernabé and Jiménez San Cristóbal 2001:279–280 no. L16k; Bernabé 2005, fr. 496k; Graf and Johnston 2007:46–47 no. 37; Edmonds forthcoming-2.

Φιλίστη Φερσεφόνηι χαίρειν.

Group D

	Provenance	Date BCE	Gender	Shape	Position in grave	Coin	Burial and grave-goods
D1	Poseidonia (Paestum), Italy	VI c.	unknown	*silver* lamella	unknown	unknown	unknown
D2	Pelinna, Thessaly	ca. 275	female	two ivy-leaves	two on chest	*danake* in mouth with gorgon; coin of Antigonos Gonatas	Inhumation in marble sarcophagus: in the cranium: a wreath of lead stem, clay gilt berries and gilt bronze myrtle leaves with gold ornament; near the cranium: a clay *aryter*, a clay bowl, two gold spirals ending in snake-heads; near the feet: clay *aryter* with a lamp inside, clay unguentarium, two bowls, a shallow *skyphos*; by the feet bronze *lebes* with bones of a neonate. On the cover slab of sarcophagus: two clay bowls and fragments of a third, clay feeder and clay figurine of comic actor sitting on an altar
D3	Pherai, Thessaly	ca. 300	unknown	rectangular	on chest?	unknown	unknown
D4	Amphipolis, Macedonia	320–280	female	rectangular	folded on chest	silver coin of Philip II	Inhumation in stone sarcophagus, looted. Gold ring and finger-ring; stone-constructed exedra for funeral rituals
D5	Pherai, Thessaly	ca. 300	unknown	rectangular	unknown	unknown	Cremation? In marble cylindrical(?) *osteotheke* with few bones and ashes

E3   Pella, Macedonia.
Bibliography: Lilibaki-Akamati 1989:95 pl. 9; 1989–1991:73–80 pl. 27a; SEG 42.619b, 45.782, 48.819; EBGR 1994–95.218, 1998.69; Riedweg 1998:389–398, and 2002; Bernabé and Jiménez San Cristóbal 2001:279–280 no. L16b; Bernabé 2005, fr. 496b; Graf and Johnston 2007:42–43 no. 31; Edmonds forthcoming-2.

> Φερσεφόνηι
> Ποσείδιππος μύστης
> 3   εὐσεβής.

E4   Sfakaki, Crete.
Bibliography: Above no. 8; SEG 48.1227; EBGR 1998.89; Riedweg 2002; Bernabé and Jiménez San Cristóbal 2001:277–278 no. L16l; Bernabé 2005, fr. 494; Graf and Johnston 2007:26–27 no. 17; Edmonds forthcoming-2.

> Πλούτωνι ...
> Φερσεφόνη.

E5   Agios Athanassios, Macedonia.
Bibliography: Petsas 1967a, 399–403, esp. 400 figure 21 (drawing); Petsas 1967b, 75b (photograph); Tsimpidou-Auloniti 1992:369–370 (mention); Bernabé 2005, fr. 496l; Graf and Johnston 2007:46–47 no. 38; Hatzopoulos 2002, 2006, and 2008 (text); EBGR 2003.68; Edmonds forthcoming-2.

> Φιλωτήρα
> τῶι Δεσπ<ό>-
> 3   τε<ι> {α} χέρε<ν>.
>
> B   ΕΙΜΩ.

Group E

	Provenance	Date BCE	Gender	Shape	Position in grave	Coin	Burial and grave-goods
E1	Eleutherna, Crete	III–I c.	un-known	rectangular	unknown	unknown	unknown (above no. 7)
E2	Aigai (Vergina), Macedonia	III–I c.	female	unknown	unknown	unknown	Cremation under tumulus looted? Hellenistic pottery
E3	Pella, Macedonia	ca. 300	male	laurel? or myrtle?	on bench of the grave's W side	no	Many glass and bone fragments from the decoration of the wooden bier and its legs with incised representation of griffin tearing a deer; iron fragments from bier or small box; part of iron strigil, iron pin; gilt clay myrtle-berries from a wreath. On the bench of the grave's W side: 41 gilt clay pebbles in the shape of acorn; 46 bone astragaloi and a bone pebble; fragment of alabaster and a clay fragment of female figurine
E4	Sfakaki, Crete	20 BCE– 40 CE	male?	*epistomion*	in the mouth	bronze on chest	Inhumation in cist-grave (above no. 8). Clay and bronze *prochous*, clay *unguentarium*, *lekythion*, two glass *phialae*, a bronze strigil, obsidian flake
E5	Agios Athanassios, Macedonia	III c.	female	rectangular	unknown	unknown	Unknown. From a looted Macedonian tomb. Trapezoid construction at the entrance for the funeral supper; gold earrings, Illyrian type pin, clay figurines

Group F Texts

F1   Elis, Peloponnese.
Bibliography: Papathanassopoulos 1969:153 pl. 153b; Michaud 1971:901, 906 pl. 228; SEG 31.354, 52.471; Yalouris 1996:128–129; Riedweg 2002; Bernabé and Jiménez San Cristóbal 2001:279–280 no. L16i; Bernabé 2005, fr. 496i; Zoumbaki 2005:169; Graf and Johnston 2007:38–39 no. 27; Edmonds forthcoming-2.

Εὐξένη.

Εὐξένα Bernabé and Jiménez San Cristóbal; Bernabé; Graf and Johnston.

F2   Aigeion, Peloponnese.
Bibliography: Papapostolou 1977:94 pl. 63b; SEG 34.338; Riedweg 1998:389–398, and 2002; Bernabé and Jiménez San Cristóbal 2001:279–280 no. L16e; Bernabé 2005, fr. 496e; Graf and Johnston 2007:30–31 no. 20; Edmonds forthcoming-2.

μύστης.

F3   Methone, Pieria, Macedonia.
Bibliography: Above no. 15; Besios 1986:142–143; SEG 40.541, 45.777; Riedweg 1998:389–398, and 2002; Bernabé and Jiménez San Cristóbal 2001:279–280 no. L16h; Bernabé 2005, fr. 496h; Graf and Johnston 2007:44–45 no. 35; Edmonds forthcoming-2.

Φυλομάγα.

F4   Aigeion, Peloponnese.
Bibliography: Papakosta 1987:153; SEG 41.401; Riedweg 1998:389–398, and 2002; Bernabé and Jiménez San Cristóbal 2001:279–280 no. L16c; Bernabé 2005, fr. 496c; Graf and Johnston 2007:30–31 no. 21; Edmonds forthcoming-2.

Δεξίλαος μύστας.

F5   Aigeion, Peloponnese.
Bibliography: Papakosta 1987:153; SEG 41.401; Riedweg 1998:389–398, and 2002; Bernabé and Jiménez San Cristóbal 2001:279–280 no. L16d; Bernabé 2005, fr. 496d; Graf and Johnston 2007:30–31 no. 22; Edmonds forthcoming-2.

Φίλων μύστας.

F6   Pella, Macedonia.

Bibliography: Lilibaki-Akamati 1989:95 pl. 8; 1989–1991:82–84 pl. 29a; SEG 42.619a; Riedweg 1998:389–398, and 2002; Bernabé and Jiménez San Cristóbal 2001:279–280 no. L16a; Bernabé 2005, fr. 496a; Graf and Johnston 2007:42–43 no. 32; Edmonds forthcoming-2.

Φιλοξένα.

F7   Elis, Peloponnese.

Bibliography: Themelis 1994:146–149, 154 no. 15 pl. 82b; SEG 46.456, 52.470; Riedweg 1998:389–398, and 2002; Bernabé and Jiménez San Cristóbal 2001:279–280 no. L16j; Bernabé 2005, fr. 496j; Zoumbaki 2005:354–355; Graf and Johnston 2007:32–33 no. 32; Edmonds forthcoming-2.

Φιλημήνα.

F8   Pydna, Pieria, Macedonia.

Bibliography: Above no. 13; Besios 1992:247; SEG 45.803; Riedweg 1998:389–398, and 2002; Bernabé and Jiménez San Cristóbal 2001:279–280 no. L16e; Bernabé 2005, fr. 496e; Graf and Johnston 2007:30–31 no. 20; Edmonds forthcoming-2.

Obverse: ῎Ανδ-
          ρων.

Reverse: ῎Ανδ-
          ρων.

F9   Pydna, Pieria, Macedonia.

Bibliography: Above no. 14; Besios 1992:247; SEG 45.803; Riedweg 1998:389–398, and 2002; Bernabé and Jiménez San Cristóbal 2001:279–280 no. L16e; Bernabé 2005, fr. 496e; Graf and Johnston 2007:30–31 no. 20; Edmonds forthcoming-2.

Obverse: Ξενα-
          ρίστη.

F10   Europos, Kilkis, Macedonia.

Bibliography: Savvopoulou 1992:427 pl. 4; SEG 45.762; Riedweg 1998:389–398, and 2002; Bernabé and Jiménez San Cristóbal 2001:279–280 no. L16g; Bernabé 2005, fr. 496g; Graf and Johnston 2007:44–45 no. 36; Edmonds forthcoming-2.

Βοττακός.

F11   Pella, Macedonia.
Bibliography: Lilibaki-Akamati 1992:127–128; SEG 45.783, 47.928; BE 1996.257; Riedweg 1998:389–398, and 2002; Bernabé and Jiménez San Cristóbal 2001:279–280 no. L16f; Bernabé 2005, fr. 496f; Graf and Johnston 2007:30–31 no. 20; Edmonds forthcoming-2.

      Ἡγησίσκα.

F12   Dion, Pieria, Macedonia.
Bibliography: Pantermalis 1999:271; SEG 49.703; Graf and Johnston 2007:42–43 no. 33; Edmonds forthcoming-2.

      Ἐπιγέ-
      νης.

Group F

	Provenance	Date BCE	Gender	Shape	Position in grave	Coin	Burial and grave-goods
F1	Elis, Peloponnese	300–275	female	leaf	unknown	unknown	Inhumation in pithos. Clay vases?, gold necklace, gold earrings, fragments of gold foils from a diadem
F2	Aigeion, Peloponnese	II–I c.	male	laurel? or myrtle?	unknown	gold *danake*	Inhumation in cist-grave, looted. Iron strigil, two gold finger-rings, two gold Nike-earrings, fragments of silver and clay vase
F3	Methone, Pieria, Macedonia	ca. 300	female	rectangular	on the body	no	Inhumation in cist-grave, looted, above no. 15. Ivory fragments of bier's decoration of floral patterns and of figures of the Dionysiac cycle; two gold earrings, two gold finger-rings, seven clay vessels, a bronze *phiale*, an iron scissor, a bronze gilt wreath
F4	Aigeion, Peloponnese	III–I c.	male	leaf	unknown	two gold *danake*	Inhumation in cist-grave. Six clay vessels, iron strigil, two fragments of bronze objects
F5	Aigeion, Peloponnese	III–I c.	male	almond? or myrtle?	unknown	gold *danake*	Inhumation in cist-grave. Three craniums and a number of bones; twelve gold lance-shape leaves, gold finger-ring for burial use, two silver bowls, two *unguentaria*
F6	Pella, Macedonia	ca. 300	female	laurel? or myrtle?	unknown	no	Inhumation in cist-grave. Clay myrtle-berries from a wreath; fragments of bone gilt small *chous*; bronze gilt leaves; forty-three bronze nail-heads; two small bronze rings; three pieces of bone tool; eight glass eyes; two small clay *skyphoi*; clay lamp; inscribed clay plate; gold finger-ring; gold earrings

Group F, cont.

	Provenance	Date BCE	Gender	Shape	Position in grave	Coin	Burial and grave-goods
F7	Elis, Peloponnese	III c.	female	myrtle	under the cranium	leaf as danake	Inhumation in cist-grave. Gold finger-ring, gold earrings, clay *pyxis* to the left of cranium; small *skyphos* between the legs, small amphora, four clay *unguentaria*, clay cup, lamp; bronze, iron, silver, and bone fragments from a small wooden box in which a bronze folding mirror, iron tweezers, iron scissors, clay *unguentarium*, clay *pyxis*
F8	Pydna, Pieria, Macedonia	336–300	male	gold coin of Philip II	in the mouth	gold coin of Philip II	Inhumation in pit-grave (above no. 13) immediately to the N of cist grave (below F9). Ivory fragments from the bier, two bronze gilt wreaths, and four clay vessels
F9	Pydna, Pieria, Macedonia	336–300	female	gold coin of Philip II	in the mouth	gold coin of Philip II	Inhumation in cist grave (above no. 14) with pit-grave immediately to the S (above F8). Ivory fragments from the bier, bronze ladle, a small bronze bell, a lead *pyxis*, and seven clay vessels

	Provenance	Date BCE	Gender	Shape	Position in grave	Coin	Burial and grave-goods
F10	Europos, Kilkis, Macedonia	ca. 300	male	rectangular	unknown	unknown	Inhumation? in cist grave, looted. Glass eyes, bone fragments and bronze nails from bier's decoration; clay vases, alabasters, Phoenician vase, iron strigils, bronze gilt wreath with berries. Outside the grave, to the NE: trapezoid construction for funeral supper, where pottery fragments, and fragments of *kantharos*, bones, and shells; traces of *enagismos* in later times NW of the construction, bronze gilt wreath with clay gilt berries, bronze coin badly worn, red-figure *pelike* with amazon, griffin, and youths in gymnasium
F11	Pella, Macedonia	ca. 300	small girl	leaf	unknown	unknown	Inhumation in cist grave. Gold finger-ring with incised animal; gold earrings of Cupids
F12	Dion, Pieria, Macedonia	ca. 300?	male	small disc	unknown	the small disc?	unknown, from Macedonian tomb V

Group G

	Provenance	Date BCE	Gender	Shape	Position in grave	Coin	Burial and grave-goods
G1	Pella, Macedonia	200–150	female	olive?	inside the larnax	gold stater of Philip II	No text (written in ink?, now lost, Chryssostomou 1992). Cremation in chamber tomb. On the dromos pottery and amphora-handle with seal. Inside marble sarcophagus: wooden larnax with cremated bones covered with gold-purple cloth; two gold myrtle-wreaths (24 and 30 leaves each); gold jewel shoe-shaped; burnt bone object. On the floor of the chamber: bronze *phiale*, small clay *pyxis*, two clay *unguentaria*, a small bone object, clay Thasian amphora, clay lamp, iron lamp-stand, glass *skyphos*
G2	Sfakaki, Crete	1–50 CE	male?	epistomion	mouth	silver coin	No text. Inhumation (above no. 10). Around the feet from the knees down: clay *prochous*, four glass cups, glass *phiale*, bronze *lekythion*, and bronze strigil
G3	Sfakaki, Crete	50–100 CE	female?	rectangular *epistomion*	mouth	no	No text. Inhumation (above no. 11). Around the feet: a clay *kylix*, a clay *prochous*, four clay *unguentaria*, glass cup, bronze mirror, lead *pyxis*, and bronze nails
G4	Sfakaki, Crete	I c. CE	female?	rectangular *epistomion*	mouth	no	No text. Inhumation (above no. 12). Deceased A buried later than deceased B to the N, and B (an older burial probably of a female) to the S. Around the feet of both: a clay *prochous*, three *aryballos*-shaped *lekythia*, a clay *unguentarium*, a clay cup, and a glass *phiale*; deceased A also a bronze coin; deceased B also bronze foils (from a wooden *pyxis*?)

Appendix 2

Long- or Short-Text *Epistomia,* and Provenance

Epistomia Engraved with Long Texts

	Group	Provenance	Date BCE	Leaves/Coins
1	A1	Thourioi, Italy	IV c.	
2	A2	Thourioi, Italy	IV c.	
3	A3	Thourioi, Italy	IV c.	
4	A4	Thourioi, Italy	IV c.	
5	C1	Thourioi, Italy	IV c.	
6	B1	Petelia, Italy	IV c.	
7	B10	Hipponion, Italy	ca. 400	
8	B2	Pharsalos, Thessaly	360–340	
9	B9	Thessaly	350–300	
10	D3	Pherai, Thessaly	350–300	
11	D5	Pherai, Thessaly	ca. 300	
12	B11	Entella?, West Sicily	III c.?	
13	D2	Pelinna Thessaly	ca. 275	yes
14	B3	Eleutherna, Crete	III–I c.	
15	B4	Eleutherna, Crete	III–I c.	
16	B5	Eleutherna, Crete	III–I c.	
17	B6	Eleutherna, Crete	III–I c.	
18	B7	Eleutherna, Crete	III–I c.	
19	B8	Eleutherna, Crete	III–I c.	
20	B12	Sfakaki, Crete	II–early I c.	
21	A5	Rome, Italy	II c. CE	

Epistomia Engraved with Short or No Texts

	Group	Provenance	Date BCE	Leaves/ Coins
1	D1	Poseidonia, Italy	VI c.?	
2	F8	Pydna, Pieria, Macedonia	336–300	coin
3	F9	Pydna, Pieria, Macedonia	336–300	coin
4	E3	Pella, Macedonia	ca. 300	yes
5	F3	Methone, Pieria, Macedonia	ca. 300	
6	F6	Pella, Macedonia	ca. 300	yes
7	F10	Europos, Kilkis, Macedonia	ca. 300	
8	F11	Pella, Macedonia	ca. 300	yes
9	E2	Aigai (Vergina), Macedonia	ca. 300	
10	E5	Agios Athanassios, Macedonia	ca. 300	
11	D4	Amphipolis, Macedonia	320–280	
12	F12	Dion, Pieria, Macedonia	325–250?	pseudo-coin
13	F1	Elis, Peloponnese	300–275	
14	F7	Elis, Peloponnese	III c.	yes
15	E1	Eleutherna, Crete	III–I c.	
16	F2	Aigeion, Peloponnese	III–I c.	yes
17	F4	Aigeion, Peloponnese	III–I c.	yes
18	F5	Aigeion, Peloponnese	III–I c.	yes
19	E4	Sfakaki, Crete	20 BCE–40 CE	
20	G1	Pella, Macedonia	200–150	yes
21	G2	Sfakaki, Crete	1–50 CE	
22	G3	Sfakaki, Crete	50–100 CE	
23	G4	Sfakaki, Crete	I c. CE	

Provenance

South Italy and Sicily

	Provenance	Group	Date BCE	Leaves/Coins
1	Poseidonia, Italy	D1	VI c.?	
2	Thourioi, Italy	A1	IV c.	
3	Thourioi, Italy	A2	IV c.	
4	Thourioi, Italy	A3	IV c.	
5	Thourioi, Italy	A4	IV c.	
6	Thourioi, Italy	C1	IV c.	
7	Petelia, Italy	B1	IV c.	
8	Hipponion, Italy	B10	ca. 400	
9	Entella?, West Sicily	B11	III c.?	
10	Rome, Italy	A5	II c. CE	

Crete

	Provenance	Group	Date BCE	Leaves/Coins
1	Eleutherna	B3	III–I c.	
2	Eleutherna	B4	III–I c.	
3	Eleutherna	B5	III–I c.	
4	Eleutherna	B6	III–I c.	
5	Eleutherna	B7	III–I c.	
6	Eleutherna	B8	III–I c.	
7	Eleutherna	E1	III I c.	
8	Sfakaki	B12	II–early I c.	
9	Sfakaki	E4	20 BCE–40 CE	
10	Sfakaki	G2	1–50 CE	
11	Sfakaki	G3	50–100 CE	
12	Sfakaki	G4	I c. CE	

Macedonia

	Provenance	Group	Date BCE	Leaves/Coins
1	Pydna, Pieria	F8	336–300	coin
2	Pydna, Pieria	F9	336–300	coin
3	Methone, Pieria	F3	ca. 300	
4	Europos, Kilkis	F10	ca. 300	
5	Pella	E3	ca. 300	yes
6	Pella	F6	ca. 300	yes
7	Pella	F11	ca. 300	yes
8	Aigai (Vergina)	E2	ca. 300	
8	Agios Athanassios	E5	ca. 300	
10	Dion, Pieria	F12	325–250?	pseudo-coin
11	Amphipolis	D4	320–280	
12	Pella	G1	200–150	yes

Thessaly

	Provenance	Group	Date BCE	Leaves/Coins
1	Pharsalos	B2	360–340	
2	Thessaly	B9	350–320	
3	Pherai	D3	ca. 300	
4	Pherai	D5	ca. 300	
5	Pelinna	D2	ca. 275	yes

Peloponnese

	Provenance	Group	Date BCE	Leaves/Coins
1	Elis	F1	300–275	
2	Elis	F7	III c.	yes
3	Aigeion	F2	III–I c.	yes
4	Aigeion	F4	III–I c.	yes
5	Aigeion	F5	III–I c.	yes

Bibliography

Acosta-Hughes, Benjamin, Kosmetatou, Elizabeth, and Baumbach, Manuel, eds. 2004. *Labored in Papyrus Leaves: Perspectives on an Epigram Collection Attributed to Posidippus (P.Mil.Vogl. VIII 309)*. Center for Hellenic Studies, Hellenic Studies Series 2. Washington, DC and Cambridge, MA.

Adam-Veleni, Polyxeni. 2000. "Απολλωνία η Μυγδονική." *Το Αρχαιολογικό Έργο στη Μακεδονία και Θράκη* 14:273–290.

———. 2002. *Μακεδονικοί βωμοί. Τιμητικοί και ταφικοί βωμοί αυτοκρατορικών χρόνων στη Θεσσαλονίκη, πρωτεύουσα της επαρχίας Μακεδονίας, και στη Βέροια, πρωτεύουσα του Κοινού των Μακεδόνων*. Δημοσιεύματα Αρχαιολογικού Δελτίου 84. Athens.

Albinus, Lars. 2000. *The House of Hades: Studies in Ancient Greek Eschatology*. Studies in Religion 2. Aarhus.

Alexiou, Evangelos. 1998. "'Οὐκ ἀπὸ δρυὸς οὐδ' ἀπὸ πέτρης': Plutarch *Consolatio ad Uxorem* 608C und die Umdeutung eines Homersverses." *Mnemosyne* 51:72–75.

Alexiou, Margaret. 2002. *Ὁ τελετουργικὸς θρῆνος στὴν νεοελληνικὴ παράδοση*. Ed. Dimitrios Yatromanolakis and Panagiotis Roilos. Athens.

———. 2004. "Not by Words Alone: Ritual Approaches to Greek Literature." In *Greek Ritual Poetics*. Center for Hellenic Studies, Hellenic Studies Series 3, ed. Dimitrios Yatromanolakis and Panagiotis Roilos, 94–120. Washington, DC and Cambridge, MA.

Alexiou, Stylianos. 1966. "Αρχαιότητες και μνημεία Κεντρικής και Ανατολικής Κρήτης." *Αρχαιολογικό Δελτίο Χρονικά* 21:407–408, plates 437α–γ.

———. 2002a. "Nouvelle identification de villes crétoises." In Στυλιανός Αλεξίου, *Μινωικά και Ελληνικά: Αρχαιολογικές μελέτες*, 145–156. Athens.

———. 2002b. "Une nouvelle inscription de Agia Pelagia." In Στυλιανός Αλεξίου, *Μινωικά και Ελληνικά: Αρχαιολογικές μελέτες*, 157–163. Athens.

———. 2002c. "Απολλωνία – Πάνορμος." In Στυλιανός Αλεξίου, *Μινωικά και Ελληνικά: Αρχαιολογικές μελέτες*, 191–204. Athens.

——. 2006. "Τοπωνυμικά του Μυλοποτάμου: Πάνορμος, Παντομάτριον και άλλα." In *Ο Μυλοπόταμος από την Αρχαιότητα ως Σήμερα: Περιβάλλον, Αρχαιολογία, Ιστορία, Λαογραφία, Κοινωνιολογία: Πρακτικά Διεθνούς Συνεδρίου (Πάνορμο, 24–30 Οκτωβρίου 2003)*. Vol. 2: *Αρχαίοι Χρόνοι*, ed. Irene Gavrilaki and Yannis Tzifopoulos, 277–287. Rethymno.

Allamani, Viktoria, Chatzinikolaou, Kalliopi, Tzanakouli, Viki, and Galiniki, Styliana. 1999. "Θέρμη 1999. Η ανασκαφή στο νεκροταφείο και στοιχεία για την οργάνωση του χώρου του." *Το Αρχαιολογικό Έργο στη Μακεδονία και Θράκη* 13:153–166.

Allen, Thomas W., Halliday, William R., and Sikes, Edward E. 1936. *The Homeric Hymns*. Oxford. Repr. Amsterdam 1980.

Alonge, Mark. 2005. "The Palaikastro Hymn and the Modern Myth of the Cretan Zeus." *Princeton/Stanford Working Papers in Classics* December 2005. http://www.princeton.edu/~pswpc/papers/papers.html.

Aly, Wolf. 1912. "Ursprung und Entwicklung der kretischen Zeusreligion." *Philologus* 71:457–478.

Amandry, Pierre. 1950. *La mantique Apollinienne à Delphes: Essai sur le fonctionnement de l'oracle*. Bibliothèque des Écoles françaises d'Athènes et de Rome 170. Paris.

——. 1953. *Collection Hélène Stathatos*. Vol. 1: *Les bijoux antiques*. Strasbourg.

Anagnostopoulos, Ioannis S. 1984. *Ο θάνατος και ο κάτω κόσμος στη δημοτική ποίηση (εσχατολογία της δημοτικής ποίησης)*. Διδακτορική διατριβή του Φιλοσοφικού Τμήματος του Εθνικού και Καποδιστριακού Πανεπιστημίου Αθηνών. Athens.

Anderson, Peter. 2005. "A Verse-Scrap on a Kylix by Epiktetos." *Transactions of the American Philological Association* 135:267–277.

Andreadaki-Vlazaki, Maria. 1994–1996. "Αρχαιολογικές ειδήσεις 1992–1994. Νομός Ρεθύμνης, Σφακάκι Παγκαλοχωρίου, οικόπεδο αδελφών Μυτιληναίου." *Κρητική Εστία* 5:251.

——. 1995. "Το αρχαιολογικό ενδιαφέρον στην περιοχή Σταυρωμένου/ Χαμαλευρίου Ρεθύμνου." *Κρητολογικά Γράμματα* 11:367–379.

——. 2002. "Αρχαιολογικές ειδήσεις. Νομός Ρεθύμνης, Επαρχία Ρεθύμνης, Χαμαλεύρι." *Κρητική Εστία* 9:272–274.

——. 2004. "Η περιοχή του Μυλοποτάμου κατά την αρχαιότητα." In *Ελεύθερνα, Πόλη - Ακρόπολη - Νεκρόπολη*, ed. Nicholas Stampolidis, 26–43. Athens. (= 2006. "Η περιοχή του Μυλοποτάμου κατά την αρχαιότητα." In *Ο Μυλοπόταμος από την Αρχαιότητα ως Σήμερα: Περιβάλλον, Αρχαιολογία, Ιστορία, Λαογραφία, Κοινωνιολογία: Πρακτικά Διεθνούς Συνεδρίου [Πάνορμο,*

24–30 Οκτωβρίου 2003]. Vol. 2: *Αρχαίοι Χρόνοι,* ed. Irene Gavrilaki and Yannis Tzifopoulos, 11–34. Rethymno.)

Andreadaki-Vlazaki, Maria, and Papadopoulou, Eleni. 1997. "LMIIIA1: Pottery, Chronology and Terminology." *Monographs of the Danish Institute at Athens* 1:111–155.

Andronikos, Manolis. 1994. *Βεργίνα ΙΙ: Ο τάφος της Περσεφόνης.* Βιβλιοθήκη τῆς ἐν Ἀθήναις Ἀρχαιολογικῆς Ἑταιρείας 138. Athens.

Antonaccio, Carla. 1995. *An Archaeology of Ancestors: Tomb Cult and Hero Cult in Early Greece.* Greek Studies: Interdisciplinary Approaches. Lanham, MD.

Antonelli, Carlo. 1995. "Dioniso e la religione Minoica." In *Πεπραγμένα του Ζ΄ Διεθνούς Κρητολογικού Συνεδρίου (Ρέθυμνο, 25–31 Αυγούστου 1991).* Vol. A1: Νέα Χριστιανική Κρήτη 11–14 (1994–1995), ed. Nikolaos E. Papadogiannakis, 25–32. Rethymno.

Antzoulatou-Retsila, Eurydiki. 2004. *Μνήμης Τεκμήρια.* Athens.

Aposkitou, Martha. 1960. "Κρήτη καὶ Ὅμηρος." *Κρητικά Χρονικά* 14:147–172.

Apostolakou, Vili. 2003. *Λατώ.* Athens.

Apurimac. 1998. *Μάνα Γη, ινδιάνικα ποιήματα. Mother Earth, Indian Poems. Madre tierra, terre notre mère.* Athens.

Arnaoutoglou, Ilias N. 2003. *Thusias heneka kai sunousias: Private Religious Associations in Hellenistic Athens.* Academy of Athens Yearbook of the Research Centre for the History of Greek Law 37.4. Athens.

Arnott, Robert. 2002. "Before Machaon and Podalirius: Minoan and Mycenaean Healers." *Cretan Studies* 7:1–19.

Arrighetti, Graziano. 2001. "Fra purificazioni e produzione letteraria: La teogonia di Epimenide." In *Epimenide Cretese: Quaderni del Dipartimento di discipline storiche "E. Lepore," Università "Federico II,"* ed. Alfonso Mele et al., 217–225. Naples.

Assmann, Jan. 2005. *Death and Salvation in Ancient Egypt.* Trans. David Lorton. Ithaca, NY.

Athanassaki, Lucia. 1996. "Προφητεία και πολιτική: Η ερμηνεία των θεϊκών μηνυμάτων στους Πέρσες του Αισχύλου." In *Ιεροί λόγοι: Προφητείες και μαντείες στην ιουδαϊκή, την ελληνική και τη ρωμαϊκή αρχαιότητα,* ed. Dimitris I. Kyrtatas, 79–111. Athens.

Athanassakis, Apostolos N. 2004. *The Homeric Hymns.* Translation, introduction, and notes. 2nd ed. Baltimore, MD and London.

Athanassiadi, Polymnia. 2005. *Ἰουλιανός: Μία βιογραφία.* Athens.

Avagianou, Aphrodite A. 1991. *Sacred Marriage in the Rituals of Greek Religion.* European University Studies XV.54. Bern.

———. 2000. "Ephorus on the Founding of Delphi's Oracle." *Greek, Roman, and Byzantine Studies* 39:121–136.

———. 2002. "Ἑρμῆι χθονίωι· θρησκεία και άνθρωπος στη Θεσσαλία." In *Λατρείες στην 'Περιφέρεια' του Αρχαίου Ελληνικού Κόσμου*, ed. Aphrodite A. Avagianou, 11–29. Athens.

Aversa, Gregorio. 2006. "The Site of Axos: Italian Excavations and Researches at the End of the 19th Century." In *Ο Μυλοπόταμος από την Αρχαιότητα ως Σήμερα: Περιβάλλον, Αρχαιολογία, Ιστορία, Λαογραφία, Κοινωνιολογία: Πρακτικά Διεθνούς Συνεδρίου (Πάνορμο, 24–30 Οκτωβρίου 2003)*. Vol. 4: *Ελεύθερνα - Αξός*, ed. Irene Gavrilaki and Yannis Tzifopoulos, 103–116. Rethymno.

Babbitt, Frank C. 1931, 1936. *Plutarch's Moralia*. Vols. 3, 5. Loeb Classical Library. Cambridge, MA.

Bachvarova, Mary B. 2005. "The Eastern Mediterranean Epic Tradition from *Bilgames* and *Akka* to the *Song of Release* to Homer's *Iliad*." *Greek, Roman, and Byzantine Studies* 45:131–151.

Bakker, Egbert J. 1997. *Poetry in Speech: Orality and Homeric Discourse*. Myth and Poetics. Ithaca, NY and London.

———2001. "The Greek Gilgamesh, or the Immortality of Return." In *ΕΡΑΝΟΣ: Πρακτικά του Θ´ Συνεδρίου για την Οδύσσεια (2-7 Σεπτεμβρίου 2000)*, 331–353. Ithaca.

———. 2002. "The Making of History: Herodotus' *Histories Apodexis*." In *Brill's Companion to Herodotus*, ed. Egbert J. Bakker, Irene J. F. de Jong, and Hans van Wees, 3–32. Leiden.

———. 2005. *Pointing at the Past: From Formula to Performance in Homeric Poetics*. Center for Hellenic Studies, Hellenic Studies Series 12. Washington, DC and Cambridge, MA.

Baldwin Bowsky, Martha W. 1995. "Roman Crete: No Provincial Backwater." In *Πεπραγμένα του Ζ´ Διεθνούς Κρητολογικού Συνεδρίου (Ρέθυμνο, 25–31 Αυγούστου 1991)*. Vol. A1: Νέα Χριστιανική Κρήτη 11–14 (1994–1995), ed. Nikolaos E. Papadogiannakis, 33–67. Rethymno.

———. 1999. "The Business of Being Roman: The Prosopographical Evidence." In *From Minoan Farmers to Roman Traders: Sidelights on the Economy of Ancient Crete*, ed. Angelos Chaniotis, 305–347. Stuttgart.

———. 2000. "Pasiphae's Granddaughters: Identifying Local Traditions for Cretan Women Responding to Roman Influence." In *Πεπραγμένα του Η´ Διεθνούς Κρητολογικού Συνεδρίου (Ηράκλειο, 9–14 Σεπτεμβρίου 1996)*. Vol. A1, ed. Alexis Kalokairinos, 51–70. Herakleio.

———. 2001a. "A Temple of Hermes at Sybritos: On the Road from Gortyn to the Diktynnaion (Crete)." *Annuario della Scuola Archeologica di Atene e delle Missioni Italiane in Oriente* 79:263–276.

———. 2001b. "When the Flag Follows Trade: Metellus, Pompey, and Crete." In *Roman Military Studies.* Electrum, Studies in Ancient History 5, ed. Edward Dabrowa, 31–72. Kraków.

———. 2002a. "Colonia Iulia Nobilis Cnosus (Creta)." In *Πρακτικὰ ΙΑ´ Διεθνοῦς Συνεδρίου Κλασσικῶν Σπουδῶν (Καβάλα, 24–30 Αὐγούστου 1999)*, ed. Nicholaos A. Livadaras, vol. B:75–89. Athens.

———. 2002b. "Reasons to Reorganize: Antony, Augustus, and Central Crete." In *Tradition and Innovation in the Ancient World.* Electrum, Studies in Ancient History 6, ed. Edward Dabrowa, 25–65. Kraków.

———. 2004a. "From Traders to Landowners: Acculturation in Roman Gortyn." In *Creta romana e protobizantina: Atti del congresso internazionale organizzato dalla Scuola Archeologica Italiana di Atene (Iraklion, 23–30 settembre 2000)*, ed. Antonino Di Vita, Monica Livadioti, and Ilaria Simiakaki, vol. 1:33–47. Padua.

———. 2004b. "Of Two Tongues: Acculturation at Roman Knossos." In *Colonie romane nel mondo greco.* Minima Epigraphica et Papyrologica Separata III, ed. Giovanni Salmeri, Andrea Raggi, and Anselmo Baroni, 95–150. Rome.

———. 2006. "Territorial Reorganization West of Mt. Ida: From Worry to Worship." In *Ο Μυλοπόταμος από την Αρχαιότητα ως Σήμερα: Περιβάλλον, Αρχαιολογία, Ιστορία, Λαογραφία, Κοινωνιολογία: Πρακτικά Διεθνούς Συνεδρίου (Πάνορμο, 24–30 Οκτωβρίου 2003)*. Vol. 2: *Αρχαίοι Χρόνοι*, ed. Irene Gavrilaki and Yannis Tzifopoulos, 253–275, Rethymno.

———. Forthcoming. "From Territory to Town Zone: An Extra-Mural Sanctuary of Aptera (Crete)?"

Baldwin Bowsky, Martha W. and Niniou-Kindeli, Vana. 2006. "On the Road Again: A Trajanic Milestone and the Road Connections of Aptera, Crete." *Hesperia* 75:405–433.

Bandy, Anastassius C. 1970. *The Greek Christian Inscriptions of Crete.* Vol. 10, part I: *IV–IX A.D.* Athens.

Banou, Eleni S. 1994–96. "Αρχαιολογικές ειδήσεις 1992–1994. Νομός Ρεθύμνης, Επαρχία Μυλοποτάμου, Αλφά." *Κρητική Εστία* 5:290–291.

Barbantani, Silvia. 2005. "Notes on a Hellenistic Hymn to Arsinoe-Aphrodite (*P. Lit. Goodsp.* 2, I–IV)." *Ancient Society* 35:135–165.

Barker, Elton. 2006. "Paging the Oracle: Interpretation, Identity, and Performance in Herodotus' *History*." *Greece & Rome* 53:1–28.

Barr-Sharrar, Beryl. 1982. "Macedonian Metal Vases in Perspective: Some Observations in Context and Tradition." In *Macedonia and Greece in Late Classical and Hellenistic Times.* Studies in the History of Art 10, ed. Beryl Barr-Sharrar and Eugene N. Borza, 122–139. Washington, DC.

Barrington Atlas. 2000. Richard J. A. Talbert, ed. *Barrington Atlas of the Greek and Roman World.* Princeton, NJ.

Baumgarten, Roland 1998. *Heiliges Wort und Heilige Schrift bei den Griechen: Hieroi Logoi und verwandte Erscheinungen.* ScriptOralia 110. Tübingen.

BE. "Bulletin épigraphique 1938–2004." *Revue des Études Grecques* 51–117.

Beaulieu, Marie-Claire. 2004. "L'héroïsation du poète Hésiode en Grèce ancienne." *Kernos* 17:103–117.

Beaumont, Lesley A. 1995. "Mythological Childhood: A Male Preserve? An Interpretation of Classical Athenian Iconography." *Annual of the British School at Athens* 90:339–361.

Bechtel, Friedrich. 1917. *Die historischen Personennamen des Griechischen bis zur Kaiserzeit.* Halle.

Becker, Andrew S. 1995. *The Shield of Achilles and the Poetics of Ekphrasis.* Greek Studies: Interdisciplinary Approaches. Lanham, MD.

Benardete, Seth. 1969. *Herodotean Inquiries.* The Hague.

Bernabé, Alberto. 2000. "Nuove frammenti orfici e una nuova edizione degli Ὀρφικά." In *Tra Orfeo e Pitagora: Origini e incontri di culture nell'antichità. Atti dei Seminari Napoletani 1996-1998,* ed. Marisa Tortorelli Ghidini, Alfredina Storchi Marino, and Amedeo Visconti, 43–80. Naples.

———. 2001. "La teogonia di Epimenide: Saggio di ricostruzione." In *Epimenide Cretese: Quaderni del Dipartimento di discipline storiche "E. Lepore," Università "Federico II,"* ed. Alfonso Mele et al., 195–216. Naples.

———. 2002a. "Orphisme et Présocratiques: Bilan et perspectives d'un dialogue complexe." In *Qu'est-ce que la philosophie présocratique?* Cahiers de Philologie 20, ed. André Laks and Claire Louguet, 205–247. Villeneuve-d'Ascq.

———. 2002b. "La toile de Pénélope: A-t-il existé un mythe orphique sur Dionysos et les Titans." *Revue de l'histoire des religions* 219:401–433.

———. 2004, 2005. *Poetae epici graeci testimonia et fragmenta.* Pars II: *Orphicorum et orphicis similium testimonia et fragmenta,* fasc. 1–2. Monachii et Lipsiae.

———. Forthcoming. "The Hittite Myth 'The Voyage of the Immortal Human Soul' and the Orphic Gold Tablets: Analogies and Differences." In *Ritual Texts for the Afterlife: A Gold Tablets Conference at the Ohio State University, April 28-30, 2006,* ed. Fritz Graf and Sarah Iles Johnston.

Bernabé, Alberto and Jiménez San Cristóbal, Ana Isabel. 2001. *Instrucciones para el más allá: Las laminillas órficas de oro*. With iconographic appendix by Ricardo Olmos and illustrations by Sara Olmos. Madrid. (= 2007. *Instructions for the Netherworld: The Orphic Gold Tablets*. Trans. Michael Chase. Religions in the Graeco-Roman World 162. Leiden.)

———. Forthcoming. "Are the Orphic Gold Leaves Orphic?" In *Further Along the Path: Recent Approaches to the 'Orphic' Gold Tablets*, ed. Radcliffe G. Edmonds III. Cambridge.

Bernand, André. 2003. Ἕλληνες μάγοι. Trans. Iosif Kamaris. 2nd ed. Athens. (= 1991. *Sorciers grecs*. Paris)

Bernand, Etienne. 1984. "À propos de l'épitaphe métrique de la crétoise Juliana (I. Métriques, 50)." *Zeitschrift für Papyrologie und Epigraphik* 55:137–140.

Berti, Irene. 2002. "Epigraphical Documentary Evidence for the Themis Cult: Prophecy and Politics." *Kernos* 15:225–234.

Berve, Helmut. 1926. *Das Alexanderreich auf prosopographischer Grundlage*. Vol. 1: *Darstellung*, Vol. 2: *Prosopographie*. Munich.

Bessi, Benedetta. 2004. "Due capsule bronzee da Gortina e da Sabratha: Portasigilli o amuleti?" In *Creta romana e protobizantina: Atti del congresso internazionale organizzato dalla Scuola Archeologica Italiana di Atene (Iraklion, 23-30 settembre 2000)*, ed. Antonino Di Vita, Monica Livadioti, and Ilaria Simiakaki, vol. 3.2:1193–1203. Padua.

Bessios, Matthaios. 1986. "ΙΣΤ΄ Εφορεία Προϊστορικών και Κλασικών Αρχαιοτήτων, Μεθώνη." *Αρχαιολογικό Δελτίο Χρονικά* 41:142–143.

———. 1992. "Ανασκαφές στη βόρεια Πιερία, 1992." *Το Αρχαιολογικό Έργο στη Μακεδονία και Θράκη* 6:245–248.

Betegh, Gábor. 2004. *The Derveni Papyrus: Cosmology, Theology, and Interpretation*. Cambridge.

———. Forthcoming. "Speculating on Tablet C." In *Ritual Texts for the Afterlife: A Gold Tablets Conference at the Ohio State University, April 28-30, 2006*, ed. Fritz Graf and Sarah Iles Johnston.

Betz, Hans Dieter. Forthcoming. "'A Child of Earth Am I and of Starry Heaven': Concerning the Anthropology of Man in the Orphic Gold Tablets." In *Further Along the Path: Recent Approaches to the 'Orphic' Gold Tablets*, ed. Radcliffe G. Edmonds III. (translation of: 1998. "'Der Erde Kind bin ich und des gestirnten Himmels': Zur Lehre vom Menschen in der orphischen Goldplättchen." In *Ansichten griechischer Rituale: Geburstags-Symposium für Walter Burkert, Castelen bei Basel 15. bis 18. März 1996*, ed. Fritz Graf, 399–419. Stuttgart and Leipzig).

Bezantakos, Nicholaos P. 2006. "Ησίοδος και Ανατολή." In *Μουσάων αρχώμεθα: Ο Ησίοδος και η αρχαϊκή επική ποίηση*, ed. Nicholaos P. Bezantakos and Christos Tsagalis, with an introduction by Glenn W. Most, 21–138. Athens.

BGU. *Ägyptische Urkunden aus den Königlichen/Staatlichen Museen zu Berlin, Griechische Urkunden.* http://scriptorium.lib.duke.edu/papyrus/texts/clist.html.

Bieber, Margarete. 1930. "Maske." *Realencyclopädie* 14.2:2070–2120.

Bierl, Anton F. Harald. 1991. *Dionysos und die griechische Tragödie: Politische und "metatheatralische" Aspekte im Text.* Classica Monacensia 1. Tübingen.

Bile, Monique. 1988. *Le dialecte crétois ancien.* École française d'Athènes, Études crétoises 27. Paris.

———. 1992. "Les termes relatifs à l'initiation dans les inscriptions crétoises (VIIe–Ier siècles av. J.C.)." In *L'initiation: Actes du colloque international de Montpellier, 11–14 Avril 1991.* Tome 1: *Les rites d'adolescence et les mystères,* ed. Alain Moreau, 11–18. Montpellier.

Bloom, Antonios, Bishop of Sourozh. 2006. "Θάνατος και απώλεια." http://www.myriobiblos.gr/texts/greek/souroz_thanatos.html.

Bodel, John. 2001. "Epigraphy and the Ancient Historian." In *Epigraphic Evidence: Ancient History from Inscriptions,* ed. John Bodel, 1–56. London and New York.

Boegehold, Alan L. 1999. *When a Gesture was Expected: A Selection of Examples from Archaic and Classical Greek Literature.* Princeton, NJ.

Boehringer, David. 2001. *Heroenkulte in Griechenland von der geometrischen bis zur klassischen Zeit.* Klio Beihefte 3. Berlin.

Böhme, Robert. 1992. "Der Lykomide im Homer." *Zeitschrift für Papyrologie und Epigraphik* 94:51–57.

Bommas, Martin. 2005. *Heiligtum und Mysterium: Griechenland und seine ägyptischen Gottheiten.* Zaberns Bildbände zur Archäologie. Mainz am Rhein.

Bonnechere, Pierre. 2003a. "Trophonius of Lebadea: Mystery Aspects of an Oracular Cult in Boeotia." In *Greek Mysteries: The Archaeology and Ritual of Ancient Greek Secret Cults,* ed. Michael B. Cosmopoulos, 169–192. London and New York.

Bonnechere, Pierre. 2003b. *Trophonios de Lébadée: Cultes et mythes d'une cité béotienne au miroir de la mentalité antique.* Religions in the Graeco-Roman World 150. Leiden.

Bonner, Campbell. 1910. "Dionysiac Magic and the Greek Land of the Cockaigne." *Transactions and Proceedings of the American Philological Association* 41:175–185.

Borgeaud, Philippe. 2001. *Η Μητέρα των θεών: Από την Κυβέλη στην Παρθένο Μαρία.* Trans. Anastasia Karastathi and Mina Kardamitsa. Athens. (= 1996. *La Mère des dieux: de Cybèle à la Vierge Marie.* Paris.)

Bosanquet, Robert C. 1908–1909. "The Palaikastro Hymn of the Kouretes." *Annual of the British School at Athens* 15:339–356.

Bosnakis, Dimitrios. 1994–95. "Οι αιγυπτιακές θεότητες στη Ρόδο και την Κω από τους ελληνιστικούς χρόνους μέχρι και τη ρωμαιοκρατία." *Αρχαιολογικό Δελτίο Μελέτες* 49–50:43–74, plates 7–10.

Bottini, Angelo. 1992. *Archeologia della salvezza: L'escatologia greca nelle testimonianze archeologiche.* Milan.

———. 2000. "Forme di religiosità salvifica in Magna Grecia: La documentazione archeologica." In *Tra Orfeo e Pitagora: Origini e incontri di culture nell'antichità; Atti dei Seminari Napoletani 1996-1998,* ed. Marisa Tortorelli Ghidini, Alfredina Storchi Marino, and Amedeo Visconti, 127–137. Naples.

Bowden, Hugh. 2003. "Oracles for Sale." In *Herodotus and his World: Essays from a Conference in Memory of George Forrest,* ed. Peter Derow and Robert Parker, 256–274. Oxford.

———. 2005. *Classical Athens and the Delphic Oracle: Divination and Democracy.* Cambridge.

———. 2009. "Cults of Demeter Eleusinia and the Transmission of Religious Ideas." In *Greek and Roman Networks in the Mediterranean,* ed. Irad Malkin, Christy Constantakopoulou, and Katerina Panagopoulou, 70–82. London and New York.

Braccesi, Lorenzo. 2004. "Creta nella letteratura augustea." In *Creta romana e protobizantina: Atti del congresso internazionale organizzato dalla Scuola Archeologica Italiana di Atene (Iraklion, 23-30 settembre 2000),* ed. Antonino Di Vita, Monica Livadioti, and Ilaria Simiakaki, vol. 1:3–6. Padua.

Bragantini, Irene. 1995. "La raffigurazione di Caronte in età romana." *La Parola del Passato* 50:395–413.

Brécoulaki, Hariclia. 2006. *La peinture funéraire de Macédoine: Emplois et fonctions de la couleur, IVe-IIe s. av. J.-C.* Vols. 1–2. Meletemata 48. Athens. (= a summary version in "La peinture funéraire de Macédoine [pl. 55–56]." In *Rois, Cités, Nécropoles: Institutions, Rites et Monuments en Macédoine: Actes des Colloques de Nanterre [Décembre 2002] et d'Athènes [Janvier 2004].* Meletemata 45, ed. Anne Marie Guimier-Sorbets, et al., 47–61. Athens.)

Breglia Pulci Doria, Luisa. 2001. "Osservazioni sulla Teogonia di Epimenide." In *Epimenide Cretese: Quaderni del Dipartimento di discipline storiche "E. Lepore," Università "Federico II,"* ed. Alfonso Mele et al., 279–311. Naples.

Bremer, Jan M. 1981. "Greek Hymns." In *Faith, Hope and Worship: Aspects of Religious Mentality in the Ancient World*. Studies in Greek and Roman Religion 2, ed. Henk S. Versnel, 193–215. Leiden.

———. 1994. "Death and Immortality in Some Greek Poems." In *Hidden Futures: Death and Immortality in Ancient Egypt, Anatolia, the Classical, Biblical, and Arabic-Islamic World*, ed. Jan M. Bremer, Theo P. J. van den Hout, and Rudolph Peters, 109–124. Amsterdam.

Bremer, Jan M., van den Hout, Theo P. J., and Peters, Rudolph, eds. 1994. *Hidden Futures: Death and Immortality in Ancient Egypt, Anatolia, the Classical, Biblical, and Arabic-Islamic World*. Amsterdam.

Bremmer, Jan N. 1984. "Greek Maenadism Reconsidered." *Zeitschrift für Papyrologie und Epigraphik* 55:267–286.

———. 1991. "Orpheus: From Guru to Gay." In *Orphisme et Orphée en l'honneur de Jean Rudhardt*. Recherchers et Rencontres, Publications de la Faculté des Lettres de Genève 3, ed. Philippe Borgeaud, 13–30. Geneva.

———. 1994a. "The Soul, Death, and the Afterlife in Early and Classical Greece." In *Hidden Futures: Death and Immortality in Ancient Egypt, Anatolia, the Classical, Biblical, and Arabic-Islamic World*, ed. Jan M. Bremer, Theo P. J. van den Hout, and Rudolph Peters, 91–106. Amsterdam.

———. 1994b. *Greek Religion*. Greece & Rome New Surveys in the Classics 24. Oxford.

———. 1996. "The Status and Symbolic Capital of the Seer." In *The Role of Religion in the Early Greek Polis: Proceedings of the Third International Seminar on Ancient Greek Cult, organized by the Swedish Institute at Athens, 16–18 October 1992*. Skrifter Utgivna av Svenska Institutet i Athen 8.14, ed. Robin Hägg, 97–109. Stockholm.

———. 1998. "'Religion', 'Ritual' and the Opposition 'Sacred vs. Profane': Notes towards a Terminological 'Genealogy.'" In *Ansichten griechischer Rituale: Geburstags-Symposium für Walter Burkert, Castelen bei Basel 15. bis 18. März 1996*, ed. Fritz Graf, 9–32. Stuttgart and Leipzig.

———. 1999. "Rationalization and Disenchatment in Ancient Greece: Max Weber among the Pythagoreans and Orphics?" In *From Myth to Reason? Studies in the Development of Greek Thought*, ed. Richard Buxton, 71–83. Oxford.

———. 2002. *The Rise and Fall of the Afterlife: The 1995 Read-Tuckwell Lectures at the University of Bristol*. London.

———. 2004. "Ritual." In *Religions of the Ancient World: A Guide*, ed. Sarah Iles Johnston, 32–44. Cambridge, MA.

———. 2006. "The Rise of the Hero Cult and the New Simonides." *Zeitschrift für Papyrologie und Epigraphik* 158:15–26.

———. Forthcoming. "Divinities in the Gold Leaves: Brimo, Eukles, Eubouleus and Persephone." In *Ritual Texts for the Afterlife: A Gold Tablets Conference at the Ohio State University, April 28-30, 2006*, ed. Fritz Graf and Sarah Iles Johnston.

Breslin, Joseph. 1977. *A Greek Prayer*. Pasadena, CA.

Brisson, Luc. 1995. *Orphée et l'Orphisme dans l'Antiquité gréco-romaine*. Aldershot.

———. 2002. "La figure du Kronos orphique chez Proclus. De l'orphisme au néoplatonisme, sur l'origine de l'être humain." *Revue de l'histoire des religions* 219:435–458.

Brixhe, Claude and Panayotou, Anna. 1995. "Le plomb magique de Phalasarna." In *Hellènika Symmikta: Histoire, Linguistique, Épigraphie, II*. Études d'Archéologie Classique 8, ed. Claude Brixhe, 23–39. Nancy.

Brown, A. S. 1998. "From the Golden Age to the Isles of the Blest." *Mnemosyne* 51:385–410.

Broze, Michèle, Busine, Aude, and Inowlocki, Sabrina. 2006. "Les catalogues de peuples grecs. Fonctions et contexts d'utilisation." *Kernos* 19:131–144.

Budin, Stephanie Lynn. 2003. *The Origin of Aphrodite*. Bethesda, MD.

Bultrighini, Umberto. 1993. "Divinità della salute nella Creta ellenistica e romana: Ricerche preliminari." *Rivista di Cultura Classica e Medioevale* 35:49–118.

Burgess, Jonathan S. 2004. "Performance and the Epic Cycle." *Classical Journal* 100:1–23.

———. 2005. "The Epic Cycle and Fragments." In *A Companion to Ancient Epic*, ed. John M. Foley, 344–352. Oxford.

Burkert, Walter. 1968. "Orpheus und die Vorsokratiker: Bemerkungen zum Derveni-Papyrus und zur pythagoreischen Zahlenlehre." *Antike und Abendland* 14:93–114 (= 2006. In *Walter Burkert Kleine Schriften III: Mystica, Orphica, Pythagorica*. Hypomnemata Supplement-Reihe 2.3, ed. Fritz Graf, 62–88. Göttingen.)

———. 1975. "Le laminette auree: Da Orfeo a Lampone." In *Orfismo in Magna Grecia: Atti del quattordicesimo convegno di studi sulla Magna Grecia, Taranto, 6-10 Ottobre 1974*, 81–104. Naples. (= 2006. In *Walter Burkert Kleine Schriften III: Mystica, Orphica, Pythagorica*. Hypomnemata Supplement-Reihe 2.3, ed. Fritz Graf, 21–36. Göttingen.)

———. 1977. "Orphism and Bacchic Mysteries: New Evidence and Old Problems of Interpretation." In *Protocol of the 28th Colloquy of the Center for Hermeneutical Studies in Hellenistic and Modern Culture*, ed. Wilhelm Wuellner, 1–8. Berkeley, CA. (= 2006. In *Walter Burkert Kleine Schriften III:*

Mystica, Orphica, Pythagorica. Hypomnemata Supplement-Reihe 2.3, ed. Fritz Graf, 37–46. Göttingen.)

———. 1982. "Craft Versus Sect: The Problem of Orphics and Pythagoreans." In *Jewish and Christian Self-Definition.* Vol 3: *Self-Definition in the Greco-Roman World*, ed. Ben F. Meyers and Ed P. Sanders, 1–22, 183–189. Philadelphia, PA. (= 2006. In *Walter Burkert Kleine Schriften III: Mystica, Orphica, Pythagorica.* Hypomnemata Supplement-Reihe 2.3, ed. Fritz Graf, 191–216. Göttingen.)

———. 1985. *Greek Religion.* Trans. John Raffan. Cambridge, MA.

———. 1987. *Ancient Mystery Cults.* Cambridge, MA.

———. 1992. *The Orientalizing Revolution: Near Eastern Influence on Greek Culture in the Early Archaic Age.* Trans. Margaret E. Pinder and Walter Burkert. Revealing Antiquity 5. Cambridge, MA and London.

———. 1993. "Bacchic Teletai in the Hellenistic Age." In *Masks of Dionysus*, ed. Thomas H. Carpenter and Christopher A. Faraone, 259–275. Myth and Poetics. Ithaca, NY. (= 2006. In *Walter Burkert Kleine Schriften III: Mystica, Orphica, Pythagorica.* Hypomnemata Supplement-Reihe 2.3, ed. Fritz Graf, 120–136. Göttingen.)

———. 1994a. "Olbia and Apollo of Didyma: a New Oracle Text." In *Apollo, Origins and Influences*, ed. Jon Solomon, 49–60. Tucson, AZ and London.

———. 1994b. "Orpheus, Dionysos und die Euneiden in Athen: Das Zeugnis von Euripides' *Hypsipyle.*" In *Orchestra: Drama, Mythos, Bühne*, ed. Anton F. H. Bierl and Peter Möllendorff, with Sabine Vogt, 44–49. Stuttgart and Leipzig. (= 2006. In *Walter Burkert Kleine Schriften III: Mystica, Orphica, Pythagorica.* Hypomnemata Supplement-Reihe 2.3, ed. Fritz Graf, 112–119. Göttingen.)

———. 1995. "Greek Poleis and Civic Cults: Some Further Thoughts." In *Studies in the Ancient Greek Polis: Papers from the Copenhagen Polis Centre 2.* Historia Einzelschriften 95, ed. Mogens H. Hansen and Kurt Raaflaub, 201–210. Stuttgart.

———. 1997. "Star Wars or One Stable World? A Problem of Presocratic Cosmogony (*PDerv.* Col. XXV)." In *Studies on the Derveni Papyrus*, ed. André Laks and Glenn W. Most, 167–174. Oxford.

———. 1998. "Die neuen orphischen Texte: Fragmente, Varianten, 'Sitz im Leben'." In *Fragmentsammlungen philosophischer Texte der Antike: Atti del Seminario Internazionale, Ascona, Centro Stefano Franscini, 22-27 Settembre 1996.* Aporemata 3, ed. Walter Burkert et al., 387–400. Göttingen. (= 2006. In *Walter Burkert Kleine Schriften III: Mystica, Orphica, Pythagorica.* Hypomnemata Supplement-Reihe 2.3, ed. Fritz Graf, 47–61. Göttingen.)

———. 2001a. "The Formation of Greek Religion at the Close of the Dark Ages." In *Walter Burkert Kleine Schriften I: Homerica.* Hypomnemata Supplement-Reihe 2.1, ed. Christoph Riedweg et al., 13–29. Göttingen.

———. 2001b. "Der Odyssee-Dichter und Kreta." In *Walter Burkert Kleine Schriften I: Homerica.* Hypomnemata Supplement-Reihe 2.1, ed. Christoph Riedweg et al., 127–137. Göttingen.

———. 2001c. "Die Leistung eines Kreophylos: Kreophyleer, Homeriden und die archaische Heraklesepik." In *Walter Burkert Kleine Schriften I: Homerica.* Hypomnemata Supplement-Reihe 2.1, ed. Christoph Riedweg et al., 138–149. Göttingen.

———. 2001d. "The Making of Homer in the Sixth Century B.C.: Rhapsodes versus Stesichoros." In *Walter Burkert Kleine Schriften I: Homerica.* Hypomnemata Supplement-Reihe 2.1, ed. Christoph Riedweg et al., 198–217. Göttingen.

———. 2004a. "Epiphanies and Signs of Power: Minoan Suggestions and Comparative Evidence." In *Divine Epiphanies in the Ancient World.* Illinois Classical Studies 29, ed. Danuta Shanzer, guest ed. Nanno Marinatos, 1–23. Urbana Champaign, IL.

———. 2004b. *Babylon, Memphis, Persepolis: Eastern Contexts of Greek Culture.* Cambridge, MA.

———. 2005a. "Near Eastern Connections." In *A Companion to Ancient Epic*, ed. John M. Foley, 291–301. Oxford.

———. 2005b. "Signs, Commands, and Knowledge: Ancient Divination between Enigma and Epiphany." In *Mantike: Studies in Ancient Divination.* Religions in the Graeco-Roman World 155, ed. Sarah Iles Johnston and Peter T. Struck, 29–49. Leiden.

Burnett, Anne Pippin. 1983. *Three Archaic Poets: Archilochus, Alcaeus, Sappho.* Cambridge, MA.

Bury, Rev. Robert G. 1929. *Plato.* Vol. 9: *Timaeus, Critias, Cleitophon, Menexenus, Epistles.* Loeb Classical Library. Cambridge, MA.

Buxton, Richard. 1992. "Imaginary Greek Mountains." *Journal of Hellenic Studies* 112:1–15.

———. 1994. *Imaginary Greece: The Contexts of Mythology.* Cambridge.

Cairon, Élodie. 2006. "Une vie bienheureuse dans l'au-delà: L'épigramme pour Prôté, *IGUR*, 3, no 1146." *Revue des Études Grecques* 119:776–781.

Calame, Claude. 1991. "Eros initiatique et la cosmogonie orphique." In *Orphisme et Orphée en l'honneur de Jean Rudhardt.* Recherchers et Rencontres. Publications de la Faculté des Lettres de Genève 3, ed. Philippe Borgeaud, 227–247. Geneva.

———. 1995. *The Craft of Poetic Speech in Ancient Greece*. Trans. Janice Orion, preface by Jean-Claude Coquet. Myth and Poetics. Ithaca, NY.

———. 1996. *Thésée et l'imaginaire athénien: Légende et culte en Grèce antique*. Preface by Pierre Vidal-Naquet. 2nd ed. Lausanne.

———. 1997. "Figures of Sexuality and Initiatiatory Transition in the Derveni Theogony and Commentary." In *Studies on the Derveni Papyrus*, ed. André Laks and Glenn W. Most, 65–80. Oxford.

———. 1998. "Mort heroïque et culte à mystère dans l'*Oedipe à Colone* de Sophocle: Actes rituels au service de la création mythique." In *Ansichten griechischer Rituale: Geburtstags-Symposium für Walter Burkert; Castelen bei Basel 15. bis 18. März 1996*, ed. Fritz Graf, 326–356. Stuttgart and Leipzig.

———. 2002. "Qu'est-ce qui est orphique dans les Orphica? Un mise au point introductive." *Revue de l'histoire des religions* 219:385–400.

———. 2003. *Myth and History in Ancient Greece: The Symbolic Creation of a Colony*. Trans. Daniel W. Berman. Princeton, NJ.

———. 2004. "Succesion des âges et pragmatique poétique de la justice: Le récit hésiodique des cinq espèces humaines." *Kernos* 17:67–102.

———. Forthcoming. "'Orphic' Invocations and Commentaries: Funerary Transpositions of Religious Discourse." In *Further Along the Path: Recent Approaches to the 'Orphic' Gold Tablets*, ed. Radcliffe G. Edmonds III. Cambridge.

Camassa, Giorgio. 1995. "Passione e rigenerazione. Dioniso e Persefone nelle lamine 'orfiche'." In *Forme di religiosità e tradizioni sapienziali in Magna Grecia: Atti del Convegno, Napoli 14–15 dicembre 1993*. Annali dell'Istituto Universitario Orientale di Napoli XVI (1994), ed. Albio C. Cassio and Paolo Poccetti, 171–182. Pisa and Rome.

Cantilena, Renata. 1995. "Un obolo per Caronte?" *La Parola del Passato* 50:165–177.

Capdeville, Gérard. 1990. "L'oracle de l'Ida crétois." *Kernos* 3:89–101.

Capriglione, Jolanda C. 2001. "La malva e l'asphodelo." In *Epimenide Cretese: Quaderni del Dipartimento di discipline storiche "E. Lepore," Università "Federico II,"* ed. Alfonso Mele et al., 37–51. Naples.

Caraveli, Anna. 1986. "The Bitter Wounding: The Lament as Social Protest in Rural Greece." In *Gender & Power in Rural Greece*, ed. Jill Dubisch, 169–194. Princeton, NJ.

Carington Smith, Jill. 1982. "A Roman Chamber Tomb on the South-East Slopes of Monasteriaki Kephala, Knossos." *Annual of the British School at Athens* 77:255–293.

Carpenter, Thomas H. 1993. "On the Beardless Dionysus." In *Masks of Dionysus*, ed. Thomas H. Carpenter and Christopher A. Faraone, 185–206. Myth and Poetics. Ithaca, NY.

———. 1997. *Dionysiac Imagery in Fifth-Century Athens*. Oxford.

———. Forthcoming. "Apulian Dionysus and the Afterlife." In *Ritual Texts for the Afterlife: A Gold Tablets Conference at the Ohio State University, April 28–30, 2006*, ed. Fritz Graf and Sarah Iles Johnston.

Carpenter, Thomas H. and Faraone, Christopher A., eds. 1993. *Masks of Dionysus*. Myth and Poetics. Ithaca, NY.

Casadio, Giovanni. 1994. *Storia del culto di Dioniso in Argolide*. Rome.

———. 1995. "Dioniso Italiota: Un dio greco in Italia meridionale." In *Forme di religiosità e tradizioni sapienziali in Magna Grecia: Atti del Convegno, Napoli 14-15 dicembre 1993*. Annali dell'Istituto Universitario Orientale di Napoli XVI (1994), ed. Albio C. Cassio and Paolo Poccetti, 79–107. Pisa and Rome.

———. 1999. *Il vino dell'anima: Storia del culto di Dioniso a Corinto, Sicione, Trezene*. Biblioteca di storia delle religioni 1. Rome.

Casertano, Giovanni. 2000. "Orfismo e Pitagorismo in Empedocle?" In *Tra Orfeo e Pitagora: Origini e incontri di culture nell'antichità: Atti dei Seminari Napoletani 1996-1998*, ed. Marisa Tortorelli Ghidini et al., 195–236. Naples.

———. 2001. "Che cosa ha 'veramente' detto Epimenide." In *Epimenide Cretese: Quaderni del Dipartimento di discipline storiche "E. Lepore," Università "Federico II,"* ed. Alfonso Mele et al., 357–390. Naples.

Cassio, Albio C. 1987. "ΠΙΕΝ nella laminetta di Hipponion." *Rivista di filologia e d'istruzione classica* 115:314–316.

———. 1995. "ΠΙΕΝΑΙ e il modello ionico della laminetta di Hipponion." In *Forme di religiosità e tradizioni sapienziali in Magna Grecia: Atti del Convegno, Napoli 14-15 dicembre 1993*. Annali dell'Istituto Universitario Orientale di Napoli XVI (1994), ed. Albio C. Cassio and Paolo Poccetti, 183–205. Pisa and Rome.

———. 1996. "Da Elea a Hipponion e Leontinoi: Lingua di Parmenide e testi epigrafici." *Zeitschrift für Papyrologie und Epigraphik* 113:14–20.

Castriota, David. 1992. *Myth, Ethos, and Actuality: Official Art in Fifth-Century B.C. Athens*. Madison, WI.

Catarzi, Marcello. 2001. "Epimenide e il tempo." In *Epimenide Cretese: Quaderni del Dipartimento di discipline storiche "E. Lepore," Università "Federico II,"* ed. Alfonso Mele et al., 315–356. Naples.

Cerchiai, Luca. 1995. "Daimones e Caronte sulle stele felsinee." *La Parola del Passato* 50:376–394.

Cerri, Giovanni. 1995. "Cosmologia dell'Ade in Omero, Esiodo e Parmenide." *La Parola del Passato* 50:437–467.

Chaniotis, Angelos. 1986. "Review of H. Verbruggen, Le Zeus Crétois, Paris 1981." *Κρητικά Χρονικά* 26:290–307.

———. 1987. "Ploutarchos, praeses insularum (Prosopography of the Later Roman Empire I Plutarchus 4)." *Zeitschrift für Papyrologie und Epigraphik* 68:227–231.

———. 1988. "Als die Diplomaten noch tanzten und sangen. Zu zwei Dekreten kretischer Städte in Mylasa." *Zeitschrift für Papyrologie und Epigraphik* 71:154–156.

———. 1990. "Μιὰ ἄγνωστη πηγὴ γιὰ τὴ λατρεία στὸ Ἰδαῖο Ἄντρο στὴν ὕστατη ἀρχαιότητα." In *Πεπραγμένα του ΣΤ´ Διεθνούς Κρητολογικού Συνεδρίου (Χανιά 24-30 Αυγούστου 1986)*. Vol. A2, ed. Vana Niniou-Kindeli, 393–401. Chania.

———. 1993. "Τα δάση στην αρχαία Κρήτη." *Διάλογος* 11–12:59–70.

———. 1995. "Kretischen Inschriften." *Tekmeria* 1:15–37.

———. 1996a. *Die Verträge zwischen kretischen Poleis in der hellenistischen Zeit.* Heidelberger Althistorische Beiträge und Epigraphische Studien 24. Stuttgart.

———. 1996b. "Bemerkungen zum Kalender kretischer Städte in hellenistischer Zeit." *Tekmeria* 2:16–41.

———. 1999. "Milking the Mountains: Economic Activities on the Cretan Uplands in the Classical and Hellenistic Period." In *From Minoan Farmers to Roman Traders: Sidelights on the Economy of Ancient Crete*, ed. Angelos Chaniotis, 181–220. Stuttgart.

———. 2000. "Das Jenseits: Eine Gegenwelt?" In *Gegenwelten zu den Kulturen Griechenlands und Roms in der Antike*, ed. Tonio Hölscher, 159–181. Munich.

———. 2001a. "Heiligtum und Stadtgemeinde im klassischen und hellenistischen Kreta." In *Kreta und Zypern: Religion und Schrift von der Frühgeschichte bis zum Ende der archaischen Zeit; Tagung in Ohlstadt, Oberbayern, 26.-28. 2. 1999*, ed. A. Kyriatsoulis, 319–332. Altenburg.

———. 2001b. "Ein Alexandrinischer Dichter und Kreta: Mythische Vergangenheit und gegenwärtige Kultpraxis bei Kallimachos." In *ΙΘΑΚΗ: Festschrift für Jörg Schäfer zum 75. Geburtstag am 25. April 2001*, ed. Stephanie Böhm and Klaus-Valtin von Eickstedt, 213–217. Würzburg.

———. 2002. "Ritual Dynamics: The Boiotian Festival of the Daidala." In *KYKEON: Studies in Honour of H. S. Versnel*. Religions in the Graeco-Roman World 142, ed. Hermans F. J. Horstmanshoff et al., 23–48. Leiden.

———. 2003. "Negotiating Religion in the Cities of the Eastern Roman Empire." *Kernos* 16:177–190.

———. 2004. "From Communal Spirit to Individuality: The Epigraphic Habit in Hellenistic and Roman Crete." In *Creta romana e protobizantina: Atti del congresso internazionale organizzato dalla Scuola Archeologica Italiana di Atene (Iraklion, 23-30 settembre 2000)*, ed. Antonino Di Vita, Monica Livadioti, and Ilaria Simiakaki, vol. 1:75–87. Padua.

———. 2005a. "Inscribed Instrumenta Domestica and the Economy of Hellenistic and Roman Crete." In *Making, Moving and Managing: The New World of Ancient Economies 323-31 BC*, ed. Zofia H. Archibald et al., 92–116. Oxford.

———. 2005b. "Ritual Dynamics in the Eastern Mediterranean: Case Studies in Ancient Greece and Asia Minor." In *Rethinking the Mediterranean*, ed. William V. Harris, 141–166. Oxford.

———. 2005c. "Griechische Rituale der Statusänderung und ihre Dynamik." In *Investitur- und Krönungsrituale: Herrschaftseinsetzungen im kulturellen Vergleich*, ed. Marion Steinicke and Stefan Weinfurter, 43–61. Cologne.

———. 2006a. "A Dodecahedron of Rock Crystal from the Idaean Cave and Evidence for Divination in the Sacred Cave of Zeus." In *Ο Μυλοπόταμος από την Αρχαιότητα ως Σήμερα: Περιβάλλον, Αρχαιολογία, Ιστορία, Λαογραφία, Κοινωνιολογία: Πρακτικά Διεθνούς Συνεδρίου (Πάνορμο, 24-30 Οκτωβρίου 2003)*. Vol. 3: *Αρχαίοι Χρόνοι. Ιδαίο Άντρο*, ed. Irene Gavrilaki and Yannis Tzifopoulos, 205–216. Rethymno.

———. 2006b. "Rituals between Norms and Emotions: Rituals as Shared Experience and Memory." In *Ritual and Communication in the Graeco-Roman World*. Kernos Supplément 16, ed. Eftychia Stavrianopoulou, 211–238. Liège.

———. 2006c. "Heiligtümer ueberregionaler Bedeutung auf Kreta." In *Kult - Politik - Ethnos: Überregionale Heiligtümer im Spannungsfeld von Kult und Politik; Kolloquium, Münster, 23.-24. November 2001*. Historia Einzelschriften 189, ed. Klaus Freitag et al., 197–210. Stuttgart.

———. Forthcoming. *Οἱ ἐπιγραφὲς τοῦ Ἰδαίου*.

Chantraine, Pierre. 1980. *Dictionnaire étymologique de la langue grecque: Histoire des mots*. Paris.

Chappell, Mike. 2006. "Delphi and the *Homeric Hymn to Apollo*." *Classical Quarterly* 56:331–348.

Chatzitaki-Kapsomenou, Chryssoula. 1997. "Η λογική του παραλόγου στον αινιγματικό λόγο." In *Γλώσσα και Μαγεία. Κείμενα από την αρχαιότητα*, ed. Anastassios-Phoibos Christidis and David Jordan, 138–146. Athens.

Chester, Stephen J. 2005. "Divine Madness? Speaking in Tongues in 1 Corinthians 14.23." *Journal for the Study of the New Testament* 27.4:417–446.

Chicoteau, Marcel. 1997. "The 'Orphic' Tablets Depicted in a Roman Catacomb (c. 250 AD?)." *Zeitschrift für Papyrologie und Epigraphik* 119:81–83.

Chirassi Colombo, Ileana. 1991. "Le Dionysos oraculaire." *Kernos* 4:205–217.

Christidis, Anastassios-Phoibos. 1996. "Ο προφητικός λόγος." In *Ιεροί λόγοι: Προφητείες και μαντείες στην ιουδαϊκή, την ελληνική και τη ρωμαϊκή αρχαιότητα*, ed. Dimitris I. Kyrtatas, 25–46. Athens.

———. 1997. "Η μαγική χρήση της γλώσσας." In *Γλώσσα και Μαγεία: Κείμενα από την αρχαιότητα*, ed. Anastassios-Phoibos Christidis and David Jordan, 53–64. Athens.

Christidis, Anastassios-Phoibos and Jordan, David, eds. 1997. *Γλώσσα και Μαγεία: Κείμενα από την αρχαιότητα*. Athens.

Chryssostomou, Anastassia. 1996–1997. "Στοιχεία καθημερινής ζωής και λαϊκής λατρείας από την Πέλλα των ελληνιστικών χρόνων. Η σωστική ανασκαφή στο οικόπεδο Γεωργίου Παππά." *Αρχαιολογικό Δελτίο Μελέτες* 51–52:197–230, plates 55–64.

Chryssostomou, Pavlos. 1992. "Ο Μακεδονικός τάφος Β´ της Πέλλας." *Το Αρχαιολογικό Έργο στη Μακεδονία και Θράκη* 6:137–149.

———. 1998. *Η Θεσσαλική θεά Εν(ν)οδία ή Φεραία θεά. Δημοσιεύματα του Αρχαιολογικού Δελτίου* 64. Athens.

———. 1999–2001. "Ταφικό ιερό μυστών του Διονύσου στη Μενηίδα Βοττιαίας." *Αρχαιολογικά Ανάλεκτα εξ Αθηνών* 32–34:195–220.

———. 2000. "Το ταφικό ιερό μυστών του Διονύσου στη Μενηίδα Βοττιαίας: η ανασκαφή του έτους 2000." *Το Αρχαιολογικό Έργο στη Μακεδονία και Θράκη* 14:455–471.

Chryssostomou, Anastassia and Chryssostomou, Pavlos. 2001. "Ανασκαφή στη δυτική νεκρόπολη του Αρχοντικού της Πέλλας κατά το 2001." *Το Αρχαιολογικό Έργο στη Μακεδονία και Θράκη* 15:477–488.

———. 2002. "Ανασκαφή στη δυτική νεκρόπολη του Αρχοντικού της Πέλλας κατά το 2002." *Το Αρχαιολογικό Έργο στη Μακεδονία και Θράκη* 16:465–478.

Chryssanthaki-Nagle, Katérina. 2006. "La monnaie funéraire dans les nécropoles de Macédoine." In *Rois, Cités, Nécropoles: Institutions, Rites et Monuments en Macédoine; Actes des Colloques de Nanterre (Décembre 2002) et d'Athènes (Janvier 2004)*. Meletemata 45, ed. Anne Marie Guimier-Sorbets et al., 89–103. Athens.

Clay, Diskin. 2004. *Archilochos Heros: The Cult of Poets in the Greek Polis*. Center for Hellenic Studies, Hellenic Studies Series 6. Washington, DC and Cambridge, MA.

Bibliography

Clay, Jenny Strauss. 1983. *The Wrath of Athena: Gods and Men in the Odyssey.* Princeton, NJ.

———. 1989. *The Politics of Olympus: Form and Meaning in the Major Homeric Hymns.* Princeton, NJ.

———. 1996. "Fusing the Boundaries: Apollo and Dionysos at Delphi." *Métis* 11:83–100.

———. 1997. "Ἡ συγχώνευση τῶν ὁρίων. Ὁ Ἀπόλλων καὶ ὁ Διόνυσος στοὺς Δελφούς." In *Acta of the First Panhellenic and International Conference on Ancient Greek Literature (23-26 May 1994).* International Centre for Humanistic Research Studies and Researches 38, ed. John-Th. A. Papademetriou, 261–272. Athens.

———. 2003. *Hesiod's Cosmos.* Cambridge.

Clinton, Kevin. 1986. "The Author of the Homeric Hymn to Demeter." *Opuscula Atheniensia* 16.4:43–49.

———. 2003. "Stages of Initiation in the Eleusinian and Samothracian Mysteries." In *Greek Mysteries: The Archaeology and Ritual of Ancient Greek Secret Cults*, ed. Michael B. Cosmopoulos, 50–78. London and New York.

Coldstream, J. Nicolas. 1973. *Knossos: The Sanctuary of Demeter.* Annual of the British School at Athens Supplement 8. London.

Cole, Susan G. 1980. "New Evidence for the Mysteries of Dionysus." *Greek, Roman, and Byzantine Studies* 21:223–238.

———. 1993. "Voices from Beyond the Grave: Dionysus and the Dead." In *Masks of Dionysus*, ed. Thomas H. Carpenter and Christopher A. Faraone, 276–295. Myth and Poetics. Ithaca, NY.

———. 1995. "Civic Cult and Civic Identity." In *Sources for the Ancient Greek City-State: Acts of the Copenhagen Polis Centre 2.* Det Kongelige Danske Videnskabernes Selskab, Historisk-filosofiske Meddelelser 74, ed. Mogens H. Hansen and Kurt Raaflaub, 292–325. Copenhagen.

———. 2003. "Landscapes of Dionysos and Elysian Fields." In *Greek Mysteries: The Archaeology and Ritual of Ancient Greek Secret Cults*, ed. Michael B. Cosmopoulos, 193–217. London and New York.

———. 2004. *Landscapes, Gender, and Ritual Space: The Ancient Greek Experience.* Berkeley, CA.

———. Forthcoming. "Something to Do with Dionysos." In *Ritual Texts for the Afterlife: A Gold Tablets Conference at the Ohio State University, April 28-30, 2006*, ed. Fritz Graf and Sarah Iles Johnston.

Coleman, Simon and Elsner, Jaś, eds. 1995. *Pilgrimage Past and Present: Sacred Travel and Sacred Space in the World Religions.* London.

Collard, Christopher, Cropp, Martin J., and Lee, Kevin H., eds. 1995. *Euripides: Selected Fragmentary Plays with Introductions, Translations and Commentaries.* Vol. 1: *Telephus, Cretans, Stheneboea, Bellerophon, Cresphontes, Erechtheus, Phaethon, Wise Melanippe, Captive Melanippe.* Warminster.

Colli, Giorgio. 1981. *La sapienza greca.* Vol. 1: *Dioniso, Apollo, Eleusi, Orfeo, Museo, Iperborei, Enigma.* 3rd ed. Milan.

Collins, Derek. 2003. "Nature, Cause, and Agency in Greek Magic." *Transactions of the American Philological Association* 133:17–49.

———. 2004. *Master of the Game: Competition and Performance in Greek Poetry.* Center for Hellenic Studies, Hellenic Studies Series 7. Washington, DC and Cambridge, MA.

———. Forthcoming. "Theocritus and Zuntz's Group B Tablets: Copies or Models." In *Ritual Texts for the Afterlife: A Gold Tablets Conference at the Ohio State University, April 28-30, 2006*, ed. Fritz Graf and Sarah Iles Johnston.

Comparetti, Domenico. 1910. *Laminette orfiche, edite e illustrate.* Firenze.

Compton, Todd M. 2006. *Victim of the Muses: Poet as Scapegoat, Warrior, and Hero in the Greco-Roman and Indo-European Myth and History.* Center for Hellenic Studies, Hellenic Studies Series 11. Washington, DC and Cambridge, MA.

Connelly, Joan Breton. 2007. *Portrait of a Priestess: Women and Ritual in Ancient Greece.* Princeton and Oxford.

Cook, Erwin F. 1992. "Ferrymen of Elysium and the Homeric Phaeacians." *Journal of Indo-European Studies* 20:239–267.

———. 1995. *The Odyssey in Athens: Myths of Cultural Origins.* Myth and Poetics. Ithaca, NY.

———. 2004. "Near Eastern Sources for the Palace of Alkinoos." *American Journal of Archaeology* 108:43–77.

COrdPtol 29. *Corpus des Ordonnances des Ptolémées.* Ed. M.-Th. Lenger. Mémoires 64.2. Brussels 1980. http://scriptorium.lib.duke.edu/papyrus/texts/clist.html.

Cosi, Dario M. 2000. "Orfeo e l'Orfismo: Tra continuità e innovazione." In *Tra Orfeo e Pitagora: Origini e incontri di culture nell'antichità: Atti dei Seminari Napoletani 1996-1998*, ed. Marisa Tortorelli Ghidini et al., 139–159. Naples.

Cosmopoulos, Michael B., ed. 2003. *Greek Mysteries: The Archaeology and Ritual of Ancient Greek Secret Cults.* London.

Cozzoli, Adele-Teresa. 2001. *Euripide, Cretesi: Introduzione, testimonianze, testo critico, traduzione e commento.* Testi e Commenti 15. Pisa and Rome.

CPG. Corpus Paroemiographorum Graecorum. Ed. Ernst L. von Leutsch and Friedrich G. Schneidewin. Vols. 1–2, 1839, 1851. Göttingen.

Craik, Elizabeth. 2002. "Euripides Hippolytos and Cretan Cults: Transitions to Manhood and Marriage." *Cretan Studies* 7:59–65.

Crane, Gregory. 1988. *Calypso: Backgrounds and Conventions of the Odyssey.* Beiträge zur klassischen Philologie 191. Frankfurt.

Csapo, Eric. 1997. "Riding the Phallus for Dionysus: Iconology, Ritual, and Gender-Role De/Construction." *Phoenix* 51:253–295, plates 1–8.

Cucuzza, Nicola. 1993. "Leto e il cosiddetto tempio di Rhea di Festós." *Quaderni dell'Istituto di Archeologia della Facoltà di Lettere e Filosofia Università di Messina* 8:21–27.

Cullyer, Helen. 2005. "A Wind that Blows from Thrace: Dionysus in the Fifth Stasimon of Sophocles' *Antigone*." *Classical World* 99:3–20.

Currie, Bruno G. F. 2005. *Pindar and the Cult of Heroes.* Oxford.

Dalby, Andrew. 1998. "Homer's Enemies: Lyric and Epic in the Seventh Century." In *Archaic Greece: New Approaches and New Evidence*, ed. Nick Fisher and Hans van Wees, 195–211. London.

Danforth, Loring M. 1982. *The Death Rituals of Rural Greece.* Photography by Alexander Tsiaras. Princeton, NJ.

Daraki, Maria. 1997. Ὁ Διόνυσος καὶ ἡ θεὰ Γῆ. Athens.

Daux, George. 1955. "Chronique des fouilles et découvertes archéologiques en Grèce en 1954: Épire, Nome d'Arta." *Bulletin de Correspondance Hellénique* 79:267.

———. 1976. "Notes de lecture: En Crète Hermès Kédritès." *Bulletin de Correspondance Hellénique* 100:211–213.

Davaras, Kostis. 1985. "Ρωμαϊκό νεκροταφείο Αγίου Νικολάου." Ἀρχαιολογικὴ Ἐφημερίς 1985:130–216, plates 35–59.

Davesne, Alain and Le Rider, Georges. 1989. *Gülnar II: Le trésor de Meydancıkkale (Cilicie Trachée, 1980).* With the contributions of Françoise de Cénival et al. Institut Français d'Études Anatoliennes. Paris.

Day, Joseph W. 2000. "Epigram and Reader: Generic Force as (Re-)Activation of Ritual." In *Matrices of Genre: Authors, Canons, and Society*, ed. Mary Depew and Dirk Obbink 37–57, 248–254. Cambridge, MA.

De Araújo Caldas, Marcos J. 2003. *Delphi - Orakel der Mächtigen: Untersuchungen zur Geschichte, Funktion und Bedeutung des delphischen Orakels in archaischen Zeit.* Bonn.

Defradas, Jean. 1972. *Les thèmes de la propagande delphique.* 2nd ed. Collection d'Études Anciennes. Paris.

De Heer, Cornelis. 1969. Μάκαρ, εὐδαίμων, ὄλβιος, εὐτυχής: *A Study of the Semantic Field Denoting Happiness in Ancient Greek to the End of the 5th Century B.C.* Amsterdam.

Delia, Diana. 1992. "The Refreshing Water of Osiris." *Journal of the American Research Center in Egypt* 29:181–190.

Demakopoulou, Kaiti. 1998. "Ο νεολιθικός θησαυρός." In *Κοσμήματα της ελληνικής προϊστορίας: Ο νεολιθικός θησαυρός: Εθνικό Αρχαιολογικό Μουσείο 15 Δεκεμβρίου 1998 - 28 Φεβρουαρίου 1999*, ed. Kaiti Demakopoulou, 15–19. Athens.

Dempsey, Rev. T. 1918. *The Delphic Oracle: Its Early History, Influence, and Fall*. With a prefatory note by R. S. Conway. Oxford.

Denniston, John D. 1950. *The Greek Particles*. 2nd ed. Oxford.

Depew, Mary. 1993. "Mimesis and Aetiology in Callimachus' *Hymns*." In *Callimachus: Proceedings of the Groningen Workshops on Hellenistic Poetry*. Hellenistica Groningana I, ed. M. Annette Harder, Remco F. Regtuit, and Gerry C. Wakker, 57–77. Groningen.

———. 2000. "Enacted and Represented Dedications: Genre and Greek Hymn." In *Matrices of Genre: Authors, Canons, and Society*, ed. Mary Depew and Dirk Obbink, 59–79, 254–263. Cambridge, MA.

De Polignac, François. 1996. "Entre les dieux et les morts: Statut individuel et rites collectifs dans la cité archaïque." In *The Role of Religion in the Early Greek Polis: Proceedings of the Third International Seminar on Ancient Greek Cult, organized by the Swedish Institute at Athens, 16–18 October 1992*. Skrifter Utgivna av Svenska Institutet i Athen 8.14, ed. Robin Hägg, 31–40. Stockholm.

———. 2000. *Ἡ γέννηση τῆς ἀρχαίας ἑλληνικῆς πόλης: Λατρεῖες, χῶρος καὶ κοινωνία (8ος-7ος αἰώνας)*. Introd. Claude Mossé. Trans. Nassos Kyriazopoulos. Athens. (= 1995. *La naissance de la cité grecque: cultes, espace et societé*. Paris.)

Derrett, J. Duncan M. 1984. "Whatever Happpened to the Land Flowing with Milk and Honey?" *Vigiliae Christianae* 38:178–184.

De Souza, Philip. 1999. *Piracy in the Graeco-Roman World*. Cambridge.

Despoini, Aikaterini. 1996. *Ελληνική Τέχνη: Αρχαία χρυσά κοσμήματα*. Athens.

———. 1998. "Χρυσά επιστόμια." In *Μνείας Χάριν: Τόμος στη μνήμη Μαίρης Σιγανίδου*, ed. Maria Lilibaki-Akamati and Katerina Tsakalou-Tzanavari, 65–80. Thessaloniki.

Detienne, Marcel. 1975. "Les chemins de la déviance: Orphisme, dionysisme et pythagorisme." In *Orfismo in Magna Grecia: Atti del quattordicesimo convegno di studi sulla Magna Grecia, Taranto, 6–10 Ottobre 1974*, 49–79. Naples.

———. 1979. *Dionysos Slain*. Trans. Mireille Muellner and Leonard Muellner. Baltimore, MD.

———. 1989. *Dionysos at Large*. Trans. Arthur Goldhammer. Cambridge, MA.

———. 1996. *The Masters of Truth in Archaic Greece*. Forward by Pierre Vidal-Naquet. Trans. Janet Lloyd. New York.

———. 2001. "Forgetting Delphi between Apollo and Dionysos." *Classical Philology* 96:147–158.

———. 2003. *The Writing of Orpheus: Greek Myth in Cultural Contact*. Trans. Janet Lloyd. Baltimore, MD.

Dettori, Emanuele. 1996. "Testi 'orfici' dalla Magna Grecia al Mar Nero." *La Parola del Passato* 51:292–310.

Diamantis, Nikitas. 1998. "Επιγραφές από το παλαιοχριστιανικό νεκροταφείο Κισάμου." *Αρχαιολογικό Δελτίο Μελέτες* 53:313–330.

Di Benedeto, Vincenzo. 2004. "Fra Hipponion e Petelia." *La Parola del Passato* 59:293–306.

Di Branco, Marco. 2004. "Pellegrinaggi a Creta. Tradizioni e culti cretesi in epoca tardoantica." In *Creta romana e protobizantina: Atti del congresso internazionale organizzato dalla Scuola Archeologica Italiana di Atene (Iraklion, 23-30 settembre 2000)*, ed. Antonino Di Vita, Monica Livadioti, and Ilaria Simiakaki, vol. 1:7–15. Padua.

Dickey, Eleanor. 1996. *Greek Forms of Address from Herodotus to Lucian*. Oxford and New York.

Dickie, Matthew W. 1994. "Which Poseidippus?" *Greek, Roman, and Byzantine Studies* 35:373–383.

———. 1995a. "The Dionysiac Mysteries in Pella." *Zeitschrift für Papyrologie und Epigraphik* 109:81–86.

———. 1995b. "A New Epigram by Poseidippus on an Irritable Dead Cretan." *Bulletin of the American Society of Papyrologists* 32:5–12.

———. 1998. "Poets as Initiates in the Mysteries: Euphorion, Philicus and Posidippus." *Antike und Abendland* 44:49–77.

———. 2001. *Magic and Magicians in the Greco-Roman World*. London.

Dieterich, Albrecht. 1911. *Kleine Schriften mit einem Bildnis und zwei Tafeln*. Leipzig and Berlin.

———. 1969. *Nekyia: Beiträge zur Erklärung der neuentdeckten Petrusapokapypse*. 2nd ed. Stuttgart. Orig. pub. Leipzig, 1913.

Dietrich, Bernard C. 1992. "Divine Madness and Conflict at Delphi." *Kernos* 5:41–58.

Dignas, Beate. 2004. "Posidippus and the Mysteries: *Epitymbia* Read by the Ancient Historian." In *Labored in Papyrus Leaves: Perspectives on an Epigram Collection Attributed to Posidippus (P.Mil.Vogl. VIII 309)*. Center for Hellenic Studies, Hellenic Studies Series 2, ed. Benjamin Acosta-Hughes et al., 177–186. Washington, DC and Cambridge, MA.

Dillery, John. 2005. "Chresmologues and Manteis: Diviners and the Problem of Authority." In *Mantike: Studies in Ancient Divination*. Religions in the Graeco-Roman World 155, ed. Sarah Iles Johnston and Peter T. Struck, 167–231. Leiden.

Dillon, Matthew. 1997. *Pilgrims and Pilgrimage in Ancient Greece*. London and New York.

Di Marco, Massimo. 1993. "Dioniso ed Orfeo nelle *Bassaridi* di Eschilo." In *Orfeo e l'Orfismo: Atti del Seminario Nazionale (Roma-Perugia 1985-1991)*, ed. Agostino Masaracchia, 101–153. Rome.

Dodds, Eric R. 1951. *The Greeks and the Irrational*. Sather Classical Lectures 25. Berkeley, CA.

———. 1960. *Euripides. Bacchae*. Edited with introduction and commentary. Oxford.

Donohue, Alice A. 2005. *Greek Sculpture and the Problem of Description*. Cambridge.

Dousa, Thomas M. Forthcoming. "Common Motifs in the 'Orphic' B Tablets and Egyptian Funerary Texts: Continuity or Convergence?" In *Further Along the Path: Recent Approaches to the 'Orphic' Gold Tablets*, ed. Radcliffe G. Edmonds III. Cambridge.

Dova, Stamatia. 2000. "Who is μακάρτατος in the *Odyssey*?" *Harvard Studies in Classical Philology* 100:53–65.

Dover, Kenneth J. 1997. *Aristophanes. Frogs*. Abridged from the 1993 edition. Oxford.

Drosinou, Paraskevi. 1992. "ΚΕ΄ Εφορεία Προϊστορικών και Κλασικών Αρχαιοτήτων. Νομός Χανίων, Κίσαμος, Οικόπεδο Αλέξ. και Γεωργίου Ραϊσάκη." *Αρχαιολογικό Δελτίο Χρονικά* 47 B2:579–581.

Drozdek, Adam. 2001. "Heraclitus' Theology." *Classica et Mediaevalia* 52:37–56.

Dubois, Laurent. 1996. *Inscriptions grecques dialectales d'Olbia du Pont*. Geneva.

Dué, Casey. 2001. "Achilles' Golden Amphora in Aeschines' *Against Timarchus* and the Afterlife of Oral Tradition." *Classical Philology* 96:33–47.

Dunkle, Roger. 1997. "Swift-Footed Achilles." *Classical World* 90:227–34.

Dunn, Francis M. 2000. "Euripedean Aetiologies." *Classical Bulletin* 76:3–27.

Durán, Martí. 1996. "Pamfos." *Anuari de filologia, Secció D, Studia Graeca et Latina (Universitat de Barcelona, Facultat de Filologia)* 19:45–63.

Easterling, Pat. 2004. "Now and Forever in Greek Drama and Ritual." In *Greek Ritual Poetics*. Center for Hellenic Studies, Hellenic Studies Series 3, ed. Dimitrios Yatromanolakis and Panagiotis Roilos, 149–160. Washington, DC and Cambridge, MA.

EBGR. Angelos Chaniotis et al. "Epigraphic Bulletin for Greek Religion 1987–2002." *Kernos* 4–18 (1991–2005).

Edmonds III, Radcliffe G. 1999. "Tearing Apart the Zagreus Myth: A Few Disparaging Remarks on Orphism and Original Sin." *Classical Antiquity* 18:35–73.

———. 2004. *Myths of the Underworld Journey: Plato, Aristophanes, and the 'Orphic' Gold Tablets*. Cambridge.

———. Forthcoming-1. "Who Are You? A Brief History of Scholarship." In *Further Along the Path: Recent Approaches to the 'Orphic' Gold Tablets*, ed. Radcliff G. Edmonds III. Cambridge.

———. Forthcoming-2. "Texts and Translations of the Gold Tablets, with Critical Apparatus and Tables." In *Further Along the Path: Recent Approaches to the 'Orphic' Gold Tablets*, ed. Radcliff G. Edmonds III. Cambridge.

———. Forthcoming-3. "Sacred Scripture or Oracles for the Dead? The Semiotic Situation of the 'Orphic' Gold Tablets." In *Further Along the Path: Recent Approaches to the 'Orphic' Gold Tablets*, ed. Radcliffe G. Edmonds III. Cambridge.

———. Forthcoming-4. "Persephone and *poinê*: Recompense for the Powers of the Underworld in the 'Orphic' Gold Tablets and Pindar fr. 133." In *Ritual Texts for the Afterlife: A Gold Tablets Conference at the Ohio State University, April 28-30, 2006*, ed. Fritz Graf and Sarah Iles Johnston.

Edwards, Mark. 2004. *Hesiod's Ascra*. Berkeley, CA.

Efraim. 1990. Εὐφραίμ, ἀρχιμανδρίτης καὶ καθηγούμενος Ἱερᾶς Μονῆς Φιλοθέου. Ἱερὰ Μονὴ Φιλοθέου. Hagion Oros.

Ekroth, Gunnel. 2002. *The Sacrificial Rituals of Greek Hero-Cults in the Archaic to the Early Hellenistic Period*. Kernos Supplément 12. Liège.

Elsner, Jaś and Rutherford, Ian, eds. 2005. *Pilgrimage in Graeco-Roman and Early Christian Antiquity*. Oxford.

Erickson, Brice L. 2000. *Late Archaic and Classical Crete: Island Pottery Styles in an Age of Historical Transition*. Ph.D. Dissertation, University of Texas at Austin. Ann Arbor, MI.

———. 2002. "Aphrati and Kato Syme: Pottery, Continuity, and Cult in Late Archaic and Classical Crete." *Hesperia* 71:41–90.

———. 2004. "Eleutherna and the Greek World, ca. 600–400 B.C." In *Crete Beyond the Palaces: Proceedings of the Crete 2000 Conference*. Prehistory Monographs 10, ed. Leslie Preston Day et al., 199–212. Philadelphia.

———. 2005. "Archaeology of Empire: Athens and Crete in the Fifth Century B.C." *American Journal of Archaeology* 109:619–663.

———. 2006. "Cretan Austerity in the Sixth Century BC." In *Ο Μυλοπόταμος από την Αρχαιότητα ως Σήμερα: Περιβάλλον, Αρχαιολογία, Ιστορία, Λαογραφία, Κοινωνιολογία: Πρακτικά Διεθνούς Συνεδρίου (Πάνορμο, 24-30 Οκτωβρίου 2003)*. Vol. 4: *Ελεύθερνα - Αξός*, ed. Irene Gavrilaki and Yannis Tzifopoulos, 69–92. Rethymno.

Evans, Rhiannon. 2003. "Searching for Paradise: Landscape, Utopia, and Rome." *Arethusa* 36:285–307.

Exler, Francis X. J. 1976. *The Form of the Ancient Greek Letter of the Epistolary Papyri (3rd c. B.C.-3rd c. A.D.): A Study in Greek Epistolography*. Chicago. Orig. pub. Washington, DC, 1923.

Falconer, William A., ed. 1923. *Cicero*. Vol. 20: *De senecture, de amicitia, de divinatione*. Loeb Classical Library. Cambridge, MA.

Fantuzzi, Marco. 2006. "The Myths of Dolon and Rhesus from Homer to the 'Homeric/Cyclic' Tragedy *Rhesus*." In *La poésie épique grecque: Métamorphoses d'un genre littéraire (Vandoevres-Genève, 22-26 Août 2005)*. Entretiens sur l'antiquité classique 52, ed. Franco Montanari and Antonios Rengakos, 135–182. Geneva.

Fantuzzi, Marco and Hunter, Richard. 2005. *Ο Ελικώνας και το Μουσείο: Η ελληνιστική ποίηση από την εποχή του Μεγάλου Αλεξάνδρου έως την εποχή του Αυγούστου*. Trans. Dimitra Koukouzika and Maria Nousia. Ed. Theodoros Papangelis and Antonios Rengakos. Athens. (= 2002. *Muse e modelli: La poesia ellenistica da Alessandro Magno ad Augusto*. Rome and Bari.)

Faraklas, Nikolas, et al. 1998. Νικόλας Φαράκλας, Έφη Κατάκη, Αγγελική Κόσσυβα, Ναπολέων Ξιφαράς, Εμμανουήλ Παναγιωτόπουλος, Γιώργος Τασούλας, Νίκη Τσατσάκη, Μαρία Χατζηπαναγιώτη. *Οι επικράτειες των αρχαίων πόλεων της Κρήτης*. Σειρά Ρίθυμνα 6. Rethymno.

Faraone, Christopher A. 2002. "A Drink from the Daughters of Mnemosyne: Poetry, Eschatology, and Memory at the End of Pindar's *Isthmian 6*." In *Vertis in usum: Studies in Honor of Edward Courtney*. Beiträge zur Altertumskunde 161, ed. John F. Miller et al., 259–270. Munich and Leipzig.

———. 2004. "Orpheus' Final Performance: Necromancy and a Singing Head on Lesbos." *Studi Italiani di Filologia Classica* 97:5–27.

———. 2005. "Necromancy Goes Underground: The Disguise of Skull- and Corpse-Divination in the Paris Magical Papyri (PGM IV 1928-2144)." In *Mantike: Studies in Ancient Divination*. Religions of the Graeco-Roman World 155, ed. Sarah Iles Johnston and Peter T. Struck, 255–282. Leiden.

———. Forthcoming-1. "Rushing Into Milk: New Perspectives on the Gold Tablets." In *Further Along the Path: Recent Approaches to the 'Orphic' Gold Tablets*, ed. Radcliffe G. Edmonds III. Cambridge.

———. Forthcoming-2. "Mystery Cults and Incantations: Evidence for Orphic Charms in Euripides' *Cyclops*?" In *Ritual Texts for the Afterlife: A Gold Tablets Conference at the Ohio State University, April 28-30, 2006*, ed. Fritz Graf and Sarah Iles Johnston.

Faraone, Christopher A. and Obbink, Dirk, eds. 1991. *Magika Hiera: Ancient Greek Magic and Religion*. New York.

Farnell, Lewis R. 1995. *Greek Hero Cults and Ideas of Immortality: The Gifford Lectures Delivered in the University of St. Andrewes in the Year 1920*. Chicago. Orig. pub. Oxford, 1921.

———. 2004. *The Cults of the Greek States*. 5 vols. Chicago. Orig. pub. Oxford, 1896–1909.

Faure, Paul. 2000a. *Οδυσσέας ο Κρητικός (13ος αιώνας π.Χ.)*. Trans. Stavros Vlontakis. Athens. (= 1998. *Ulysse le crétois*. Paris.)

———. 2000b. "Ports et mouillages minoens de la côte nord de Crète." *Πεπραγμένα του Η΄ Διεθνούς Κρητολογικού Συνεδρίου (Ηράκλειο, 9–14 Σεπτεμβρίου 1996)*, ed. Alexis Kalokairinos, vol. A1:457–469. Heraklio.

Fauriel, Claude. 1999. *Ελληνικά δημοτικά τραγούδια*. Vols. A–B. 2nd ed. Ed. Alexis Politis. Heraklio.

Federico, Eduardo. 2001. "La Katharsis di Epimenide ad Atene: La vicenda, gli usi e gli abusi ateniesi." In *Epimenide Cretese: Quaderni del Dipartimento di discipline storiche "E. Lepore," Università "Federico II,"* ed. Alfonso Mele et al., 77–128. Naples.

Ferrari, Gloria. 2003. "Myth and Genre on Athenian Vases." *Classical Antiquity* 22:37–54.

FGrHist. Fragmente der griechischen Historiker. Ed. Felix Jacoby et al. Leiden.

Finkelberg, Margalit. 2006. "Regional Texts and the Circulation of Books: The Case of Homer." *Greek, Roman, and Byzantine Studies* 46:231–248.

Fol, Alexander. 2004. "Die thrakische Orphik oder zwei Wege zur Unsterblich-keit." *Die Thraker: Das goldene Reich des Orpheus, 23. Juli bis 28. November 2004*, 177–186. Bonn.

Fontenrose, Joseph. 1974. "Work, Justice, and Hesiod's Five Ages." *Classical Philology* 69:1–16.

———. 1980. *Python: A Study of Delphic Myth and its Origins*. Berkeley, CA.

———. 1981. *The Delphic Oracle: Its Responses and Operations with a Catalogue of Responses*. Berkeley, CA.

Foti, Giuseppe and Pugliese Carratelli, Giovanni. 1974. "Un sepolcro di Hipponion e un nuovo testo orfico." *La Parola del Passato* 29:91–126.

Fountoulakis, Andreas. 2002. "Herondas 8.66–79: Generic Self-Consciousness and Artistic Claims in Herondas' Mimiambs." *Mnemosyne* 55:301–319.

Fowler, Don. 2000. "The Didactic Plot." In *Matrices of Genre: Authors, Canons, and Society*, ed. Mary Depew and Dirk Obbink, 205–219, 299–302. Cambridge, MA.

Fowler, Robert L. 2000. "Greek Magic, Greek Religion." In *Oxford Readings in Greek Religion*, ed. Richard Buxton, 317–343. Oxford.

Frangoulidis, Stavros A. 1993. "Polyphemus' Prayer to Poseidon: Homer, *Odyssey* 9.528–35." *Quaderni Urbinati di Cultura Classica* 43:45–49.

Franke, Peter R. and Marathaki, Irini. 1999. *Οίνος και νόμισμα στην αρχαία Ελλάδα*. Athens.

Frankfurter, David. 1998. *Religion in Roman Egypt: Assimilation and Resistance.* Princeton, NJ.

——. 2002. "Dynamics of Ritual Expertise in Antiquity and Beyond: Towards a New Taxonomy of 'Magicians.'" In *Magic and Ritual in the Ancient World*. Religions in the Graeco-Roman World 141, ed. Paul Mirecki and Marvin Meyer, 159–178. Leiden.

——. 2004. "Sacred Texts and Canonicity: Introduction." In *Religions of the Ancient World: A Guide*, ed. Sarah Iles Johnston, 622–623. Cambridge, MA.

Frazer, James G. 1965. *Pausanias's Description of Greece.* 6 vols. New York. Orig. pub. London, 1989.

Freese, John H., ed. 1926. *Aristotle.* Vol. 22: *The 'Art' of Rhetoric.* Loeb Classical Library. Cambridge, MA.

Fridh-Haneson, Britt Marie. 1987. "Votive Terracottas from Italy: Types and Problems." In *Gifts to the Gods: Proceedings of the Upsala Symposium 1985*. Acta Universitatis Upsaliensis Boreas 15, ed. Tulia Linders and Gullog Nordquist, 67–75. Uppsala.

Furley, William D. 1995. "Praise and Persuasion in Greek Hymns." *Journal of Hellenic Studies* 115:29–46.

Furley, William D. and Bremer, Jan M. 2001. *Greek Hymns: Selected Cult Songs from the Archaic to the Hellenistic Period.* Vol. 1: *The Texts in Translation.* Vol. 2: *Greek Texts and Commentary.* Studien und Texte zu Antike und Christentum 9–10. Tübingen.

Furtwängler, Andreas and Spanou, Niki. 2004. "Χάλκινο νόμισμα 3ος αι. π.Χ., Χάλκινο νόμισμα μέσα 2ου αι. π.Χ." In *Ελεύθερνα, Πόλη - Ακρόπολη - Νεκρόπολη*, ed. Nicholas C. Stampolidis, 161 no. 23, 162 no. 27. Athens.

Gager, John G., ed. 1992. *Curse Tablets and Binding Spells from the Ancient World.* New York and Oxford.

Galanaki, Kalliopi. 2001. *Θεοί, δαίμονες και θνητοί σε χάλκινα τορεύματα από το Ιδαίο Άντρο.* Διδακτορική διατριβή, Πανεπιστήμιο Κρήτης. Rethymno.

———. 2006. "Χάλκινες ανάγλυφες ομφαλωτές φιάλες της πρώιμης αρχαϊκής περιόδου από το Ιδαίο Άντρο." *Ο Μυλοπόταμος από την Αρχαιότητα ως Σήμερα: Περιβάλλον, Αρχαιολογία, Ιστορία, Λαογραφία, Κοινωνιολογία: Πρακτικά Διεθνούς Συνεδρίου (Πάνορμο, 24-30 Οκτωβρίου 2003).* Vol. 3: *Αρχαίοι Χρόνοι. Ιδαίο Άντρο,* ed. Irene Gavrilaki and Yannis Tzifopoulos, 85–136. Rethymno.

Gallavotti, Carlo. 1978-1979. "Il documento orfico di Hipponion e altri testi affini." *Museum Criticum* 13-14:337–359.

———. 1988. "Revisione di testi epigrafici 25: Un'aurea lamella di Creta." *Bollettino dei Classici* 9:28–31.

García, John F. 2002. "Symbolic Action in the *Homeric Hymns*: The Theme of Recognition." *Classical Antiquity* 21:5–39.

Garland, Robert. 1985. *The Greek Way of Death.* Ithaca, NY.

———. 1989. "The Well-Ordered Corpse: An Investigation into the Motives Behind Greek Funerary Legislation." *Bulletin of the Institute of Classical Studies* 36:1–15.

Garner, R. Scott. 2005. "Epic and Other Genres in the Ancient Greek World." In *A Companion to Ancient Epic*, ed. John M. Foley, 386–396. Oxford.

Gartziou-Tatti, Ariadni. 1999. "Θάνατος και ταφή του Ορφέα στη Μακεδονία και τη Θράκη." *Ancient Macedonia VI: Papers Read at the Sixth International Symposium Held in Thessaloniki, October 15-19, 1996.* Vol. 1:439–451. Institute for Balkan Studies 272. Thessaloniki.

Gavrilaki, Irene. 1989. "ΚΕ΄ Εφορεία Προϊστορικών και Κλασικών Αρχαιοτήτων. Σφακάκι Παγκαλοχωρίου, οικόπεδο Πολιουδάκη." *Αρχαιολογικό Δελτίο Χρονικά* 44 Β2:457–460, plates 253β–254α.

———. 1991-1993. "Αρχαιολογικές ειδήσεις 1989-1991, Νομός Ρεθύμνης, Σφακάκι Παγκαλοχωρίου, οικόπεδο Μ. Πολιουδάκη." *Κρητική Εστία* 4:239–241, plate 2β.

———. 2004. "Νεκροταφεία ρωμαϊκών χρόνων στην Αργυρούπολη Ρεθύμνης." In *Creta romana e protobizantina: Atti del congresso internazionale organizzato dalla Scuola Archeologica Italiana di Atene (Iraklion, 23-30 settembre 2000),* ed. Antonino Di Vita, Monica Livadioti, and Ilaria Simiakaki, vol. 2:301–312. Padua.

Gavrilaki-Nikoloudaki, Irene. 1988. "ΚΕ΄ Εφορεία Προϊστορικών και Κλασικών Αρχαιοτήτων: Σταυρωμένος Ρεθύμνου, θέση Σφακάκι (οικόπεδο Πολιουδάκη)." *Αρχαιολογικό Δελτίο Χρονικά* 43 Β2:557–558, plates 346γ–δ.

Gavrilaki, Irene and Tzifopoulos, Yannis Z. 1998. "An 'Orphic-Dionysiac' Gold *Epistomion* from Sfakaki near Rethymno." *Bulletin de Correspondance Hellénique* 122:343–355.

Gehrke, Hans-Joachim. 1997. "Gewalt und Gesetz: Die soziale und politische Ordnung Kretas in der archaischen und klassischen Zeit." *Klio* 79:23–68.

George, David. 2006. "These First in Crete at Ida Known: The Reception of Mylopotamos in Latin Literature." In *Ο Μυλοπόταμος από την Αρχαιότητα ως Σήμερα: Περιβάλλον, Αρχαιολογία, Ιστορία, Λαογραφία, Κοινωνιολογία: Πρακτικά Διεθνούς Συνεδρίου (Πάνορμο, 24-30 Οκτωβρίου 2003)*. Vol. 3: *Αρχαίοι Χρόνοι. Ιδαίο Άντρο*, ed. Irene Gavrilaki and Yannis Tzifopoulos, 229–237. Rethymno.

Georgoudi, Stella. 2002. "Gaia/Gê: Entre mythe, culte et idéologie." In *Myth and Symbol I: Symbolic Phenomena in Ancient Greek Culture; Papers from the First International Symposium on Symbolism at the University of Tromsø, June 4-7, 1998*. Papers from the Norwegian Institute at Athens 5, ed. Synnøve des Bouvrie, 113–134. Bergen.

Georgoulaki, Eleni. 1996. "Religious and Socio-Political Implications of Mortuary Evidence: Case Studies in Ancient Greece." *Kernos* 9:95–120.

———. 2002. "Discerning Early Minoan Cultic Trends: The Archaeological Evidence." *Kernos* 15:19–29.

Gera, Deborah L. 2003. *Ancient Greek Ideas on Speech, Language, and Civilization.* Oxford.

Gerhard, Gustav A. 1905. "Untersuchungen zur Geschichte des griechischen Briefes, I. Die Formel 'ὁ δεῖνα τῷ δεῖνι χαίρειν.'" *Philologus* 64:27–65.

Ghinatti, Franco. 2004. "L'epigrafia della koiné." In *Creta romana e protobizantina: Atti del congresso internazionale organizzato dalla Scuola Archeologica Italiana di Atene (Iraklion, 23-30 settembre 2000)*, ed. Antonino Di Vita, Monica Livadioti, and Ilaria Simiakaki, vol. 1:57–74. Padua.

Giangiulo, Maurizio. 1995. "Sapienza pitagorica e religiosità apolline." In *Forme di religiosità e tradizioni sapienziali in Magna Grecia: Atti del Convegno, Napoli 14-15 dicembre 1993*. Annali dell'Istituto Universitario Orientale di Napoli XVI (1994), ed. Albio C. Cassio and Paolo Poccetti, 9–27. Pisa and Rome.

Giangrande, Giuseppe. 1993. "La lamina orfica di Hipponion." In *Orfeo e l'Orfismo: Atti del Seminario Nazionale (Roma-Perugia 1985-1991)*, ed. Agostino Masaracchia, 235–248. Rome.

Giannobile, Sergio and Jordan, David R. 2006. "A Lead Phylactery from Colle San Basilio (Sicily)." *Greek, Roman, and Byzantine Studies* 46:73–86.

Giannopoulou, Mimika and Demesticha, Stella. 1998. *Τσκαλαριά: Τα εργαστήρια αγγειοπλαστικής της περιοχής Μανταμάδου Λέσβου.* Athens.

Gigante, Marcello. 2001. "Bios laerziano di Epimenide." In *Epimenide Cretese: Quaderni del Dipartimento di discipline storiche "E. Lepore," Università "Federico II,"* ed. Alfonso Mele et al., 7–24. Naples.

Girone, Maria. 2004. "Dediche votive cretesi." In *Creta romana e protobizantina: Atti del congresso internazionale organizzato dalla Scuola Archeologica Italiana di Atene (Iraklion, 23–30 settembre 2000),* ed. Antonino Di Vita, Monica Livadioti, and Ilaria Simiakaki, vol. 1:119–130. Padua.

Godley, Alfred D., ed. 1920–1925. *Herodotus. The Histories.* 4 vols. Loeb Classical Library. Cambridge, MA.

Goula, Eleni. 2006. "Παρατηρήσεις σχετικά με την παραγωγή των πρωτο-ανατολιζόντων τεχνέργων του Ιδαίου." In *Ο Μυλοπόταμος από την Αρχαιότητα ως Σήμερα: Περιβάλλον, Αρχαιολογία, Ιστορία, Λαογραφία, Κοινωνιολογία: Πρακτικά Διεθνούς Συνεδρίου (Πάνορμο, 24–30 Οκτωβρίου 2003).* Vol. 3: *Αρχαίοι Χρόνοι. Ιδαίο Άντρο,* ed. Irene Gavrilaki and Yannis Tzifopoulos, 31–83. Rethymno.

Graf, Fritz. 1974. *Eleusis und die orphische Dichtung Athens in vorhellenistischer Zeit.* Religions Geschichtliche Versuche und Vorarbeiten 33. Berlin.

———. 1979. "Apollon Delphinios." *Museum Helveticum* 36:2–22.

———. 1980. "Milch, Honig und Wein: Zum Verständnis der Libation im griechischen Ritual." *Perennitas: Studi in onore di Angelo Brelich promossi dalla Cattedra di Religioni del mondo classico dell'Università degli Studi di Roma,* 209–221. Rome.

———. 1985. *Nordionische Kulte: Religionsgeschichtliche und epigraphische Untersuchungen zu den Kulten von Chios, Erythrai, Klazomenai und Phokaia.* Bibliotheca Helvetica Romana 21. Rome.

———. 1987. "Orpheus: A Poet among Men." In *Interpretations of Greek Mythology,* ed. Jan N. Bremmer, 80–106. London and Sydney.

———. 1991. "Textes orphiques et rituel bacchique. A propos des lamelles de Pélinna." In *Orphisme et Orphée en l'honneur de Jean Rudhardt.* Recherchers et Rencontres, Publications de la Faculté des Lettres de Genève 3, ed. Philippe Borgeaud, 87–102. Geneva.

———. 1993. "Dionysiac and Orphic Eschatology: New Texts and Old Questions." In *Masks of Dionysus,* ed. Thomas H. Carpenter and Christopher A. Faraone, 239–258. Myth and Poetics. Ithaca, NY.

———. 1997. *Magic in the Ancient World.* Trans. Franklin Philip. Revealing Antiquity 10. Cambridge, MA.

———. 2004a. "What is Ancient Mediterranean Religion." In *Religions of the Ancient World: A Guide*, ed. Sarah Iles Johnston, 3–16. Cambridge, MA.

———. 2004b. "Myth." In *Religions of the Ancient World: A Guide*, ed. Sarah Iles Johnston, 45–58. Cambridge, MA.

———. Forthcoming-1. "Editing the Gold Tablets." In *Ritual Texts for the Afterlife: A Gold Tablets Conference at the Ohio State University, April 28-30, 2006*, ed. Fritz Graf and Sarah Iles Johnston.

———. Forthcoming-2. "Text and Ritual: The Corpus Eschatologicum of the Orphics." In *Further Along the Path: Recent Approaches to the 'Orphic' Gold Tablets*, ed. Radcliffe G. Edmonds III. Cambridge.

Graf, Fritz and Johnston, Sarah Iles, eds. 2007. *Ritual Texts for the Afterlife: Orpheus and the Bacchic Gold Tablets.* London and New York.

Grammatikaki, Eva and Litinas, Nikos. 2000. "Μαγικός κατάδεσμος." *Eulimene* 1:61–69.

Granger, Herbert. 2000. "Death's Other Kingdom: Heraclitus on the Life of the Foolish and the Wise." *Classical Philology* 95:260–281.

Griffith, R. Drew. 2001. "Sailing to Elysium: Menelaus' Afterlife (*Odyssey* 4.561–569) and Egyptian Religion." *Phoenix* 55:213–243.

Grinder-Hansen, Keld. 1991. "Charon's Fee in Ancient Greece? Some Remarks on a Well-Known Death Rite." *Acta Hyperborea* 3:207–218.

Grossardt, Peter. 1998. *Die Trugreden in der Odyssee und ihre Rezeption in der antiken Literatur.* Sapheneia. Beiträge zur klassischen Philologie 2. Bern.

Guarducci, Margherita. 1939. "Le laminette auree con iscrizioni orfiche e l'obolo di Caronte.'" *Atti della Pontificia Accademia Romana di Archeologia. Rendiconti* 15:87–95.

———. 1943-1946. "Creta e Delfi." *Studi e Materiali di Storia delle Religioni* 19:85–114.

———. 1972. "Il cipresso dell'oltre tomba." *Rivista di Filologia e d'Istruzione Classica* 100:323–327.

———. 1973. "Corone d'oro." *Epigraphica* 35:7–23.

———. 1974a. "Laminette auree orfiche: Alcuni problemi." *Epigraphica* 36:7–32.

———. 1974b. "Ancora sull'inno cretese a Zeus Dicteo." In *Antichità Cretesi: Studi in onore di Doro Levi*, vol. 2:32–38. Catania.

———. 1975. "In margine alle corone d'oro: Armento e Grumentum." *Epigraphica* 37:209–212.

———. 1977. "La corona d'oro di Mnasistratos messenio." *Epigraphica* 39:140–142.

———. 1985. "Nuove riflessioni sulla laminetta 'orfica' di Hipponion." *Rivista di Filologia e d'Istruzione Classica* 113:385–397.

Guimier-Sorbets, Anne-Marie. 2004. "Les mosaiques de Crète et d'Alexandrie: Rapports et influences." In *Creta romana e protobizantina: Atti del congresso internazionale organizzato dalla Scuola Archeologica Italiana di Atene (Iraklion, 23–30 settembre 2000)*, ed. Antonino Di Vita, Monica Livadioti, and Ilaria Simiakaki, vol. 3.2:1163–1172. Padua.

Guimier-Sorbets, Anne Marie and Morizot, Yvette. 2006. "Construire l'identité du mort: L'architecture funéraire en Macédoine (pl. 45–53)." In *Rois, Cités, Nécropoles: Institutions, Rites et Monuments en Macédoine: Actes des Colloques de Nanterre (Décembre 2002) et d'Athènes (Janvier 2004)*. Meletemata 45, ed. Anne Marie Guimier-Sorbets et al., 117–130. Athens.

Guizzi, Francesco. 2001. *Hierapytna: Storia di una polis cretese dalla fondazione alla conquista romana.* Atti della Accademia Nazionale dei Lincei, Anno CCCXCVIII, 2001. Classe di scienze morali, storiche e filologiche, Memorie Serie IX. Vol. XIII.3. Rome.

———. 2003. "Devenir Courète." *Kernos* 16:171–175.

———. 2006. "Eleutherna and its Territory from the Archaic to Hellenistic Age: Some Notes." In *Ο Μυλοπόταμος από την Αρχαιότητα ως Σήμερα: Περιβάλλον, Αρχαιολογία, Ιστορία, Λαογραφία, Κοινωνιολογία: Πρακτικά Διεθνούς Συνεδρίου (Πάνορμο, 24–30 Οκτωβρίου 2003)*. Vol. 4: *Ελεύθερνα - Αξός*, ed. Irene Gavrilaki and Yannis Tzifopoulos, 93–101. Rethymno.

Günther, Wolfgang. 2003. "'Unsterbliche Kränze': Zur Selbstdarstellung milesischer Propheten in didymeischen Inschriftendenkmälern." *Chiron* 33:447–457.

Guthrie, William K. C. 1993. *Orpheus and Greek Religion: A Study of the Orphic Movement.* Princeton, NJ.

Gutzwiller, Kathryn, ed. 2005a. *The New Posidippus: A Hellenistic Poetry Book.* Oxford.

———. 2005b. "The Literariness of the Milan Papyrus, or 'What Difference a Book?'" In *The New Posidippus: A Hellenistic Poetry Book*, ed. Kathryn Gutzwiller, 287–319. Oxford.

Haft, Adele J. 1984. "Odysseus, Idomeneus, and Meriones: The Cretan Lies of *Odyssey* 13–19." *Classical Journal* 79:289–306.

Haider, Peter. 2001. "Minoan Deities in an Egyptian Medical Text." In *POTNIA: Deities and Religion in the Aegean Bronze Age; Proceedings of the 8th International Aegean Conference, Göteborg University, 12–15 April 2000.* Aegaeum 22, ed. Robert Laffineur and Robin Hägg, 479–482. Liège.

Hallager, Erik, Andreadaki-Vlazaki, Maria, and Hallager, Birgitta P. 1992. "New Linear B Tablets from Khania." *Kadmos* 32:61–87.

Halm-Tisserant, Monique. 2004. "Le sparagmos, un rite de magie fécondant." *Kernos* 17:119–142.

Hamilakis, Yannis, and Momigliano, Nicoletta, eds. 2006. *Archaeology and European Modernity: Producing and Consuming the 'Minoans'; Atti del convegno, Venezia, 25-27 novembre 2005.* Creta Antica 7. Padua.

Hardie, Philip R. 1985. "*Imago Mundi*: Cosmological and Ideological Aspects of the Shield of Achilles." *Journal of Hellenic Studies* 105:11–31.

Harrison, Jane E. 1908–1909. "The Kouretes and Zeus Kouros." *Annual of the British School at Athens* 15:308–338.

Harrison, Thomas. 2000. *Divinity and History: The Religion of Herodotus.* Oxford.

———. 2003. "'Prophecy in Reverse'? Herodotus and the Origins of History." In *Herodotus and his World: Essays from a Conference in Memory of George Forrest*, ed. Peter Derow and Robert Parker, 237–255. Oxford.

Haslam, Michael W. 1993. "Callimachus' Hymns." In *Callimachus: Proceedings of the Groningen Workshops on Hellenistic Poetry.* Hellenistica Groningana I, ed. M. Annette Harder, Remco F. Regtuit, and Gerry C. Wakker, 111–125. Groningen.

Hatzopoulos, Miltiade B. 1994. *Cultes et rites de passage en Macédoine.* Meletemata 19. Athens.

———. 2002. "Λατρεῖες τῆς Μακεδονίας· τελετὲς μεταβάσεως καὶ μυήσεις." In *Λατρείες στην 'Περιφέρεια' του Αρχαίου Ελληνικού Κόσμου*, ed. Aphrodite Avagianou, 11–29. Athens.

———. 2006. "De la vie à trépas: Rites de passage, lamelles dionysiaques et tombes macédoniennes (pl. 57)." In *Rois, Cités, Nécropoles: Institutions, Rites et Monuments en Macédoine; Actes des Colloques de Nanterre (Décembre 2002) et d'Athènes (Janvier 2004).* Meletemata 45, ed. Anne Marie Guimier-Sorbets, et al., 131–141. Athens.

———. 2008. "Οἱ ἐπιγραφὲς τῆς Ἡράκλειας τῆς Μυγδονικῆς (Ἅγιος Ἀθανάσιος – Γέφυρα) μεταξὺ ἀρχαιολογίας καὶ ἀρχαιοκαπηλίας." In *Πρακτικὰ Β´ Πανελληνίου Συνεδρίου Ἐπιγραφικῆς (Θεσσαλονίκη, 24-25 Νοεμβρίου 2001)*, ed. Ilias Sverkos, 237-253. Thessaloniki.

Heiden, Bruce. 1991. "Tragedy and Comedy in the *Frogs* of Aristophanes." *Ramus* 20:95–111.

Heintz, Jean-Georges, ed. 1997. *Oracles et prophéties dans l'Antiquité: Actes du Colloque de Strasbourg, 15-17 juin 1995.* Université des Sciences Humaines de Strasbourg, Travaux du Centre de Recherche sur le Proche-Orient et la Grèce antique 15. Paris.

318

Henrichs, Albert. 1978. "Greek Maenadism from Olympias to Messalina." *Harvard Studies in Classical Philology* 82:121–160.

———. 1984a. "Loss of Self, Suffering, Violence: The Modern View of Dionysos from Nietzsche to Girard." *Harvard Studies in Classical Philology* 101:207–266.

———. 1984b. "Male Intruders Among the Maenads: The So-Called Male Celebrant." In *MNEMAI: Classical Studies in Memory of Karl K. Hulley*, ed. Harold D. Evjen, 69–91. Chico, CA.

———. 1990. "Between Country and City: Cultic Dimensions of Dionysus in Athens and Attica." In *Cabinet of the Muses: Essays on Classical and Comparative Literature in Honor of Thomas G. Rosenmeyer*, ed. Mark Griffith and Donald J. Mastronarde, 257–277. Atlanta, GA.

———. 1993a. "'He Has a God in Him': Human and Divine in the Modern Perception of Dionysus." In *Masks of Dionysus*, ed. Thomas H. Carpenter and Christopher A. Faraone, 13–43. Myth and Poetics. Ithaca, NY.

———. 1993b. "Gods in Action: The Poetics of Divine Performance in the Hymns of Callimachus." In *Callimachus: Proceedings of the Groningen Workshops on Hellenistic Poetry*. Hellenistica Groningana I, ed. M. Annette Harder, Remco F. Regtuit, and Gerry C. Wakker, 127–147. Groningen.

———. 1995. "'Why Should I Dance?': Choral Self-Referentiality in Greek Tragedy." *Arion* 3:56–111.

———. 1998. "Dromena und Legomena: Zum rituellen Selbstverständnis der Griechen." In *Ansichten griechischer Rituale: Geburstags-Symposium für Walter Burkert, Castelen bei Basel 15. bis 18. März 1996*, ed. Fritz Graf, 33–71. Stuttgart and Leipzig.

———. 2000. "Drama and Dromena: Bloodshed, Violence, and Sacrificial Metaphor in Euripides." *Harvard Studies in Classical Philology* 100:173–188.

———. 2003a. "*Hieroi Logoi* and *Hierai Bibloi*: The (Un)written Margins of the Sacred in Ancient Greece." *Harvard Studies in Classical Philology* 88:205–240.

———. 2003b. "Writing Religion: Inscribed Texts, Ritual Authority, and the Religious Discourse of the Polis." In *Written Texts and the Rise of Literate Culture in Ancient Greece*, ed. Harvey Yunis, 38–58. Cambridge and New York.

———. 2004a. "Sacred Texts and Canonicity: Greece." In *Religions of the Ancient World: A Guide*, ed. Sarah Iles Johnston, 633–635. Cambridge, MA.

———. 2004b. "'Let the Good Prevail': Perversions of the Ritual Process in Greek Tragedy." In *Greek Ritual Poetics*. Center for Hellenic Studies, Hellenic Studies Series 3, ed. Dimitrios Yatromanolakis and Panagiotis Roilos, 189–198. Washington, DC and Cambridge, MA.

Herrero de Jáuregui, Miguel. Forthcoming-1. "Dialogues of Immortality from the *Iliad* to the Golden Leaves." In *Further Along the Path: Recent Approaches to the 'Orphic' Gold Tablets*, ed. Radcliffe G. Edmonds III. Cambridge.

———. Forthcoming-2. "The Poetics of Supplication in the Katabasis of the Soul." In *Ritual Texts for the Afterlife: A Gold Tablets Conference at the Ohio State University, April 28–30, 2006*, ed. Fritz Graf and Sarah Iles Johnston.

Hershbell, Jackson P. 2007. "Plutarch and Plato's Cretan City." *Ariadne* 12:113–122.

Higgins, Reynold A. 1961. *Greek and Roman Jewellery*. London.

———. 1982. "Macedonian Royal Jewelry." In *Macedonia and Greece in Late Classical and Hellenistic Times.* Studies in the History of Art 10, ed. Beryl Barr-Sharrar and Eugene N. Borza, 140–151. Washington, DC.

Hinz, Valentina. 1998. *Der Kult von Demeter und Kore auf Sizilien und in der Magna Graecia*. Palilia 4. Wiesbaden.

Hodos, Tamar. 2006. *Local Responses to Colonization in the Iron Age Mediterranean*. London and New York.

Hoffmann, Herbert. 2002. "Focusing on the Invisible: Greek Myth and Symbol Contemplation." In *Myth and Symbol I: Symbolic Phenomena in Ancient Greek Culture; Papers from the First International Symposium on Symbolism at the University of Tromsø, June 4–7, 1998*. Papers from the Norwegian Institute at Athens 5, ed. Synnøve des Bouvrie, 73–88. Bergen.

Holger, Thesleff. 1986. "Notes on the Paradise Myth in Ancient Greece." *Temenos* 22:129–139.

Hollmann, Alexander. 2005. "The Manipulation of Signs in Herodotos' *Histories*." *Transactions of the American Philological Association* 135:279–327.

Hood, Sinclair, Warren, Peter, and Cadogan, Gerald. 1964. "Travels in Crete, 1962." *Annual of the British School at Athens* 59:50–99, plates 9–17.

Höper, Hermann-Josef. 1992. "Zwei Statuenbasen als Reste einer Opferstätte auf dem Hl. Antonios, einem der Olympgipfel (Griechenland)." In Μουσικός ἀνήρ: *Festschrift für Max Wegner zum 90. Geburstag*. Antiquitas. Reihe 3, Abhandlungen zur Vor- und Frühgeschichte, zur klassischen und provinzial-römischen Archäologie und zur Geschichte des Altertums 32, ed. Oliver Brehm and Sascha Klie, 213–222. Bonn.

Hopkinson, Neil. 1984. "Callimachus' *Hymn to Zeus*." *Classical Quarterly* 34:139–148.

Hopman-Govers, Marianne. 2001. "Le jeu des épithètes dans les *Hymnes orphiques*." *Kernos* 14:35–49.

Hordern, James. 2000. "Notes on the Orphic Papyrus from Gurob (*P.Gurob* 1: Pack^2 2464)." *Zeitschrift für Papyrologie und Epigraphik* 129:81–86.

Howgego, Christopher J. 1995. *Ancient History from Coins*. 2nd ed. London.

Hubbard, Thomas K. 1992. "Nature and Art in the Shield of Achilles." *Arion* 3:16–41.

Humphreys, Sally C. 2004. *The Strangeness of Gods: Historical Perspectives on the Interpretation of Athenian Religion*. Oxford.

Hunter, Richard. 2005. "Generic Consciousness in the Orphic *Argonautica*?" In *Roman and Greek Imperial Epic*. Rethymnon Classical Studies 2, ed. Michael Paschalis, 149–168. Herakleio.

Huxley, George. 1975. "Cretan Paiawones." *Greek, Roman, and Byzantine Studies* 16:119–124.

Iacobacci, Gabriela. 1993. "La laminetta aurea di Hipponion: Osservazioni dialettologiche." In *Orfeo e l'Orfismo: Atti del Seminario Nazionale (Roma-Perugia 1985-1991)*, ed. Agostino Masaracchia, 249–264. Rome.

Iakov, Daniel. 2004. "Είναι οι Βάκχες του Ευριπίδη μετατραγωδία." In Θυμέλη: Μελέτες χαρισμένες στον καθηγητή Ν. Χ. Χουρμουζιάδη, ed. Daniel Iakov and Eleni Papazoglou, 49–62. Herakleio.

——. 2005. "Ο Πίνδαρος και η μεταθανάτια ζωή: ξαναδιαβάζοντας τον δεύτερο Ολυμπιόνικο." *Ελληνικά* 55:7–18.

——. Forthcoming. "Milk in the Gold Tablets from Pelinna." *Trends in Classics 2*.

IC. *Inscriptiones Creticae*, ed. Margarita Guarducci, *opera et consilio Friderici Halbherr collectae*. Vols. I–IV. Rome 1935–1950.

IG II². *Inscriptiones Graecae*. Vol. II: *Inscriptiones Atticae Euclidis anno posteriores, editio altera*, ed. Johannes Kirchner. Berlin 1913–1940, repr. editio minor Chicago 1974.

IG IV.1². *Inscriptiones Graecae*. Vol. IV: *Inscriptiones Argolidis*, fasc. 1: *Inscriptiones Epidauri, editio altera*, ed. Friedrich Hiller von Gaertringen. Berlin 1929, repr. Chicago 1977.

IG XII.2. *Inscriptiones Graecae*. Vol. XII: *Inscriptiones Insularum Maris Aegaei Praeter Delum*, fasc. 2: *Inscriptiones Lesbi, Nesi Tenedi*, ed. William R. Paton. Berlin 1899.

IG XIV. *Inscriptiones Graecae*. Vol. XIV: *Inscriptiones Italiae et Siciliae, additis Galliae, Hispaniae, Britanniae, Germaniae inscriptionibus*, ed. Georg Kaibel (*Inscriptiones Galliae*, ed. Albert Lebèque). Berlin 1890.

Intrieri, Maria. 2002. "La preghiera di fronte alla morte nel mondo greco." *Les Études Classiques* 70:257–275.

Jameson, Michael. 1993. "The Asexuality of Dionysus." In *Masks of Dionysus*, ed. Thomas H. Carpenter and Christopher A. Faraone, 44–64. Myth and Poetics. Ithaca, NY.

Jameson, Michael H., Jordan, David R., and Kotansky, Roy D. 1993. *A Lex Sacra from Selinous.* Greek, Roman, and Byzantine Studies Monograph 11. Durham, NC.

Janda, Michael. 2005. *Elysion: Entstehung und Entwicklung der griechischen Religion.* Innsbrucker Beiträge zur Sprachwissenschaft 119. Innsbruck.

Janko, Richard. 1984. "Forgetfulness in the Golden Tablets of Memory." *Classical Quarterly* 34:89–100.

———. 1997. "The Physicist as Hierophant: Aristophanes, Socrates and the Authorship of the Derveni Papyrus." *Zeitschrift für Papyrologie und Epigraphik* 118:61–94.

———. 2001. "The Derveni Papyrus (Diagoras of Melos, *Apopyrgizontes Logoi?*): A New Translation." *Classical Philology* 96:1–32.

———. Forthcoming. "Reconstructing an Archetype of the Golden Tablets of Memory in Light of the New Evidence." In *Ritual Texts for the Afterlife: A Gold Tablets Conference at the Ohio State University, April 28–30, 2006,* ed. Fritz Graf and Sarah Iles Johnston.

Jeanmaire, Henri. 1951. *Dionysos: Histoire du culte de Bacchus.* Paris.

Jeannaraki, Anton. 2005. Ἄισματα κρητικὰ μετὰ διστίχων καὶ παροιμιῶν: *Kretas Volkslieder nebst Distichen und Sprichwörtern.* Repr. Rethymno. Orig. pub. Leipzig, 1876.

Jesnick, Ilona Julia. 1997. *The Image of Orpheus in Roman Mosaic: An Exploration of the Figure of Orpheus in Graeco-Roman Art and Culture with Special Reference to its Expression in the Medium of Mosaic in Late Antiquity.* BAR International Series 671. Oxford.

Johnston, Sarah Iles. 1999. *Restless Dead: Encounters between the Living and the Dead in Ancient Greece.* Berkeley, CA.

———. 2002. "Sacrifice in the Greek Magical Papyri." In *Magic and Ritual in the Ancient World.* Religions in the Graeco-Roman World 141, ed. Paul Mirecki and Marvin Meyer, 344–358. Leiden.

———. 2004a. "Mysteries." In *Religions of the Ancient World: A Guide,* ed. Sarah Iles Johnston, 98–111. Cambridge, MA.

———. 2004b. "Magic." In *Religions of the Ancient World: A Guide,* ed. Sarah Iles Johnston, 139–152. Cambridge, MA.

———. 2004c. "Divination and Prophecy: Greece." In *Religions of the Ancient World: A Guide,* ed. Sarah Iles Johnston, 383–386. Cambridge, MA.

———. 2005. "Delphi and the Dead." In *Mantike: Studies in Ancient Divination.* Religions of the Graeco-Roman World 155, ed. Sarah Iles Johnston and Peter T. Struck, 283–306. Leiden.

Johnston, Sarah Iles and McNiven, Timothy. 1996. "Dionysos and the Underworld in Toledo." *Museum Helveticum* 53:25–36.

Jordan, David R. 1985a. "The Inscribed Gold Tablet from the Vigna Codini." *American Journal of Archaeology* 89:162–167.

———. 1985b. "A Survey of Greek Defixiones Not Included in the Special Corpora." *Greek, Roman, and Byzantine Studies* 26:151–197.

———. 1989. "A Note on the Gold Tablet from Thessaly." *Horos* 7:129–130.

———. 1997a. "Πρώιμη γραφή ως μαγεία." In *Γλώσσα και Μαγεία: Κείμενα από την αρχαιότητα*, ed. Anastassios-Phoibos Christidis and David Jordan, 65–74. Athens.

———. 1997b. "Μια εισαγωγή στις εκδόσεις αρχαίων μαγικών κειμένων." In *Γλώσσα και Μαγεία: Κείμενα από την αρχαιότητα*, ed. Anastassios-Phoibos Christidis and David Jordan, 147–152. Athens.

———. 2000. "New Greek Curse Tablets (1985–2000)." *Greek, Roman, and Byzantine Studies* 41:5–46.

———. 2001. "'Written' Instructions for the Dead: An Example from Mordovia." *Zeitschrift für Papyrologie und Epigraphik* 134:80.

Jouan, François. 1992. "Dionysos chez Eschyle." *Kernos* 5:71–86.

Joubin, André. 1893. "Inscription crétoise relative à l'orphisme." *Bulletin de Correspondance Hellénique* 17:121–124.

Kahn, Charles H. 1997. "Was Euthyphro the Author of the Derveni Papyrus?" In *Studies on the Derveni Papyrus*, ed. André Laks and Glenn W. Most, 55–63. Oxford.

———. 2001. *Pythagoras and the Pythagoreans: A Brief History*. Indianapolis, IN.

Kaizer, Ted. 2006. "In Search of Oriental Cults: Methodological Problems Concerning 'the Particular' and 'the General' in Near Eastern Religion in the Hellenistic and Roman Periods." *Historia* 55:26–47.

Kalaïssakis, Georgios I. 1892. "Περὶ τῆς ἐν Κρήτῃ Λάππας ἢ Ἀργυρουπόλεως." *Παρνασσός* 15:615–621.

Kalfas, Vassilis. 1995. *Πλάτων Τίμαιος: Εισαγωγή, μετάφραση, σχόλια.* Athens.

Kalléris, Jean N. 1988. *Les anciens Macédoniens: Étude linguistique et historique.* 2 vols. Collection de l'Institut Français d'Athènes. Athens.

Kallintzi, Konstandina. 2006. "Les nécropoles d'Abdère: Organisation de l'éspace et rites funéraires (pl. 17–21)." In *Rois, Cités, Nécropoles: Institutions, Rites et Monuments en Macédoine. Actes des Colloques de Nanterre (Décembre 2002) et d'Athènes (Janvier 2004).* Meletemata 45, ed. Anne Marie Guimier-Sorbets et al., 143–153. Athens.

Kalpaxis, Thanassis. 2004. "Οι 'Ακροπόλεις' της Ελεύθερνας: Κεντρικός ανασκαφικός τομέας II." In *Ελεύθερνα, Πόλη - Ακρόπολη - Νεκρόπολη*, ed. Nicholas C. Stampolidis, 104–115. Athens.

Kalpaxis, Thanassis, Furtwängler, Andreas, Schnapp, Alain, Γεωργιάδου, Αναστασία, Γιαλούρη, Ελεάνα, Guy, Max, Ιωαννίδου, Ρόζα, Καραμαλίκη, Νότα, Neisius, Desirée, Matheron, Marie-France, Sahm, Birgit, Σαρπάκη, Ανάγια, Seilheimer, Horst, Τσατσάκη, Νίκη, Τσιγωνάκη, Χριστίνα, and Villa, Emmanuelle. 1994. *Ελεύθερνα Τομέας II.2: Ένα ελληνιστικό Σπίτι (Σπίτι "Α") στη θέση Νησί*. Rethymno.

Kalpaxis, Thanassis and Tsatsaki, Niki. 2000. "Eleutherna: Zufallsfunde aus einer der hellenistischen Nekropolen der Stadt." *Archäologisher Anzeiger* 2000:117–128.

Kanatsoulis, Dimitrios. 1955. *Μακεδονικὴ προσωπογραφία (ἀπὸ τοῦ 148 π.Χ. μέχρι τοῦ Μ. Κωνσταντίνου)*. Ἑλληνικὰ Παράρτημα 8. Thessaloniki.

Kaninia, Eriphyli. 1994–95. "Χρυσά στεφάνια από τη νεκρόπολη της αρχαίας Ρόδου." *Αρχαιολογικό Δελτίο* 49–50:97–132, plates 17–30.

Kanonidis, Ioannis. 1990. "Σωστική ανασκαφή στο χώρο της πλατείας Κυπρίων Αγωνιστών (Διοικητηρίου)." *Το Αρχαιολογικό Έργο στη Μακεδονία και Θράκη* 4:259–267.

Kapsomenos, Eratosthenes G. 2000–2001. "Η προμηθεϊκή ιδέα στο κρητικό δημοτικό τραγούδι." *Κρητική Εστία* 8:233–247.

Karadima-Matsa, Chryssa and Dimitrova, Nora. 2003. "Epitaph for an Initiate at Samothrace and Eleusis." *Chiron* 33:335–345.

Karageorghis, Vassos and Stampolidis, Nicholas C., eds. 1998. *Eastern Mediterranean: Cyprus - Dodecanese - Crete 16th-6th cent. B.C.: Proceedings of the International Symposium held at Rethymnon, Crete in May 1997*. Athens.

Karamitrou-Medessidi, Georgia. 2000. "Νομός Κοζάνης 2000: Ανασκαφές εν οδοίς και παροδίως." *Το Αρχαιολογικό Έργο στη Μακεδονία και Θράκη* 14:607–640.

Karetsou, Alexandra, ed. 2000. *Κρήτη - Αίγυπτος: Πολιτισμικοί δεσμοί τριών χιλιετιών*. Athens.

———. 2003. "Juktas Peak Sanctuary: Notes on the 12th Century Material." *Mitteilungen des Deutschen Archäologischen Instituts, Athenische Abteilung* 118:49–65.

Karetsou, Alexandra, Andreadaki-Vlazaki, Maria, and Papadakis, Nikos, eds. 2000. *Κρήτη - Αίγυπτος. Πολιτισμικοί δεσμοί τριών χιλιετιών: Κατάλογος, Αρχαιολογικό Μουσείο Ηρακλείου, 21 Νοεμβρίου 1999–21 Σεπτεμβρίου 2000*. Herakleio.

Katsoulakos, Dimitris Th. 2001. Ἡ νότια κοίλη Λακεδαίμων καὶ τὰ μοιρολόγια της: Συμβολὴ στὴν μελέτη τῆς ἱστορίας καὶ τοῦ ψυχικοῦ κόσμου τῶν ἀνθρώπων της. Athens.

Katz, Joshua T. and Volk, Katharina. 2000. "'Mere bellies'?: A New Look at *Theogony* 26–28." *Journal of Hellenic Studies* 120:122–131.

Kefalidou, Eurydice. 1996. *ΝΙΚΗΤΗΣ: Εικονογραφική μελέτη του αρχαίου ελληνικού αθλητισμού*. Διδακτορική διατριβή Αριστοτελείου Πανεπιστημίου Θεσσαλονίκης, Ενυάλειο Κληροδότημα στη μνήμη Λάμπρου Ενυάλη. Thessalonkiki.

———. 2005–2006. "Καταβάσεις και άνοδοι του Διονύσου. Παρατηρήσεις στην αττική και κατωιταλιωτική αγγειογραφία." *Eulimene* 6–7:13–44.

———. 2006. "Ιερά του ανατολικού Μυλοποτάμου: οι μαρτυρίες των ειδωλίων." In *Ο Μυλοπόταμος από την Αρχαιότητα ως Σήμερα: Περιβάλλον, Αρχαιολογία, Ιστορία, Λαογραφία, Κοινωνιολογία: Πρακτικά Διεθνούς Συνεδρίου (Πάνορμο, 24-30 Οκτωβρίου 2003)*. Vol. 4: *Ελεύθερνα - Αξός*, ed. Irene Gavrilaki and Yannis Tzifopoulos, 227–273. Rethymno.

Kelhoffer, James A. 2005. "John the Baptist's 'Wild Honey' and 'Honey' in Antiquity." *Greek, Roman, and Byzantine Studies* 45:59–73.

Kelly, Amanda. 2006. "The Roman Baths of Mylopotamos: A Distribution Study." In *Ο Μυλοπόταμος από την Αρχαιότητα ως Σήμερα: Περιβάλλον, Αρχαιολογία, Ιστορία, Λαογραφία, Κοινωνιολογία: Πρακτικά Διεθνούς Συνεδρίου (Πάνορμο, 24-30 Οκτωβρίου 2003)*. Vol. 2: *Αρχαίοι Χρόνοι*, ed. Irene Gavrilaki and Yannis Tzifopoulos, 239–252. Rethymno.

Keramaris, Anastassios, Protopsalti, Soultana, and Tsolakis, Stefanos. 2002. "Η ανασκαφική έρευνα στη ΒΙ.ΠΕ.Θ. Σίνδου 2002." *Το Αρχαιολογικό Έργο στη Μακεδονία και Θράκη* 16:233–240.

Kern, Otto. 1916. "Orphiker auf Kreta." *Hermes* 51:554–567.

Kindt, Julia. 2006. "Delphic Oracle Stories and the Beginning of Historiography: Herodotus' *Croesus Logos*." *Classical Philology* 101:34–51.

Kingsley, Peter. 1995. *Ancient Philosophy, Mystery, and Magic: Empedocles and Pythagorean Tradition*. Oxford.

Kiourtzian, Georges. 2000. *Recueil des inscriptions grecques chrétiennes des Cyclades de la fin du IIIe au VIIe siècle après J.-C.* Travaux et Mémoires du Centre de Recherche d'Histoire et Civilisation de Byzance. Collège de France Monographies 12. Paris.

Kirk, Geoffrey S., Raven, John E., and Schofield, Malcolm. 1988. *Οἱ Προσωκρατικοὶ φιλόσοφοι*. Trans. Demosthenes Kourtovik. Athens. (= 1983. *The Presocratic Philosophers: A Critical History with a Selection of Texts*. 2nd ed. Cambridge.)

Kitchell, Kenneth F. 1977. *Topographica Cretica: Topoi of Classical Crete with Testimonia*. Ph.D. Dissertation, Loyola University of Chicago. Ann Arbor, MI.

Kitov, Georgi. 2005. "Thracian Tumular Burial with a Gold Mask Near the City of Shipka, K Central Bulgaria." *Archaeologia Bulgarica* 9:23–37.

Kokkinia, Christina. 1999. "Rosen für die Toten im griechischen Raum und eine neue ῥοδισμός-Inschrift aus Bithynien." *Museum Helveticum* 56:202–221.

Kokolakis, Minos. 1995a. "Zeus' Tomb: An Object of Pride and Reproach." *Kernos* 8:123–138.

———. 1995b. "'Ο τάφος τοῦ κρηταγενοῦς Διός: Ἀγλάϊσμα καὶ ὄνειδος." In *Πεπραγμένα του Ζ΄ Διεθνούς Κρητολογικού Συνεδρίου (Ρέθυμνο, 25–31 Αυγούστου 1991)*. Vol. Α1: Νέα Χριστιανική Κρήτη 11–14 (1994–1995), ed. Nikolaos E. Papadogiannakis, 483–500. Rethymno.

Konis, Polyvios. 2006. "The Post-Resurrection Appearances of Christ: The Case of the *Chairete* or 'All Hail'." *Rosetta* 1:31–40. http://www.rosetta.bham.ac.uk/Issue_01/Konis.htm.

Konstantinopoulos, Grigorios. 1994–95. "Ἔργα πλαστικής και επιγραφές από το 'Διονύσιον' τέμενος της αρχαίας Ρόδου." *Αρχαιολογικό Δελτίο Μελέτες* 49–50 A:75–82, plates 11–12.

Kotansky, Roy D. 1991. "Incantations and Prayers for Salvation on Inscribed Greek Amulets." In *Magika Hiera: Ancient Greek Magic and Religion*, ed. Christopher A. Faraone and Dirk Obbink, 107–137. New York.

———. 1994. *Greek Magical Amulets: The Inscribed Gold, Silver, Copper and Bronze Lamellae. Part I: Published Texts of Known Provenance*. Abhandlungen der Rheinisch-Westfälischen Akademie der Wissenschaften, Sonderreihe Papyrologica Coloniensia 22.3. Opladen.

Kotsonas, Antonios. 2002. "The Rise of the Polis in Central Crete." *Eulimene* 3:37–74.

Kottaridou, Angéliki. 2006. "Couleur et sens: L'emploi de la couleur dans la tombe de la reine Eurydice (pl. 59–62)." In *Rois, Cités, Nécropoles: Institutions, Rites et Monuments en Macédoine; Actes des Colloques de Nanterre (Décembre 2002) et d'Athènes (Janvier 2004)*. Meletemata 45, ed. Anne Marie Guimier-Sorbets et al., 155–168. Athens.

Koukouli-Chryssanthaki, Chaïdo. 1992. "Ο αρχαίος οικισμός της Δράμας και το ιερό του Διονύσου." In *Η Δράμα και η περιοχή της: ιστορία και πολιτισμός· επιστημονική συνάντηση 24–25 1989*. Drama.

Kouremenos, Theokritos, Parássoglou Georgios P., and Tsantsanoglou, Kyriakos. 2006. *The Derveni Papyrus*. Edited with introduction and commentary. Studi e Testi per il Corpus dei Papiri Filosofici Greci e Latini 13. Florence.

Kourinou, Eleni. 2000. *Σπάρτη: Συμβολὴ στὴ μνημειακὴ τοπογραφία της.* Διδακτορικὴ διατριβή. Horos Ἡ Μεγάλη Βιβλιοθήκη 3. Athens.

Kraay, Colin M. 1976. *Archaic and Classical Greek Coins.* London.

Kritzas, Charalampos. 1992–1993. "Nouvelle inscription provenant de l'Asclépiéion de Lebena (Crète)." *Annuario della Scuola Archeologica di Atene e delle Missioni Italiane in Oriente* 70–71:275–290.

———. 2004. "Ρωμαϊκό επιτύμβιο ανάγλυφο από την περιοχή Τυμπακίου-Γόρτυνος." In *Creta romana e protobizantina: Atti del congresso internazionale organizzato dalla Scuola Archeologica Italiana di Atene (Iraklion, 23-30 settembre 2000)*, ed. Antonino Di Vita, Monica Livadioti, and Ilaria Simiakaki, vol. 3.2:1089–1102. Padua.

———. 2006. "Ενδείξεις αρχαίας λατρείας στην κορυφή της Ἴδης." In *Ο Μυλοπόταμος από την Αρχαιότητα ως Σήμερα: Περιβάλλον, Αρχαιολογία, Ιστορία, Λαογραφία, Κοινωνιολογία: Πρακτικά Διεθνούς Συνεδρίου (Πάνορμο, 24-30 Οκτωβρίου 2003)*. Vol. 3: *Αρχαίοι Χρόνοι. Ιδαίο Άντρο*, ed. Irene Gavrilaki and Yannis Tzifopoulos, 183–202. Rethymno.

Kurke, Leslie. 2003. "Aesop and the Contestation of Delphic Authority." In *The Cultures within Ancient Greek Culture: Contact, Conflict, Collaboration*, ed. Carol Dougherty and Leslie Kurke, 77–100. Cambridge.

Kurtz, Donna C. and Boardman, John. 1994. *Ἔθιμα ταφῆς στον αρχαίο ελληνικό κόσμο*. Trans. Ourania Vizyinou and Theodoros Xenos. Athens. (= 1971. *Greek Burial Customs*. London.)

Kurz, Marcel. 2003. *Ὄλυμπος*. Trans. Ourania A. Katsamaka. Katerini. (= 1923. *Le mont Olympe*. Paris.)

Kvist, Kirsten. 2003. "Cretan Grants of Asylia: Violence and Protection as Interstate Relations." *Classica et Mediaevalia* 54:185–222.

Kyparissi-Apostolika, Nina. 1998. "Τα προϊστορικά κοσμήματα." In *Κοσμήματα της ελληνικής προϊστορίας: Ο νεολιθικός θησαυρός· Εθνικό Αρχαιολογικό Μουσείο 15, Δεκεμβρίου 1998-28 Φεβρουαρίου 1999*, ed. Kaiti Demakopoulou, 29–34. Athens.

———. 2001. *Τα προϊστορικά κοσμήματα της Θεσσαλίας*. Δημοσιεύματα του Αρχαιολογικού Δελτίου 76. Athens.

Kyriazopoulos, Vassilios D. and Livadas, Georgios. 1967. "Ἀρχαιολογικὰ εὑρήματα ἐπὶ τῆς κορυφῆς τοῦ Ὀλύμπου Ἅγιος Ἀντώνιος." *Ἀρχαιολογικὸν Δελτίον* 22:6–14, plates 5–15.

Lada-Richards, Ismene. 1999. *Initiating Dionysus: Ritual and Theatre in Aristophanes' Frogs*. Oxford.

Ladianou, Katerina. 2005. "The Poetics of *Choreia*: Imitation and Dance in the *Anacreonteia*." *Quaderni Urbinati di Cultura Classica* 80:47–58.

Laffineur, Robert. 1980. "Collection Paul Canellopoulos (XV): Bijoux en or grecs et romains." *Bulletin de Correspondance Hellénique* 104:345–457.

Lalonde, Gerald V. 2005. "Pagan Cult to Christian Ritual: The Case of Agia Marina Theseiou." *Greek, Roman, and Byzantine Studies* 45:91–125.

Lamberton, Robert. 1986. *Homer the Theologian: Neoplatonist Allegorical Reading and the Growth of the Epic Tradition.* Berkeley, CA.

Lambrinoudakis, Vassilios D. 1971. Μηροτραφής: Μελέται περὶ τῆς γονιμοποιοῦ τρώσεως ἢ δεσμεύσεως τοῦ ποδὸς ἐν τῇ ἀρχαίᾳ ἑλληνικῇ μυθολογίᾳ. Ἐθνικὸν καὶ Καποδιστριακὸν Πανεπιστήμιον Ἀθηνῶν, Βιβλιοθήκη Σοφίας Ν. Σαριπόλου 12. Athens.

———. 1972. "Τὰ Ἐκδύσια τῆς Φαιστοῦ." Ἀρχαιολογικὴ Ἐφημερίς 1972:99–112.

Langdon, Merle K. 2000. "Mountains in Greek Religion." *Classical World* 93:461–470.

Larivée, Annie. 2003. "Du vin pour le Collège de veille? Mise en lumière d'un lien occulté entre le Choeur de Dionysos et le νυκτερινὸς σύλλογος dans les *Lois* de Platon." *Phronesis* 48:29–53.

Larson, Jennifer. 2001. *Greek Nymphs: Myth, Cult, Lore.* New York and Oxford.

Lateiner, Donald. 1989. *The Historical Method of Herodotus.* Phoenix Supplement 23. Toronto.

Le Rider, Georges. 1975. "Contremarques et sufrappes dans l'antiquité grecque." In *Numismatique antique: Problèmes et méthodes; Actes du colloque organisé à Nancy du 27 septembre au 2 octobre 1971 par l'Université de Nancy II et l'Université de Louvain,* vol. 2, ed. Jean-Marie Dentzer, Philippe Gauthier, Tony Hackens, 27–56. Nancy-Louvain.

———. 1977. *Le monnayage d'argent et d'or de Philippe II frappé en Macédoine de 359 à 294.* Paris.

———. 1996. *Monnayage et finances de Philippe II: Un état de la question.* Meletemata 23. Athens.

Lebedev, Andrei. 1996a. "Pharnabazos, the Diviner of Hermes: Two Ostraca with Curse Letters from Olbia." *Zeitschrift für Papyrologie und Epigraphik* 112:268–278.

———. 1996b. "The Devotio of Xanthippos: Magic and Mystery Cults in Olbia." *Zeitschrift für Papyrologie und Epigraphik* 112:279–283.

Lebessi, Aggeliki. 1976. Οἱ στῆλες του Πρινιᾶ: Δημοσιεύματα τοῦ Ἀρχαιολογικοῦ Δελτίου 22. Athens.

———. 1981. "Ἡ συνέχεια τῆς κρητομυκηναϊκῆς λατρείας: Ἐπιβιώσεις καὶ ἀναβιώσεις." Ἀρχαιολογικὴ Ἐφημερίς 1981:1–24.

———. 1985. *Τὸ ἱερὸ τοῦ Ἑρμῆ καὶ τῆς Ἀφροδίτης στὴ Σύμη Βιάννου.* Vol. I1: *Χάλκινα Κρητικὰ τορεύματα.* Βιβλιοθήκη τῆς ἐν Ἀθήναις Ἀρχαιολογικῆς Ἑταιρείας 102. Athens.

———. 1989. "Ὁ κρητικὸς αὐλός." *Ariadne (Ἀφιέρωμα στὸν Στυλιανὸ Ἀλεξίου)* 5:55–61.

———. 2002. *Τὸ ἱερὸ τοῦ Ἑρμῆ καὶ τῆς Ἀφροδίτης στὴ Σύμη Βιάννου.* Vol. III: *Τὰ χάλκινα ἀνθρωπόμορφα εἰδώλια.* Βιβλιοθήκη τῆς ἐν Ἀθήναις Ἀρχαιολογικῆς Ἑταιρείας 225. Athens.

Lebessi, Aggeliki and Muhly, Polymnia. 2003. "Ideology and Cultural Interaction: Evidence from the Syme Sanctuary, Crete." *Cretan Studies* 9:95–103.

Leclerc, Marie-Christine. 1992. "Épiménide sans paradoxe." *Kernos* 5:221–233.

Ledbetter, Grace M. 2003. *Poetics Before Plato: Interpretation and Authority in Early Greek Theories of Poetry.* Princeton, NJ.

Lefèvre-Novaro, Daniela. 2004. "Les offrandes d'époque géométrique-orientalisante dans les tombes crétoises de l'âge du bronze: Problèmes et hypotheses." *Creta antica* 5:181–197.

Leitao, David. 1995. "The Perils of Leukippos: Initiatory Transvestism and Male Gender Ideology in the *Ekdusia* at Phaistos." *Classical Antiquity* 14:130–163.

Lekatsas, Panagis. 1985. *Διόνυσος: Καταγωγὴ καὶ ἐξέλιξη τῆς Διονυσιακῆς Θρησκείας.* 2nd ed. Athens.

———. 1996. *Τὸ θεῖον βρέφος: Θρησκειολογικὴ θεώρηση.* Athens.

Létoublon, Françoise. 1995. "Said over the Dead or Tant de marbre parlant sur tant d'ombres." *Arethusa* 28:1–19.

Levaniouk, Olga. 2000. "Aithôn, Aithon, and Odysseus." *Harvard Studies in Classical Philology* 100:25–51.

Lévêque, Pierre. 2000. "Apollon et l'Orphisme à Olbia du Pont." In *Tra Orfeo e Pitagora: Origini e incontri di culture nell'antichità; Atti dei Seminari Napoletani 1996–1998*, ed. Marisa Tortorelli Ghidini et al., 81–90. Naples.

Lewis, Naphtali. 1990. "The 'Ivy of Liberation' Inscription." *Greek, Roman, and Byzantine Studies* 31:197–202.

LGPN. 1987, 1994, 1997, 2000, 2005. *A Lexicon of Greek Personal Names.* Peter M. Fraser and Elaine Matthews, eds. Vol. I: *The Aegean Islands, Cyprus, Cyrenaica*; Michael J. Osborne and Shawn G. Byrne, eds. Vol. II: *Attica*; Peter M. Fraser and Elaine Matthews, eds. Vol. IIIA: *The Peloponnese, Western Greece, Sicily and Magna Graecia*; Peter M. Fraser and Elaine Matthews, eds. Vol. IIIB: *Central Greece: From the Megarid to Thessaly.* Peter

M. Fraser and Elaine Matthews, eds. R. W. V. Catling (assistant ed.). Vol. IV: *Macedonia, Thrace, Northern Regions of the Black Sea.* Oxford.

Liapis, Vayos J. 2003. Ἄγνωστος θεός: Ὅρια τῆς ἀνθρώπινης γνώσης στοὺς Προσωκρατικοὺς καὶ στὸν Οἰδίποδα Τύραννο. Athens.

———. 2004. "They Do it with Mirrors: The Mystery of the Two *Rhesus* Plays." In Θυμέλη: Μελέτες χαρισμένες στον καθηγητή Ν. Χ. Χουρμουζιάδη, ed. Daniel Iakov and Eleni Papazoglou, 159–188. Herakleio.

Lilibaki-Akamati, Maria. 1989. "Ἀπό τα νεκροταφεία της Πέλλας." *Το Αρχαιολογικό Έργο στη Μακεδονία και Θράκη* 3:91–101.

———. 1989–1991. "Ανατολικό νεκροταφείο Πέλλας. Ανασκαφή 1989." *Αρχαιολογικό Δελτίο* 44–46:73–80, 82–83, pl. 15–17, 19, 24–29.

———. 1992. "Ἀπό την τοπογραφία και τα νεκροταφεία της Πέλλας." *Το Αρχαιολογικό Έργο στη Μακεδονία και Θράκη* 6:127–136.

LIMC. 1981–1997. *Lexicon Iconographicum Mythologiae Classicae,* ed. John Boardman et al. Zürich.

Link, Stefan. 2002. "100 Städte – 100 Verfassungen? Einheitlichkeit und Vielfalt in den griechischen Städten Kretas." *Cretan Studies* 7:149–175.

Lioutas, Asterios. 1997. "ΙΣΤ´ Εφορεία Προϊστορικών και Κλασικών Αρχαιοτήτων. Θεσσαλονίκη, Δίκτυο φυσικού αερίου." *Αρχαιολογικό Δελτίο Χρονικά* 52:635–637, plates 231δ.

Litinas, Nikos. 2006. "'Ατάλιον Κρήτης." In *Ο Μυλοπόταμος από την Αρχαιότητα ως Σήμερα: Περιβάλλον, Αρχαιολογία, Ιστορία, Λαογραφία, Κοινωνιολογία: Πρακτικά Διεθνούς Συνεδρίου (Πάνορμο, 24–30 Οκτωβρίου 2003).* Vol. 2: *Αρχαίοι Χρόνοι,* ed. Irene Gavrilaki and Yannis Tzifopoulos, 289–293. Rethymno.

Llewelyn, Stephen R. 1998. *New Documents Illustrating Early Christianity.* Vol. 8: *A Review of the Greek Inscriptions and Papyri Published 1984–1985.* Grand Rapids, MI.

Lloyd-Jones, Sir Hugh. 1976. "The Delphic Oracle." *Greece & Rome* 23:60–73.

———. 1990. "Pindar and the Afterlife: Addendum (1989)." In *Greek Epic, Lyric, and Tragedy: The Academic Papers of Sir Hugh Lloyd-Jones,* 80–109. Oxford. (= 1985. *Pindare.* Entretiens sur l'antiquité classique 17, 245–283. Geneva.)

———. 1998. "Ritual and Tragedy." In *Ansichten griechischer Rituale: Geburstags-Symposium für Walter Burkert, Castelen bei Basel 15. bis 18. März 1996,* ed. Fritz Graf, 271–295. Stuttgart and Leipzig.

Lonsdale, Steven H. 1993. *Dance and Ritual Play in Greek Religion.* Baltimore, MD.

———. 1995. "A Dancing Floor for Ariadne (*Iliad* 18.590–592): Aspects of Ritual Movement in Homer and Minoan Religion." In *The Ages of Homer: A*

Tribute to Emily Townsend Vermeule, ed. Jane B. Carter and Sarah P. Morris, 273–284. Austin.

López-Ruiz, Carolina. Forthcoming. "The Symbolism of Milk in the Gold Tablets: A Near Eastern Perspective." In *Ritual Texts for the Afterlife: A Gold Tablets Conference at the Ohio State University, April 28–30, 2006*, ed. Fritz Graf and Sarah Iles Johnston.

Loraux, Nicole. 2002. *The Mourning Voice: An Essay on Greek Tragedy*. Trans. Elizabeth T. Rawlings. Foreword by Pietro Pucci. Ithaca, NY and London.

Loscalzo, Donato. 2003. "Il poeta non è un indovino: A proposito di Hes. *Th.* 31–2." *Hermes* 131:358–363.

LSAG. Lilian H. Jeffery. 1990. *The Local Scripts of Archaic Greece: A Study of the Origin of the Greek Alphabet and its Development from the Eighth to the Fifth Centuries B.C.* Rev. ed. with supplement by Alan W. Johnston. Oxford Monographs on Classical Archaeology. Oxford.

LSJ. Henry G. Liddell, Robert Scott, and Henry. S. Jones, eds. 1968. *A Greek-English Lexicon with a Supplement*. With the assistance of Roderick McKenzie. 9th ed. Oxford.

Lupi, Marcello. 2001. "Epimenide a Sparta: Note sulla tradizione." In *Epimenide Cretese: Quaderni del Dipartimento di discipline storiche "E. Lepore," Università "Federico II,"* ed. Alfonso Mele et al., 169–191. Naples.

Lyons, Deborah. 1999. "Manto and Manteia: Prophecy in the Myths and Cults of Heroines." In *Sibille e linguaggi oracolari: Mito, storia, tradizione; Atti del Convegno Macerata-Norcia, Settembre 1994*. Ichnia 3, ed. Ileana Chirassi Colombo and Tullio Seppilli, 227–237. Pisa and Rome.

MacDowell, Douglas M. 2002. *Demosthenes Against Meidias (Oration 21)*. Edited with introduction, translation and commentary. London.

MacGillivray, Alexander, Driessen, Jan M., and Sackett, Hugh. 2000. *The Palaikastro Kouros: A Minoan Chryselephantine Statuette and its Aegean Bronze Age Context*. British School at Athens Studies 6. London.

Maddoli, Gianfranco. 1996. "Cults and Religious Doctrines of the Western Greeks." In *The Western Greeks: Classical Civilization in the Western Mediterranean*, ed. Giovanni Pugliese Carratelli, 481–498. London.

Makris, Konstandinos. 2001. *Πορφυρίου Πυθαγόρου βίος: Εισαγωγή, μετάφραση, σχόλια*. Athens.

Malama, Penelope. 2000. "Νεότερα στοιχεία από το ανατολικό νεκροταφείο της Αμφίπολης στα πλαίσια του έργου 'Διαπλάτυνση του δρόμου Αμφίπολης-Μεσολακκιάς'." *Το Αρχαιολογικό Έργο στη Μακεδονία και Θράκη* 14:55–70.

———. 2001. "Νεότερα στοιχεία από το ανατολικό νεκροταφείο της Αμφίπολης." *Το Αρχαιολογικό Έργο στη Μακεδονία και Θράκη* 15:111–126.

Malamidou, Dimitria. 2006. "Les nécropoles d'Amphipolis: Nouvelles données archéologiques et anthropologiques (pl. 29–32)." In *Rois, Cités, Nécropole: Institutions, Rites et Monuments en Macédoine; Actes des Colloques de Nanterre (Décembre 2002) et d'Athènes (Janvier 2004).* Meletemata 45, ed. Anne Marie Guimier-Sorbets et al., 199–208. Athens.

Malkin, Irad. 1998. *The Returns of Odysseus: Colonization and Ethnicity.* Berkeley, CA.

Maltomini, Franco. 2006. "Una lamella d'oro del Museo Archeologico Nazionale di Cividale del Friuli." *Zeitschrift für Papyrologie und Epigraphik* 156:103–108.

Mandalaki, Aikaterini. 2000. "Ο 'Κρητικός νόμος' του Πλάτωνος και τα συναφή προβλήματα (Πλατ. 'Νόμοι' VIII 847e–848c)." In *Πεπραγμένα του Η' Διεθνούς Κρητολογικού Συνεδρίου (Ηράκλειο, 9-14 Σεπτεμβρίου 1996).* Vol. A2, ed. Alexis Kalokairinos, 215–231. Herakleio.

———. 2006. "Αξός: ιστορία μιας κρητικής πόλης από την αρχαϊκή μέχρι την ελληνιστική εποχή." In *Ο Μυλοπόταμος από την Αρχαιότητα ως Σήμερα: Περιβάλλον, Αρχαιολογία, Ιστορία, Λαογραφία, Κοινωνιολογία: Πρακτικά Διεθνούς Συνεδρίου (Πάνορμο, 24-30 Οκτωβρίου 2003).* Vol. 4: *Ελεύθερνα - Αξός,* ed. Irene Gavrilaki and Yannis Tzifopoulos, 187–204. Rethymno.

Mandeli, Katia. 2006. "Τελετουργική χρήση του Ιδαίου Άντρου ήδη από τη νεολιθική εποχή;" In *Ο Μυλοπόταμος από την Αρχαιότητα ως Σήμερα: Περιβάλλον, Αρχαιολογία, Ιστορία, Λαογραφία, Κοινωνιολογία: Πρακτικά Διεθνούς Συνεδρίου (Πάνορμο, 24-30 Οκτωβρίου 2003).* Vol. 3: *Αρχαίοι Χρόνοι. Ιδαίο Άντρο,* ed. Irene Gavrilaki and Yannis Tzifopoulos, 11–19. Rethymno.

Manoledakis, Manolis. 2003. *"Νέκυια": Ερμηνευτική προσέγγιση της σύνθεσης του Πολυγνώτου στη "Λέσχη των Κνιδίων" στους Δελφούς.* Thessaloniki.

Marangou-Lerat, Antigone. 1995. *Le vin et les amphores de Crète de l'époque classique à l'époque imperial.* École française d'Athènes, Études crétoises 30. Paris.

Marinatos, Nanno. 2000. *The Goddess and the Warrior: The Naked Goddess and Mistress of Animals in Early Greek Religion.* London.

———. 2001. "The Adventures of Odysseus and the East Mediterranean Tradition." In *Kreta und Zypern: Religion und Schrift von der Frühgeschichte bis zum Ende der archaischen Zeit: Tagung in Ohlstadt, Oberbayern, 26.-28. 2. 1999,* ed. A. Kyriatsoulis, 319–332. Altenburg.

———. 2004. "The Character of Minoan Epiphanies." In *Divine Epiphanies in the Ancient World.* Illinois Classical Studies 29, ed. Danuta Shanzer, guest ed. Nanno Marinatos, 25–42. Urbana Champaign, IL.

Markantonatos, Andreas. 2002. *Tragic Narrative: A Narratological Study of Sophocles' Oedipus at Colonus.* Untersuchungen zur antiken Literatur and Geschichte 63. Berlin and New York.

———. 2004. "Mystic Filters for Tragedy: Orphism and Euripides' *Rhesus.*" *Ariadne* 10:15–48.

Marki, Efterpi. 1990. "Παρατηρήσεις στον οικισμό της αρχαίας Πύδνας." In *Μνήμη Δ. Λαζαρίδη: Πρακτικά Αρχαιολογικού Συνεδρίου "Πόλις και Χώρα στην Αρχαία Μακεδονία και Θράκη," Καβάλα, 9-11 Μαΐου 1986,* 45–50, plates 1–13. Thessaloniki.

Markoulaki, Stavroula. 1987a. "ΚΕ´ Εφορεία Προϊστορικών και Κλασικών Αρχαιοτήτων: Νομός Χανίων, Καστέλλι Κισάμου, Οικόπεδο Κέντρου Υγείας." *Αρχαιολογικό Δελτίο Χρονικά* 42 Β2:558–564, plates 324β–331.

———. 1987b. "Οι Ώρες και οι Εποχές σε ψηφιδωτό από το Καστέλλι Κισάμου." *Κρητική Εστία* 1:33–59, plates 9–20.

———. 1994. "ΚΕ´ Εφορεία Προϊστορικών και Κλασικών Αρχαιοτήτων: Νομός Χανίων, Καστέλλι, Κέντρο Υγείας." *Αρχαιολογικό Δελτίο Χρονικά* 49 Β2:724–725.

———. 1995. "ΚΕ´ Εφορεία Προϊστορικών και Κλασικών Αρχαιοτήτων: Νομός Χανίων, Καστέλλι Κισάμου, Κέντρο Υγείας." *Αρχαιολογικό Δελτίο Χρονικά* 50 Β2:736–739.

Markoulaki, Stavroula, Christodoulakos, Yannis, and Fragonikolaki, Christina. 2004. "Η αρχαία Κίσαμος και η πολεοδομική της οργάνωση." In *Creta romana e protobizantina: Atti del congresso internazionale organizzato dalla Scuola Archeologica Italiana di Atene (Iraklion, 23-30 settembre 2000),* ed. Antonino Di Vita, Monica Livadioti, and Ilaria Simiakaki, vol. 2:355–373. Padua.

Markoulaki, Stavroula and Niniou-Kindeli, Vana. 1982. "Ἑλληνιστικὸς οἰκογενειακὸς τάφος Χανίων. Ἀνασκαφὴ οἰκοπέδου Μαθιουλάκη." *Αρχαιολογικό Δελτίο Μελέτες* 37:7–118, plates 27–40.

———. 1985. "Ἑλληνιστικὸς οἰκογενειακὸς τάφος οἱὰ Χανιά." In *Πεπραγμένα τοῦ Ε´ Διεθνοῦς Κρητολογικοῦ Συνεδρίου (Ἅγιος Νικόλαος, 25 Σεπτεμβρίου - 1 Ὀκτωβρίου 1981).* Vol. Α, ed. Theocharis Detorakis, 216 226. Herakleio,

Marks, Jim. 2003. "Alternative Odysseys: The Case of Thoas and Odysseus." *Transactions of the American Philological Association* 133:209–226.

Maronitis, Dimitris N. 1999. *Ὁμηρικὰ Μεγαθέματα: πόλεμος - ὁμιλία - νόστος.* Athens.

Martin, Richard P. 1983. *Healing, Sacrifice, and Battle: Amechania and Related Concepts in Early Greek Poetry.* Innsbrucker Beiträge zur Sprachwissenschaft 41. Innsbruck.

———. 1993. "The Seven Sages as Performers of Wisdom." In *Cultural Poetics in Archaic Greece: Cult, Performance, Politics*, ed. Carol Dougherty and Leslie Kurke, 108–128. Cambridge.

———. 2001. "Rhapsodizing Orpheus." *Kernos* 14:23–33.

———. 2005a. "Cretan Homers: Tradition, Politics, Fieldwork." *Abstract The Homerizon: Conceptual Interrogations in Homeric Studies, June 27–July 1, 2005.* http://chs.harvard.edu/chs/files/classics_issue3_martin.pdf.

———. 2005b. "Epic as Genre." In *A Companion to Ancient Epic*, ed. John M. Foley, 9–19. Oxford.

———. 2007. "Golden Verses: Voice and Authority in the Tablets." *Princeton/ Stanford Working Papers in Classics* 2007. http://www.princeton. edu/~pswpc/pdfs/rpmartin/040701.pdf. (= Fritz Graf and Sarah Iles Johnston, eds. *Ritual Texts for the Afterlife: A Gold Tablets Conference at the Ohio State University, April 28–30, 2006*, forthcoming.)

Martínez Nieto, Roxana Beatriz. 2001. "La Θεογονία de Museo: Fragmentos inéditos e intento de reconstrucción." *Emerita* 69:115–152.

Martínez-Fernández, Ángel. 2003. "Una nueva inscripción votiva de Lisos, Creta." *Zeitschrift für Papyrologie und Epigraphik* 145:131–132.

———. 2006a. "Αρχαία επιγράμματα της Αξού." In *Ο Μυλοπόταμος από την Αρχαιότητα ως Σήμερα: Περιβάλλον, Αρχαιολογία, Ιστορία, Λαογραφία, Κοινωνιολογία: Πρακτικά Διεθνούς Συνεδρίου (Πάνορμο, 24–30 Οκτωβρίου 2003)*. Vol. 4: *Ελεύθερνα - Αξός*, ed. Irene Gavrilaki and Yannis Tzifopoulos, 167–186. Rethymno.

———. 2006b. *Epigramas Helenísticos de Creta.* Manueles y Anejos de «Emerita» 48. Madrid.

Martínez-Fernández, Ángel and Niniou-Kindeli, Vana. 2000–2001. "El heroon de Aptera (Creta) y sus inscripciones." *Fortunatae* 12:145–159.

Martínez-Fernández, Ángel, Tsatsaki, Niki, and Kapranos, Epaminondas. 2006. "Una inscripción inédita de Chamalevri, Creta." *Zeitschrift für Papyrologie und Epigraphik* 157:87–94.

Mastrocinque, Attilio. 1993. "Orpheos Bakchikos." *Zeitschrift für Papyrologie und Epigraphik* 97:16–24.

———. 2002. "Zeus Kretagenès seleucidico: Da Seleucia a Praeneste (e in Giudea)." *Klio* 84:355–372.

Matthaiou, Angelos P. and Papadopoulos, Georgios K. 2003. Ἐπιγραφὲς Ἰκαρίας. Ἐπιγραφικὸν πιττάκιον 1. Athens.

Maurizio, Lisa. 1995. "Anthropology and Spirit Possession: A Reconsideration of the Pythia's Role at Delphi." *Journal of Hellenic Studies* 115:69–86.

———. 1997. "Delphic Oracles as Oral Performances: Authenticity and Historical Evidence." *Classical Antiquity* 16:308–334.

———. 1999. "Narrative, Biographical and Ritual Conventions at Delphi." In *Sibille e linguaggi oracolari: Mito, storia, tradizione; Atti del Convegno Macerata-Norcia, Settembre 1994.* Ichnia 3, ed. Ileana Chirassi Colombo and Tullio Seppilli, 133–158. Pisa and Rome.

Mazzoldi, Sabina. 2002. "Cassandra's Prophecy between Ecstasy and Rational Mediation." *Kernos* 15:145–154.

McDonald, Marianne. 1978. *Terms for Happiness in Euripides.* Hypomnemata 54. Göttingen.

McLennan, George R. 1977. *Callimachus. Hymn to Zeus.* Introduction and commentary. Testi e commenti. Rome.

Megas, Georgios A. 1940. "Ζητήματα ἑλληνικῆς λαογραφίας, κεφάλαιον Στ΄: Τὰ κατὰ τὴν τελευτήν." Ἐπετηρὶς τοῦ Λαογραφικοῦ Ἀρχείου 2:166–205.

Meimaris, Yannis E. and Kritikakou-Nikolaropoulou, Kalliope I. 2005. *Inscriptions from Palaestina Tertia.* Vol. Ia: *The Greek Inscriptions from Ghor es-Safi (Byzantine Zoora).* Meletemata 41. Athens.

Mele, Alfonso. 2001. "Il corpus epimenideo. Appendice. Afrodite e le Erinni." In *Epimenide Cretese: Quaderni del Dipartimento di discipline storiche "E. Lepore," Università "Federico II,"* ed. Alfonso Mele et al., 227–278. Naples.

Mele, Alfonso, Tortorelli Ghidini, Marisa, Federico, Eduardo, Visconti, Amedeo, eds. 2001. *Epimenide Cretese: Quaderni del Dipartimento di discipline storiche "E. Lepore," Università "Federico II."* Naples.

Melfi, Milena. 2001. "Filostrato, *Vita di Apollonio di Tiana* IV.34, ed il terremoto di Lebena." *Creta antica* 2:225–236.

———. 2004. "Il santuario di Lebena e la rinascita del culto di Asclepio nel II sec. d.C." In *Creta romana e protobizantina: Atti del congresso internazionale organizzato dalla Scuola Archeologica Italiana di Atene (Iraklion, 23–30 settembre 2000),* ed. Antonino Di Vita, Monica Livadioti, and Ilaria Simiakaki, vol. 2:515–529. Padua.

———. 2006. "The Idaean Cave in Roman Times: Cult, Politics and Propaganda." In *Ο Μυλοπόταμος από την Αρχαιότητα ως Σήμερα. Περιβάλλον, Αρχαιολογία, Ιστορία, Λαογραφία, Κοινωνιολογία: Πρακτικά Διεθνούς Συνεδρίου (Πάνορμο, 24–30 Οκτωβρίου 2003).* Vol. 3: *Αρχαίοι Χρόνοι. Ιδαίο Άντρο,* ed. Irene Gavrilaki and Yannis Tzifopoulos, 217–227. Rethymno.

Merkelbach, Reinhold. 1988. *Die Hirten des Dionysos: Die Dionysos-Mysterien der römischen Kaiserzeit und der bukolische Roman des Longus.* Stuttgart.

———. 1995. *Isis Regina, Zeus Sarapis: Die griechisch-ägyptische Religion nach den Quellen dargestellt.* Stuttgart and Leipzig.

———. 1999. "Die goldenen Totenpässe: Ägyptisch, orphisch, bakchisch." *Zeitschrift für Papyrologie und Epigraphik* 128:1–13.

Mikalson, Jon D. 2005. *Ancient Greek Religion.* Oxford.

Miliadis, Giannis. 1926. "Ἀμβρακίας τάφοι." Ἀρχαιολογικὸν Δελτίον 10:63–77.

Miller, Andrew M. 1986. *From Delos to Delphi: A Literary Study of the Homeric Hymn to Apollo.* Mnemosyne Supplement 93. Leiden.

Miller, Stella G. 1982. "Macedonian Tombs: Their Architecture and Architectural Decoration." In *Macedonia and Greece in Late Classical and Hellenistic Times.* Studies in the History of Art 10, ed. Beryl Barr-Sharrar and Eugene N. Borza, 152–171. Washington, DC.

———. 1992. *The Tomb of Lyson and Kallikes: A Painted Macedonian Tomb.* Mainz.

Mills, Sophie. 1997. *Theseus, Tragedy, and the Athenian Empire.* Oxford.

Minchin, Elizabeth. 2001. *Homer and the Resources of Memory: Some Applications of Cognitive Theory to the Iliad and the Odyssey.* Oxford.

Mirecki, Paul and Meyer, Marvin, eds. 2002. *Magic and Ritual in the Ancient World.* Religions in the Graeco-Roman World 141. Leiden.

Misaïlidou-Despotidou, Vassiliki. 1995. "Ανασκαφή στη Νέα Φιλαδέλφεια το 1995." *Το Αρχαιολογικό Έργο στη Μακεδονία και Θράκη* 9:311–320.

Mitsopoulos-Leon, Veronica. 1984. "Zur Verehrung des Dionysos in Elis noch-mals: ΑΞΙΕ ΤΑΥΡΕ und die sechzehn heiligen Frauen." *Mitteilungen des Deutschen Archäologischen Instituts, Athenische Abteilung* 99:275–290.

Moatti, Claudia. 2006. "Translation, Migration, and Communication in the Roman Empire: Three Aspects of Movement in History." *Classical Antiquity* 25:109–140.

Monaco, Maria Chiara. 2006. "Αξός: Ιδέες και παρατηρήσεις σχετικά με την ομάδα των όπλων από τον ναό της Αφροδίτης της Αξού." In *Ο Μυλοπόταμος από την Αρχαιότητα ως Σήμερα: Περιβάλλον, Αρχαιολογία, Ιστορία, Λαογραφία, Κοινωνιολογία: Πρακτικά Διεθνούς Συνεδρίου (Πάνορμο, 24-30 Οκτωβρίου 2003).* Vol. 4: *Ελεύθερνα - Αξός,* ed. Irene Gavrilaki and Yannis Tzifopoulos, 117–136. Rethymno.

Morante Mediavilla, Bibiana. 2006. "La glossa Hesiquea γάνος y su aceptión ὕαινα ὑπὸ Φρυγῶν καὶ Βιθυνῶν." *Emerita* 74:321–340.

Mørkholm, Otto. 1991. *Early Hellenistic Coinage: From the Accession of Alexander to the Peace of Apamea (336-188 BC).* Ed. Philip Grierson and Ulla Westermark. Cambridge.

Morris, Ian. 1987. *Burial and Ancient Society: The Rise of the Greek City-State.* Cambridge.

Morris, Sarah P. 1992. *Daidalos and the Origins of Greek Art.* Princeton, NJ.

———. 1997. "Homer and the Near East." In *A New Companion to Homer*, ed. Ian Morris and Barry Powell, 599–623. Leiden.

Most, Glenn W. 1997a. "Hesiod's Myth of the Five (or Three or Four) Races." *Proceedings of the Cambridge Philological Society* 43:104–127.

———. 1997b. "The Fire Next Time: Cosmology, Allegoresis, and Salvation in the Derveni Papyrus." *Journal of Hellenic Studies* 117:117–135.

———. 2006. *Hesiod. Theogony, Works and Days, Testimonia.* Loeb Classical Library. Cambridge, MA.

Motte, André and Pirenne-Delforge, Vincianne. 1992. "Le mot et les rites: Aperçu des significations de ὄργια et de quelque dérivés." *Kernos* 5:119–140.

Mourelatos, Alexander-Phoibos. 2002. Ὁδοί τῆς γνώσης καὶ τῆς πλάνης: Λόγος καὶ εἰκόνα στα ἀποσπάσματα του Παρμενίδη. Trans. Spyros A. Moschonas. Herakleio. (= 2008. *The Route of Parmenides.* Revised and expanded edition, with a new introduction, three supplemental essays, and an essay by Gregory Vlastos. Las Vegas.)

Moustaka, Aliki. 2004. "Δακτυλιόλιθοι ἀπό το Ιδαίο Ἄντρο." In *Creta romana e protobizantina: Atti del congresso internazionale organizzato dalla Scuola Archeologica Italiana di Atene (Iraklion, 23-30 settembre 2000)*, ed. Antonino Di Vita, Monica Livadioti, and Ilaria Simiakaki, vol. 1:225–242. Padua.

Moutsopoulos, Evangelos. 1992. "Prévinir ou guérir? Musique et états orgiastiques chez Platon." *Kernos* 5:141–151.

Muellner, Leonard C. 1974. *The Meaning of Homeric EYXOMAI through its Formulas.* Innsbrucker Beiträge zur Sprachwissenschaft 13. Innsbruck.

———. 1998. "Glaucus Redivivus." *Harvard Studies in Classical Philology* 98:1–30.

Mugione, Eliana. 1995. "La raffigurazione di Caronte in età greca." *La Parola del Passato* 50:357–375.

Munson, Rosaria Vignolo. 2005. *Black Doves Speak: Herodotus and the Language of Barbarians.* Center for Hellenic Studies Series, Hellenic Studies Series 9. Washington, DC and Cambridge, MA.

Murray, Gilbert. 1908–1909. "The Hymn of the Kouretes." *Annual of the British School at Athens* 15:357–365.

Mylonas, George E. 1961. *Eleusis and the Eleusinian Mysteries.* Princeton, NJ.

Myres, John L. 1893. "Nouvelles et correspondance: Éleuthernae." *Bulletin de Correspondance Hellénique* 17:629.

Nagler, Michael L. 1996. "Dread Goddess Revisited." In *Reading the Odyssey: Selected Interpretive Essays*, ed. with an introduction by Seth L. Schein, 141–161. Princeton, NJ.

Nagy, Gregory. 1979. *The Best of the Achaeans: Concepts of the Hero in Archaic Greek Poetry*. Baltimore, MD.

———. 1990a. "Ancient Greek Poetry, Prophecy, and Concepts of Theory." In *Poetry and Prophecy: The Beginnings of a Literary Tradition*, ed. James L. Kugel, 56–64. Ithaca, NY.

———. 1990b. *Pindar's Homer: The Lyric Possession of an Epic Past*. Baltimore, MD and London.

———. 1994. "The Name of Apollo: Etymology and Essence." In *Apollo, Origins and Influences*, ed. Jon Solomon, 3–7. Tucson, AZ and London. Repr. in *Homer's Text and Language*, 138–143. Urbana Champaign, IL and Chicago, 2004.

———. 2004a. "Éléments orphiques chez Homère." *Kernos* 14:1–9.

———. 2004b. *Homer's Text and Language*. Traditions. Urbana Champaign, IL and Chicago.

———. 2005. "The Epic Hero." In *A Companion to Ancient Epic*, ed. John M. Foley, 71–89. Oxford.

Nakassis, Dimitri. 2004. "Gemination at the Horizons: East and West in the Mythical Geography of Archaic Greek Epic." *Transactions of the American Philological Association* 134:215–233.

Νεκρώσιμοι καὶ ἐπιμνημόσυνοι ἀκολουθίαι, n.d. Official version of the Greek Orthodox Church. Athens.

Nelis, Damien P. 2005. "The Reading of Orpheus: The Orphic *Argonautica* and the Epic Tradition." In *Roman and Greek Imperial Epic*, ed. Michael Paschalis, 170–192. Herakleio.

Niafas, Konstantinos. 1997. "A Note on Ep. Adesp. 9.X.14 Powell (*PChicag.* Pack^2 1620)." *Zeitschrift für Papyrologie und Epigraphik* 119:55–56.

Nikolaïdis, Anastassios. 1989. "Οἱ Κρῆτες στὴν ἀρχαία καὶ νεότερη ἑλληνικὴ παροιμιογραφία." *Ariadne (Ἀφιέρωμα στὸν Στυλιανὸ Ἀλεξίου)* 5:399–406.

Nikolidaki, Eleni. 2003. "Apollonius Rhodius and Crete." *Cretan Studies* 8:154–165.

Nilsson, Martin P. 1950. *The Minoan-Mycenaean Religion and its Survival in Greek Religion*. 2nd rev. ed. Skrifter Utgivna av Kungl: Humanistiska Vetenskapssamfundet i Lund 9. Lund.

———. 1985. *The Dionysiac Mysteries of the Hellenistic and Roman Age*. Skrifter Utgivna av Svenska Institutet i Athen 8.5. Lund 1957. Repr. Salem, NH.

Niniou-Kindeli, Vana. 1987. "Κιβωτιόσχημος τάφος της Ρωμαιοκρατίας στο Επανοχώρι Σελίνου." *Κρητική Εστία* 1:16–32, plates 1–8.

———. 1991-1993. "Κεφαλές Διονύσου στο Αρχαιολογικό Μουσείο Χανίων." *Κρητική Εστία* 4:25–37, plates 1–9.

———. 1993. "ΚΕ´ Εφορεία Προϊστορικών και Κλασικών Αρχαιοτήτων. Καστέλλι Κισάμου, Β´ Δημοτικό Σχολείο." *Αρχαιολογικό Δελτίο Χρονικά* 48:475–476.

———. 2002. "Αρχαιολογικές ειδήσεις. Νομός Ρεθύμνης, Επαρχία Αμαρίου, Πατσός." *Κρητική Εστία* 9:301–304.

Niniou-Kindeli, Vanna and Christodoulakos, Yannis. 2004. "Ρωμαϊκή Απτέρα. Μια πρώτη προσέγγιση." In *Creta romana e protobizantina: Atti del congresso internazionale organizzato dalla Scuola Archeologica Italiana di Atene (Iraklion, 23-30 settembre 2000)*, ed. Antonino Di Vita, Monica Livadioti, and Ilaria Simiakaki, vol. 2:313–334. Padua.

O'Bryhim, Shawn. 1996. "A New Interpretation of Hesiod, *Theogony* 35." *Hermes* 124:131–139.

———. 1997. "Hesiod and the Cretan Cave." *Rheinisches Museum für Philologie* 140:95–96.

Obbink, Dirk. 1993. "Dionysus Poured Out: Ancient and Modern Theories of Sacrifice and Cultural Formation." In *Masks of Dionysus,* ed. Thomas H. Carpenter and Christopher A. Faraone, 65–86. Myth and Poetics. Ithaca, NY.

———. 1997. "Cosmology as Initiation vs. the Critique of Orphic Mysteries." In *Studies on the Derveni Papyrus,* ed. André Laks and Glenn W. Most, 39–54. Oxford.

———. 2005. "New Old Posidippus and Old New Posidippus: From Occasion to Edition in the Epigrams." In *The New Posidippus: A Hellenistic Poetry Book,* ed. Kathryn Gutzwiller, 97–115. Oxford.

———. Forthcoming. "Poetry and Performance in the Orphic Gold Leaves." In *Further Along the Path: Recent Approaches to the 'Orphic' Gold Tablets,* ed. Radcliffe G. Edmonds III. Cambridge.

Obsomer, Claude. 2003. "Hérodote II 148 à l'origine du mot Labyrinthos? La Minotauromachie revisitée." *Cretan Studies* 9:105–186.

Oikonomou, Stavroula. 2002. *Χρυσά και αργυρά επιστόμια.* MA thesis, University of Crete. Σειρά Ρίθυμνα 17. Rethymno.

———. 2004. "Νεκρικά κοσμήματα: τα ελάσματα κάλυψης του στόματος." *Eulimene* 5:91–133.

Olck, Franz. 1901. "Cypresse." *Realencyclopädie* 4.2:1909–1938.

Oldfather, Charles. H., ed. 1939. *Diodorus of Sicily.* Vol. 3. Loeb Classical Library. Cambridge, MA.

Olivieri, Alexander. 1915. *Lamellae aureae orphicae, edidit, commentario instruxit.* Kleine Texte für Vorlesungen und Übungen 133. Bonn.

Orlandos, Anastasios K. and Vranousis, Leandros. 1973. *Τὰ χαράγματα τοῦ Παρθενῶνος.* Athens.

Otto, Walter F. 1991. *Διόνυσος: Μύθος και λατρεία.* Trans. Theodoros Loupassakis. Athens. (= 1960. *Dionysos, Mythos und Kultus.* Darmstad.)

Overbeck, Bernhard and Overbeck, Mechtild. 2005. *Οίνου σφραγίς: Ο Διόνυσος και ο κόσμος του στους αρχαίους σφραγιδόλιθους.* Athens.

Paisios. 1935. *Παϊσίου Μοναχοῦ, Ἀκολουθία νεκρώσιμος τοῦ ἐξοδιαστικοῦ τῶν μοναχῶν τῶν ἐν Ἁγίῳ Ὄρει Ἱερῶν Μονῶν.* Hagion Oros.

Pakannen, Petra. 1996. *Interpreting Early Hellenistic Religion: A Study on the Mystery Cult of Demeter and the Cult of Isis.* Papers and Monographs of the Finnish Institute at Athens 3. Helsinki.

Palermo, Dario. 2001. "Luoghi di culto sulla Patela di Priniàs: Per la storia della città fra la tarda età del Bronzo e il VII sec. a.C." *Creta antica* 2:159–167.

Pallas, Dimitrios. 1971. "Ἀνασκαφὴ τῆς βυζαντινῆς βασιλικῆς τοῦ Γλυκέος ἐν Ἠπείρῳ (πίν. 163–178)." *Πρακτικὰ τῆς ἐν Ἀθήναις Ἀρχαιολογικῆς Ἑταιρείας* 1971:130–145.

Panagopoulos, Andreas. 1981. *Πλάτων καὶ Κρήτη.* Ἑλληνικὴ Ἀνθρωπιστικὴ Ἑταιρεία, Διεθνὲς Κέντρον Ἀνθρωπιστικῶν Κλασσικῶν Ἐρευνῶν, Σειρὰ Β΄: Μελέται καὶ Ἔρευναι 33. Athens.

———. 1987. *Ἀριστοτέλης καὶ Κρήτη.* Athens.

Pantermalis, Dimitrios. 1999. *Δίον, η Ανακάλυψη.* Athens.

PAntinoopolis I 18 (= MP^3 2466). http://scriptorium.lib.duke.edu/papyrus/texts/clist.html.

Papachatzis, Nicholaos D. 1979. *Παυσανίου Ἑλλάδος περιήγησις.* Vol. 3: *Μεσσηνιακὰ καὶ Ἠλειακά.* Athens.

———. 1986. "Ορφέας." In *Ελληνική Μυθολογία,* vol. 3, ed. Ioannis T. Kakridis, 293–299. Athens.

———. 1990. "Ἡ λαϊκὴ θρησκεία στὴν ἀρχαία Ἑλλάδα τῶν ἱστορικῶν χρόνων." *Ἀρχαιολογικὴ Ἐφημερίς* 1990:1–82.

———. 1993. "Ἡ ἑλληνικὴ θεὰ Ρέα καὶ ἡ φρυγικὴ 'Μητέρα τῶν θεῶν' ἢ Μεγάλη Μητέρα." *Ἀρχαιολογικὴ Ἐφημερίς* 1993:49–82.

Papachristodoulou, Ioannis. 2000. "Σχέσεις των κρητικών πόλεων με τη Ρόδο στην Ελληνιστική περίοδο. Μια οικογένεια καλλιτεχνών από την Ελεύθερνα." In *Πεπραγμένα του Η΄ Διεθνούς Κρητολογικού Συνεδρίου (Ηράκλειο, 9-14 Σεπτεμβρίου 1996).* Vol. A2, ed. Alexis Kalokairinos, 541–551. Herakleio.

Papadopoulou, Eleni. 2000–2001. "Αρχαιολογικές ειδήσεις 1995-97, Νομός Ρεθύμνης, Επαρχία Ρεθύμνης, Σφακάκι Παγκαλοχωρίου." *Κρητική Εστία* 8:288–290.

———. 2006. "Υστερομινωικός θολωτός τάφος στις Μαργαρίτες Μυλοποτάμου." In *Ο Μυλοπόταμος από την Αρχαιότητα ως Σήμερα: Περιβάλλον, Αρχαιολογία,*

Ιστορία, Λαογραφία, Κοινωνιολογία: Πρακτικά Διεθνούς Συνεδρίου (Πάνορμο, 24-30 Οκτωβρίου 2003). Vol. 2: *Αρχαίοι Χρόνοι,* ed. Irene Gavrilaki and Yannis Tzifopoulos, 129–152. Rethymno.

Papadopoulou, Thalia. 2001. "The Prophetic Figure in Euripides' 'Phoenissae' and 'Bacchae.'" *Hermes* 129:21–31.

Papagiorgis, Kostis. 1995. *Ζῶντες καὶ τεθνεῶτες.* 3rd ed. Athens.

Papaïkonomou, Irini-Despina. 2006. "L'interpretation des 'jouets' trouvés dans les tombes d'enfants d'Abdère (pl. 33–36)." In *Rois, Cités, Nécropoles: Institutions, Rites et Monuments en Macédoine; Actes des Colloques de Nanterre (Décembre 2002) et d'Athènes (Janvier 2004).* Meletemata 45, ed. Anne Marie Guimier-Sorbets et al., 239–249. Athens.

Papakosta, Lambrini. 1987. "ΣΤ´ Εφορεία Προϊστορικῶν καὶ Κλασικῶν Ἀρχαιοτήτων, Αἴγιο, Ὁδός Σοφοκλέους 8." *Αρχαιολογικό Δελτίο Χρονικά* 42 Β1:153.

Papamichael, Anni. 1962–1963. "Χρῆσις τῶν μετάλλων εἰς μαγικάς, δεισιδαίμονας καὶ ἄλλας ἐνεργείας εἰς τὸν κοινωνικὸν βίον τοῦ λαοῦ." *Ἐπετηρὶς τοῦ Λαογραφικοῦ Ἀρχείου* 15–16:62–91.

Papapostolou, Ioannis A. 1977. "ΣΤ´ Εφορεία Προϊστορικῶν καὶ Κλασικῶν Ἀρχαιοτήτων, Αἴγιο, Ὁδός Ἀγαμέμνονος 16 (Διαμαντή Ράχη)." *Αρχαιολογικό Δελτίο* 32 Β1–Β2:94, plate 63β.

Papathanassopoulos, Giorgos A. 1969. "Ἀρχαιότητες καὶ Μνημεῖα Ἠλείας· Ἀρχαία Ἦλις." *Αρχαιολογικό Δελτίο Χρονικά* 24 Β1:152–154, plates 149–157.

Pape, Wilhelm and Benseler, Gustav E. 1959. *Wörterbuch der griechischen Eigennamen.* Vol. 1–2. 3rd ed. Braunschweig 1911. Repr. Graz.

Pappalardo, Eleonora. 2001. "I bronzi dell'antro Ideo nel contesto della produzione cretese coeva." *Creta antica* 2:169–198.

———. 2004. "Avori orientali da Creta: Il ruolo di Creta nella distribuzione degli avori nel mediterraneo orientale." *Creta antica* 5:205–247.

Paraskevaïdis, Christodoulos, Archbishop of Athens and all Greece. 2005. *Ἑλληνισμὸς προσήλυτος: Ἡ μετάβαση τοῦ Ἑλληνισμοῦ ἀπὸ τὴν ἀρχαιότητα στὸ Χριστιανισμό.* Athens.

Parise, Nicola F. 1995. "'Segni premonetari' ed obolo di Caronte." *La Parola del Passato* 50:178–184.

Parke, Herbert W. 1940. "A Note on the Delphic Priesthood." *Classical Quarterly* 34:85–89.

Parke, Herbert W. and Wormell, Donald E. W. 2004. *The Delphic Oracle.* 2 vols. Chicago. Orig. pub. Oxford, 1956.

Parker, Robert. 1983. *Miasma: Pollution and Purification in Early Greek Religion.* Oxford.

———. 1991. "The *Hymn to Demeter* and the *Homeric Hymns*." *Greece & Rome* 38:1–17.

———. 1995. "Early Orphism." In *The Greek World*, ed. Anton Powell, 483–510. London.

———. 1996. *Athenian Religion: A History*. Oxford.

———. 2000a. "Greek States and Greek Oracles." In *Oxford Readings in Greek Religion*, ed. Richard Buxton, 76–108. Oxford.

———. 2000b. "Review of Roland Baumgarten, Heiliges Wort und Heilige Schrift bei den Griechen: Hieroi Logoi und verwandte Erscheinungen." *Bryn Mawr Classical Review* 2000.01.12.

———. 2005. *Polytheism and Society in Ancient Athens*. Oxford.

Parker, Robert and Stamatopoulou, Maria. 2004. "A New Funerary Gold Leaf from Pherai." Ἀρχαιολογικὴ Ἐφημερίς 143:1–32.

Passagianis, Kostas. 1928. Μανιάτικα. Μοιρολόγια καὶ τραγούδια. Ἱστορικὴ καὶ Λαογραφικὴ Βιβλιοθήκη τοῦ Συλλόγου πρὸς Διάδοσιν Ὠφελίμων Βιβλίων 3. Athens.

Paton, Sara. 2004. "The Villa Dionysos at Knossos: Recent Work." In *Creta romana e protobizantina: Atti del congresso internazionale organizzato dalla Scuola Archeologica Italiana di Atene (Iraklion, 23-30 settembre 2000)*, ed. Antonino Di Vita, Monica Livadioti, and Ilaria Simiakaki, vol. 2:281–285. Padua.

PDerveni. See Kouremenos, Parássoglou, and Tsantsanoglou.

Peponi, Anastassia-Erasmia. 2004. "Χωρογραφία θεάτρου: Ὁμηρικός Ὕμνος εις Ἀπόλλωνα (στ. 146–206)." In Θυμέλη: Μελέτες χαρισμένες στον καθηγητή Ν. Χ. Χουρμουζιάδη, ed. Daniel Iakov and Eleni Papazoglou, 303–321. Herakleio.

Perlman, Paula J. 1992. "One Hundred-Citied Crete and the 'Cretan Πολιτεία'." *Classical Philology* 87:193–205.

———. 1995. "*Invocatio* and *Imprecatio*: The Hymn to the Greatest Kouros from Palaikastro and the Oath in Ancient Crete." *Journal of Hellenic Studies* 115:161–167.

———. 1996. "Πόλις Ὑπήκοος: The Dependent Polis and Crete." In *Introduction to an Inventory of Poleis: Symposium August 23-26, 1995; Acts of the Copenhagen Polis Centre 3*. Det Kongelige Danske Videnskabernes Selskab, Historisk-filosofiske Meddelelser 74, ed. Mogens H. Hansen, 233–287. Copenhagen.

———. 2000. "KRETES AEI LEISTAI? The Marginalization of Crete in Greek Thought and the Role of Piracy in the Outbreak of the First Cretan War."

In *Hellenistic Rhodes: Politics, Culture, and Society.* Studies in Hellenistic Civilization 9, ed. Per Bilde et al., 132–161. Aarhus.

———. 2002. "The Cretan Colonists of Sicily: Prosopography, Onomastics and Myths of Colonization." *Cretan Studies* 7:177–211.

———. 2004a. "Tinker, Tailor, Soldier, Sailor: The Economies of Archaic Eleutherna, Crete." *Classical Antiquity* 23:95–137.

———. 2004b. "Crete." In *An Inventory of Archaic and Greek Poleis: An Investigation Conducted by the Copenhagen Polis Centre for the Danish National Research Foundation*, ed. Mogens H. Hansen and Thomas H. Nielsen, 1144–1195. Oxford.

Petridou, Georgia. 2004. "Adopted by Persephone: Adoption and Initiation Ritual in A1–A3 Zuntz and Pelinna 1–2." In *Cult and Death: Proceedings of the Third Annual Meeting of Postgraduate Researchers, The University of Liverpool, May 2002.* BAR International Series 1282, ed. Danai-Christina Naoum, Georgina Muskett, and Mercourios Georgiadis, 69–76. Oxford.

Petsas, Photios M. 1961–62. "Ἀνασκαφὴ ἀρχαίου νεκροταφείου Βεργίνης (1960/61)· Τύμβος LI." *Ἀρχαιολογικὸν Δελτίον* 17 A:259.

———. 1966. *Ὁ τάφος τῶν Λευκαδίων.* Βιβλιοθήκη τῆς ἐν Ἀθήναις Ἀρχαιολογικῆς Ἑταιρείας 57. Athens.

———. 1967a. "Μακεδονία, Νομὸς Θεσσαλονίκης, Ἅγιος Ἀθανάσιος." *Ἀρχαιολογικὸν Δελτίον Χρονικά* 22:399–400, σχ. 21.

———. 1967b. "Χρονικὰ ἀρχαιολογικὰ 1966–1967: 68: Ἅγιος Ἀθανάσιος – Γέφυρα." *Μακεδονικά* 9:167–168, plate 75β.

Picard, Charles. 1946. "La triade Zeus-Héra-Dionysos dans l'Orient hellénique d'après les nouveaux fragments d'Alcée." *Bulletin de Correspondance Hellénique* 70:455–473.

———. 1961. "Éleusinisme ou orphisme? Les nouvelles lamelles d'or inscrites d'Éleutherna (Crète)." *Revue de l'histoire des religions* 159:127–130.

Piérart, Marcel. 1996. "La mort de Dionysos à Argos." In *The Role of Religion in the Early Greek Polis: Proceedings of the Third International Seminar on Ancient Greek Cult, organized by the Swedish Institute at Athens, 16–18 October 1992.* Skrifter Utgivna av Svenska Institutet i Athen 8.14, ed. Robin Hägg, 141–151. Stockholm.

Pierris, Apostolos L. 1992. "Origin and Nature of Early Pythagorean Cosmogony." In *Pythagorean Philosophy*, ed. Konstantine J. Boudouris, 126–163. Athens.

———. 1996. *Περὶ τέλους: Φιλοσοφικὴ τετραλογία.* Patra.

Pikoulas, Yanis A. 2001. *Ἡ χώρα τῶν Πιέρων: Συμβολὴ στὴν τοπογραφία της.* Athens.

Pingiatoglou, Semeli. 2004. "Ἀφροδίτης ἄνοδοι." In *Θυμέλη: Μελέτες χαρισμένες στον καθηγητή Ν. Χ. Χουρμουζιάδη*, ed. Daniel Iakov and Eleni Papazoglou, 369–388. Herakleio.

Pirenne-Delforge, Vincianne. 1994. *L'Aphrodite grecque: Contribution à l'étude de ses cultes et de sa personnalité dans le panthéon archaïque et classique.* Kernos Supplément 4. Liège.

Pirenne-Delforge, Vincianne and Suárez de la Torre, E., eds. 2000. *Héros et héroïnes dans les mythes et les cultes grecs: Actes du Colloque organisé à l'Université de Valladolid, du 26 au 29 mai 1999.* Kernos Supplément 10. Liège.

Platon, Nicholaos. 1958. "Χρονικά, ἀνασκαφὴ Ἀσκληπιείου Λισσοῦ." *Κρητικὰ Χρονικά* 12:465–467.

Poccetti, Paolo. 1995. "Per un dossier documentario dei riflessi di dottrine misteriche e sapienziali nelle culture indigene dell'Italia antica: Note sulle iscrizioni Osche Ve 161, 185; Po 103." In *Forme di religiosità e tradizioni sapienziali in Magna Grecia: Atti del Convegno, Napoli 14-15 dicembre 1993.* Annali dell'Istituto Universitario Orientale di Napoli XVI (1994), ed. Albio C. Cassio and Paolo Poccetti, 109–136. Pisa and Rome.

———. 2000. "La diffusione di dottrine misteriche e sapienziali nelle culture indigene dell'Italia antica: Appunti per un dossier." In *Tra Orfeo e Pitagora: Origini e incontri di culture nell'antichità; Atti dei Seminari Napoletani 1996-1998,* ed. Marisa Tortorelli Ghidini et al., 91–126. Naples.

Politis, Nicholaos G. 1931. "Τὰ κατὰ τὴν τελευτήν." In *Λαογραφικὰ Σύμμεικτα.* Vol. 3. Δημοσιεύματα Λαογραφικοῦ Ἀρχείου 6, 323–365. Athens.

———. 1932. *Ἐκλογαὶ ἀπὸ τὰ τραγούδια τοῦ ἑλληνικοῦ λαοῦ.* 3rd ed. Athens.

Pologiorgi, Melpo. 1985. "Ἀπό το κλασικό και ελληνιστικό νεκροταφείο της Κυδωνίας." *Ἀρχαιολογικό Δελτίο Μελέτες* 40 A:162–177, plates 59–68.

Pontrandolfo, Angela. 1995. "Olinto e Corinto: Considerazioni sul rituale funerario." *La Parola del Passato* 50:483–508.

Pope, Maurice. 2003. "Perceptions of Crete: From Cadmus to Kadmos." *Cretan Studies* 8:217–227.

Postlethwaite, Norman. 1999. "The Death of Zeus Kretagenes." *Kernos* 12:85–98.

Poulaki-Pantermali, Eftychia. 1987. "Ἀνασκαφή Αγ. Δημητρίου Ολύμπου." *Το Ἀρχαιολογικό Ἔργο στη Μακεδονία και Θράκη* 1:201–208.

———. 1990. "Ὄλυμπος 3: μια παλιά ιστορία." *Οι αρχαιολόγοι μιλούν για την Πιερία, Καλοκαίρι* 1986, 84–95. Katerini.

Pratt, Louise H. 1993. *Lying and Poetry from Homer to Pindar: Falsehood and Deception in Archaic Greek Poetics.* Michigan Monographs in Classical Antiquity. Ann Arbor, MI.

Prent, Mieke. 2005. *Cretan Sanctuaries and Cults: Continuity and Change from Late Minoan IIIC to the Archaic Period*. Religions in the Graeco-Roman World 154. Leiden.

Price, Simon. 1999. *Religions of the Ancient Greeks*. Cambridge.

Psaropoulou, Betty. 1986. *Οι τελευταίοι τσουκαλάδες του ανατολικού Αιγαίου*. Nauplio.

Psaroudakis, Kyriakos. 1999–2000. "Διόνυσος και μέταλλα: Η σχέση θρησκείας, μαγείας και τεχνολογίας στην αρχαιότητα." *Αρχαιογνωσία* 10:179–207, plates 30–33.

Psilakis, Nikos. 2002. "Σκύλλις, Κληματίς, Σκυλλίτας Διόνυσος: επιβιώσεις σε αμπελουργικό οικισμό της Κρήτης." In *Οίνος παλαιός ηδύποτος: Το Κρητικό κρασί από τα προϊστορικά ως τα νεότερα χρόνια: Πρακτικά του Διεθνούς Επιστημονικού Συμποσίου, Κουνάβοι, Δήμος "Ν. Καζαντζάκης," 24–26 Απριλίου 1998*, ed. Aikaterini K. Mylopotamitaki. Herakleio.

Psychogiou, Eleni. 2003. "Μοιρολοΐστρες, νεκροί και σιτάρι: Αντιλήψεις για τη μεταθανάτια ζωή στις επιμνημόσυνες γυναικείες τελετουργίες." In *Θάνατος και εσχατολογικά οράματα, θρησκειοϊστορικές προοπτικές*, ed. Photis Terzakis, 364–403. Athens.

Pucci, Pietro. 1977. *Hesiod and the Language of Poetry*. Baltimore, MD and London.

Pugliese Carratelli, Giovanni. 1974. "Epimenide." *Antichità Cretesi: Studi in onore di Doro Levi*. Vol. 2:9–15. Catania.

———. 2001. *Le lamine d'oro orfiche: Istruzioni per il viaggio oltremondano degli iniziati greci*. Biblioteca Adelphi 419. Milan. (= 1993. *Le lamine d'oro 'orfiche': Istruzioni per il viaggio oltremondano degli iniziati greci*. Edizione e commento. Milan.)

Quinn, Jerome D. 1961. "Cape Phokas, Lesbos—Site of an Archaic Sanctuary for Zeus, Hera and Dionysus?" *American Journal of Archaeology* 65:391–393.

Rangos, Spiros. 2003. "Θάνατος και ψυχή από την Ιλιάδα στον Φαίδωνα: η 'ορφική μετάλλαξη'." In *Θάνατος και εσχατολογικά οράματα, θρησκειοϊστορικές προοπτικές*, ed. Photis Terzakis, 130–187. Athens.

Rauch, Marion. 1999. *Bacchische Themen und Nilbilder auf Campanarelleſs*. Rahden/Westf.

Redfield, James. 1991. "The Politics of Immortality." In *Orphisme et Orphée en l'honneur de Jean Rudhardt*. Recherchers et Rencontres, Publications de la Faculté des Lettres de Genève 3, ed. Philippe Borgeaud, 103–117. Geneva.

Reece, Steve. 1994. "The Cretan Odyssey: A Lie Truer than Truth." *American Journal of Philology* 115:157–173.

Rengakos, Antonios. 2006. *Το χαμόγελο του Αχιλλέα. Θέματα αφήγησης και ποιητικής στα ομηρικά έπη.* Prologue by Gregory Nagy. Athens.

Rhode, Erwin. 1987. *Psyche: The Cult of Souls and Belief in Immortality Among the Ancient Greeks.* Trans. W. B. Hillis. London 1925. Repr. Chicago.

Rhomiopoulou, Katerina. 1997. *Lefkadia, Ancient Mieza.* Athens.

———. 2006. "Nécropoles macédoniennes du littoral et de l'arrière-pays (pl. 39)." In *Rois, Cités, Nécropoles: Institutions, Rites et Monuments en Macédoine: Actes des Colloques de Nanterre (Décembre 2002) et d'Athènes (Janvier 2004).* Meletemata 45, ed. Anne Marie Guimier-Sorbets et al., 301–309. Athens.

Ricci, Serafino. 1893. "Miscellanea epigrafica (Atene, Keos, Amorgos, Melos, Thera, Creta)." *Monumenti antichi* 2:253–316.

Ricciardelli, Gabriella. 1992. "Le lamelle di Pelinna." *Studi e Materiali di Storia delle Religioni* 58:27–39.

———. 2000. "Mito e performance nelle associazioni dionisiache." In *Tra Orfeo e Pitagora: Origini e incontri di culture nell'antichità; Atti dei Seminari Napoletani 1996-1998,* ed. Marisa Tortorelli Ghidini et al., 265–283. Naples.

Richardson, Nicholas J. 1974. *The Homeric Hymn to Demeter.* Oxford.

———. 2005. *Ομήρου Ιλιάδα, κείμενο και ερμηνευτικό υπόμνημα.* Vol. Στ': Ραψωδίες Φ-Ω. Trans. Maria Nousia. Ed. Antonios Rengakos. Thessaloniki. (= 1993. *The Iliad: A Commentary.* Vol. VI: Books 21–24. Cambridge.)

Richter, Gisela M. A. 1946. "A Fourth-Century Bronze Hydria in New York." *American Journal of Archaeology* 50:361–367.

Riedweg, Christoph. 1987. *Mysterienterminologie bei Platon, Philon und Klemens von Alexandrien.* Untersuchungen zur antiken Literatur und Geschichte 26. Berlin and New York.

———. 1993. *Jüdisch-hellenistische Imitation eines orphischen Hieros Logos: Beobachtungen zu OF 245 und 247 (sog. Testament des Orpheus).* Classica Monacensia 7. Tübingen.

———. 1995. "Orphisches bei Empedokles." *Antike und Abendland* 41:34–59.

———. 1998. "Initiation – Tod – Unterwelt. Beobachtungen zur Kommunikationssituation und narrativen Technik der orphisch-bakchischen Goldblättschen." In *Ansichten griechischer Rituale: Geburstags-Symposium für Walter Burkert, Castelen bei Basel 15. bis 18. März 1996,* ed. Fritz Graf, 359–398. Stuttgart and Leipzig. (= forthcoming. "Initiation – Death – Underworld: Narrative and Ritual in the Gold Leaves." In *Further Along the Path: Recent Approaches to the 'Orphic' Gold Tablets,* ed. Radcliffe G. Edmonds III. Cambridge.)

———. 2002. "Poésie orphique et rituel initiatique: Éléments d'un 'Discours sacré' dans les lamelles d'or." *Revue de l'histoire des religions* 219:459–481.

———. 2005. *Pythagoras: His Life, Teaching, and Influence*. Trans. Steven Rendall et al. Ithaca, NY.

Rigsby, Kent J. 1996. *Asylia: Territorial Inviolability in the Hellenistic World*. Berkeley, CA and London.

Rinon, Yoav. 2006. "Tragic Hephaestus: The Humanized God in the *Iliad* and the *Odyssey*." *Phoenix* 60:1–20.

Rizakis, Athanassios and Touratsoglou, Ioannis P. 2000. "*Mors Macedonica*: Ὁ θάνατος στὰ ἐπιτάφια μνημεῖα τῆς Ἄνω Μακεδονίας." Ἀρχαιολογικὴ Ἐφημερίς 139:237–281.

Robertson, Noel D. 1990. "Some Recent Work in Greek Religion and Mythology." *Echos du Monde Classique* 34:419–442.

———. 1991. "Some Recent Work in Greek Religion and Mythology (continued)." *Echos du Monde Classique* 35:57–79.

———. 1998. "The Two Processions to Eleusis and the Program of the Mysteries." *American Journal of Philology* 119:547–575.

———. 2002. "The Religious Criterion in Greek Ethnicity: The Dorians and the Festival Carneia." *American Journal of Ancient History* NS 1.2:5–74.

———. 2003. "Orphic Mysteries and Dionysiac Ritual." In *Greek Mysteries: The Archaeology and Ritual of Ancient Greek Secret Cults*, ed. Michael B. Cosmopoulos, 218–240. London and New York.

Romm, James S. 1992. *The Edges of the Earth in Ancient Thought: Geography, Exploration, and Fiction*. Princeton, NJ.

Rosenberger, Veit. 2001. *Griechische Orakel: Ein Kulturgeschichte*. Darmstadt.

Ross, Shawn A. 2005. "Barbarophonos: Language and Panhellenism in the *Iliad*." *Classical Philology* 100:299–316.

Rossi, Laura. 1996. "Il testamento di Posidippo e le laminette auree di Pella." *Zeitschrift für Papyrologie und Epigraphik* 112:59–65.

———. 1999. "Lamentazioni su pietra e letteratura 'trenodica': Motivi topici dei canti funerari." *Zeitschrift für Papyrologie und Epigraphik* 126:29–42.

Roth, Paul. 1984. "Teiresias as Mantis and Intellectual in Euripides' *Bacchae*." *Transactions of the American Philological Association* 114:59–69.

RouECHÉ, Charlotte. 1989. *Aphrodisias in Late Antiquity: The Late Roman and Byzantine Inscriptions Including Texts from the Excavations at Aphrodisias conducted by Kenan T. Erim*. With contributions by Joyce M. Reynolds. Journal of Roman Studies Monographs 5. London.

Rudhardt, Jean. 1991. "Quelques réflexions sur les hymnes orphiques." In *Orphisme et Orphée en l'honneur de Jean Rudhardt*. Recherchers et Rencontres, Publications de la Faculté des Lettres de Genève 3, ed. Philippe Borgeaud, 263–288. Geneva.

————. 2002. "Les deux mères de Dionysos, Perséphone et Sémélé, dans les Hymnes orphiques." *Revue de l'histoire des religions* 219:483–501.

Ruotolo, Giuseppe. 2005. "Dionysos nella monetazione antica." *Invigilata Lucernis* 27:275–295.

Russo, Joseph, et al. 2005. *Ομήρου Οδύσσεια, κείμενο και ερμηνευτικό υπόμνημα.* Vol. Γ΄: Ραψωδίες Ρ–Ω. Trans. Philio Philippou. Ed. Antonios Rengakos. Thessaloniki. (= 1993. *A Commentary on Homer's Odyssey.* Vol. 3: Books XVII–XXIV. Oxford.)

Rusten, Jeffrey and Cunningham, Ian C., eds. 1993. *Theophrastus.* Vol. 6: *Theophrastus, Characters. Herodas, Mimes. Sophron and Other Mime Fragments.* 2nd ed. Loeb Classical Library. Cambridge, MA.

Rutherford, Ian. 2001. *Pindar's Paeans: A Reading of the Fragments with a Survey of the Genre.* Oxford.

Rutkowski, Bogdan. 1986. *The Cult Places of the Aegean.* New Haven, CT and London.

Sacco, Giulia. 2001. "ΓΗΣ ΠΑΙΣ ΗΜΙ. Sul v. 10 della laminetta di Hipponion." *Zeitschrift für Papyrologie und Epigraphik* 137:27–33, plates xii–xiv.

Sakellarakis, Jannis A. 1983. "Ἀνασκαφὴ Ἰδαίου Ἄντρου (παρένθ. πίν. ΙΖ΄ καὶ πίν. 252–282)." *Πρακτικὰ τῆς ἐν Ἀθήναις Ἀρχαιολογικῆς Ἑταιρείας* 1983 B:415–500.

————. 1988. "The Idaean Cave: Minoan and Greek Worship." *Kernos* 1:207–214.

————. 1988–89. "Ἰδαῖο Ἄντρο: ἡ Μινωικὴ καὶ ἡ Ἑλληνικὴ λατρεία." *Κρητικὰ Χρονικά* 28–29:22–27.

————. 1998. *Ἀρχαιολογικὲς ἀγωνίες στὴν Κρήτη τοῦ 19ου αἰώνα. 51 ἔγγραφα γιὰ τὶς κρητικὲς ἀρχαιότητες (1883–1898).* Herakleio.

————. 2006. "Με αφορμή κάποια λείψανα επίπλων στο Ιδαίο Άντρο." In *Ο Μυλοπόταμος από την Αρχαιότητα ως Σήμερα: Περιβάλλον, Αρχαιολογία, Ιστορία, Λαογραφία, Κοινωνιολογία: Πρακτικά Διεθνούς Συνεδρίου (Πάνορμο, 24–30 Οκτωβρίου 2003). Vol. 3: Αρχαίοι Χρόνοι. Ιδαίο Άντρο,* ed. Irene Gavrilaki and Yannis Tzifopoulos, 137–181. Rethymno.

Sakellarakis, Jannis A. and Panagiotopoulos, Diamantis. 2006. "Minoan Zominthos." In *Ο Μυλοπόταμος από την Αρχαιότητα ως Σήμερα: Περιβάλλον, Αρχαιολογία, Ιστορία, Λαογραφία, Κοινωνιολογία: Πρακτικά Διεθνούς Συνεδρίου (Πάνορμο, 24–30 Οκτωβρίου 2003). Vol. 2: Αρχαίοι Χρόνοι,* ed. Irene Gavrilaki and Yannis Tzifopoulos, 47–75. Rethymno.

Sakellarakis, Jannis A. and Sapouna-Sakellaraki, Efi. 1997. *Archanes: Minoan Crete in a New Light.* Athens.

Salskov Roberts, Helle. 2002. "Pots for the Living, Pots for the Dead. Were Pots Purpose-Made for the Funeral or Reused? Can Inscriptions Throw Light on the Problem?" In *Pots for the Living, Pots for the Dead*. Acta Hyperborea 9, ed. Annette Rathje, Marjatta Nielsen, and Bodil Bundgaard Rasmussen, 9–31. Copenhagen.

Santamaria Álvarez, Marco Antonio. 2006. "El Edén griego: Las Islas de los Bienaventurados, de Hesíodo a Platón." *Respublica Litterarum (Suplemento Monográfico Utopia)* 15:1–20. http://hdl.handle.net/10016/690.

Sapouna, Polina. 1998. *Die Bildlampen römischen Zeit aus der Idäischen Zeusgrotte auf Kreta*. BAR International Series 696. Oxford.

———. 2004. "Ταυροκαθάψια σε ρωμαϊκούς λύχνους. Μινωική παράδοση ή τυχαία αντιγραφή." In *Creta romana e protobizantina: Atti del congresso internazionale organizzato dalla Scuola Archeologica Italiana di Atene (Iraklion, 23-30 settembre 2000)*, ed. Antonino Di Vita, Monica Livadioti, and Ilaria Simiakaki, vol. 3.1:945–958. Padua.

Sarinaki, Maria. Forthcoming. *The Literary Cretan Goddess: Female Deities Associated with Crete in Literary Sources of the Archaic and Classical Period*. Ph.D. Dissertation, University of Texas at Austin.

Saunier, Guy. 1999. *Ἑλληνικά δημοτικά τραγούδια: Τὰ μοιρολόγια*. Athens.

SB. *Sammelbuch griechischer Urkunden aus Ägypten*. http://scriptorium.lib.duke.edu/papyrus/texts/clist.html.

Savvopoulou, Thomi. 1992. "Ο Β΄ ταφικός τύμβος της Τούμπας Παιονίας." *Το Αρχαιολογικό Έργο στη Μακεδονία και Θράκη* 6:425–431.

———. 1995. "Ευρωπός 1995." *Το Αρχαιολογικό Έργο στη Μακεδονία και Θράκη* 9:395–404.

Savvopoulou, Thomi, Giannakis, Giannis, and Niaouris, Giannis. 2000. "Προστασία και διαμόρφωση του αρχαιολογικού χώρου της Ευρωπού." *Το Αρχαιολογικό Έργο στη Μακεδονία και Θράκη* 14:291–298.

Scafuro, Adele. 2005. "The Crowning of Gods and Citizens in Fourth Century Athens." Paper delivered at the University of Crete, Rethymno, May 23, 2005.

Scanlon, Thomas F. 1999. "Women, Bull Sports, Cults, and Initiation in Minoan Crete." *Nikephoros* 12:33–70.

Scarpi, Paolo. 2001. "Il grande sonno di Epimenide: Ovvero vivere sulla linea di confine." In *Epimenide Cretese: Quaderni del Dipartimento di discipline storiche "E. Lepore," Università "Federico II,"* ed. Alfonso Mele et al., 25–35. Naples.

Schefer, Christina. 2000. "'Nur für Eingeweihte!' Heraklit und die Mysterien (Zu Fragment B1)." *Antike und Abendland* 46:46–75.

Scheinberg, Susan. 1979. "The Bee Maidens of the *Homeric Hymn to Hermes*." *Harvard Studies in Classical Philology* 83:1–28.

Schiering, Wolfgang, Müller, Walter, and Niemeier, Wolf-Dietrich. 1982. "Landbegebung in Rethymnon und Umgebung." *Archäologischer Anzeiger* 1982:15–54.

Schlesier, Renate. 1993. "Mixtures of Masks: Maenads as Tragic Models." In *Masks of Dionysus*, ed. Thomas H. Carpenter and Christopher A. Faraone, 89–114. Myth and Poetics. Ithaca, NY.

———. 1994. "Das Löwenjunge in der Milch: Zu Alkman, Fragment 56 P. [=125 Calame]." In *Orchestra: Drama, Mythos, Bühne*, ed. Anton F. H. Bierl and Peter Möllendorff, with Sabine Vogt, 19–29. Stuttgart and Leipzig.

Schmidt, Margot. 1991. "Bemerkungen zu Orpheus in Unterwelts- und Thrakerdarstellungen." In *Orphisme et Orphée en l'honneur de Jean Rudhardt*. Rechercers et Rencontres, Publications de la Faculté des Lettres de Genève 3, ed. Philippe Borgeaud, 31–50. Geneva.

———. 1996. "South Italian and Sicilian Vases." In *The Western Greeks: Classical Civilization in the Western Mediterranean*, ed. Giovanni Pugliese Carratelli, 443–456. London.

———. 2000. "Aufbruch oder Verharren in der Unterwelt? Nocmals zu den apulischen Vasenbildern mit Darstellungen des Hades." *Antike Kunst* 43:86–101.

Schröder, Stefan. 1999. "Zwei Überlegungen zu den Liedern vom Athener-schatzhaus in Delphi." *Zeitschrift für Papyrologie und Epigraphik* 128:65–75.

Schürmann, W. 1996. *Das Heiligtum des Hermes und der Aphrodite in Syme Viannou*. Vol. 2: *Die Tierstatuetten aus Metall*. Bibliothek der Archäologischen Gessellschaft zu Athen 159. Athens.

Scullion, Scott. 1994. "Olympian and Chthonian." *Classical Antiquity* 13:75–119.

———. 1998. "Dionysos and Katharsis in *Antigone*." *Classical Antiquity* 17:96–122.

———. 2000a. "Heroic and Chthonian Sacrifice: New Evidence from Selinous." *Zeitschrift für Papyrologie und Epigraphik* 132:163–171.

———. 2000b. "Tradition and Invention in Euripidean Aitiology." In *Euripides and Tragic Theatre in the Late Fifth Century*. Illinois Classical Studies 24–25, ed. Martin J. Cropp et al., 217–233. Urbana Champaign, IL.

———. 2001. "Dionysos at Elis." *Philologus* 145:203–218.

———. 2002. "'Nothing to Do with Dionysos': Tragedy Misconceived as Ritual." *Classical Quarterly* 52:102–137.

Scully, Stephen. 2003. "Reading the Shield of Achilles: Terror, Anger, Delight." *Harvard Studies in Classical Philology* 101:29–47.

Seaford, Richard. 1981. "Dionysiac Drama and the Dionysiac Mysteries." *Classical Quarterly* 31:252–275.

———. 1986. "Immortality, Salvation, and the Elements." *Harvard Studies in Classical Philology* 90:1–26.

———. 1993. "Dionysus as Destroyer of the Household: Homer, Tragedy, and the Polis." In *Masks of Dionysus*, ed. Thomas H. Carpenter and Christopher A. Faraone, 115–146. Myth and Poetics. Ithaca, NY.

———. 1994. "Sophokles and the Mysteries." *Hermes* 122:275–288.

———. 1996. *Euripides. Bacchae*. With an introduction, translation and commentary. Warminster.

———. 2003a. Ἀνταπόδοση καὶ τελετουργία: Ὁ Ὅμηρος καὶ ἡ τραγῳδία στὴν ἀναπτυσσόμενη πόλη-κράτος. Trans. Vayos Liapis. Athens. (= 1994. *Reciprocity and Ritual: Homer and Tragedy in the Developing City-State*. Oxford.)

———. 2003b. "Aeschylus and the Unity of Opposites." *Journal of Hellenic Studies* 123:141–163.

———. 2004a. *Money and the Early Greek Mind: Homer, Philosophy, Tragedy*. Cambridge.

———. 2004b. "Tragedy, Ritual, and Money." In *Greek Ritual Poetics*. Center for Hellenic Studies, Hellenic Studies Series 3, ed. Dimitrios Yatromanolakis and Panagiotis Roilos, 71–93. Washington, DC and Cambridge, MA.

———. 2005. "Mystic Light in Aeschylus' *Bassarai*." *Classical Quarterly* 55:602–606.

———. 2006. *Dionysos: Gods and Heroes of the Ancient World*. London and New York.

Seelinger, Robert A. 1998. "The Dionysiac Context of the Cult of Melikertes/Palaimon at the Isthmian Sanctuary of Poseidon." *Maia* 50:271–280.

SEG. *Supplementum Epigraphicum Graecum* 1–52 (1923–2002).

Segal, Charles. 1982. *Dionysiac Poetics and Euripides' Bacchae*. Princeton, NJ.

———. 1986. *Interpreting Greek Tragedy: Myth, Poetry, Text*. Ithaca, NY and London.

———. 1989. *Orpheus: The Myth of the Poet*. Baltimore, MD and London.

———. 1990. "Dionysos and the Gold Tablets from Pelinna." *Greek, Roman, and Byzantine Studies* 31:411–419.

Seremetakis, K. Nantia. 1994. Ἡ τελευταία λέξη στῆς Εὐρώπης τα ἄκρα: Δι-αίσθηση, θάνατος, γυναίκες. Athens.

Sharankov, Nicolay. 2001. "A Dedicatory Inscription from Odessos." *Zeitschrift für Papyrologie und Epigraphik* 137:174–178.

Sherratt, Susan. 1996. "With Us but Not of Us: The Role of Crete in Homeric Epic." In *Minotaur and Centaur: Studies in the Archaeology of Crete and Euboea Presented to Mervyn Popham*. BAR International Series 638, ed. Doniert Evely et al., 87–99. Oxford.

Shorey, Paul. 1937. Plato. Vol. 5: *The Republic. Books 1-5*. Rev. ed. Loeb Classical Library. Cambridge, MA.

Sider, David. 1997. "Heraclitus in the Derveni Papyrus." In *Studies on the Derveni Papyrus*, ed. André Laks and Glenn W. Most, 129–148. Oxford.

Sidiropoulos, Kleanthis. 2000. "Νομισματικά ευρήματα." In *Πρωτοβυζαντινή Ελεύθερνα Τομέας I*, vol. B, ed. Petros G. Themelis, 261–287. Rethymno.

———. 2004. "Χάλκινο νόμισμα μέσα 3ου αι. π.Χ., Χάλκινο νόμισμα 235–200 π.Χ." In *Ελεύθερνα, Πόλη - Ακρόπολη - Νεκρόπολη*, ed. Nicholas C. Stampolidis, 161 nos. 21–22. Athens.

———. 2006. "Ἀργύριον ἀξικόν: νομισματικές εκδόσεις και θησαυροί." In *Ο Μυλοπόταμος από την Αρχαιότητα ως Σήμερα: Περιβάλλον, Αρχαιολογία, Ιστορία, Λαογραφία, Κοινωνιολογία: Πρακτικά Διεθνούς Συνεδρίου (Πάνορμο, 24-30 Οκτωβρίου 2003)*. Vol. 4: *Ελεύθερνα - Αξός*, ed. Irene Gavrilaki and Yannis Tzifopoulos, 147–165. Rethymno.

Simms, Robert M. 1990. "Myesis, Telete, and Mysteria." *Greek, Roman, and Byzantine Studies* 31:183–195.

Sismanidis, Kostas L. 1997. *Κλίνες και κλινοειδείς κατασκευές των μακεδονικών τάφων. Δημοσιεύματα του Αρχαιολογικού Δελτίου* 58. Athens.

Sistakou, Evina. 2005. *Ἡ γεωγραφία τοῦ Καλλιμάχου καὶ ἡ νεωτερικὴ ποίηση τῶν ἑλληνιστικῶν χρόνων*. Athens.

Skafte Jensen, Minna. 2005. "Performance." In *A Companion to Ancient Epic*, ed. John M. Foley, 45–54. Oxford.

Skarlatidou, Eudokia. 2007. *Θέρμη: Το αρχαίο νεκροταφείο κάτω από τη σύγχρονη πόλη. Thermi: The Ancient Cemetery beneath the Modern Town*. Thessaloniki.

Skoulikas, Michaïl E. 2000. *Οι Κρήτες τοξότες: Από τα μινωικά χρόνια έως τον 17ο αι. μ.Χ.* Athens.

Skouteri-Didaskalou, Eleonora. 1997. "Το στίγμα της 'μαγείας': Περιδινήσεις ενός σημείου αναφοράς στην ανθρωπολογική θεωρία." In *Γλώσσα και Μαγεία: Κείμενα από την αρχαιότητα*, ed. Anastassios-Phoibos Christidis and David Jordan, 11–51. Athens.

Slatkin, Laura M. 2005. "Homer's *Odyssey*." In *A Companion to Ancient Epic*, ed. John M. Foley, 315–329. Oxford.

Small, David B., ed. 1994. *Methods in the Mediterranean: Historical and Archaeological Views on Texts and Archaeology*. Mnemosyne Supplement 135. Leiden.

SNG Kopenhagen. *Sylloge nummorum graecorum Kopenhagen: The Royal Collection of Coins and Medals*. Copenhagen.

Snodgrass, Anthony. 2000. "The Archaeology of the Hero." In *Oxford Readings in Greek Religion*, ed. Richard Buxton, 180–190. Oxford.

Sokolowski, Franciszek. 1962. *Lois sacrées de cités grecques. Supplément.* École française d'Athènes. Travaux et mémoires des anciens membres étrangers de l'École et de divers savants 11. Paris.

Sommerstein, Alan H. 1989. *Aeschylus Eumenides.* Cambridge.

———, ed. 1996. *The Comedies of Aristophanes.* Vol. 9: *Frogs*, with translation and notes. Warminster.

Somville, Pierre. 1992. "Le signe d'extase et la musique." *Kernos* 5:173–181.

Sonnabend, Holger. 2004. "Roman Rule and Cretan Identity: The Impact on Society and Culture." In *Creta romana e protobizantina: Atti del congresso internazionale organizzato dalla Scuola Archeologica Italiana di Atene (Iraklion, 23-30 settembre 2000)*, ed. Antonino Di Vita, Monica Livadioti, and Ilaria Simiakaki, vol. 1:25–28. Padua.

Sorel, Reynal. 2002. *Ορφέας και Ορφισμός.* Trans. Ilias Nikoloudis. Athens. (= 1994. *Orphée et l'Orphisme.* Paris.)

Soueref, Kostas. 2002. "Τούμπα Θεσσαλονίκης 2002: Το αρχαίο νεκροταφείο στην 'Αλάνα.'" *Το Αρχαιολογικό Έργο στη Μακεδονία και Θράκη* 16:277–289.

Sourvinou-Inwood, Christiane. 1987. "Myth as History: The Previous Owners of the Delphic Oracle." In *Interpretations of Greek Mythology*, ed. Jan N. Bremmer, 215–241. London and Sydney.

———. 1995. *Reading Greek Death to the End of the Classical Period.* Oxford.

———. 1997. "The Hesiodic Myth of the Five Races and the Tolerance of Plurality in Greek Mythology." In *Greek Offerings: Essays on Greek Art in Honour of John Boardman.* Oxbow Monograph 89, ed. Olga Palagia, 1–21. Oxford.

———. 2000a. "What is Polis Religion?" In *Oxford Readings in Greek Religion*, ed. Richard Buxton, 13–37. Oxford.

———. 2000b. "Further Aspects of Polis Religion." In *Oxford Readings in Greek Religion*, ed. Richard Buxton, 38–55. Oxford.

———. 2003. *Tragedy and Athenian Religion.* Greek Studies: Interdisciplinary Approaches. Lanham, MD.

———. 2004. "Gendering the Athenian Funeral: Ritual Reality and Tragic Manipulations." In *Greek Ritual Poetics.* Center for Hellenic Studies, Hellenic Studies Series 3, ed. Dimitrios Yatromanolakis and Panagiotis Roilos, 161–188. Washington, DC and Cambridge, MA.

———. 2005. *Hylas, the Nymphs, Dionysos and Others: Myth, Ritual, Ethnicity.* Skrifter Utgivna av Svenska Institutet i Athen 8.19. Stockholm.

Sporn, Katja. 2001. "Auf den Spuren der kretischen Diktynna." In *IΘΑΚΗ: Festschrift für Jörg Schäfer zum 75. Geburtstag am 25. April 2001*, ed. Stephanie Böhm and Klaus-Valtin von Eickstedt, 225–233. Würzburg.

———. 2002. *Heiligtümer und Kulte Kretas in klassischer und hellenistischer Zeit*. Studien zur Antiken Heiligtümern 3. Heidelberg.

———. 2004. "Pan- und Nymphenreliefs auf Kreta." In *Creta romana e protobizantina: Atti del congresso internazionale organizzato dalla Scuola Archeologica Italiana di Atene (Iraklion, 23-30 settembre 2000)*, ed. Antonino Di Vita, Monica Livadioti, and Ilaria Simiakaki, vol. 3.2:1103–1119. Padua.

———. 2006. "Πήλινα ειδώλια από τη Δροσιά Μυλοποτάμου." In *Ο Μυλοπόταμος από την Αρχαιότητα ως Σήμερα: Περιβάλλον, Αρχαιολογία, Ιστορία, Λαογραφία, Κοινωνιολογία: Πρακτικά Διεθνούς Συνεδρίου (Πάνορμο, 24-30 Οκτωβρίου 2003)*. Vol. 4: *Ελεύθερνα - Αξός*, ed. Irene Gavrilaki and Yannis Tzifopoulos, 205–226. Rethymno.

Spyridakis, Georgios K. 1941-1942. "Ἐξορκισμοὶ καὶ μαγικοὶ κατάδεσμοι ἐκ κρητικῶν χειρογράφων." Ἐπετηρὶς τοῦ Λαογραφικοῦ Ἀρχείου 3–4:60–76.

Stampolidis, Nicholas C. 1987. *Ο βωμός του Διονύσου στην Κω*. Δημοσιεύματα του Αρχαιολογικού Δελτίου 34. Athens.

———. 1993. *Ελεύθερνα, Τομέας III, 1: Γεωμετρικά - αρχαϊκά χρόνια και Οδηγός στην Έκθεση "Το γεωμετρικό-αρχαϊκό νεκροταφείο της Ορθής Πέτρας."* Rethymno.

———. 1994. *Ελεύθερνα: Από τη γεωμετρική και αρχαϊκή νεκρόπολη. Ταφικές πυρές και ομηρικά έπη*. Rethymno.

———. 1996a. *Ἀντίποινα, 'Reprisals': Contribution to the Study of Customs of the Geometric-Archaic Period*. Rethymno.

———. 1996b. "Μια υπόθεση εργασίας." *Ariadne* 8:65–69.

———. 1998a. "Εισαγωγή 11ος-6ος αι. π.Χ." In *Ανατολική Μεσόγειος: Κύπρος - Δωδεκάνησα - Κρήτη, 16ος-6ος αι. π.Χ. Αρχαιολογικό Μουσείο Ηρακλείου, Μάρτιος-Ιούνιος 1998*, ed. Nicholas C. Stampolidis and Alexandra Karetsou, 102–134. Herakleio.

———. 1998b. "Imports and Amalgamata: The Eleutherna Experience." In *Eastern Mediterranean: Cyprus - Dodecanese - Crete, 16th-6th cent. B.C.; Proceedings of the International Symposium held at Rethymnon, Crete in May 1997*, ed. Vassos Karageorghis and Nicholas C. Stampolidis, 175–185. Athens.

———. 2001. "Οι ταφικές πυρές στην αρχαία Ελεύθερνα: Αφορμή για επανεξέταση." In *Οι καύσεις στην Εποχή του Χαλκού και την Πρώιμη Εποχή του Σιδήρου: Πρακτικά του Συμποσίου, Ρόδος, 29 Απριλίου-2 Μαΐου 1999*, ed. Nicholas C. Stampolidis, 187–199. Athens.

———. 2003a. "On the Phoenician Presence in the Aegean." In *ΠΛΟΕΣ, Sea Routes: Interconnections in the Mediterranean, 16th-6th c. B.C.; Proceedings of the International Symposium held at Rethymnon, Crete in September 29th-October 2nd 2002*, ed. Nicholas C. Stampolidis and Vassos Karageorghis, 217-232. Athens.

———. 2003b. "Μια περιληπτική ματιά στη Μεσόγειο της Πρώιμης Εποχής του Σιδήρου (11ος-6ος αι. π.Χ.)". In *Πλόες... Από τη Σιδώνα στη Χουέλβα. Σχέσεις λαών της Μεσογείου, 16ος-6ος αι. π.Χ. Κατάλογος της ΄Εκθεσης*, ed. Nicholas C. Stampolidis, 41-79. Athens.

———, ed. 2003c. *Πλόες... Από τη Σιδώνα στη Χουέλβα: Σχέσεις λαών της Μεσογείου, 16ος-6ος αι. π.Χ. Κατάλογος της ΄Εκθεσης*. Athens.

———. 2004a. "Ελεύθερνα. Η θέση: Η νεότερη έρευνα," "Η πόλη: δυτικός ανασκαφικός τομέας III," "Οι νεκροπόλεις." In *Ελεύθερνα, Πόλη - Ακρόπολη - Νεκρόπολη*, ed. Nicholas C. Stampolidis, 18-25, 82-103, 116-143. Athens.

———. 2004b. "Κατάλογος αντικειμένων αριθμοί: 24, 25, 26, 250, 251, 252, 253, 257." In *Ελεύθερνα, Πόλη - Ακρόπολη - Νεκρόπολη*, ed. Nicholas C. Stampolidis, 161-162, 234-236, 238. Athens.

———. 2004c. "Ελεύθερνα: Πρώιμη Εποχή του Σιδήρου." In *Το Αιγαίο στην Πρώιμη Εποχή του Σιδήρου: Πρακτικά του Διεθνούς Συμποσίου, Ρόδος, 1-4 Νοεμβρίου 2002*, ed. Nicholas C. Stampolidis and Angeliki Giannikouri, 51-75. Athens.

———. 2004d. "Ελεύθερνα: Ιστορικές και ετυμολογικές επισημάνσεις." *Eleftherna (Scientific Yearbook of the Department of Psychology, University of Crete)* 1:29-31.

———. 2006. "Herodotean locus and Eleuthernian locus." In *Ο Μυλοπόταμος από την Αρχαιότητα ως Σήμερα: Περιβάλλον, Αρχαιολογία, Ιστορία, Λαογραφία, Κοινωνιολογία: Πρακτικά Διεθνούς Συνεδρίου (Πάνορμο, 24-30 Οκτωβρίου 2003)*. Vol. 4: *Ελεύθερνα - Αξός*, ed. Irene Gavrilaki and Yannis Tzifopoulos, 53-67. Rethymno.

Stampolidis, Nicholas C. and Karageorghis, Vassos, eds. 2003. *ΠΛΟΕΣ, Sea Routes: Interconnections in the Mediterranean, 16th-6th c. B.C.; Proceedings of the International Symposium held at Rethymnon, Crete in September 29th-October 2nd 2002*. Athens.

Stampolidis, Nicholas C. and Karetsou, Alexandra, eds. 1998. *Ανατολική Μεσόγειος: Κύπρος - Δωδεκάνησα - Κρήτη, 16ος - 6ος αι. π.Χ., Αρχαιολογικό Μουσείο Ηρακλείου, Μάρτιος-Ιούνιος 1998*. Herakleio.

Stanley, D. Keith. 1993. *The Shield of Homer: Narrative Structure in the Iliad*. Princeton, NJ.

Stansbury-O'Donnell, Mark D. 1999. *Pictorial Narrative in Ancient Greek Art.* Cambridge.

Stavrianopoulou, Eftychia. 1991. "Ἡμερολόγιο θυσιῶν τῆς Ἐλεύθερνας." In *Ἐλεύθερνα, Τομέας II.* Vol. 1: *Ἐπιγραφές από το Πυργί και το Νησί,* ed. Henri van Effenterre et al., 31–50. Rethymno.

——. 1993. "Der ΜΑΤΕΡΕΣ-Kult in Eleutherna und der ΜΗΤΕΡΕΣ-kult in Engyon." *La Parola del Passato* 48:161–175.

Stefanakis, Manolis I. 1998. "A Mid-Fourth Century BC Alliance Coinage on Crete? The Case of Kytaion Reassessed." In *Post-Minoan Crete: Proceedings of the First Colloquium on Post-Minoan Crete Held by the British School at Athens and the Institute of Archaeology, University College London, 10–11 November 1995.* British School at Athens Studies 2, ed. William G. Cavanaugh and Mike Curtis, with J. Nicolas Coldstream and Alan W. Johnston, 96–104. Athens.

Steinbichler, Walter. 1995. "Meriones, der ποιμὴν Κρητῶν, als Ἰδομενέως θεράπων. Zu AP 12, 97 (Antipatros von Sidon) und 12, 247 (Straton von Sardes)." *Quaderni Urbinati di Cultura Classica* 49:81–90.

Stevens, Susan T. 1991. "Charon's Obol and Other Coins in Ancient Funerary Practice." *Phoenix* 45:215–229.

Stewart, Andrew. 1982. "Dionysos at Delphi: The Pediments of the Sixth Temple of Apollo and Religious Reform in the Age of Alexander." In *Macedonia and Greece in Late Classical and Hellenistic Times.* Studies in the History of Art 10, ed. Beryl Barr-Sharrar and Eugene N. Borza, 204–227. Washington, DC.

Stibbe, Conrad M. 1991. "Dionysos in Sparta." *Belletin Antieke Beschaving* 66:1–44.

Strataridaki, Anna. 1988. *The Historians of Ancient Crete: A Study in Regional Historiography.* Ph.D. Dissertation, University of California at Davis. Ann Arbor, MI.

——. 1988–1989. "The Historians of Ancient Crete: A Study in Regional Historiography." *Κρητικά Χρονικά* 28–29:137–193.

——. 1991. "Epimenides of Crete: Some Notes on His Life, Works, and the Verse 'Κρῆτες ἀεὶ ψεῦσται'." *Fortunatae* 2:207–223.

——. 1998. "Theopompus of Chios, Epimenides, and Einstein's Theory of Relativity." *La Parola del Passato* 53:352–358.

——. 2003. "Epimenides: What is in a Name?" *Cretan Studies* 8:189–198.

Stroumsa, Guy. Forthcoming. "The Afterlife of Orphism: Jewish, Christian and Gnostic Perspectives." In *Ritual Texts for the Afterlife: A Gold Tablets*

Conference at the Ohio State University, April 28–30, 2006, ed. Fritz Graf and Sarah Iles Johnston.

Strubbe, Johan H. M. 1991. "Cursed be He that Moves my Bones." In *Magika Hiera: Ancient Greek Magic and Religion*, ed. Christopher A. Faraone and Dirk Obbink, 33–59. New York.

———. 1997. *APAI ΕΠΙΤΥΜΒΙΟΙ: Imprecations Against Desecrators of the Grave in the Greek Epitaphs of Asia Minor; A Catalogue.* Inschriften griechischer Städte aus Kleinasien 52. Bonn.

Suárez de la Torre, Emilio. 2002. "La 'rationalité' des mythes de Delphes: Les dieux, les héros, les médiateurs." *Kernos* 15:155–178.

Suter, Ann. 2002. *The Narcissus and the Pomegranate: An Archaeology of the Homeric Hymn to Demeter.* Ann Arbor, MI.

Svenbro, Jesper. 1992. "'Ton luth, a quoi bon?' La lyre et la pierre tombale dans la pensée grecque." *Métis* 7:135–160.

———. 2002. *Φρασίκλεια: Ανθρωπολογία της ανάγνωσης στην ἀρχαία Ἑλλάδα.* Trans. Stephanos Oikonomou. Athens. (= 1993. *Phrasikleia: An Anthropology of Reading in Ancient Greece.* Trans. Janet Lloyd. Myth and Poetics. Ithaca, NY.)

Svoronos, Joannes N. 1890. *Numismatique de la Crète ancienne, accompagnée de l'histoire, la géographie et la mythologie de l'ile.* Vol. 1: *Description de monnaies: Histoire et géographie.* Macon.

Sweetman, Rebecca. 2004. "The Mosaics of Roman and Early Christian Knossos: Interpreting their Contexts and Workshop Production." In *Creta romana e protobizantina: Atti del congresso internazionale organizzato dalla Scuola Archeologica Italiana di Atene (Iraklion, 23–30 settembre 2000)*, ed. Antonino Di Vita, Monica Livadioti, and Ilaria Simiakaki, vol. 3.2:1173–1185. Padua.

Swindler, Mary H. 1913. *Cretan Elements in the Cults and Ritual of Apollo.* Ph.D. Dissertation, Bryn Mawr College. Bryn Mawr College Monographs 13. Bryn Mawr, PA.

Sygkollitis, Spiros. 1934. "Ὁ νεκρὸς εἰς τὴν Ἀνασελίτσα." *Λαογραφία* 11:387–414.

Tataki, Argyro B. 1988. *Ancient Beroea Prosopography and Society.* Meletemata 8. Athens.

———. 1998. *Macedonians Abroad: A Contribution to the Prosopography of Ancient Macedonia.* Meletemata 26. Athens.

Tegou, Eva. 1998. "Νομός Ρεθύμνης, Επαρχία Ρεθύμνης, Χαμαλεύρι, θέση Γρολάδες (αγρός N. Αγαθάγγελου)." *Αρχαιολογικό Δελτίο Χρονικά* 53 B3:873.

———. 2002. "Αρχαιολογικές ειδήσεις. Νομός Ρεθύμνης, Επαρχία Ρεθύμνης, Χαμαλεύρι, αγρός Νικ. Αγαθάγγελου." *Κρητική Εστία* 9:275.

———. 2004. "Κατάλογος αντικειμένων αριθμοί: 1, 2, 8." In *Ελεύθερνα, Πόλη - Ακρόπολη - Νεκρόπολη*, ed. Nicholas C. Stampolidis, 147, 151. Athens.

———. 2006. "Ένα ιερό ιστορικών χρόνων στη θέση Γερακάρω της Αξού." In *Ο Μυλοπόταμος από την Αρχαιότητα ως Σήμερα: Περιβάλλον, Αρχαιολογία, Ιστορία, Λαογραφία, Κοινωνιολογία: Πρακτικά Διεθνούς Συνεδρίου (Πάνορμο, 24-30 Οκτωβρίου 2003)*. Vol. 4: *Ελεύθερνα - Αξός*, ed. Irene Gavrilaki and Yannis Tzifopoulos, 275-293. Rethymno.

Teodorsson, Sven-Tage. 2006. "Eastern Literacy, Greek Alphabet, and Homer." *Mnemosyne* 59:161-187.

Terzakis, Fotis. 1997. *Μελέτες γιὰ τὸ ιερό*. Athens.

Tessier, Andrea. 1987. "La struttura metrica della laminetta di Hipponion: Rassegna di interpretazioni." *Museum Patavinum* 5:232-241.

Themelis, Petros G. 1989-1990. "Αρχαιολογικές ειδήσεις 1988, Νομός Ρεθύμνης, Επαρχία Μυλοποτάμου, Ελεύθερνα." *Κρητική Εστία* 3:266-270.

———. 1994. "Ὁ τάφος τῆς Ἠλείας Φιλημήνας." In *Γ' Ἐπιστημονικὴ Συνάντηση γιὰ τὴν Ἑλληνιστικὴ Κεραμική: Χρονολογημένα σύνολα - ἐργαστήρια, 24-27 Σεπτεμβρίου 1991, Θεσσαλονίκη: Κείμενα, Πίνακες*. Βιβλιοθήκη τῆς ἐν Ἀθήναις Ἀρχαιολογικῆς Ἑταιρείας 137, 146-158, plates 75-88. Athens.

———, ed. 2000a. *Πρωτοβυζαντινή Ελεύθερνα Τομέας I*. Vol. 2. Athens.

———. 2000b. *Ἥρωες καὶ ἡρῶα στὴ Μεσσήνη: Βιβλιοθήκη τῆς ἐν Ἀθήναις Ἀρχαιολογικῆς Ἑταιρείας 210*. Athens.

———. 2002. *Αρχαία Ελεύθερνα, Ανατολικός Τομέας*. Athens.

———. 2004a. "Η πόλη: Ανατολικός ανασκαφικός τομέας I." In *Ελεύθερνα, Πόλη - Ακρόπολη - Νεκρόπολη*, ed. Nicholas C. Stampolidis, 46-80. Athens.

———. 2004b. "Κατάλογος αντικειμένων αριθμοί: 71, 72, 77, 78, 81, 86, 87, 88, 162, 163, 164, 191, 219, 224, 246, 248, 411." In *Ελεύθερνα, Πόλη - Ακρόπολη - Νεκρόπολη*, ed. Nicholas C. Stampolidis, 178-180, 182-187, 210, 218, 224-225, 230-232, 300. Athens.

———. 2004c. "Υστερορωμαϊκή-πρωτοβυζαντινή Ελεύθερνα, Τομέας I." In *Creta romana e protobizantina: Atti del congresso internazionale organizzato dalla Scuola Archeologica Italiana di Atene (Iraklion, 23-30 settembre 2000)*, ed. Antonino Di Vita, Monica Livadioti, and Ilaria Simiakaki, vol. 2:445-458. Padua.

———. 2006. "Γλυπτά από την Ελεύθερνα." In *Ο Μυλοπόταμος από την Αρχαιότητα ως Σήμερα: Περιβάλλον, Αρχαιολογία, Ιστορία, Λαογραφία, Κοινωνιολογία: Πρακτικά Διεθνούς Συνεδρίου (Πάνορμο, 24-30 Οκτωβρίου 2003)*. Vol. 4:

Ελεύθερνα - Αξός, ed. Irene Gavrilaki and Yannis Tzifopoulos, 11–51. Rethymno.

Themelis, Petros G. and Matthaiou, Angelos P. 2004. "Ενεπίγραφη αετωματική στήλη, 3ος αι. π.Χ." In *Ελεύθερνα, Πόλη - Ακρόπολη - Νεκρόπολη*, ed. Nicholas C. Stampolidis, 156 no. 12. Athens.

Themelis, Petros G. and Touratsoglou, Ioannis P. 1997. *Οι τάφοι του Δερβενίου*. Δημοσιεύματα του Αρχαιολογικού Δελτίου 59. Athens.

Theochari, Maria D. 2003. "Κατάλογος αντικειμένων αριθμοί: 146 (χρυσά φύλλα), 196 (χρυσά τρίλοβα φύλλα)." In *Η πόλη κάτω από την πόλη: Ευρήματα από τις ανασκαφές του Μητροπολιτικού Σιδηροδρόμου των Αθηνών, Φεβρουάριος 2000 -Δεκέμβριος 2001*. 2nd ed., ed. Liana Parlama and Nicholas C. Stampolidis, 220–221. Athens.

Theodossiev, Nikola. 1994-1995. "Semantic Notes on the Theonyms Orpheus, Sabazios, and Salmoxis." *Beiträge zur Namenforschung* 29–30:241–246.

———. 1995. "The Sacred Mountain of the Ancient Thracians." *Thracia* 11:371–384.

———. 1996. "Cult Clay Figurines in Ancient Thrace: Archaeological Evidence for the Existence of Thracian Orphism." *Kernos* 9:220–226.

———. 1997. "Further Notes on the Mountain Theonyms (Orpheus, Dionysos, Salmoxis, etc.)." *Beiträge zur Namenforschung* 32:409–416.

———. 2002. "Mountain Goddesses in Ancient Thrace: The Broader Context." *Kernos* 15:325–329.

Thomson, George. 1999. "Τὸ πρόβλημα τῶν ʽΒακχῶνʼ." In *Τὸ ἀειθαλὲς δέντρο: Διαλέξεις καὶ ἄρθρα γιὰ τὸν ἑλληνικὸ πολιτισμό*, ed. with introduction Christos Alexiou, 135–155. Athens.

Threatte, Leslie. 1980. *The Grammar of Attic Inscriptions*. Vol. 1: *Phonology*. Berlin.

Tiverios, Michalis. 1985. *Μία "κρίσις τῶν ὅπλων" τοῦ ζωγράφου τοῦ Συλέα: Παρατηρήσεις σὲ ἑρμηνευτικὰ θέματα καὶ στὶς σχέσεις εἰκονογραφίας καὶ πολιτικῆς κατὰ τὴν Υστεροαρχαϊκὴ καὶ Πρώιμη Κλασικὴ Περίοδο*. Athens.

———. 2004. "Αισχύλος και Ελευσίνια Μυστήρια." In *Θυμέλη: Μελέτες χαρισμένες στον καθηγητή Ν. Χ. Χουρμουζιάδη*, ed. Daniel Iakov and Eleni Papazoglou, 405–426. Herakleio.

Torjussen, Stian. 2005. "Phanes and Dionysos in the Derveni Theogony." *Symbolae Osloenses* 80:7–22.

Torraca, Luigi. 1995. "Le più antiche testimonianze letterarie." *La Parola del Passato* 50:414–424.

Tortorelli Ghidini, Marisa. 1992. "Sul v. 4 della laminetta di Hipponion: ψύχονται ο ψυχοῦνται?" *La Parola del Passato* 47:177–181.

———. 1995a. "Lettere d'oro per l'Ade." *La Parola del Passato* 50:468–482.

———. 1995b. "Visioni escatologiche in Magna Grecia." In *Forme di religiosità e tradizioni sapienziali in Magna Grecia: Atti del Convegno, Napoli 14-15 dicembre 1993.* Annali dell'Istituto Universitario Orientale di Napoli XVI (1994), ed. Albio C. Cassio and Paolo Poccetti, 207–217. Pisa and Rome.

———. 2000a. "Da Orfeo gli Orfici." In *Tra Orfeo e Pitagora: Origini e incontri di culture nell'antichità; Atti dei Seminari Napoletani 1996-1998,* ed. Marisa Tortorelli Ghidini et al., 11–41. Naples.

———. 2000b. "I giocattolo di Dioniso tra mito e rituale." In *Tra Orfeo e Pitagora: Origini e incontri di culture nell'antichità; Atti dei Seminari Napoletani 1996-1998,* ed. Marisa Tortorelli Ghidini et al., 255–263. Naples.

———. 2001. "Epimenide a Creta: Tra biografia e teogonia." In *Epimenide Cretese: Quaderni del Dipartimento di discipline storiche "E. Lepore," Università "Federico II,"* ed. Alfonso Mele et al., 53–76. Naples.

Tracy, Stephen V. 1975. *The Lettering of an Athenian Mason.* Hesperia Supplement 15. Princeton, NJ.

———. 1982. *IG II² 2336: Contributors of First Fruits for the Pythaïs.* Beiträge zur klassischen Philologie 15. Meisenheim am Glan.

———. 1990a. *Attic Letter-Cutters of 229 to 86 B.C.* Hellenistic Culture and Society 6. Berkeley, CA and London.

———. 1990b. *The Story of the Odyssey.* Princeton, NJ.

———. 1995. *Athenian Democracy in Transition: Attic Letter-Cutters of 340 to 290 B.C.* Hellenistic Culture and Society 20. Berkeley, CA and London.

———. 2003. *Athens and Macedon: Attic Letter-Cutters of 300 to 229 B.C.* Hellenistic Culture and Society 38. Berkeley, CA and London.

Trendall, Arthur D. and Cambitoglou, Alexander. 1992. *Second Supplement to the Red-Figured Vases of Apulia,* Part III: *Post-Script.* Bulletin of the Institute of Classical Studies 60. London.

Trümpy, Catherine. 1997. *Untersuchungen zu den altgriechischen Monatsnamen und Monatsfolgen.* Bibliothek der klassischen Altertumswissenschaften 98. Heidelberg.

———. 2004. "Die Thesmophoria, Brimo, Deo und das Anaktoron: Beobachtungen zur Vorgeschichte des Demeterkults." *Kernos* 17:13–42.

Tsagalis, Christos C. 2002. "Ανδρομάχη μαινομένη: Το διονυσιακό στοιχείο στην Ιλιάδα." *Ελληνικά* 52:199–225.

———. 2006. "Ποίηση και ποιητική στην Θεογονία και στα Έργα και Ημέραι." In *Μουσάων αρχώμεθα: Ο Ησίοδος και η αρχαϊκή επική ποίηση,* ed. Nicholaos P. Bezantakos and Christos K. Tsagalis, with an introduction by Glenn W. Most, 139–255. Athens.

Tsagarakis, Odysseas. 1989. "Ἑκατόμπολις Κρήτη." *Ariadne (Ἀφιέρωμα στὸν Στυλιανὸ Ἀλεξίου)* 5:79–83.

———. 1995a. "*Odyssey* 11: The Question of the Sources." In *Homer's World*. Papers from the Norwegian Institute at Athens 3, ed. Øivind Anderson and Matthew Dickie, 123–131. Bergen.

———. 1995b. "The Two Views of the Afterlife." *Εὐχὴν Ὀδυσσεῖ: Πρακτικά του Ζ΄ Συνεδρίου για την Οδύσσεια (3-8 Σεπτεμβρίου 1993)*, 275–285. Ithaca.

———. 1997. "Το θεματικό μοτίβο της κατάβασης στην *Οδύσσεια*: Προέλευση, πηγές." In *Acta of the First Panhellenic and International Conference on Ancient Greek Literature (23-26 May 1994)*. International Centre for Humanistic Research Studies and Researches 38, ed. John-Th. A. Papademetriou, 29–43. Athens.

———. 2000. *Studies in Odyssey 11*. Hermes Einzelschriften 82. Stuttgart.

———. 2001. "Η λογοτεχνία στη δωρική Κρήτη και ο ευρωπαϊκός προσανατο-λισμός της." *Πρακτικά του Α΄ Διεθνούς Επιστημονικού Συνεδρίου "Κρήτη και Ευρώπη: Συγκρίσεις, Συγκλίσεις και Αποκλίσεις στη Λογοτεχνία," Βαρβάροι, 30 Ιουνίου έως 2 Ιουλίου 2000*, 1–8. Barbaroi.

———. 2006. "Η ποίηση στη μινωική Κρήτη." In *Πεπραγμένα του Θ΄ Διεθνούς Κρητολογικού Συνεδρίου (Ελούντα, 1-6 Οκτωβρίου 2001)*. Vol. A4, ed. Theocharis Detorakis and Alexis Kalokairinos, 245–253. Herakleio.

Tsantsanoglou, Kyriakos. 1997. "The First Columns of the Derveni Papyrus and their Religious Significance." In *Studies on the Derveni Papyrus*, ed. André Laks and Glenn W. Most, 93–128. Oxford.

Tsantsanoglou, Kyriakos and Parássoglou, Giorgos M. 1987. "Two Gold Lamellae from Thessaly." *Hellenika* 38:3–16.

Tsatsaki, Niki. 2004. "Κεραμική από ελληνιστικούς τάφους στο Σφακάκι και στον Σταυρωμένο Ρεθύμνου." *ΣΤ΄ Επιστημονική Συνάντηση για την Ελληνιστική Κεραμική: Προβλήματα χρονολόγησης, κλειστά σύνολα, εργαστήρια, Βόλος, 17-23 Απριλίου 2000*, 739–750 plates 343–346. Athens.

Tsigarida, Elissavet-Bettina. 1999. "Παρατηρήσεις πάνω στα μετάλλινα στεφάνια της Μακεδονίας." *Ancient Macedonia V: Papers read at the Fifth International Symposium held in Thessaloniki, October 10-15, 1989 (Manolis Andronikos in Memoriam)*. Vol. 3. Institute for Balkan Studies 240, 1631–1643. Thessaloniki.

Tsimbidou-Avloniti, Maria. 1992. "Ταφικός τύμβος στον Αγ. Αθανάσιο Θεσσαλονίκης: Νέα ανασκαφικά στοιχεία." *Το Αρχαιολογικό Έργο στη Μακεδονία και Θράκη* 6:369–382.

———. 2000. "'Λάρνακ' ἐς ἀργυρέην ...' (Ιλ. Σ, 413)." In *Μύρτος: Μνήμη Ιουλίας Βοκοτοπούλου*, ed. Polyxeni Adam-Veleni, 543–575. Thessaloniki.

———. 2006. "La tombe macédonienne d'Hagios Athanasios près de Thessalonique (pl. 63–65)." In *Rois, Cités, Nécropoles: Institutions, Rites et Monuments en Macédoine; Actes des Colloques de Nanterre (Décembre 2002) et d'Athènes (Janvier 2004)*. Meletemata 45, ed. Anne Marie Guimier-Sorbets et al., 321–331. Athens.

Tsirivakos, Ilias K. 1965. "Ἤπειρος, Νομὸς Θεσπρωτίας, ἀνασκαφὴ ἐν Ἀμβρακίᾳ." *Ἀρχαιολογικὸν Δελτίον* 20 Β:355–360, plates 422–426.

Tsochos, Haralambos. 2002. "Το ιερό των Αιγυπτίων θεών και η λατρεία τους στους Φιλίππους μέσα από το επιγραφικό υλικό." *Το Αρχαιολογικό Έργο στη Μακεδονία και Θράκη* 16:83–94.

Tsouderos, Giannis E. 2002. "Θάνατος, Χάρος Ἄδης, Απάνω και Κάτω Κόσμος, μαύρη γης στην παλιά Κρητική μαντινάδα." In *Πεπραγμένα Συνεδρίου "Η Κρητική Μαντινάδα" (Κουνουπιδιανά Ακρωτηρίου, 4–5 Αυγούστου 2001)*, ed. Kostas Moutzouris, 269–286. Akrotiri Chanion.

Tsougarakis, Dimitris. 1987. "Ἡ Βυζαντινὴ Κρήτη." In *Κρήτη Ἱστορία καὶ Πολιτισμός*, vol. 1, ed. Nicholaos M. Panagiotakis, 339–404. Herakleio.

———. 1988. *Byzantine Crete: From the 5th Century to the Venetian Conquest.* Athens.

Tzedakis, Yannis. 1979. "Εφορεία Προϊστορικών και Κλασικών Αρχαιοτήτων Χανίων: Καστέλλι Κισάμου, οικόπεδο Καλογριδάκη." *Αρχαιολογικό Δελτίο* 34:394.

Tzedakis, Yannis, Hallager, Eric, and Andreadaki-Vlazaki, Maria. 1989–1991. "Αρχαιολογικές ειδήσεις 1992–1994: Νομός Χανίων, Επαρχία Κυδωνίας, πόλη Χανίων, Μινωικός και Κλασικός οικισμός, λόφος Καστέλλι." *Κρητική Εστία* 4:199–202, plate 1.

Tzifopoulos, Yannis Z. 1998a. "*Hemerodromoi* and Cretan *Dromeis*: Athletes or Military Personnel? The Case of the Cretan Philonides." *Nikephoros* 11:137–170.

———. 1998b. "Ο 'Ορφισμός' στην Κρήτη." *Θαλλώ* 10:81–96.

———. 1999. "Παρατηρήσεις σὲ τέσσερις ἐπιγραφές σπηλαίων τοῦ Νομοῦ Ρεθύμνης (IC II.v.37, 38, xxviii.1, SEG xxxvi 808)." *Horos* 13:213–224.

———. 2000. "The Inscriptions." In *Πρωτοβυζαντινή Ελεύθερνα Τομέας I*, vol. B, ed. Petros G. Themelis, 237–259. Rethymno.

———. 2002. "Λατρείες στην Κρήτη: Η περίπτωση των ορφικο-διονυσιακών ελασμάτων." In *Λατρείες στην 'Περιφέρεια' του Αρχαίου Ελληνικού Κόσμου*, ed. Aphrodite Avagianou, 147–171. Athens.

———. 2004. "Pecunia sacra deae Dictynnae: Τα μιλιάρια από τη Βιράν Επισκοπή και το Ροδοπού και άλλες επιγραφικές μαρτυρίες." In *Creta romana e protobizantina: Atti del congresso internazionale organizzato dalla Scuola*

Archeologica Italiana di Atene (Iraklion, 23-30 settembre 2000), ed. Antonino Di Vita, Monica Livadioti, and Ilaria Simiakaki, vol. 1:94–108. Padua.

———. 2006a. "The Archive of Inscriptions of the Rethymno Prefecture: Results and Prospects." In *Πεπραγμένα του Θ΄ Διεθνούς Κρητολογικού Συνεδρίου (Ελούντα, 1-6 Οκτωβρίου 2001).* Vol. A5, ed. Theocharis Detorakis and Alexis Kalokairinos, 207–214. Herakleio.

———. 2006b. "The Archive of Inscriptions of the Rethymno Prefecture: Results, Prospects and New Discoveries in Axos, Crete." In *Ο Μυλοπόταμος από την Αρχαιότητα ως Σήμερα: Περιβάλλον, Αρχαιολογία, Ιστορία, Λαογραφία, Κοινωνιολογία: Πρακτικά Διεθνούς Συνεδρίου (Πάνορμο, 24-30 Οκτωβρίου 2003).* Vol. 4: *Ελεύθερνα - Αξός,* ed. Irene Gavrilaki and Yannis Tzifopoulos, 137–145. Rethymno.

———. 2007. "The Archive of Inscriptions of the Rethymno Nome: Results, Prospects and New Discoveries in Lappa, Crete." In *Acta XII Congressus Internationalis Epigraphiae Graecae et Latinae, Barcelona, 3-8 Septembris 2002.* Monografies de la Secció Històrico-Arqueològica X, ed. Marc Mayer i Olivé, Giulia Baratta, Alejandra Guzmán Almagro, 1461–1466. Barcelona.

———. Forthcoming-1. "The Inscriptions." In *Ελεύθερνα Τομέας I,* ed. Petros G. Themelis. Rethymno.

———. Forthcoming-2. "Ἐπιγραφὲς Συβρίτου Νομοῦ Ρεθύμνης." *Horos.*

Usener, Hermann. 1902. "Milch und Honig." *Rheinisches Museum für Philologie* 57:177–195.

Ustinova, Yulia. 1996. "Orgeones in Phratries: A Mechanism of Social Integration in Attica." *Kernos* 6:227–242.

———. 2002. "'Either a Daimon, or a Hero, or Perhaps a God': Mythical Residents of Subterranean Chambers." *Kernos* 15:267–288.

———. 2004. "Truth Lies at the Bottom of a Cave: Apollo Pholeuterios, the Pholarchs of the Eleats, and Subterranean Oracles." *La Parola del Passato* 59:25–44.

Vamvouri Ruffy, Maria. 2004. *La fabrique du divin: Les* Hymnes *de Callimaque à la lumière des* Hymnes *homériques et des* Hymnes *épigraphiques.* Kernos Supplément 14. Liège.

Van Effenterre, Henri. 1991. "Loi archaïque sur l'excès de boisson: Les deux inscriptions de Nési." In *Ελεύθερνα, Τομέας II.* Vol. 1: *Επιγραφές από το Πυργί και το Νησί,* ed. Henri van Effenterre et al., 17–21, 24–30. Rethymno.

Van Effenterre, Henri, Kalpaxis, Thanassis, Petropoulou, Aggeliki B., and Stavrianopoulou, Eftychia, eds. 1991. *Ελεύθερνα, Τομέας II.* Vol. 1: *Επιγραφές από το Πυργί και το Νησί.* Rethymno.

Van Effenterre, Henri and Ruzé, Françoise. 1994, 1995. *Nomima: Recueil d'inscriptions politiques et juridiques de l'archaïsme grec.* 2 vols. Collection de l'École française de Rome 188. Paris.

Vassilakis, Antonis. 2004. "Ρωμαϊκά μαυσωλεία Κνωσού και Γόρτυνας." In *Creta romana e protobizantina: Atti del congresso internazionale organizzato dalla Scuola Archeologica Italiana di Atene (Iraklion, 23-30 settembre 2000)*, ed. Antonino Di Vita, Monica Livadioti, and Ilaria Simiakaki, vol. 3.1:699–708. Padua.

———. 2006. "Το Ιδαίο Άντρο στη μινωική εποχή." In *Ο Μυλοπόταμος από την Αρχαιότητα ως Σήμερα: Περιβάλλον, Αρχαιολογία, Ιστορία, Λαογραφία, Κοινωνιολογία: Πρακτικά Διεθνούς Συνεδρίου (Πάνορμο, 24-30 Οκτωβρίου 2003)*. Vol. 3: *Αρχαίοι Χρόνοι. Ιδαίο Άντρο*, ed. Irene Gavrilaki and Yannis Tzifopoulos, 21–30. Rethymno.

Vassilika, Eleni. 2004. "A New Egyptian God in Roman Crete." In *Creta romana e protobizantina: Atti del congresso internazionale organizzato dalla Scuola Archeologica Italiana di Atene (Iraklion, 23-30 settembre 2000)*, ed. Antonino Di Vita, Monica Livadioti, and Ilaria Simiakaki, vol. 3.2:1083–1087. Padua.

Velasco Lopez, Maria de Henar. 1992. "Le vin, la mort et les bienheureux (à propos des lamelles orphiques)." *Kernos* 5:209–220.

Verbruggen, Henri. 1981. *Le Zeus Crétois.* Collection d'Études Mythologiques. Paris.

Verdelis, Nicholaos M. 1950–1951. "Χαλκῆ τεφροδόχος κάλπις ἐκ Φαρσάλων." Ἀρχαιολογικὴ Ἐφημερίς 1950–1951:80–105.

———. 1953–1954. "Ὀρφικὰ ἐλάσματα ἐκ Κρήτης: Προσφορὰ Ἐλένης Ἀ. Σταθάτου." Ἀρχαιολογικὴ Ἐφημερίς (Εἰς μνήμην Γεωργίου Π. Οἰκονόμου) 1953–1954 II:56–60. (= 1963. "Tablettes orphiques de Crète." In *Collection Hélène Stathatos.* Vol. 3: *Objets antiques et byzantins*, 256–259. Strasbourg.)

Vermeule, Emily. 1979. *Aspects of Death in Early Greek Art and Poetry.* Sather Classical Lectures 46. Berkeley, CA and London.

Vernant, Jean Pierre. 1976. *Μύθος καὶ σκέψη στὴν ἀρχαία Ἑλλάδα: Μελέτες ἱστορικῆς ψυχολογίας.* Trans. Stella Georgoudi. Thessaloniki. (= 1983. *Myth and Thought among the Greeks.* Trans. Janet Lloyd. London and Boston, MA.)

Versnel, Henk S. 1981. "Religious Mentality in Ancient Prayer." In *Faith, Hope and Worship: Aspects of Religious Mentality in the Ancient World.* Studies in Greek and Roman Religion 2, ed. Henk S. Versnel, 1–64. Leiden.

———. 2002. "The Poetics of the Magical Charm: An Essay in the Power of Words." In *Magic and Ritual in the Ancient World.* Religions in the Graeco-Roman World 141, ed. Paul Mirecki and Marvin Meyer, 105–158. Leiden.

Vertoudakis, Vassilios. 2000a. *Epigrammata Cretica: Λογοτεχνικοὶ τόποι καὶ μύθοι τῆς Κρήτης στὸ ἀρχαῖο ἑλληνικὸ ἐπίγραμμα.* Herakleio.

———. 2000b. "Ἡ θέση τῆς Κρήτης στην ἐπιγραμματικὴ ποίηση της ελληνιστικής και αυτοκρατορικής περιόδου." In *Πεπραγμένα του Η´ Διεθνούς Κρητολογικού Συνεδρίου (Ηράκλειο, 9-14 Σεπτεμβρίου 1996).* Vol. Α1, ed. Alexis Kalokairinos, 83–89. Herakleio.

Vian, Francis. 1998. "L'histoire d'Astérios le Crétois: Nonnos tributaire des Bassariques des Dionysios?" *Zeitschrift für Papyrologie und Epigraphik* 122:71–78.

Vikela, Evgenia. 2003. "Continuity in Greek Religion: The Case of Zeus Cretagenes." *Cretan Studies* 8:199–216.

Vinogradov, Jurij G. 1991. "Zur sachlichen und geschichtlichen Deutung der Orphiker-Plättchen von Olbia." In *Orphisme et Orphée en l'honneur de Jean Rudhardt.* Recherchers et Rencontres, Publications de la Faculté des Lettres de Genève 3, ed. Philippe Borgeaud, 77–86. Geneva.

Vinogradov, Jurij G. and Kryžickij, Sergej D. 1995. *Olbia: Eine altgriechischen Stadt im nordwestlichen Schwarzmeerraum.* Mnemosyne Supplement 149. Leiden.

Virvidakis, Stelios. 1996. "Ἡ προφητεία του φιλοσόφου: Πολιτικές εξαγγελίες στην πλατωνική *Πολιτεία.*" In *Ιεροί λόγοι: Προφητείες και μαντείες στην ιουδαϊκή, την ελληνική και τη ρωμαϊκή αρχαιότητα,* ed. Dimitris I. Kyrtatas, 115–132. Athens.

Visconti, Amedeo. 2001. "Epimenide bouzyges." In *Epimenide Cretese: Quaderni del Dipartimento di discipline storiche "E. Lepore," Università "Federico II,"* ed. Alfonso Mele et al., 129–167. Naples.

Viviers, Didier. 1995. "Hérodote et la neutralité des Crétois en 480 avant notre ère. La trace d'un débate athénien?" *Hermes* 122:257–269.

———. 2004. "Rome face aux cités crétoises: Trafics insulaires et organisation de la province." In *Creta romana e protobizantina: Atti del congresso internazionale organizzato dalla Scuola Archeologica Italiana di Atene (Iraklion, 23-30 settembre 2000),* ed. Antonino Di Vita, Monica Livadioti, and Ilaria Simiakaki, vol. 1:17–24. Padua.

Vogliano, Achille. 1913. "Analecta epigraphica Graeco-latina." *Atti del Academia Archeologica di Napoli* 2:269.

Von Salis, Arnold. 1957. "Antiker Bestattungsbrauch." *Museum Helveticum* 14:89–99.

Voutiras, Emmanuel. 1984. "ΕΡΜΑΣ ΚΥΦΑΡΙΣΣΙΤΑΣ auf Kreta." *Philologus* 128:142–144.

———. 1998. *ΔΙΟΝΥΣΟΦΩΝΤΟΣ ΓΑΜΟΙ: Marital Life and Magic in Fourth Century Pella.* Amsterdam.

———. 2000. "Το ιερό του Διονύσου στην Άφυτη." In *Μύρτος: Μνήμη Ιουλίας Βοκοτοπούλου*, ed. Polyxeni Adam-Veleni, 631–540. Thessaloniki.

———. 2006. "Le culte de Zeus en Macédoine avant la conquête romaine." In *Rois, Cités, Nécropoles: Institutions, Rites et Monuments en Macédoine; Actes des Colloques de Nanterre (Décembre 2002) et d'Athènes (Janvier 2004)*. Meletemata 45, ed. Anne Marie Guimier-Sorbets et al., 333–346. Athens.

Wachter, Rudolf. 1998. "Griechisch χαῖρε: Vorgeschichte eines Grusswortes." *Museum Helveticum* 55:65–75.

Waldner, Katharina. 2000. *Geburt und Hochzeit des Krieges: Geschlechterdifferenz und Initiation in Mythos und Ritual der griechischen Polis*. Religions Geschichtliche Versuche und Vorarbeiten 46. Berlin.

Walker, Henry J. 1995. *Theseus and Athens*. Oxford.

Wallace, Robert W. 2003. "An Early Fifth-Century Athenian Revolution in Aulos Music." *Harvard Studies in Classical Philology* 101:73–92.

Walsh, George B. 1984. *The Varieties of Enchantment: Early Greek Views of the Nature and Function of Poetry*. Chapel Hill, NC and London.

Watkins, Calvert. 1995. "Orphic Gold Leaves and the Great Way of the Soul: Strophic Style, Funerary Ritual Formula, and Eschatology." In *How to Kill a Dragon: Aspects of Indo-European Poetics*. New York and Oxford.

Weber, Berthold F. 2004. *Milet*. Band I: *Bauwerke in Milet*, Teil 10: *Die römischen Heroa von Milet*. Herausgegeben im Auftrag des Deutsches Archäologisches Instituts von Volkmar von Graeve. Berlin and New York.

West, Martin L. 1965. "The Dictaean Hymn to the Kouros." *Journal of Hellenic Studies* 85:149–159.

———. 1966. *Hesiod. Theogony*. Edited with prolegomena and commentary. Oxford.

———. 1975. "Zum neuen Goldblättchen aus Hipponion." *Zeitschrift für Papyrologie und Epigraphik* 18:229–236.

———. 1978. *Hesiod Works and Days*. Edited with prolegomena and commentary. Oxford.

———. 1983. *The Orphic Poems*. Oxford.

———. 1997a. "Hocus-Pocus in East and West: Theogony, Ritual, and the Tradition of Esoteric Commentary." In *Studies on the Derveni Papyrus*, ed. André Laks and Glenn W. Most, 81–90. Oxford.

———. 1997b. *The East Face of Helicon: West Asiatic Elements in Greek Poetry and Myth*. Oxford.

———, ed. 2003. *Homeric Hymns, Homeric Apocrypha, Lives of Homer*. Loeb Classical Library. Cambridge, MA.

Willetts, Ronald F. 1962. *Cretan Cults and Festivals*. New York.

Williams, A. R. 2006. "Bulgaria's Gold Rush." *National Geographic*, December: 2–21.

Winkler, John J. 1990. *The Constraints of Desire: The Anthropology of Sex and Gender in Ancient Greece.* New York and London.

Xifaras, Napoleon. 2002. *Οικιστική της Πρωτογεωμετρικής και Γεωμετρικής Κρήτης: Η μετάβαση από τη "μινωική" στην "ελληνική" κοινωνία.* Διδακτορική διατριβή, Πανεπιστήμιο Κρήτης. Rethymno.

Yalouris, Nicholaos. 1996. *Αρχαία Ἤλις: Το λίκνο των Ολυμπιακών αγώνων.* Athens.

Yangaki, Anastassia. 2004. "Τα χρυσά φυλακτά." In *Πρωτοβυζαντινή Ελεύθερνα Τομέας Ι*, vol. A, ed. Petros G. Themelis, 187–204. Rethymno.

Yatromanolakis, Dimitrios and Roilos, Panagiotis. 2003. *Towards a Ritual Poetics.* Athens.

———, eds. 2004. *Greek Ritual Poetics.* Center for Hellenic Studies, Hellenic Studies Series 3. Washington, DC and Cambridge, MA.

Yiouri, Evgenia. 1978. *Ὁ κρατήρας τοῦ Δερβενίου.* Βιβλιοθήκη τῆς ἐν Ἀθήναις Ἀρχαιολογικῆς Ἑταιρείας 89. Athens.

Yunis, Harvey. 2003. "Writing for Reading: Thucydides, Plato, and the Emergence of the Critical Reader." In *Written Texts and the Rise of Literate Culture in Ancient Greece*, ed. Harvey Yunis, 189–212. Cambridge.

Zacharia, Katerina. 2004. "Sophocles and the West: The Evidence of the Fragments." In *Shards from Kolonos: Studies in Sophoclean Fragments*, ed. Alan Sommerstein, 57–76. Bari.

Zeitlin, Froma I. 1993. "Staging Dionysus between Thebes and Athens." In *Masks of Dionysus*, ed. Thomas H. Carpenter and Christopher A. Faraone, 147–182. Myth and Poetics. Ithaca, NY.

Zimmermann, Bernhard. 1992. *Dithyrambos: Geschichte einer Gattung.* Hypomnemata 98. Göttingen.

Zizioulas, Ioannis, Metropolitan of Pergamos. 2003. *Ελληνισμός και Χριστιανισμός, η συνάντηση των δύο κόσμων.* Athens.

Zoes, Antonis A. 1996. *Κνωσός, το εκστατικό όραμα: Σημειωτική και ψυχολογία μιας αρχαιολογικής περιπέτειας.* Herakleio.

Zographou, Gerasimoula. 1995. "L'argumentation d'Hérodote concernant les emprunts faits par les Grecs à la religion égyptienne." *Kernos* 8:187–203.

Zoumbaki, Sophia B. 1987. "Θεατρικά προσωπεία του Εθνικού Αρχαιολογικού Μουσείου." *Αρχαιολογικό Δελτίο Μελέτες* 42 A:354–66, plates 3–14.

———. 2005. *Prosopographie der Eleer bis zum 1. Jh. V. Chr.* Meletemata 40. Athens.

Zuntz, Günther. 1971. *Persephone: Three Essays on Religion and Thought in Magna Graecia.* Oxford.

Figure Credits

Map. Courtesy of Dr. Katja Sporn; plotting by Hans P. Birk. Map modified by Jill Curry Robbins, after Sporn 2002, Tafeln 2–4.

Figure 1a. Photograph by Stephanos N. Stournaras.

Figure 1b. Drawing by Federico Halbherr, in Comparetti 1910:31.

Figure 2a. Photograph by Stephanos N. Stournaras.

Figure 2b. Drawing by Federico Halbherr, in Comparetti 1910:38.

Figure 3a. Photograph by Stephanos N. Stournaras.

Figure 3b. Drawing by Federico Halbherr, in Comparetti 1910:38.

Figure 4a. Photograph by Yannis Ploumidis Papadakis.

Figure 4b. Drawing by Margarita Guarducci, in IC II.xxx.4, p. 314.

Figure 5a. Photograph by Stephanos N. Stournaras.

Figure 5b. Drawing by Nikolaos Verdelis 1953–1954:57.

Figure 6a. Photograph by Stephanos N. Stournaras.

Figure 6b. Drawing by Nikolaos Verdelis 1953–1954:58.

Figure 7a. Photograph by Stephanos N. Stournaras.

Figure 7b. Drawing by Federico Halbherr, in Comparetti 1910:41.

Figure 8. Photograph by the author.

Figure 9a. Photograph by Stephanos Alexandrou.

Figure 9b. Drawing by Amanda Kelly.

Figure 10a. Photograph by Stephanos Alexandrou.

Figure 10b. Drawing by Katerina Kaklamanou.

Figures 11–13. Photographs by Aris Tsantiropoulos.

Figures 14–16. Photographs by Matthaios Bessios.

Figures 17a-g. Photographs by Yannis Ploumidis Papadakis.

Figures 18. Photographs by the author.

Figures 19–22. Photographs by Yannis Ploumidis Papadakis.

Figure 23. Photograph by Betty Psaropoulou.

Figures 24–39. Photographs by Nikos Litinas.

Figure 40. Drawing by Arnold von Salis 1957:98, Abb. 8.

Figure 41. By permission of The J. Paul Getty Museum, Malibu, CA.

Figures 42a–c. Gift of Edward Drummond Libbey, Florence Scott Libbey, and the Egypt Exploration Society, by exchange. Photos reproduced by permission of the Toledo Museum of Art.

Figures 43–44. Photographs by Yannis Ploumidis Papadakis.

Figures 45–46. Photographs by the author.

Figure 47. Drawing by Federico Halbherr, in Ricci 1893:304–305, no. 13.

Figure 48. Drawing by Federico Halbherr, in IC I.xii.1.

Figure 49. Drawing by Federico Halbherr, in IC I.xii.8.

Figures 50a–b. Photographs by Petros Themelis.

Index of Passages

CPSIA information can be obtained
at www.ICGtesting.com
Printed in the USA
JSHW050928180723
44958JS00002B/9

9 780674 023796